S0-BDP-037

'When people are in danger, everyone has a duty to speak out. This book is a good example. Here the health profession shows its expertise in a responsible way. I hope their book can help us to change our way of thinking as well as our way of acting.'
Kofi Annan, Secretary-General, United Nations

'Medical textbooks too often neglect the consequences of war to human health: it makes this book all the more important.'
Gro Harlem Brundtland, Director-General, WHO

'Once more we owe a debt of gratitude to the medical world. This time it is due to the Finnish "Physicians for Social Responsibility". Their new publication, *War or Health*, is an encyclopaedia of peaceful information about war – its history, its weaponry, its destructiveness, its consequences for civilians and the environment and current hopes for its eventual abolition. A very useful resource book for all who are serious about peace.'
Bruce Kent, Past President, The International Peace Bureau

THIS BOOK IS ALSO AVAILABLE IN THE FOLLOWING COUNTRIES

FIJI
University Book Centre
University of South Pacific,
Suva
Tel: 679 313 900
Fax: 679 303 265

GHANA
EPP Book Services
P O Box TF 490
Trade Fair
Accra
Tel: 21 778347
Fax: 21 779099

MOZAMBIQUE
Sul Sensacoes
PO Box 2242,
Maputo
258 1 421 974
258 1 423 414

NAMIBIA
Book Den
PO Box 3469
Shop 4, Frans Indongo Gardens
Windhoek
Tel: 264 61 239 976
Fax: 264 61 234248

NEPAL
Everest Media Services
GPO Box 5443, Dillibazar
Putalisadak Chowk
Kathmandu
977 1 416026
977 1 250176

PAKISTAN
Vanguard Books
45 The Mall,
Lahore
92 42 735 5079
92 42 735 5197

PAPUA NEW GUINEA
Unisearch PNG Pty Ltd
Box 320, University
National Capital District
675 326 0130
675 326 0127

RWANDA
Librairie Ikirezi
PO Box 443,
Kigali
Tel/Fax: 250 71314

SUDAN
The Nile Bookshop
New Extension St 41
PO BOX 8036
Khartoum
Tel: 249 11 463749

TANZANIA
TEMA Publishing Co Ltd
PO Box 63115
Dar Es Salaam
255 22 2113608
255 22 2110472

UGANDA
Aristoc Booklex Ltd
PO Box 5130, Kampala Rd
Diamond Trust Building
Kampala
Tel: 256 41 344381/349052
Fax: 256 41 254867

ZAMBIA
UNZA Press
PO Box 32379
Lusaka
Zambia
260 1 290409
260 1 253952

WAR OR HEALTH?
a reader

EDITORIAL BOARD
Ilkka Taipale with P. Helena Mäkelä, Kati Juva,
Vappu Taipale, Sergei Kolesnikov, Raj Mutalik, Michael Christ

EDITORIAL ASSISTANT
Hanna Tapanainen

PREFACE BY
KOFI ANNAN, Secretary-General of the United Nations

University Press
DHAKA

White Lotus
BANGKOK

NAE
CAPE TOWN

Zed Books
LONDON & NEW YORK

in association with

Physicians for Social Responsibility (Finland)
HELSINKI

and

IPPNW
CAMBRIDGE, MASS.

War or Health? A Reader was first published in 2002 by

In Bangladesh
University Press Ltd, Red Crescent Building, 114 Motijheel C/A, Dhaka 1000

In Burma, Cambodia, Laos, Thailand and Vietnam
White Lotus, GPO Box 1141, Bangkok 10501, Thailand

In Southern Africa
New Africa Education (a division of New Africa Books),
201 Werdmuller Centre, Newry Street, Claremont 7708, South Africa

In the Rest of the World
Zed Books Ltd., 7 Cynthia Street, London N1 9JF, UK
and Room 400, 175 Fifth Avenue, New York, NY 10010, USA

in association with

Physicians for Social Responsibility (Finland),
P O Box 722, SF-00101 Helsinki, Finland

and

International Physicians for the Prevention of Nuclear War,
727 Massachusetts Avenue, Cambridge, MA 02139, USA

Distributed in the United States exclusively by Palgrave, a division
of St. Martin's Press, LLC, 175 Fifth Avenue, New York, NY 10010, USA.

Copyright © Physicians for Social Responsibility (Finland), 2001

Artist: Oliver Whitehead

Cover designed by Andrew Corbett
Designed and set in 10/12 pt Garamond by Long House, Cumbria, UK
Printed and bound by Bookcraft Ltd, Radstock, Bath

The rights of the authors of this work have been asserted by them
in accordance with the Copyright, Designs and Patents Act, 1988

All rights reserved

A catalogue record for this book is available from the British Library
US CIP data is available from the Library of Congress

ISBN 1 85649 950 2 Cased
ISBN 1 85649 951 0 Limp

In Southern Africa
ISBN 1 919876 59 6 Limp

CONTENTS

I HISTORICAL VIEW   5

II DIFFERENT ARMS SYSTEMS   63

III   HEALTH AND SOCIAL EFFECTS OF WARFARE

TO THE READER

EDITORIAL BOARD

In spite of the amount of human suffering caused by wars there has been a lack of discussion on the broad implications of warfare for human well-being and for the state of our environment and culture. It is our hope that *War or Health?* will serve as a stimulus for such debate. The book presents warfare in a new profile, demonstrating its consequences for the whole civilian population, including important special groups such as children, women, old people and the mentally handicapped. It highlights the changing nature of wars, currently with a focus on prolonged local conflicts taking place in the midst of civilian life, but with the possibility of new weapons of mass destruction never excluded. On the other hand, it describes the efforts of nations, inter-governmental agencies and non-governmental organizations (NGOs) to prevent the damage associated with warfare, finding non-violent means of solving conflicts and establishing confidence and solidarity.

This reader is a part of such non-governmental actions. It was commissioned by the NGO Physicians for Social Responsibility (PSR), Finland, which was established in 1982 and whose membership now includes some 6 per cent of the country's physicians. From the start PSR adopted a broad agenda: prevention of wars in general and opposition to inequalities in health and well-being between different parts of the world. It builds on a strong professional background and sets great store by knowledge-based action. It has a tradition of writing, editing and publishing textbooks and readers, including the major international reader *Health and Disease in Developing Countries* (Lankinen *et al.*, eds, MacMillan, 1994).

PSR, Finland is the national affiliate of International Physicians for the Prevention of Nuclear War (IPPNW), recipient of the 1985 Nobel Peace Prize for its efforts at making the human consequences of nuclear warfare widely known. IPPNW has a history of collaboration between physicians from the two post-war superpowers, the USA and the Soviet Union, personified in the co-presidents, Drs Lown and Chazov. It gives us great pleasure, therefore, to have physicians from both the USA and Russia among the editors of this reader and to present as its opening chapter a joint article by Drs Lown and Chazov.

This book would not have been possible without the expertise and diligence of its many international and national authors. The editors wish to extend their heartfelt thanks to them. A very special thank you is due to the artist of the book, Oliver Whitehead, whose thought-provoking pictures may remain in the minds of the readers longer than the written ideas. Editorial assistant Hanna Tapanainen MD has done a tremendous job in keeping together all the manuscripts and in persuading the authors to deliver on time – thank you, Hanna. Finally Lena Hyppönen deserves warm thanks for copy-editing and sometimes retyping all the manuscripts.

We, the Finnish editors, are very glad to see the book at this stage, and proud of having had the opportunity to participate in its publication. We are especially pleased to present our contribution to the global peace process from a small country that survived the Second World War and now has no enemies.

Ilkka Taipale, P. Helena Mäkelä, Kati Juva and Vappu Taipale

ABOUT THE ILLUSTRATIONS
BEHIND THE LINES

A series of linear white chalk drawings was made on the sidewalks in different locations in Helsinki, using familiar military images and symbols. The drawings were made only for the duration needed to photograph them in black and white.

I wanted to portray the fact that the effects of war filter through society continuously with images that bring attention to the aspects of war close to everyday public life. Sidewalks are areas common to all people: areas where children draw, graffiti are made and officials map out our boundaries.

Creating these drawings signifies both obedience and defiance, so from the artist's point of view the images convey a way of drawing attention to the fact that all people are in some way constantly involved with war.

Oliver Whitehead

LIST OF ABBREVIATIONS

ABM Anti-Ballistic Missile (Treaty)
ACHR American Committee for Human Rights
ADR Alternative dispute resolution
AGARD Advisory Group For Aerospace Research and Development
AI Amnesty International
ANC African National Congress
APEC Asia–Pacific Economic Cooperation
APIM Association Professionelle Internationale des Médecins APLM Antipersonnel landmines
ASD Acute stress disorder
BICEPS brevity–simplicity–centrality
BiH Bosnia and Herzegovina
BMA British Medical Association
BMJ *British Medical Journal*
BW Biological warfare
BTWC Biological and Toxin Weapons Convention
BWC Biological Weapons Convention
CBR Community-based rehabilitation
CBU Cluster Bomb Unit
CBW Chemical and biological warfare
CCW Convention on Conventional Weapons
CFE Conventional Armed Forces in Europe (Treaty)
CFS Chronic fatigue syndrome
CINAP Intercongregational Commission for Justice and Peace
CIS Commonwealth of Independent States
Cls confidence limits
CNI St Louis Committee for Nuclear Information
CTBT Comprehensive Test Ban Treaty
CIA Central Intelligence Agency
CTBT Comprehensive Test Ban Treaty
CTR Cooperative Threat Reduction
CW Chemical warfare
CWC Chemical Weapons Convention
DESNOS Disorder of extreme stress not otherwise specified
DHS Demographic and Health Survey
DNS Deep-sea navigable ship
DS86 Dosimetry System 1986
DU Depleted uranium
DZ Dom Zdravlja (health centre)

ECRP Ethnic Conflict Resolution Project
ECTF European Community Task Force
EMP Electromagnetic pulse
EU European Union
EZLN Zapatista National Liberation Army
FAE Fuel–Air Explosive
FAS Federation of American Scientists
FBiH Federation of Bosnia & Herzegovina
FMCT Fissile Material Cut-Off Treaty
FMLN Farabundo Martí National Liberation Front (El Salvador)
FMS Fibromyalgia syndrome
Frelimo Front for the Liberation of Mozambique
FTAA Free Trade Agreement of the Americas
GATT General Agreement on Tariffs and Trade
GDP Gross domestic product
GIPRI Geneva International Peace Research Institute
GNP Gross national product
GP General practitioner
GWI Gulf War illnesses
HEU Highly-enriched uranium
HI Handicap International
HPM High-power microwaves
HRW Human Rights Watch
IAEA International Atomic Energy Agency
IALANA International Association of Lawyers against Nuclear Arms
ICBL International Campaign to Ban Landmines
ICC International Criminal Court
ICJ International Court of Justice
ICRC International Committee of the Red Cross
IEBL Inter-Entity Boundary Line
IGO International governmental organizations
IHL International humanitarian law
ILO International Labour Organization
IMAW International Medical Association against War
IMF International Monetary Fund
INF Intermediate-range Nuclear Forces agreement
IPB International Peace Bureau
IPC International Peace Campaign
IPPNW International Physicians for Prevention of Nuclear War

IPRA International Peace Research Association
ISDN Integrated Systems of Digital Network
ITU International Telecommunication Union
IUCN International Union for the Conservation
of Nature (now World Conservation Union)
KE Kinetic energy
KLA Kosovo Liberation Army
KTO Kuwaiti Theatre of Operations
LCNP Lawyers' Committee on Nuclear Policy
MAPW Medical Association for the Prevention
of War
MCANW Medical Campaign against Nuclear
Weapons
MCS Multiple chemical sensitivity syndrome
MECS Middle East Cancer Society
MLRS Multiple Launch Rocket System
MPC Medical Peace Campaign
MPC&A Material Protection Control and
Accounting
MPI Middle Powers Initiative
MRTA Tupac Amaru Revolutionary Movement
(Peru)
MSF Médecins sans Frontières
NA nuclear ammunition
NAFTA North American Free Trade Agreement
NAM Non-Aligned Movement
NATO North Atlantic Treaty Organization
NCI National Cancer Institute
NGO Non-governmental organization
NIH National Institutes of Health
NLW Non-lethal weapon
NOD Non-offensive defence
NPS Nuclear-powered submarine
NPT Nuclear Non-Proliferation Treaty
NWC Nuclear Weapons Convention
NZ New Zealand
OAS Organization of American States
ODS Operation Desert Storm
OECD Organization for Economic
Cooperation and Development
OOTW Operations Other Than War
OPIDN Organophosphate-induced delayed
neurotoxicity
OTA Office of Technology Assessment
PCB polychlorinated biphenyl
PGA Parliamentarians for Global Action
PHR Physicians for Human Rights
PINRO Polar Institute of Fishing and
Oceanography
PIOOM Interdisciplinary Research Programme
on the Root Causes of Human Rights
Violations (based at University of Leiden,
Netherlands)
PLO Palestine Liberation Organization
PrepCom Preparatory Committee for a Global
Campaign on Small Arms and Light Weapons
PRIO International Peace Research Institute of
Oslo

PSR Physicians for Social Responsibility
PTBT Partial Test Ban Treaty
PTSD Post-traumatic stress disorder
RAW Radioactive waste
Renamo Mozambique National Resistance
RERF Radiation Effects Research Foundation
RMA Revolution in Military Affairs
RNB Radioactive noble gases
RS Republika Srpska
RSK Republic of Serbian Krajina
SALT Strategic Arms Limitation Treaty
SANE National Committee for a Sane Nuclear
Policy
SCP Siberian chemical plant
SIPRI Stockholm International Peace Research
Institute
START Strategic Arms Reduction Treaties
TBq Terabequerel
UAV Unmanned aerial vehicle
UDHR Universal Declaration of Human Rights
UN United Nations
UNCHS United Nations Centre for Human
Settlements (Habitats)
UNDP United Nations Development
Programme
UNEP United Nations Environmental
Programme
UNESCO United Nations Educational,
Scientific and Cultural Organization
UNHCR United Nations High Commissioner
for Refugees
UNICEF United Nations Children's Fund
UNIDIR United Nations Institute for
Disarmament Research
UNMIK United Nations Mission in Kosovo
UNPA United Nations Protected Area
UNITA National Union for the Total Indepen-
dence of Angola
UNRWA United Nations Relief and Works
Agency for Palestine Refugees in the Near East
UNSCOM United Nations Special Commission
URNG National Revolutionary Union of
Guatemala
US United States
USAID United States Agency for International
Development
WCMC World Conservation Monitoring Centre
WCP World Court Project
WFP World Food Programme
WG war gas
WHA World Health Assembly
WHO World Health Organization
WTO World Trade Organization
WWF World Wildlife Fund
ZAPU Zimbabwe African People's Union
ZANU Zimbabwe African National Union

PREFACE

KOFI ANNAN

Secretary-General, United Nations

The United Nations Charter excludes the UN from intervening in matters within the domestic jurisdiction of member states. However, even national sovereignty can be set aside if it affects the duty of the Security Council to preserve international peace and security and prevent genocide.

Most wars nowadays are civil wars, and in many of today's conflicts civilians have become the main targets of violence. Armies count their own losses, but there is no agency whose job it is to keep a tally of civilians killed. In many cases, the conflict eventually becomes so dangerous that the international community finds itself obliged to intervene. But the most effective interventions are not military. Wherever possible intervention should consist in preventive diplomacy and correcting the causes of conflict such as ethnic tension and poverty.

In the final analysis the UN exists to uphold the rights of peoples. But when we ask 'Why didn't someone intervene?' the question should not be addressed only to the United Nations. All of us have the obligation to halt or prevent injustice and suffering.

The United Nations is an association of sovereign states, and states do tend to be extremely jealous of their sovereignty. Small states especially are fearful of intervention in their affairs by great powers. Our century has indeed seen many examples of the strong 'intervening' – or interfering – in the affairs of the weak, from the allied intervention in the Russian civil war in 1918 to the Soviet interventions in Hungary, Czechoslovakia and Afghanistan. Others might refer to the American intervention in Vietnam, or even the Turkish intervention in Cyprus in 1974. The motives and the legal justification may be better in some cases than others, but the word intervention has come to be used almost as a synonym for invasion.

The Charter of the United Nations gives responsibilities to great powers in their capacity as permanent members of the Security Council. But as a safeguard against abuse of those powers, Article 2.7 of the Charter protects national sovereignty even from intervention by the UN itself. The article forbids the United Nations to intervene 'in matters which are essentially within the domestic jurisdiction of any state'.

That prohibition is just as relevant today as it was in 1945: violations of sovereignty remain violations of the global order. Yet, in other contexts the word intervention has a more benign meaning. We all applaud the policeman who intervenes to stop a fight, or the teacher who prevents big boys from bullying smaller ones, and medicine uses the word intervention to describe the act of the surgeon, who saves life by intervening to remove malignant growth or to repair damaged organs. Of course, the most intrusive methods of treatment are not always to be recommended. A wise doctor knows when to let nature take its course. But a doctor who never intervened would have few admirers, and probably even fewer patients. So it is in international affairs. Why was the United Nations established, if not to act as a benign policeman or doctor? Our job is to intervene: to prevent conflict where we can, to put a stop to it when it has broken out, or, when neither of those things is possible, at least to contain it and prevent it from spreading. That is what the world expects of us, even though, sadly, the UN by no means always lives up to such expectations. It is also what the Charter requires of us, particularly in Chapter VI, which deals with the peaceful settlement of disputes, and Chapter VII which describes the action the UN must take when peace comes under threat, or is actually broken.

International conflict or domestic dispute?

The purpose of Article 2.7 was to confine such interventions to situations where international peace is threatened or broken, and to keep the UN from interfering in purely domestic disputes. Yet even that article carries the important rider that 'this principle shall not prejudice the application of enforcement measures under Chapter VII'. In other words, even national sovereignty can be set aside if it stands in the way of the Security Council's overriding duty to preserve international peace and security. On the face of it, there is a simple distinction between international conflict, which is clearly the UN's business, and domestic disputes, which are not. The very phrase 'domestic dispute' sounds reassuring. It suggests a little local difficulty which the state in question can easily settle if only it is left alone to do so.

We all know that in recent years it has not been like that. Most wars nowadays are civil wars – at least that is how they start – and are anything but benign. They are 'civil' only in the sense that civilians – non-combatants – have become the main victims. In the First World War roughly 90 per cent of those killed were soldiers, and only 10 per cent civilians. In the Second World War, even if we count all the victims of the Nazi death camps as war casualties, civilians made up about half of all those killed. But in many of today's conflicts civilians have become the main targets of violence. It is now conventional to put the proportion of civilian casualties somewhere in the region of 75 per cent. I say conventional because the truth is that no one really knows. Relief agencies such as the UN High Commissioner for Refugees and the Red Cross rightly devote their resources to helping the living rather than counting the dead.

Armies count their own losses, and sometimes boast about the number of the enemy they have killed. But there is no agency whose job it is to keep a tally of civilians killed. The victims of today's brutal conflicts are not merely anonymous but literally countless. Yet so long as the conflict rages within the borders of a single state, the old othodoxy would require us to let it rage. In reality, this old orthodoxy was never absolute. The UN

Charter was, after all, issued in the name of 'the peoples', not the governments, of the United Nation. Its aim is not only to preserve international peace – vitally important though that is – but also 'to reaffirm faith in fundamental human rights, in the dignity and worth of the human person'. The Charter protects the sovereignty of peoples. It was never meant as a licence for governments to trample on human rights and human dignity. Sovereignty implies responsibility, not just power.

In the year 1998 we celebrated the 50th anniversary of the Universal Declaration of Human Rights. That declaration was not meant as a purely rhetorical statement. The UN General Assembly that adopted it also decided that it had the right to express its concern about the apartheid system in South Africa. The principle of international concern for human rights took precedence over the claim of non-interference in internal affairs. And the day before it adopted the Universal Declaration, the General Assembly had adopted the Convention on the Prevention and Punishment of the Crime of Genocide, which puts all states under an obligation to 'prevent and punish' this most heinous of crimes. It also allows them to 'call upon the competent organs of the United Nations' to take action for this purpose. Since genocide is almost always committed with the connivance, if not the direct participation, of state authorities, it is hard to see how the United Nations could prevent it without intervening in a state's internal affairs. As for punishment, a very important attempt is now being made to fulfil this obligation through the ad hoc tribunals for the former Yugoslavia and Rwanda, and in 1998 in Rome I had the honour to open the conference that adopted the statute of the permanent International Criminal Court. This court will have the competence to try cases of war crimes and crimes against humanity wherever, and by whomsoever, they are committed.

Frontiers old and new

State frontiers should no longer be seen as a watertight protection for war criminals or mass murderers. The fact that a conflict is internal does not give the parties any right to disregard the most basic rules of human conduct. Besides, most internal conflicts do not remain so for very long. They soon spill over into neighbouring countries. The most obvious and tragic way this happens is through the flow of refugees. But there are others, one of which is the spread of knowledge. News today travels around the world more rapidly than we could imagine even a few years ago. Human suffering on a large scale has become impossible to keep secret. People in far-off countries not only hear about it, but often see it on their television screens.

That in turn leads to public outrage and pressure on governments to do something – in other words, to intervene. Moreover, today's conflicts not only spread across existing frontiers but sometimes give birth to new states, which of course means new frontiers. In such cases, what started as an internal conflict becomes an international one, when peoples who formerly lived together in one state find each other's behaviour so threatening, or so offensive, that they can no longer do so.

Such separations are seldom as smooth and trouble-free as the famous 'velvet divorce' between Czechs and Slovaks. All too often they happen in the midst of, or at the end of, a long and bitter conflict, as was the case with Pakistan and Bangladesh, with the former Yugoslav republics, and with Ethiopia and Eritrea. In other cases, such as the former Soviet Union, the initial separation may be largely non-violent, yet it soon gives rise to new conflicts, which pose new problems for the international community.

In many cases, the conflict eventually becomes so dangerous that the international community finds itself obliged to intervene. By then it can only do so in the most intrusive and expensive way, that is through military intervention. But the most effective interventions are not military. It is much better, from every point of view, if action can be taken to resolve or manage a conflict before it reaches the military stage.

Sometimes this action may take the form of economic advice and assistance. In so many cases ethnic tensions are exacerbated by poverty and famine, or by uneven economic development which brings wealth to one section of a community while destroying the homes and livelihood of another. If outsiders can help avert this by suitably targeted aid and investment, by giving information and training to local entrepreneurs, or by suggesting more appropriate state policies, their intervention should surely be welcomed by all concerned. That is why I see the work of the UN Development Programme, and of our sister Bretton Woods institutions in Washington, as organically linked to the UN's work on peace and security.

Preventive diplomacy

In other cases what is most needed is skilful and timely diplomacy. The United Nations does its best to 'intervene' in such effective but non-military ways. The organization was established in the first place to prevent unnecessary conflict, to seek international solutions to international problems, and to obtain respect for international law and agreements from a recalcitrant party without destroying forever that party's dignity and willingness to cooperate. When the moment is ripe, diplomacy through the United Nations can achieve the will of the international community. We much prefer to see disputes settled under Chapter VI, rather than move to the drastic and expensive means available under Chapter VII.

For many years the UN has been conducting successful peacekeeping operations, both of the traditional variety, monitoring ceasefires and buffer zones, as well as the more complex multidimensional operations that helped bring peace to Namibia, Mozambique and El Salvador. And in recent years there has been an increasing emphasis on the UN's political work. Early diplomatic intervention can, at its best, avert bloodshed altogether. But our resources are limited, and we are strong believers in the principle of subsidiarity, which Europeans are so fond of. In other words, we are more than happy if disputes can be dealt with peacefully at the regional level, without the UN needing to be involved.

Who should intervene – and why?

We must assume, however, that there will always be some tragic cases where peaceful means have failed: where extreme violence is being used, and only forceful intervention can stop it. Even during the Cold War, when the UN's own enforcement capacity was largely paralyzed by divisions in the Security Council, there were cases where extreme violations of human rights in one country led to military intervention by one of its neighbours. In 1971 Indian intervention ended the civil war in east Pakistan, allowing Bangladesh to achieve independence. In 1978 Vietnam intervened in Cambodia, putting an end to the genocidal rule of the Khmer Rouge. In 1979 Tanzania intervened to overthrow Idi Amin's erratic dictatorship in Uganda.

In all three of those cases the intervening states gave refugee flows across the border as the reason why they had to act. But what justified their action in the eyes of the world was the internal character of the regimes they acted against. And history has by and large ratified that verdict. Few would now deny that in those cases intervention was a lesser evil than allowing massacre and extreme oppression to continue. Yet at the time, in all three cases, the international community was divided and disturbed. Why? Because these interventions were unilateral. The states in question had no mandate from anyone else to act as they did. And that sets an uncomfortable precedent.

Can we really afford to let each state be the judge of its own right, or duty, to intervene in another state's internal conflict? If we do, will we not be forced to legitimize Hitler's championship of the Sudeten Germans, or Soviet intervention in Afghanistan? Most of us would prefer, I think, especially now that the Cold War is over, to see such decisions taken collectively, by an international institution whose authority is generally respected. And surely the only institution competent to assume that role is the Security Council of the United Nations? The UN Charter clearly assigns responsibility to the Council for maintaining international peace and security. I would argue, therefore, that only the Council has the authority to decide that the internal situation in any state is so grave as to justify forceful intervention.

The Security Council

As you know, many member states feel that the Council's authority now needs to be strengthened by an increase in its membership, bringing in new permanent members or possibly adding a new category of members. Unfortunately a consensus on the details of such a reform has yet to be reached.

This is a matter for the member states. As Secretary-General I would make only three points. First, the Security Council must become more representative, to reflect today's realities rather than those of 1945. Second, the Council's authority depends not only on the representative character of its membership but also on the quality and speed of its decisions. Humanity is ill-served when the Council is unable to react quickly and decisively in a crisis. Third, the delay in reaching agreement on reform, however regrettable, must not be allowed to detract from the Council's authority and responsibility in the meanwhile.

The Council in its present form derives its authority from the Charter. That gives it a unique legitimacy as the linchpin of world order, which all member states should value and respect. It also places a unique responsibility on Council members, both permanent and non-permanent, a responsibility of which their governments and indeed their citizens should be fully conscious.

Of course the fact that the Council has this unique responsibility does not mean that the intervention itself should always be undertaken directly by the United Nations, in the sense of forces wearing blue helmets and controlled by the UN Secretariat. No one knows better than I do, as a former Under-Secretary-General in charge of peacekeeping, that the UN lacks the capacity for directing large-scale military enforcement operations. At least for the foreseeable future, such operations will have to be undertaken by member states, or by regional organizations. But they need to have the authority of the Security Council behind them, expressed in an authorizing resolution. That formula, developed in 1990 to deal with the Iraqi aggression against Kuwait, has proved its usefulness and will no doubt be used again in future crises. But we should not assume that intervention always needs to be on a massive scale.

There are cases where the speed of the action may be far more crucial than the size of the force. Personally I am haunted by the experience of Rwanda in 1994: a terrible demonstration of what can happen when there is no intervention, or at least none in the crucial early weeks of a crisis. General Romeo Dallaire, the commander of the UN mission, has indicated that with a force of even modest size and means he could have prevented much of the killing. Indeed he has said that 5000 peacekeepers could have saved 500,000 lives. It is tragic that at the crucial moment the opposite course was chosen, and the size of the force reduced. Surely things would have been different if the Security Council had had at its disposal a small rapid reaction force, ready to move at a few days' notice. I believe that if we are to avert further such disasters in the future we need such a capacity; that member states must have appropriately trained stand-by forces immediately available, and must be willing to send them quickly when the Security Council requests.

Some have even suggested that private security firms, like the one that recently helped restore the elected president to power in Sierra Leone, might play a role in providing the United Nations with the rapid reaction capacity it needs. When we had need of skilled soldiers to separate fighters from refugees in the Rwandan refugee camps in Goma, I even considered the possibility of engaging a private firm. But the world may not be ready to privatize peace.

In any case, let me stress that I am not asking for a standing army at the beck and call of the Secretary-General. The decision to intervene, I repeat, can be taken only by the Security Council. But at present the Council's authority is diminished, because it lacks the means to intervene effectively even when it wishes to do so.

Who is responsible?

The UN is an association of sovereign states, but the rights it exists to uphold belong to peoples, not governments. By the same token, it is wrong to think that the obligations of UN membership fall only on states. Each one of us, whether as workers in government, in intergovernmental or non-governmental organizations – in business, in the media, or simply as human beings – has an obligation to do whatever she or he can to correct injustice. Each of us has a duty to halt – or, better, to prevent – the infliction of suffering.

Much has been written about the 'duty to interfere' (*le devoir d'ingerence*). We should remember that the inventor of this phrase, Bernard Kouchner, coined it not as a minister in the French government but when he was still running the charity Médecins du Monde. He argued that non-governmental organizations had a duty to cross national boundaries, with or without the consent of governments, in order to reach the victims of natural disasters and other emergencies. Their right to do this has since been recognized by two resolutions of the UN General Assembly in 1988 (after the earthquake in Armenia) and again in 1991 (when conflict broke out in the Balkans). Both these resolutions, while paying full respect to state sovereignty, assert the overriding right of people in desperate situations to receive help, and the right of international bodies to provide it.

So when we recall tragic events such as those of Bosnia or Rwanda and ask 'why did not someone intervene?' the question should be addressed not only to the United Nations, or even to its member states. Each of us as an individual has to take her or his share of responsibility. No one can claim ignorance of what happened. All of us should recall how we responded, and ask: what did I do? Could I have done more? Did I let my prejudice, my indifference or my fear overwhelm my reasoning? Above all, how would I react next time? 'Next time' may already be here.

We have a duty to speak out

When people are in danger, everyone has a duty to speak out. No one has a right to pass by on the other side. If we are tempted to do so, we should call to mind the unforgettable warning of Martin Niemöller, the German Protestant theologian who lived through the Nazi persecution:

> in Germany they came first for the Communists. And I did not speak up, because I was not a Communist. Then they came for the Jews. And I did not speak up, because I was not a Jew. Then they came for the trade unionists. And I did not speak up because I was not a trade unionist. Then they came for the Catholics. And I did not speak up, because I was a Protestant. Then they came for me. And by that time there was no one left to speak up.

This book, *War or Health*, is in my opinion a good example of speaking out. There have been many physicians and groups of physicians actively speaking out to save human lives endangered by violence. IPPNW, International Physicians for the Prevention of Nuclear War, has even received the Nobel Peace Price because of its activities. However, nuclear war is not the only danger in the world today. The book is an overview of many different consequences of wars and conflicts. It has a strong medical ethos but it is also written for anyone interested in the complicated issues of war and peace. Health is highly valued by everyone and in all parts of the world. Here the health profession shows its expertise in a responsible way, and this knowledge is supplemented by that of the best experts from other disciplines.

This year, in July, when opening a meeting of the Security Council on conflict prevention, I said: 'We must make conflict prevention the cornerstone of collective security in the twenty-first century. That will be not achieved by grand gestures, or by short-term thinking. It requires us to change deeply ingrained attitudes'. I hope this book can help us to change our way of thinking as well as our way of acting.

ACKNOWLEDGEMENT

The text is an edited version of the 35th Ditchley Foundation Lecture, delivered on 26 June 1998, and later printed in *Medicine, Conflict and Survival*, vol. 15: 115–25 (1999). We are grateful to the Ditchley Foundation, to *Medicine, Conflict and Survival* and to the Secretary-General's Office for permission to publish it here.

Address for Correspondence

Executive Office of the Secretary-General, United Nations Plaza, New York, NY

INTRODUCTION

Health and Peace for Mankind

BERNARD LOWN AND EVGENI CHAZOV

We have just crossed the threshold of a new century. Looking back, how was the advent of the 20th century perceived one hundred years ago? A leading medical personality in the English-speaking world, Sir William Osler, reflecting on the 19th century, wrote: 'The century now drawing to a close has seen realization of much that the wise of old longed for, much of which the earnest spirits of the past have dreamt. It has been a century of real progress'. And Victor Hugo waxed lyrical about the promise just over the horizon: 'In the 20th century, war will be dead, royalty will be dead, and dogmas will be dead; but man will live. For all there will be but one country – that country will be the whole earth; for all there will be but one hope – that hope the whole heaven. All hail, then, to that noble 20th century, which shall own our children and which our children shall inherit'.

One hundred years later such noble expectations sound hallucinatory. We, who have just exited the most brutal century of a millennium notorious for barbarism, can only murmur with shame, guilt, despair and even revulsion. Yet we have not profited from the tragic lesson of our ill-fated times. We are bringing with us into the new age the verminous baggage of violence and war. Most shameful is that our belongings include nuclear weapons, the ultimate instruments of genocide, now stockpiled in the arsenals of many nations.

From the outset of the atomic age, the doomsday clock on the mast-head of the *Bulletin of Atomic Scientists* provided a measure of our proximity to nuclear catastrophe. Begun in 1947, the clock's minute hand has moved forward and back like a seismographic needle informing on the quavering instability of our times. The symbolic hand now hovers at nine minutes to midnight, where it has been for nearly a quarter of a century. While an imprecise measure of the nuclear danger, it reflects the sobering reality that both the USA and Russia are still brimming with nuclear overkill, that proliferation is ongoing and that nuclear abolition continues to be a remote dream.

At present Russia has 6000 and the United States around 7500 operational strategic warheads. In late 1997, President Clinton signed Presidential Decision directive 60, which reserves to the United States the right to the first use of nuclear weapons. It furthermore widens latitude for the Pentagon to retaliate against a non-nuclear weapons state that might resort to chemical and biological weapons against the United States or its allies. The Russians, who have previously renounced a first-use nuclear policy, not to be outdone, have now readopted this same malign strategy. In March 1999, on the occasion of the 40th anniversary of Russian nuclear forces, Vladimir Yakovlev, chief of the missile programme, stressed that Russia's economic crisis and new security threats prompted a review of nuclear deterrence. He stated unequivocally: 'Russia, for objective reasons, is forced to lower the threshold for using nuclear weapons, extend the nuclear deterrent to smaller-scale conflicts, and openly warn potential opponents about this'.

One would have hoped that ending the Cold War would be reflected in the nuclear stance of the two powers. In fact, the pact reached by presidents Clinton and Yeltsin in 1994, to stop aiming nuclear missiles at one another, remains unimplemented. Nuclear warheads are still attached to missiles and remain on high alert to be launched on a few minutes' warning. Incomprehensibly, the friendly relations between the two powers have not stopped them from targeting one another. Actually, the American strategic war plan presently includes 3000 targets in Russia, a 20 per cent increase since 1995. The unnerving paradox is that though the mindless ideological confrontation of the Cold War and its bilious rhetoric have been abandoned, dangerous nuclear postures are firmly in place. Moth-eaten, fatuous doctrines are the basis for holding millions of people hostage for their lives. Rationalizations of current nuclear policies are nothing but a charade attempting to explain the inexplicable, defend the indefensible and justify the insane. This moral depravity is a legacy of Hitlerism. From the smouldering embers of the Nazi defeat, the victors plucked a perverse mindset that legitimizes actions not unlike those practised in concentration camps where gassed victims were stoked into crematoria. Nuclear weapons are proverbial portable gas chambers, though of far greater efficiency, and inflict mass murder on a far larger scale. Their acceptance defines and amplifies the moral sickness of our age.

So why are genocidal weapons being maintained? It may relate to another major issue of our times, namely the growing divide between affluent and impoverished. At a time when prodigious fortunes are being amassed, the wealth gap within industrialized nations is ever growing. But the divide is far more marked between the developed nations. As the latest UN Development Report (1999) concludes: 'Global inequalities in income and living standards have reached grotesque proportions'.

The industrialized countries, with 21 per cent of the world's population, account for 85 per cent of the world's gross national product, 85 per cent of world trade and 85 per cent of global energy consumption. The poorest quintile contributes a meagre 1.4 per cent to the global gross national product and engages in only 0.9 per cent of world trade. In an age when information and communication are the coinage of progress and affluence, the world's top ten telecommunication companies control 86 per cent of the US$262 billion world market, and all are in the North. The gap is not only large, but is widening rapidly. In 1997 the richest 20 per cent of the world's inhabitants had 74-fold the annual income of the poorest 20 per cent. This represents more than a doubling of the income gap in less than 40 years.

The consequences of such disparities are expressed tragically in health statistics. Far too many of the world's 6 billion people live in grinding, unremitting and hopeless poverty that strips their human dignity and shunts them to an early grave. On average, 32 per cent of people born in 42 of the world's poorest countries will die before they reach the age of forty.

As the world races ever onwards towards globalization, for those left behind there is a mounting crisis of identity. Homogenization pressured from above spurs tribalism and ethnic wars as people desperately try to maintain some semblance of human individuality and preserve some control over their lives.

The inequities of the present world order are not God-given. They derive from rigidly enforced unequal economic playing fields wherein the products of poor countries are sold cheap, while those of rich countries are sold dear. The result is a world seething with unrest and readily destabilized. Poverty, ill-health, inadequate housing, joblessness and hopelessness promote desperation in the young, who become ready fodder for fanaticism.

Against these growing desperate multitudes, nuclear weapons are intended by the rich to contain the impoverished. The constant drum-beat in northern media of an increasing threat of biological weapons has equated them in the public mind to the genocidal potential of nuclear weapons. Such information, in addition to promoting support for the maintainenance of atomic stockpiles, contributes to legitimizing a lowered threshold for a nuclear response.

The present global order is not immutable. If the forces that shape it appear formidable, far more formidable is the force of informed public opinion when aroused to action. This mighty Gulliver cannot be tied down with Lilliputian ropes. Waiting in the wings are enormous social constellations working to forge a world civil society. The aim is for a global world order organized from below responsive to the basic needs of people. Included on the agenda are health care, adequate housing, literacy and education as well as the outlawing of governmental violence and the assurance of a sustainable environment for generations yet unborn. These objectives are supported by thousands of organizations working for a new world consensus based on international law and intended to constrain the strong while defending the weak. This stirring of the popular will was exhibited recently in Seattle when protesters from many walks of life, headed by American trade unionists, shut down the World Trade Organization conference.

In shaping a new global agenda, the role of the peace movements and particularly that of the International Physicians for the Prevention of Nuclear War (IPPNW) is especially instructive. When IPPNW was launched in 1981, the Soviet Union and the United States were in a headlong rush toward nuclear confrontation. An uninformed public stood by as helpless and frightened spectators. IPPNW's response was to disseminate information on the essential issues and to empower people to act on behalf of their own survival. Without a doubt our greatest contribution was the stimulation of open dialogue with physician counterparts in the two hostile camps and educating millions on the danger and medical consequences of nuclear war. Doctors contributed substantially to ending the Cold War. The world is now a safer place as a result of their engagement.

Those involved in the decisive shaping of IPPNW rapidly learned that ruling establishments are unmoved by high-sounding principles, by historic necessities or by moral imperatives. Politicians respond only sluggishly to the prompting of danger or to the future unfolding of urgent problems. Motion and change are compelled by an aroused public opinion which has been denied legitimate rights.

Another lesson from the Cold War period is that a small group of deeply committed individuals can reach a wide public and thereby make a substantial difference. Herein lies the great value of *War or Health?*, an ambitious and encyclopedic book loaded with a distillation of knowledge on war and how it damages health. This creative text will contribute to keeping the medical profession informed and help promote its involvement in activities consonant with the highest principles of the health profession. Few groups can play as decisive a role in wresting human destiny from the cult-keepers of militarism.

Human history is yet to begin, and for it to do so an abandonment of organized state-sponsored violence in adjudicating differences between nations and peoples is required. The start of a new millennium is a reason for an innovative and determined resolve to this end.

I

HISTORICAL VIEW

Barbed wire
Oliver Whitehead

MEDICINE AGAINST WAR

An Historical Review of the Anti-War Activities of Physicians

CHRISTIAN JENSSEN

With the development of efficient military sanitary services, physicians became aware of the ethical dilemma between the humanization and the prevention of war. The most outstanding of the physicians who stood at the cradle of the peace movement in the second half of the 19th century was the German pathologist Rudolf Virchow. A first International Medical Association against War was founded in 1905 by the French radiologist Joseph Alexandre Rivière, and after the First World War (WWI) the German cardiologist Georg Friedrich Nicolai gave impetus to the development of the scientific basics of pacifism. The experiences of WWI initiated a discussion on the dualistic role of medical professionals with respect to war: the Committee for War Prophylaxis of the Dutch medical association (founded in 1932) drew attention to the psychological causes of warfare, while the Association Internationale des Médecins contre la Guerre (1932) as well as the Medical Peace Campaign (1936) brought into focus the medical consequences of war and the problem of the involvement of medicine and physicians in its preparation and prolongation. Albert Schweitzer and Physicians for Social Responsibility, founded in the US in 1961 together with physician groups in other countries, played a key role in the anti-atomic movement in the years 1954 to 1963 which resulted in the Partial Test Ban Treaty, and in 1980 the American and Soviet cardiologists Bernard Lown and Eugene Chazov founded International Physicians for the Prevention of Nuclear War. This organization, with about 200,000 members from more than 80 countries, was successful in educating the medical profession and the general public on the medical consequences of nuclear war and in uniting physicians across the dividing lines of the Cold War to work for the prevention of what was called the 'final epidemic'.

> Physicians, more than the representatives of other professions, are obliged to be messengers of peace and humanity.
>
> Rudolf Virchow[1]

In the Napoleonic era, war seemed to have become a continuous mass European experience and formed the norm for international relationships. The rapid economic and technological development of the age was accompanied by conflicting interests within and between countries. These erupted in an almost incessant series of wars, which shook Central Europe and North America between 1792 and 1815. The early pacifist utopia of a free confederation of free nations, of a 'golden age' of peaceful relationships between peoples, developed in response to this. The idea that it was possible to avoid or even abolish war was growing. Between 1814 and 1815 the first peace associations were founded in North America, and in 1816 the London Peace Society was formed as the first European peace association.[2]

The official sanitary service that had been developed in the event of war was completely insufficient. Care of the wounded was accomplished mainly by voluntary women's societies. The sanitary losses were high. In the three-day battle of Leipzig (1813) 180,000 soldiers participated, and as many as 100,000 died or were injured. Of the 34,000 casualties that were brought to the town of Leipzig, 11,000 died because of poor sanitary and medical conditions.[3] Protection and treatment of the wounded were regulated through single contracts between the belligerent parties, not a generally binding part of international law.

The first medical statements about war and peace can be found at the beginning of the 19th century. In 1805 the physician to the count of Bückeburg Faust demanded a convention for the protection of wounded men, at the same time condemning war as an 'enemy of mankind'.[4] One can understand the history of medical anti-war activities only in the light of this ethical dilemma between the fundamental rejection of war as a source of avoidable human suffering, on the one hand, and the obligation to fulfil the humanitarian duty of medicine even in times of war on the other. This history is embedded in the eventful developments of the past two centuries with their incessant series of wars. It is necessary to examine the interaction of this history with the peace movement and other critical social developments as well as its part in the contradictory social role of medicine and the medical profession.

Physicians as pioneers of the European peace movement (1848–69)

The four international peace congresses from 1848 to 1851[5] brought the ideas of peace and mutual understanding between nations to a broader public, and stimulated the foundation of peace societies in several countries. Some physicians stood at the cradle of the continental peace movement. Robert Motherby as a delegate of the Free Protestant Church of Königsberg took part in the Frankfurt International Peace Congress in 1850. In the same year he founded the first German peace society in Königsberg, which was already disorganized by the police in May 1851.[6] Another physician from Königsberg, the left-wing liberal Johann Jacoby, was a member of the central committee of the Ligue Internationale de la Paix et de la Liberté.[7] He was one of the few strong opponents of the wars between Prussia and Austria and between the North German confederation and France, and became a nucleus of international contacts of the friends of peace. Two of the founders of social medicine and public health in Germany, Georg Varrentrapp and Gustav-Adolf Spiess, were members of the local organizing committee of the Frankfurt International Peace Congress in 1850. Spiess saw progress in education, arts, science and trade as the source of mutual understanding and peace, but was unsuccessful in bringing local peace committees to life in Germany.[8] Varrentrapp was a member of the executive committee of the Ligue Internationale et Permanente de la Paix[9] and honorary member of the Union de la Paix.[10] As a participant in the International Congress of the International Association for the Advancement of Social Sciences (1865) and of the 7th International Congress of Statistics (1869) he urged that research on the social consequences of armaments be undertaken. On the other hand he did not use his membership of several international scientific societies and his editorship of the German *Quarterly for Public Health* to promote the idea of peace in Germany by specific medical, social and scientific arguments.[11]

The only example of the use of facts on the medical consequences of warfare at this early stage of peace propaganda is a booklet on the epidemics of war based on the journals of the Medical Society of Metz and published as the third volume of the *Bibliotheque de la Paix* by the Ligue Internationale et Permanente de la Paix in 1868. Beginning with the year 586, the author describes the history of the epidemics of Metz as the bitter harvest of the many battles that were fought around this town over the centuries. To accept war as an inevitable evil would be a blasphemy against humankind and the Creator and would mean renouncing any idea of progress. On the contrary, the challenge of war is that it harbours the seeds of progress in all the other fields of human endeavour.[12]

Rudolf Virchow: medicine is a social science

The most outstanding of the physicians who in the second half of the 19th century opposed the increasing militarization of social life was the German pathologist Rudolf Virchow, one of the principal architects of modern scientific medicine, the father of cellular pathology as well as a pioneer of public health, anthropology and ethnology.[13] The crucial event of his life was his participation in the Prussian governmental commission to investigate the causes of the Silesian typhus epidemic in the spring of 1848. Here he established his basic medical, scientific, social and political positions. He now felt a 'whole man': 'my medical creed merges with my political and social creed'.[14] He explained the causes of common diseases as due to the insufficiency of society and living conditions which he considered it necessary to change. During the revolution of 1848 he mounted the barricades for a democratic and peaceful German republic and fought for medicine to become recognized as a social science. Virchow understood the state as a community of equal individuals which has the task of providing welfare and securing healthy conditions for all citizens. Medicine should become a part of political and social life; politics should, in reverse, become 'medicine on a large scale'. Medicine and politics should finally meet 'at a cosmopolitical point of view, that of human, scientific politics, that of anthropology and physiology (in a broader sense)'.[15] Pacifist ideas became an integral part of this concept. As one of the founders of the Deutsche Fortschrittspartei (German Progressive Party) Virchow returned to politics in 1861. As a member of the Prussian Chamber of Deputies he became a famous opponent of Bismarck's politics of 'blood and iron' . On 20 October 1869 he initiated the idea of general disarmament by introducing the following motion in the Prussian Chamber:

Considering that the reduction of the expenses of the North German Confederation is quite necessary to balance the Prussian budget without a further burden on the people and in order to acquire the means for those essential purposes that, according to the acknowledgement of the royal government itself, have been for years neglected... Finally considering that the permanent state of war-readiness in almost all the European countries is not the result of the rivalry between their peoples, but solely the conduct of the cabinets, we request the royal government to use all its influence to reduce the expenses of the military administration of the Northern Confederacy, and to bring about a general disarmament through diplomatic negotiations.[16]

This motion was part of a planned coordinated action by members of parliaments in several European countries initiated by the secretary of the London Peace Society Henry Richard. On 5 November 1869 it was rejected by the Prussian Chamber by 215 votes to 99. Only eight months later the German–French War, which resulted in the death of 182,000 French and German people, began. Virchow now pleaded for a realistic medical history of this war in order that all readers of this history should become 'ardent supporters of the doctrine of peace being necessary for the prosperity of the peoples'.[17] Nevertheless Virchow was a patriot and helped decisively to build up the German sanitary services. Moreover, he was susceptible also to nationalist feelings as can be seen in his publications during the war: 'We have to gain victory in order to have peace in our own house after all'.[18] In later life he remained an eager advocate of a peaceful mission for medicine and science. Physicians should be 'apostles of peace and reconciliation'.[19] Virchow strongly supported the idea of international medical congresses because such meetings would be

one of the means that serve and should serve to bring people closer together and to promote mutual understanding; and in that respect they appear to be a way to peace. By appreciating and experiencing one another, one gets used to opposing each other with arguments and reasons instead of weaponry or insults.[20]

As a president of the 10th International Congress of Medicine in 1890 in Berlin he pleaded for reconciliation with members of the French scientific and medical professions. Over and over he urged international meetings of people and concordant work in the fields of science and communal and social practice in order to 'develop strong guarantees of peace'.[21] In later years, in political speeches and interviews and at meetings, Virchow defended disarmament, international courts of arbitration and a United States of Europe – all objectives he had identified as early as 1848 as pre-conditions for the solution of the social question. He was a member of the German committee of the Interparliamentary Union, founded the German committee of the International Arbitration and Peace Association[22] and supported the foundation of the Deutsche Friedensgesellschaft (German Peace Society) by Alfred Hermann Fried and others in 1891.[23] He fought against racism and national egoism in his scientific and political field of activity. He believed in 'the great pedagogical course of events' inevitably leading Europe to a civilizational 'unity of variety' and putting an end to the arms race and to wars.[24] For him 'Disarm or perish' seemed to be the bleak dilemma of European peoples towards the end of the 19th century. At the end of his life Virchow did not rely on the capabilities of parliaments or governments but on informed public opinion:

Let's not lose a day, not even a hour... Let's organise a horrible war on war. Let's demand disarmament with loud voice! Let's appeal to our people. Let's talk with the language that wins heart and soul. Let's inform the public of its rights and duties. If it wants to, it will learn to guide governments to work in favour of the public needs.[25]

Humanization versus prevention of war: physicians at the crossroads around 1900

Around the turn of the century the peace movement experienced an impetus world-wide. It founded international organizations like the International Peace Bureau in Bern (1892) and the Interparliamentary Union (1889). In 1901, at the 10th International Peace Congress in Glasgow, it published a common programme under the new term 'Pacifism'. The traditional 19th-century ideology of the 'friends of peace', which had been based on ethical, religious and pedagogic arguments, was completed by this effort to emphasize pacifist ideas scientifically and theoretically. Principal examples are the voluminous work of the Russian banker, tycoon and privy councillor Jan Bloch on the technical, economical and political consequences of the *War of the Future* (6 vols, 1898), the books of the Russian sociologist Jakob Nowikow criticizing the social-Darwinist legitimization of war, and the numerous papers and books of the Austrian journalist Alfred Hermann Fried, especially his handbook of the peace movement (1911/1913).[26] The Russian initiative at the 1st Conference of The Hague (1899) and some success in the settlement of international conflicts by arbitration awoke a common hope that the elementary pacifist demands for a court of arbitration and disarmament would forge ahead politically step by step. The increasing internationalization in science and economics, and the breathtaking development of transportation, communication and world trade which accompanied the industrial revolution, led to war and anarchy in international relationships appearing as an anachronisms. The world seemed to have become smaller; man, in contrast, seemed to have grown to be a cosmopolitan.

On the other hand the costs of weaponry and armaments in Europe increased by 83 per cent in 25 years and amounted to 50 per cent of the Continent's total budget; expenditure on social welfare, on the other hand, was equivalent to only 5 per cent of direct military expenses. Simultaneously a revolution in military technology took place. The analysis of Bloch and others suggested that a future war would be a suicide without a victor. The extent of the sanitary losses and war damage caused by the modern weapons was assumed to exceed any previous aftermath of war.[27]

By the mid-19th century, in the great European wars[28] as well as in the North American civil war (1861–65), the discrepancies between the numbers of casualties and sick persons on the one hand and the opportunities for medical help by the sanitary services on the other had grown rapidly. Some private persons, affected by their experience of the horrors of these wars, for example the Swiss banker Henri Dunant, the English nurse Florence Nightingale and physicians like Friedrich von Esmarch and Theodor Billroth, were initiators of public support for the care of victims of war and for the improvement of the sanitary services in the armies. This resulted in the Geneva Convention of 1864 and also in the establishment of functioning sanitary services in the armies of the European nations. The underlying conception of the 'humanization of war' by international law, voluntary help and sanitary services was based on the belief that war is an unavoidable evil. This conviction was questioned only by minorities in society.[29] Esmarch, for example, at the time of the 1st Conference of The Hague wrote that he did not believe in the idea of 'eternal peace' and in the feasibility of the general disarmament of the great powers. That's why he saw it as a duty of governments to develop the sanitary services in the same measure as they developed the weapons destined for the destruction of the enemy. He preferred the establishment of aid societies to the foundation of peace organizations because – in the case of the outbreak of a new war – the old experience would corroborate that the better is the enemy of the good.[30]

In the literature of the second half of the 19th and the beginning of the 20th century there are few critical comments on this principle of the humanization of war. Interestingly they all come from outside the medical profession. Referring to a congress of the Red Cross societies in Vienna, for example, the pioneer of the peace movement in Germany and Austria, Alfred Hermann Fried, wrote in 1897: 'To alleviate the consequences of war means to render war possible and to facilitate its outbreak'.[31]

Another Austrian peace activist of this time, Moritz Adler, responded in 1892 to the proposals of Billroth to reinforce the medical service of the armies by speaking of a 'medical arms race', which would be no better than the 'arms race in weapons'. Each physician irrespective of his political point of view should be a friend of peace and an opponent of war. Adler extended the medical principle of prevention to the problem of war and proposed a corporate anti-war action by the medical profession.[32] This criticism of sanitary ideology was not reflected in medical-ethical discussion until the end of the First World War. The continuity of the physicians' mission and of traditional medical ethics in war was an unquestioned paradigm. Despite the fact that the insufficiency of medical services in times of war had been experienced personally by many physicians, the majority of the medical profession neglected or accepted the contradiction between the medical mission to preserve life and the annihilation of life through war.[33]

Nevertheless physicians played an increasing role within the scientific field of pacifism as well as in the institutions and international associations of the peace movement.[34] The public-health physician Nils August Nilson was the chairman of the Swedish Peace and Arbitration Association and of the Swedish Peace Alliance, and headed the Bureau Internationale et Permanente de la Paix in Bern. In Great Britain the professor of ophthalmology at London University, Sir William Collins, was a member of the British National Peace Council, and the physician Henry Hodgkin was chairman of the National Council against Conscription and founder of the International Fellowship of Reconciliation.

Three Swiss physicians represented very contrasting positions within the peace movement. The surgeon and lecturer at the University of Zurich Henri Monnier was a member of the central committee of the Swiss Peace Society and the Carnegie Foundation. The professor of psychiatry at the University of Zurich August Forel, despite his social Darwinist outlook, was a famous exponent of international pacifism. In 1914 he published a book, *The United States of the World,* and after the First World War he vehemently supported the idea of the League of Nations. In 1905 the Zurich general practitioner Fritz Brupbacher founded the Swiss Antimilitarist League which demanded, in contradiction to the position of official social democracy, the abolition of the armed forces as a means of power of the bourgeois class. Inspired by the pacifist theories of Jan Bloch, in 1905 the Polish public-health physician Józéf Polak founded the Polish Society of the Friends of Peace. He proposed that pacifism should examine not only war but also the conditions for peaceful coexistence of peoples.[35] The Dutch physician Pieter Hendrick Eijkman ran the Bureau préliminaire de la fondation pour l'internationalisme, which had the objective of interlocking all national pacifist organizations. Around 1910 the most influential member of a Russian physicians' group, which saw the 'prevention of war and promotion of the holy work of peace' as 'an occupational duty of the medical profession', was the editor of the medical weekly *Wratsch* (Physician), Professor Vladimir Alexejewitsch Manassein.

In France, around the turn of the century the physiologist and Nobel Prize winner for medicine (1913), Charles Richet, became one of the most famous war opponents. In 1888 Richet followed Frédéric Passy as the president of the Societé Francaise pour l'Arbitrage entre Nations and the permanent council of French peace societies. His books *Les guerres et la paix* (1899) and *Le passé de la guerre et l' avenir de la paix* (1907) became almanacs for the peace movement and were translated into several languages. Richet chaired the editorial board of the peace journal *La paix par le droit*, and in 1895, together with two other leading pacifists, bought the influential newsletter *L'Independence Belge*, which in the following years was a mouthpiece for the ideas of peace and international understanding.[36] He saw the establishment of a strong international central authority and arbitration court, rather than disarmament, as the most important goal of the peace movement.[37]

A first international medical association against war (1905–14)

In 1904 the Parisian Joseph Alexandre Rivière, an internationally renowned radiologist, specialist in physical therapy and pioneer in cancer radiotherapy,[38] called upon his colleagues at a banquet of the Continental Anglo-American Medical Society to support the idea of universal peace.

In early March 1905, in the middle of the Russian-Japanese War, Rivière invited his colleagues to join 'an International Congress of medical men who, in the name of their mission of humanity, would meet to protest against armed conflicts, thus bringing a powerful assistance to the work of peace by arbitration'.[39] Six months later, on 21 September 1905, Rivière and 23 colleagues founded the Association Médicale Internationale contre la Guerre (International Medical Association against War, IMAW). The basic principles of IMAW were the abolition of war and respect for human life.

The medical and scientific approach of Riviére, first developed in his doctoral thesis in 1884, also deeply influenced his philosophical, social and political convictions as well as the programme of IMAW. He believed in recognizing the 'philosophic principle' of physiology, namely the 'subordination of the elements of our organism' under the hierarchy of the nervous system, also in social life. This biologistic approach, which had similarly been represented by Virchow and later by Georg Friedrich Nicolai, led him to see the transportation and communication systems ensuring national and international life as analogous to the nerves, arteries and veins ensuring the psychic and physical life of the human body. The central nervous system as the 'sovereign who rules the whole organism'[41] had to be supplemented at the level of international relations by a central principle regulating interests between social groups and nations. An international tribunal composed of all elements which constitute nations as professional groups and corporations should form an obligatory common opinion and deliver a judgement on international questions. A humanitarian tribunal, elected by the citizens of each country as a world parliament, would have the task of supreme jurisdiction. An international police force would replace national ones. Palliative measures urged by the IMAW were: the 'prohibition of certain murderous arms'; 'control of the manufacture of all instruments of destruction'; 'unification of weights, measures, money, languages and religions, which will ensure universal harmony'; and the education of the people in the ways of peace.[42]

Rivière's *Annales de Physicotherapiè* (circulation 15,000), the *Gazette Médicale de Paris,* the *Lancet,*[43] the *British Medical Journal* and the *Journal of Advanced Therapeutics* reported on the annual meetings and other events of the IMAW. *Le Figaro, Daily Mail, Daily Telegraph* and *Courier Européen* brought the addresses of IMAW to the attention of the Interparliamentary Union, to the 2nd Conference of The Hague (1907), to King Edward VII, to US President Theodore Roosevelt and to the conference of Algeciras.[44] Until the year 1910 the organization grew very rapidly. Strong groups existed in France, Italy, Belgium, Great Britain, Russia, Spain, and Central and North America. In the United States in 1907 an American Medical Association for Aid in the Prevention of War was founded. In 1910 the IMAW could enlist 1089 adherents in 21 European nations, in 18 countries of South and Latin America, in Canada and in the United States of America. At the last of its annual meetings on 21 March 1914, Rivière again urged the ostracism of the declaration of war. On 10 March at the last Peace Banquet in Paris he had predicted the 'annihilation of the belligerents' and the destruction of all achievements 'the peoples have built up in centuries'.[45] The outbreak of WWI sealed the downfall of the IMAW, which would continue to exist formally and in the personal capacity of Rivière until the mid-1930s. As the first international organization of physicians against war, the Association Médicale Internationale contre la Guerre had failed to make a specific professional contribution to the theoretical concepts of the peace movement and to discuss the role of physicians in war. Rivière himself, in his Physicotherapeutical Institute in Paris, helped in the rehabilitation of injured Canadian and French soldiers.[46] In 1927, looking back to this time, he wrote that in times of war it would be the mission of the physician 'to repair the human machine and to restore it for new battles'.[47]

Georg Friedrich Nicolai: 'the biology of war' and scientific pacifism

The collapse of IMAW due to the outbreak of WW I is characteristic of the débâcle of the pacifist utopia in Europe, which was based predominantly on ethical and religious arguments as well as on deterministic ideologies of progress. It was the German physician Georg Friedrich Nicolai who, among others in this situation, tried to give the pacifist idea and movement new, stable foundations.[48] Before WW I, the professor of physiology and internal medicine at the Berlin Charité had gained some scientific stature from his pioneering work in electrocardiography and clinical electrophysiology but had not engaged in political debates. He had been the student or associate of some of the greatest scientists of his era, including Virchow, Ivan Petrovitsch Pavlov, Willem Eint-hooven and Max Planck. Trained in Germany, France, Italy, the Netherlands and in Russia, shaped by international scientific cooperation and having grown up in a demo-cratic family tradition, the outbreak of war seemed to the cosmopolitan Nicolai to be an anachronism. Moreover he was outraged at the uniform chauvinistic justifications of war by German intelligence, which were expressed especially in the 'Manifesto to the Civilised World'.[49] Nevertheless Nicolai felt obliged to volunteer as a civil physician for the military sanitary services. At the same time, together with the physicist Albert Einstein and the astronomer Wilhelm Foerster he demanded, in an 'Appeal to the Europeans', an alliance of European scholars for the conclusion of the war and the foundation of a peaceful Europe.[50] That was the beginning of a series of arguments with his military authority. These came to a provisional end on 20 June 1918 with his spectacular escape to Scandinavia in a stolen military aeroplane. The series of events resumed with his return to Germany on 25 November 1918, continuing with the deprivation of his *venia legendi* (lectureship) by Berlin University, on account of desertion and treason, on 5 March 1920. In 1921 it ended with his resignation and subsequent emigration to South America.

His courage to stand up for his convictions in those years, his steadfastness in the face of his demotion from professor of medicine to mere military male nurse on the basis of his antimilitaristic attitude, but above all his theoretical contribution to the peace movement made him a symbol of German pacifism. With his voluminous book *The Biology of War*,[51] which was translated into eight different languages, he made the first attempt at a comprehensive analysis of the biological, psychological, historical and political roots of the social phenomenon of war as well as of its effects and the way to overcome it. Nicolai's work differs from other peace books because of the unremitting scientific argument with which he tried to invalidate the social Darwinist justification of war. Nicolai found the behavioural roots of human belligerence in tribal, racial and family instincts which led, in interaction with the development of poverty, to patriotism, nationalism and war. His vision of the abolition of war was based on the typical bio-logistic perception of mankind as a homogeneous organism with its individual members being like 'falling leaves of an oaktree, which survives centuries'.[52] Continuing the socio-biological analogy already developed by Virchow, Nicolai saw 'the thousands of secret fibres of technics and traffic, science and a common way of thinking' as the phenotype of the collective organism of humankind.[53] The abolition of war would be a logical consequence of evolution. On the one hand mankind had developed the weapons of destruction, swelling war to its extremes. On the other hand war had no biological value, causing 'negative selection' and wasting energy.[54] That is why the task of pacifism should be to accelerate the evolutionary process of mankind, 'passionately taking side with justice against violence' and by promoting a change of the paradigm from 'force before justice' to 'justice before force'.[55] Nicolai derived his concept of humanity and his vision of a world without war from the natural history of mankind's development and from the evolutionary interest of the '*genus humanum*'. Although his pacifistic arguments were based on scientific and especially on biological-medical arguments, we do not find in his work any analysis of the medical consequences of modern warfare nor a critical discussion of the physicians' role in war.

Medical opposition to militarization and preparation for war: the inter-war period

After WWI other physicians, from very different perspectives, had already reached a more differentiated view of the importance and the responsibility of medical personnel in war than had Nicolai.

In the years between 1914 and 1918 about 38,000 physicians, dentists and pharmacists offered their support to the German sanitary services, and 1325 physicians lost their lives in the battlefields. The army sanitary services as well as the personnel of the Red Cross made their contribution to lowering the mortality of the 10 million war-disabled to 3 per cent (1866: 8.6 per cent, 1870/71: 4.5 per cent). In contrast to earlier wars, with the help of the sanitary services many of the wounded got fit again for active service.[56] The German specialist in internal medicine Wilhelm His proudly wrote: 'Behind the front of weapons there fought a second front, which did not murder, but save, which did not destroy, but secure: the front of physicians'.[57] Referring to an extreme result of this understanding of the medical mission in war, namely the treatment of 'war neurosis' by electro-shock,[58] in 1920 Sigmund Freud criticized this view: the physicians had the role of

> machine guns behind the front line, the role of repulsing the runaways... The physician first of all should be an advocate of the patient, not of another... There cannot be a compromise between the submission to humanity and universal conscription.[59]

The Carnegie Foundation for International Peace published a wide-ranging economic and social history of WW I intended to promote a healthy public opinion in favour of peace. In the book *Public Health in War* the Austrian-Hungarian medical officer Karl Kassowitz discussed the 'dualistic role' of medical men in war. The perception of the medical mission in war as an 'essentially important part of the war machinery' had gained victory over the 'idea of an impartial and helpful humanitarian, not involved in the battle'. Kassowitz saw war as a severe disease that had afflicted mankind for over a thousand years with only short remissions.

> The position of the physician in the presence of this disease must not be doubtful. Also in this case the principle of prevention being more important than healing has to be applied. The prophylaxis of the war pandemic, this insidious mass epidemic, is called pacifism. All measures which are appropriate to stop the exacerbation of this disease must be supported by the physician.[60]

When in the 1930s the danger of a new big war began to grow, there was a renewed international effort to form medical opposition to militarization and preparation for war. In 1930 the Dutch family practitioner J. Roorda and four colleagues urged an international initiative by the Dutch Medical Association in favour of the prevention of war.

This idea resulted in the foundation of the Committee for War Prophylaxis of the Dutch Medical Association.[61] For the first time in history an official professional organization of physicians discussed the relation between medicine and war, and called upon 39 other national medical associations and the Association Professionelle Internationale des Médecins (APIM) to cooperate in the prophylaxis of war. By informing the public on the causes and consequences of war and on the insufficiency of medical help in modern warfare the medical profession could help to transform individual aversion to war into a collective one. The medical associations should restrict their efforts in war prophylaxis to their own professional field and not join the peace societies. Roorda proposed to the APIM five fields of activity: to influence patients to study the problem of war and to become active; appeals by medical associations to governments; encouragement of other professions; medical congresses on war; and the establishment of an international medical movement against war.[62] The committee was most interested in the psychological causes of war. In 1935 it launched the Letter to the Statesmen addressing the problem of war-psychosis, which in a short time was signed by about 350 psychiatrists from 39 nations and was published and commented on in several medical journals in 21 countries. The letter called attention to the 'seeming contradiction between the conscious individual aversion to war and the collective preparedness to wage war' and to the difference between the popular image of war and its reality.[63] Although some groups of physicians, for example in Great Britain, Switzerland, Sweden and Hungary, supported this initiative, the Committee for War Prophylaxis was not successful in organizing a joint peace campaign amongst the various national medical organizations.

Whereas the Dutch committee drew attention in particular to the psychology of war two other international medical efforts at this time brought into focus the medical consequences of war as well as the problem of the involvement of medicine and medical persons in the preparation for and the prolongation of war. In 1932 the German specialist in internal medicine Felix Boenheim issued an 'Appeal to the World's Physicians' to unite in the work against the impending war and to support the initiative of Henri Barbusse for an international anti-war convention.[64] Hundreds of doctors from at least 14 countries signed the appeal, among them Sigmund Freud, Carl Gustav Jung, Fritz Brupbacher and the famous French obstetrician Jean Dalsace. In 1932 Boenheim published several articles in newsletters and journals criticizing the rise in military expenditures, warning against the risk of war and disillusioning people on the efficacy of medical help and civil defence in the case of chemical and aerial warfare.[65] At the World Congress against War and Fascism in August 1932 in Amsterdam[66] the participating physicians in two special workshops discussed the medical consequences of war, the refusal of physicians to take part in preparations for war, chemical war in particular, and the transfer of resources from the military to health and social welfare systems. They founded the Association Internationale des Médecins contre la Guerre (International Physicians Association against War) with 11 national groups in Europe. Very active national sections existed in Germany, France and Austria. The 268 members of the international association came from 45 nations, among them Bernard Zondek, Erwin Ackerknecht, Albert Döderlein, Friedrich Wolf, Jean Dalsace and Julius Tandler. But the victory of National Socialism in Germany destroyed the organization, which had had its centre in Berlin.[67]

After the meeting in Amsterdam, which had some communist bias, a politically broader-based second large International Peace Congress took place in September 1936 in Brussels. It was initiated by Lord Robert Cecil, the president of the International Peace Campaign (IPC) and the International Federation of League of Nations Societies. Lord Cecil had been the initiator of the National Peace Ballot (1934), where more than 11 million British people answered five questions related to security policy. More than 90 per cent spoke out in favour of the League of Nations, disarmament and nationalization of the armaments industry, but only 1 out of 660 supported a radical pacifistic point of view.[68] Lord Cecil invited several professional groups to take part in the congress. Because several attempts to form a Committee for War Prophylaxis of the British Medical Association (BMA) had failed,[69] in August 1936 a group of British physicians in London founded the Medical Peace Campaign (MPC), presided over by the general surgeon Cecile Booysen. This group found support from renowned medical scientists, for example the Regius Professor of Physic at Cambridge University and Medical Research Council member John Alfred Ryle, who after the death of Cecile Booysen was elected president of MPC, the professor of anatomy Sir Wilfrid Edward Le Gros Clark, and the professor of surgery at the University of Leeds, Lord Berkeley George Moynihan.[70] In a letter of support to Cecile Booysen, which was published in the second bulletin of the MPC in December 1936, Ryle described the medical profession as 'the only profession pledged by its own creed as well as by international agreement to pacifism in action'.[71] Together with colleagues from the Dutch Committee for War Prophylaxis the Medical Peace Campaign organized a special physicians' conference at the Brussels Peace Congress, presided over by Professor E. Gorter, a paediatrician from Leyden. It was attended by physicians and psychologists from Australia, Belgium, Czechoslovakia, Finland, France, Great Britain and the Netherlands.[72] They decided to found an International Medical Association for the Prevention of War, and set up commissions to study the causes of war as a social phenomenon, the best ways to win public opinion to the cause of peace, and the medical consequences of war. At the physicians' meeting, papers were presented and discussed on the rise of the mortality from tuberculosis as a consequence of WWI, on the interrelation of war and epidemics and on the disrespect of the Red Cross in the Abyssinian War (1935–36). In a statement issued after the congress the British section of the MPC commented:

> We view the work of preserving peace as a prophylactic task of the first order rather than as an intrusion into the sphere of politics; or, if we objected that war is a political event, then we say that the whole field of social medicine and of the public health services has become an integral part of politics. The profession is already committed to politics, in the sense that its functions are no longer merely curative but in a high degree preventive; and it is only a logical extension of these functions to make them embrace the task of preventing the miserable consequences of war by forestalling the outbreak of the war itself.[73]

The discussions of the medical commission at the Brussels Peace Congress and its six resolutions showed a distinct contradiction between the psychologically-oriented concept of the Dutch Committee for War Prophylaxis and some of its supporters from Great Britain and other countries, on the one hand, and the aim of the majority of the members of the MPC to show the consequences of war and to take into account a refusal of physicians to take part in war preparations on the other.[74] The International

Peace Campaign at the Brussels Congress founded two scientific committees to study the causes and consequences of war and the role of science in its preparation or prevention.

Stimulated by the correspondence of Siegmund Freud and Albert Einstein on the causes of war and hopes for peace (*Why War?*),[75] the psychological commission of the IPC, chaired by John Rickman of the London Hospital of Psychoanalysis, was sure 'that the precipitating causes of war are mainly psychological'. It outlined several subjects of psychological research on the causes of war and its prevention.[76] The result of this research was the book *Medical Opinions on War*, which was published in 1939 on behalf of the Committee for War Prophylaxis of the Dutch Medical Association. Nine of the 15 authors of the book were British. The book was a collection of ideas about how to prevent war from very different psychological viewpoints based, for example on the concepts of individual psychology as well as those of family and social psychology.[77] Public discussion on the psychological aspects of peace and war was also stimulated by several activities of the National Council for Mental Hygiene of Great Britain,[78] through radio addresses, letters to newspapers and the essays of several psychologists and psychiatrists.[79]

The Medical Peace Campaign concentrated on the problems of air-raid precautions and chemical warfare.[80] Starting in the summer of 1936 the British government in co-operation, for example, with the British Medical Association was active in training medical professionals for the event of aerial and chemical warfare. In this situation the MPC, referring for example to the scientific analysis made by John Desmond Bernal and the Cambridge Scientists' Anti-War Group,[81] initiated a letter-campaign in the *Lancet* and in the *British Medical Journal* to draw the attention of the profession and the broader public to the insufficiency and the ambivalence of such war preparations.[82] The MPC, together with the Cambridge group, criticized very seriously the governmental plans for air-raid precaution and civil defence and rejected the National Emergency Inquiry of the Committee for Imperial Defence as an attempt to turn physicians into helpless cogs in the war machine.[83] At the Annual Representative Meeting of the British Medical Association in Oxford in July 1936 and again at the Annual Representative Meeting in Belfast in July 1937, a member of the MPC, A.T. Jones, proposed taking the initiative for the prohibition of chemical weapons. A modified version of this resolution was adopted.[84] The most important result of the work of the MPC was the book *The Doctors' View of War*, published in 1938 but still well worth reading today.[85] It describes the 'diseases of war' and examines critically the thesis of social Darwinism that war could be 'nature's pruning hook'. Based on an analysis of the role of medical men on the battlefields and in civil defence, the authors finally discuss political attitudes to war prophylaxis. Most impressive is the foreword, written by the president of the MPC, J. A. Ryle, outlining a vision of the physician refusing to accept his accustomed role in war.[86]

Of course, at this time this was only a dream. In 1939 the MPC had no more than 200–300 members. At its second general assembly on 22 February 1939, Ryle stated that the situation was now too close to war for the quiet development of an anti-war policy. For that reason the campaign was devoting itself rather to preparedness in a medical sense.[87] A last appeal by the MPC in May 1939 to colleagues around the world to make war impossible by their joint action[88] was doomed to failure. The great outcry of the physicians of the world against the impending Second World War did not occur. Sixty million people did not survive the battles and bombings of the years 1939–45.

New challenge: doctors and the bomb

When the Korean War looked like developing into a third world war, a group of seven British physicians, among them members of the Medical Peace Campaign of the 1930s, published a letter in the *Lancet*. It outlined the medical consequences of WW II, warned of the horrors of a new war and discussed the consequences of the arms race for public health and social welfare. The group appealed to their medical colleagues to join in a common effort to stop the preparations for war.[89] Several letters of reply and a leading article 'Prospect of War' were published in the *Lancet*, most of them supportive.[90] As a result of this public discussion, on 16 March 1951 130 doctors joined in a first meeting and founded the Medical Association for the Prevention of War (MAPW). By the middle of that year, MAPW had 230 members and one year later 370, with groups in London, Birmingham and Oxford. Three working parties were set up to discuss the misuse of science, for example in the development of biological weapons, to study the psychology of war and to promote international links between physicians of several countries. There were contacts with several doctors and medical groups in the USA, the Netherlands, Denmark, Belgium, France, the Soviet Union, Italy, India, Poland and Hungary.[91] In 1952 in Denmark the Danish Physicians' Union against War was founded with about 200–300 members and held some well attended meetings.[92] In 1953, it was again Felix Boenheim who, in the then-German Democratic Republic (East Germany), assembled doctors in the Peace Community of Physicians. At conferences university committees informed colleagues and the public on the medical consequences of the Second World War and especially on the effects of the atomic bombing of Hiroshima and Nagasaki.[93] In May 1953 delegates of these groups, together with about 200 physicians from 32 nations, met in Vienna at the World Congress of Physicians, focusing their deliberations on actual living conditions. They discussed the consequences of the Second World War on public health in these terms, as well as the physicians' responsibility in face of the danger of a new war. Among the participants were several doctors who had been active against war two decades earlier, for example Felix Boenheim, chairman of the physicians' conference at the Amsterdam Congress against War and Fascism in 1932, and Professor Gorter, who was the president of the Physicians Commission of the international convention of the IPC in Brussels in 1936.[94]

In 1954 nuclear weapons testing became an object of major public concern. On March 1 the Bravo test of a 15mt hydrogen bomb at the Bikini Atoll exposed the crew of the Japanese fish trawler *Lucky Dragon* and inhabitants of the Marshall Islands to nuclear fallout. The suffering of the 23 Japanese fishermen and the death of one of them aroused an international storm of protest.

Sir Alexander Haddow, director of the Chester Beatty Cancer Research Institute and later chairman of MAPW, appealed in a letter to *The Times* for the intervention of scientists against the nuclear arms race and proposed a world council of natural scientists and physicians on the subject of nuclear weapons.[95] In April 1954, MAPW organized an informal session on the consequences of the explosions of thermonuclear weapons which was attended by about 700 people. It published the booklets *Do you Know... ?* and *Facts on Fall Out*, and a list of 27 studies on the medical consequences of nuclear fallout.[96]

As a reaction to governmental plans for the deployment of atomic weapons and the establishment of an army in 1956 in the Federal Republic of Germany (West Germany) the obstetrician Bodo Manstein founded the multiprofessional Fighting Union Against Atomic Damage with about 2000 members of the medical profession. One year later Fritz Katz initiated the Physicians Association for the Outlawing of Atomic War with about 800 members. These groups played an important role in the broad public movement Kampf dem Atomtod (Fight Against Atomic Death). Physicians informed their patients, through leaflets and posters, on the medical effects of atomic weapons and test explosions.[97] The well-known medical journals *Medizinische Klinik* and *Medizinische Welt* ran articles on the physics and technology of atomic bombs, the biological effects of radiation, radiation injuries and radiation protection, and critically discussed the atomic escalation of politics.[98] In March 1958, 936 physicians from Hamburg signed an appeal to stop atomic testing and to stop the deployment of atomic weapons on German soil.[99] In 1957 the general session of the German physicians (Deutscher Ärztetag) founded a scientific commission to study the effects of radiation pollution. One year later, in June 1958, the general session of the German physicians discussed the report of its atomic commission in great depth and issued a resolution condemning the misuse of atomic energy, urging the proscription of all weapons of mass destruction and calling for an international convention to stop nuclear testing. The general assembly as well as the medical journals did not, on the other hand, discuss the misuse of medicine and medical persons in the medical preparations for an atomic war.[100]

These efforts by physicians in several countries were strongly influenced by: the famous Göttinger Manifest of 18 German atomic scientists issued on 12 April 1957 against participation in the production, testing or use of atomic weapons; the appeal of Linus Pauling for an international convention to stop atomic testing, which by 13 January 1958 was signed by 9235 scientists, and not least by the voice of the famous jungle doctor from Lambaréné, Albert Schweitzer (1875–1965). The creator of the ethics of 'reverence for life' and bearer of the Nobel Peace Prize (1952, awarded in 1953) was, until the mid-1950s, an idealistic, silent pioneer of peace between people, humankind and nature, trusting in the capability of the actors of history to renew their ethical way of thinking. Responding to Norman Cousins, the editor of the *Saturday Review*, in January 1957 Schweitzer still resisted all requests, for example from Bertrand Russell and UN secretary-general Dag Hammarskjöld, to take a public stand on the question of atomic weapons. But Cousins insisted and persuaded Schweitzer that he was one of the very few individuals whose voice would be widely heard.[100] On 23 April 1957 millions of people world-wide listened to Schweitzer's message, which was broadcast by the radio station of Oslo, the town of the Nobel Peace Prize, as well as by more than 150 other stations. Basing his stand on sober medical and scientific arguments, the physician Schweitzer warned against the terrible consequences of radioactivity caused by the atomic tests for the health of present and future generations. He called eloquently for public opinion in all nations, East and West, to inspire and accept an agreement to stop atomic testing:

> A public opinion of this kind stands in no need of plebiscites or of the forming of committees to express itself. It works through just being there. The end of further experiments with atom bombs would be like the early sunrays of hope which suffering humanity is longing for.

This 'Declaration of Conscience'[102] was met by a lively response world-wide. For the first time in the United States of America the calming propaganda of the Atomic Energy Commission was questioned with moral and scientific authority. Together with Linus Pauling and Bertrand Russell, Schweitzer felt like 'a ringleader of a conspiracy' in the anti-atomic movement.[103] Several politicians, for example US presidential candidate Adlai Stevenson and senator Richard Neuenberger, and peace groups, for example the National Committee for a Sane Nuclear Policy (SANE), took up the arguments of Schweitzer,[104] which were detailed in three further broadcast appeals, 'Peace and Atomic War', on Radio Oslo and 90 other stations on 28, 29 and 30 April 1958. In the middle of 1958, the deadlock in the negotiations to stop nuclear testing seemed to have been overcome. A UN scientific commission came to the conclusion that an agreement to stop nuclear testing could be verified effectively. The Soviet Union and later on the US and Great Britain observed a test moratorium until at the end of 1959, after 137 meetings, the Geneva negotiations got bogged down. The political events of the summer of 1961 – the Berlin Wall, new atmospheric testing by the Soviet Union and new underground testing by the US – again alarmed the now 86-year-old Schweitzer. Again he signed appeals. After the start of large atmospheric tests by the United States in April 1962 he wrote in a very personal and urgent way to President John F. Kennedy informing him of the possible consequences of exposure to radioactivity.[105] At the crucial point of the Cuban missile crisis in November 1962, he again wrote to Kennedy urging him to renounce the use of atomic weapons.[106]

The words and the personal example of Schweitzer were like matches igniting blazes of public and medical concern. In Great Britain in 1961 Professor Lionel Penrose and his wife Margaret reactivated MAPW, which in the years between 1961 and 1965 held conferences on the Pathogenesis of War and on Physicians and the Prevention of War at several universities in Great Britain. In the US the cardiologist Bernard Lown and several colleagues from the Harvard Medical School founded Physicians for Social Responsibility (PSR) at the end of 1961:

> to provide for the medical community and the general public the scientific data on which political decisions must in general be based; to alert physicians to the dangerous implications of the arms race; to involve physicians in serious exploration of peaceful alternatives; and to develop support for programmes promoting effective disarmament and peace.[107]

A project group of PSR studied the effects of a limited thermonuclear attack on Massachusetts, the physicians' role in the post-attack period and the efficacy of the administration's shelter programme. The results of this research were published in the *New England Journal of Medicine* in May 1962[108] and were presented before a sub-committee of the House Armed Services Committee in June 1963.[109] An analysis of the St Louis Committee for Nuclear Information (CNI) on the accumulation of strontium 90 in children's deciduous teeth[110] and other scientific evidence on the exposure to radioactive isotopes by nuclear testing gained much public interest. In the nuclear test-ban treaty hearings of the Senate Foreign Relations Committee on 27 August 1963, PSR presented an estimation of the health hazards of continued atmospheric testing.[111] They wrote to every senator urging ratification of the Partial Test Ban Treaty (PTB). In September 1963, prominent members of PSR launched advertisements in the *Washington*

Post and in newsletters expressing their deep concern about the dangers to children of radiation from continuing tests and asking 'all parents, all citizens, to express their feelings to their senators'.[112]

In the mid-1960s psychiatrists and psychologists in the United States also investigated the psychological roots of war, the psychological fallout of nuclear testing as well as the responses of children and adults to the nuclear arms race and the government's nuclear shelter programmes.[113]

One can only speculate about the influence that Albert Schweitzer, the PSR and the other activities of physicians had on the political processes leading to the PTB of 5 August 1963, and its ratification. But after the successful negotiations Kennedy released Schweitzer's letter of congratulation to the world press. Linus Pauling spoke of the 'significant influence' of Schweitzer's messages to Kennedy.[114] Cousins reported that on the occasion of a banquet after the signing of the PTB many governmental and congressional officials had spoken of Schweitzer's role as having been of decisive importance.[115] No doubt partly as a result of the activities of the PSR, the concern about radioactive fallout became the most important factor accounting for the massive public support of the PTB in the US. The majority of the senators' questions at the ratification hearings referred to the health hazards of nuclear fallout.[116]

International physicians for the prevention of nuclear war

In 1963, Albert Schweitzer saw the PTB as 'a rosy dawn', knowing that 'the sun can only rise, if all nuclear explosions including the underground ones cease'.[117] But two decades later, and 40 years since peoples and physicians were first confronted with the medical consequences of nuclear weapons, the world was still waiting for this sunrise. The superpowers had stored more than 50,000 strategic and tactical nuclear weapons with a destructive power of 15 billion tons of TNT, more than four tons of TNT for every person on earth. The nations' resources were worn out by the Cold War, and an uncontrolled arms race with a steady risk of intended and unintended nuclear destruction was maintained. In 1978, the Australian paediatrician Helen Caldicott together with several young American doctors in Boston refounded Physicians for Social Responsibility (PSR). Later on Caldicott and others were successful in activating physicians not only in the USA but also in several European countries. They organized symposia on the consequences of nuclear explosions on towns where the symposia were held (The Final Epidemic).[118] In the USA, the PSR grew very rapidly and at the beginning of the 1980s already had about 20,000 members. In the United Kingdom the Medical Campaign against Nuclear Weapons (MCANW) was founded and the MAPW reactivated. In the Federal Republic of Germany a new movement, Physicians' Initiative against Atomic Energy, very crucially discussed government plans for civil defence and physicians' involvement in the medical preparation for nuclear war.[119] In an advertisement 'Danger: nuclear war' in the *New York Times* on 3 March 1980, the PSR appealed to the leaders of the USSR and the USA to prohibit the use of nuclear weapons. Moreover they invited their colleagues in both countries to meet and to discuss the consequences of thermonuclear war from the viewpoint of medicine.

Following an exchange of letters between the two cardiologists Bernard Lown and Evgeni Chazov, six American and Soviet physicians met in Geneva in December 1980 and founded International Physicians for the Prevention of Nuclear War (IPPNW) as a non-political federation of national physicians' organizations dedicated to evaluation of the medical implications of nuclear weapons and nuclear warfare, and to the education of the medical profession, the general public and political leaders on this subject.[120] At the first congress of IPPNW in March 1981, which was attended by 72 physicians from 12 countries, Lown said:

> We are here because the world is moving inexorably toward the use of nuclear weapons. The atomic age and space flight have crystallised as never before the enormous power of science and technology. These developments have also brought humankind to a bifurcation – one road of unlimited opportunity for improving the quality of life, the other of unmitigated misery, devastation and death. In the throes of decision is the question whether humankind has a future.[121]

Under the co-presidency of Lown and Chazov the IPPNW discussed the nuclear issue primarily as a public health issue of the greatest importance and avoided the linkage with the ideological and political problems that had embittered relations between the confronting political blocs. So the organization was able to attract the interest and support of doctors from East and West and from various political viewpoints, as well as the attention of the broad public. These efforts to educate colleagues and the public on the medical consequences of nuclear war united physicians across the dividing lines of the Cold War to work for the prevention of 'the final epidemic'.

Important national and international medical professional organizations (for example the American Medical Association, the British Medical Association and the medical associations of other countries as well as several medical science societies) took over the medical concerns of the IPPNW. The World Health Organization (WHO) addressed 'the role of physicians and other health workers in the preservation and promotion of peace as the most significant factor for the attainment of health for all'. A working group of WHO investigated the 'effects of nuclear war on health and health services' and came to the conclusion that 'the only approach to the treatment of health effects of nuclear warfare is primary prevention, that is, the prevention of nuclear war'.[122]

At the yearly international congresses, national congresses and symposia, in medical curricula and in prestigious medical journals, the scientific facts on the medical implications of nuclear war and the nuclear arms race, including the psychological impact of living with the nuclear threat and the public health consequences of the arms race to the world's health, were studied and became a matter of international concern. Because the message had been heard, all political concepts based on the perceptions of keeping nuclear war limited and of being able to win or prevail in a nuclear conflict were rendered incredible. In 1985 the IPPNW, which now represented 135,000 physicians in 41 national affiliates, was awarded the Nobel Peace Prize for 'considerable service to mankind by spreading authoritative information and in creating an awareness of the catastrophic consequences of atomic warfare'.[123]

But the IPPNW did not restrict itself to the mere description of the fatal prognosis of a continued nuclear arms race. In 1984, it offered a 'medical prescription' calling for a comprehensive moratorium on all nuclear explosions as a simple and readily verifiable first step in slowing and reversing the arms race. An International Commission to Investigate the Health and Environmental Consequences of Nuclear Weapons Testing and Production was set up, and the Ceasefire Campaign coordinated the protests against all nuclear tests. Projects like SatelLife, the East–West Physicians Campaign, the Concert Tour for Peace and the international congresses of the IPPNW demonstrated the opportunities of a free-flowing dialogue of physicians from the East, West and South as well as the sound alternatives to the Cold War and arms race, and made a significant contribution to a changed political climate world-wide. As the Cold War drew to its end in 1989, the IPPNW had about 200,000 members in more than 80 countries and was able to broaden its agenda. At the beginning of the new millennium, it is still advocating a world without nuclear weapons (Abolition 2000), not only because they are weapons of mass destruction but also because they are symptoms of a world order based on insecurity, violence, war, inequity, ruinous exploitation of natural resources and environmental pollution. In the tradition of Rudolf Virchow, IPPNW, together with the various medical associations against war and Physicians for Social Responsibility, currently calls upon physicians to promote and protect health at a social level and to accept their medical responsibility for the survival of life on earth and for peace through health.[124]

ACKNOWLEDGEMENTS

The author wishes to thank Dr Kerstin Werner and Mrs Noëlle Gielen for their assistance in translation of the text and Drs Thomas M. Ruprecht and Patricia Craig for fruitful cooperation in researching the history of the anti-war activities of physicians.

REFERENCES AND NOTES

1. Opening remarks at the 11th International congress of Medicine, Rome 1894, quoted from *Vossische Zeitung*, 31 March 1894.
2. See van der Linden, Wilhelm Hubertus (1987), *The International Peace Movement 1815–1874*, Amsterdam; Hetzel, Hermann (1891), *Die Humanisirung des Krieges in den letzten hundert Jahren, 1789–1889*, Frankfurt; and Ruprecht, Thomas M. and Christian Jenssen (eds) (1991), *Äskulap oder Mars? Ärtze gegen den Krieg*, Bremen.
3. von Esmarch, Friedrich (1899), *Ueber den Kampf der Humanität gegen die Schrecken des Kriege*, Kiel-Stuttgart.
4. See Hetzel, n. 2 above.
5. 1848 in Brussels, 1849 in Paris, 1850 in Frankfurt, 1851 in London. The main subjects were: arbitration, disarmament, congress of nations, a United States of Europe and an international code (see van der Linden, n. 2 above).
6. See van der Linden, n. 2 above.
7. Founded in 1867 in Geneva at an international peace congress which was attended by about 6000 people. Well-known members of this left-wing, democratic organization were Victor Hugo, Giuseppe Garibaldi and Mikhail Bakunin (see van der Linden, n. 2 above).
8. See van der Linden; and Ruprecht and Jenssen, n. 2 above.
9. Founded on 30 May 1867 at the World Exhibition in Paris on the initiative of Frédéric Passy (Nobel Peace Prize 1901) by advocates of free trade, clergymen and industrialists.

10. One of the vice-presidents of this more conservative league was the German chemist Justus von Liebig. A member of the Swiss committee of the league was Gustave Moynier, the first president of the International Committee of the Red Cross societies (see van der Linden, n. 2 above), founded in 1869 by Felix Santallier in Le Havre.

11. See van der Linden, n. 2 above; and Bleker, Johanna, and Heinz-Peter Schmiedebach (eds) (1987), *Medizin und Krieg. Vom Dilemma der Heilberufe 1865–1985*, Frankfurt/M.

12. Guilhaumon, M.F. (1868), *La guerre et les epidemies d'après les memoires de la société des sciences medicales de Metz*, Paris: Bibliotheque de la Paix, Livr. 3. Vol 1.

13. See Ruprecht and Jenssen, n. 2 above.

14. Ibid.

15. Eisenberg, L. (1986), *Medicine and War* 2, 243–50; Eisenberg, L. (1984), *American Journal of Medicine*, 524–32; Virchow, R. (1848) *Die Medizinische Reform* 1, Nos 5, 21; Virchow, R. (1849) *Die Einheitsbestrebungen in der wissenschaftlichen Medicin*, Berlin.

16. Ruprecht and Jenssen, n. 2 above; Eisenberg (1984), n. 15, and Jenssen, C. (1989), *Zeitschrift für klinische Medizin*, 44, 2141–4.

17. Virchow, R. (1879), *Gesammelte Abhandlungen auf dem Gebiete der öffentlichen Medicin und der Seuchenlehre* (2 vols), Berlin (Engl: *Collected Essays on Public Health and Epidemiology*, 2 vols, ed. L.J. Rather, Canton MA 1985).

18. See n. 17 above; Ruprecht and Jenssen, n. 2 above; and n. 11.

19. Sudhoff, Karl (1922), *Rudolf Virchow und die Deutschen Naturforscherversammlungen*, Leipzig.

20. Virchow, R. (1890), *Archiv für Pathologie, Anatomie und klinische Medicin*, 120: 1–6.

21. Virchow, R. (1891/1892), *Die Nation* 10: 760–61.

22. Founded in 1880 by Hodgson Pratt. Pratt urged Virchow to accept the chairmanship of the German committee (letter from Pratt to Virchow, 19 February 1886; Virchow archives in Berlin, Germany).

23. See Ruprecht and Jenssen, n. 2 above; and Chickering, Roger (1975), *Imperial Germany and a World Without War. The peace movement and German society, 1892–1914*, Princeton.

24. 'Etats-Unis d'Europe, Une Interview avec le Professeur Virchow', *Le Matin* (Paris), 11 November 1895: 1–2.

25. See Ruprecht and Jenssen, n. 2 above; and Jenssen, C. and Thomas Ruprecht (1990), *Medizinhistorisches Journal* 25: 252–67.

26. See Chickering, n. 23 above; and Fried, Alfred Hermann (1911/1913) *Handbuch der Friedensbewegung* (2 vols), Berlin-Leipzig .

27. See Fried, n. 26 above.

28. 1859 France–Austria; 1854–56 Crimean War England/France–Russia; 1866 Prussia–Austria; 1870–71 Germany–France.

29. See Hetzel, n. 2 above; and n. 11.

30. See n. 3 above.

31. Fried, Alfred Hermann (1901), *Unter der weissen Fahne! Aus der Mappe eines Friedensjournalisten. Gesammelte Artikel und Aufsätze von Alfred Hermann Fried*, Berlin.

32. Billroth, discussing the horrible medical effects of new types of guns, for example, at the Assembly of Austrian Physicians in 1890 and in 1891 in a speech to the Austrian-Hungary Parliamentary Delegations, proposed that the sanitary services should have the same number as the fighting troops. Adler answered in the role of a physician (Adler, Moritz (1892) *Offenes Sendenschreiben an PT Herrn Professor Theodor Billroth von Moritz Adler. Mit einem Vorwort von Bertha von Suttner,* Berlin-Leipzig).

33. See n. 11 above.

34. See Ruprecht and Jenssen, n. 2 above; and Fried, n. 26.

35. See Ruprecht and Jenssen, n. 2 above.

36. See Chickering, n. 23 above.

37. See Ruprecht and Jenssen, n. 2 above.

38. See Ruprecht and Jenssen, n. 2 above; and Lewer, N. and P. van den Dungen. (1990), *Medicine and War* 6: 94–104.

39. Rivière, Joseph Alexandre (1937), *Un demi-siecle de physicotherapie, Organisation mondiale de la paix. Souvenirs documentaires*, Tome III. Paris.

40. Ibid.

41. Ibid.
42. Ibid.
43. See, for example, *Lancet* i (1905): 945; *Lancet* ii (1905): 1946-47; *Lancet* i (1906): 617 and 985; *Lancet* i (1908): 953; *Lancet* ii (1908): 1338; *Lancet* ii (1910): 1107; *Lancet* i (1911): 357.
44. See n. 39 above.
45. Rivière, Joseph Alexandre (1934), *Un demi-siècle de physicotherapie, ses conceptions – son oeuvre*, Tome IV,. Paris.
46. See Ruprecht and Jenssen, n. 2 above; and Lewer and van den Dungen, n. 38.
47. See n. 39 above.
48. See Ruprecht and Jenssen, n. 2 above; and n. 11.
49. 'Aufruf an die Kulturwelt', an address of solidarity to the German government that was signed by the most famous German scientists, writers and artists, among them physicians and medical scientists like Emil von Behring, Paul Ehrlich, Albert Neisser and Wilhelm von Waldeyer-Hartz; quoted in Nicolai, Georg Friedrich (1919), *Die Biologie des Krieges. Betrachtungen eines Deutschen Naturforschers den Deutschen zur Besinnung* (erste originalausgabe), Zürich (Engl: *The Biology of War* London, 1919) and Ruprecht and Jenssen, n. 2 above.
50. See Nicolai, n. 49 above, and Nicolai, Georg Friedrich (1922), *Aufruf an die Europäer. Gesammelte Aufsätze zum Wiederaufbau Europas. Herausgegeben und eingeleitet von Dr Hans Wehberg*, Leipzig–Wien-Zürich.
51. See Nicolai, n. 49 above.
52. Ibid.
53. See Nicolai (1922), n. 50 above.
54. See Nicolai, n. 49 above.
55. Speech 'Pazifismus als Weltanschaung' and resolution 'Pazifistisches Manifest' at the general assembly of the Deutsche Friedensgesellschaft (German Peace Society), Kassel 1919, quoted in Nicolai (1922) n. 50 above.
56. See n. 11 above and Wilhelm His (1931), *Die Front der Ärzte*, Bielefeld-Leipzig.
57. His, ibid.
58. The Austrian psychiatrist Julius Wagner von Jauregg, Nobel laureate 1927, was a member of a commission of medical scientists at the front line of Isonzo. He and other psychiatrists tried to treat soldiers with psychiatric symptoms caused by their horrible experiences at the battlefield with electroshocks. After the war there were instituted legal proceedings against Wagner von Jauregg because of unmedical methods of treatment. On 14 October 1920, Freud gave evidence to the Austrian Parliamentary Commission for the Investigation of Derelictions of Military Duties (see Riedesser, Peter and Axel Verderber (1985), *Aufrüstung der Seelen. Militärpsychiatrie und Militärpsychologie in Deutschland und Amerika*, Freiburg/Br.; and n. 11 above; and Ruprecht and Jenssen, n. 2 above.
59. The text of the expert opinion of Freud (23 February 1920) and the testimony of Freud at the hearing of the parliamentary commission were published by R. Gicklhorn: *Psyche* XXVI (1972): 939–51 (quotation from the oral testimony, p. 947); the English translation of the expert opinion only was published in the *International Journal of Psychoanalysis* 27 (1956): 16–18.
60. Pirquet, Clemens (ed.) (1926) *Volksgesundheit im Krieg* (2 vols), Wien, New Havre.
61. Ruprecht and Jenssen, n. 2 above.
62. Roorda, J. *et al.* (1930), *Nederlandse Tijdschrift voor Geneeskunde* 74: 4689–99; *PHJW* (1932) 'Drooglever Fortuijn', *Nederlandse Tijdschrift voor Geneeskunde* 76: 758–60; 'A Medical Movement against War', *British Medical Journal* (1933) (Suppl): 250–1.
63. Roorda, J. (1935), *Ned Tijdschr Geneesk.* 79: 4818–28; 'The War Mentality: an address to statesmen', *Lancet* ii (1935): 907; 'Psychiatrists Warn against Insanity of War', *Mental Hygiene*, 20 (1936): 167–9.
64. The Amsterdam Congress (27–29 August 1932) was initiated by Romain Rolland and Henri Barbusse, supported for example by Albert Einstein, Heinrich Mann, Bertrand Russell, Paul Langevin, Martin Andersen-Nexö, Maxim Gorki and Upton Sinclair. More than 4000 people from 35 nations participated (see Ruprecht and Jenssen, n. 2 above).
65. Ruprecht and Jenssen, n. 2 above.
66. See n. 64 above.
67. Ruprecht and Jenssen, n. 2 above.

68. The four general principles of the International Peace Campaign (Rassemblement Universel pour la Paix) were: (i) the recognition of the sanctity of treaty obligations; (ii) reduction and limitations of armaments by international agreement and the suppression of profit from the manufacture of and trade in arms; (iii) strengthening of the League of Nations for the prevention and stopping of war by the organization of collective security and mutual assistance; and (iv) establishment within the framework of the League of Nations of effective machinery for remedying international conditions which might lead to war. The Brussels congress (3–6 September 1936) was attended by about 4900 delegates from 35 nations, representing 750 national and 40 international organizations. Rassemblement pour la Paix (1937): pp. 6/13–15/36/215–20.

69. *Lancet* ii (1935): 265/ 1031; *Lancet* ii (1936): 217; *Mental Hygiene* 20 (1936): 167–9.

70. Ruprecht and Jenssen, n. 2 above, and *Lancet* ii (1936): 465–6.

71. Medical Peace Campaign Bulletin No. 2, December 1936: pp. 111–12. Ryle favoured a medical-scientific approach of MPC: *Lancet* i (1937): 1250–1 and *British Medical Journal* i (1938): 1092.

72. *Lancet* ii (1936): 465–6 and 761.

73. Memorandum on War Prevention and on the Medical Characteristics and Consequences of Modern Warfare, issued by the Medical Committee to be called the International Medical Association for the Prevention of War (British Section), (University College London, Penrose Papers 40/3).

74. Ibid.; and *Lancet* ii (1936): 761; *Rassemblement Universel pour la Paix* (1937), pp. 134–5.

75. Ruprecht and Jenssen, n. 2 above. Freud discussed the ways to divert human aggressive impulses so that they don't need to find expression in war. He came to the conclusion that 'anything that encourages the growth of emotional ties between men must operate against war'.

76. *Medican Peace Campaign Bulletin*, No. 5, January 1938.

77. Roorda, J. (ed.) (1939), *Medical Opinions on War*, published on behalf of the Netherlands Medical Association (Committee for War-Prophylaxis), Amsterdam.

78. 'Mental Hygiene and International Relations', *Mental Hygiene* 20 (1936): 332–4; *Lancet* i (1936): 274–7.

79. Ruprecht and Jenssen, n. 2 above.

80. *Lancet* ii (1936): 1075, 1340, 1355–7.

81. *Lancet* i (1937): 458 and 541–2.

82. *British Medical Journal* i (1937): 1091–2, 1179, 1230, 1282–83, 1339–40; *British Medical Journal* ii (1937): 90, 140; *British Medical Journal* ii (1937): 90, 139–40; *Lancet* ii (1936): 1295–6, 1340; *Lancet* i (1937): 158–9, 1542–4; *Lancet* ii (1937): 1338–9; *Lancet* i (1938): 293, 346–7 and 1291.

83. *Lancet* ii (1937): 1338–9; i (1938): 346–7.

84. *Lancet* ii (1936): 216–17; *Lancet* ii (1937/Suppl): 56.

85. Joules, Horace (ed.) (1938), *The Doctor's View of War*, London.

86. Ibid.

87. *Lancet* i (1939): 538.

88. *Lancet* i (1939): 1127 and *British Medical Journal* i (1939): 1014.

89. Doll, Richard, *et al.* (1951) *Lancet* i: 170.

90. 'Prospect of War' (correspondence), *Lancet* i (1951): 235–6; 292–4; 353–4; 396; 414–15.

91. The first meeting was chaired by Horace Joules. Lionel Penrose proposed the foundation of MAPW and Duncan Leys was elected the first president (*Lancet* i (1951): 804; *British Medical Journal* i (1951): 769; see also Ruprecht and Jenssen, n. 2 above).

92. Arnung, K., personal communication (February 1990), leaflet of *Danske Laegers Sammenslutning Mod Krig* (1952).

93. *Friedensgemeinschaft Deutscher Ärzte* (1953).

94. See ns 92 and 93 above.

95. *The Times*, 30 March 1954, p. 7; see also the leading article ('The Bomb') in *Lancet* i (1954): 815–16 and the discussion in *Lancet* i (1954): 887; 932; 1030; 1084; 1135.

96. See Ruprecht and Jenssen, n. 2 above.

97. Ibid.

98. *Medizinische Welt* (1952): 1396–9; (1955): 100, 512; (1956): 1118, 1156; (1957): 506, 738, 1092, 1476; (1958): 896, 1934; (1959): 1506; *Medizinische Klinik* 52 (1957): 7, 34, 242, 1430–1.

99. *Blätter für deutsche und internationale Politik* 3 (1958): 282–3.

100. *Ärztliche Mitteilungen/Deutsches Ärzteblatt* 42 (1957): 625–6; 43 (1958): 758; 768–77.

101. Ruprecht and Jenssen, n. 2 above; and Cousins, Norman (1985), *Albert Schweitzer's Mission: Healing and Peace*, New York, London.

102. Cousins, n. 101 above.

103. Letter of Schweitzer to Haustein, 22 September 1958, Albert Schweitzer Archives, Gunsbach (France).

104. Cousins, n. 101 above.

105. Ibid.

106. Letter from Schweitzer to Kennedy, 203 November 1962, Albert Schweitzer Archives, Gunsbach.

107. Ruprecht and Jenssen, n. 2 above.

108. Aronow, S., Erwin, F. and V. Sidel (eds) (1963) *The Fallen Sky. Medical consequences of thermonuclear war*, New York; and Ervin, F.R. *et al.*, *New England Journal of Medicine* (1962): 266: 1127–37; Sidel, V., Geiger, J. and B. Lown, *New England Journal of Medicine* (1962): 266, 1137–45; Leiderman, P.H.and J.H. Mendelson, *New England Journal of Medicine* 266 (1962): 1149–55; Aronow S., *New England Journal of Medicine* 266 (1962): 1145–9.

109. Mentioned in Statement prepared by Physicians for Social Responsibility for the Nuclear Test-ban Treaty hearings of the United States Senate Foreign Relations Committee, 27 August 1963 (typescript, Archives of PSR, Boston, MA).

110. The results of this Baby Tooth Survey, in which over 80,000 teeth were accumulated, were published later: Rosenthal, L. *et al.*, *Journal of Dental Research* 45 (1966): 343–9. In CNI some physicians were active members, for example the pathologist Walter Bauer, the physiologist Barry Commoner and the paediatrician Alfred Schwartz. The CNI also published an account of the effects of a nuclear attack on St Louis: see Boyer, B., *Journal of the American Medical Association* 253 (1985): 633–43.

111. See n. 109 above.

112. Haines, A. and M. Hartog, *British Medical Journal* 297 (1988): 408–11.

113. The psychiatrist J.D. Frank was a director of SANE and member of MAPW. He described denial as a typical reaction of people to the nuclear threat: Frank, J.D., *Psychiatry* 23 (1960): 245–66; Frank, J.D. *Journal of Nervous and Mental Disease* 144 (1967): 479–84; members of the American Association for Orthopsychiatry investigated the behavioural reactions of children and high school students to the Cuban missile and Berlin crises: S.K. Escalona, *Children* 10 (1963): 137–42, and M. Schwebel (ed.), *Behavioral Science and Human Survival*, Palo Alto (California), 1965. An interesting scientific paper dealt with the effects of fallout shelter confinement on family adjustment: S.E. Cleveland, *Archives of Genetic Psychiatry* 8 (1963): 43. In 1964 the Group for the Advancement of Psychiatry published findings on the psychiatric aspects of the prevention of nuclear war: P. Boyer,. *Journal of the American Medical Association* 253 (1985): 633–43; R.A. Clark, *American Journal of Psychotherapy* 19 (1965): 540–58.

114. Letter, Pauling to Schweitzer, 1 October 1963, Albert Schweitzer Archives, Gunsbach (France).

115. Cousins, n. 101 above.

116. See n. 112 above.

117. Ruprecht and Jenssen, n. 2 above.

118. Adams, Ruth and Susan Cullen (eds) (1981), *The Final Epidemic. Physicians and scientists on nuclear war*, Chicago.

119. SeeRuprecht and Jenssen, n. 2 above, and n. 11 above.

120. Ruprecht and Jenssen, n. 2 above; IPPNW (1986) *International Physicians for the Prevention of Nuclear War, description and brief history*, Boston, MA; and Chazov, Evgeni I., Ilyin, Leonid A. and Angelina K. Guskova (1984), *Nuclear War: The medical and biological consequences. Soviet physicians' viewpoint*, Moscow.

121. Lown, B., *Lancet* ii (1988): 203–4.

122. World Health Organization (1984/1987), *Effect of Nuclear War on Health and Health Services*. Report of the WHO Management Group on follow-up of WHA resolution 36.28, Geneva.

123. See IPPNW, n. 120 above, and Ruprecht and Jenssen, n. 2 above.

124. IPPNW Internet information: http://www.ippnw.org./12th World Congress. IPNNW History. 1985 Nobel Peace Prize. Peace through Health. Abolition of Nuclear Weapons. Affiliates. IPPNW Mission. htlm.

2 THE IMAGE OF WAR IN MEDICAL JOURNALS

A Case Study

LAURI VUORENKOSKI, ILKKA TAIPALE
and VAPPU TAIPALE

To assess the characteristics of the medical image of war we chose the internationally-renowned *British Medical Journal* (*BMJ*) as our source and explored all the entries referring to war from 1920 to 1996. We wanted to avoid the military medical journals and the more specialized journals of surgery or psychiatry reflecting the interest and expertise of their authors. The *BMJ* is one of the most highly-regarded medical magazines, it is read world-wide by medical specialists of all types, and it tends to react rapidly but professionally to the findings of medical and social research. It is clear that the *BMJ* doesn't represent, either qualitatively or quantitatively, all the facts about war available to the medical profession, but our presumption was that it gives a good overview of the general spread of information available to critical medical readers, be they general practitioners or specialists.

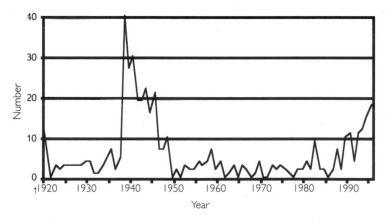

Figure 2.1 Number of medical articles and editorials referring to war in the BMJ

A total of 458 articles referring to war, published in the *BMJ* between 1920 and 1996, were collected and analysed. This number clearly reflected Britain's war situation at the time, as most of the entries were published in the years 1939–46. Later wars and conflicts were not so widely covered: Nigerian wars were reflected on, the Falklands war produced one article and the situation in former Yugoslavia provoked different reactions. The most frequently-mentioned military conflict since the Second World War (WW II) was the 1991 Gulf War, which created an outburst of letters, opinions, editorials and research throughout the 1990s (Figure 2.1) We didn't compare the number of our selected articles to the total number of *BMJ* entries – the *BMJ* has become more and more voluminous over the decades – but primarily assessed the qualitative aspects of medical information they contained, and screened the availability of data on some central topics.

Chemical, bacterial and nuclear warfare

Discussion of chemical warfare began in 1921. The editorial for 24 December (1921: 1087) stated that 'a great field of research has been opened…in the main, we cannot but regard it as a degradation of medical science'. Gas warfare, several poison gases and their possible use in warfare were discussed on the topic and the 1929 Disarmament Conference referred to. One of the rare British parliamentary discussions referred to in the *BMJ* was 'Medical Notes in Parliament' (8 November 1930: 803) which stated that:

> 2000 horses had been handed over for experiments in poison gas and the cultivation of bacteria for spreading plague… The experiments carried out were for preventive and curative treatment of horses affected by poison gases… In 1930, 729 animals had been used for experiments and 366 were killed by the experiments… Officers holding vivisection licences for poison gas experiments worked in strict conformity with the provisions of the Cruelty to Animals Act, 1876.

Even during WW II, the topic was rarely touched on, being mentioned mostly in individual case reports on, for instance, eye lesions. In 1946 an entry on chemical warfare experiments using human subjects[1] stated that:

> human subjects have been employed for many years to assess the value of certain types of potential chemical warfare agents, and efficacy of suggested defensive measures. All the subjects were volunteers… No one was subjected to a test without first being told the precise nature of the test and the possible consequences to himself. The tests were chiefly routine in nature and hundreds of volunteers have been used in this way.

There was no more discussion about the voluntarism and its consequences but some photographs of burns and lesions were provided. In 1959 the psychochemical aspects of the new type of nerve gases were raised.

Bacterial warfare was not a popular topic. Only one editorial was found (21 June 1947, 893):

> If a third world war occurs it is likely to be even more unpleasant than the 1939–1945 disturbance. What with rocket-propelled atomic bombs, radioactive sprays, and poison gases

calculated to make mustard gas seem no more distressing than a slight overdose of sal volatile, the next war is hardly likely to see many survivors. To complete this tale of horror we are from time to time solemnly warned that bacterial warfare will be freely used... There is one ray of hope. The factors governing the epidemic spread of a particular organism are as yet but little known.

Radioactivity, radiation and fallout were the leading topics from 1947 onwards. A rich collection of articles emerged, exploring amongst other issues the risks of leukaemia, the effects of strontium 90, and radioactive contaminants. Although the atomic bomb was mentioned in 1947, the first dedicated article found on this topic was an editorial, 'Defence Against Atom Bombs' (21 May 1955: 1263). An interesting detail is that one of the rare debates on medical aspects of war technology referred to briefly in the *BMJ* under 'Medical Notes in Parliament' was in 1957, when opposition leader Aneurin Bevan and Prime Minister Harold Macmillan argued about nuclear fallout following the British nuclear explosions in the Pacific (15 June 1957: 1423). The prime minister said that 'the fallout was insignificant', but the opposition directed attention to the reported protest of 2000 US scientists as showing the real concern felt in informed quarters about the danger of continuing these tests. The evidence was studied later:[2] the long-term effects of the participation of more than 22,000 men in the United Kingdom's atmospheric nuclear weapons tests and experimental programmes were assessed. Researchers concluded that participation had had no detectable effect but the possibility that it may have caused a small risk of leukaemia in the early years afterwards cannot be ruled out.

Nuclear warfare and the treatment of mass casualties were discussed in 1958. The *BMJ* followed the physicians' movement against nuclear war, which started anew in the 1980s and led to the 1985 Nobel Peace Prize. The journal reported early on about new war technology and the medical profession: the effects of new explosive bullets were discussed, and medical arguments against new and old landmines clearly stated. The use of torture was opposed, and many articles emphasized human rights.

Psychiatric aspects of war

An interesting feature of our selected entries is the voluminous and widely-based collection of psychiatric texts, which make up the majority of the contributions. War neuroses and war psychoses, much more infrequent than neurotic symptoms, were regularly reported; studies and findings were published from the First World War (WW I) on, and the late sequelae of war stress provoked interest in the 1920s. The publication of mental health articles almost certainly enhanced the position of psychiatry among clinical disciplines. For instance, psychiatric experiences in the Spanish Civil War were reported in 1939, with another article on the general medical situation. The frequent reporting of psychiatric symptoms produced articles about depressive states and hysteria in wartime, and even some innovative psychotherapeutic solutions of using air-raid noises. This pre-occupation with mental health was evident even up to the 1990s when the question arose as to whether the symptoms of the Gulf War were psychosomatic or the effects of some chemical agent.

Alongside the reactions and circumstances of the soldiers on the battlefield, the needs and reactions on the home front were considered. 'Psychiatric Preparations for War Emergencies' was the title of a 1938 editorial (31 December: 1375). Panic states of the general population, the mental health of children and the consequences of their compulsory evacuation were discussed in 1941 (editorial, 25 January: 1982) (see also Chapter 22 in this book). An analysis in 1942 of German psychological warfare (2 April: 445–8), reviewing a survey by the American Committee on National Morale, exposed the psychological methods of the German army. In 1944 an official assessment of WW II and mental health was published by the UK health authorities and referred to in an editorial (19 December: 762), which stated: 'the [health] Board finds no evidence that the war has brought about any increase in serious cases of mental breakdown'. These assessments were repeated later on. Post-traumatic stress disorder (PTSD) was also touched on in the earlier editions, but was never developed at any length.

One rare and nearly forgotten document can be found in the *BMJ* for 12 October 1935. A manifesto signed by 350 psychiatrists from various countries stated that:

> There is a seeming contradiction between the conscious individual aversion to war and the collective preparedness to wage war… We psychiatrists declare that our science is sufficiently advanced for us to distinguish between real, pretended and unconscious motives, even in statesmen. The desire to disguise national militarism by continual talk about peace will not protect political leaders from the judgement of history.

This detailed document reflects the way the psychiatrists were in touch with the mental atmosphere of the time and wanted to do their best to avoid the big calamity then openly planned.

Prisoners of war

Prisoners of war did not need much space until WW II. Italian troops in Libya attracted some attention in 1943 but the scope is more hygienic (war wounds, etc.) than anything else.[3] The prisoner-of-war mentality and the after-effects of repatriation are studied: emphasis is on typical mental reactions following release as opposed to those shown while in detention.

The 1945 invasion of Belsen, with more than 67,000 internees, was a shock to the medical community. This is well reflected by W.R.F. Collis, who abandons neutral medical language to reflect the horrors of reality.[4] His article is

> an appreciation of the situation by the senior medical officer after 24 hours contact…it is impossible to give an adequate description on paper. No word can describe the stench of decaying faeces, rotting bodies, and burning rags…an enormous task lies ahead if these poor people are to be cured and rehabilitated.

Many subsequent contributions described living conditions and mental states in different camps where, for example, Polish, Belgian and German prisoners had been held, as well as those of women war captives, repatriated allied prisoners of war, and medical experiments on concentration camp victims in Nazi Germany.

Health of the conscripts and soldiers

In 1920, the editorial for 16 October (601) speaks of the 'sick wastages of war':

> [T]he enormous importance of the wastage of men from medical causes, as opposed to that from battle casualties… Sick admissions to casualty clearing stations for one year 1917, [reveals that]…no fewer than 25 per cent of the cases originated from scabies or pyodermia, and… nearly 20 per cent were due directly or indirectly to trench fever.

No wonder that the topic 'War as an educator in Hygiene' was directly or indirectly referred to on several separate occasions.

In subsequent years, the *BMJ* regularly published a report called 'The Health of the Army'. In 1922, (21 March: 563–5) it problematized the fact that

> 20 per cent of the cases brought before the medical board were suffering from tachycardia for which no cause…could be found… The chief cause of admissions to hospital was venereal disease, with a ratio of 70.7 per 1000 of strength.

These reports were no longer published during or after WWII.

Although the traditional material of war medicine has always been surgical wounds and hygiene problems, these do not outnumber the other important topics in our sample. The hygienic aspects of the El Alamein victory convinced the *BMJ*'s readers of the importance of standards of cleanliness. The concept of social hygiene in wartime stressed once again the importance of venereal diseases. Enuresis in the army was noticed as a problem in 1944.[5]

Waging war, facing problems

The second most common topic in our *BMJ* selection was air raids and their consequences. After their first mention in 1935, there follows a continual flow of reports and studies, with a series of 27 articles in 1939 on war wounds and air raid casualties. Living on an island had made the population adapt to a type of warfare which always occurred overseas or in a naval battle. Now, during the 20th century, modern warfare intruded into the everyday life of ordinary people with aeroplanes and air raids, changing the situation totally. No one could be safe any more.

The nutritional and food-intake requirements of the civilian population were often discussed, especially during WW II. Iron-deficiency anaemia was studied carefully year after year and detailed recommendations on how to feed an infant and a child during wartime were made. Child health was an important topic.

The medical profession

The editorial, 'War and the Medical Profession', 9 September 1939 (571) states: 'to-day, the profession is fully organised against emergency… In recent months this work has intensified in readiness for the calamity of European war'; the following week's editorial, 16 September 1939 (610) was already called 'London Hospitals in Wartime'. The war had become a reality, the needs of civilians were set aside and outpatient clinics closed except for war casualties. In 1942 the editorial 'Medicine at War' (21 February: 262–3) stated that:

> the difficulties with which medicine has been faced in the present war – and, it may fairly be added, its relative failure to overcome them – are of interest in that they represent in a microcosm the experience of the democratic peoples as a whole in this struggle... The new problems are not obviously medical problems. They lie on the borderlands of medicine and sociology, of medicine and psychology, of medicine and physical invention.

Social needs and modern war was not an unknown topic for the *BMJ*, which referred in 1951 to the famous British sociologist Richard Titmuss. In 1954 the journal simply reported on new, emerging social problems such as: 'illegitimacy and the war: it was one of the social consequences of the war that the government accepted new responsibilities for the welfare of unmarried mothers and their babies' (editorial, 7 August: 350).

Conclusion

Compared to their Finnish colleagues, the readers of the *BMJ* were provided with a more comprehensive and balanced image of war and warfare, yet the *BMJ* was only one of several important journals in English. It is remarkable that much of the information was provided in the editorials, which gave the issues more importance and authority. Topics covered a range of issues, from chemical warfare to prisoners of war. Contributions were made by different specialists, but psychiatry and mental health issues were conspicuously frequent. The civilian population, especially children, was discussed in the medical reviews in order to remind the profession of this group's needs. The combatants, on the other hand, were hardly mentioned at all. Assessments were regularly presented on the state of medical research in time of war, and also on the wartime situation of public health, and the moral aspects of war were occasionally discussed.

REFERENCES

A list of the 458 *BMJ* articles and editorials is available from the authors.

1. Cullumbine, H. (1946), 'Chemical Warfare Experiments Using Human Subjects', *BMJ*: 19 October: 576–8.
2. Beral, V. *et al.* (1988), 'Mortality of Employees of the Atomic Weapons Establishment, 1951–82', *BMJ* 297 (6651) 24 September: 757–70; Darby, S.C., *et al.* (1993), 'Further Follow-up of Mortality and Incidence of Cancer in Men From the United Kingdom who Participated in the United Kingdom's Atmospheric Nuclear Weapon Tests and Experimental Programmes', *BMJ* 307 (6918) 11 December: 1530–5.
3. Boyd, J.S.K. (1943), 'Enteric Group Fevers in Prisoners of War from the Western Desert', *BMJ* 12 June: 719.
4. Collis, W.R.F. (1945), 'Belsen Camp: A Preliminary Report', *BMJ*, 9 June: 814.
5. Backus, P.I., McGill, C.M. and G.S. Mansell (1944), 'Investigation and Treatment of Enuresis in the Army', *BMJ*, 7 October: 462–5.

Address for correspondence

National Research and Development Centre for Welfare and Health (STAKES), Siltasaanrenkatu 18, PO Box 220,00531 Helsinki, Finland.

3 THE IMPACT OF WARFARE ON MEDICINE

MATTI PONTEVA

Warfare normally has a devastating effect on general health, but the situation is more complicated for medicine and medical research. There are historical examples that show connections between the needs of warfare and pressures to improve or develop medical care methods, organizations and procedures. Such impact is easiest to see in the advanced first care and treatment of those wounded in war and in the prevention and care of infectious diseases, but present also in many other medical specialities. The social consequences of war may extend widely and also make necessary medical innovations, novel organizational solutions and rationalizations to retain an acceptable level of public health services. Depending on our philosophic conception of the causes of wars it is also possible to think that wars could in some cases be prevented by the medical treatment of factors that increase the need to resort to war.

Although effective warfare usually has a devastating effect on the health of the population of both sides, it can sometimes have a stimulating and profitable effect on medicine. This is possible through a mechanism of reaction: more effective medicine is needed to ensure the survival of the population. Military leaders say this more roughly: they need enough 'living' or 'fighting' power. Connections between warfare and the development of medicine have not been a popular branch of research, partly because of the difficulties in such kind of analysis and partly because of unnecessary secrecy.

Chapter 3 discusses the theme quite generally, because the influence of warfare on the need for medical care is discussed in many other chapters in this reader. The public health aspects of warfare are also omitted in the main because these have been the focus of other recent publications.[1]

Historical trends

The powerful regulators of human population have through the ages been famine, epidemics, war and death, the four Apocalyptic equestrians. The first two are often a consequence of war and an untimely death a consequence of some of the three other factors. The most important mission of medicine has often been seen as a fight against untimely death. So it is easy to deduce that the fight against war is also a medical mission although it would be more precise to speak about the fight against the negative effects of warfare on human beings.

Until the First World War (WW I), more deaths among fighting troops occurred from infectious diseases than from wounds on the battlefield.[2] There were some exceptions in shorter wars and when there had been practically only one major battle. One considerable exception was the war between Germany and France in the years 1870–71 on the German side. This was due to a systematic vaccination against smallpox but also because of a higher medical and hygienic standard. The importance of vaccination was demonstrated in practice among the civilians after the war, when thousands of the unvaccinated died in a smallpox epidemic and the vaccination was soon made obligatory in Prussia.[3] In many armies mortality from infectious diseases still exceeded that of the battlefield even in the later stages of WW I owing to the pandemic influenza of 1918.[4] The spread of this pandemic was estimated to have been enhanced by wartime or post-war circumstances, so this situation also stimulated the development of preventive means against epidemics.

The military importance of infectious diseases has also led to the idea of biological weapons (Chapter 10). Primitive attempts at such use are known from long ago, and it is probable that the first spread of Black Death to Europe in the 14th century was due to the deliberate throwing of infected corpses into a besieged enemy camp.

The importance of warfare as a straight cause of untimely death is self-evident. Therefore it is logical that the ancient surgeons made many attempts to save soldiers from the effects of battle traumas. Some of their inventions have stimulated later developments, such as the ideas of bone elevation and trepanation in cranial traumas, or some methods of splinting in fractures of extremities, but the influence on civilian surgery remained mainly insignificant. Considering the methods of caring for serious wounds on the battlefield up to the late 19th century, we can say that this was a great piece of good luck for the civilians. Later the situation has changed and many steps in surgical advancement and anaesthesiology during the 20th century owe a debt to military medicine.

The big historical change in the impact of warfare or potential warfare has been the escalation of the threat to civilians. Percentages of war-related deaths among civilians are estimated to have risen from 19 per cent of all such deaths in WW I to 90 per cent during the 1990s.[5] Though wars are usually not comparable as far as their nature, methods, locality and indirect effects are concerned, a possible global threat must seriously be taken into consideration. The use and threat of nuclear weapons has been one factor in this escalation, but of a more psychological nature in the light of absolute or proportional numbers directly affected.

The possibilities of classical curative medicine resisting this kind of change and development are poor. This situation calls for concentrating on preventive health and social care and extensive social support arrangements in the actual event of war. The importance of curative medicine will naturally turn out to be smaller than previously, but the differences between general and military medicine will also decrease.

Impact of some specialities

The division of medicine into specialities is quite young. Before the 20th century it was enough to separate internal medicine and surgery or physicians and surgeons. After WW I extensive division into specialities and subspecialities took place. At the same time the impact of wartime medicine and surgery on public health has become clear.

In surgery and anaesthesiology (specialized first care included) the need of rapid and massive blood transfusions, and later also infusions of plasma expanders and clear solutions, was verified in WW I and proved in WW II to be inevitable in all traumas where circulatory schock was threatening. The use of infusions is now a routine method in advanced first care and during transport to emergency stations. The proper treatment of infected wounds is nowadays mainly derived from experience on the battlefield, after the principles of radical wound revision (debridement) and delayed closure were accepted. Especially in injuries caused by high velocity bullets it is very important to follow the treatment principles of military surgeons.

Other examples of the military influence on the treatment of trauma patients are external fixation of limb fractures and methods of treating special forms of gangrenes, trench foot, cold injuries and burns. Battle injuries have also caused a great demand to develop brain and neurosurgery as well as reconstructive surgery as a whole.

Infectious diseases are still important as a cause of death in war and also during peace in most parts of the world. Though the invention of antibiotics just before WW II has changed the possibilities of treating bacterial diseases, global prevention is still impossible because of economic problems and the lack of vaccination possibilities. The military applications of strict control of contaminated persons, the use of quarantine and reasonable use of antibiotics could be good principles among civilians. A special branch of infectious diseases is venereal diseases, which have often been a particular problem in the military. Prevention is the only way to keep this problem under control and these methods could also be beneficial in civilian society.

The impact of warfare on non-infectious diseases is more indirect and obscure. Though the general connection between social humiliation and deficiency diseases is obvious, the special influence of war is not usually possible to demonstrate. We can be sure that experiences with wartime patients have stimulated the research and care of complications and after-effects of infectious and dietary diseases, but development in this area could have been intensive without war. Branches that seem clearly to have benefited from war experience are cardiology and pulmonology.

In psychiatry the big change on the battlefield was the expansion of firepower, but especially the far-reaching effects of the increase in arms in the form of artillery, armoured troops and air force. A special condition, known as shell shock, with mainly psychic symptoms was named in WW I, but the possible contribution of brain concussion or explosion pressure to the condition is still obscure. After WW II the understanding of stress reactions and disorders has profited much from military experiences as well as from some of the methods of quick support in critical situations.

Within military medicine itself some procedures are clearly an outcome of wartime demands, for example the medical selection of soldiers in conjunction with psychological and administrative procedures. Many military medical procedures could be applicable in other circumstances. On the battlefield it is clear that prioritization in medical treatment is inevitable to maximize the number of wounded that can be saved. Classification according to the prognosis of injury or injuries (triage) is an established method also in general disaster medicine.

In the area of diagnostics the needs of wartime medicine have mainly been directed towards simplicity without great innovations. The lesson of war is often how to get along with meagre resources. Some of the rapid development in this sector after the great wars may be due to the requirements for the care of the war veterans. A more important link between the consequences of war and social medicine is found in rehabilitation. This word was generally unknown in its medical sense before WW II, but nowadays is a central part of the aftercare of war veterans as well as of many civilian patients.

A straight connection between warfare and the development of pharmacology is weak, though the need for special drugs grows considerably during wartime. The invention of such things as new analgesics, antibiotics and infusion solutions takes place usually in peacetime; only their production increases in war. The inhuman testing of risky preparations during the WW II in Germany did not yield any useful medicines. Some chemical compounds or compound groups were developed for chemical warfare, but later on almost similar compounds were observed to be modifiable for medical use.

Some other areas of impact

Though the principal effect of warfare on public health is negative, there are some exceptions. Usually the benefactor is not war itself but the change of circumstances and living conditions. In countries where excess weight is a national problem general health may improve during war as long as there is no real malnutrition. Dietary factors may, for example, have caused the decline of diabetes mortality in many countries during WW II. The danger of epidemics grows but the possibility of catching an infection diminishes when movement is restricted. However, war-caused deprivation will usually proceed and the general health situation weaken; the decline is worst among groups whose health was already poor before the outbreak of hostilities. Corrective measures are often more needed after the war than during it, a clear challenge to public health organizations.

Wars yield plenty of material for epidemiologic research. Depending on the level of medical reporting and statistics in different armies and states, such material can be well-suited and practical for scientific studies. In these cases it is possible to say that the impact on research work has been positive. Such observations also form a natural basis for later preventive measures. Regrettably possibilities of following the impact of war on the morbidity and mortality of noncombatant populations are often considered trivial and the military and political leaders have little interest in these questions.

The development of catastrophe or disaster medicine owes much to wartime observations and experiences. Principles applied to advanced primary care in disasters are derived mainly from military experience. The origin of social research of disasters is said to have been the collision and explosion in Halifax harbour in the year 1917 and the origin of corresponding medical research the Cocoanut Grove fire in Boston in the year

1942. Neither of these incidents was caused by war, but they and the research which followed them were possible because of the state of war in Canada and USA.

War has always also had an influence on the structure and organization of medical and social services in any country or state. The solutions may be quite diverse but sometimes they indicate distinct progress when compared with some confused peacetime situation. The impact of war could then be profitable, even in the long run. War naturally also has an effect on medical employees and workers. Despite many debilitating factors it is possible that shared responsibility, experiences and survival have a supportive effect and personal growth has happened even under war conditions. Wars have also stimulated many voluntary activities, especially in the medical and social fields. The origin of the International Red Cross after Henri Dunant's experiences on the battlefield of Solferino is a well-known example.

General estimation of impact

As stated earlier, the impact of warfare on public health is negative in most cases, but the impact on medical research can be stimulating and demanding, leading sometimes to real achievements. The impact on medical services can sometimes be simplifying and rationalizing, but is mostly restrictive and reduces the standard of care. Sometimes war can lead to a medical catastrophe, a situation in which care needs considerably exceed available medical resources.

The impact of war on society as a whole and especially on economics and the standard of living also has a secondary effect on physical and mental health. In this sense war can be compared to a widespread epidemic or large natural disaster. The long-term social and political consequences of even a rather destructive, lost war need not be very injurious as it is possible to see after WW II in, for example, Germany, Japan and Finland. When compared with old catastrophes it should be remembered that the general depression after the Black Death in the 14th century lasted more than a hundred years. Consequences of incidents on this scale usually remain outside the possibilities of proper medical help. In poor developing countries the social catastrophe threshold may lie much lower.

To draw a parallel between war and natural disasters is characteristic of the cataclysmic philosophy of war.[6] This is an obvious opposite to the very general political philosophy of war. In both cases it seems that the task of medicine is to resist wars; they cannot have any common objectives. War as a cataclysm is a threat that can neither be mastered nor predicted. It could be valuable to widen this interpretation by seeing war as a possible control mechanism on a human population which does not have natural enemies any more. Then we could find a common objective and try to reduce wars by increasing the use of medical means in controlling the human population explosion. Possibly this implies that at least temporarily we have to accept a change in our conceptions of the main tasks of medicine: to resist single human deaths is not as important as to promote the diversity of nature and human dignity during life.

REFERENCES

1. Levy, B.S. and V.W. Sidel (eds) (1997), *War and Public Health*, New York: Oxford University Press and the American Public Health Association, 1997.
2. Urlanis, B. (1971), *Wars and Populations* (trans. Leo Lempert), Moscow: Progress Publishers.
3. Linden, V.F. (1932), 'Ihmisen ikuinen taistelu sairautta ja kuolemaa vastaan' (Man's everlasting struggle against disease and death); available only in Finnish, *Annales Medicinae Militaris Fenniae* 7: 103–40.
4. Garfield, R.M. and A.I. Neugut (1991), 'Epidemiologic Analysis of Warfare. A Historical Review', *JAMA* 266: 688–92.
5. Garfield, R.M. and A.I. Neugut (1997), 'The Human Consequences of War', in B. S. Levy and V. W. Sidel (eds), *War and Public Health*, New York: Oxford University Press and the American Public Health Association, 27–38.
6. Rapaport, A. (1971), editor's introduction to the abridged translation of *On War* by Carl von Clausewitz, London: Penguin Books, 11–80.

Address for correspondence

Central Military Hospital and Defence Staff, P.O. Box 50, FIN-00301 HELSINKI
Tel: 358-9-1812 5761, Fax: 358-9-1812 5617

4 PROBLEMS OF ASSISTANCE AND PROTECTION IN MODERN CONFLICTS

GUNNAR ROSÉN

The origins of protecting victims of war can be traced back thousands of years. In a simplified way its roots can be divided into three branches:

- instinctive human compassion, expressed particularly by women,
- moral norms, derived from religion or ideology, and
- practical or political appropriateness, based primarily on reciprocity.

Temples, churches and monasteries were the first to offer asylum, protection and care to wounded fighters and persecuted civilians. Since parties to a conflict often shared the same beliefs and moral norms, religious personnel remained neutral. If God or gods had granted asylum to those who had fled to the sanctuaries, violating those sanctuaries and trespassing on holy ground would be to challenge the gods themselves. Religion also set the first rules for warfare itself, often combined with sensible practices and wise politics. Holy men and women, often at the same time healers, were needed by all, and in addition to their status as intermediaries between men and gods they were often intermediaries between men themselves. Status and profession made them untouchable, and this state was transferred also to the secular medical profession.

In negotiations between the parties, reciprocity was often the key issue. Surprisingly early on there were treaties and customs for protection of prisoners of war which benefited all parties, if not out of humanity, then as hostages requiring reciprocity, or at least as slaves and members of a labour force. Ancient rulers of India and Persia ordered lenient treatment of conquered peoples in order to avoid unnecessary hate and to make them allies. Among some African tribes women, children and slaves were kept out of the fighting because they represented the property for which one was fighting. By common understanding some methods of warfare were forbidden, for example the poisoning of wells in dry regions on which all were dependent.

In the western tradition Christianity has been the strongest factor influencing the formulation of the laws and customs of war, later followed by treaties on general human rights. Canonic laws preceded secular laws and were much more respected than the latter. The fact that the main rules of ethics are more or less the same in all major religions has facilitated efforts to find common ground for universal humanitarian conventions.

Legal support

National laws and bilateral treaties between some states preceded international laws for which Hugo Grotius (1583–1645) was the foremost spokesman. Influenced by him, the Swedish king Gustavus Adolphus proclaimed in his War Articles of 1621 that an act which was a crime in the home country was also so in enemy land. Particularly protected were churches, schools and hospitals, as well as priests, the elderly, women and children. Unfortunately the early death of the king shortly after led to anarchy and atrocities in the Thirty Years' War. The same has been the fate of the laws of war on numerous later occasions. Nevertheless, a universal law and code of conduct exists today, namely the Geneva Convention, ratified by all states of the world except the newest. The big question is, as it always has been, how to strengthen respect for it. The War Articles of Gustavus Adolphus stated that they had to be read aloud before each regiment once a month so that nobody could claim that he had violated them out of ignorance. More than ever this should be demanded of all armed forces today.

The first concern of the international law was the wounded and sick soldiers in enemy hands. As witness to the sufferings of the victims of the battle of Solferino in North Italy in 1859, the Swiss Henry Dunant took the initiative for the first Geneva Convention for the protection of wounded soldiers, which was signed originally in 1864 by 12 European states. Today there exist four Geneva conventions of 1949 and two Additional Protocols of 1977. These latter are in fact two new conventions, the first regulating warfare itself in international conflicts, the second extending the basic rules of international conflicts to civil wars. Several other international treaties to limit the means of warfare and to protect human rights complement the Geneva conventions.

Problems in practice

Based on reciprocity, the basic rules of the original Geneva conventions have functioned reasonably well in conflicts and wars between states, and saved millions of lives, particularly of those prisoners of war. Prohibitions of the use of indiscriminate weapons, totalitarian warfare and certain arms were included first in the 1977 Protocols and later in certain other treaties, but have not yet come under real test in international conflicts.

The main problem of international law today is that old-style wars between states have become rare and the majority of modern armed conflicts consist of a vast scale of basically internal or semi-internal conflicts which are more or less outside the law of war. In general soldiers are today the best-protected people, and the vast majority of victims in need of assistance are civilians: people oppressed by their own governments, local villagers caught in crossfire between fighting parties and often terrorized by them all, displaced people within the borders of their own countries or as refugees outside, political detainees and target groups of terrorists who may be living far from the actual scene of the conflict. In many of the modern conflicts the only law applied has been the law of the jungle, resulting in senseless destroying of everything, leaving only ruins and deserted land even to the winners.

Former Yugoslavia, Chechnya, Afghanistan, Somalia, Rwanda and Angola are some examples of the situations and circumstances in which medical and relief missions have to be carried out today. Idealism and professional medical training alone are not enough. Training is needed in many new aspects of these conflict situations. Sometimes the mission takes place in the framework of a big multinational operation, and one has to know and understand the workings and division of work of a vast international machinery. Sometimes one is almost alone amidst an unknown people and culture, walking on a tightrope in order not to get in conflict with corrupt local warlords or with popular religious taboos. Training in negotiation and diplomacy is essential, as is the ability to deal with the all-present media.

Relief agencies and organizations

In spite of many difficulties and setbacks international relief work and protection activities are today larger than ever, and even the most hard-boiled governments and parties to conflict are often in pressing need of assistance offered to their people from the outside. The bargaining power this gives to the humanitarian agencies, intergovernmental bodies as well as NGOs, has given good results but could still be made much more effective. Lack of coordination and cooperation remains the greatest problem. Open discussion between the agencies and organizations on division of work, different strategies, new approaches and training of personnel is sorely needed.

The concept of protection is wide-ranging, from protection of political detainees to keeping alive masses of displaced people and refugees. There is also a large range of organizations and agencies with different backgrounds and aims and partial to different, sometimes conflicting, strategies and working methods. One question of coordination is which agency is best suited for what.

In the background there are the big UN and other intergovernmental agencies, working in the first place on a high diplomatic level and providing resources and logistic support: the UN High Commissioner for Refugees (UNHCR), the United Nations Development Programme (UNDP), the World Food Programme (WFP), the United Nations Children Fund (UNICEF) and others. The International Committee of the Red Cross (ICRC) is the official guardian of the Geneva conventions and the humanitarian intermediary between the parties. Supported by the national Red Cross societies and their world federation, it is most often the central agency in the heart of the conflict itself.

The religious organizations, through their missionary work, often have deep roots in the conflict areas and the best knowledge of their ethnological and political conditions, health and social problems and local languages. They often also have intimate and good relations with the people and will commonly take a strong political stand for them. Western organizations often forget that there are also strong Moslem, Buddhist, Jewish and other organizations. Cooperation with them would be fruitful in many ways, not least in avoiding mistakes in regard to local customs and taboos.

Algonside the old and established organizations, there is an increasing number of NGOs, some of them full of enthusiasm but lacking experience. New dimensions of protection and relief work must also be carefully considered, particularly relations with the strongest of the new gods, the media.

The role of medical personnel

To a considerable degree the medical personnel have preserved their historical esteem and authority. Medical work, relief and protection activities are always needed and in that way are reasonably well protected. Intentional attacks against international medical personnel and their institutions have remained relatively few, even if supplies have been robbed and mainly local personnel have died in crossfire. The recent killing of six ICRC workers in Chechnya was a provocation for local reasons. Ordinarily, keeping strictly to its policy of impartiality and neutrality, the ICRC has succeeded in most places in keeping its hospital and relief work going without interruption even under the changing governments of Kabul.

Medical personnel usually work in the front line of events. Many times recently they have become the first and closest eyewitnesses to atrocities of different degrees and dimensions.

Hazards of the work

Any organization wanting honestly to assist and protect people under their care should always consider some basic questions:

- why are we here and what do we want to accomplish?
- what short- and long-term consequences may our decisions and actions have for those people we want to assist?
- how may our action affect the work of others, those working at our side as well as the larger operation of which our work is a part?

It is obvious that the truth about atrocities and corruption must be told to someone – grave violations against humanity must come out and be corrected – but by whom, when and by what means? More than once honest but outspoken organizations have been thrown out of the country at the cost that thousands of people have been left in distress.

The presence of foreign relief personnel itself most often gives considerable protection to the people. Nevertheless the fieldwork might be a daily exercise in tightrope walking between conflicting interests and endeavours. How to deal with local chiefs asking for gifts and favours before letting relief through? How to pacify hostile local people who are as poor or poorer than the refugees you are supposed to assist? Should the relief be stopped and your protégées left unaided when clearly part of the assistance is used to feed soldiers? How to handle the mafia in the camps discriminating against some groups and selling relief goods at nearby city markets? Time and again the question arises: whom to tell and what measures to take? A wrong move might put the whole operation in jeopardy and also alienate donors, who constantly ask, 'does my contribution truly reach the needy people?'

Relations to the media

Relief work has recently gained a powerful new ally in the all-present modern media. In the old days, when the big boys were beating the small boys in the backyards of the world, nobody knew. Today even the warlords of the jungle must take into consideration what effect their actions might have on world opinion and on outside support. Victories and defeats in the information war have become more important than victories in the field. The big question of conscience and policy is how to deal with the media, which can give enormous support to an action or totally destroy it.

In regard to the media different agencies use different policies, sometimes conflicting but nevertheless working together to the benefit of a common goal. A good example is the silent – not official – understanding and interaction between activities of the ICRC and Amnesty International. Amnesty uses publicity and public pressure against govern-ments which violate human rights as its main tool. Understandably Amnesty is seldom itself permitted to visit prisons but its pressure has on many occasions played an important role in forcing the governments to open the prison gates to the ICRC. ICRC keeps absolutely silent on the observations of its delegates, reporting only to the detaining power, but jointly these two separate actions have led to the improvement of the conditions of tens of thousands of detainees.

In other kinds of situations more consideration could be given as to which agency is best suited for which action. In every major operation one of the first tasks should be the formation of a coordination committee in which all intergovernmental agencies as well as NGOs participate. Policies towards the media are an important issue which have to be decided.

There is a natural rivalry between the organizations themselves for the attention of the press. Every agency needs publicity in order to get support for its work and to give feedback to its donors. Most often the independent press is also the right medium to which to reveal the violations against humanity, corruption and other problems in the operation area. Many organizations invite journalists to follow their work. As correct as this might be, a proper briefing of the correspondents on the sensitive situations in which the work often takes place is also important.

Some agents have even commercialized relief. Not to speak of actual business, ranging from buying and selling such thing as supplies and logistic services to the smuggling of refugees, some relief actions themselves are tainted with the smell of money. Honest and hard-working organizations and their field personnel sometimes feel frustrated on discovering that publicity seems to be the main concern of certain operators. Groups arrive with their own TV teams already on the plane, deliver some supplies with cameras running, make statements which might put the whole action in jeopardy, and disappear.

Mistakes are also sometimes made by some inexperienced and idealistic newcomers who, wanting no harm done, are manipulated by the ruthless media into speaking their minds on matters which have shocked them – and, in so doing, cutting their own wings. Time and again the question must be repeated: what are the consequences to the people I am supposed to aid?

The heart of the matter

Doctors, nurses and other health workers returning from the field have often seen the worst of what a man can do to other human beings. In modern civil wars and other internal conflicts all common sense seems frequently to have been lost, nobody is in control and pure self-interest and hate blind the parties from realizing that they are engaged in total self-destruction. The shocking discovery for an outsider is to see how thin is the veneer of culture and education in these situations.

To speak of the Geneva conventions and human rights may sound like a bad joke in these circumstances. When hate blinds people, not even the sound principle of reciprocity in good and bad enters the minds of the fighting parties. Nevertheless the primary duty of medical personnel is to preserve good sense even when all others seem to have lost it. Trustworthy allies are usually to be found amongst their local medical colleagues. The time to speak sense to the fighters might come when they themselves lie wounded and maimed on the hospital bed.

Summary

In the present world situation the medical profession needs not only a good training in many new things – in the workings of international machinery, ethnology, politics, logistics, communication, negotiation, the handling of the media – but also a deep insight into its own historical role and a conviction of its importance. The fundamental principles of humanity and impartiality, as well as neutrality as a tool to realize them, are easy to adopt in theory, but much courage is often needed to stand up for them in the midst of the fighting parties. When the norm should be that only medical priority or the grade of vulnerability of groups to be fed should decide the order of assistance, warlords in the area may demand something quite different. The medical profession and relief workers are often left alone to speak out for universal norms of humanity.

5 THE CHANGING CHARACTER OF WAR

ARTO NOKKALA

War is a form of intentional conflict behaviour between at least two parties using intensive organized physical violence against each other. The character of war is affected both by technology and politics. Although the primary perspective is political, the technological perspective highlights essential changes in the conduct of war. Armed conflict is intrastate and, so far, fought outside the euroatlantic security community. Peace operations are not outside the definition of war, if the intervener uses intensive force. Most war actors are small and non-state, motivated by a variety of interests. Nevertheless, war is still predominantly a political act to change the distribution of power. Technological development has led to a bifurcation of military capabilities and, in the short run, a mixed image of war in terms of action strategies. Most developed countries present an image of war with a non-linear battlefield, where fighting occurs between highly mobile integrated forces with cap- abilities to concentrate accurate firepower at great distances. The dominant image of recent wars, however, includes mass armies. Their action strategies have often changed only little, in spite of some new technology. Development of information management supports visions of infrastructure warfare, where damage is caused using cumulative effects of relatively minor violence targeted on vulnerable nodes. This may give a softer image of war than is characteristic of traditional conflicts, and future wars may be less total. But they are no less destructive, since the separation of civilians and soldiers becomes more difficult, territorial borders less important and more violent means are still available. Nevertheless, the dominant image of war at the beginning of the 21st century seems to remain that of an armed intrastate conflict, with a relatively strong international dimension and some more highly sophisticated technology coming into play.

What is war?

Politics, international law and science give a variety of answers to the question 'What is war?'. Common to many definitions, however, is that the dominant feature of war is large-scale organized violence, employed for political ends.[1] The ancient war theoretician

Sun Tzu claimed, though, that subjugating one's enemy by a threat of violence represents the height of martial skills.[2] Nevertheless the basic character of war includes fighting, and with it suffering, loss of life and material destruction. Fighting is the organized use of force, mutual systematic physical violence, where opposing actors tend to treat each other as a group of dehumanized objects.

To underline the physicality of violence is to reject the idea, supported by the almost pervasive presence of structural violence, that human society needs continuously to be at war.[3] In spite of that, there is no reason to overrule the assumption that structural violence may lead to physical violence and vice versa. But the physicality of violence highlights the fact that human collectivities use technology in order to damage each other. Its qualities affect the magnitude of harm caused. Yet war, like any human action, remains intentional, even when the fighting has unintended consequences. These belong to the essential character of war in spite of efforts to limit violence.

War is a form of conflict behaviour between at least two parties. Military intervention means backing a spectrum of international political measures to manage a violent conflict in a contested area, depending on the role and intensity of violence from the viewpoint of the parties involved.

It can be argued that so-called peace enforcement is not necessarily non-war, even if its legitimation might make a difference. This argument points out that the motivational basis, objectives, intensity and norms of violence also vary in armed two-party confrontations. War is *always* somehow politically limited and ends sooner or later. It is misleading to exclude outright all modern interventions from the definition of war, even if they claim to be aimed at stopping the killing and restoring peace between the primary parties. This is even clearer in cases where the intervener chooses a side.

Factors affecting the character of war: technology or politics?

Scientific-technical development produces equipment and technologies that may be used in warfare. Man-made technology creates both opportunities for and restrictions to warfare, and changes its character. In principle, every material item can be used as a weapon, a tool for physical violence. Production of items intended to be used as weapons depends on many technologies. The modern military organization uses a lot of civilian technology, which is integrated in actual weapons. Dual-use technology is ever more problematic from the viewpoint of arms control and disarmament. The technological perspective focuses especially on how the physical, largely measurable qualities of the equipment affect its impact on a target. The production, dissemination and quality of technology can introduce incentives or restrictions to its damaging use. Technological development that changes the character of war usually increases its destructive capacity, even if some technologies may offer opportunities to limit the damage.

During the 20th century humankind has developed a level of technology that might result in the self-destruction of most of global society. Yet the development of weapons of mass destruction has not increased the fear of war sufficiently to surpass the fear of defeat at war, which might have led to disarmament and a universal denouncement of war. In this sense, the impact of technology has turned out to be limited.

The 1991 Gulf War has often been presented as an example of new technologies at war. On the other hand, its representative value from the technological perspective must not be overemphasized. Security developments and other aspects of the conflict situation matter more.

From a political perspective the main focus is on asking how collective choices produce a quest for destructive technology. Armaments are developed and purchased according to the requirements and understanding of the political situation. The appearance and character of war changes along with policies. From this perspective, social incentives and non-incentives to acquire weapons and resort to their use are most important. Technological capability matters, but the framing of arguments about ends and means is crucial. Essential questions concern the perceptions of the actors of the threat and possibility of war, as well as of others and themselves, and of different interests and their compatibility. Cultural norms affect the conduct of war even when basic principles of military organizations are shared.

In describing the background, appearance, objectives, cessation, consequences and avoidance of war the perspective of politics is primary. But in order to highlight changes in the essential character of war at the level of violence used, the technological perspective is also needed, as we shall see below.

Changes of appearance and agency

Since the Second World War (WW II) more and more armed conflict has been intrastate, even if one of the warring parties is a government. Wars have mostly appeared outside the euroatlantic security community, which has led to the conclusion that democracies don't fight each other. But countries within that community have used weapons in the management of conflicts in Somalia, Bosnia and Kosovo, and played a central role in defeating Iraq in 1991. Inside the community, the only recent conflict counting as a war has been fought in Northern Ireland.

Wars in which both the two primary parties are states have turned out to be rare, in spite of the ever-increasing number of states in the world. The other trend in the Cold War period is intervention by a state or a coalition of states in a war or lesser armed conflict as a third, interested party under the mandate of an international organization. The character of intervention has changed not only in its legitimation and number of actors, but in its actual conduct. The intervener does not necessarily choose to support one side, but certainly departs from traditional peacekeeping methods in readiness to use even large-scale force.

In addition to the already-mentioned fact that the protagonists of war are often rather small and non-state, a somewhat new trait is that they may involve private armies and be motivated by a variety of factional, economic, religious, criminal and sometimes markedly private interests.[4] Intervening states, on the other hand, argue that their use of force is motivated by human rights concerns and the need to restore peace and law and order, or to rebuild the state and society – even if their own interests of security, prestige and profit are also involved.

In all situations war remains a political act with an interest in changing the distribution of power. Primary actors usually also have a territorial interest in the conflict that goes beyond having a base from which to launch the violence. Politically motivated terrorism can also be understood as war, if the violence is large-scale and the conflict can be systematized between definable parties. At present, however, most terrorism does not qualify for that definition.

Technologies and action strategies

Changes in the character of war are illuminated in action strategies, which lump together military strategy, operational doctrines and tactics. Their nature is largely determined by the technology available. In evaluating the current scene, attention must be paid both to recent wars and to projections of future wars, which are used to support political decisions, affect the reproduction of military organizations and may form self-fulfilling prophecies in social processes.

Especially since the 1991 Gulf War , the effects of technological development on the character of war and the strategic environment have been called a 'revolution in military affairs' (RMA).This image largely contradicts actual performance in current wars. It is also highly problematic because of its technological enthusiasm. The RMA has been a tool of policies to legitimate military planning, especially in the United States. With the Gulf War cited as an example, the RMA has been widely propagated, rather as the Strategic Defence Initiative (Star Wars) was during the 1980s.

In spite of its deficiencies and the fact that it is only the latest in a long line of 'military revolutions', the RMA represents the present military-technological and strategic-operational trend. It describes a war scenario between two technologically developed state actors, or a conflict in which at least one of the parties has the technology. But it can also be used as a yardstick to highlight some effects of high technology in less-intensive intrastate wars.

The RMA results partly from the diminishing political utility of nuclear weapons. It is also largely a strategy preferred by democratic countries, gaining impetus from their intrinsic reluctance to send soldiers abroad on international conflict-management tasks. But for many other countries and social groups, the RMA presents both the 21st-century technology-based military threat and capabilities which they have to consider in their military policies.

Plainly, in the arms dynamic of the world, the RMA is about utilizing new highly sophisticated technology in qualitative armaments, largely replacing the large numbers of soldiers and weapons in modern military organizations. Military efficiency is believed to increase and personnel costs to be reduced. The increasing output appears as improved opportunities to concentrate devastating firepower from great distances on the enemy's centre of gravity. The new approach is supported by developments in information technology, improved logistics and increased mobility of forces. The qualitative arms dynamic is promoted by countries which have the most advanced production of superior technology and access to it.[5]

Opportunities of states to keep up with the technological development of arms become uneven, at least in the short run. Globalization, the end of the Cold War and changes in superpower status have resulted in a situation in which, more clearly than ever, the world forms a strategic unit for some actors, like the United States and the North Atlantic Treaty Organization (NATO). This gives them opportunities to project military force, while seeking to avoid actual involvement in wars. At the same time, they can restrict flows of new weapons if they want to.

Of the prominent military actors of the past, Russia obviously cannot participate in the RMA because of its lack of resources, even if it has for a long time been aware of the consequences of the new technology. Non-state actors and most of the developing countries, but also large and medium-sized powers like China and North Korea, still depend on large numbers of soldiers. In their arms production, these two countries are outside the newest developments. China is expected to technologize its military during the economic rise of the country.

Today, military-technological and strategic differentiation is determined in the first place by military capabilities, even if almost every military organization tries to draw something out of the new technology. Countries that have been successful in the qualitative arms race are in a technological sense more ready to fight 'third-wave wars'[6] by professionals and advanced conventional weapons. Other states and non-state actors still have mass armies which lack computers, electronics, communications and integrated weapons systems.

Divergent military capabilities lead in the short run to a mixed image of war in terms of action strategies. Much depends on who the actors in the specific war are, and to what extent they are supported by an actor with technologically-advanced arms, but local conditions also play a part.

The image of recent post-Cold War wars is predominantly one of fighting in which parties use traditional infantry and artillery tactics. The army is the most important force. It is in a relatively independent role in relation to the air force or navy. Parties have usually tried to improve their intelligence, command, firepower and mobility with some new technology. On the other hand, several intrastate wars have involved mainly protracted, localized and occasional fighting between small units. They use light arms such as assault and sniper rifles and hand-grenades, random mortar and artillery fire, and antipersonnel mines.

In intrastate wars parties often have close to equal military capabilities. The inferior party strengthens its position by guerrilla-type action. Knowledge of local conditions of terrain and weather, and the availability of supplies and popular support form central ingredients of the tactics, without any major change since the time of the Cold War. The presence of small and rather independent units, the lack of centralized leadership, shifting loyalties and motivations, often loose norms regarding the use of weapons and locally-changing balances of forces contribute to situations in which civilians have become deeply involved and are intentionally targeted.

Built-up areas like towns still represent a military advantage for the defending side in spite of technological developments. But urban warfare is characterized by attrition, occasional high casualty rates and material destruction, depending on the intensity of fighting. This was evidenced especially in Chechnya, but on a smaller scale also in Bosnia.

In the image of an interstate war the qualitatively advanced military can be expected to have a penetrating versatile intelligence, great flexibility and mobility of forces, and several opportunities to concentrate firepower on relatively small targets even from great distances. Instead of sending in troops, aerial bombing and missiles may be used to provoke the desired changes in the behaviour of the adversary. Defence and offence are more difficult to separate from each other than in fighting situations between less technical armies.

The battlefield becomes non-linear. Fighting is more a series of fast encounters between mobile units instead of fixed positions of troops and long periods of relative inactivity. Army, air force and navy act in an integrated fashion. The army is increasingly air-mechanized, taking the airspace close to ground for its use by a variety of helicopters and assault aircraft. The battlefield is also extended horizontally in the sense that the military organization may be dependent on foreign support and access to information sources more widely than is usual in intrastate wars.

The new technology is also stressed in the peace operations of international conflict management. Air power is demonstrated and used, not least because the intervener often finds it politically less costly than sending in the army. Non-lethal weapons[7] and automation will increasingly be used in the future.

The development and inclusion of new technologies is increasingly motivated by efforts to avoid media setbacks in the information age. Democratic states especially try to legitimize their war efforts through global communication in front of ever-larger audiences. Media and networks are also carefully used for propaganda and psychological warfare in conflict management operations. Modern technology helps to create a tidy image of warfare compared with a dirty one produced by less sophisticated technology. In the Gulf War the 'less favourable effects' of the coalition's weapons were efficiently censored. Parties to intrastate conflicts, on the other hand, use close-range weapons whose effects come easily to the attention of people outside the conflict zone if the media are present.

It is true that some new military technology has an accuracy that makes it possible to avoid so-called collateral damage. On the other hand, war with new weapons in urbanized environments may have consequences that are extremely difficult to evaluate in advance. An almost total lack of civil defence often increases the damage. A relatively new phenomenon of war is major local destruction and high casualties in a very short time caused by air-strikes and artillery fire. It may be deliberately sought, even if the targeted force has lost its ability to take cover or its will to fight.

Obtaining information and processing it, while preventing the opponent from doing the same, have become important means for warring parties to avoid their own casualties. Informational superiority is often presented as a blueprint for victory. Developments in intelligence and information management improve the opportunities of most developed countries to acquire versatile and real-time knowledge about the enemy. The more advanced military can increase its opportunities to surprise and concentrate its destructive force. At the same time, it can free up troops and firepower and substitute for them by complicating the information management of the adversary. All the while, however, it preserves its capability for maximizing firepower if and when it decides to strike.

A soft image of war: no less destructive

The development of information management not only affects the character of single military operations but also has wider consequences, to the extent that the definition of war must be questioned. Intelligence, psychological and information warfare form an integrated totality. Along with technological developments, this trend applies increasingly to intrastate wars, even if methods are much more context-dependent and technical means often less sophisticated.

The party which is more capable of information warfare, or the intervener in a conflict, may use force less visibly or at a greater distance, multiplying it with information manipulation. A strong party can also unite information attacks with air strikes, sabotage, the deployment of special forces and other subversive means, all tailored together in a civil–military operation.

In developed segments of society, using information as a weapon is encouraged by access to largely commercial information networks. Actors try to affect the direction of crisis development to their own perceived advantage. On the other hand, the global character and uncontrollability of networks make their wide systematic use difficult. Several niches offer opportunities for weak actors to challenge state military and police forces, generating mistrust of their capacity to offer protection.[8]

In many parts of the world, state borders become ever more porous as urbanization continues and social mobility increases. Social systems have more nodes that are physically vulnerable. For military planners, such conditions provide the incentive to inflict wide-ranging damage on the potential adversary by relatively restricted but directed violence. This kind of warfare, focused simultaneously on material resources and information management, can be called infrastructure war. The adversary's important communications systems will be cut; disinformation will be sown; information retrieval may be restricted. Information warfare and preparation for it are strongly linked to a preoccupation with information safety in normal times. Unilateral peacetime efforts to gain control of networks at the expense of other actors go hand in hand with opportunities for information superiority in war.

In infrastructure war, armed action will be directed first of all at those targets which would be most crucial to the opponent's technical ability to mount an organized response. Preparation for such a war stimulates the development of highly specialized forces to take advantage of the situation before the actual outbreak of open hostilities. A disincentive to infrastructure offensives is the possible negative economic, environmental or social feedback effects, which are difficult to control in an interdependent world.

The ability to plan and execute an information war will become increasingly available to small and non-state actors, who would then be able to extend their military activities globally. Theoretically, a form of future war might find a relatively small group, either in concert with or independently of territorially-based interests, fighting a long-term, long-range war against some other group by recourse to terrorism and information networks. Inevitably, this kind of warfare might often be mixed with violent international criminal activity.

Information and infrastructure wars present a softer image of war than do traditional armed conflicts, and are harder to understand – during the calmer passages of their duration, at any rate – as the large-scale application of physical force. Even if such a war may present less instant killing, it is nevertheless no less destructive in terms of suffering than old-style military conflict. It is also true that new applications of action strategies and war technologies often coexist alongside the old options.

Conclusions

The present bifurcation of military capabilities may not necessarily continue in the future if military actors in conflict regions have the interests and resources to acquire new technology. Leading military actors like the United States have long prepared themselves for a wide selection of different contingencies. The term 'military operations other than war' is illustrative of this thinking. Such operations may include intensive violence from the viewpoint of the actor targeted by them. Military organizations also tend to underline connections between real war and other activities.

The dominant image of war at the beginning of the 21st century slowly but not necessarily turns into a more high-tech intrastate armed conflict with a relatively dense international dimension. Wars may be fewer in the future than today but at the same time their variety will increase, with interventions of various kinds. War will not be restricted to the least-developed states. Most states still use and create images of intensive interstate wars as the basis of their military policies, even if militaries seem to be given a wider spectrum of tasks. Indeed, many of them do not have much to do with classical warfare.

War may be less 'total' for all the parties involved, but clearly separating civilians and soldiers becomes increasingly difficult. Civilians are not only deliberately targeted, as in numerous recent conflicts and terrorist attacks. They are also increasingly used for war efforts. Territorial borders will become less important for the military actions of the future. In spite of some opposing trends, like the professionalization of armies and increasing accuracy of high-tech weapons, all of this points to a transition from a counterforce to a countervalue strategy.

Low-intensity warfare, prominence of intrastate armed conflicts and visions of information and infrastructure war together point to more complicated definitions of war and peace. As such they challenge the politics of disarmament and international law and all those in the medical and other professions interested in alleviating suffering and promoting human rights and responsibilities.

NOTES AND REFERENCES

1. One possible way of rating the intensity of violence is to consider the number of deaths it causes. If an armed conflict causes, for example, at least 1000 deaths per year, it can be understood as a war. A very different possibility is to understand the phenomenon and its scale as a socially-constructed matter of judgement, and as such continuously changing.
2. Sun Tzu (1963), *The Art of War*, with a Preface by Samuel Griffith, Oxford: Oxford University Press.
3. Galtung, Johan (1984) *There Are Alternatives! Four Roads to Peace and Security*, Nottingham: Spokesman.

4. Kaldor, Mary (1999), *New and Old Wars. Organized Violence in a Global Era*, Cambridge: Polity Press.

5. Buzan, Barry and Eric Herring (1998), *The Arms Dynamic in World Politics*, Boulder: Lynne Rienner.

6. Toffler, Alvin and Heidi (1993), *War and Anti-War. Survival at the Dawn of the Twenty-first Century*, Boston: Little, Brown & Company.

7 Dando, Malcolm (1998), *A New Form of Warfare. The Rise of Non-lethal Weapons*, London: Brassey's.

8. Kushner, Harvey W. (ed.) (1998), *The Future of Terrorism. Violence in the New Millennium*, London: Sage.

Address for correspondence

Koivukatu 9 C, 11710 Riihimäki, Finland
Tel: +358 19 719 988; email: arto.nokkala@kolumbus.fi.

6 MILITARY MEDICINE

MATTI PONTEVA

The role of military medicine in the management of the medical consequences of war is quite unambiguous, but problematic when estimating the general possibilities of primary prevention of wars. In practice it is very important to keep up the humane principles of the medical profession and obey both the ratified international conventions and laws and the national laws. Central areas in military medicine are advanced first care and surgery, control of infectious diseases and the medical part of stress management. Preventive measures are emphasized. Though the efficiency of military medicine has been satisfactory in the developed countries and the possibilities of managing most war situations are still good there are alarming signs concerning the future. From the standpoint of prevention there always remains the basic dilemma: efficient military medical services in the operational area increase the possibilities of continuing warfare.

The moral of military medicine

The role of military medicine in the prevention of wars is confusing because it can be said that the primary prevention of war has already failed when medicine is needed. However, this is not a reason to neglect the medical care of war victims, be they armed or unarmed. Most wars break out independently of any deliberate estimation of their consequences to human beings, but without organized medical care the consequences could be much more devastating. In severe circumstances the military medical organization is often the only one that is able to act satisfactorily.

Members of the medical or any other health care profession have the basic obligation to act in the best interests of the patient.[1] As members of the armed services of some country they also have commitments to serve military goals determined by their commanders. Sometimes this may lead to very severe moral conflicts, especially when it does not seem ethical to obey only the rule of conserving the own 'fighting strength'.[2] It may be easier to think that medical obligations should always take precedence over military ones, but in practice this is not always possible and can sometimes endanger patients or reduce the care results.

A general rule must be to follow the generally accepted medical principles, especially the unconditional ones. Many restrictions are inevitable in the field but, nevertheless, the wartime patient has the right to be treated in the best possible way. Sometimes this may only be the proper prioritizing, depending on the prognosis in the real circumstances, followed by palliative care. Compromising with such things as autonomy, privacy and alternativity cannot be avoided, but principles of impartiality and equity should be followed as far as possible.

In this connection the significance of international conventions[3] must not be underestimated. They are described in Chapter 44 of this book: here I will only reassert that the principles of impartiality and the right to specific protection are very generally accepted. They also give the health professionals the moral justification to perform their medical duties in circumstances where their freedom of action is restricted for military reasons. Naturally there are many other internationally ratified and national laws that are to be obeyed. As a matter of principle, military medical personnel are obliged to obey only lawful orders.

Moral aspects are also essential in resisting the use of inhuman warfare methods. Conventions, laws and preventive information are often not sufficient; continuous observation and reporting during the situation is needed, disregarding the possibility of becoming personally endangered. Refusal to participate in torture and inhuman medical trials should be self-evident for all who participate in medical work in the military.

Medical care in the military

Military medicine is not actually a separate branch of medicine but a common frame for general and special medical methods that are applied in certain circumstances. Its role can vary widely from the helper of an individual soldier in the west to the theory and practice of public health service in the former eastern bloc.

The possibilities of curative military medicine were relatively weak up to the late 19th century. From then onwards the general development of surgery and medicine brought along new methods that were applicable also in the field. When they turned out to be life-saving or function-saving the consequence was some kind of chain reaction: soldiers received new hope and their leaders new possibilities to conserve the fighting strength, and pressure to promote curative military medicine came from both sides. Naturally the humane ideas of Henri Dunant and others operated similarily and had a particular influence on the organization of impartial medical care. However, without the development of medicine the impact of humane activities would have been much less significant.

During active fighting the most important sector of military medicine is advanced first care and surgery near the place of incident. The number of victims is often so large that optimizing the quantity of those who are savable inevitably requires some conventional prioritizing principles for setting the individual prognosis at different levels of treatment and evacuation. This has resulted in the development of the principles of triage, which are more or less followed also in civilian mass catastrophes or disasters. In modern war a constantly increasing proportion of the victims have been civilians. They are to be treated and evacuated in accordance with the same principles as soldiers, and in most circumstances the field medical organization is the only functional one. Lack of resources, both in personnel and in materials, is a rule when extensive battlefield medical care is considered; these resources must be used equally.

Another central feature in military medicine through the ages has been the fight against infectious diseases. Up to the 20th century infections killed more soldiers than weapons and still cause more sick days and inability to serve than physical traumas, even in fighting troops. The most important medical discovery of the 20th century, anti-biotics, was not made by military physicians, but was desperately needed in military medicine. A proper restrictiveness in the use of antibiotics is essential in hard and defect-ive circumstances and, again, the principles must be the same for soldiers and civilians.

The third central area in military medicine nowadays is psychiatry or mental health work. The area may be divided into psychiatric prevention, care and rehabilitation, which belong self-evidently to medicine, and stress management, which is a much wider con-cept and concerns, in addition to medical personnel, all military leaders, chaplains and behavioural experts among the troops. General field-care principles originating in the Russo–Japanese war of 1904–5, namely proximity–immediacy–expectancy, are seen as very important in military psychiatry. Later they were widened to include the principles of brevity–simplicity–centrality (BICEPS). Such managing principles to promote rapid recovery from psychic trauma in time of war are also valuable in the care of civilian victims.

The development of medical and social rehabilitation also owes much to military medicine because the need to promote the recovery of war veterans has in many cases been the starting-point for wider rehabilitation arrangements and organizations. The basic idea may be more humane and psychological, aimed not only at retaining the fighting strength, as rehabilitation can sometimes take years. A well-functioning rehabilitation system is a signal to veterans that society will take care of them, and also of the civilian victims of war, in the name of impartiality and equity.

It is impossible to imagine that the previously mentioned functions of medical care in fighting troops could be realized without an expert body which is an organic part of military forces. Therefore it is not seen as unethical to care for victims of war by serving in military medical organizations, but an ethical dilemma can arise if professional medical measures begin to look as if they are supporting the continuation of war. Strictly to observe the international conventions may be the military medical professional's best way to avoid conflicts of conscience.

Possibilities of curative medicine in war

Management of the immediate medical consequences of war depends in the first place on the professional skills, on the technical and material premises as well as on the quantitative personnel resources of the medical organization. In addition, changes in the methods of warfare – the increase of firepower and mobility, increasing numbers of civilians left at the target area of military operations, amongst other factors – have a growing influence on the success of medical work in the field. Between the Crimean War of 1854–56 and the 1950–53 Korean War (US troops) the proportion of combatants who died from wounds decreased from 20 to 2.5 per cent,[4] which reflects the general development of advanced first care and the possibilities of a developed western society. Changes in the correlation between site and fatality of wound have been surprisingly small, e.g. head, face and neck wounds accounted for 41 per cent of all fatal wounds in the US Civil War and 42 per cent in the Second World War. A small proportional decrease in the lethality percentage of thoracic and abdominal wounds has been achieved through arduous and expensive methods: intravenous infusion, rapid evacuation and operation together with special surgical methods. In economically poor countries such advanced first care and field surgery is not possible.

An important change has also been the increase of multiple wounds which is not yet clearly seen in the statistics of great wars. Presumably this tendency will continue. Use of high-velocity projectiles will make wound treatment more difficult and time-consuming. The growing proportion of civilian victims in operational areas will be an aspect of refugee problems. Thus it is probable that possibilities of managing the immediate medical consequences of warfare through the procedures of military medicine, even though these are intensified and advanced, will in the future diminish in most countries.

Preventive medicine in the military

Before the era of antibiotics, prophylactic methods were the only effective ones in resisting infectious diseases. Therefore it is logical that many old military medical orders deal with primitive measures of field hygiene, some of them still being almost up to date. Application of vaccination, quarantine and comprehensive desinfection in the military has often been an example to civil authorities of how to administer preventive measures. In exceptional circumstances strict cooperation is needed and the protection of the civil population is not practically possible without exchanging timely epidemiological data with the military. During war the hygienic level as a rule decreases and the first warnings of threatening epidemics usually come from the military.

Resisting the use of weapons of mass destruction and other forbidden weapons also belongs to preventive military medicine. In this connection it is very important to separate promotion of a forbidden arms system from the development of methods for treating the possible victims of such arms. The difference may, however, be quite small, especially for some biological and chemical weapons.

Most military forces have special orders of field health-care to resist the dangers of decreasing hygiene and possible epidemics. If there are civilians in the area of operations, it is always best to obey the same orders. Naturally the conventional principles of equal rights to medical care are the same, also in the question of prophylactic measures.

Application of medical services in the military way

Military medical professionals are working within an organization which is hierachical and formal and has the central obligation to prepare for war. Nevertheless, it is possible to maintain the principles of medical ethics if the leaders obey laws and international conventions. Therefore it is probable that the same kinds of arrangements are also applicable in other organizations that have the same kind of structure and operate in difficult circumstances. A good example is the peacekeeping operations of the United Nations, where the organization of forces and their medical services is military practically without any exception; this is even more so for the peace-enforcing operations. As Dag Hammarskiöld said: 'Peacekeeping is not a job for soldiers, but no one else can do it', so we can say that there are many demanding international tasks in which organizing the medical services according to the military model is the best and sometimes the only way. The situation is often the same in purely humanitarian operations, especially when the external circumstances are severe. Occasionally the formal organization is not as important as the military medical knowledge of operating in primitive conditions.

Military medicine in the prevention of wars

Possibilities for a total prevention of wars through military medical actions are small, but intervening in the social causes of war by socio-medical research and information is possible. The matters in question are in fact extensive and global, such as population explosion, social injustice, exploitation and structural poverty: these are not matters for a restricted branch of medicine.

Military medicine has nevertheless its own role in the management of the consequences of war. It is clear that refusal to help the soldier victims of war is not a solution and could be against the physician's responsibility to treat those who are in medical need. Medical professionals in the military must retain their professionality and obey in the first place both internationally-ratified conventions and laws and the national laws. They must not discriminate against anybody who needs medical help; they treat human beings, not enemies. Strict adherence to humane principles also means psychological prevention of the demoralizing effects of warfare.

From the point of view of war prevention the basic dilemma remains: effective activity of military medicine improves the chances of continuing warfare. This undesired outcome seems to be unavoidable.

REFERENCES

1. Howe, E.G. (1981), 'Medical Ethics – Are They Different for the Military Physician?', *Military Medicine* 146: 837–41; Moskop, J.C. (1998) 'A Moral Analysis of Military Medicine', *Military Medicine* 163: 76–9.
2. Sidel, V.W. (1997), 'The Roles and Ethics of Health Professionals in War', in B.S. Levy and V.W. Sidel (eds) *War and Public Health*, New York: Oxford University Press and the American Public Health Association, 281–92 (Chapter 18).
3. Basic Rules of the Geneva Conventions and their Additional Protocols (1983), Geneva: ICRC.
4. Garfield, R.M. and A.I. Neugut (1991), 'Epidemiologic Analysis of Warfare. A Historical Review', *JAMA* 266: 688–92.

Address for correspondence: see Chapter 3.

DIFFERENT ARMS SYSTEMS

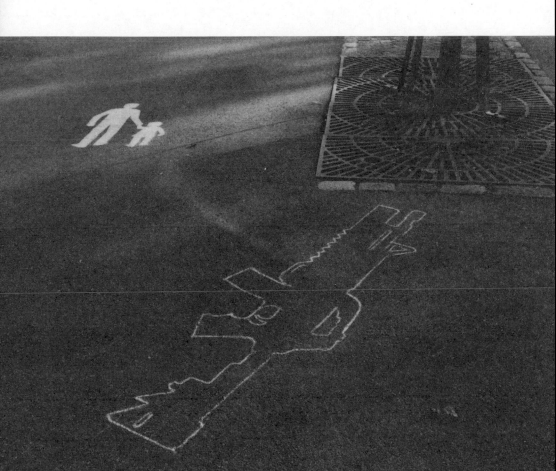

Machine gun
Oliver Whitehead

7 ANTIPERSONNEL WEAPONS

ERIC PROKOSCH AND ERNST JAN HOGENDOORN

'Antipersonnel' weapons are weapons designed for use against people. One defini tion of antipersonnel is that of *The United States Air Force Dictionary* (1966): 'designed to destroy or obstruct personnel'. They are distinguished in military terminology from wea- pons to be used against other targets, such as antitank, antiaircraft, or antimateriel weapons.

'Conventional' weapons are weapons other than chemical, biological, or nuclear weapons; incendiary and smoke munitions are normally considered 'conventional'. Although various military powers retain stockpiles of chemical, biological or nuclear weapons, virtually all armaments used on today's battlefields are conventional.

Most antipersonnel weapons are conventional. Most of them wound or kill through the violent transfer of energy to the body by a small piece of metal, typically a bullet, or a fragment thrown off by the explosion of a bomb or shell. Other sources of wounding by conventional weapons include blast and fire.

The distinction between antipersonnel and other munitions is not always clear, as often the same weapon can be used against various targets. Sometimes several effects are built into the same weapon: an antitank warhead may, for example, incorporate an anti- personnel feature. Some weapons have dual, multiple or non-specific military designa- tions because of such multiplicity of use (for example, 'antipersonnel/antimateriel', or 'general purpose' to denote a high-explosive bomb which is intended for use against various targets). The use of antipersonnel weapons in warfare presents two basic kinds of health problems: wounding, and other effects which are secondary to the destruction which the weapons are meant to cause.

This chapter offers a survey of trends in modern antipersonnel weaponry and an examination of the health consequences. The weapons are grouped according to wounding mechanisms and other basic design features, and the wounding process is described in terms of the main factors producing wounds of greater or lesser severity. Some reference is made to the problems posed by other conventional weapons also. (Antipersonnel mines are discussed in a separate chapter of this book.)

Since the second half of the 19th century, attempts have been made to restrict or ban the use of various weapons in order to reduce the suffering inflicted in war. In the 1970s, in response to international concern over weaponry introduced in the US–Indochina war, Sweden and other countries proposed a new series of bans and restrictions. The proposals led to the adoption in 1980 of the Convention on Prohibitions or Restrictions on the Use of Certain Conventional Weapons Which May be Deemed to be Excessively Injurious or to have Indiscriminate Effects ('Convention on Conventional Weapons', cited below as the 'CCW'). Further bans and restrictions were adopted at the first Review Conference of the CCW, held in 1995 and 1996.

The existing international bans and restrictions on the use of conventional weapons and the prospects for adopting further ones are discussed in this chapter, along with their bases under international humanitarian law, particularly as set forth in the 1977 Protocol Additional to the Geneva Conventions of 12 August 1949, and Relating to the Protection of Victims of International Armed Conflicts (Protocol I) (cited here as 1977 Protocol I).

The chapter also considers ethical questions for members of the medical profession who engage in antipersonnel weapons research.

Small-calibre weapons systems

Most small-calibre weapons are rifled guns. A spiral groove (rifling) on the inside of the barrel imparts spin to the bullet, stabilising the bullet in flight.

Exterior ballistics, the study of the motion of projectiles in flight, shows that a spinning bullet experiences a periodic yawing motion, a deviation of the longitudinal axis of the bullet from the tangent of the trajectory. During the first part of its flight, the maximum angle of yaw may be of the order of 3 to 5 degrees. Later along the trajectory, the yawing decreases.

If the angle of yaw is relatively large when the bullet hits the body, the yaw will be magnified in the body and the bullet will undergo a rapid periodic turning movement, often popularly described as tumbling. If the yaw is small, the bullet may start turning at some point further along its trajectory inside the body, or it may travel through and emerge from the other side without turning.

As a bullet starts to turn, an increasingly larger surface of the bullet presses against the tissues and an increasingly greater amount of its kinetic energy is transferred to the tissues, thrusting them aside from the bullet path extremely fast and producing a 'temporary cavity' which lasts a few milliseconds. The displaced tissues are stretched, damaged, or destroyed. Broadly speaking, the greater the kinetic energy transfer, the more extensive the wound. The sooner a bullet starts to turn on entering the body, the greater its wounding capacity.

Recent research by the late professor of forensic medicine Karl G. Sellier and the ballistic scientist Beat P. Kneubuehl has yielded a comprehensive and convincing account of the process of bullet wounding and the design parameters producing different degrees of severity of injury.[1] The turning motion is described by these authors as one where the bullet turns approximately 180 degrees, so that it is travelling with the base forward, then turns broadside and oscillates around this position as it continues to travel. According to Sellier and Kneubuehl, the tendency of a bullet to start turning early after striking the body is dependent on the angle of yaw on impact, the shape of the bullet nose, and the gyroscopic stability of the bullet. Gyroscopic stability is, in turn, dependent on such factors as the rate of spin, the moments of inertia and the geometry of the bullet. In general, the greater the gyroscopic stability of a bullet (for example, because of a higher spin rate), the further it will go in the body before starting to turn; and the shorter a bullet is in relation to its diameter, the less likely it is to turn.

Knowledge of these factors can permit the designer of a small-calibre weapons system to increase its wounding capacity and thus the level of suffering which the weapon is likely to inflict or, on the contrary, to decrease it.

In 1899 the Hague Peace Conference, in reaction to the British use of mushrooming 'dum-dum' bullets, adopted a Declaration prohibiting the use in war of 'bullets which expand or flatten easily in the human body, such as bullets with a hard envelope which does not entirely cover the core or is pierced with incisions'. Since then, the Hague Declaration Concerning the Prohibition of Dum-Dum Bullets has been largely respected, at least in the letter of the law: as far as is known, the bullets specifically described in the declaration have never been fielded in a military weapons system and have been used in war only by individual soldiers in isolated incidents.

Modern military rifle bullets are fully enclosed in a hard metal jacket and therefore will not mushroom on hitting the body, unless someone has tampered with them by cutting or otherwise weakening the nose, which would make their use illegal under the Hague Declaration. But if a bullet starts turning, there will be massive energy transfer to the tissues, comparable to what happens at the surface of the body when it is struck by a mushrooming bullet; and the earlier a bullet starts to turn after entering the body, the greater the likelihood of a large wound. Furthermore, depending on the bullet construction, the stresses on a bullet as it turns can cause the bullet to deform or break up, adding to the potential wounding effect because of the increase in the surface area of bullet material pressing against the tissues.

Concern over the potentially devastating effects of rifle bullets revived in the 1960s with reports of the lethality of the AR-15 5.56mm rifle (later designated M16) used by US forces in Indochina. Prompted by the concern, in 1974 seven states presented a proposal for a new ban on the use of especially injurious bullets. The proposal came under attack by the NATO countries and is not reflected in the CCW. However, in 1979 the UN conference which was drafting the Convention adopted a resolution inviting governments to carry out further research on the wounding effects of small-calibre weapons systems and appealing to all governments 'to exercise the utmost care in the development of small-calibre weapon systems, so as to avoid an unnecessary escalation of the injurious effects of such systems'.

The research envisioned in the resolution had already begun. In 1975 Sweden convened an international interdisciplinary symposium on wound ballistics. Further symposia were held in 1977, 1978, 1981, 1985 and 1988 (the last of them in China). Many papers were presented by military and medical experts from different countries and many topics were discussed, including not only the physical process of wounding but complex physiological effects, the treatment of injuries and techniques of testing and observation. One of the benefits of the symposia was that a body of knowledge was being built up, available in the open literature and reflecting the approaches of different national research traditions.

In a presentation to the fourth International Symposium on Wound Ballistics in 1981, a representative of the Belgian Fabrique Nationale Herstal (FN Herstal), developer of the new NATO standard SS109 5.56mm rifle bullet, described the design factors resulting in a bullet which would be relatively unlikely to turn. He made clear that the SS109 design programme had been heavily influenced by the appeal in the 1979 resolution of the UN conference to avoid unnecessarily increasing the injurious effects of small-calibre weapon systems.

In August 1994, at the third session of the group of governmental experts preparing the first Review Conference of the CCW, Switzerland introduced a proposal for a new protocol to the convention aimed at prohibiting the use of excessively injurious small-calibre arms and ammunition. The formula offered had several advantages over the seven states' proposal of 1974 and the modifications of that proposal introduced by the sponsoring states later in the 1970s. Most importantly, it specified a minimum length for the 'narrow channel' corresponding to the wound track from the point of entrance into the body to the point where the bullet starts to turn. (From a humanitarian point of view, the narrow channel should be as long as possible.)[2]

The Review Conference did not take action on the Swiss proposal, but in the Final Declaration adopted by the conference it proposed that the question of preparing a new protocol on small-calibre weapons and ammunition could be considered at the next Review Conference of the CCW, due to be held not later than 2001. As a preparatory step, over 40 states sent experts to an International Workshop on Wound Ballistics, convened by the Swiss Government on 7–8 October 1997. A second workshop, focusing on methods which could be used to test the wounding effects of different projectiles, was held in March 1999. Ultimately, internationally-agreed testing methods will be needed if a new ban on excessively injurious small-calibre weapons systems is to be based on objective criteria relating to their effects.

Weapons already fielded such as the Russian AK-74 rifle, reported to cause severe wounds, and possible future developments in small-calibre weapons systems need to be kept under scrutiny in the interest of reducing battlefield suffering as far as possible. One of these is the 'personal defence weapon', a new concept for replacing the traditional handgun with a weapon which is small and light but has some of the characteristics of a submachine gun. One company, the Belgian FN Herstal, has produced such a weapon, the P90 personal defence weapon, and is pressing for NATO standardization based on the bullet used in the weapon. Several other companies are developing similar weapons.

The P90 personal defence weapon fires a 5.7mm bullet, the SS90, which the manufacturer claims will penetrate body armour or a ballistic fibre helmet at a range of 100m or more and still retain enough kinetic energy to inacapacitate a soldier. Particularly troubling is the manufacturer's statement that the SS90 bullet and a similar 5.7mm handgun bullet, the SS190, will start tumbling after about 5cm of penetration in NATO gelatin, used for ballistic tests; the SS190 is also said to create a wound cavity 8cm in diameter. In advertising materials, the manufacturer has claimed that the P90 has been designed for 'maximum wound profile'.

Other weapons and ammunition under development in recent years which could have an impact on patterns of battlefield wounding include: new shotguns capable of semiautomatic fire; small-calibre weapons firing flechettes (nail-like darts), which could potentially be designed to deform or turn in the body; and rifle and handgun ammunition of various sorts including duplex ammunition (a cartridge containing two bullets which diverge in flight) and cartridges containing both a bullet and shotgun pellets.

High-explosive fragmentation munitions

A high-explosive munition consists of a metal case with a high explosive filler and a detonating device. Detonation of the explosive produces gases which expand with explosive rapidity, shattering the casing and producing fragments of metal flying outwards from the point of explosion.

Damage from a high-explosive munition is caused by the blast and by the fragments. The amount of damage produced by a fragment is closely related to its mass, its shape, and its velocity when it hits the target (impact velocity). The impact velocity equals the velocity imparted by the explosion (the initial velocity) minus the velocity lost in flight. Initial velocity is a function of the charge-to-mass ratio – the ratio of the mass of explosive to the mass of the metal casing, and to the *brisance* (shattering power, linked to the rate of detonation) of the explosive. The higher the *brisance* or the greater the charge-to-mass ratio, the greater the initial velocity.

As with small-calibre projectiles, the severity of the wound is generally a function of the amount of energy which the wounding missile transfers to the tissues as it travels through the body. It follows that the greater the energy which a fragment possesses when it hits the body, the greater its wounding capacity. The kinetic energy of a fragment or other missile is proportional to its mass multiplied by the square of its velocity ($KE = \frac{1}{2}Mv^2$). This formula shows the relative importance of mass and velocity as factors in wounding.

In the early 1950s, US government military laboratories began a programme of redesign of conventional munitions, largely in response to the Korean War experience and largely directed at improving the efficiency of antipersonnel munitions. There were related developments in other countries. One important line of research and development was to obtain more control over the size, shape and number of fragments produced by explosive munitions. It was found that this could be achieved in three ways:

• *Natural fragmentation*, the fragmentation of a casing which has not been specially scored or shaped for fragmentation effect. It was found that special materials could be used for munition casings, producing smaller fragments. Mortar shells and rocket warheads made of specially worked cast iron were introduced into the inventory of the US Army in the 1960s. Later, high-fragmentation steels were developed for use in artillery shells.

• *Controlled fragmentation*, in which the size and shape of the fragments is predetermined by such techniques as scoring the metal case or making the casing out of notched wire wound around a metal shell.

- *Pre-fragmentation* (sometimes regarded as a subcategory of controlled fragmentation), in which the fragments themselves, typically metal balls or cubes, are manufactured beforehand and embedded in the case.

Munition effectiveness has been enhanced also through the increasing use of higher-*brisance* explosives. Many post-Second World War (WW II) munitions in the US and other countries are filled with cyclotol, a mixture of the higher-*brisance* explosive RDX with the more stable TNT.

A controlled fragmentation or pre-fragmentation casing is generally weaker than one which employs natural fragmentation. These techniques tend to be used in smaller munitions, such as hand grenades or bomblets (see next section), while an artillery shell will be made of naturally fragmenting steel strong enough to withstand the stresses of being propelled through a gun barrel.

An important overall trend in the design of high-explosive munitions since WW II has been a reduction in fragment size. The impetus for this development came from the findings of WW II wound ballistics research that a small fragment can cause a wound many times its diameter if it hits the body at a high enough speed. This finding was confirmed by battlefield casualty surveys in which the bodies and medical records of thousands of US casualties were examined and the wounds related to the missiles which had caused them.

It was realized that the fragments produced by WW II-era high-explosive munitions were much larger than what was needed to attack personnel or light materiel. The implication of the WW II studies was that the efficiency of high-explosive munitions could be greatly improved if the fragment size was reduced and the number of fragments correspondingly increased.

Striking the body with high kinetic energy, a fragment imparts its energy extremely quickly, thrusting the tissues aside from its path and creating a temporary cavity lasting a few milliseconds, with resultant tissue damage or destruction. As fragments lack the sleek aerodynamic shape of a bullet, the energy transfer will tend to be greatest at the point of entrance and to diminish as the fragment slows down inside the body.

High-explosive munitions are used with many delivery systems. They include hand grenades, aerial bombs, rocket warheads, landmines and ammunition for small arms, automatic guns, mortars and artillery.

The relative simplicity and low cost of some of these weapons systems make them prone to abuse: far more rounds are fired than should be necessary in purely military terms. These weapons also lend themselves to the purposes of armed forces bent not merely on defeating the opposing force but on terrorizing the civilian population. The over-use and misuse of artillery and other weapons have resulted in much gratuitous suffering and destruction in recent decades.[3]

Cluster weapons

The idea of a weapon comprising a cluster of smaller munitions (submunitions) is not new. Bomb clusters comprising a number of small high-explosive or incendiary bombs were used extensively in WW II. Since then there have been many refinements in the design of cluster weapons.

Modern cluster munitions were first used in the 1960s in the US–Indochina war. Of them, the most widely used in that war was the CBU-24. This munition resembles a conventional 750-lb (340kg) bomb in shape and size. It consists of a metal case or dispenser containing some 640 to 670 1–lb (0.45kg), spherical high-explosive bomblets. Dropped from an airplane, the CBU-24 opens in the air, releasing the bomblets, which are aerodynamically designed to scatter in a pattern. When the bomblets hit the ground, they explode.

The CBU-24 bomblets employ the principle of pre-fragmentation described above. Each bomblet has some 300 5.56mm steel balls embedded in its casing. Thus, the use of one CBU-24 results in some 200,000 steel balls shooting in all directions over a wide area. The bomblets can also be fitted with delayed-action fuses so that some of them explode at random intervals after the attack, making it unsafe to enter the area.

Many approaches to the design of cluster weapons have been taken since the 1960s. Besides free-fall dispensers like that used in the CBU-24, there are dispensers fixed to an aircraft, from which the bomblets or other submunitions are ejected downwards, rearwards or sideways as the aircraft flies along. Different types of bomblets can be used: high explosive (either antipersonnel or antimateriel, the main distinction being in the size of fragments), antitank, incendiary, or bomblets with combined effects. Chemical and biological bomblets have also been designed. Cluster munitions have been developed for other delivery systems: artillery shells and rocket and missile warheads containing submunitions. Some of the newest cluster bomb designs are modular (allowing different combinations of dispensers and bomblets) and give the pilot considerable control over how the bomblets are ejected.

One problem posed by antipersonnel cluster weapons is the risk that a person hit by them will suffer multiple injuries, which are more difficult to treat than single wounds. Clearly a 0.7g fragment from a CBU-24 bomblet is likely to cause a less severe wound than a typical 60 to 80g fragment from a 9kg WW II fragmentation bomb, but with many more fragments emanating from the explosion of bomblets throughout the target area there will be a greater risk of multiple injury. As the area coverage of the cluster bomb is much greater, more soldiers are likely to be injured.

Greater area coverage brings a greater risk of indiscriminate effects. Some cluster weapons have a very wide area of coverage, greater than what might be envisioned as the area occupied by most tactical military targets. Two modern cluster weapons, the Multiple Launch Rocket System (MLRS), a vehicle-mounted 12-rocket system with cluster warheads, first used in the 1991 Gulf War, and the German MW-1 aircraft-mounted cluster weapon, under development, are reported to have the capacity to disseminate submunitions over areas of approximately 45 hectares at maximum range from the MLRS and up to 13 hectares from the MW-1.

The sheer number of submunitions brings problems akin to those posed by land-mines, particularly the problem of unexploded ordnance (see below). Cluster weapons tend to employ a principle of overkill to compensate for difficulties of target acquisition: there are many more submunitions than what would be needed if it were known that they would all hit the intended targets.

The US–Indochina war saw the appearance of the Hayes dispenser, a huge boxlike container filled with bomblets. Two Hayes dispensers fitted in the bomb bay of a B-52 aircraft could dispense 77,040 M40 0.14kg high-explosive submunitions over a wide area. This may have been an all-time high in the quantity of bomblets contained in a cluster weapon but some modern designs also allow for large numbers of submunitions to be dispensed: 7728 antitank/antipersonnel bomblets from a salvo of MLRS rockets, for example, or 4536 antitank bomblets from an MW-1 dispenser.

Since the appearance of the first modern cluster bombs, there has been an order of magnitude increase in area coverage and bomblet numbers. Not all cluster weapons have such large numbers of submunitions or cover such large areas as those cited above, but the potential for large numbers and large area coverage exists. Since the US–Indochina war, cluster weapon technologies have proliferated. As of 1994 there were over 60 high-explosive cluster bombs in production or under development in at least 14 countries. Cluster weapons have become an important part of the arsenals of various countries. In the US alone, some US$3 billion was due to be spent on cluster weapons in the Department of Defense budget over the five fiscal years from 1995 to 1999, according to figures compiled by the Mennonite Central Committee.

In 1974, seven states proposed an international ban on the use in warfare of 'cluster warheads with bomblets which act through the ejection of a great number of small-calibred fragments or pellets'. The proposal was strongly opposed by other states during the discussions leading to the adoption of the CCW in 1980. The only reflection of this proposal is in Protocol I to the Hague Convention, which prohibits the use of 'any weapon the primary effect of which is to injure by fragments which in the human body escape detection by X-rays'.[4]

Canister and cartridge rounds for artillery, tanks and aircraft

An ancient form of artillery ammunition, canister rounds, received renewed interest during the Korean War when a need for close-range, cannon-fired munitions to defend against 'human-wave' attacks was perceived. Canister and cartridge rounds for artillery and tanks are larger, more sophisticated versions of the shotgun cartridge. Thousands of small metal balls, slugs or flechettes are packed inside a shell which opens after leaving the gun barrel, dispersing the contents in a cone-shaped spray. The antipersonnel effect of such a large number of projectiles is enormous.

Canister rounds are designed to break up on leaving the gun barrel, whereas cartridge rounds are fused to break up explosively at a certain time interval after being fired. In both cases, the round will rupture, freeing the packed projectiles which are dispersed by centrifugal force (gun barrels are rifled to impart a spin to the rounds) in a cone that at the maximum effective range may be more than 100m wide. Canister rounds are intended for close-in position defence, while cartridge rounds are designed for use at greater distances.

Canister and cartridge antipersonnel rounds are produced in many countries. Most models are filled with metal balls or slugs, but the United States was the first to develop a number of canister and cartridge rounds (the latter called 'Beehive' ammunition) filled with flechettes. China, Israel and Russia are also known to have developed and produced flechette-filled antipersonnel shells and rockets. (Flechette-filled shotgun shells have also been produced and are available on the open market.)

Antipersonnel canister and cartridge rounds can be problematic on two grounds: because of their large dispersal areas, their use can be indiscriminate in areas populated by civilians; while the likelihood of multiple wounding increases the seriousness of the injury and the difficulty of treating casualties.

A further problem would arise if the missiles inside a canister or cartridge round were specially formed to increase the wounding effect. Flechettes, for example, can be specially made to deform, break up or turn after hitting the body. Flechettes producing these effects have been designed for use in experimental small-calibre weapons but up to now they do not appear to have been used in artillery, tank or rocket munitions, probably because the extra manufacturing cost would make such shells uneconomical. Flechettes will also turn if they hit the body above a certain velocity. Flechette-filled artillery rounds developed to date appear to be below the velocity threshold for turning, but a flechette-filled antipersonnel 2.75-inch (70mm) air-to-ground rocket warhead, used in the US–Indochina war, was above the threshold. Tumbling flechettes may thus have already appeared on the battlefield.

Seven states presented a proposal in 1974 to ban the use of weapons releasing multiple flechettes. The proposal was opposed by other states and is not reflected in the CCW.

Incendiary weapons

Incendiary weapons are weapons that use flame or heat to set fire to or scorch targets. Although incendiary weapons have existed for thousands of years, many new and more destructive incendiary devices were developed and used during WW II. In WW II, incendiary bullets, grenades, shells, bombs and flamethrowers were used on the battle-field and large numbers of incendiary bombs were used to attack cities in the latter half of the war. The fire bombings of Dresden and Tokyo remain potent symbols of the civilian destruction that incendiary agents can wreak. Despite attempts to restrict their use, incendiary munitions remain in military inventories.

Incendiary weapons include a wide range of agents and delivery systems. Aerial incendiary bombs are commonly filled with thickened oil, often called napalm, or with oil-and-metal mixtures called pyrogels. Similar thickened fuels are used for flame-throwers. Ignitable metals and metallic compounds like magnesium and thermite (a compound of ground ferric oxide and aluminum), and pyrophoric (self-igniting) materials such as sodium and white phosphorus, are commonly packed into bullets, grenades, artillery shells and rocket warheads, aircraft rocket warheads, and cluster munitions. (White phosphorus shells are generally considered 'smoke' munitions, used for marking targets or obscuring the battlefield, but because phosphorus particles are dispersed on impact and burn at a very high temperature on contact with atmospheric oxygen, white phosphorus is also used to start fires and to attack personnel.) Depleted uranium (see below), used in antitank projectiles, pulverises when it penetrates armour; as it is pyrophoric in this state, such projectiles have an incendiary effect.

Since WW II, the development of more effective munitions has continued. Current incendiary munitions cover wider areas and burn longer and at hotter temperatures than did WW II models. One of the most important incendiary materials developed by the United States and used in the US–Indochina war was napalm-B. Napalm-B uses polystyrene as a thickener; it is more viscous than earlier napalms, covering a greater area, and burns longer and more hotly. This not only makes it more effective at burning vegetation and buildings but can also be expected to result in more severe injuries. The former Soviet Union is also reported to have improved an aerial incendiary spray device first fielded in WW II. According to one report, one such improved device, the VAP-500, contains granulated phosphorus mixed with water or a calcium chloride solution. This substance is released in conjunction with a smoke mixture, a mixture of chloro-sulphuric acid and sulphur trioxide, which dries the phosphorus and hastens its ignition. After the phosphorus dries sufficiently, it ignites and forms a flaming cloud. This weapon was reported to have been used in Afghanistan.

Incendiary weapons can be extremely injurious. The types of burns caused are dependent on the incendiary agent used. Metallic incendiaries such as magnesium and thermite cause small but deep burns (magnesium burns often produce ulcers as well) and expose the victims to extremely high temperatures. White phosphorus also causes deep burns (the particles can burn for hours until they are neutralized), and the injuries are further complicated by the toxic properties of white phosphorus, which may be absorbed into the body and cause renal or cardiac failure and liver damage.

Thickened fuel-based incendiaries like napalm adhere to and burn clothing, skin, vegetation and other materials. Injuries can also be caused by flame or vapour inhalation, carbon monoxide and lack of oxygen. Napalm burns often cover large areas of the body. Because of the high burning temperature and extended burning time, the resulting wounds are typically deep. Mortality from the burns depends on the degree and extent of burns as well as on the victim's general health. Burn victims are also at risk from shock and later infection.

Burn injuries from incendiary weapons are difficult to treat and often require advanced medical facilities and treatment beyond the capacity of many developing countries. Serious burns often result in lifelong incapacitation or death after protracted illness and extreme suffering. If the victim's life is saved, he or she may have to live with scarring (sometimes with very thick keloids), disabilities, chronic pain, lowered resistance to disease and the social stigma suffered by people with extensive scarring and deformities. Long-term treatment with multiple skin grafts or reconstructive surgery is possible but is often unavailable or far beyond the means of the victim or of those responsible for the provision of medical services.[5]

The first attempt to restrict the use of incendiary weapons was in the 1868 St Petersburg *Declaration Renouncing the Use, in Time of War, of Explosive Projectiles under 400 Grammes Weight* (St Petersburg Declaration), which prohibited contracting parties from using any projectile weighing less than 400g filled with explosive or 'fulminating or inflammable substances'. In 1972, prompted by international concern over the widespread use of napalm and other incendiaries in the US–Indochina war, the UN General Assembly adopted resolution 2932A (XXVII) deploring the use of napalm and other incendiary weapons in all conflicts. Later in the 1970s, 21 states presented a proposal for an outright ban on the use of incendiaries in war. The proposal led to the adoption in 1980 of Protocol III to the CCW, whose most important feature is a prohibition in all circumstances of attacks by air-delivered incendiary weapons against 'any military objective located within a concentration of civilians'. This prohibition, if observed by all states, would prevent civilians being indiscriminately burned in aerial incendiary attacks on ostensibly military targets within civilian areas, as occurred in the fire bombing of cities in WW II. It is unfortunate that the majority of states participating in the drafting of Protocol III were not willing also to protect soldiers by banning the use of incendiary weapons altogether.

Enhanced-blast munitions

The term enhanced-blast munition can be used to refer to blast munitions in which the explosive material is dispersed in the atmosphere before the process of detonation is completed. This improves the effectiveness of the munitions in two ways. First, the explosion occurs over a wider area, creating a blast wave which is destructive throughout the area; if the munition is a fuel–air explosive, there is the added advantage that the explosive mixture will flow into any spaces that are not sealed. Second, the air provides the oxygen for combustion, whereas a conventional explosive has to contain an oxidizing agent. The reaction with atmospheric oxygen greatly increases the total energy released per mass of explosive. For example, a propylene oxide fuel–air explosive reportedly releases 7.9 times as much energy as the same mass of TNT. [6]

Enhanced-blast munitions are effective against 'soft' targets and targets open to the atmosphere, including unreinforced buildings, aircraft on the ground, aircraft hangars, radar antennas, antipersonnel mines and some antivehicle mines, woody vegetation, personnel and surface ships. They are less effective than ordinary high-explosive munitions against reinforced targets. Tactical uses include minefield clearance, the clearing of helicopter landing zones and attacking personnel.

Three types of enhanced-blast munitions have been developed and produced: (i) fuel–air explosives (FAEs), containing highly combustible liquid, gaseous or powdered fuels, usually hydrocarbon fuels, which are dispersed in a cloud or an aerosol; (ii) reactive-surround warheads, a term used to refer to a Russian munition consisting of a thin-walled steel container filled with aluminum and nitrocellulose; and (iii) slurry-explosive munitions, containing a mixture of a high explosive or other highly combustible solid with a combustible liquid. The latter include a 6800kg US bomb called the 'daisy cutter' which was used in the US–Indochina war and reportedly produces a concussive blast greater than that of the smallest nuclear device. Its lethal range is said to be 74m, and the total casualty zone is said to extend outwards for 396m, giving an area of 49 hectares in flat terrain over which there will be casualties. [7]

As a result of wound research during WW II and subsequent research into the effects of nuclear weapons, there is now a considerable literature on blast injury. [8] But details of enhanced-blast munitions remain classified, and there appear to be no reliable scientific descriptions of battlefield injuries in the published literature. The wounding effects of these munitions therefore remain the subject of some speculation outside military circles.

According to a 1993 study by the US Defense Intelligence Agency and the US Army

Foreign Science and Technology Center, released to Human Rights Watch under the US Freedom of Information Act:

> fuel–air explosions generate alternating waves of positive and negative pressure, mild in comparison to high explosives (HE) but of much longer duration and therefore higher impulse. Nonliving targets are destroyed or damaged by the initial positive overpressure, but the subsequent negative pressure (rarefaction) is most lethal to live targets, as it causes blood vessels in the lungs to rupture.

The study continues:

> The kill mechanism [of fuel–air explosives] against living targets is unique – and unpleasant... What kills is the pressure wave and, more importantly, the subsequent rarefaction, which ruptures the lungs... If the fuel deflagrates but does not detonate, victims will be severely burned and will probably also inhale the burning fuel. Since the most common FAE fuels, ethylene oxide and propylene oxide, are highly toxic, undetonated FAE should prove as lethal to personnel caught within the cloud as most chemical agents.
>
> Lethality is a function of degree of confinement. Personnel in foxholes will be hit harder than personnel in the open, and wearing flak jackets or body armour also increases the degree of bodily injury.

The study contains figures for the lethal radius of a Russian FAE munition which, like earlier reports of other FAEs, shows how quickly the antipersonnel effect falls away outside a circumscribed area of destruction. The weapon is reported to produce 99 per cent antipersonnel lethality at a radius of 7.6–8.2m, 50 per cent lethality and 100 per cent incapacitation at 8.2–9.1m, 1 per cent lethality and 50 per cent incapacitation at 9.1–10.1m, and 1 per cent incapacitation at 16.8–22.9m.[9]

Not only will an FAE damage targets above ground, but the cloud of fuel enters foxholes, trenches and other shelters open to the atmosphere. In the words of a 1991 US Central Intelligence Agency (CIA) study entitled 'Conventional Weapons Producing Chemical-Warfare-Agent-like Injuries', the fuel–air mixture 'will enter any space not totally sealed, creep into houses, seep into ventilation systems, be drawn into the air intakes of engines, and settle in any depression the terrain offers'. In a confined space, the blast effect is magnified because the pressure wave is reflected off the walls. According to the CIA study,

> The effect of an FAE explosion within confined spaces is immense. Those near the ignition point are obliterated. Those at the fringe are likely to suffer many internal, and thus invisible, injuries, including burst eardrums and crushed inner ear organs, severe concussions, ruptured lungs and internal organs, and possibly blindness.

Emphasizing the superficial similarity of effects to those produced by nerve gases, the CIA study continues:

> Lung injuries and resulting nerve injuries may mimic CW [chemical warfare] agents. A blast will damage tissue in the lungs, which produces swelling and bleeding both into the tissue and the air passages. Tears in the lung walls can occur in many locations and allow air to enter the circulating blood. These air bubbles (emboli) in the blood may produce a variety of symptoms in multiple body parts. Air emboli may be forced into the veins and may travel through the left side of the heart into the systemic circulation. These bubbles can embolize to such critical areas of the circulation as the brain and heart and are a likely cause of damage to the heart muscle. Air emboli may also cause abnormal nervous system symptoms.

An FAE weapon can also cause a variety of other CW-like effects. Injuries to the nervous system usually include concussion, and brain damage can produce mental changes like some CW agents. CW-like lung effects can be produced by the presence of air in the chest cavity and in the surrounding tissues. These symptoms include difficult breathing, chest pain, and bleeding from the nose and mouth. In victims with severe lung damage, the skin has a bluish tint caused by a lack of oxygen.

Blast injuries, unlike any CW-agent injury, produce a unique injury to the ear. Blast usually causes rupture of the eardrum, as well as possible dislocation of the middle ear bones and bleeding from the ear. Rupture of the eardrum also causes loss of hearing, ringing in the ears, and possible balance defects. The inner ear may also be damaged, producing a hearing loss in all frequencies.

FAEs were first developed by the United States in the early 1960s, but the Soviet Union soon fielded its own versions. The technology to produce FAEs has proliferated to other states including Chile, China, France, Iraq, Japan, Spain, and possibly also Germany, India, Israel and North Korea. Some of these munitions are available on the arms market.

FAEs have reportedly been used by the Soviet Union, primarily as an antipersonnel weapon, in a border conflict with China in 1969 and in Afghanistan; by US forces in the Gulf War of 1991; and in Bosnia-Herzegovina, Chechnya, and Sierra Leone (here reportedly used by the mercenary firm Executive Outcomes).

In 1979, at the UN Conference which was drafting the CCW, Mexico, Sweden and Switzerland submitted a proposal to ban the antipersonnel use of FAEs. No action was taken on the proposal.

FAEs and other enhanced-blast munitions are now fielded in a wide variety of air-to-surface and surface-to-surface weapon systems. The United States and Russia have reportedly developed third-generation enhanced-blast munition warheads.

Directed-energy weapons

Directed-energy weapons (DEWs) are weapons in which various forms of energy are concentrated and directed at a target. Because some of them can be used to disable without killing, or to damage materiel, DEWs are often referred to as 'nonlethal' weapons, along with incapacitating chemicals and other devices which are beyond the scope of this chapter. One type of DEW, blinding lasers, has become the object of an international ban, as described below.

Laser devices are available for various military uses, such as rangefinding and target designation. Even these devices are dangerous to the eyes, and there have been accidents. In addition, considerable work has gone into the development of laser weapons to destroy optical sensors (sensors simulating human eyesight which are mounted on tanks, vehicles or aircraft) and for antipersonnel use. The intense concentration of light energy in a laser beam pinpoints the damaging effect on the eyes, causing temporary or permanent blindness. The eye focuses the laser beam on to a small point on the retina, magnifying the brightness of the beam by a factor of approximately 100,000. The effect is further multiplied if the victim is using magnifying or light-collecting optics in front of the eyes, such as binoculars.

Concerned by the humanitarian implications of these developments, between 1989 and 1991 the International Committee of the Red Cross (ICRC) convened four expert meetings attended by specialists in laser technology, ophthalmology, military medicine and psychiatry, and international humanitarian law. As summarized by the ICRC, the meetings found that:

- Lasers can be very small and very inexpensive. Clip-on devices that can now be fitted to rifles for training purposes could easily be made non-eye safe. Laser rangefinders could be misused to blind intentionally, and 'as the energy and wavelength of the laser necessary to destroy sensors is similar to those necessary to damage eyes, laser systems said to be designed for anti-sensor purposes could also be used for anti-personnel purposes'.
- It is not easy to produce a laser which will dazzle but not blind. For dazzling systems to be effective over long ranges, it is inevitable that at shorter ranges eye damage will result. The exact range for dazzling as against permanent blindness is unpredictable as, in battlefield conditions, factors such as smoke, dust and humidity will cause variations. Most infrared wavelengths cannot produce temporary effects (dazzling or flash blindness) but only permanent effects.
- It is difficult to protect soldiers by means of special goggles. Goggles 'would only screen out a limited range of known wavelengths, whereas lasers can operate over a wide range of wavelengths'.
- Blinding was characterized by the experts as an especially severe form of disability, permanent and incurable, often causing severe long-term depression, and placing a heavy burden on the victim's family and on a country's medical and social services.[10]

Prompted by the concern of the ICRC, other non-governmental organizations and governments, the first Review Conference of the CCW adopted at its first session in 1995 a new Protocol IV (Protocol on Blinding Laser Weapons) to the CCW. This prohibits the use in warfare of 'laser weapons specifically designed, as their sole combat function or as one of their combat functions, to cause permanent blindness to unenhanced vision, that is to the naked eye or to the eye with corrective eyesight devices'. It states further that in using laser systems, states parties to the Protocol 'shall take all feasible precautions to avoid the incidence of permanent blindness to unenhanced vision'. In an important loophole, the Protocol does not prohibit '[b]linding as an incidental or collateral effect of the legitimate military employment of laser systems, including laser systems used against optical equipment'.

Other laser weapons have aroused a great deal of interest throughout the world. Many of these systems are currently being developed for antimissile purposes but they could also take on antimaterial and antipersonnel roles. The US Armament Research, Development and Engineering Center and the Los Alamos Laboratories are two US military research centres investigating the use of high-powered laser pulses (causing a plasma and blast wave) against sensors, vehicles and the crew inside. In a similar vein, the US Navy is apparently investigating charged-particle beam weapons that would project a stream of electrons at close to the speed of light.

Another potential DEW system that has generated interest in the United States uses acoustic beam technology. Experiments conducted with high-powered acoustical sources have revealed what have been described as profoundly incapacitating and lethal effects upon personnel. According to a 1995 study, 'Selective Area/Facility Denial Using High Power Acoustic Beam Technology', prepared for the US Advanced Research Projects Agency and the US Army Missile Command by Scientific Applications and Research Associates and obtained by William M. Arkin under the Freedom of Information Act, the antipersonnel effects of acoustical fields vary with frequency. At infrasound frequencies (of about 5–200Hz) the sound resonates within or between bodily organs, producing discomfort, intestinal pain and nausea; at mid-audio frequencies (500–2500Hz) the sound resonates within air cavities in the body producing nausea and internal organ damage; at high frequencies (5–30 kHz) the sound is absorbed in the body and can produce a moderate to lethal rise in body temperature, tissue burns, and dehydration. The degree of incapacitation or injury varies with intensity. At about 90–120dB it produces extreme levels of annoyance or distraction; at about 150dB it produces severe incapacitating effects, physical trauma an damage to tissue; and levels greater than about 170dB it can cause instantaneous blast-wave-type trauma.

Because sound waves are tunable, they have generated a great deal of interest for less-than-lethal purposes. The most advanced systems appear to use infrasound. It does not appear that these systems will become portable but infrasound weapons have been proposed for crowd control and area denial purposes. These weapons would be mounted on helicopters or trucks, air-delivered or emplaced as fixed barriers. Russian scientists apparently have developed a portable device that can propel a 10Hz sonic packet over hundreds of metres. The device can reportedly moderate the sonic packet for either lethal or less-than-lethal effect.

Although the intended purpose of most acoustical weapon development is non-lethal, little research has been conducted on the weapons' long-term effects. Because sound waves primarily affect the ears, high-powered acoustical fields can cause permanent hearing loss. Depending on the intensity and duration of exposure, these weapons can also cause permanent injury and death.

Other less-than-lethal directed-energy systems are also reported to be under development. US researchers are working on microwave, thermal, and magneto-phosphene guns. Microwave weapons would direct microwave energy that can cause progressive incapacitation by increasing the body temperature. (High-frequency microwaves could also enter structures through cracks and seams.) The developers of a thermal gun are proceeding on a similar principle of progressive incapacitation. The magnetophosphene gun is designed around a biophysical mechanism that evokes a visual response, known as magnetophosphenes. This effect is experienced when someone received a blow to the head and sees stars.

It is unclear how these different directed-energy systems would be fielded and if they would ever be portable. Many are being developed under the rubric of non-lethal weapons but potentially all could be misused or have as yet unknown harmful effects. Interest in less-than-lethal weapons is increasing, especially those using directed energy; unlike chemical and biological weapons, they are not prohibited under international law.

The increased interest in non-lethal technologies has generated controversy: would these technologies only be used in a less-than-lethal manner? would they be used to increase the efficiency of deadly weapons? would they cause unnecessary suffering?

Does the presence of less-than-lethal weapons lower the threshold for military intervention?[11]

Development efforts in the realm of DEWs need to be monitored to ensure that these weapons are not indiscriminate or excessively injurious.

Secondary effects of modern warfare

The secondary effects of modern warfare are often unintended, but can cause harm to combatants and civilians often long after the hostilities have ended. They can be divided into six somewhat overlapping and non-exclusive broad categories: (i) weapons that continue to remain active and able to injure and kill; (ii) weapons that have secondary injurious effects; (iii) weapons and their ancillary equipment that can produce deleterious effects to those employing them; (iv) the psychological effect of modern warfare on combatants and civilians; (v) weapons that can leave long-term human and environmental hazards; and (vi) indiscriminate weapons or tactics that affect civilian populations.

The explosive material remnants of war are the most dramatic legacy of the modern battlefield. They include landmines and other forms of unexploded ordnance, often referred to as duds (munitions which fail to explode). Unexploded ordnance has been a major affliction of war since the early part of the 20th century. To this day there are areas in France and Belgium that remain unsafe because of unexploded artillery shells from WW I, and many places in other countries are afflicted by the explosive remnants of subsequent wars.[12] The modern trend to employ ever greater numbers of munitions, especially in the form of cluster weapons, has only compounded the problem.

As described above, most major military powers have numerous surface- and air-delivered cluster weapons. Imperfections resulting from mass production techniques mean that in none of these systems can all the submunitions be expected to function as required. For example, the US armed forces require a 'functional reliability' of at least 95 per cent for submunitions. It follows that up to 5 per cent of the submunitions will fail to explode. This unreliability is further affected by the age of the submunitions, the delivery technique, the ambient air temperature and the impact medium. Given a 95 per cent rate of reliability, the US military has calculated that a typical fire mission of 36 Multiple Launched Rocket System rockets with 644 submunitions per rocket would produce 1364 unexploded submunitions. A typical artillery mission with 24 artillery pieces firing two cluster shells each would produce 212 unexploded submunitions. A B-52 bomber dropping a full load of 45 CBU-59/CBU-71 cluster bombs (each containing 650 submunitions) would produce 1710 unexploded submunitions.

The prolonged or intense use of cluster weapons will thus produce an enormous quantity of unexploded submunitions in the battlefield, some portion of which can later be set off by contact or vibration. This presents a serious hazard not only to combatants but to civilians. Limited efforts are now being made to identify where cluster munitions are being released, but, as stated in a 1996 US military manual on 'Multiservice procedures for operations in an unexploded ordnance environment' no system now exists to provide accurate tracking of unexploded submunitions.

As shown by the problem of landmines, the dissemination of great numbers of explosive munitions can render large areas unsafe for civilians long after a war has ended. Next to landmines it is cluster weapons which most clearly bring this risk. US procurement figures over the period of the US–Indochina war suggest that over 300,000,000 bomblets were dropped on Indochina during the war, in addition to some 60,000,000 or more aerially emplaced antipersonnel mines. If five per cent of the bomblets failed to explode, the attacks would have left some 15 million unexploded bomblets as a long-term hazard. More than 20 years after the end of the war, the hazard is still present.

It has been estimated that a minimum of 24,000,000 bomblets and mines were dropped from cluster weapons during the 1991 Gulf War. A five per cent rate of unreliability would mean that this short war left over a million unexploded munitions.[13]

Realization of these problems, arising from the Gulf War, led in 1996 to the US armed forces publishing a manual on 'Multiservice procedures for operations in an unexploded ordnance environment' (US Army field manual FM 100-38). 'Saturation of unexploded submunitions has become a characteristic of the modern battlefield', the manual begins. It states that there is an increasing potential for 'fratricide': casualties to one's forces caused by unexploded ordnance (UXO) deployed by one's own side. Commanders at all levels face a twofold challenge: 'one, to reduce the potential for fratricide from UXO hazards and two, to minimize the impact that UXO may have on the conduct of combat operations'. The manual deals with these purely military challenges, but the challenge of clearing unexploded submunitions and protecting civilians after the end of hostilities will be far greater.

Besides the problem of weapons that lie in wait for unsuspecting combatants or civilians, some modern military weapons can cause injury beyond their primary purpose. Prime examples are laser rangefinders and target designators that can be maliciously or accidentally targeted against personnel and, depending on their strength and wave length, can temporarily or permanently blind. With the deployment of high-energy weapons systems such as lasers, infrasound, microwave and electromagnetic pulse weapons, all of which have potential antipersonnel applications, the probability of serious misuse against people is likely to increase.

Along with the hazards of high-energy weapons, the modern battlefield has become a cauldron of harmful chemicals. Propellants and other chemicals used in modern weapon systems can be toxic, especially if used within confined spaces. The increased use of advanced materials (graphite composites, artificial fibres and fabrics, advanced coatings, synthetic lubricants, adhesives and matrix systems) introduces chemicals to the battlefield which are potentially toxic, especially if heated or burned.

The products of propellant combustion, nitric oxide and nitrogen dioxide, which can precipitate methemoglobinemia, a dangerous condition that limits the blood's capacity to carry oxygen, have long been identified as a serious concern for military gunners. The modern military need for transportation and electricity has also led to the prevalence of electric generators, fixed and rotary wing aircraft, and diesel-fuelled trucks and tracked vehicles. Hydrocarbon exhaust exposure has been associated with allergic conditions and asthma and may facilitate the development of cancer. Whereas in ordinary life civilians may be warned of the presence of smog and pollution and advised to stay indoors, soldiers have little choice, especially during war, and must work in this environment.

As noted in an earlier section of this chapter, fuel–air explosives also contain chemicals that have severe toxic effects as do other enhanced-blast munitions and missile-propulsion systems These chemicals include propylene oxide, ethyl oxide, fluid heptane and its derivatives mixed with propylene or butylene nitrates, and 1,2 dimethyl-hydrazine.

Compounds such as propylene and ethylene oxide irritate the respiratory tract and lungs, skin and eyes. They may also have a toxic effect on the liver and kidneys. Large doses may cause immediate respiratory difficulties and induce a state of shock that can progress to convulsions and pulmonary edema. Nitro-explosive compounds, also found in blast weapons, may produce long-term toxic effects on the liver, kidneys and other organs. High concentrations may cause convulsions, severe pulmonary oedema, and heart failure.

Smoke munitions also introduce toxic chemicals into the battlefield. Concentrated smokes can produce fever, muscle pain, nausea, abdominal pain, kidney and liver damage, and pulmonary oedema. Newer smoke mixtures contain fibrous and particulate materials that are potentially harmful to human health.

Modern warfare is also hazardous psychologically. With the advent of intense, mechanized warfare, the stresses of combat have increased and exacted a heavy toll. During WW I shell shock or 'war neurosis' became a common occurrence. After the war it was thought that prior screening could identify and exclude most soldiers prone to psychoneurosis and breakdown during combat, but WW II proved this wrong. In heavy fighting, some divisions suffered one 'battlefield fatigue' casualty for every five, three or even two wounded in action. This average has not changed significantly and is the basis for US combat stress control estimates for mid-intensity conflict, as outlined in the 1994 US Army field manual FM 8-51, 'Combat stress control in a theater of operations: tactics, techniques and procedures'. The increased destructiveness of modern weapons, fear of chemical, biological and nuclear warfare, and fear of injuries such as blinding have become major sources of stress on the battlefield. The psychological effects can be long-lasting. Many war veterans today suffer from post-traumatic stress disorder.

Many of these stresses are also experienced by civilians caught up in armed conflicts. These helpless victims must live with death and destruction or become refugees with no home and few or no possessions. In addition, in many recent conflicts civilians have become a prime target of hostilities. Usually little or no psychiatric care is available for civilians.

After the cessation of hostilities, many of the effects of war remain. In addition to the deaths, the destruction of homes and other features of the physical environment and the hazards of unexploded ordnance, chemicals used or released in war may remain long-term human and environmental hazards. For example, in a massive herbicidal programme lasting nearly a decade during the US–Indochina war, US forces expended nearly 55 million kilograms of active herbicidal agents, including the dioxin-containing Agent Orange. This left an enduring legacy for soldiers and civilians exposed to the herbicides. Exposure to heavy doses of phenoxy herbicides and their contaminates increased the risk of neurophysical dysfunctions, congenital defects and cancers. The cost to the environment was also enormous. Large areas of Vietnam have not yet fully recovered from the wartime attacks. Many fragile ecosystems were devastated, not to recover substantially for many decades.[14]

In the 1991 Gulf War, chemical compounds – pesticides like DEET and permethrin, chemical decontamination agents, vaccines and prophylactics, and perhaps trace amounts of chemical warfare agents – are suspected of causing the persistent illnesses suffered by Gulf War veterans since the conflict.

The US use of herbicides in the US–Indochina war led to the inclusion in the 1977 Protocol I of Article 35(3) prohibiting methods or means of warfare which are intended or may be expected to cause widespread, long-term and severe damage to the natural environment. Such damage can prejudice the health or survival of the population, as noted in Article 55(1) of the same Protocol. This prohibition is, however, only binding on states parties to 1977 Protocol I and did not prevent Iraq (not a party to the protocol) from intentionally releasing oil into the Persian Gulf and starting hundreds of oil fires, producing large amounts of harmful pollutants (cadmium, lead, mercury and nickel) and soot.

Also during the Gulf War, the US armed forces fielded munitions containing depleted uranium (DU), a new type of weapon presenting a potential long-term health hazard. Although concerns had been raised about the possible health hazards of these munitions, they were dismissed by the military as negligible compared to the substantial increase in effectiveness that DU munitions would provide.

DU is a dense and mildly radioactive byproduct of the process of production of fissionable uranium for weapons. Because it is dense and ignites on impact, it is used as a kinetic energy penetrator in antitank ammunition. DU is also used as a component of tank armour. Safe disposal of DU is expensive.

According to a recent study by members of the US Army Chemical School entitled 'Introduction to depleted uranium', the use of DU for armour or munitions exposes soldiers to two primary health hazards: (i) the heavy metal toxicity of DU. Soldiers can be exposed to DU through inhalation, ingestion or penetration into the body. DU, like lead, is a heavy metal poison and if left in the body may cause kidney failure; (ii) ionizing radiation consisting primarily of alpha particles. During impacts or upon combustion, DU fragmentation or spalling (detachment of fragments of the inner surface of the wall of an armoured vehicle) and DU oxide (a very heavy black dust) are formed and released into the interior of the vehicle or into the surrounding environment. Ingestion, inhalation or injection of DU dust, fragments or spalling will result in internal exposure to the ionizing effects of alpha radiation.

US regulations classify DU as low-level waste and require clean-up (at great expense) of areas where the munitions were tested. US military manuals require troops to avoid DU-contaminated areas: when it is necessary to cross a 'radiation contamination control line', soldiers are instructed to wear protective coveralls, gloves, rubberized boots, protective masks with filters, and accompanying head covers.

There are indications that DU munitions are becoming standard weapons. In addition to the US, it is believed that France, Israel, Pakistan, Russia, Saudi Arabia, Thailand, Turkey, the United Kingdom and other countries possess or are developing weapons systems containing DU. DU munitions are now available on the international arms market.

DU munitions and other hazardous weapons systems are being fielded without any clear understanding of their long-term effects. It is clear that insufficient research is being conducted on the secondary hazards of modern warfare. Long-term effects of the use of modern conventional weapons are commonly dismissed as unimportant if the new weapons are believed to provide a tactical advantage. The possible harm to soldiers is discounted or ignored. Little thought is given to the welfare of the civilian population that must live in the area after the cessation of hostilities.

Although international humanitarian law has been formulated to protect civilians and civilian objects, indiscriminate bombing and attacks on civilians, including refugees, continue to occur with depressing frequency. Attacks on objects of military value can also have significant effects on the civilian population. During the Gulf War, coalition bomber aircraft attacked Iraqi chemical and biological research, production and storage facilities which were close to civilian populations. The risk of release of at least some of this material could not be excluded. Attacks in armed conflicts are also regularly carried out against the infrastructure on which the survival of civilians depends. These include electrical generating facilities, water supplies, sanitation systems, transportation systems and food and energy supplies.

As modern weapons become more numerous and complex, greater effort must be expended on ensuring that they are safe to use and do not have indiscriminate effects. These efforts must include a decision to investigate and limit possible harmful secondary effects. The effort must be made when a weapon is developed, when it is fielded and when it is used.

Ethical questions for medical personnel

The design of antipersonnel weapons draws from medical science. Extensive research programmes in WW II led to the establishment of the science of wound ballistics, the study of the motion of projectiles in the body and the damage caused. Postwar work has yielded criteria for producing different levels of incapacitation; these criteria are used as standards for the expected performance of antipersonnel weapons. In general, the more rapid the incapacitation which a missile is required to produce, the more severe the wound will have to be. Similarly, studies of blast and burn wounds on human beings and laboratory animals are used in designing the corresponding weapons. Where possible, laboratory findings are compared with battlefield casualty surveys and studies of the accidental discharge of weapons encompassing such matters as the nature and location of wounds, the circumstances in which they were inflicted, the wounding agent and the course of the victim's condition.[15]

The study of war wounds and wound management cannot be regarded as a neutral science. One purpose is to improve treatment, but treatment will be used to return soldiers to the battlefield, and the provision of good treatment is an important element in maintaining the morale of fighting forces. Another purpose is to develop more effective and often more destructive weaponry.

From the point of view of the armed forces, these aims may be laudable. From the perspective of the overall interests of humanity, the judgment is less clear. An increase in antipersonnel destructiveness achieved by one side of a conflict can be quickly emulated by the other and proliferate further, raising the overall antipersonnel destructiveness of warfare or, at least, the ease and efficiency with which it is accomplished. A medical professional who engages in weapons research is obliged by the ethics of his or her profession never to do harm, yet the research can result in a great deal of harm. The ethical problems posed by medical research and the use of medical knowledge in weapon design are not easy to resolve. They need to be considered and debated within the medical profession.

In 1996 the ICRC convened a seminar in Montreux on the medical profession and the effects of weapons. Among other things, the seminar noted in its recommendations that members of the medical profession involved in work relating to the design or development of weapons should recognize that they may face an ethical dilemma. It recommended that military medical research should be reviewed by non-military ethical committees.

The seminar concluded that 'the effects of weapons are a public health issue'. It recommended that the effects of weapons on health should be incorporated as a recognized subject in courses at university level and other educational agendas. It discussed the development of a communication strategy to inform and mobilize target audiences in a factual manner about the issues surrounding the medical effects of weapons.

The seminar also recommended that 'weapons of the future, especially those developed on the basis of knowledge of the human genome and of genetic engineering, should be given serious consideration by a group of knowledgeable professionals'.[16]

Restricting antipersonnel weapons

Over the years, the community of nations has been able to agree to outlaw or restrict a few weapons of warfare on humanitarian grounds. Early important bans were the 1899 Hague Declaration concerning the Prohibition of Dum-Dum Bullets and the 1925 Geneva Protocol for the Prohibition of the Use of Asphyxiating, Poisonous or Other Gases, and of Bacteriological Methods of Warfare.

In 1980 the CCW was adopted at a UN conference. Its three protocols, respectively: (i) ban the use of antipersonnel weapons using nonmetallic fragments; (ii) provide safeguards against the indiscriminate use of landmines; and (iii) restrict the use of incendiary weapons to avoid indiscriminate effects. As mentioned in this chapter, proposals for bans and restrictions on other antipersonnel weapons were discussed in the 1970s but not included in the convention.

The first Review Conference of the CCW, held in 1995 and 1996, adopted amendments to Protocol II on landmines, and a new Protocol IV on blinding laser weapons. Both the amendments and Protocol IV entered into force in 1998. The next Review Conference is due to be held not later than 2001. At present only one formal proposal has been made, that of the Swiss for a new protocol on small-calibre weapon systems.

International humanitarian law – the body of international law which governs the conduct of armed conflicts – offers two principal grounds for banning or restricting the use of specific weapons: (i) the prohibition of use of weapons of a nature to cause superfluous injury or unnecessary suffering to combatants, enshrined in Article 35(2) of 1977 Protocol I; and (ii) the prohibition of indiscriminate attacks, set forth in Article 51 of the same Protocol. Under Article 51, indiscriminate attacks are attacks of a nature to strike military objectives and civilians or civilian objects without distinction. A third possible ground is the prohibition of methods or means of warfare causing widespread, long-term and severe damage to the natural environment.

The prohibition of use of weapons causing superfluous injury in particular is based on the principle set forth in international humanitarian law that the permitted means of injuring the enemy are not unlimited. As stated in the 1868 St Petersburg Declaration, the use of 'arms which uselessly aggravate the sufferings of disabled men, or render their death inevitable' would be contrary to the laws of humanity.

One of the subjects discussed at the 1996 ICRC seminar on the medical profession and the effects of weapons, referred to above, was the possibility of formulating objective criteria which could lead to a judgement that a given weapon causes superfluous injury. The discussion of this question has continued since the seminar.[17]

The Swiss proposal for a protocol on small-calibre weapons systems is an example of an initiative to impose restrictions on a specific weapon system in order to avoid superfluous injury. Incendiary weapons should be banned on the same grounds. Consideration should be given to the possible banning or restriction of use of enhanced-blast munitions, especially fuel–air explosives.

On grounds of avoiding indiscriminate effects, the highest priority for the community of nations in recent years has been the effort to achieve a ban on the use of antipersonnel mines. Cluster weapons are another type of armament which needs to be scrutinized from this point of view. A case might also be made for banning polluting munitions such as depleted uranium projectiles because of their potential long-term health hazards.

Other existing and future weapons, including directed-energy weapons, need to be kept under review to avoid superfluous injury or indiscriminate effects. Under Article 36 of the 1977 Protocol I, states parties are required to determine whether any new weapon, means or method of warfare is prohibited under the protocol or any other rule of international law applicable to the state party. This determination must be made not just at the moment of adoption or acquisition of a weapon, but during the process of study and development as well.

Medical personnel and others with knowledge of the effects of weapons should contribute this knowledge to the review process required under Article 36 of the 1977 Protocol I and to the general public debate over the use of particular weapons. The control of weapons is exercised not only through the arduous process of adoption of international rules but through the political process and through public debate both nationally and internationally. In keeping with international humanitarian law, the aim must be to reduce as far as possible the suffering inflicted on both civilians and combatants in warfare.

ACKNOWLEDGEMENT

The authors wish to express their appreciation to Ove Bring, Robin M. Coupland, Jonathan E. Fine, Beat P. Kneubuehl, Dominique Loye, James Welsh and Arthur H. Westing for their valuable comments on Chapter 7.

REFERENCES

1. Sellier, K.G. and B.P. Kneubuehl (1995), *Wound Ballistics and the Scientific Background*, Amsterdam: Elsevier.
2. Prokosch, E. (1995), S*mall-calibre Weapon Systems: bringing the dum-dum ban up to date*. Colchester, United Kingdom: University of Essex Papers in the Theory and Practice of Human Rights, No. 11.
3. Prokosch, E. (1995), *The Technology of Killing: a military and political history of antipersonnel weapons*, London: Zed Books. International Committee of the Red Cross (1996) 'The Medical Profession and the Effects of Weapons: report of the symposium, Montreux, Switzerland, 8–10 March 1996, held under the auspices of the International Committee of the Red Cross. Geneva.
4. Prokosch, E. (1995), *Cluster Weapons*, Colchester, United Kingdom: University of Essex Papers in the Theory and Practice of Human Rights, No. 15.
5. Stockholm International Peace Research Institute (1975), *Incendiary Weapons*, Stockholm: Almqvist & Wiksell.
6. Lavoie, L. (1989), 'fuel–air Explosives, Weapons, and Effects', *Military Technology*, No. 9: 64–70.
7. Stockholm International Peace Research Institute (1976), *Ecological Consequences of the Second Indochina War*, Stockholm: Almqvist & Wiksell; Stockholm International Peace Research Institute (1978), *Anti-personnel Weapons*, London: Taylor & Francis.
8. See n. 7 (1978) above; and S. Glasstone and P.J. Dolan (eds) (1977), *The Effects of Nuclear Weapons*, Washington: US Department of Defense and US Department of Energy.
9. US Defense Intelligence Agency, US Army Foreign Science and Technology Center (1993) 'fuel–air and enhanced-blast explosives technology – foreign', DST-1850S-207-93. Washington.
10. International Committee of the Red Cross (1993), *Blinding Weapons: reports of the meetings of experts convened by the International Committee of the Red Cross on battlefield laser weapons, 1989–1991*, Geneva.
11. Dando, M. (1996) *A New Form of Warfare: the rise of non-lethal weapons*, London, Washington: Brassey's; Lewer, N. and S. Schofield (1997), *Non-lethal Weapons: a Fatal Attraction? Military strategies and technologies for 21st-century conflict*, London: Zed Books.
12. Westing, A.H. (ed.) (1985), *Explosive Remnants of War: mitigating the environmental effects*, Stockholm International Peace Research Institute, London: Taylor & Francis.
13. See n. 4 above.
14. See n. 7 above.
15. See n. 3 above.
16. See n. 3 (1996) above.
17. See n. 3 (1996) above; and R.M. Coupland (ed.) (1997), *The SirUS Project: towards a determination of which weapons cause 'superfluous injury or unnecessary suffering'*, Geneva: International Committee of the Red Cross.

Address for correspondence

Amnesty International, 1 Easton Street, London WC1X 0DW, United Kingdom
Human Rights Watch Arms Division, 1630 Connecticut Avenue NW, Suite 500, Washington DC 20009, USA

8 SMALL ARMS

MICHAEL RENNER

The category of weapons known as 'small arms' covers a broad spectrum from pistols to shoulder-fired surface-to-air missiles. These weapons are typically used in the most common contemporary zones of conflict: small wars within rather than between countries, and not necessarily involving regular government troops. Reliance on small arms does not limit the potential danger of these non-conventional conflicts, which have a tendency to persist and escalate while arms remain available. Insurgent guerrilla groups, paramilitary forces, organized criminal bands, warlord armies and vigilante hit squads are typical end users of small arms. Particularly in southern Africa and Central America a seamless transition has occurred between politically motivated and criminal conflict sustained by poverty, unemployment and a persistent culture of violence. These conditions make the flow of arms especially difficult to track and control. Small arms are supplied in direct government-to-government transfers, by government-sponsored private arms companies, and by black market arms networks; they are captured by insurgents and stolen by criminal gangs. Their easy availability encourages violence to persist and hampers reconstruction, development and democratic structures in war-ravaged societies.

Decommissioning and collection of small arms by peacekeeping forces and through buy-back schemes have shown some positive results, though techniques need to be refined; political will and support are crucial. The success of the anti-landmine campaign has drawn attention to the wider small arms issue and represents a positive example.

Small arms are the weapons of choice in today's typical conflict, in which fighting rages within rather than between countries. The wide availability of these easily-carried and concealed weapons is contributing both to the intensity and the duration of conflicts. Although the firepower, reach and precision-targeting of major conventional weapons systems and nuclear weapons dwarf the capacities of assault rifles and other small arms, the hundreds of millions of these low-tech, inexpensive, sturdy and easy-to-use weapons are the tools for most of the killing in contemporary conflicts, causing as much as 90 per cent of the deaths. Small-arms proliferation also threatens the consolidation of still-weak democracies, compromises the reconstruction of war-torn societies and obstructs social and economic development.

'Small arms and light weapons', the term used in the literature, usually includes weapons that can be carried by an individual or by a pack animal. This class of weapons encompasses such items as pistols and revolvers, rifles and assault rifles, hand grenades, machine guns, light mortars and light antitank weapons like grenade launchers and recoilless rifles. Another important category is antipersonnel landmines (not discussed here). Because they are portable, shoulder-fired surface-to-air missiles are also included even though they are far more high-tech and complex than most other small arms. The term therefore covers a broad spectrum, from weapons with exclusive military application, to firearms used by police forces, to handguns or hunting rifles in the legitimate possession of civilians.[1]

The same characteristics that have long led policymakers to underestimate their importance also make small arms easy to acquire and handle, and harder to track and control:

(1) Because small weapons do not carry nearly as large a price tag as big-ticket military items, their importance is all too easily underestimated. Worldwide, perhaps US$3 billion worth of small arms and light weapons are being shipped across international borders each year (due to the lack of reliable data, this is a rough estimate); that would be equivalent to about one-eighth of all international arms sales.[2]

(2) The relatively low cost of most small arms also means that they are affordable to many sub-state groups. For just US$50 millon, roughly the cost of a single modern jet fighter, one can equip a small army with some 200,000 assault rifles at today's 'fire-sale' prices.[3]

(3) Unlike major weapons, small arms do not require any complex organizational, logistical or training capacities to maintain and operate. Hence they are usable by a large number of groups and are the preferred kind of equipment of the armed forces of many poor countries and of guerrilla and other armed sub-state groups.[4]

(4) Many small weapons are so lightweight and can be assembled and reassembled with such ease that children as young as ten can use them. While the phenomenon of child soldiers is not a new one, the easy availability of lightweight small arms in the contemporary era has boosted the ability of children to participate in armed conflicts.[5]

(5) Their light weight and small size make small arms easy to conceal and smuggle. Small arms are readily available on a burgeoning black market, and therefore easy for guerrilla groups, criminal organizations and other interested buyers to obtain.[6]

(6) Major weapons become obsolete relatively quickly and are in constant need of new spare parts and maintenance. By contrast, small arms are sturdy enough to have a long life, making it possible for them to be circulated from one conflict to another. For example, an F-5 jet fighter requires an inventory of about 60,000 spare parts, but an AK-47 Kalashnikov has only 16 moving parts. Small arms of Second World War (WW II) vintage and some even of First World War (WW I) vintage are still used in today's conflicts.[7]

Small arms in contemporary conflicts

The overall number of wars and organized armed conflicts defined as involving government forces at least on one side, and either another government or an opposition group on the other – appears to have declined in recent years, following virtually uninterrupted growth since WW II (see Figure 8.1.) According to AKUF, a University of Hamburg research group analysing the causes of war, there were 25 active armed conflicts in 1997, down from a peak of 51 in 1992.[8]

According to a detailed analysis by researchers at the University of Uppsala in Sweden, only 6 out of 101 conflicts in the period 1989–96 were international, that is involving the forces or territory of more than one state. The 101 armed conflicts had as many as 254 separate conflict parties. The combatants typically are not only uniformed soldiers but also guerrilla groups of various stripes, paramilitary forces, drug and organized crime bands, warlords and vigilante hit squads.[9]

Yet the Hamburg and Uppsala projects define war in ways that seem to exclude a potentially large number of armed conflicts from consideration. The Uppsala group restricts itself to those armed conflicts that involve at least one party representing a sovereign state and that revolve around a contested government or territory. The criteria used by the Hamburg group require the presence of a certain degree of central organization among the fighting forces and a degree of continuity and strategy.

A large number of armed conflicts today do not, however, fully meet these criteria. Clashes may be spontaneous and erratic, violence may ebb and flow and be employed randomly, the fighting may not involve any government forces and the combatants may be motivated by causes other than overthrowing a government or redrawing a border. In the post-Cold War period, as many Third World governments and guerrilla forces have lost the military aid they previously received from the big powers, armies and other fighting forces have begun to fragment; with heavily-armed splinter groups, accountable to no one, abounding, new violence arises out of the old patterns of militarization. In other words, the nature of conflicts has changed. But it is precisely these non-conventional conflicts, which today may be too small to elicit much concern but may turn into tomorrow's big flare-ups, in which small arms play a key role.

Researchers with the PIOOM Foundation in Leiden, The Netherlands, use far broader criteria than the Hamburg and Uppsala projects and report far higher numbers of armed conflicts (see Table 8.1.) PIOOM also argues that greater monitoring is needed of roughly 100 'tension situations' around the world, in which little or no violence has occurred to date or where violence has abated from past wars but where major fighting may reoccur. PIOOM data suggest that while high-intensity conflicts (major wars) have indeed declined in recent years, low-intensity and violent political conflicts have sharply increased in number.

Table 8.1: Trends in armed conflicts, 1993–97[10]

	1993	1995	1996	1997
High-intensity conflicts (HIC)	22	20	19	17
Low-intensity conflicts (LIC)		39	42	70
Violent political conflicts (VPC)	84	40	75	74
Total	106	99	136	161

Note: High-intensity conflicts involve more than 1000 deaths per year, low-intensity conflicts 100–1000 deaths and violent political conflicts 25–100 deaths.

Privatization of violence

Such near-war violence may stem from a broad variety of causal factors but is sustained primarily by one: the easy availability of large numbers of weapons, especially small weapons. Michael Klare, director of the Five College Program in Peace and World Security Studies in Amherst, Massachusetts, argues that 'the abundance of arms *at every level of society* means that any increase in inter-communal tensions and hostility will entail an increased likelihood of armed violence and bloodshed'.[11]

The dispersal of arms to private armies and militias, insurgent groups, criminal organisations and other non-state actors feeds a cycle of violence at work in many societies that in turn causes even greater demand for guns. A variety of motivations spawns different kinds of violence, including: political violence, pitting governments against insurgent forces fighting to overthrow the government or to achieve a separate state; communal violence, involving different ethnic, religious or other identity-based groups; and criminal violence, involving drug traffickers, organized criminal groups or petty individual crime. And ordinary citizens in many countries are increasingly arming themselves in self-defence against widespread crime and violence.

Southern Africa and several Central American countries, among others, experienced a seamless transition from politically motivated to criminal violence in the early 1990s. These and other countries had only begun to recover from years of fighting with conditions conducive to crime: severe economic and social inequalities, endemic poverty, a pervasive lack of jobs and a culture of violence. Recently demobilized soldiers and former guerrilla fighters in particular find themselves often poorly equipped to make a living in the civilian world; not surprisingly, many tend to fall back on the tools and skills they acquired during years of conflict, leading to rising banditry, in several countries, while weak or corrupt judiciary systems and ineffective police forces have given rise to vigilante squads intent on what they call 'social cleansing' – killing individuals suspected of crimes or otherwise perceived as unwanted.

These are factors that feed what Klare calls the privatization of security and violence: 'a growing tendency of individuals, groups, and organizations to rely on private security forces rather than on the state's police and paramilitary formations'.[12] Indeed, private security formations are on the rise and civilian police are becoming more militarized at the same time as national armies are shrinking in size. Private security forces come in several colours, sometimes blurring the distinction between policing, paramilitary functions and mercenary activity. In several countries, private security forces rival or outstrip the size of the public police, and in some – among them Australia, South Africa and the United States – they outnumber even the national army. In the United States, there are now roughly three times as many private security guards as there are police officers. Growing to almost 2 million persons, private security forces are more numerous than the 1.6 million strong national armed forces.

Easy availability of small arms

Small arms are so ubiquitous that many regions of the world find themselves awash in them. One analyst put the number of firearms in worldwide circulation at 500 million.[13]

Even though this estimate apparently includes only military-style firearms, and not those that might commonly be in the possession of police forces, private security guards or the general population, it must surely be a conservative figure. In all likelihood, civilian-type firearms also number in the hundreds of millions. No one really knows how many weapons are in circulation among the general population of most countries. A 1997 survey by the UN Commission on Crime Prevention and Criminal Justice provided only part of the global picture and perhaps little more than the tip of the iceberg.[14]

Some rough quantitative data exist for military rifles. The most notorious assault rifle is the AK-47, also known by its inventor's name, Kalashnikov. Manufactured in the former Soviet Union and in nine other countries, more than 70 million Kalashnikovs have been produced in some 100 different versions since 1947; most of these are still in use and are in service in the armies of 78 countries and in countless guerrilla groups the world over. A number of other assault rifles are also in use by a large number of national armed forces (see Table 8.2). In addition to licensed production of these and other small weapons, several countries are apparently flooding the world market with counterfeit (unauthorized) versions. All in all, more than 100 million military-style rifles are thought to exist worldwide.[15]

Table 8.2: Production and deployment of major types of assault rifles[16]

Type	Country of origin	Number manufactured (millions)	Number of countries using the weapon	manufacturing the weapon
AK-47/-72	USSR/Russia	70+*	78	14+
M-16	United States	8	67	7
FN-FAL	Belgium	5–7	94	15
G-3	Germany	7+	64+	18

*Some sources report a range of 35–50 million produced.

Note: The numbers of countries in which these assault rifles are in use include only those where the national armed forces are armed with them. In many countries, guerrilla forces, organized gangs, and other groups may also have one or the other model in their possession, so the numbers reported here are likely to be underestimated.

The danger that easy availability of weapons may translate into impulsive recourse to violence is probably greatest in societies that are struggling to rebuild themselves after long years of warfare and to shake off the legacy of a culture of violence. They face the particular challenge of reintegrating large numbers of former soldiers or guerrillas into civilian life in a situation where warfare has destroyed a large portion of their public infrastructure, economic activity remains handicapped, national treasuries are depleted, and foreign lenders are demanding belt-tightening. Though political violence may finally be absent, social and criminal violence is often ascendant. That kind of violence may in turn provoke countermeasures that could well rekindle political confrontations. Peace, so difficult to attain in the first place, rests on a shaky foundation.

Among the regions that are of particular concern are Central America and southern Africa. Emerging from its devastating civil war of the 1980s, El Salvador has been formally at peace since 1992, yet some 20,000 violent deaths since that year comes close, on an annual basis, to rivalling the number of people killed during the war, some 75,000 over a period of 13 years. The postwar violence stems from several factors.

The large majority of 40,000 demobilized soldiers and guerrillas have been unable to establish themselves in civilian society. Some of them have taken up arms left over from the war. Formed by former soldiers and by disoriented youth, heavily armed Salvadoran criminal groups are responsible for murders, kidnappings and robberies nation-wide. Gang members are buying and smuggling weapons left over from the civil war into neighbouring countries and the United States, and there is evidence that some of them have formed alliances with Mexican and Colombian drug traffickers.

With unemployment running at an estimated 50 per cent and roughly two-thirds of the Salvadoran population living in extreme poverty, crime is rampant. Furthermore, because of corruption and an ineffective judicial system, vigilante justice has been on the rise; new death squads have emerged that target people considered to be criminals or anti-social elements. In reaction to rising crime and violence, ordinary citizens are also arming themselves.[17]

Southern Africa confronts similar challenges. On the order of 9 million small arms are thought to be in the arsenals of the armies of South Africa, Angola, Mozambique and Zimbabwe, but substantial additional numbers of weapons are in private hands, in hidden caches or flowing in secret arms-trading channels that cross borders with impunity. Although no one knows for sure just how many firearms are in circulation, there is no doubt that the region is flooded with weapons. Some 4 million firearms are licensed to private citizens in South Africa but illegal weapons are estimated to number 5–8 million. 'Light weapons have become a form of currency throughout the region', writes Jacklyn Cock of the University of Witwatersrand.[18]

In South Africa, the political violence of the years of transition away from apartheid (1990–93), during which some 10,000 people were killed, has declined dramatically. But according to Cock there has been a parallel, equally dramatic increase in criminal violence fuelled by high unemployment and economic hardship. Military-style weapons such as the AK-47 and the G-3 are increasingly used in robberies and in the so-called taxi wars, clashes between competing taxi owners who have employed hitmen to kill passengers and drivers of their rivals. In a sense South Africa is being hit by an arms boomerang: the instability that South Africa's apartheid regime sowed in Mozambique by supporting the ruthless Mozambique National Resistance (Renamo) rebels and supplying them with weapons is now hitting home. Many of these weapons are being smuggled back into South Africa, joining other arms flowing in from Namibia and Angola and those leaking from weapons depots inside South Africa.[19]

A top official of the Mozambique Defence Force, Lazaro Mathe, has said that Mozambique, with a population of 15 million, has more weapons than people. Others have estimated the number at 10 million. During the country's civil war, both the government and the rebels were supplied with large amounts of small weapons by South Africa and the Soviet Union. The protagonists in turn 'passed out weapons almost indiscriminately, arming not just soldiers but everyone they could find', as Suzanne Daley, a reporter for the *New York Times* put it. It is widely believed that weapons collection by a UN peacekeeping force in the mid-1990s was limited and ulimately ineffectual because combatants retained their best weapons and there was no attempt to collect weapons held by civilians. Now, poorly-paid soldiers and police officers are selling weapons, the one commodity that seems boundless, to what appears to be an insatiable market in South Africa.

The Mozambican experience seems bound to repeat itself in Angola, another of the countries that apartheid-era South Africa sought to destabilize and one that has been at war from 1975 to 1994. Perhaps as many as 90 per cent of Angolans privately possess firearms. The government's campaign to recover arms from civilians as required under the country's peace accord has so far made little more than a small dent.

The picture that emerges globally is one where individual countries and entire regions are inundated with both military-style small weapons and civilian firearms. To the extent they exist at all, current controls appear hopelessly inadequate for dealing with what is an unencumbered flow of arms. Many countries are just beginning to recognize the potential for large-scale violence and instability that this massive availability of firepower implies.

Supply channels

That small weapons are so ubiquitous should not come as a surprise: a multitude of seemingly inexhaustible sources feed the market. Some of the weapons produced each year never cross any borders, destined instead for domestic recipients. But international transfers play a crucial role. These run the gamut from direct government-to-government sales and government-approved exports by private arms manufacturers to: covert deliveries by government agencies and a variety of black market deals involving private arms merchants; to capture of arms by insurgent forces or theft from government arsenals; and finally to the often-illicit passing of weapons from one area of conflict to another. Governments may decry the latter kinds of deals but government sales are by far the most important source of arms proliferation. Officials in Washington and Moscow like to think that the Cold War period is now history ; but the extensive arms transfers carried out by the two superpowers during those decades continue to have a deadly impact.

Among the most important producers are the former Soviet Union, the United States, China, Germany, Italy, Belgium, Switzerland, the Czech Republic and Israel. But the United Nations Institute for Disarmament Research (UNIDIR) in Geneva has identified close to 300 companies in 52 countries that were manufacturing small arms and related equipment in 1994, a 25 per cent increase in the number of such countries since the mid-1980s. Although no statistics are available, it would appear that world-wide production of small arms easily runs to several million, if not tens of millions, of units each year.[20]

Most international transfers take place in the form of either direct government-to-government transfers or commercial sales involving private companies (the most important source of transfers since the end of the Cold War). Unfortunately, available statistics for such transactions do not distinguish between major and small arms. Michael Klare estimates that of US$25.9 billion worth of arms that US firms were authorized to export in 1989–93, small arms accounted for perhaps one-third, US$8.6 billion worth.

He reckons that anywhere from 10 to 20 per cent of US grant transfers of arms and ammunition (worth US$55.2 billion in 1950–94) involved small arms.[21]

While too little information is available even about these official, 'legal' sales authorized and acknowledged by governments, there are a multitude of secret and illegal deals by governments and others about which, owing to their very nature, very little is known. In addition to clandestine supplies by government agencies, the international black market is being fed by legions of private arms merchants and criminal organizations. According to Klare, black market sales have greatly expanded in recent years.[22]

Table 8.3: Selected examples of commodities-for-arms transactions, 1980s and 1990s[23]

Country/region	Observation
Liberia/Sierra Leone	Charles Taylor and other Liberian warlords have traded timber, iron ore and agricultural products for small arms and military training since 1990; Taylor earned up to US$100 million* a year. In early 1990s, government and rebel soldiers in neighbouring Sierra Leone plundered diamond mines. Rebels exchanged diamonds for rocket launchers and Kalashnikovs from Taylor's forces.
Rwanda	In 1992, Egypt accepted future Rwandan tea harvests as collateral for US$6 million worth of artillery, mortars, landmines and assault rifles sent to the government; Egypt took delivery of US$1 million in Rwandan tea before fighting in Rwanda's civil war damaged the tea bushes.
Southern Africa	Many ivory and rhino horn poachers in Zimbabwe and Mozambique are ex-soldiers involved in both buying and selling small arms on the black market. UNITA rebel forces in Angola earn US$450–500 million a year in diamond sales. Also, UNITA paid for South African military support with ivory, slaughtering tens of thousands of elephants. Renamo rebels in Mozambique bartered game (meat, hides, ivory) for guns.
Cambodia	Khmer Rouge financed their military effort by trading timber and gems to 'renegades' in the Thai military who control the Cambodian–Thai border, earning US$100–250 million a year. Other Cambodian factions also finance their armies with timber sales.
China	Pingyuan in Yunnan province is a major drugs and arms trafficking centre. Most of the weapons used in criminal activities in 24 of China's 31 provinces come in via Pingyuan from Burma and Vietnam.
Central America	Black-market arms sales are linked to the illicit drugs trade. Traffickers of guns and drugs often combine their operations and use the same Mexico routes and transportation systems.

*For comparative purposes, US$100 million might purchase up to 400,000 assault rifles at typical, discounted prices.

Black-market deals often involve the barter of weapons for natural resources, animal products, drugs and other commodities, or at least the financing of arms purchases through the sale of such commodities (see Table 8.3.) Other important sources of weapons flows are the capture of arms by insurgent forces, the looting of military depots and leaks from government arsenals (that is, the theft and sell-off of weapons by soldiers), as has happened in Somalia, South Africa, Russia, Albania and other countries. Even in the United States, small arms' parts are apparently systematically stolen from the Pentagon's repair shops and warehouses and sold off to gun dealers.

A source of growing importance for both legal and illegal arms sales are surplus stocks, now that the end of the Cold War has left many countries of NATO and the former Warsaw Pact with far more military hardware than they need. Narrow cost–benefit considerations have led several governments to sell off surplus equipment, often at bargain rates, instead of dismantling or destroying it. For instance, Turkey received 304,000 formerly East German Kalashnikovs and 83 million rounds of ammunition from Germany.[24]

A different kind of surplus arms are those that get transferred, illicitly, from one hotspot of the world to another. Often, when a conflict in one country comes to an end, the weapons, particularly the small weapons, are sold or donated by former protagonists to belligerents in other countries. The US supply of arms to the Afghan Mujahideen during the 1980s provides one of the most striking examples. Of an estimated US$6–9 billion worth of arms, the Mujahideen fighters may have received as little as 30–40 per cent, the remainder being diverted to other destinations. Weapons from the Afghan pipeline turned Pakistan's North West Frontier Province into a massive arms bazaar, and aggravated violence in Pakistan's Sindh province. And they have been smuggled into civil war–plagued Tajikistan, into India's Punjab region, to Muslims in northern India who feel increasingly threatened by Hindu extremists and into Kashmir, where they increased the severity of the violence between Indian forces and pro-independence militants. Furthermore, there are reports of some of these weapons turning up in Sri Lanka, Burma and Algeria.[25]

The story of the leaky Afghanistan arms pipeline is far from an aberration. Weapons left behind by the United States in Vietnam in the 1970s showed up in the Middle East and Central America; US armaments pumped into Central America in the 1980s are now part of a regional black market; weapons from Lebanon's civil war of the 1970s and 1980s have been shipped to Bosnia; and surplus arms from Mozambique's civil war are being smuggled by former rebel soldiers to bands of criminals in Zimbabwe and South Africa. Other examples abound (see Table 8.4).

Peacekeeping and buy-backs

The most immediate challenge in coping with small arms is to reduce the number of weapons that are already in circulation. First, weapons that are now surplus to the needs of armies in industrialized countries will need to be dismantled instead of being sold off cheaply. Second, arms that are left over at the end of civil wars in developing countries need to be collected before they fall into the hands of domestic or international smugglers.

Table 8.4: Selected examples of arms transfers from hotspot to hotspot, 1980s and 1990s[26]

Initial recipient	Subsequent recipient(s)
Vietnam	Vietnam inherited 1.8 million US-made small arms and close to 150,000 tons of ammunition following the withdrawal of US troops in 1975. Much of this was acquired by Cuba, and then by the Sandinista government in Nicaragua and the FMLN rebels in El Salvador. Leftover US arms also went to Chilean rebels.
Palestine Liberation Organization	The CIA obtained several tons of Soviet-made munitions that had been confiscated from PLO forces by the Israelis in 1982, and transferred them to the Nicaraguan Contras.
Nicaragua, El Salvador	Weapons remaining from civil wars of the 1980s are being shipped to new areas of conflict. Contra arms are being sold to drug cartels and rebels in Colombia (via Panama). Some AK-47s and rocket-propelled grenades formerly held by the Contras and FMLN found their way to Zapatista rebels in Chiapas, Mexico. Some ex-FMLN guns went to Peru's MRTA rebels and to Salvadoran gangs in the United States.
Ethiopia, Sudan, Somalia	The Mengistu government offered several thousand U.S.-made weapons inherited from the previous, pro-Western government to the FMLN rebels in El Salvador. Following the collapse of the Mengistu regime in Ethiopia, weapons flooded into Somalia. Surplus weapons left over from recent conflicts in Sudan and Somalia flowed into Kenya, where they are used in deadly confrontations by rival cattle herders.
Mozambique, Angola	Large amounts of leftover weapons from conflicts in Mozambique and Angola (many of them originally supplied to rebel forces by South Africa's apartheid regime) are being smuggled into South Africa, Namibia, Zimbabwe and Zambia.

Since 1989, several UN peacekeeping operations have become involved in disarming ex-combatants. But there are several handicaps. Typically, at the end of a conflict there is no firm or reliable inventory of the total number of weapons in the possession of combatants, so that it is difficult to assess to what extent disarmament is actually taking place. A substantial portion of the weapons handed in by ex-combatants tends to be of inferior quality; by implication, the best armaments are retained or hidden. Another difficulty arises from the fact that in countries with civil wars, government and insurgent forces alike often pass out large amounts of small arms to the civilian population. Yet peacekeeping operations either have no mandate to disarm civilians, or they do not have

Table 8.5. Selected examples of gun-buyback programmes, 1990s[27]

Country	Observation
Colombia	Nationwide food-for-guns programme established (those with legally-owned weapons receive a cheque for the value of the weapon). Bogotá cash-for-weapons programme helped cause a sharp drop in 1997 homicides.
El Salvador	Goods-for-guns programme run by the Patriotic Movement Against Crime collected close to 5000 weapons during 1996 and early 1997. Yet the acquisition of new weapons – 1500 registered arms per month – far outpaces this effort. Another programme (sponsored by New York-based Guns for Goods) exchanges vouchers to buy food and clothes for guns in three cities. In both cases, lack of funding limits effectiveness.
Nicaragua	Buy-back programme incorporated cash and food incentives and an Italian-sponsored micro-enterprise programme. During 1992–93, about 64,000 weapons were bought back and 78,000 confiscated, and all were destroyed. 250,000 pieces of ammunition were also collected. Total cost US$6 million.
Haiti	A US army gun buy-back programme paid cash for functional weapons and confiscated non-functional ones. By March 1995, more than 33,000 weapons had been taken in, at a cost of US$1.9 million. The weapons in good condition were passed on to the Haitian police, the remainder melted down.
Mozambique	A programme sponsored by the Christian Council of Mozambique allows people to exchange weapons for cows, sewing machines, plows and other goods. Programme began in 1996 with a US$1.2 million grant from Germany and Japan.
Britain	A 1996 law requires that all handguns larger than 0.22 calibre must be turned in to police stations or taken out of the country, affecting some 200,000 legally held guns. New legislation will ban private ownership of handguns. Cost of compensating owners estimated at US$250–850 million.
Australia	The massacre of 35 people by a gunman in April 1996 prompted the government to enact a broadly-supported ban on automatic and semi-automatic weapons. More than 600,000 arms were handed in. The government paid more than US$200 million in compensation.
United States	More than 80 local programmes with widely-differing incentives. A Seattle effort in 1992 took in 1772 guns, fewer than 1 per cent of the guns in Seattle homes; a St Louis, Missouri, programme collected over 7500 weapons in 1991. In both cases the impact on gun-related violence was minimal.

the requisite resources and political back-up to do so. In all the UN operations, only some of the arms in circulation were collected; in some cases, all the collected weapons were destroyed, but in others many were actually passed on to the new army (integrating government and rebel soldiers) that emerged after a country's peace accord. The volume of arms is often several times larger than needed to outfit these smaller-sized forces. Weak controls over these arms and the fact that many soldiers subsist on low salaries are a virtual invitation to steal and sell arms.[28] Lessons need to be learned from this experience in order to make future efforts more effective.

In addition to disarmament efforts in the context of peacekeeping operations, several countries have tried so-called gun buy-back programmes. Even some nations that have not had recent wars on their soil have chosen this route in an effort to reduce the number of weapons in circulation. Under the buy-back schemes, individuals are encouraged to turn in arms voluntarily in return for monetary or in-kind compensation (see Table 8.5).

The experience has been quite varied, teaching important lessons that can help to improve and fine-tune future programmes. One possible pitfall of buy-backs is that monetary compensation in return for guns may provide an incentive to steal guns in order to turn them in for cash. Pricing can be the crucial factor: at compensation levels that are too far below the black-market value, few firearms will be turned in; but at levels that are too high, the black market will be stimulated. Particularly in developing countries where many ex-fighters are expected to return to homes in rural areas, Peter Batchelor points out, buy-back programmes that provide food or agricultural implements are more appropriate than programmes that offer cash for weapons. Generally speaking, buy-back schemes will tend to be more successful if they are embedded in broader community programmes.[29]

The tools to reduce the number of weapons in circulation are not in serious question. What needs attention and improvement, however, is the ways in which they are wielded. The experience of the last few years has shown that programmes to collect arms will need considerable refinement and more substantial financial and political support if they are to succeed.

Tracking down illegal transfers

To tackle the challenge of small arms, a multitude of approaches can be pursued. These include creating greater transparency, restricting both legal and illegal international transfers, establishing restrictions on new production and banning particular types of weapons.

In addition to restricting governmentally-approved sales to recipients that respect human rights and democratic governance and unambiguously adhere to norms of international law through the adoption of a code of conduct, as many nongovernmental organizations have urged – a greater effort is also needed to clamp down on illegal transfers. Although it may appear futile to try to restrict clandestine flows of small arms, it may well be sufficient to block the biggest transfers and interrupt the most important transfer routes. And such efforts might particularly focus on flows of ammunition, argues Edward Laurance: not only is the capacity to manufacture ammunition less widespread than that to produce the small weapons themselves (making transfers a potential choke-point), but because ammunition is heavy and bulky. It is less easy to transfer clandestinely.[30]

Restricting illicit transfers of weapons and ammunition alike would involve enhancing national customs controls and other measures to improve the monitoring of cross-border flows of goods. But arms traffickers will be able to circumvent strict regulations in one country so long as others have weak laws. Hence, there is a need to harmonize export regulations, and to step up international cooperation, for instance by establishing shared databases on known or suspected traffickers and illicit end-users.

Several regional efforts to counter gun-smuggling are under way. The Organization of American States has adopted a regional convention against illicit firearms trafficking.[31] In southern Africa, a tripartite agreement was signed between South Africa, Swaziland and Mozambique in June 1993 in an attempt to deal with problem of illegal arms flows into South Africa. In January 1995, South Africa and Mozambique signed an agreement to facilitate cross-border police cooperation to track down illegal weaponry; by late 1997, the accord had led to three joint operations in which several thousand small arms and several million rounds of ammunition were seized and destroyed. The success of this cooperation is likely to lead to similar missions between South Africa and other countries in the region. Finally, in Europe, the Netherlands has launched an initiative to develop a European Union database on illicit arms trafficking.

In early 1998, 15 West African governments gathered to consider a voluntary moratorium on the export, import and manufacture of light weapons. The moratorium, which was likely be formally endorsed in July 1998, is to last for three years before an assessment of its success is undertaken. Although focused on West Africa, all African nations are invited to join. Moreover, its sponsors hope that the moratorium could become a model for other regions of the world.

Discussions have also taken place on the global level, at the United Nations. The UN Commission on Crime Prevention and Criminal Justice drafted a resolution to

> work towards the elaboration of a binding international legal instrument to combat the illicit manufacturing of and trafficking in firearms, their parts and components and ammunition within the context of a United Nations convention on organised crime.

Sponsors of the initiative hoped that a binding convention could be concluded by year-end 2000. Firearms could then be exported from one country only with the permission of the destination country, and they would be marked at the time of import so they could be traced. That outcome is still awaited.

Outlook

Restricting the flow of weaponry without addressing the issue of continued production is, however, like stopping the flow of water from a hose by holding the nozzle closed; before too long, the water pressure will cause leaks. The longer that large-scale production continues, the greater the future supply of weapons and ammunition whose whereabouts and use will be of concern.

Thanks largely to the efforts of human rights, humanitarian, gun control and other grassroots groups, small arms control has become an issue with much greater visibility than even a few years ago. Several governments, such as those of Canada, Belgium, and Japan, for example, have stepped forward to endorse stricter regulation of arms transfers. Non-governmental organizations and governments that were centrally involved in the struggle for an agreement banning antipersonnel landmines feel that the momentum of the landmine discussion can help them make progress on small arms more generally. In many societies, no matter what their position on landmines may be, the lethal impact of firearms proliferation is becoming clearer. There are now many campaigns in countries around the world, raising awareness and building coalitions. These campaigns will proceed along their own tracks, but they may also coalesce into a global campaign.[32]

A strong constituency can be brought to life by making clear the horrendous effects of the virtually unlimited availability of small arms: the suffering of victims, the endless cycle of violence, the persistent insecurity. Once people understand the repercussions, the political dynamic changes: what was previously unthinkable begins to come within reach. For a long time, small arms and light weapons have escaped thorough scrutiny; their ubiquitous presence has been accepted as a necessary evil or even welcomed as a guarantor of security and a symbol of freedom. But this is beginning to change as growing numbers of people realize that excessive quantities of small arms can have devastating consequences. Progress will not come easily, given that small arms are already so widely available and that gun lobbies and other vested interests can be expected to work hard to prevent change. But, as the anti-landmine campaign demonstrates, change is possible.

ACKNOWLEDGEMENT

Chapter 8 is based on the author's *Small Arms. Big Impact: the Next Challenge of Disarmament*, Worldwatch Paper, 137, Washington DC: Worldwatch Institute, October 1997.

REFERENCES

1. Michael Klare (1995), 'Stemming the Lethal Trade in Small Arms and Light Weapons', *Issues in Science and Technology*, Fall; Rana, Swadesh (1995), *Small Arms and Intra-State Conflicts*, UNIDIR Research Paper No. 34, Geneva and New York: United Nations Institute for Disarmament Research.
2. See Klare, n. 1 above.
3. Ibid.
4. Edward Laurance (1996), *The New Field of Micro-Disarmament: addressing the proliferation and buildup of small arms and light weapons*, BICC Brief 7, Bonn: Bonn International Centre for Conversion (BICC), September; Christopher Smith (1996), 'Light Weapons and the International Arms Trade', in Christopher Smith, Peter Batchelor and Jakkie Potgieter, UNIDIR Disarmament and Conflict Resolution Project, *Small Arms Management and Peacekeeping in Southern Africa*, New York and Geneva: United Nations.
5. Brett, Rachel and Margaret McCallin (1996), *Children: The Invisible Soldiers*, Växjö, Sweden: Rädda Barnen – Swedish Save the Children.

6. Goldring, Natalie J. (1997), 'Bridging the Gap: light and major conventional weapons in recent conflicts', paper prepared for the annual meeeting of the International Studies Association, Toronto, Ontario, 18–21 March, British-American Security Information Council (BASIC).

7. Gantzel, Klaus Jürgen and Torsten Schwinghammer (1995), *Die Kriege nach dem Zweiten Weltkrieg 1945 bis 1992. Daten und Tendenzen*, Münster and Hamburg, Germany: Lit Verlag.

8. See n. 7 above; and Jung, Dietrich, Schlichte, Klaus and Jens Siegelberg (1996), *Das Kriegsgeschehen 1995. Daten und Tendenzen der Kriege und bewaffneten Konflikte im Jahr 1995*, Bonn, Germany: Stiftung Entwicklung und Frieden.

9. Sollenberg, Margareta (ed.) (1997), *States in Armed Conflict 1996*, Uppsala University, Department of Peace and Conflict Research, Report No. 46.

10. Jongman, A.J. and A.P. Schmid (1997), 'PIOOM's World Conflict Map 1997. A comparison with previous years', *PIOOM Newsletter and Progress Report*, Leiden, Netherlands, Winter; PIOOM (1996), 'World Conflict Map 1996', Leiden, Netherlands.

11. Klare, Michael T. (1995), 'Light Weapons Diffusion and Global Violence in the Post-Cold War Era', in Jasjit Singh (ed.), *Light Weapons and International Security*, Delhi: Indian Pugwash Society and British American Security Information Council, December.

12. Klare, Michael T. (1995), 'The Global Trade in Light Weapons and the International System in the Post-Cold War Era,' in Jeffrey Boutwell, Michael T. Klare and Laura Reed (eds), *Lethal Commerce: The Global Trade in Small Arms and Light Weapons*, Cambridge, MA: Committee on International Security Studies, American Academy of Arts and Sciences.

13. Singh, Jasjit (1995), 'Introduction', in Jasjit Singh (ed.), *Light Weapons and International Security*, Delhi: Indian Pugwash Society and British American Security Information Council, December.

14. UN Commission on Crime Prevention and Criminal Justice (1997), 'Draft United Nations International Study on Firearm Regulation', E/CN.15/1997/CRP.6, Vienna.

15. Bonn International Centre for Conversion (BICC) (1997), *Conversion Survey 1997*, New York: Oxford University Press.

16. Singh, Jasjit (ed.), *Light Weapons and International Security*, Delhi: Indian Pugwash Society and British American Security Information Council, December; United Nations (1997), 'Report of the Panel of Governmental Experts on Small Arms', New York, July; 'Russia: Kalashnikov anniversary', *Omri Daily Digest*, 21 February 1997; BICC (1997) *Conversion Survey 1997: global disarmament and disposal of surplus arms*, New York: Oxford University Press.

17. See Laurance (1996), n. 1 above.

18. Jacklyn Cock (1995), 'A Sociological Account of Light Weapons Proliferation in Southern Africa,' in Jasjit Singh (ed.), *Light Weapons and International Security*, Delhi: Indian Pugwash Society and British American Security Information Council, December.

19. See Smith (1996), n. 4 above, and ibid.

20. See Rana (1995), n. 1 above.

21. See n. 11 above.

22. See n. 12 above.

23. Renner, Michael (1997), *Small Arms, Big Impact: the next challenge of disarmament*, Worldwatch Paper 137, Washington DC: Worldwatch Institute, October.

24. See ns 11 and 15 above, and Pineo, Paul F. and Lora Lumpe (1996), *Recycled Weapons. American Exports of Surplus Arms, 1990–1995*, Washington, DC: Arms Sales Monitoring Project, Federation of American Scientists, May.

25. Smith, Christopher (1995), 'Light Weapons and Ethnic Conflict in South Asia', in Jeffrey Boutwell, Michael T. Klare and Laura Reed (eds), *Lethal Commerce: The global trade in small arms and light weapons*, Cambridge, MA: Committee on International Security Studies, American Academy of Arts and Sciences; and Singh, Jasjit (1995), 'Light Weapons and Conflict in Southern Asia', in Jasjit Singh (ed.), *Light Weapons and International Security*, Delhi: Indian Pugwash Society and British American Security Information Council, December.

26. See n. 23.

27. Ibid.

28. Zawels, Estanislao Angel, Stedman, Stephen John, Donald C.F. Daniel, *et al.* (1996), *Managing Arms in Peace Processes: the issues*, United Nations Institute for Disarmament Research (UNIDIR),

Disarmament and Conflict Resolution Project, New York and Geneva: United Nations.

29. See Laurance (1996), n. 4 above.

30. Ibid.

31. Organization of American States (1997), 'Inter-American Convention Against the Illicit Manufacturing of and Trafficking in Firearms, Ammunition, Explosives, and Other related Materials,' 13 November, as posted on <http://www.prepcom.org/low/pc2/pc2a1.html>.

32. The Preparatory Committee for a Global Campaign on Small Arms and Light Weapons (PrepCom), World Wide Web site <http://www.prepcom.org>. PrepCom was established as an Internet community of NGOs and individuals dedicated to preparing for a global campaign to alleviate the problems associated with the proliferation, accumulation and misuse of small arms and light weapons. The web site contains many important documents relating to small arms' issues.

Address for correspondence

25 Treasure Road, Riverhead, NY 11901, United States; Tel:/Fax: 001 - 516 - 369 6896; E-mail: mrenner@worldwatch.org

9 ANTIPERSONNEL LANDMINES

IAN MADDOCKS

A physician's responsibility

In the face of the threat of nuclear war in the 1980s, physicians sought to spell out the true human consequences of a nuclear explosion over a centre of population, warning of mega-death and injury beyond the capacity of any treatment, and affirming prevention as the only appropriate medical response. In the 1990s, against the strong opposition of the nuclear powers, IPPNW joined other non-governmental (NGO) groups in an approach to the World Court, requesting an opinion on the legality of the use of nuclear weapons, claiming that there was no situation in which the explosion of a nuclear weapon could be justified.

In the same way, physicians have recognized the impossibility of restoring a limb lost through the explosion of an antipersonnel mine, and have counted the enormous cost to families and communities affected by mine injury or threatened by future injury from the millions of mines which still lie in wait for their innocent victims. Joining an international campaign, they have claimed that the deployment of antipersonnel land mines (APLMs) cannot be excused in any situation, and requires complete elimination from military arsenals as the only acceptable medical response.[1]

It is no hyperbole to include landmines among the weapons of mass destruction; the trajectory of their damage is nevertheless slow, so slow that they will affect even those who are not yet born.

Telling the reality

The injury
Medical graduates bring a professional objectivity to the description of injuries caused by antipersonnel mines, and may look dispassionately at the horrible mutilation they cause.

But it is necessary that all be reminded that the injury caused by a mine presents a major challenge to the most skilled modern surgery. The contamination of these wounds by soil, the thrombosis initiated in intact blood vessels contused by blast, the delay which so often ensues because injury occurs far from medical help in difficult terrain – all these factors conspire to reduce blood supply to the affected area and promote infection, making unavoidable an incidence of amputation high above the apparent level of injury. Delayed closure of wounds, multiple surgical procedures and difficulty in achieving good skin closure with a stable scar and a shape suitable for a prosthesis are common consequences of these injuries.[2]

The context

We should make no apology for showing such pictures in their full detail, for describing the physical and medical reality of mine trauma, nor for telling the anecdotes which place the physical effects in a broader human context:

- A grandmother, injured as she led her young granddaughter by the hand, was blinded in the left eye as the child was killed instantly. At operation, the fragment removed from her eye was skin, her grandchild's skin flayed from the child's leg.
- A boy whose thigh wound high on his injured leg remained unhealed and infected, and when probed to its very depth, proved to contain embedded material – the tip of his own big toe.

Such simple stories make the horror topical and relevant to those whose daily lives are lived far from these threats.

Imagine that your city has been mined by terrorists. They lay mines at night, in likely public places: parks, walks by the river, playing fields, beaches. You go for a dawn walk by the beach. A child is splashing in the shallows then runs up the sand, to be suddenly thrown down, bleeding and screaming on the sand, horribly injured. You start towards him, but someone holds you back – where there is one mine there are likely to be others, don't risk it. What will you do?

Most who read this will live in a country with well-developed health services and will have ready access to skilled help in cases of injury. Imagine that you are a peasant farmer in one of the many developing countries affected by these insidious weapons. As you work in your small field, your foot triggers a mine and suddenly you are lying on the ground with a shocking injury, bleeding profusely and in terrible pain.

- *If you are lucky*, someone has heard the explosion.
- *If you are lucky*, a friend or family member is able to come to your aid.
- *If you are lucky*, that person is confident in first aid and can do something to stop the bleeding.
- *If you are lucky*, help can be found to carry you to the roadside.
- *If you are lucky*, a truck will come along soon, and
- *If you are lucky*, your family can find enough money to pay for transport to a hospital.
- *If you are lucky*, the hospital will admit you.
- *If you are lucky*, you have family members willing to give blood for you.
- *If you are lucky*, there is a surgeon with sufficient skill to manage your injury.

- *If you are lucky*, you have money to pay for the antibiotics and analgesics you require.
- and so on…

No wonder that so many mine injuries result in death. The Red Cross has estimated that 75 per cent of those injured by a mine who do not receive medical treatment within six hours of the injury will die.

The epidemiology

It has variously been estimated that between 60–70 million landmines are already in place in the soil of more than 50 nations. But many of these estimates are no more than guesses. As the *Landmine Monitor Report 1999* points out, however, the number of mines is not as important as the number of persons affected by the presence of mines in their daily lives.[3] The risk to a population posed by mines will depend, for example, on what kind of mines they are (whether self-destruct, how readily detected, how easily removed, etc.), how they have been laid (whether in distinct minefields or randomly scattered) and whether they are liable to move by flooding. The suspected presence of even one mine in a field is sufficient to stop the use of that land.

Which individuals are most at risk will depend on many factors such as culture, gender roles, or the nature of rural activity. Where women go out to gardens or to gather firewood it is they and the small children who will suffer most. If men are engaged in land clearance and preparation they will be at risk of mine injury.

The numbers of mine explosion survivors cannot be estimated with a greater accuracy, so that planning for victim relief is difficult, and this is the reason for the latest focus of the International Campaign to Ban Landmines (ICBL) which in its *Landmine Monitor Report 1999* sets out in considerable detail a country-by-country account of what is known about landmine contamination and victim needs.[4]

Military rationale for the use of antipersonnel landmines

The military strategists and field commanders have given persuasive arguments for using mines. Compared with wire, ditches or directed fields of fire, mines are claimed to be a cost-effective method for 'moulding the terrain', constraining the enemy into predetermined lines. Early international agreements (achieved through the so-called Inhumane Weapons Convention) sought to establish rules for the use of mines, but there is an urgency in military needs which carries a persuasive authority to override such rules. Mines are laid for immediate advantage, ignoring the later consequences for the generations which will hope to occupy that land in coming decades and centuries. The rules require that mines laid in battle be marked and mapped and later removed. But the battle shifts, the maps are mislaid, the immediacy moves to another arena – and the mines remain.

Five reasons against the military utility of land mines

Robert G. Gard, retired US General, has written persuasively against the military utility of land mines:[5]

- *They are not effective.* 'The effectiveness of mine barriers in channelling the enemy is highly suspect. Techniques to breach minefields are well-developed (flails, rollers, ploughs, explosive-filled hoses, fuel–air explosives). US forces had little difficulty in penetrating Iraqi minefields (sown with over 9 million mines!) in the Gulf War. Both the Chinese and the Iranians have cleared corridors in war simply by running columns of foot troops through them'.
- *They limit modern field tactics:* Gard argues that 'the widespread employment of land-mines threatens to neutralise US advantages in fire power and mobility... limiting our tactical manoeuvrability and slowing our operational tempo'.
- *They damage friendly forces:* Mines constitute a major threat to the forces which lay them. General Gray, former commandant of the US Marine Corps, is quoted: 'What the hell is the use of sowing all this if you're going to move through it? We kill more Americans with our own mines than we do anyone else'.
- *Modern techniques of deployment of mines make marking fields impossible.* In the Gulf War the use of the Gator system of canisters containing 72 anti-tank mines and 22 anti-personnel mines scattered over wide areas made it necessary to use great caution in advance.
- *They are an expensive and inefficient way of maintaining border security.* Minefields are dangerous to the citizens of the country that lays them, expensive to maintain, and require frequent maintenance when mines are triggered by animals. To be effective, they must be accompanied by observation and aimed fire.

Commander-in-Chief in the Gulf War Norman Schwartzkopf joined 14 other senior officers in an open letter to the president urging him to fulfil his commitment to ban all antipersonnel (AP) mines, as an action not only humanely but militarily responsible.

What can replace minefields?

General Gard notes that there are discriminating weapons which are as effective as minefields, even for static defence or close-in protection of facilities. He refers to non-lethal sensors, trip flares, aimed fire and observer-detonated munitions. There are radars able to identify a person's approach at a considerable distance and night-vision equip-ment which makes persons visible several hundreds of metres away.

Who is 'the enemy'?

If mines are not necessary components of military arsenals for war, they remain effective instruments for terrorizing civilian populations:

> On the other hand, AP mines have proved highly effective when used to terrorize or control civilians... Precisely because AP mines are indiscriminate and can be concealed easily, they are inherently weapons of terror.

Population control has been all too effective.[6]

As the years go by, over and over again children foraging for food or gathering firewood on the hillsides are mutilated and murdered by mines which were never marked and were never intended to be removed. Are those children the enemy? What was the quarrel with them?

What was initially a protection for an antitank field or a defensive shield of a military camp has become an instrument for spreading terror within an opponent's forces, and also within any supporting civilian population:

> The mine has been designed to disable personnel. Operating research has shown that it is better to disable the enemy than to kill him. A wounded man requires medical attention, conveyance and evacuation to the rear, and thus causes disturbances in the traffic lines of the combat areas. Also a wounded person has a detrimental psychological effect on his fellow soldiers.[7]

From that intention it is a short step to creating widespread terror in civilian populations so that they will provide no support for the opposing forces, and flee their homelands in a chaos of refugee displacement, with a long-term abandonment of productive farmland.

A military strategist will count 'casualties', review numbers and statistics and award different types of mines their 'damage ratios': which models have greatest impact for least cost in purchase or deployment. Mines which at first were like home-made rabbit traps are now sleek, smooth and symmetrical, for all the world like a lady's powder pack. Take the Misar 33, of which John Ryle, writing in *The New Yorker*, noted:

> ...a startlingly seductive object: palm size, rounded, subtly a-symmetrical, with a synthetic skin like shagreen leather. The neoprene cover over the pressure plate has a gentle resistance to touch, like a computer keyboard. It is a true designer mine, the Sony Walkman of weaponry.[8]

A technological marvel. A sanitization of terror. In just the same way have nuclear planners spoken of mega-tonnage and missile throw-weights, avoiding consideration of the terrible cost in blast injury, multiple burns and radiation damage to individuals and families. Nuclear missiles have phallic shapes and are given fine strong names: *Minuteman* and *Patriot*. The canon of landmines includes *flutter-babies* – deadly mines brightly coloured – which spiral down in their thousands from helicopters to excite the interest of children.

'Once laid, the mine has no friends'

Individual soldiers who risk engagement in the front line of battle clearly do not like antipersonnel mines. Consider this account from the Armed Forces Journal *Stars and Stripes*:

> Any veteran who's been there knows the frightening sequence. Some place down the line there is a loud explosion followed by cries of 'Medic! Medic!' All realise that some poor guy has stepped on a mine. Later, if the victim survives, his wounded companions back in the hospital soon realise that their own arm and leg wounds are minor compared to the ravages caused by an exploding mine.[9]

Because the combatants who most often use APLMs are insurgent forces, guerrilla bands or forces engaged in internal conflicts, no agreement among official representatives of sovereign states can be effective in achieving a ban on their use. Only a complete cessation of the commercial manufacture of weapons will support a ban on their export, purchase and inclusion in national arsenals or use in the field. In a world which wishes to be ruled by market forces, you sell where you can. As long as these weapons are made they will be sought and prepared for use, whether by blatant disregard of the law, clandestine cover-up or generous corruption. Wherever they are stockpiled in national armies, leakage into intra-national conflict will occur.

The protocol of the convention on inhumane weapons

The United Nations had in place, by 1981, a Convention which aimed to limit the use of anti-personnel mines, with a 'Protocol on Prohibitions or Restrictions on the Use of Mines, Booby Traps and Other Devices'. It included articles which prohibited the use of weapons directed against individual civilians or the civilian population, including indiscriminate use not directed at a military objective and liable to cause incidental loss of civilian life. Mines therefore should not be used in areas containing a concentration of civilians in which combat between ground forces is not taking place. Remote delivery of mines is not permitted unless accurate recording of placement can be done or the mines effectively neutralized when their miliary use is not longer served. Booby traps, in the form of apparently harmless objects, or attached to everyday items, are prohibited, and both the recording of minefield locations and the removal of mines after hostilities cease are required.

The Convention was the first modern attempt to control the damage caused by anti-personnel mines. But the provisions it enjoined were not being followed, it contained no process for sanctions, and it remained ratified by only 47 countries. The Protocol failed to address adequately the delayed-action damage to civilians of mines scattered in war. A major problem of the Convention on Inhumane Weapons was that it did not to apply to internal conflicts, only to conflicts between states.

The process of review
In 1993, a meeting of the International Committee of the Red Cross, held at Montreux, suggested ways in which useful moves might be made through multilateral negotiation and agreement to limit the use of landmines, offering a number of possible levels of legal amendment of the protocol, while affirming that a total ban on all such weapons was the desirable change.

In such deliberations it began to be recognized that the only final acceptable solution to the terrible damage which antipersonnel mines were causing was their complete abolition. It was also clear, however, that there were strong forces within military agencies and mine-producing countries against a ban.

Meetings of government experts were conducted in late 1994 and early 1995 to prepare for a Review Conference of the Inhumane Weapons Convention and Protocols, in Vienna, 25 September –13 October 1995. Of the 47 states which had become parties to the convention, 44 participated and 40 other countries were represented as observers. There were also delegations from the UN agencies UNHCR, UNICEF and the Department of Humanitarian Affairs. Non-governmental organizations (NGOs) were present in force, and were invited to participate in formal plenary sessions but were excluded from working groups.

The Vienna Conference was suspended without reaching any definitive agreements. Another session was held from 15–19 January 1996, and a concluding session from 22

April–2 May the same year, in Geneva. NGO groups and a number of official delegations went away very disappointed that little more had been achieved than a tightening of
the rules by which mines may be used. There was no support for the complete ban which
they affirmed.

Items discussed during the review meetings:
- *The scope of the convention.* It did not cover non-international conflicts, even though 79
  of 82 recent conflicts were not international in nature. Most countries agreed that
  non-international conflicts should be covered, and this provision was included in the
  final text.
- *Detectability.* All antipersonnel mines should be detectable, i.e. by the usual methods of
  metal detection. Some mines with mainly ceramic and plastic components have so
  little metal that they avoid the usual mine-detector.
- All antipersonnel landmines should be *short-lived, self-destructive and self-deactivating.* If
  this can be achieved, the toll of injury which goes on for many years, long after the
  original conflict has been resolved and even been forgotten, will be avoided.
- *Transfers of mines* should be prohibited to non-states and to states that are not
  signatories to the convention and protocols.
- Some system of *verification and compliance* should be established
- *Reviews* of the convention should be held every five years.

Several states had begun to advocate a complete ban on the production, stockpiling,
transfer and use of antipersonnel mines. They included Sweden, Mexico, Italy (production), Cambodia, New Zealand, Ireland, Colombia, Switzerland, Afghanistan, Belgium
and the Netherlands.

The position of many other countries remained ambivalent, affirming a commitment to
the elimination of all antipersonnel landmines as an ultimate goal but focusing on a slow
step-by-step process to reach agreement on a selective ban on long-lived and non-
detectable mines and sales to rebel or insurgent groups. The climate of world agreement
appeared to maintain that the use of antipersonnel mines may be legitimate in certain
situations.

An Australian NGO delegate, Patricia Pak Poy, put it as follows:

> Goodwill is there...but goodwill is not enough. There is a need for moral courage, political
> leadership and the will to take the required action together, which will only happen if the good
> of the people is kept uppermost in the debates.

A new initiative to break the deadlock

Mounting throughout the 1990s, a tremendous surge of protest developed around the
world against the use of these terrible weapons. The International Campaign to Ban
Landmines (ICBL) grew out of discussion in 1991 between the Medico International of
Frankfurt, Germany, and Vietnam Veterans of America. Quickly a number of other
NGOs joined the campaign, including:

- International Committee of the Red Cross

- UN Department of Humanitarian Affairs,
- Mines Action Canada
- Handicap International
- Human Rights Watch
- Mines Advisory Group
- Physicians for Human Rights
- International Physicians for the Prevention of Nuclear War.

During 1996–97 a series of constructive meetings took place between several middle powers (including Canada, Belgium, Norway and Austria) and the ICBL. They were strongly supported by a number of smaller nations which had been much affected by antipersonnel mines. At the conclusion of one of the meetings in October 1996, the Canadian representative, Ambassador Lloyd Axworthy, made a dramatic announcement that Canada would call the nations of the world together in the following year to sign a treaty banning antipersonnel landmines.

This was an unusual demonstration of moral courage and political leadership by a national government. It was a bold step which cut through established UN processes, and freed up a campaign which had threatened to become bogged down under conventional multilateral diplomacy.

In spite of vigorous opposition from major powers – the US, Russia, China, UK – the process initiated by Canada rolled on and gathered increasing momentum. A preliminary text was negotiated and adopted at the International Conference on an International Ban of Antipersonnel Mines held in Oslo, Norway from 1 to 18 September 1997, and culminated in the gathering of over 100 nations in Ottawa in December 1997, where a treaty was signed. Its long title, A Convention on the Prohibition of the Use, Stockpiling, Production and Transfer of Antipersonnel Mines and on their Destruction' has led to the common use of Ottawa Treaty as a shorthand term to designate this important international agreement.

The Ottawa Treaty

There are 17 Articles in the treaty, but its intent is well-represented in the opening article:

Article 1: General Obligations
- Each State Party undertakes never under any circumstances:
  - To use antipersonnel mines
  - To develop, produce, otherwise acquire, stockpile, retain or transfer to anyone, directly or indirectly, antipersonnel mines
  - To assist, encourage or induce, in any way, anyone to engage in any activity prohibited to a State Party under this Convention
- Each State Party undertakes to destroy or ensure the destruction of all antipersonnel mines…

The various provisions of the Ottawa Treaty form a comprehensive approach to the threat of landmines and cover most of the areas which were left unsatisfactory in the earlier multinational negotiations:

- It is not limited to particular conflicts – all use of these weapons is prohibited.
- Signatories agree not to develop, produce, otherwise acquire, stockpile, retain or transfer to anyone, directly or indirectly, antipersonnel mines or encourage others to do so.
- All stockpiles are to be destroyed within an agreed timeframe, apart from 'minimal' numbers allowed for training in de-mining.
- It demands the clearance of mines areas within an agreed timeframe, and greater efforts at assisting in mine clearance everywhere.
- It contains provisions for transparency and for sanctions against those who fail to comply.

Issues outstanding after Ottawa

The convention achieved ratification by 40 states on 16 September 1998, which resulted in its coming into force on 1 March 1999. This was a cause for much satisfaction among the many NGO groups which had worked to bring the convention into being. Nevertheless, many diplomats who address the issue of landmines see major remaining complexities and are inclined to label NGO enthusiasm as naïve. The reality which enthusiastic advocacy for a complete ban on antipersonnel landmines must confront is that many nations, while paying lip-service to elimination as an ultimate goal, continue to advocate exclusions, exceptions and special circumstances which serve to circumvent the Ottawa Treaty. These include:

Ottawa Treaty vs Conference on Disarmament
Only in the Committee on Disarmament, the diplomats of several influential countries maintain, will the main players in this grim business come together to negotiate; meantime, to use a classical military metaphor, they must keep their powder dry and maintain their right to use landmines.

The Canadians achieved a fast-track process which clearly encouraged a majority of nations to agree quickly to a treaty banning antipersonnel mines, recognizing the urgency of stopping a continuing carnage at its source. The enthusiastic response by 131 nations (as of March 1999) affirms that the Canadians were reading general world opinion accurately.

But an effective treaty must also involve the major players, and usually can only reach a binding agreement through achieving consensus. The Ottawa Treaty did not involve the United States, China, Russia, India or Pakistan. For this reason the US and several other countries have discounted the value of the Ottawa process and look to the more inclusive but frustratingly slow negotiations of the UN Conference on Disarmament.

Exceptions
The US insisted that the Korean Peninsula must be an exception to any global ban, arguing that:

- the military situation in Korea is under UN command and supervision, and so does not represent a narrow sectional interest;

- North Korea maintains a huge army in a state of border readiness and that hostilities could start with minimal notice; and that
- APLMs are an integral part of military force structure.

But former US Lieutenant-General Hollingsworth is quoted as saying: 'To be blunt, if we are relying on these weapons to defend the Korean peninsula we are in big trouble'.

Exclusions

As with nuclear weapons, any delays to the conclusion of a treaty may mean the intensive pursuit of clever ways to circumvent definitions and agreements. An example is the so-called 'systems' which include antipersonnel mines linked with antitank mines to protect the antitank mines from being easily discovered and removed.

The United States has developed several systems – some go under the names of Gator, Volcano, MOPM – in which APLMs are placed alongside other devices in order to protect them.

Definitions: directional mines and antitank systems

The US has sought a change in the definition of 'mine' so that mines which self-destruct within 15 days, as well as those which are included along with, for example, antitank mines (to block vehicles, not damage people), are permitted within the terms of the treaty.

The Ottawa Treaty rejected any exclusions and maintained an inclusive definition, fearing that any specific exclusion would encourage a removal of all 'smart mines' from the treaty and weaken it alarmingly.

Deferral of implementation of treaty

The US sought delays in the implementation of various provisions of the treaty, namely:

- destruction of stockpiles;
- clearance of mines already laid; and
- entry into force of the treaty.

The argument proposed was that tight timetables are unrealistic and that military forces need time for the development of alternative means for protecting such things as territory, camps and borders. There is no doubt that under the impetus of the unforeseen success of the landmines campaign, intensive work is now going on in many military establishments to find better ways both to detect and remove landmines, and alternative technologies to replace them.

The value of the Ottawa process

The Ottawa Treaty was significant as much for its process as for its outcomes. It demonstrated an effective initiative taken by smaller nations against the opposition of the great powers. At the Oslo Preparatory meeting in September 1997, the chairman, a South African, cut through traditional routines and protocols to get business going quickly, and an NGO, the International Campaign to Ban Landmines, was welcomed as a participant in the meeting of governments, along with the International Committee of the Red Cross. It was essentially a movement of middle powers, one which by-passed the objections of the superpowers, the Security Council and the conventional UN mechanisms. Also, it was a close alliance of dedicated nations and their diplomats with NGOs, the ICRC and the ICBL in particular, but many others also, including International Physicians for the Prevention of Nuclear War.

An important role for international NGOs such as the IPPNW is keeping up pressure on the powerful nations which have not yet signed or supported the Ottawa Treaty. The IPPNW has been able to facilitate an important conference in Russia[10] and has member affiliates also in China and in South Asia, where India and Pakistan maintain strong border controls involving landmines. In these ways the IPPNW seeks to further the process of Ottawa. Other regional meetings have extended the advocacy against antipersonnel landmines in affected areas, the Middle East, for example.[11]

Even though there remains a huge task ahead to convince the nations which felt upstaged and bypassed in this process that they must join and comply with the Ottawa Treaty, the treaty's achievements have been huge, and the example of its process persuasive. If that process can operate for landmines, might it not be a pathway to more effective international agreement over other pressing issues: nuclear, environmental, human rights, for example?

This remains to be seen. In the meantime, the issue of landmines remains on the Agenda of the Conference for Disarmament, where consensus must operate and where the major powers still standing back from the Ottawa process are represented.

Towards a mine-free world

A comprehensive approach to implementation of the ideal of a mine-free world involves many components.

Making the ban on antipersonnel land mines universal
By the year 2000, many countries had neither signed nor ratified the 1997 Convention on the Prohibition of the Use, Stockpiling, Production and Transfer of Antipersonnel Mines and on Their Destruction:

- *in the Americas:* Cuba and the USA;
- *in Europe and Central Asia:* 13 countries, including Russia and six countries of the CIS, Turkey and Yugoslavia;
- *in North Africa and the Middle East:* 13 countries, including Egypt, Israel, Iraq, Iran, and Libya;
- *in sub-Saharan Africa:* only 5 countries – Central African Republic, Comoros, the Democratic Republic of Congo, Nigeria and Somalia; and
- *in East Asia and the Pacific:* 21 countries, including China, India, North Korea, South Korea, Pakistan, Singapore and Vietnam.

Since 1999, some of these countries have moved to sign the 1997 Convention, but the key players – the USA, China, India, Pakistan, the two Koreas, Israel, Iran and Iraq remain outside the convention.

Monitoring progress in adherence to the treaty

'Landmine Monitor' is an initiative of the International Campaign to Ban Landmines which aims to monitor implementation of and compliance with the 1997 Mine Ban Treaty. It brings together a wide range of NGOs to create a systematic and continuing review of progress and problems on the path towards a mine-free world. It will build a global reporting network, maintain a central database and issue an annual report. The first of these, *Landmine Monitor Report 1999* is a 1100-page documentation of progress in every country of the world.[12] A brief 40-page summary, *Landmine Monitor Executive Report*, has been made widely available.

These documents record, for example, that several countries (Angola, Guinea-Bissau and Senegal) appear to have used antipersonnel mines since signing the Treaty. It also records probable new use of APLMs in Djibouti and Uganda by rebel groups, in Somalia by various factions, in Turkey, Yugoslavia, Burma and Sri Lanka by both government troops and rebel groups, and in Lebanon by Israel.

Antipersonnel mines and booby traps were employed commonly in the conflict in Kosovo, but nowhere in the world are APLMs now being laid on any major scale. The number of countries still producing APLMs has fallen to sixteen, and those which have stopped production include most of the former major manufacturers: Belgium, Bosnia, Bulgaria, Czech Republic, France, Hungary, Italy and the UK.

Production was thought to continue (during 1999) in:

- *Asia*: Burma, China, India, North Korea, South Korea, Pakistan, Singapore and Vietnam;
- *Europe*: Russia, Turkey, Yugoslavia;
- *the Middle East*: Egypt, Iraq, Iran; and
- *the Americas*: Cuba and the USA.

All these countries expect Iraq, however, have made a statement that they are no longer exporting APLMs.

Destroying stockpiles of APLMs

It is estimated that there are 250 million APLMs held by 108 countries. Some of the largest stocks are held by countries which have not signed the treaty:

- China: 110 million
- Russia: 60 million
- Belarus: ?>10 million
- the US: 11 million and
- India: 4 million.

Several holders of large stocks are in the process of destroying them: Italy (7 million), Sweden, UK, France, Spain, and Ukraine (11 million). The following countries have completed destruction of stocks: Australia, Austria, Belgium, Canada, El Salvador, Germany, Guatemala, Luxembourg, Namibia, Norway, Philippines, South Africa and Switzerland.

Humanitarian mine action

This is a multi-pronged approach to dealing with the actual effects of APLMs on human populations. It includes:

Surveys. Too little is known of where mines are laid and what needs to be done about them in each affected community. Although the earliest removal of mines now in the ground is an urgent task, this must be placed into the context of the total needs of affected communities. Questions such as which areas receive priority for de-mining, and how will clearance work relate to other aspects of development must be addressed.

Humanitarian mine clearance. Humanitarian mine clearance is different from military clearance. The military can afford to leave some mines behind and may aim for (say) 99.6 per cent clearance; for a civilian population even that remaining 0.4 per cent – four mines in 1000 – is unsatisfactory, retaining a real fear for the population which must use the area. The quick and effective ways of clearance favoured by commercial operators, such as mechanical devices and dogs, will not do for total clearance.

Mine awareness. Many local populations will have to live with the daily threat of APLMs for many years. While there are universal messages about learning of the threat, how to protect oneself and others and what to do if you unknowingly enter a mined area, those messages need to be adapted to local needs, cultures and traditions. Local people will usually be the best teachers of awareness, and they will need training and equipment – dummy mines and dummy unexploded ordinance, posters, leaflets, photos, tapes, videos, etc. Theatre is a powerful means to communicate, and dances and games have also been devised. Whatever means are adopted need to be evaluated before they are used more widely. Mass media reach many people, but direct, on-the-spot, local courses are recognized as the most effective teaching.

Victim assistance. Article 6 of the Ottawa Treaty requires each state party to 'provide assistance for the care and rehabilitation, and social and economic reintegration of mine victims'. It remains unclear how many survivors of an APLM explosion there are. Clear data about numbers, types of injury, location, age and sex of known victims are essential for adequate planning of interventions.

Aspects of victim assistance include:

- Emergency and primary care;
- surgical care, including amputation;
- physical rehabilitation;
- prosthetics;
- wheelchairs and crutches;
- assistance for non-amputees (blinded, deafened etc.);
- psychological rehabilitation;
- confronting social stigmatization; and
- encouraging economic productivity.

Whatever is done for APLM victims should be integrated with local health policies so that landmine victims are not seen as different or special, or apart from the many other needy persons in any community.

But landmine injuries have common features and these need to be thoroughly understood. For this reason, the IPPNW has developed a small surgical primer, *Primary Care of Landmine Injuries in Africa*, aimed at the staff of rural clinics and hospitals, and prepared in cooperation with a representative group of African surgeons.[13]

Funding for mine action

The costs which the world faces, even if no further APLMs are ever laid, are enormous, whether for the clearance of mines already in the ground or for the rehabilitation and lifetime support of those victims of mines who have already been injured, but survived, and the many thousands who will be injured in the future until every APLM is removed from its hiding-place. Two examples (taken from the *Landmine Monitor*) are shown in Table 9.1.

Table 9.1 The costs of mine clearance

	Area cleared km²	Cost US$	Cost/km² US$	De-miners employed	De-miners killed
Kuwait	728	700m	961,538	4,000	84
Afghanistan	145	90m	621,889	4,000	?

The cost of lifetime support. A child injured at the age of 10, with a life expectancy of 40–50 years, will need 25 new appliances in his or her lifetime. Even the cheapest prosthesis will cost over US$100, so that the total cost will be over $2500. Where the average family income is US$10–$20 per month, family finances will soon be exhausted. Crutches will, therefore, become the usual aid employed.

Funding mine action. Seventeen countries have made major commitments to the funding of mine action programmes, and somewhere between US$500million and US$1billion has been committed for the coming five years. This is far short of what will be needed for all aspects of mine action.

Conclusion

The agreements achieved within the international community concerning antipersonnel mines are most encouraging. In a world where international, community and domestic violence seems prone to escalation, here is an example of a potential for control over military technology and random human damage which deserves applause. But it will also need much more universal and intensive support than has been achieved so far. The emphasis has shifted from achieving a complete ban (though this has still to be attained) towards a coordinated international programme for mine clearance and victim assistance. As the *Landmine Monitor* notes: 'A world free of mines, but not free of the suffering of their victims, is hardly a goal to strive for'.[14] Continuing energy for advocacy is needed –

by physicians and by everyone concerned to see removal of this persisting scourge of human health and well-being.

REFERENCES

1. International Physicians for the Prevention of Nuclear War (IPPNW) (1997), *Landmines: a global health crisis*, IPPNW Global Health Watch Report Number 2, Boston: International Physicians for the Prevention of Nuclear War.
2. Coupland, R.M. and A. Korver (1991), 'Injuries from Antipersonnel Mines: the experience of the international committee of the Red Cross', *BMJ* 303: 1509–12; Cobey, J.C., Stover, E. and J. Fine (1995), 'Civilian Injuries Due to War Mines', *Techniques in Orthopedics* 10: 259–64.
3. ICBL (1999), *Landmine Monitor Report 1999. Towards a mine-free world*, New York: International Campaign to Ban Landmines, Human Rights Watch.
4. Ibid.
5. Gard, R.G. (1999), *Alternatives to Antipersonnel Landmines*, Washington DC: Vietnam Veterans of America.
6. Ibid.
7. Specification sheet, P4 Mk2 mine, Pakistan Ordnance Factories, Islamabad (exported to Somalia and Afghanistan, price US$6.75).
8. Ryle, J. (1993), "The Invisible Enemy. Reporter at large', *The New Yorker*, 29 November: 119–35.
9. 'The National Tribune', editorial, *Stars and Stripes*, 17 January: 6.
10. IPPNW–ICBL (1999), *New Steps towards a Mine-Free Future*. Report of the First International Conference on Landmines in Russia and the CIS, Moscow 27–28 May 1998, International Physicians for the Prevention of Nuclear War.
11. Landmine Survivors Network (1999), *Surviving the Scourge of Landmines*, The First Middle East Conference on Landmine Injury and Rehabilitation, Amman, Jordan, 11–12 July 1998, Washington DC: The Landmine Survivors Network.
12. See n. 3 above.
13. IPPNW (2000), *Primary Care of Landmine Injuries in Africa*, Cambridge MA: International Physicians for the Prevention of Nuclear War.
14. See n. 3 above.

Address for correspondence
215A The Esplanade, Seacliff, South Australia 5049
Tel: 61.8.8296 6618; Fax: 61.8.8296 6493; email: pvim@flinders.edu.au

10 CHEMICAL WEAPONS

JULIAN P. PERRY ROBINSON

The status of chemical weapons today is defined from historical, political and military considerations with a focus on underlying dynamic processes. That status requires medical preparedness against use of the weapons notwithstanding the entry into force, for 129 states so far, of the 1993 Convention on the Prohibition of Chemical Weapons. The following analysis is also used to derive a list of the chemical-warfare agents of primary concern: mustard gas, sarin and VX nerve gas, some of their congeners, and an as-yet-unrealized category of disabling chemicals. A brief summary is given of the effects on the human body of mustard and nerve gases.

Introduction

Many types of weapon use chemicals to damage their targets. Chemicals can, for example, release energy in forms which armed forces can easily direct against an enemy, such as heat or blast. Trinitrotoluene high-explosive is an aggressive chemical of this type. So are the propellants that discharge bullets from rifles. So are the substances used in flame and incendiary munitions, or to generate smokescreens. The lithium deuteride of a hydrogen bomb is a chemical. None of these, however, are what most people think of as chemical weapons. There was a time when the expression extended to napalm bombs and to white-phosphorus artillery shell, but that time has passed. 'Chemical weapon' in today's parlance means only the particular type of chemical weapon in which chemicals are used for their toxic properties, in other words for their ability to interfere with life processes through direct chemical action.

This differentiation is now to be found in the 1993 Convention on the Prohibition of Chemical Weapons, which is a disarmament-*cum*-antiproliferation treaty signed by 170 nations, and in force for 129 of them. The weapons whose development, production, stockpiling and use are banned under the treaty include all munitions and devices specifically designed to cause death or other harm through the toxic properties of chemicals: 'any chemical which through its chemical action on life processes can cause death, temporary incapacitation or permanent harm to humans or animals'.

Historical aspects

This prohibition builds upon an earlier treaty, the 1925 Geneva Protocol, which forbad the use in war of chemical (and biological) weapons, these being defined in the language and concepts of the time as 'asphyxiating, poisonous or other gases, and [...] all analogous liquids, materials or devices'. The protocol itself built upon a succession of earlier prohibitions of poison warfare that reached back down the generations and across cultures, by way of Roman law and the code of warfare which the Saracens derived from the Koran, back even to the Manu laws of India three millennia ago.

In fact, so pervasive and persistent is the prohibition of fighting with poison and disease (disease being a latter-day conceptual sub-set of poison) that we may regard it as an expression of an ancient taboo: a means whereby the human race has sought, through a societal mechanism, to protect itself against a form of danger that cannot usually be perceived until too late: a threat, therefore, that could ultimately jeopardize the species itself. This notion is worth pondering as we enter the new age of biotechnology, whose dual-use character, for good or for evil, may lead us to value that mechanism as never before and, if we are wise, to service and develop it, and protect it against deterioration.

For there is, in the world history of weapons, a recurring tendency among those who prepare for the fighting of wars initially to reject major innovations in weaponry, but later gradually to withdraw their opposition and then to assimilate the innovation into their war-fighting doctrine and into their forces. The cross-bow, for example, was denounced as un-Christian by the Second Lateran Council in 1135, but it soon became a conventional weapon. Much the same sequence of obloquy and acceptance affected gunpowder, Greek Fire, artillery and bomb-dropping aircraft. Assimilative pressures against the taboo on chemical warfare have been clearly discernible.

The rise of industrial chemistry in the 19th century brought with it new accessibilities and feasibilities for poison weapons. 'Poison gas', for example, was brought within much closer reach than it had been when Hunyadi so laboriously used clouds of arsenical smoke in his defence of Belgrade in 1456 or when the Bishop of Munster contrived to use arsenical projectiles as a siege weapon against Groningen in 1672. Moreover, through high-explosive artillery shell and through the smokeless powder that made machine-guns possible, industrial chemistry also created battlefield circumstances in which poison gas could become a uniquely powerful weapon, for it could seep into the dugouts and fortifications which otherwise protected ground forces engaged in the new trench warfare. Come the First World War (WW I), Germany and then all the other major belligerents overcame their scruples about poison weapons (despite reaffirmation of the taboo in the 1899 Hague Gas Projectile Declaration and in the 1899 and 1907 Hague Land Warfare Regulations) and turned to poison gas. By the end of the war it had almost become conventional.

So by 1918 the march of scientific discovery, technological change and adaptive military tactics were rapidly bringing about the *banalization*, as the French say, of poison weapons, and these had now become available in unprecedented variety. Prior to the 1914–18 war, use of poison as a weapon had mostly been limited to the contamination of water supplies or the smoke of burning fires and to the smearing of toxic agents onto the tips of projectiles or other piercing weapons. To these techniques had now been added a new way of dangerously contaminating the environment of enemies: through the discharge of pressure-cylinders containing choking gases such as chlorine into the air breathed by the enemy, or through the spreading of skin-burning mustard gas onto the ground over which the enemy moved. The old ways of poison warfare still lived on as, for example, in such weapons as the DIACBA rounds developed at the time of the Vietnam War in the 1960s: large artillery shells discharging many hundreds of tiny darts, each coated with a poison especially toxic when injected through the skin. The toxicants studied for these and other such devices included naturally occurring poisons (toxins) such as traditional users of poison arrows would recognize. They also included such synthetic poisons as the VX nerve-gas described later in this chapter, as well as the even more toxic acetylcholinesterase-inhibiting bisquaternary carbamates first reported from France by Funke, Depierre and Krucker in 1952. Chemical weapons of this direct-injection type had by then become insignificant, however, in comparison with the toxic vapour, aerosol and spray dissemination devices first seen on the battlefields of the Great War (WW I). Those were the original weapons of modern chemical warfare. They were, in later terminology, the first weapons of mass destruction.

Political aspects

Two mutually countervailing tendencies then set in which acted, it has now transpired, to dominate the future of chemical weapons. One was the familiar military–technological tendency to extend as far as budgets allowed lines of development initiated in response to earlier military demands. This was a tendency not confined to the victors of the war. Indeed, it became especially marked within the nascent Soviet Union, which engaged with German scientists in a decade-long secret programme of chemical-weapons development in defiance of the Treaty of Versailles. German chemical-warfare specialists were also then active in spreading the technology to numerous other countries, notably to Spain, which then used the weapons in its war against Abd el Krim in Morocco, to Sweden, to Yugoslavia and to Brazil. In France, Italy, Japan, the United Kingdom and the United States such work also progressed, and these countries too had their exporters of the technology. By the time of the Second World War (WW II), chemical weapons had proliferated greatly. Since 1945 the picture has been one of further proliferation but also, for the more industrialized countries, deproliferation. Factories for chemical weapons have been declared, in accordance with a stipulation of the 1993 Convention on the Prohibition of Chemical Weapons, by nine countries: China, France, India, Iran, Japan, Russia, South Korea, the United Kingdom and the United States. The factory identified in the Japanese declaration was owned not by the state but by a religious cult, the Aum Shinrikyo, which in June 1994 and March 1995 had released sarin nerve-gas for purposes of murder and terrorism in Matsumoto and within the Tokyo subway. Countries still outside the 1993 treaty evidently include other possessor states, notably Iraq, much, perhaps all, of whose arsenal of chemical weapons has now been destroyed under United Nations supervision in accordance with the ceasefire agreement that ended the 1991 Gulf War. Other such possessor states are widely supposed to include Egypt, Israel, Libya, North Korea, Serbia and Syria.

The second of the two opposing tendencies became evident in the way in which descriptions and images of poison-gas warfare came to symbolize the horrors of the Great War, serving as banners behind which anti-war and humanitarian sentiment could advance during those optimistic times at the outset of the League of Nations. The inter-governmental negotiation which led to the 1925 Geneva Protocol was one consequence and, in a number of countries, the new treaty caused a sharp reduction in the scale on which public resources were devoted to the study of chemical weapons. The protocol did not eliminate the need for countries to protect themselves against disregard of the treaty by potential enemies; and the possibility of some sort of technological surprise that could circumvent existing measures of protection was an inevitable concomitant of the post-war burgeoning of academic science and science-based industry. So, despite the protocol, even in the most law-abiding countries the technology of chemical warfare continued to be studied, even advanced, notwithstanding the illegality of resort to it. The same is still true today, even after conclusion of the 1993 treaty.

Yet the protocol was much more than public show; it was also a reaffirmation of the taboo. By the time Hitler had precipitated the WW II, the protocol had thus reduced the preparedness of the belligerents, even Germany, actually to initiate chemical warfare were the fortunes of war to force them to take so extreme a measure. The protocol had operated to attenuate the flow of resources into chemical-weapons programmes, which were necessarily in competition with military programmes that had not been outlawed. To be sure, substantial stockpiles of the weapons were nevertheless built up on all sides, but there was no really dedicated effort to integrate them into strategy and tactics, and they remained largely unassimilated, justified only as some sort of deterrent.

Military aspects

There were also technical and military reasons for this incomplete assimilation. The unique feature of chemical weaponry – its environmental mediation, and hence its capacity for harming an enemy over wide areas – was also a source of discouraging opportunity cost and some disadvantage in comparison with other weapons. Above all, environmental dependence made the effects of chemical weapons relatively easy to protect against: a simple filter interposed between a soldier's lungs and the air he breathed, as in a gas mask; and protective clothing to shield the soldier's skin. It was this characteristic, one may now see, which largely reduced chemical weapons to instruments of Third World warfare: of fighting in which the prevailing level of technology did not extend to anti-chemical protection on both sides. Moreover, the mechanization of warfare and its restoration of mobility to the battlefield had further diminished the tactical utility of chemical warfare between technologically-advanced belligerents. The phosgene and mustard-gas weapons of WW I were far too cumbersome and slow-acting to be of much use in the blitzkrieg or other tank battles of WW II. The organophosphorus nerve gases could have provided weapons that were more amenable to WW II battlefields, but their discovery came too late. The non-use of chemical weapons during that war, other than in isolated episodes in China and as an instrument of mass-murder in Hitler's concentration camps, was not, therefore, an aberration. The chief military attractions of chemical weapons were as displayed by Spanish, Soviet and Italian mustard-gas aircraft-bombs in, respectively, Morocco (1923), Sinkiang (1934), and Libya and Ethiopia (1930–40). Furthermore, the proven episodes of chemical warfare after WW II also fall within that same Third World pattern: Egyptian phosgene and mustard gas in the Yemen, and American CS gas in Vietnam, in the 1960s; and Iraqi CS, mustard and nerve gases against Iran in the 1980s.

It is a pattern in which one other attribute of chemical weapons may also come to the fore: the intense effects that chemical weapons may exert upon morale, and thus their capacity to terrorize and induce panic, especially chemical weapons of the types that kill or maim, and especially when noncombatant populations become their target. Iraq has provided recent demonstrations of this in the attempts of its government to suppress Kurdish opposition, most evident in the gas-bombing of Halabja in March 1988.

Two broad conclusions may be drawn from this brief overview of the history of chemical warfare: (i) the tension between the two tendencies – the promoting influence of technological and political change, and the inhibiting influence of the taboo – seems likely to persist. It will represent a continuing challenge to the authority of the 1993 Convention on the Prohibition of Chemical Weapons; and (ii) although the technology of chemical warfare was founded, developed and spread around the world by the rich industrialized countries, it is in the poorer parts of the world that it now has its chief salience. This is not only because it is there that, on the evidence of history, the weapons are most likely to be used. It is also because, in some of those places, chemical weapons are now reportedly being viewed as a means for redressing military inferiority in possible future confrontations with richer countries seeking to 'project power'. The alarm caused among coalition forces in 1990–91 by their perceptions of Iraqi chemical (and biological) weapons was plain for the rest of the world to see, and some of those same coalition countries are now augmenting the effect still further through their new alarms about chemical and biological terrorism.

In short, however strongly the Convention on the Prohibition of Chemical Weapons may reinforce that ancient taboo against chemical warfare, use of chemical weapons in the future cannot be excluded entirely. The need to understand the possible medical consequences will remain with us.

Medical aspects

All chemicals, even water, are toxic if administered in large enough quantities, and a great number of different chemicals fall within the category of poison, as commonly conceived. Quite a large number of chemicals present in industry and other civil applications are, on some measures, highly poisonous, harmful or otherwise toxic. Yet only a few dozen different chemicals have seriously been considered for chemical-weapons' purposes. Most chemicals, even ones of high lethality, fail to display those particular characteristics of accessibility, stability and super-aggressiveness needed if the resultant weapon is to be competitive with cheaper or less obnoxious conventional weapons of comparable military utility. So, in thinking about how medical preparedness should be structured against the possibility of chemical-warfare attack, the list of threat chemicals to be taken into account is quite small. It is possible that terrorists or saboteurs might succeed in unleashing other chemicals upon civil populations, but they would necessarily be chemicals of a much lesser aggressiveness, presenting a threat not significantly different from those that confront industrial-accident emergency services.

Historical experience is the best guide to the composition of that list of threat agents. The possibility of technological surprise will always be there but, given the failure of any significant novel agents to emerge over the past 40 years, the technology of chemical weaponry now seems to be so mature that the probability of surprise is no longer large.

Disregarding antiplant chemical warfare, history indicates that four main classes of chemical-warfare agent are defined by the requirements of military utility:

(1) Agents capable of inflicting rapid mass casualties over an area larger than military units can conveniently attack with high-explosive, flame or fragmentation weapons. Superseding chlorine, phosgene, trichloromethyl chloroformate, hydrogen cyanide and cyanogen chloride, organophosphorus anticholinesterase agents of substantial vapour pressure nowadays dominate this class, greatly exceeding their predecessors in aggressiveness. The dominant agent is the so-called 'G-agent nerve gas' known as sarin (O-isopropyl methylphosphonofluoridate). Some of its close congeners have also proved attractive, notably the O-1,2,2-trimethylpropyl homologue (soman) and the O-cyclohexyl and O-1-methylcyclohexyl homologues.

(2) Agents capable of exerting similar effects upon a target population that is equipped with respirators, in other words agents that can attack on or through the skin. Two families are pre-eminent: the vesicants or blister gases that are dominated by bis-(2-chloroethyl)sulphide, otherwise known as mustard gas, and the V-agent nerve gases typified by O-ethyl S-2-N,N-diisopropylaminoethyl methylphosphonothiolate, which is the Agent VX of the former US arsenal, or its O-butyl N,N-diethyl homologue, which was preferred over VX in the former Soviet arsenal.

(3) Agents amenable to the prolonged denial of terrain by establishing a contact hazard over it. The same two families of vesicants and V-agent nerve gases (see point 2 above) also dominate the third class.

(4) Agents capable of serving one or another of the first three military applications but, in so doing, causing or threatening to cause casualties that are predominantly non-fatal, in other words agents that interfere with non-vital function to the point of incapacitation. Such agents might greatly diminish the political costs of military benefits available from chemical weapons. Although a variety of different chemicals have been procured to satisfy this fourth type of requirement, notably irritant agents such as 10-chloro-5,10-dihydrophenarsazine (adamsite) and 2-chlorobenzalmalo-nonitrile (Agent CS) and anticholinergic agents such as 3-quinuclidinyl benzilate (Agent BZ), and a great range of other incapacitating chemicals studied, including LSD, benzomorphans and fentanyls, it appears to be the case that all of them have

proved militarily deficient in one respect or another. This is, nevertheless, the class in which technological surprise is at its least unlikely and for which constraints against treaty-breakout are at their weakest.

It may thus be concluded that the priority focus of medical preparedness against chemical-warfare attack should be the threat of mass casualties from mustard gas and from the G- and V-agent nerve gases.

The diverse effects upon the human body of mustard gas (which at room temperature is actually a rather dense liquid of quite low volatility) are now extensively documented from eight decades of wartime experience, occupational exposure in factories and experimental exposure in laboratories and on simulated battlefields. Initially imperceptible, exposure to the agent may have systemic as well as local consequences, the latter occurring at much lower dosages than the former. So, overall, fatalities have accounted for only about 2 per cent of recorded battlefield casualties. The time to onset of effects is also dosage-dependent and may be as long as a day or more. Onset is faster for eye-damage than for skin-burns. Absorption through the skin into the circulation is rapid, so if decontamination is to have much preventative effect it must be done within minutes of exposure. When vesication occurs, the blisters are likely to be large, painful, liable to infection and take months to heal. Spontaneous recurrence of apparently healed skin or eye lesions has been observed after an interval of decades. Lesions following inhalation exposure predispose victims towards bronchopneumonia. Pneumonia was the proximal cause of death in most of the WW I mustard fatalities. Systemic effects include reduction in white-cell numbers following bone-marrow inhibition and damage to the gastro-intestinal tract. Mustard gas is strongly carcinogenic and may also display mutagencity and teratogencity. For so simple a molecule, it is truly a terrible chemical.

For the nerve gases, in contrast, there is less documentation of what they can do to the human body but the historical database is nevertheless substantial. Both G- and V-agents have, as the primary targets of their toxicity, tissue acetylcholinesterase, to which they bind covalently, thus inhibiting it and causing the transmitter substance acetylcholine to build up at neuroeffector junctions in the peripheral and central nerous systems. The consequent cholinergic overstimulation is rapidly manifest in a broad range of clinical signs and symptoms: in severe cases, salivation, involuntary defaecation and urination, sweating, lachrymation, bradycardia and hypotension followed by respiratory depression, collapse, convulsions and death from respiratory failure. As with mustard gas, exposure may become perceptible only through onset of initial effects, typically miosis, rhinorrhea and tightness in the chest after respiratory exposure. For an adult male, a milligram of sarin may constitute a lethal dose; for VX, less than half of that.

FURTHER INFORMATION

For access to the literature on medical management of chemical-warfare casualties, readers are referred to a recent review article (Sharon Reutter, 'Hazards of Chemical Weapons Release During War', *Environmental Health Perspectives*, Vol. 107, No. 12 (December 1999): 985–90), which is posted on the internet at:
<<http://ehpnet1.niehs.nih.gov/ docs/1999/107p985-990reutter/>], to the US Army Surgeon-General's 1997 textbook *Medical Aspects of Chemical and Biological Warfare*, and to the World Health Organization's 1970 report *Health Aspects of Chemical and Biological Weapons*, a new edition of which is currently nearing completion.

Address for correspondence
University of Sussex, Brighton, BN1 9RF, United Kingdom
Tel: **44.1273.678172; Fax: **44.1273.685865; email: j.p.p.robinson@sussex.ac.uk

11 | BIOLOGICAL WARFARE – HOW SERIOUS A THREAT?

P. HELENA MÄKELÄ

Biological warfare is always the last to be discussed when speaking about weapons of mass destruction. Why is it so? Is it not as serious a threat? Is it just less known and understood, or do we not dare to think about it? The last alternative may be the right answer. With any other weapons system the damage, however devastating, remains local, with the only exception of a 'last epidemic', a nuclear winter with smoke clouds covering the whole earth for months (see page 151). By contrast, biological warfare typically causes epidemics that may spread over the globe and remain for years. No one in the world would be spared from the fear and anxiety if biological warfare introduced an unknown microbe against which we had no treatment, vaccines or shelter. Indeed, biological warfare is most clearly the form of war that we want to prevent. But will we succeed?

Basic definitions

- Biological warfare is the use of micro-organisms (including bacteria, viruses, fungi and parasites) or toxins produced by living organisms as weapons.
- The biological weapons consist of the agent itself (micro-organism or toxin) and the mechanism of its delivery.

In the development of biological weapons it is necessary to consider both these aspects; many more agents have been identified as potential weapons than actually weaponized.

History

Before the 20th century

The use of biological agents against the enemy extends back to times for which accurate records are missing. Apparently ancient Persians, Greeks and Romans dropped cadavers into wells to poison the drinking water of the enemy. The arrow poisons used by primitive tribes were biological toxins.

An Italian historian wrote the story of the destruction in 1346 of the besieged city of Kaffa on the Black Sea coast. A deadly outbreak of plague, advancing from Central Asia, had burst out among the attacking Tartars, while the city seemed to be holding its own. Then the Tartars devised a new strategy, catapulting their corpses over the city walls. This not only resulted in a massive outbreak of plague in the city but may have played a central role in the spread of the disease to Europe when the Genoans, who had been successfully holding Kaffa until the outbreak, fled with their ships to their home towns along the Italian coast. An epidemic of plague is known to have started in this area in 1347, spread to France and then, by ship again, to England in 1349 and to Norway in 1351. This was the start of the Black Death that devastated Europe for five centuries.

The story of Kaffa illustrates several features associated with biological warfare. First, the enormous potential of an infection to kill whole populations and to spread over continents as a pandemic. Second, that it is difficult to prove that an outbreak or an epidemic was due to biological warfare rather than to natural causes. Thus the role of the active use of the corpses as biological weapons is not proven; the infection, spreading with rats and their fleas, could have reached Kaffa and the Mediterranean ships anyway. In a similar fashion, the outbreaks of plague, cholera, typhoid fever and dysentery in China during the Second World War (WW II) could never be proven to be due to biological warfare in spite of the active biological warfare programme of Japan at that time.

The use of blankets from a smallpox hospital given as 'gifts' to American Indians in 1763 is well documented, indeed proudly described. Smallpox and other epidemics among the Indians turned out to be very efficient in reducing the numbers of the native tribes. The actual role of deliberate biological warfare again remains unclear since the mere contact of the Indians with the Europeans bringing these diseases to a new population not having immunity to them could have had the same result. The power of micro-organisms to act as weapons of mass destruction, however, became clear.

The First and Second World Wars

In the second half of the 19th century techniques to handle, culture, isolate and identify bacteria were developed, with Louis Pasteur and Robert Koch as the central figures. These led, of course, to the development of vaccines and eventually of antibiotics. However, they also made it possible to start a deliberate search for agents for biological warfare. During the WW I this activity was still exploratory, although Germany already had an extensive programme aimed at infecting sheep, cattle and horses to be used by the enemy forces.

The time of the WW I was the time of introducing chemical warfare. The horrors associated with this first intentional use of weapons of mass destruction led to efforts, immediately after the war, to ban such weapons. Although the development of biological weapons was still only beginning, they were included in the 1925 Geneva Protocol for the Prohibition of the Use in War of Asphyxiating, Poisonous or Other Gases, and of Bacteriological Methods of Warfare.

The Geneva Protocol did not prohibit research on biological weapons and their development. In fact the inclusion of them in the same protocol as the chemical weapons that had already proved effective may have been one factor making them interesting to those designing improved methods of warfare. What actually happened was that many countries in Europe, North America and Japan started research and development programmes on biological weapons. The most likely agents were identified and tested in laboratory and animal experiments, and their large-scale production and possible weaponization explored.

The best known of these programmes is the Japanese, thanks to the first-hand information obtained from high-ranking officers of the programmes captured during WW II by the Soviet Union or by the USA. Indeed, a detailed description of the Japanese research, including methods and results of experiments on prisoners of war, was obtained by USA intelligence in exchange for immunity from prosecution for thousands of participants in the programme. This was considered very important since the other research programmes only had data from animal experiments.

The Second World War obviously stimulated and accelerated biological-warfare research and directed it to the actual development of weapons. The UK believed that Germany was preparing for biological warfare against it (which it was not) and started an active programme to develop a means of retaliation. A new research unit (the Biology Department, Porton) was established in 1940 and located at Porton Down, where an establishment for chemical warfare (and later for defence) had existed since WW I. The Biology Department soon focused on the bacterium *Bacillus anthracis*, and its delivery by aerosol, to be created by bursting munitions. The inhaled aerosol would cause a fatal infection, anthrax.

Bombing experiments were carried out on the remote island of Gruinard off the coast of Scotland and showed that sheep could indeed be killed in this manner. Most probably this would apply to humans, too. The technology to grow sufficient amounts of the bacteria and to manufacture the bombs did not appear feasible in wartime Britain, and thus this became a joint 'N-bomb' programme of the Allies. The plant for producing the bacteria was built in Vigo, Indiana, but the war ended before it started working. In the UK a kind of poor man's variety of biological weapons, also based on the anthrax *Bacillus*, was designed and manufactured. This involved no burst or bomb but instead cattle feed (cattle cakes) containing the anthrax spores. Five million such cakes were produced in less than a year by a very small staff at Porton. The plan was to drop them from bomber planes on to German cattle fields; the death of the animals would deal a serious blow on the malnourished people (army and civilians alike). If this plan had been realized, large areas in the centre of Europe would have been heavily contaminated by anthrax spores and thus uninhabitable for decades, as we now know from experience on the similarly-contaminated Gruinard island: there had been no signs of reduction in the amount of spores in 25 years, and the island was announced as fit for habitation only 50 years later, after intensive decontamination by irrigation with formaldehyde.

The Japanese biological-warfare programme is the only one that was actually put to use during WW II, although the attacks on China appear to have been fairly limited, more in the nature of field trials. These included the contamination of water and food and the spraying of bacteria or plague-infected fleas from flying airplanes. The fact that Japanese troops were not protected from the infections and deaths also speaks for the trial nature of these attacks.

After WW II until 1972

The success of the nuclear bomb put an end to the immediate biological-warfare plans. However, the apparent promise of the N-bomb and the amount of knowledge gained from the Japanese programme (now available to the USA) meant that further work on biological warfare was considered important, and in fact large sums of money were assigned both in the UK and the USA as well as in the Soviet Union to expand research, development and even production of biological weapons.

During this time, a variety of biological agents were evaluated for their biological warfare potential. The conditions of large-scale production were explored, paying special attention to safety measures for the staff handling them. The means of delivery were also researched. Experimental munitions were detonated in closed chambers, often using bacteria considered harmless, and the agents were spread as aerosols from airplanes and through ventilator systems (e.g. in the New York underground), resulting in a pretty good method of predicting how far an agent would spread at the required (still-infective) concentration under such things as the weather conditions. Some harm was probably caused since although the pathogenic potential of the bacteria used was low, it was, nevertheless, not nil. This, however, could not be proven.

Another, concurrent line of research aimed at improving defence against biological warfare. Protective clothing and masks resembled those used against chemical weapons; vaccines and antimicrobial/antitoxin agents were specific for biological warfare and mostly even for the individual agent to be used. Methods to identify the biological-warfare agent used or even to recognize an attack of biological warfare were likewise explored.

It appeared, therefore, that towards the end of the 1950s, biological warfare was considered amongst the superpowers as a highly-promising area in which major advantages had been gained and major investments were worth making. This was even more remarkable in a period of heavy expansion of the nuclear arms race. By and by, however, opposition to biological warfare increased: there were allegations of the use of biological weapons despite the Geneva Protocol, a growing aversion to the inhuman concept of deliberately spreading disease, and anxiety about the uncontrollable nature of the epidemics.

This probably prepared the ground for the proposals to prohibit not only the use but also the development, production and stockpiling of agents of biological warfare. Such proposals were made separately by the UK and the Warsaw Pact nations in 1969 to the UN Conference on Disarmament. The decision of US President Nixon to terminate the US biological warfare programme was of great importance to the acceptance of the Convention on the Prohibition of the Development, Production and Stockpiling of Bacteriological (Biological) and Toxin Weapons and on Their Destruction. The Biological Weapons Convention (BWC) was signed in 1972 and over a hundred nations – including both the USA and the Soviet Union as well as, for example, Iraq – have since joined.

After 1972

At first, there was much publicity about the destruction of stocks of biological weapons and the conversion of biological-warfare establishments to peaceful uses according to the BWC. This positive publicity pleased the USA, distracting attention as it did from its activities with chemical agents in Vietnam, and counteracting the adverse national and international publicity that its biological-warfare activities had caused. This may have been the real motivation behind President Nixon's termination of the USA biological warfare programme.

But soon the times changed again. Biological warfare started to look much more promising with the advent of the new microbiological techniques associated with the then-developing gene technology. These appeared to make it possible in a much shorter time and to an extent not previously possible to modify the biological agents to become more suitable, indeed tailor-made for biological warfare. This was reflected in increased investment in biological warfare-related research starting early in the 1980s, all of which was, of course, called defensive and thus not in violation of the Biological Weapons Convention. (The possibilities opened up by the new technology continue to expand, as discussed below.)

At the same time, there were numerous allegations about the use of biological weapons by either the USA or the Soviet Union. The case of the yellow rain, alleged to be a fungal toxin used by the Soviet Union in Laos, Kampuchea and Afghanistan, gained much publicity. Precise evaluation of the alleged attacks in remote regions and in the past has been understandably difficult, but the opinion of several outside expert groups has been that these allegations were ungrounded and that the yellow rain was most probably the faeces of swarming bees.

Clear-cut violations of the convention are also, however, on record. Pellets containing the plant toxin ricin were used by the Bulgarian secret service for individual assassinations. An outbreak of anthrax in 1979 in Sverdlovsk in the Soviet Union, causing 66 deaths, was long suspected and, finally, in 1992 admitted to have been due to an accident in a biological-weapons production plant. President Yeltsin has in fact admitted the existence of a large offensive biological-warfare programme in Russia, with several research centres and production facilities and some 50,000 employees, operated by the company Biopreparat under the Ministry of Medical and Microbiological Industry. Another body, listed under the Ministry of Defence, was also involved. President Yeltsin promised to end this illegal activity, but its present status is not known. Iraq was likewise believed to have an active biological-warfare programme, but proof of this was obtained only slowly during UN inspections after the 1991 Gulf War. Iraqi officials claimed that the project included research on bacterial, viral and fungal agents and toxins, with production facilities and stocks being destroyed after the war. An offensive biological-weapons programme has been uncovered in apartheid South Africa, and is suspected in several other countries.

Besides the official, although secret, governmental use of biological weapons (in contravention of the BWC) there are recorded instances of their use by terrorists. In 1984 there was an intentional contamination of restaurant salad bars by *Salmonella typhimurium* in Oregon that resulted in hundreds of casualties; the source of the outbreak could not be found by intensive epidemiological investigation, and was only revealed by a member of the religious cult that had initiated it. The Aum Shinrikyo cult is well known for its sarin (nerve-gas) attack in the Tokyo underground in 1995. Apparently, besides its chemical-weapons programme, the cult had a biological-warfare programme, with production facilities and stocks of *Bacillus anthracis* and botulinum toxin. It had already tried to spread these in the underground but without success.

What are biological weapons?

The microbes

Of the micro-organisms causing disease those that are easily transmitted and likely to cause disease in most of those infected would seem best-suited to biological warfare. Many other aspects need to be considered however: how serious is the disease (case fatality rate), how soon will the disease manifest itself, will those infected further infect others (with the potential of an epidemic), what is the route of infection (usually by inhaling or ingesting the microbes)? How difficult would it be to recognize the attack, to diagnose the disease, to treat those infected and to prevent the spread of the disease? Would the microbe survive the conditions of its application, e.g. drying, and UV irradiation in the air? How easy or difficult would it be to cultivate the microbe on a large-enough scale?

Many microbes are known to have been seriously evaluated for biological-warfare potential, resulting in a short list of agents weaponized. Interestingly, *Bacillus anthracis* is the agent present on the short list of all the known biological-warfare programmes. It is easy to culture and has the special advantage of being able to form spores and thus to survive drying and heat, and therefore being likely to survive in the aerosol. It causes a rapidly fatal infection and then infects people or animals by inoculation (e.g. through scratches) or by ingestion. Other major candidates for biological warfare are the bacteria causing plague, cholera and typhoid fever. Among viruses, the most deadly ones causing Ebola or Lassa fever are of definite interest. The smallpox virus would fulfil many of the criteria for a biological weapon now that its eradication programme has succeeded (1980) and vaccination against it has been discontinued. The USA would be especially vulnerable because it ended its smallpox vaccination programme in 1972, much earlier than most countries; now some 40 per cent of its population is estimated to be susceptible to smallpox. To prevent the use of the virus all stocks present in 1980 in many microbiological laboratories were ordered to be destroyed, with the exception of two carefully-controlled WHO-sanctioned storage sites in the USA and Moscow; whether and when to destroy these is still being debated. A particular cause for concern of worry is the fact that the former Soviet Union's biological-warfare programme had included smallpox, with large quantities produced and weaponized.

Human pathogens are not the only potential biological-warfare agents. Killing the livestock of the enemy and thus impairing its ability to feed its people has been a stated target of past biological-warfare programmes and several microbes – bacteria, viruses and fungi – suitable for this have been included in the research programmes. Microbes causing disease in crop plants would likewise affect the nutrition and economy of the enemy; again, viruses, bacteria and many fungi are among potential agents.

Toxins

Several toxins produced by microbes, plants and animals are among the most lethal agents known in orders of magnitude more active than the gases developed for chemical warfare. Because of their high activity, small amounts (a few kilograms) would be sufficient to contaminate the drinking-water of a large city. The microbes producing these toxins in their natural lifestyle contaminate a food source and cause intoxication upon feeding. However, for biological-warfare purposes the toxins would be isolated and could then be applied also as aerosols or by injection (e.g. in terrorist attacks).

The most prominent of the toxins in biological-warfare programmes is the botulinum toxin produced by the bacterium *Clostridium botulinum*. It is a neurotoxin, with death resulting from paralysis of the respiratory muscles. However, many other toxins of biological warfare potential are objects of research.

The agents of the gene-technology era

Since the 1980s, biology has entered a new era of huge new possibilities through the application of gene technology. This makes it possible to determine the full genetic blueprint of any organism. This is especially easy with microbes because of the small size of their genomes, and already many pathogens have been blueprinted. Knowing the genes makes it possible (although not yet very easy) to identify their functions and thus to find out how they cause disease.

Most important in the present context is the possibility of modifying the genes (and their products) and rearranging them by, for example, inserting a toxin gene from one species into the genome of another. The modifications that one could easily imagine leading to microbes that could be more efficiently used in biological weapons include making the bacteria resistant to all common antibiotics or changing their surface structure so that they would escape recognition by the immunity created by vaccines. This latter could apply widely not only to bacteria and viruses but even to toxins, for which antibodies would in most cases be the only antidote. These modifications would be easy to make and not likely to interfere with the survival or disease-causing properties of the microbes or toxins.

By contrast, any new combinations of genes associated with disease-causing potential (virulence) are more likely to impair than to increase the virulence; this is understandable since the present combinations of genes in the present microbes are a result of a long evolution during which many modifications and combinations have already been tested, always with the selection of the fittest and the discarding of those less good. This does not preclude, however, the possibility of being able to create a supervirulent microbe with enough effort invested. The tools of gene technology certainly make possible the creation of new combinations and modifications at faster rates than are achievable in natural evolution. It is also not out of place to point out that the evolution of a new and very efficient pathogen, the human immunodeficiency virus (HIV), has been seen to take place in our times. It may also be worth noting that this was a case of natural evolution and not, as alleged, preparation for biological warfare.

The methods of gene technology also provide the certain possibility of improving the means to produce toxins in large quantities by transferring their genes from an organism producing the toxin in small amounts and in a form difficult to purify to a new production host, mostly a bacterium or a yeast. Less likely to succeed but a not-impossible approach would be the design of selective agents which attack only individuals with a certain genetic make-up. A horror picture would be a biological weapon to eliminate one race, or all but one race.

The weapons

The biological agents need further work (weaponization) to be usable in biological warfare. In other words, means have to be developed to deliver them to the target in an active state and in such a manner that they can cause the infection or poisoning intended. Since these agents can be used either in full-scale war or in terrorist attacks, the type of weapons may be very different.

In a sabotage weapon used to assassinate two Bulgarian emigres in separate incidents in London and Paris in the 1970s, the toxin (ricin) was incorporated into a tiny pellet, which was then injected by a device disguised as an umbrella. Contamination of food sources would not necessarily require any special technology. In the salad bar incident in Oregon the bacterial cultures were simply poured on to the dishes. Several members of the cult participated in this activity in many restaurants and on several days. To gain access to the well-guarded central water supplies would be much more difficult but pouring the toxin into the water would be simple. A means available for terrorist groups to spread a biological agent active after inhalation could well include the various aerosol-spreading methods tested in the 1950s, spraying the agents into ventilation systems or from a moving truck or low-flying aeroplane.

There is less information about the kinds of biological weapons that would be used on large scale in a war situation. During WW II the Allies' joint plan was to spread spores of the anthrax *Bacillus* on major German cities by bombing. The N-bomb to be used would have been 500lb cluster bombs containing over 100 small 4lb submunitions trial-tested on the island of Gruinard. While waiting for these to be manufactured the UK relied on cattle-feed cakes to be dropped from aeroplanes for livestock to eat.

To what extent the methods of aerosol spreading tested at least by the UK and the USA after the war have been included in actual biological-warfare plans is not known. Different types of munitions filled with the biological agents were tested at this time and several agents weaponized and stockpiled by the USA biological-warfare programme. These stocks were destroyed in 1971–73. The biological-warfare programme of the former Soviet Union has been reported (by former Deputy-Chief of research and production Ken Alibek after his defection to the USA) to have mounted the smallpox virus in bombs and intercontinental ballistic missiles.

The most accurate information about a recent biological-warfare programme comes from Iraq through the investigators of the United Nations Special Commission (UNSCOM) after the Gulf War. According to United Nations Security Council reports from 1995–97, and an article written by R.A. Zilinskas, a member of the UNSCOM investigation, several types of munitions were used to package the biological agents (mostly botulinum toxin or anthrax spores). These included 400lb bombs originally designed for use as chemical weapons and filled with 85 litres of the biologiocal agent. Biological agents were also loaded on to SCUD missiles (25 such were actually deployed) and tested on rockets (not known to have been deployed). These munitions also contained an explosive charge for effective dispersal of the biological agents. The aerosol-spraying technique was also adopted. Utilizing equipment intended for spraying pesticides, sprayers and tanks for holding the biological agent were installed in some aeroplanes and land vehicles. All in all, the number of warheads and bombs containing the agents were small, probably because the Iraqi biological-warfare programme was in its infancy and the different munitions and delivery systems still at the testing phase. As we know, none of these weapons was used in the Gulf War. Iraq has reported that soon after the ceasefire all biological-warfare agents and munitions and facilities were destroyed. Verification of this, however, has not been effected.

How would the weapons be used and with what consequences?

In terrorist acts? Yes, quite probably. However, the weapons and agents available to terrorist groups may be rather crude ones, like the ones already used and discussed above. They would be easy enough to produce with fairly elementary knowledge of microbiology, biochemistry and weapons technology, and this could take place unnoticed because the quantities needed would be fairly small. It seems unlikely that the groups could undertake development of new agents based on gene technology because of the special expertise and long-term effort and investment required.

The use of a biological weapon even on a small scale would certainly give rise to much anxiety, even panic. The disease cases would start appearing only a few days after the attack, and they would certainly appear both frightening in their severity and mysterious in diagnosis, associated with no effective treatment or protection of those not yet involved. Then, when the nature of the cases had been recognized, there would be worry about who else would fall ill and whether the disease would spread and start an epidemic. All this would concur with the purposes of the terrorists, with maximal attention from the media and public demands for protection. The attack might, of course, start an epidemic, something nobody wanted, of unpredictable extent and consequences.

It is more difficult to foresee the strategies of biological warfare. In local wars, the use of biological weapons could be rather similar to that of terrorist groups, and the results similar, too. In larger-scale wars biological weapons would most likely be used against civilian targets, for two reasons: (i) because this would be most effective in producing the desired result, panic and a public outcry to stop the war by whatever means; and (ii), because the soldiers would be better protected, perhaps wearing protective masks, perhaps even vaccinated against the agent. Used this way the biological weapon would be a true weapon of mass destruction. The large number of disease cases would overwhelm the capacity of the medical services and cause serious disruption to transport infrastructure and other vital functions. The psychological effect would be immense.

At the same time, because of the large number of infected and the concomitant huge numbers of the microbes multiplying in them, there would be a high risk of uncommon events, including the emergence of highly virulent microbes and their efficient transmission. This would affect not only the population at the target site but spread without respect to national borders. In other words, the likelihood of a large epidemic or even a pandemic would be considerable.

What are the means of protection?

Treatment of those affected

Medical treatment may sound quite possible in this modern era of antibiotics and specialists of infectious diseases. This is unlikely to be the case, however:

(1) a range of antibiotics exist for bacterial diseases, whereas means to cure viral infections are much less efficient;

(2) the bacterial agents to be used as biological weapons would almost certainly have been made resistant to all common antibiotics (very easy with the tools of gene technology), thus thwarting treatment. If they would still be susceptible to some uncommon antibiotic this would not help very much because the stocks of the antibiotic would soon be exhausted. Storing a large variety of antibiotics might seem a wise precaution; it would, however, be very expensive on a scale to be helpful to more than a few, and more expensive because the stores would need frequent replacement, given the relatively short half-life of the drugs;

(3) specific antibodies would be an effective antidote to toxins, but the large quantities and the unknown specificities needed would make this treatment available to very few individuals. The suggestion of storing large supplies of these is even more impractical than storing antibiotics on a large scale;

(4) the diseases caused by biological warfare are likely to be unfamiliar to most doctors, leading to delayed diagnosis and less-than-optimal treatment. The training of medical personnel may be of help, but this requires special attention;

(5) the supportive measures, even oxygen and intravenous fluids and devices for their administration, would soon be exhausted by the large numbers of patients;

(6) the large numbers of those infected would soon become the major obstacle to all treatment, with a large number of the medical personnel ill, and transport to hospitals and the maintenance of water and electricity supplies halting.

Quick recognition of an attack

The sooner the use of a biological weapon is recognized and the agent identified, the better would the medical services be prepared to handle the patients. Diagnosis would be facilitated and the most suitable treatment recommended. At the same time the numbers of cases could be reduced by advice through the mass media to prevent contamination and further transmission from cases. All this, however, is unlikely to succeed because the tasteless, odourless biological agent would not be noticed before cases start to appear, with a delay of days. Even then correct diagnosis may be delayed because of both the unfamiliarity of the agent and the symptoms of disease caused by an unusual route of infection. The preparedness of clinical microbiology laboratories to identify potential agents of biological warfare would, however, be a possible and reasonable measure to shorten this phase.

A fair amount of research has been devoted to devising methods for recognizing an aerosol attack by sampling and analysis of air. However, this is very inefficient considering the unpredictability of the attack and the small quantities of the agent needed for it to work. Modern gene technology-based methods of identifying the expected agents could be helpful, but the feasibility of representative and continuous sampling and analysis seems questionable.

Prevention of infection

Contact with the biological-warfare agent would be necessary for it to cause the disease. If one knew of an attack it might be possible to avoid contact by staying in a shelter with a filtered air supply (viruses and toxins might come through, though) and its assured separate drinking water and food stores. A small amount of protection would even be obtained by staying indoors with windows shut. How long, however, would one need to stay in the shelter? More importantly, when would be the time to go in to the shelter since the attack would be unlikely to be recognized until days later? The same applies to the use of gas masks. Overall, these mechanical protection measures would be very cumbersome and give only partial protection, but they would reduce the number of casualties. In practice it seems likely that key troops and staff of the armed forces would use the protective devices but that the general public could not.

Preventing the disease in the infected persons could be more efficient if one had the specific means available. As discussed above, immunity obtained by vaccination could be very effective, but this would require the prediction of the biological-warfare agent that will be used and that this would not have been altered by genetic techniques. Only those individuals who had been vaccinated would be protected, and the vaccine should have been administered at least 1–2 weeks prior to the attack. Vaccines for many of the potential biological-warfare agents do not, however, exist or are unavailable to the public. Development of new vaccines might be considered a wise preparation, but it would be very expensive. The development of a vaccine requires several years of research and extensive field-testing. This would raise the question of how to determine priorities *vis-à-vis* the development of vaccines against common diseases that could in normal times save huge numbers of lives. Vaccinating the whole population with several possibly-needed vaccines would not only be very expensive but would also be likely to cause several cases of serious adverse effects and even deaths. For example the vaccine that helped to eradicate smallpox did cause serious adverse reactions and is no longer produced, nor is it available in large quantities.

Preventing the local outbreak from spreading and starting an epidemic should obviously be based on common methods of epidemic control, including extensive surveillance of cases in order to devise strategies to block the spread. These should certainly be used, but the disruption to the infrastructure in the affected area is likely to make this impossible, and the success of such methods is at best unpredictable.

Protection of the users of biological weapons

Protecting oneself is an obvious need for those developing and using biological weapons. However, risks are taken and may be considered appropriate under the exceptional circumstances of war or terrorist action. On the other hand, the unpredictability of the use of biological weapons and therefore the uncertainty of how well a nation's own troops or people would be protected may have been and may still be important factors preventing biological warfare.

Common methods in handling infectious agents are the mainstay of protection for the workers. Mechanical isolation is the rule in laboratories and production facilities handling the agents; the best-known case of failure of these is the Sverdlovsk anthrax outbreak discussed above. Adherence to the strict requirements of isolation makes the work both slow and cumbersome as well as expensive. Immunity would be the best method of protection, and therefore development of vaccines goes hand-in-hand with the development of weapons. Vaccinating the relatively small staff working in weapons' development and production could be done even with still-experimental vaccines. The secrecy maintained about all these activities will also ensure that information about the vaccines used or the agents handled is not leaked out. This becomes more of a problem when considering large-scale use of the weapons. Should all members of the armed forces be vaccinated? What about the population? The more people receiving the vaccine, the greater the danger that its identity would leak out, in which case the enemy might be able to initiate a similar vaccination procedure (if it had sufficiently prepared for defence against biological warfare and correctly guessed which agents the other side was likely to use).

International efforts at preventing biological warfare

Intergovernmental treaties

As described above, two international treaties designed to prevent biological warfare are in force: the 1925 Geneva Protocol, and the 1972 Biological Weapons Convention. Both have been signed by over 100 nations. Experience has shown their shortcomings. After the Geneva Protocol, which prohibited only the first use of biological weapons in war, extensive research programmes were established in many countries, in some cases stressing the defensive aspects, in others being openly offensive (as permitted by the protocol as long as the weapons were not used). The UK, for example, developed the anthrax weapons to be available as retaliation should Germany use biological weapons.

Obviously there was need of a more comprehensive treaty and the 1972 Biological Weapons Convention was intended to provide this. This prohibited the development, production and stockpiling of the weapons and ordered the destruction of existing stockpiles. The transfer to any other state of the capability of producing or otherwise acquiring biological weapons is also prohibited (Article III). On the other hand, Article X encourages international exchange of equipment, materials and technologies for the peaceful application of biological agents and toxins. Defensive research was also allowed to continue. This creates a problem: any work on the biological agents could be considered defensive; too bad that the same knowledge concerning virulence properties, as well as the cultivation of the microbes or production of their components, can be useful for offensive purposes. Developing a vaccine – clearly a part of defensive research – would greatly facilitate the development of the agent to be used as a weapon. Even research on the weapons could be defensive, needed to design defence measures.

The evidence since 1972 shows that the effort put into defensive biological-weapons research diminished at first and then increased, according to the political climate and the opportunities seen in the weapons. Recent revelations of actual production and stock-piling of biological weapons by both terrorist groups and sovereign nations (Iraq and the former Soviet Union for sure) have greatly increased the feeling that defensive biological-warfare research is needed, research which is then likely to increase knowledge of biological warfare.

Another problem with the Biological Weapons Convention is that it can be and has been violated. This has been facilitated by the convention's lack of measures to verify compliance. The only possibility included in the convention is a complaint to the UN Security Council that can be filed by any participant state if it suspects violation of the convention by another state. The matter has been considered by the review conferences held at intervals after the entry into force of the convention, the first in 1980, then in 1986, 1991 and 1996, with the fifth planned for 2001. The 1986 conference introduced a system of confidence-building measures as a kind of substitute for a verification system. These include voluntary declarations by participant states of certain key activities, such as: maximum safety laboratories; national defence research programmes against biological weapons, major epidemics, and vaccine production facilities. An ad hoc working group was established in 1991 to make a preliminary analysis of possible verification measures and their feasibility. On this basis a second ad hoc working group has been active since 1995, supported by the fourth review conference (1996). It aims at a definite proposal in 2001 suggesting a separate verification protocol. The verification system is planned to be based on two components: declarations and inspections. The inspections would apparently be initiated by a suspicion of violation. In addition other measures could be included, such as more routine visits as spot-checks. A global network of surveillance and reporting of unusual epidemics might be a supportive measure, perhaps in collaboration with the World Health Organization (WHO). However, these suggested verification measures are not at all foolproof. Research and even production in moderate amounts of the agents of biological warfare have no outward features distinguishing them from microbiological laboratory work done, for example, in hospitals and universities. The gene technology applied to weapons' agents does not differ in appearance or methodology from any peaceful applications. Large-scale production requires big fermentors and downstream processing equipment but these do not differ from equipment used for producing vaccines or other biotechnology products. This aspect has been demonstrated clearly by the difficulties that UNSCOM had in obtaining verification of the Iraqi biological-warfare programme.

Article III of the convention is intended to prohibit transfer of any materials or knowledge related to biological warfare to other states. Although the implementation of this article (through export controls) is the responsibility of each state, there have been international efforts to coordinate these activities. The principal actor is the Australia group initially established within the Chemical Weapons Convention (see Chapter 10) framework and expanded in 1990 to include biological weapons. The group now consists of over 30 participating nations. A result of its work is a list of technologies and materials, the export of which is controlled. This list includes many pathogenic microbes and toxins, as well as fermentors, centrifuges and other equipment used in microbiological and biotechnological production. A problem is that these are also used in peaceful microbiological work, and Article X actually encourages exchange of items of this sort. The strict implementation of Article III would, therefore, be in direct conflict with Article X and could also hamper microbiological research in general. On the other hand, the export controls will never be very effective with materials as difficult to define as these.

Non-governmental efforts

Many individual scientists have been active and outspoken about the serious dangers of biological warfare and the responsibility of scientists to work against it. These include Professor Joseph Rotblat, once a member of the Los Alamos Manhattan Project team (see Chapter 12), an initiator of the Pugwash conferences (Chapter 59) and winner of the 1995 Nobel Peace Prize, and professors Robert L Sinsheimer from the University of California, Santa Barbara and professor Keith R. Yamamoto from the University of California at San Francisco, and professor Matthew Meselson of Harvard University, all world-known experts in molecular biology and gene technology. Professor Yamamoto has coauthored *Gene Wars*, to draw attention to the increased dangers of biological warfare in the present gene-technology era.

Several non-governmental organizations have been active in biological-warfare questions. Pugwash held a Conference on Chemical and Biological Warfare as early as 1959, followed by several meetings. It worked in closed collaboration with WHO to produce the 1970 WHO report on 'Health Aspects of Chemical and Biological Weapons'; prominent scientists collaborating included three Nobel laureates: Joshua Lederberg, Niels Jerne and Andre Lwoff. The Federation of American Scientists (FAS) has a Working Group on Biological Weapons Verification; it addressed the 1996 review conference of the Biological Weapons Convention stressing the need and feasibility of verification. The World Medical Association also spoke at the same conference, stressing the need to guard against misuse of genetic research. The International Network of Engineers and Scientists for Global Responsibility also addressed the conference, asking it to appeal to the scientific community to support only activities with peaceful purposes. The International Physicians for the Prevention of Nuclear War (see Chapter 1) has expanded its agenda from nuclear weapons to all weapons of mass destruction: it has not, however, been especially vocal on the question of biological warfare.

In view of the difficulties, indeed the impossibility, of formal treaties and regulations to prevent activities related to biological warfare, two possibilities remain for its effective prevention: (i) public opinion, clearly expressed, making any biological-warfare development or activity politically unacceptable and thus impossible, and (ii) a consensus of scientists for responsibility to prevent biological warfare to the extent of refusing to participate in any research or other action related to it no matter how lucrative the proposal in terms of financial compensation or research achievement. These are strict requirements, very difficult to achieve in all countries of the world. Rigorous support would be needed to achieve this aim, both in influencing public opinion and in talking to all scientists in the field. Could such a mass action be undertaken?

REFERENCES AND ADDITIONAL READING

1. World Health Organization (1970), *Health Aspects of Chemical and Biological Weapons*, Geneva.
2. Stockholm International Peace Research Institute (SIPRI) (1971), *Allegations of Biological Warfare in China and Korea, 1951–52*, in *The Prevention of CBW*, Vol. 5, Stockholm: Almqvist & Wiksell, pp. 238–60.
3. Paxman, H.R. (1982), *A Higher Form of Killing: the secret story of gas and germ warfare*, London: Chatto & Windus.
4. Gottfried, R.S. (1983), *The Black Death. Natural and human disaster in medieval Europe,* London: Robert Hale.
5. Manchee, R.J., Broster, M.G., Anderson, I.S, and R.M. Henstridge (1983), 'Decontamination of *Bacillus Anthracis* on Gruinard Island?' *Nature* , 303: 239–40.
6. Nowicke, J.W. and M. Meselson (1984), Yellow rain – a palynological analysis. *Nature,* 309: 205–06.
7. Capps, L., Vermund, S H and C. Johnsen (1986), 'Smallpox and Biological Warfare. The case for abandoning vaccination of military personnel', *American Journal of Public Health* 76:1229–31.
8. Piller, C. and K.T. Yamamoto (1988), *Gene Wars*, New York: Beech Tree Books, William Morrow.
9. Cole, L.A. (ed.) (1990), *Clouds of Secrecy. The army's germ warfarea tests over populated areas*, Rowman & Litlefield Publishers, Inc. Maryland .
10. Wright, S. (1991), 'Biowar Treaty in Danger', *Bulletin of Atomic Scientists* September: 36–40.
11. Hendricks M. (1991), 'Biological Weapons' Treaty Review', *ASM News*: 57: 358–61.
12. Carter, G.B. (1992), *Porton Down. Seventy-five years of chemical and biological research*, London: HMSO Publications.
13. Meselson, M. *et al.* (1994), 'The Swerdlovsk Anthrax Outbreak of 1979', *Science* 266: 1202–8.
14. Kadlec, R.P., Zelicoff, A.P. and A.M. Vrtis (1997) 'Biological Weapons Control. Prospects and implications for the future', *Journal of the American Medical Association (JAMA)* 278: 351–6.
15. Török, T.J., Tauxe, R.V., Wise, R.P. *et al.* (1997), 'A Large Community Outbreak of Salmonellosis Caused by Intentional Contamination of Restaurant Salad Bars', *JAMA* 278: 389–95.
16. Franz, D.R., Jahrling, P.B., Friedlander, A.M. *et al.* (1997), 'Clinical Recognition and Management of Patients Exposed to Biological Earfare Agents', *JAMA* 278: 399–411.
17. Christopher, G.W., Cieslak, T.J., Pavlin, J.A. *et al.* (1997) 'Biological Warfare. A Historical Perspective', *JAMA* 278: 412–17.
18. Zilinskas, R.A. (1997), 'Iraq's Biological Weapons.', *JAMA* 278: 418–24.
19. Barnaby W. (1997), *The Plague Makers. The secret world of biological warfare*, London: Vision Investigation Series, Satin Publications Ltd.
20. Monath, T.P. *et al.* (1998), 'Strengthening the Biological Weapons Convention', *Science* 282: 1423.
21. Rath, J. *et al.* (1998), 'Biological Weapons Control'. *Science* 282: 2194.
22. Roberts, B. (1998), 'Export Controls and Biological Weapons: New Roles, New Challenges', *Critical Reviews in Microbiology* 24: 235–54.
23. Berns, K.I. *et al.* (1998), 'Preventing the Misuse of Microorganisms: the Role of the American Society for Microbiology in Protecting Against Biological Weapons', *Critical Reviews in Microbiology* 24: 273–80.
24. Ashraf, H. (1999), 'UK Inquiry Opened into Human Trials of Biological and Chemical Weapons', *Lancet* 354: 753.
25. Kaplan, M.M. (1999), 'The Efforts of WHO and Pugwash to Eliminate Chemical and Biological Weapons – a Memoir', *Bulletin of the WHO* 77: 149–55.
26. Meselson, M. (1999), 'The Challenge of Biological and Chemical Weapons', *Bulletin of the WHO* 77: 102–3.
27. Henderson, D.A. (1999), 'The Looming Threat of Bioterrorism', *Science* 283: 1279.
28. Davis, C.J. (1999), 'Nuclear Blindness: An Overview of the Biological Weapons Programs of the Former Soviet Union and Iraq'. *Emerging Infectious Diseases* 5: 509–12.
29. Olson, K.B. (1999), 'Aum Shinrikyo: Once and future threat?' *Emerging Infectious Diseases* 5: 513–16.
30. Kortepeter, M.G. and G.W. Parker (1999), 'Potential Biological Weapons Threats'. *Emerging Infectious Diseases* 5: 523–7.

31. Russell, P.K. (1999), 'Vaccines in Civilian Defense Against Bioterrorism', *Emerging Infectious Diseases* 5: 531–3.
32. Zoon, K.C. (1999), 'Vaccines, Pharmaceutical Products, and Bioterrorism: Challenges for the US Food and Drug Administration', *Emerging Infectious Diseases* 5: 513–36.
33. O'Toole, T. (1999), 'Smallpox: An Attack Scenario', *Emerging Infectious Diseases* 5: 540–6.
34. Inglesby, T.V., Henderson, D.A., Bartlett, J.G. *et al.* (1999), 'Anthrax as a Biological Weapon. Medical and Public Health Management'. *JAMA* 281:1735–45.
35. Henderson, D.A., Inglesby, T.V., Bartlett, J.G. *et al.* (1999), 'Smallpox as a Biological Weapon. Medical and Public Health Management', *JAMA* 281: 2127–37.
36. MacIntyre, G.A. (2000), 'Weapons of Mass Destruction Events with cContaminated Casualties: effective planning for health care facilities', *JAMA* 283: 124–9.

Address for correspondence

National Public Health Institute, Mannerheimintie 166, FIN-00300 Helsinki, Finland

12 HEALTH EFFECTS OF THE MILITARY USE AND TESTING OF NUCLEAR WEAPONS

KATI JUVA

Nuclear weapons are the most disastrous weapons mankind has ever developed. They have only been used twice in a wartime situation – against the Japanese cities Hiroshima and Nagasaki in August 1945. The number of casualties by the end of that year was 140,000 in Hiroshima and 70,000 in Nagasaki. Additional thousands have died during the following decades. The long-term effect of the radiation is still causing an excess of certain malignancies and other health hazards among the people then exposed.

Nuclear-weapons testing has been conducted until very recently: lately also new states have joined the nuclear powers. The negative health effects of nuclear tests have been estimated to be even greater than the effects of the Hiroshima and Nagasaki bombs. It has been calculated that the ionizing radiation released into the atmosphere by these tests has caused over 400,000 cancer deaths all around the world.

This chapter concentrates on the actual use, whether in a war or in a testing situation, of nuclear weapons. Nuclear weapons' production is dealt with in Chapter 14, nuclear waste in chapters 40 and 41 and possible nuclear terrorism in Chapter 15.

Principles of nuclear weapons

There are two main types of nuclear weapons, using either only fission energy or fusion reactions induced by a small fission component.

The first nuclear weapons were fission bombs. A vast amount of energy is released when nuclei of large atoms are split as a consequence of bombardment by neutrons. This can result in a chain reaction, when at least one neutron produced by the splitting induces a new splitting. When there is a critical mass of the fissile material, the chain reaction continues without further external stimulation and results in the release of a huge amount of energy in a gigantic explosion. The amount of the released energy can be calculated by Einsteins' famous formula $E = mc^2$.

The fissile materials used in fission bombs are uranium-235 and plutonium-239. Most of the resulting fission products have very short half-lives (the time when half of the element's mass has 'used' its radioactivity and decayed into another element or isotope), but some have half-lives of several hours, weeks and years. As regards the health of human beings the most important radioactive isotopes produced are iodine-131 (half-life 8 days), strontium-90 (half-life 28.8 years) and cesium-137 (half-life 30.2 years).

The radiation produced by a nuclear explosion induces radioactive changes in the environment. When the explosion takes place in the atmosphere, the most important radionuclide produced is carbon-14 as a result of a reaction in which a stable nitrogen-14 atom captures a neutron and emits a proton. Carbon-14 is a beta-emitter (see Box 12.1) with a half-life of 5,730 years. In the case of ocean testing (underwater or surface) there will be a conversion of the natural isotope sodium-23 to radioactive sodium-24 (a beta emitter, half-life 15 hours). The production of other radionuclides depends on whether the explosion takes place high in the atmosphere or near above, on or under the ground.

Thermonuclear bombs (hydrogen or H-bombs) are based on fusion of light nuclei. The main reaction is fusion between different isotopes of hydrogen (deuterium and tritium). The initiation of these reactions needs huge temperatures and therefore a small fission component with plutonium-239 or uranium-235 is used to trigger the explosion.

In the 1970s the United States also developed the so-called neutron bomb. These are hydrogen bombs with little material to absorb the neutrons produced by the fusion, so the explosion will be relatively smaller and most of the released energy will be in the form of neutrons. These are extremely lethal to all forms of life, but later there will be less radioactive contamination in the environment and buildings and other structures suffer less damage.

Ionizing radiation

There are several ways in which ionizing radiation is dangerous to health. High levels (a few hundred rems) delivered in a short period of time result in severe injury and usually death within hours or days. The symptoms of this radiation illness are general malaise, nausea and vomiting directly after the exposure, followed by high fever and diarrhoea. Soon there will be gastrointestinal bleeding resulting in hematemesis and bloody diarrhoea. Death usually comes within ten days. Somewhat smaller amounts of radiation cause radiation illness with milder symptoms. In these cases survival depends on the previous health status of the victim and on the medical care available (e.g. treatment of fluid balance and infections).

High levels of radiation can also cause mental retardation and microcephaly among unborn children. No genetic effects have been found even after the high exposure among the descendants of the surviving victims of Hiroshima and Nagasaki.

A cataract can develop in individuals who have survived high doses of ionizing radiation. This takes several years to develop. Also, some immunological effects have been found among the survivors.

The main long-term health effect of radiation is the elevated risk of different

12.1

Ionizing radiation

Radioactivity can be divided into four types, with different penetration capacities and consequently different health effects.: (i) *gamma radiation* is high-frequency electromagnetic radiation energy. It is highly penetrating through fabric and wood, but can be stopped by lead or thick concrete; (ii) *beta radiation* consists of electrons. Even high doses can penetrate only a few millimetres below the skin; (iii) *alpha radiation*, which consists of helium-nuclei, is even less penetrating; and (iv), *neutron radiation* is highly penetrative but the neutrons are rapidly converted into protons and electrons. Thus, neutron radiation causes a hazard only close to the explosion.

The measure of radioactivity is the *becquerel*, which equals one disintegration per second. The dose of radiation is measured by *rads*. It is a unit of dose equal to the deposition of 100 ergs of energy per gram of material being irradiated (100 rads = 1 gray). Röntgen is a unit to measure gamma radiation and one röntgen is equal to 0.94 rads.

To assess the relative biological damage of different types of radiation absorbed by living tissue, the *rem* has been established as the agreed measure. For gamma and beta radiation, rems and rads are essentially equivalent, but for heavy particle radiation (neutrons, protons, alpha particles) the ratio of rems to rads ranges from 2 to 40 (100 rems = 1 sievert).

Radioactivity can affect human beings by direct external radiation or by inhalation or digestion of radioactive particles. These internal particles can be especially dangerous by staying in the lungs or in the intestine a long time and inducing cancerous changes in the cells.

malignancies. The risk of leukaemia especially increases up to 15-fold after high levels of radiation. The risk of leukaemia is highest in the 6–7 years after the exposure, but continues to be higher than in the average population even 50 years later. Frequencies of thyroid cancer, breast cancer, stomach cancer, lung cancer and multiple myeloma are also higher among those exposed to ionizing radiation than among those not exposed. The peak of the increases varies: the over-representation of thyroid cancer begins ten years after exposure, while multiple myeloma usually takes more than 30 years to develop. The higher the levels of radiation exposure, the greater the risk of cancer.

In 1990 the National Research Council of the National Academy of Sciences of the United States published a report of the Committee on Biological Effects of Ionizing Radiation (BEIR V) which estimated that a 1-rem exposure of one million people will result in a total of 790 (90 per cent confidence limits (Cls) 585–1200) extra deaths from cancer.

Chronology of nuclear testing

The first nuclear-weapons test and explosion (Trinity) took place in Alamogordo, New Mexico in July 1945, followed by the explosion of a nuclear bomb over Hiroshima on 6 August 1945 and a similar one over Nagasaki three days later, by US military forces.

During the following years the United States made several atmospheric nuclear tests in the Pacific, at the atolls of Bikini and Enewetak. After this the test site was moved to Nevada. The Soviet Union made its first nuclear test in 1949 in Semipalatinsk in present Kazakhstan. Their other test site has been in Novaya Zemlya. France made several nuclear-weapons tests in Algeria between 1960 and 1965 and continued testing in the Pacific (mainly in Moruroa atoll). The British conducted atmospheric tests in Australia in 1952–57 and later (together with the USA) on Christmas Island. China made its first nuclear-weapons' test in 1964 in Lop Nor. The first thermonuclear bomb (a hydrogen bomb) was exploded by the US in 1952 and the Soviet Union followed in 1953.

The total estimated number of atmospheric tests is 518 (the US 217, the Soviet Union 210, Great Britain 21, France 48 and China 22). These figures include five underwater and three space explosions by the US.

From the late 1950s onwards the nuclear powers began to test nuclear weapons under ground. This was due to a growing awareness of the health risks of atmospheric testing and subsequent public pressure. The 1963 Limited Test Ban Treaty prohibited nuclear testing in the atmosphere, underwater and in space. France and China did not sign it, and continued atmospheric testing up until 1974 and 1980, respectively.

Underground tests are safer than atmospheric tests, especially regarding the release of long-lasting carbon-14 into the atmosphere. Nevertheless, leakage of radioactive material into the atmosphere (venting) has often occurred in underground testing, especially in the Soviet tests but also in the American tests until 1971. Huge amounts of underground rock have been converted into radioactive material, of which plutonium-239 is the most dangerous. It is more than probable that during the following thousands of years some part of this radioactivity will find its way into the human environment, mainly by dissolving into the groundwater at the continental test sites and into the ocean at the Pacific.

The number of underground nuclear weapons tests exceeds 1400. Lately also India and Pakistan have joined the nuclear powers by conducting a series of underground tests in May 1998. The Soviet Union /Russia made its last test in 1990 in Novaya Zemlya and the US in 1993 in Nevada. The French conducted their last test series in 1995–96, in the Pacific, and China in August 1996 at Lop Nor. The Comprehensive Test Ban Treaty still waits to be ratified by all nuclear powers (see Box 12.2).

Nuclear explosions over Hiroshima and Nagasaki

On 6 August 1945, the United States exploded a 15-kilotons nuclear bomb over the Japanese city Hiroshima (350,000 inhabitants), and three days later over Nagasaki (250,000 inhabitants). The Hiroshima bomb ('Little Boy') exploded 580 metres above the city centre and the Nagasaki bomb ('Fat man') 500 metres above the northeast part of the city. About half of the bombs' energy came as blast, 35 per cent as heat and 15 per cent as ionizing radiation.

The pressures produced by the bombs were several hundreds of thousand times normal atmospheric pressure, causing a wind velocity of 280 metres per second at the site of the explosion (hypocentre) and 28 metres per second 3.2 kilometres away. The

12.2

Nuclear weapons treaties

Limited Test Ban Treaty 1963
Bans nuclear-weapons tests in the atmosphere, outer space and underwater. China and France, although not parties to the treaty, adhere to its provisions.

Treaty on Non-Proliferation of Nuclear Weapons, 1968
Entered into force in 1970 for a period of 25 years; became permanent in 1995. Signed by 178 states. India and Pakistan refused to sign until 1995. Bans the transfer of nuclear weapons or weapons technology to non-nuclear states. Commits nuclear powers to negotiations on halting the arms race and a treaty on complete disarmament. Commits non-nuclear states not to acquire nuclear weapons.

Threshold Test Ban Treaty, 1974
The United States and Soviet Union; bans underground tests of over 150 kilotons.

Comprehensive Test Ban Treaty (CTBT), 1996
Bans all nuclear-weapons testing. The CTBT was opened for signature in September 1996. As of August 1999, 152 nations had signed, including all five original nuclear-weapon states. India, Pakistan and North Korea have not signed. Ratified by 43 states (August 1999) including France and the United Kingdom. The treaty names 44 states that must deposit their instruments of ratification for it to enter into force. Of these, 21 ratified in August 1999.

mushroom clouds reached up to 12,000 metres. The heat on the earth beneath the hypocentre immediately after the explosion was 7000°C. Wooden materials were charred up to 3 kilometres from the hypocentre. This enormous blast and heat resulted in extensive destruction of buildings and other structures. About 13 square kilometres of Hiroshima and 6.7 square kilometres of Nagasaki were turned into ashes. Most people within 1.0–1.5 kilometres from the hypocentres succumbed to instant death with carbonisation of the body. Severe burns occurred in exposed people up to 3.5 kilometres from the hypocentres. Direct injuries caused by the blast and destruction of buildings and other structures killed thousands of people. In Hiroshima about 40,000 victims are presumed to have been killed within the first day.

Many of those who were further from the hypocentres and survived the instant effects of the explosion developed radiation illness and died within few weeks. It is estimated that 90–100 per cent of those exposed without any shielding within 1.0 kilometres from the hypocentre died within a week. The early mortality rate of those 1.5–2.0 kilometres from the hypocentre was 14 per cent for the shielded and 83 per cent for the unshielded. The total estimated number of deaths by the end of 1945 is 140,000 in Hiroshima and 70,000 in Nagasaki.

One of the most tragic effects of these bombings has been the increased risk of micro-cephaly (small head size) and mental retardation among those exposed to the radiation in their mother's womb. The risk was highest between pregnancy weeks 8 and 15. It was shown to be clearly dose-dependent. Nearly 20 per cent of children with an estimated in utero dose of more than 100 rads suffered from mental retardation.

The long-term health effects of the Hiroshima and Nagasaki bombings consist mainly of the increased risk of leukaemia and other malignant cancers among the survivors (*hibakusha*). The elevated incidence for leukaemia started in 1948, with the highest peaks in 1951 and 1953. The higher the radiation dose and the lower the age of the exposed person, the greater the risk. An excess of leukaemia incidence is still seen among the *hibakusha*. The increased risk for other malignancies started later: For thyroid cancer the elevation was first seen in 1955. For breast cancer there was a slight increase starting ten years after, and a more significant increase 20 years after, the exposure. The risk of lung cancer, stomach cancer and brain tumours have also shown a significant increase during the decades following the bombings. Skin cancer has increased since the late 1970s. For a more detailed description of the medical and also psychological and social effects of these bombings see Chapter 14.

Nuclear testing

Enormous amounts of radioactive material have been released into the environment by nuclear-weapons testing. The atmospheric testing has been extremely hazardous because the long-lasting radioactive isotopes, such as carbon-14 and cesium-137, have been released and distributed all around the globe. In addition to the excess external radiation from the surrounding environment many radionuclides have entered the food chain. This results in 'hot particles' which can sometimes stay a long time inside an organism increasing significantly the individual risk of cancer.

It has been estimated that by the year 2000 the excess dose in million person-rems (one excess rem for one million people) of cesium-137 will have been 219 and that of carbon-14, 100. By this time most of the cesium-137 and many other radionuclides with half-lives of less than 30 years will have decayed. Carbon-14 (with a half-life of 5730 years) continues to cause excess radiation up to 2600 million person-rems for thousands of years. The total excess radiation dose due to the fallout from atmospheric testing will be 544 million person-rems by the year 2000, and 3144 million person-rems up to infinity.

All this excess radiation in our environment increases the risk of malignant diseases, especially leukaemias. The individual increase in the risk of getting a cancer is of course quite low, 1.1×10^{-4} up to the year 2000. But when we take into account the whole world's population, it can be estimated that the fallout has so far induced a cancer in 430,000 persons , and will induce 2 million more during the following thousands of years. Most of these will be in the northern hemisphere, with the greatest risk between 40 and 50 degrees latitude.

In addition to this small (but significant) global increase in the cancer risk there have been many groups of people and larger populations with much greater exposure to nuclear fallout and thus to a markedly elevated risk of malignant diseases. In March 1954 a heavy fallout cloud was carried eastwards from a US test at Bikini Atoll, heavily contaminating the Japanese fishing boat *Lucky Dragon*. All 24 crew members developed radiation illness; one died seven months later and the rest remained hospitalized under intensive care. The fallout caused visible snowing of radioactive waste at the downwind atoll of Rongelap. The inhabitants were not evacuated until two days later. It has been estimated that 86 Rongelap people were exposed to an average of 190 rems whole-body radiation, meaning an additional one-in-seven risk of developing fatal cancer.

French testing in Moruroa in June and July 1967 caused a heavy fallout on the island Tureia, from where two French meteorologists were evacuated and transferred to hospital a couple of days later. The French, though, denied any dangerous fallout and the local inhabitants were not evacuated until 1968. Large populations living downwind of the Nevada test site in the US and of the Semipalatinsk test site in the former Soviet Union (present-day Kazakhstan) have also been repeatedly exposed to radioactive fallout. As a result there has been an unusual concentration of leukaemia cases in the southwestern corner of Utah (northeast from the Nevada test site), and in Semipalatinsk the cancer risk among the 10,000 most heavily-exposed people has been reported to be 39 per cent above expected.

There have been local hot spots of radiation quite far from the testing area, where weather conditions (such as a thunderstorm) have caused much higher concentrations of radioactive fallout than average. One of the most famous is the thousand-fold increase in the radiation level in Albany, New York in April 1953 occurring a few hours after an atmospheric test in Nevada. Other similar hot spots have been noticed elsewhere after different tests, and many have probably gone unnoticed. In many of these areas there has been a high concentration of iodine-131, especially increasing the risk of thyroid cancer.

The military personnel taking part in the nuclear testing have also been exposed to excess radiation, but there is almost no public information on the actual doses or of the health effects of the radiation. In a British study conducted in 1982 on the effects of testing in Australia, a slightly increased risk of leukaemia and other related neoplasms was found among the 8000 military personnel exposed to radiation: 27 recorded deaths compared to the 17.2 expected. A Chinese senior military officer has admitted that 'a few deaths have occurred'. There is very little data about French testing. On the whole, the French and the Chinese have been the most secretive in their testing and its effects.

Nuclear testing has also caused severe socio-economic and environmental problems. In most places the tests have been conducted in areas where minorities or indigenous people live. Many local people have been evacuated from areas surrounding the test sites. In the Pacific the structure and ecosystem of the coral atolls have been damaged. This has had major health effects: ciguatera fish poisoning, a great public health problem in the South Pacific, is known to increase when the ecosystem in the coral atolls is damaged; and, as could have been anticipated, the incidence of ciguatera poisoning increased ten-fold from 1960 to 1975 as a result of the damage to the atolls caused by nuclear testing.

Possible nuclear war

The number of nuclear weapons was at its (largest more than 60,000 warheads) in the middle of the 1990s. In 1999 more than 30,000 nuclear weapons still remained, equivalent in force to 200,000 Hiroshima-sized bombs. Ninety-five per cent of these are owned by the United States or Russia.

The known effects of the nuclear explosions in Hiroshima and Nagasaki over 50 years ago and the knowledge of the much higher power and advanced mechanics of current nuclear weapons give us some understanding of what might happen in a large-scale nuclear war, where large cities will be the most probable targets.

Already in 1962 a group of physicians in Boston were writing articles in the *New England Journal of Medicine* describing the potential medical consequences of a nuclear attack on the city. They estimated that 2 million people would die and an additional 1.5 million would be injured. A cigar-shaped fallout cloud would be heading downwind, contaminating large areas relatively far from the explosion point. Most physicians and other medical staff would be killed or severely injured and medical facilities, including hospitals, health centres and ambulances, would be destroyed. In such conditions, without medical personnel, drugs and other equipment there could be no treatment for those wounded and the disposal of corpses would be very difficult if not impossible. Risk of epidemic diseases would be high. The message of these physicians was clear: there will be no cure available in a nuclear war. Prevention is the only way to take any medical responsibility for the health of the people.

Since then nuclear bombs have become even more powerful and disastrous and their number has increased. The number of casualties will thus be enormous and there will be no way to prepare for the bomb. Shelters and other means of civil defence will be useless in a nuclear attack. If they are not destroyed by the explosion, the surrounding environment will probably stay radioactive for a long period of time and the supply of electricity and water will cease. And it will be impossible for a number of people (including children and the wounded) to live in a small shelter for more than a few days, nor would there be any means of transporting the ill and the wounded to possibly preserved hospitals.

In addition to the effects of blast, fire and radiation, there may also be damage to electronic equipment by an electromagnetic pulse (EMP) resulting from a nuclear explosion. The area of an EMP on the earth's surface depends on the altitude of the explosion. High-altitude bursts (above 30 kilometres) can create source regions over 1500 kilometres in diameter, and a single hydrogen bomb exploded 300 kilometres over the central United States would create an EMP covering nearly all of North America. The electrical field produced by the EMP lasts only about a nanosecond, but its effects can be tremendous. The shielding of equipment can be done by metal enclosure, but this is difficult, expensive and seldom done.

The EMP induces large voltages and currents in power lines, communication cables, radio towers and in other long conductors, destroying them. It also affects semi-conductive chips by heating them instantly up to temperatures near the melting-point of the material, resulting in a failure of the device. By destroying computers the EMP can affect industrial processes, power and communication systems, and water supplies. All these effects will increase the disastrous consequences of nuclear attack and make efforts to help the victims extremely difficult.

There will also be global effects on the climate if a series of nuclear weapons is exploded above major cities as is the most likely scenario. The explosions and subsequent fires will cause vast amounts of soot and small particles to float in the atmosphere. This will create a large black cloud over the hemisphere, absorbing the sun's rays and thus cooling the earth's surface significantly. In the most pessimistic scenarios this nuclear winter will cause the earth's surface temperature to fall between −25 and −15°C in most parts of the northern hemisphere for months; others forecast the temperature fall to 'only' about 15°C in summer and 5°C in winter. But most meteorologists agree that a nuclear winter would cause a total climate catastrophe with the destruction of large areas of cultivated land and consequent famine. The natural world would suffer enormous damage.

It is clear, therefore, that the prevention of nuclear war is the utmost responsibility of all conscientious people world-wide. It is no less than a question of human survival.

ADDITIONAL READING

SIPRI (1981), *Nuclear Radiation in Warfare*, London: Taylor & Francis.

Chazov, Y.I., Ilyin, L.A. and A.K. Guskova (1984), *Nuclear War: The medical and biological consequences*, Moscow: Novosti Press Agency Publishing House.

IPPNW (1991), *Radioactive Heaven and Earth – The health and environmental effects of nuclear weapons testing in, on, and above the earth*, New York and London: The Apex Press and Zed Books.

Yokoro, K. and N. Kamada (1997), 'The Public Health Effects of the Use of Nuclear Weapons', in Levy, B.S. and V.W. Sidel. (eds), *War and Public Health*, Oxford University Press in cooperation with the American Public Health Association.

Address for correspondence

P.O. Box 722, SF 00101 Helsinki, Finland. email: katijuva@katto.kaapeli.fi

13 ATOMIC BOMB CASUALTY
Experiences from Hiroshima and Nagasaki

MASAO TOMONAGA

During the half-century since the first and second uses of nuclear weapons on human beings at Hiroshima and Nagasaki respectively, a number of medical consequences have emerged, mostly related to radiation exposure. More than 200,000 survivors (*hibakushas*), who had recovered from acute effects have been forced to face the fear of such consequences for the rest of their lives. Not only bodily but psychological problems have also affected them profoundly. In this chapter medical aspects of the atomic bomb casualties are described to provide basic knowledge of the effects of the nuclear weapon on human beings and to encourage readers to support demands for a world free of nuclear weapons.

Bombs

The nuclear bomb detonated over Hiroshima on 6 August 1945 at 8:17 am was a uranium-type device equivalent to 15 kilotons of TNT; that detonated over Nagasaki on 9 August at 11:02 am was a plutonium-type bomb as powerful as 20 kilotons of TNT. The former bomb destroyed over 90 per cent of Hiroshima City and the latter over 60 per cent of Nagasaki City. The physical energy of these bombs consisted of three elements: blast, heat and radiation, making up approximately 50 per cent, 35 per cent and 15 per cent of the total energy, respectively. Each blast was calculated to be 280m/sec at Ground Zero (the hypocentres), and about 30m/sec at 3 kilometres; each affected a radius of 11 kilometres after 30 minutes. The heat ray elaborated from the giant fireballs, which reached approximately one million centigrade at the moment of detonation and 7000°C on the fireball surface after 0.3 sec, radiated straight outwards. Wooden materials up to 3 kilometres distant were burnt out. Human skin was burned at distances of up to 3.5 kilometres.

The radiation energy was mainly composed of gamma and neutron rays, which radiated concentrically in air. Smaller amounts of alpha and beta particles reached the ground as fallout. According to the Dosimetry System 1986 (DS86) the open-air (kerma) dose was extremely high at 0.5 kilometres from the hypocentre in both Hiroshima and Nagasaki, approximately 4100 rad (cGy) and 10,000 rad (cGy) respectively; it declined rather rapidly in proportion to the distance, to 400 rad (cGy) and 790 rad (cGy) at 1.0 kilometres, and to 7 rad (cGy) and 12 rad (cGy) at 2.0 kilometres; it was almost negligible above 2.5 kilometres.[1] The organ doses were calculated by taking into account the shielding effects of the body thickness, providing slightly lower values compared with the kerma dose at a given distance. It was also estimated that those who entered the hypocentre area on the next day and stayed there for a week would have received approximately 10 rad (cGy) from the residual radiation due to fallout. The so-called black rain was observed in both cities on the day of bombing: a northwestern part of Hiroshima and a localized eastern part of Nagasaki. It was estimated that exposure to residual radiation due to the rains would have been 1–3 rad (cGy) in Hiroshima and 20–40 rad (cGy) in Nagasaki. Among the residents in the Nishiyama district of Nagasaki two cases of chronic myeloid leukaemia later developed .

Acute effects

Including deaths occurring within three months after the explosions, approximately 114,000 and 70,000 people in Hiroshima and Nagasaki respectively died of immediate or acute effects of the atomic bombs. The greatest number of deaths was caused by acute bodily effects of the explosions. Because of the three major components of the physical effects of the atomic bombs, those people in the proximity of the hypocentre were said to have been killed three times in a moment. Immediate deaths were caused by severe mechanical injuries due to the blast itself or by materials flown by the blast; at the same time their bodies were burnt out by the extraordinarily high temperatures. They were also exposed to lethal doses of radiation. The last component of the atomic bomb explosion would become noticeable only when a proximally-exposed person had survived, overcoming the injuries caused by the former two components.

Burns. Two types of burns were observed: flame or fire burns and flash burns. The former is a type of usual burn but the latter is unique in that the affected skin turned red immediately and became aggravated progressively within a few hours. These flash burns were typically observed as sharply demarkated areas of the exposed skin facing the direction of the hypocentre. Many *hibakushas* thus had a unilateral, anterior or posterior body-surface burn according to their positioning at the time of explosion. Any type of shielding protected the skin against burns; white clothing was a better protector for flash burns than black, and tightly-fitting clothes were less protective than loosely-fitting ones.

The flash burns were in recovery phase after 50 days, with some infections and pigmentation and frequently complicated with keloid formation. About 50 per cent of the survivors who were exposed in the proximity showed second-degree flash burns. Rare cases with burns were observed among survivors exposed at more than four kilometres in Nagasaki and two kilometres in Hiroshima. Medical care for survivors right after the explosion was largely related to this burn.

Mechanical injuries. Fractures, lacerations, contusions and abrasions were included in this category. Direct effects of the blast and indirect effects of the rumbling walls, flying debris and shattering glass caused injuries of variable degree. Glass wounds gave surgeons difficulties in excision of so many glass fragments. The relationship between these injuries and the distance from the hypocentre was not as marked as for the burns, lacerations were observed among survivors exposed beyond three kilometres. It was speculated that the mechanical injuries accounted for the largest number of immediate deaths and deaths among survivors immediately after the detonation.

Radiation. The earliest symptoms of acute radiation effects observed among the immediate survivors were nausea and vomiting, just like the symptoms observed in patients receiving intensive radiotherapy for their cancers. These acute symptoms lasted for a few hours or days depending on the exposure dose. Later on, within a few weeks, epilation, petechiae of the skin and oral cavity, and gastro-intestinal bleeding and/or diarrhoea appeared. These symptoms are typical of bone-marrow failure caused by high-dose radiation. The earliest medical surveys done by the Manhattan District Atomic Bombs Investigating Groups of the US Army and Japanese medical groups provided data that the maximum distances from the hypocentre in survivors showing epilation and/or petechiae of the skin extended to about three kilometres. According to the DS86 the estimated radiation kerma dose at two kilometres was only about 10 rad (cGy), as mentioned above, suggesting a considerable discrepancy between the observed clinical symptoms suggestive of an acute radiation effect and the dose estimated by the physical dosimetry. It is still uncertain whether the observed epilation and petechiae were actually related to the atomic bomb irradiation or not, due to the lack of a good biological dosimetry system. It could be tested by employing a very sensitive cytogenetic technique, which can detect chromosome injuries induced by radiation. Such an approach is now being undertaken for survivors.

About 15–20 per cent of deaths occurring among the immediate survivors after the detonations were considered to be due to acute radiation effects. And 40–50 per cent of all survivors showed any one of the radiation-related symptoms. The acute effects of atomic-bomb irradiation were also clearly demonstrated by hematological examinations; hemoglobin, white blood cell counts and platelet counts all declined in proportion to the exposure dose. Hematological examination was also performed for people who entered the proximity of the hypocentre for rescue early after the detonation, in order to clarify the possibility of exposure to residual radiation due to radioactive fallout from the explosions. There was no clear evidence of low white blood cell count suggestive of exposure to residual irradiation.

No first aid. It must be emphasized that those *hibakushas* who survived for a time after detonation could not have received any meaningful first aid, because almost all types of medical care centres were completely destroyed by the blast and fire in both cities. For instance Nagasaki Medical College, which had the largest hospital in Nagasaki City at that time and was located only 700 metres from the hypocentre, was 100 per cent destroyed and burnt out with the death of over 890 professors, students and nurses. Police and military rescue systems also collapsed due to the massive damage to personnel, facilities, and traffic and communications networks. Seriously-wounded *hibakushas* were transferred to naval hospitals located 30–40 km from Nagasaki. Skin burns and various types of body injury were properly treated by the standard medical care, but sulphur drugs and antibiotics were not available because of the war situation. Many survivors subsequently suffered from severe infections and died. Bone-marrow failure due to exposure to high-dose radiation further compromised the defence system of *hibakushas* after a few weeks. There were no treatment modalities for bone-marrow failure except blood transfusions for severe anemia. Thus, medical care was clearly insufficient due to the massive damage to the socio-medical structure of the two cities and the lack of knowledge about acute radiation.

Psychological effects. An extensive psychological study was performed by Lifton in the early 1960s, and was published in 1967.[2] The most intractable experience of atomic bomb explosion caused severe emotional damage to many *hibakushas*; they lost their identity for a while, because so many family members and acquaintances were lost instantaneously and they felt guilty when repeatedly seeing that they could do nothing to help those dying. Such a self-punishing sense lasted for many years. Such a psychological state made many *hibakushas* suffer from emotional numbness in daily life. Those who recovered good bodily health tended to face a lack of the will to work for a long period.

Social effects. Many *hibakushas* and their families also faced economic ruin due to the loss of their homes, all possessions, and working members. Economic incomes declined seriously, but no public aid was available due to the severe societal confusion just after the surrender of Japan to the allied forces. Thus the socio-economic fallout, persisting for several years after the bomb, prevented many *hibakushas* from recovering their previous social and economic level. Many children who lost their parents and relatives had to live and survive by themselves with serious handicaps. Young women with skin burns, especially on the face, tended to lose marriage opportunities.

Microcephaly due to in utero *exposure.* There were several hundreds cases of *in utero* exposure in both cities. Some reports indicated that spontaneous abortions were very frequent among pregnant women. However, there was no good research to clarify how many malformations were induced among foetuses exposed to the atomic bomb irradiation *in utero*. The only one evident sequel of *in utero* exposure was microcephaly (small head) which occurred among foetuses exposed at a gestational age of less than 16 weeks. They showed smaller head circumferences than fewer than half the controls. Most of them suffered from both mental and general developmental retardation.

Late effects

The most frequent medical consequences of the physical effects of the atomic bomb explosions was the occurrence of malignant diseases in organs which were exposed to high-dose radiation. Before the nuclear-weapons era, it was already well-known that ionizing radiation could be harmful enough to produce certain malignant diseases such as leukaemias and skin cancers. Since the discovery of X-rays by Dr Roentgen in 1895, a half-century had already passed and the application of X-rays to medical diagnosis and treatment had been established. In some instances occupational exposure to X-rays was apparently responsible for the occurrence of leukaemias and cancers. The same was true for the atomic bomb survivors who were subproximally (0.5–2.0km) exposed to the explosions. The first malignant disease observed among the survivors was leukaemia, which began to occur as early as two to three years after the explosions. It reached its peak after ten years and then declined. At this time solid cancers gradually began to increase. Non-malignant diseases were also induced by the radiation: cataract and hypothyroidism are representative of them.

Malignant diseases

Although the genuine molecular basis for the occurrence of leukaemias and cancers by radiation is still poorly understood, epidemiological evidence has clearly shown an increased risk for almost all types of malignant diseases. Among them leukaemias were the most threatening malignant disease among survivors who had recovered from the acute effects of the bombing because in the 1940s and 1950s leukaemia was diagnosed as fatal because of the lack of any specific therapy. After 50 years the leukaemia incidence declined to a near-normal level, whereas the increased risk of cancers continues.

Epidemiology of leukaemias. Leukaemias began to be seen in an increased number among survivors around two years after irradiation exposure, significantly observed simultaneously in both cities. The United States Academy of Sciences and the Ministry of Health and Welfare of the Japanese government started an extensive emidemiological study by creating a large-scale cohort of survivors. From 1950 onwards all leukaemias and related diseases were registered and diagnoses were confirmed by a group of expert hematologists from both countries. Professional statistics staff periodically analysed the accumulated data and calculated annual incidences of all leukaemias as a whole, and of each type of leukaemia separately.

The most important part of such an epidemiological study on the effects of atomic bomb radiation was to establish a good dosimetry system to provide a reliable estimation of the exposure dose for each *hibakusha* case of the cohort. In the early phase, the epidemiological study was based on the Dosimetry System (DS) 65 which was derived from the accumulated data of an experimental atomic bomb explosion in the Nevada Desert caused by detonating a plutonium bomb of the same size as that of Nagasaki. DS65 was later further developed to DS86 by correcting for several functions, such as the humidity of the air in the two cities at the time of the bombing and the neutron content in the radiation from the two bombs. DS86 is now accepted as the more precise and reliable dosimetry system applicable to most of the survivors.

From 1950 up until the present day the cohort study on the incidence of leukaemia as well as all other malignant diseases has provided a number of periodic reports from the Radiation Effects Research Foundation (RERF), formerly the Atomic Bomb Casualty Commission.[3] The cohorts consisted of 82,000 survivors in Hiroshima and 38,000 in Nagasaki, 120,000 in total at the start of the survey in 1950. Along with this cohort study

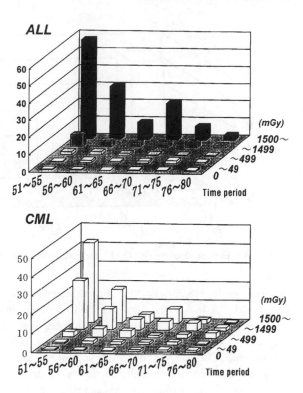

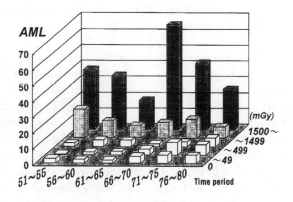

Figure 13.1 Atom bomb survivors' luekaemia: incidence by dose and period: (I) of acute lymphoid leukaemia (ALL) and chronic myeloid leukaemia (CML); and (II) of acute myeloid leukaemia (AML) and other types of leukaemia (Other).

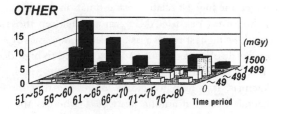

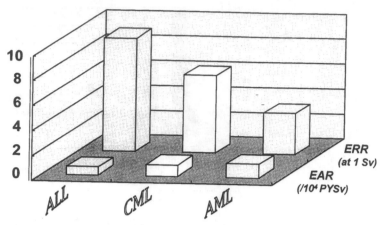

Figure 13.2 Excess absolute risk (EAR) and excess relative risk (ERR) of survivor's leukaemia

an open study which dealt with the entire *hibakusha* populations in both cities was conducted. All leukaemia cases occurring among the residents who were within 9 kilometres at the time of bombing in both cities were registered irrespective of whether they were cohort cases or not. Their exposure doses were calculated similarly as in the cohort study. Both types of epidemiological study guaranteed the quality of our leukaemia-detection programme. The following descriptions will be based mainly on the data of the RERF study; this leukaemia-incidence study was conducted with the cooperation of RERF, the Atomic Bomb Disease Institute of Nagasaki University Medical School and the Research Institute for Radiation Biology and Medicine of Hiroshima University.

Leukaemia types observed. There are four major types of human leukaemias, occurring in otherwise healthy persons (such leukaemias are called *de novo* leukaemias): (i) acute myeloid leukaemia (AML), acute lymphoid leukaemia (ALL), chronic myeloid leukaemia (CML); and chronic lymphoid leukaemia (CLL). Recently there has been an increasing number of leukaemias, mostly AML, that are considered as secondary leukaemias caused by anti-cancer drugs and/or radiation among cancer patients who had received such therapies.

As shown in Figure 13.1, among *hibakushas* three major types of leukaemia, AML, ALL, and CML, but not CLL, had a higher incidence in heavily-irradiated survivors than in minimally- or non-irradiated survivors. As shown in Figure 13.2, the cohort study provided the highest relative-risk estimation for ALL, the second highest risk for CML and the lowest risk for AML. Among children those exposed to high-dose radiation showed the highest relative risk for leukaemia, mostly ALL. In contrast CML and AML were mostly observed among adults exposed to high-dose radiation.

The leukaemias among *hibakushas* were morphologically basically similar to *de novo* leukaemias. It is hematologically interesting that three major types of human *de novo* leukaemia occurred among *hibakushas*, whereas the so-called secondary leukaemia is almost always AML. There was a famous report from the United Kingdom that the therapeutic radiation for anchylosing spondylitis caused AML as well as CML. Thus the radiation seems to be leukaemogenic on human beings in a similar way as in *de novo* leukaemias.

Dose response, incubation time and time course of leukaemias. Dose response was apparent for each type of leukaemia; the response curve was linear for ALL and CML, and quadratic for AML. The threshold dose or the lowest dose which can induce leukaemia could not be clearly determined by the statistical calculation, but it was considered a little below 50 rad (cGy).

Time from the exposure to occurrence of leukaemia was called the incubation time which means that during this period initiation of leukaemia cell transformation and the expansion of the abnormal leukaemic clone had induced clinical symptoms that led to the establishment of the diagnosis. The incubation time was shorter in proportion to increased dose; this trend was especially apparent for ALL and CML, and less distinct for AML.

For ALL and CML the increased risk reached its peak as late as ten years after exposure and declined rather quickly after that. In contrast, the AML risk did not show a peak but persisted for more than 30 years and is even now slightly elevated. Thus the time course of the increased risk is different between leukaemia types, indicating some basic difference in leukaemogenesis between them.

Treatment of the leukaemias. In the 1950s and 1960s, when the leukaemia risks among *hibakushas* were the highest, treatment modalities were still primitive; almost all cases of acute leukaemia died within a few months and of CML in a few years. Only palliative care, such as blood transfusion, was available. There was no chance to receive chemo-therapy or bone-marrow transplantation, which can now produce a considerable number of cures from leukaemia. This situation induced a profound fear for all *hibakushas* of soon developing a lethal sequel to the atomic bomb irradiation.

Cancers other than leukaemia. After ALL and CML began to show a decline around ten years after exposure, AML still persisted; in addition solid tumors such as breast cancer and thyroid cancer began to increase gradually among the survivors. The increased risk of solid tumors still persists. Cancers of the gastrointestinal tract, lung cancer, hepatocellular carcinoma, skin cancer and brain tumours are all reported to be sig-nificantly increased among heavily-irradiated survivors.[4] Cancers of the pancreas, ovaries and testes were not significantly increased. Almost all types of cancer with an increased incidence among *hibakushas* showed a linear response curve in proportion to the exposure dose, but the relative risk-estimation revealed that the risks were smaller in cancers than in leukaemias. However, it is important to recognize that the absolute risks, namely absolute numbers of patients, were larger for cancers than for leukaemia, because the cancer incidences are generally higher than leukaemia incidences.

The increased incidence for thyroid cancer observed in *hibakushas* was recently reproduced in the child population exposed to radioactive materials delivered from the accidental explosion of a nuclear power station in Chernobyl in 1986. Although the

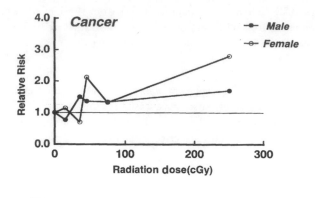

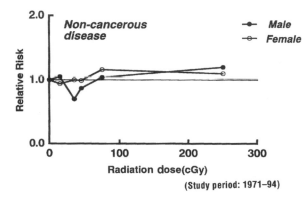

(Study period: 1971–94)

Figure 13.3 Periodic health survey for *hibakushas*: cancers (upper) and non-cancerous disease (lower)

exposure pattern is different between the two examples, external versus internal, it is apparent that the thyroid gland is highly susceptible to radiation and the sensitivity is higher in children than in adults.

Although malignant lymphoma and multiple myeloma were once reported to be increasing among heavily-irradiated populations, this remains controversial and surveys for these lymphoid malignancies are being continued by the RERF project.

General health survey and cancer-detection programme

As shown in Figure 13.3, periodic survey for causes of death among the atomic bomb survivors provided a persistently elevated risk for cancers. It is, therefore, important to conduct medical screening for various cancers which are relatively prevalent in the general Japanese population, such as gastric cancer, lung cancer, uterine cancer, and multiple myeloma. Such general health checks and the cancer-detection programme are supported by the Ministry of Health and Welfare of the Japanese government. Probably due to such an intensive health care system, the overall survival curve of *hibakushas* is slightly superior to that of non-*hibakushas* in Nagasaki City.

Non-malignant diseases/abnormalities

The biological effects of radiation are wide. At the cellular level apoptosis and necrosis occur in proportion to exposure dose. Cell death usually does not cause genetic defects that could be inherited by daughter cells. However, there seems to be a suitable range of doses that can cause genetic abnormalities in sublethally damaged cells. Many of the statistics on the morbidity of each organ showed increased risks of malignancies but some non-malignant diseases have also been reported.

Among them chronic hypothyroidism with positive auto-antibodies is representative. However, it is still not well-understood why radiation could cause autoimmune disorders. Many cases of pre-senile cataract were observed. Recently liver cirrhosis has been reported to be increased in proportion to exposure dose in the RERF cohort.

Another example of non-malignant disease is benign tumours; uterine myoma has been observed in increased incidence proportional to exposure dose. Benign thyroid nodules were also found to have increased in proportion to exposure dose. Gastric polyps or intestinal polyposis are now under investigation. These studies became feasible recently owing to the addition of echosonography, gastrofiberscopy, and colonofiberscopy and computed tomography to the routine health survey of the *hibakushas*.

Chromosome abnormalities in blood cells. It is a very important biological observation that many of the healthy *hibakushas* who were exposed to higher doses of the atomic bomb irradiation have chromosome abnormalities in their blood cells even now after half a century. The rate of chromosome abnormalities is apparently increased in proportion to the exposure dose as shown in Figure 13.4, indicating that such abnormalities were induced by the atomic bomb and have persisted until now.

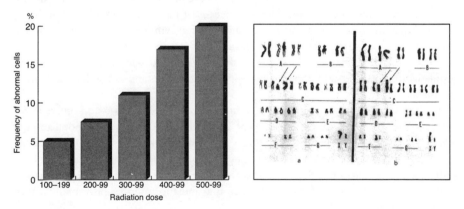

Figure 14.4 Chromosome abnormality in healthy atomic bomb survivors by exposure dose

Our study demonstrated that T lymphocytes as well as myeloid progenitor cells carried the same chromosome abnormality, providing evidence that the target cell of the radiation injury was hematopoietic stem cells. Therefore, the injured stem cells seem to have survived many years in *hibakushas'* bodies. If such chromosome abnormalities had caused genetic changes in certain important oncogens or anti-oncogenes, leukaemias or cancers could have been induced.[5]

Late psychological/psychiatric effects

The atomic bomb attacks on both cities caused a huge loss of (mainly civilian) human lives and the destruction of two city societies. Many surviving *hibakushas* lost their family members and relatives: not infrequently only one family member survived. As already described clearly in Dr Lifton's book,[6] these surviving *hibakushas* suffered from severe psychological damage induced by their extraordinary experience of the bombs.

Around 5 to 10 years after the bomb, there were many *hibakushas* who had lost interest in daily life and work, as already mentioned. This apparent psychological numbness was due to an overwhelming experience, the reaction now recognized and treated as post-traumatic stress disorder (PTSD). However, systematic psychological care was not available, because this syndrome had not been recognized by physicians and administrative officials at that time. *Hibakushas* thus fought a lonely battle against this long-lasting depressive state.

Except for some research conducted in the 1950s, there has been no systematic survey by psychologists or psychiatrists to evaluate scientifically the long-lasting psychological damage observed in many *hibakushas*. In 1995, on the occasion of the anniversary of the atomic bombings, a mass survey of the *hibakushas'* mental-health status began with a WHO screening test. More than 6,000 survivors have participated in this study. The screening questionnaire test, which consisted of ten simple questions concerning daily mental state, revealed a statistically significant increase in the proportion of people with mental problems, especially in the proximally-exposed population. A questionnaire asking them about their experiences at the time of bombing (including: loss of family members), about acute radiation-related symptoms such as hair loss and petechiae, and about the late symptoms or diseases considered to be the result of radiation exposure, further clarified that those *hibakushas* with the severest mental problems after 50 years were those whose experiences at the time of bombing were most traumatic.

It is apparent that the psychological reactions observed by Lifton and others in the 1960s persist today, 50 years after the event. Medical care for the general population of *hibakushas* has focused mainly on their bodily problems for more than a half century, but it is now clear, although unfortunately so late, that mental health care should have been addressed at the same time. Such a mental care programme has been started recently in Nagasaki. Medical care staff must recognize that radiation phobia profoundly affects many *hibakushas* even today.

Conclusion

The medical consequences of the first use of atomic bombs on human beings at Hiroshima and Nagasaki proved clearly the illegal and immoral nature of the nuclear weapons. These weapons destroy not only military facilities but also the whole of the neighbouring society. The results are overwhelming. No one in the proximity of the bombing can survive intact because of exposure to radiation. Without any visible bodily damage, many *hibakushas* died of acute radiation sickness.

Some survivors overcame the early period of radiation sickness only to suffer from late radiation effects. Most characteristically, a lethal disease, leukaemia, developed in the early period. Many survivors died of this malignancy and many more later developed solid tumours, such as breast cancer. The surviving *hibakushas* were severely affected mentally as well as bodily, leading to complicating health problems and making health care difficult.

All of these facts indicate that nuclear weapons are weapons that should never again be used. It is unfortunate that more than 30,000 nuclear warheads are still retained by the superpowers. Nuclear deterrence theory and nuclear arsenals must be seriously and intensively challenged by political, military, economic and medical arguments. The nuclear-weapons era must be overcome with the discovery of a new theory and practical plan for of international security.

REFERENCES

1. Roesch W.C. (ed.) (1987), *US-Japan Joint Reassessment of Atomic Bomb Radiation Dosimetry in Hiroshima and Nagasaki*. Radiation Effects Research Foundation, Hiroshima, Japan, 1987.
2. Lifton, R.J. (1967), *Death in Life, Survivors of Hiroshima*, New York: Random House.
3. Preston, D.L., Kusumi, S., Tomonaga, M., Izumi, S., Ron, E., Kuramoto, A., Kamada, N., Dohy, H., Matuo, T., Nonaka, H., Thompson, D.E., Soda, M. and K. Mabuchi (1994), 'Cancer Incidence in Atomic Bomb Survivors. Part III: leukaemia, lymphoma and multiple myeloma, 1950–1987'. *Radiation Research* 137: s68–97; and Shimizu, Y., Kato, H. and W.J. Schull (1990), 'Studies of the Mortality of A-bomb Survivors, 9. Mortality, 1950–1985: Part 2. Cancer mortality based on the recently revised dose (DS86)', *Radiation Research* 121: 120–41.
4. See Shimizu *et al.*, n. 3 above.
5. Amenomori, T., Honda, T., Otake, M., Tomonaga, M. and M. Ichimaru (1988), 'Growth and Differentiation of Circulating Hematopoietic Stem Cells with Atomic Bone Irradiation-induced Chromosome Abnormalties', *Experimental Hematology* 16: 849–54.
6. See n. 2 above.

Address for correspondence

Department of Hematology, Molecular Medicine Unit, Atomic Bomb Disease Institute, Nagasaki University School of Medicine, Sakamoto 1-12-4, Nagasaki, Japan.

Tel: 95-849-7109; Fax: 95-849-7113; Email: tomomasa@net.nagasaki-u.ac.jp

14 NUCLEAR TERRORISM

FRANK BARNABY

Some terrorist groups contain people with considerable scientific and technical skills. The construction of the explosive device that destroyed the PanAm jumbo jet over Lockerbie on 21 December 1988 and of the nerve-gas weapon used in the Tokyo underground by the Aum Shinrikyo group on 20 March 1997 required considerable skills. The fabrication of a primitive nuclear explosive, as opposed to a military nuclear weapon, would require no greater skill than that required to make the Lockerbie bomb or the Tokyo nerve-gas weapon. Sub-national groups now have access to professional scientific and technical skills and to large sums of money; plutonium, which can be used to fabricate nuclear explosives, is increasingly available; relatively small amounts of plutonium are needed for a nuclear explosive; the open literature makes available the technical information needed to design and fabricate a nuclear explosive: only a small number of competent people are necessary to make such a device: for all these reasons, the risk of nuclear terrorism is steadily increasing. The best (perhaps the only) way of preventing a terrorist group obtaining plutonium and fabricating a nuclear explosive would be to ban the reprocessing of spent nuclear reactor-fuel elements. If this is not done, it may be only a matter of time before nuclear terrorists destroy a city in a nuclear explosion.

The risk that sub-national groups will acquire nuclear explosives in increasing. Such groups – commonly, and usually disparagingly, called terrorists, need to move continually to higher levels of violence. Recently, we have seen the level escalate from the sabotage of jumbo jets to the Tokyo nerve-gas attack in 1997. The Tokyo incident shows that some of the leaders of these groups have considered the pros and cons of using weapons of mass destruction, nuclear, chemical and biological.

They had, until recently, decided that killing, or threatening to kill, large numbers of people indiscriminately, women and children included, or contaminating large areas, would not further their aims. But the Tokyo nerve-gas attack shows that they no longer believe this. The moral restraints on mass killing have weakened.

The next rung on the terrorist ladder of escalation may well be the acquisition and use of a nuclear weapon. As plutonium and highly-enriched uranium become more available world-wide, it is increasingly possible for a sub-national group to steal, or otherwise illegally acquire, civil or military weapon-usable fissile material and fabricate its own nuclear-explosive device to detonate it or threaten to detonate it.

Nuclear terrorism

Terrorist groups have shown themselves to be sophisticated and skilled. The construction of the explosive device that destroyed the PanAm jumbo jet over Lockerbie, for example, required considerable skill, as did the construction of the nerve-gas weapon used in the Tokyo underground. Sub-national groups now have access to professional scientific and technical skills and to large sums of money.

The combination of these with the increasing availability of the fissile materials which can be used to fabricate nuclear explosives; the relatively small amounts of fissile material, particularly plutonium, needed for a nuclear explosive; the availability in the open literature of the technical information needed to design and fabricate a nuclear explosive; and the small number of competent people necessary to fabricate a primitive nuclear explosive must give rise to considerable concern.

This is not to suggest that making a device is the only nuclear terrorist threat. Konrad Kellen lists other nuclear activities that a sub-national group may become involved in:

Making or stealing of a nuclear weapon and its detonation; the making or stealing of a nuclear weapon for blackmail; the damaging of a nuclear plant for radioactive release; the attack on a nuclear-weapons site to spread alarm; the attack on a nuclear plant to spread alarm; the holding of a nuclear plant for blackmail; the holding off-site of nuclear plant personnel; the theft of fissionable material for blackmail or radioactive release; the theft or sabotage of things nuclear for demonstration purposes; and an attack on a transporter of nuclear weapons or materials.[1]

Three designs of crude nuclear explosives would be adequate for most purposes of a terrorist group intent on nuclear terrorism:

1 *The gun using highly-enriched uranium as the fissile.* This is the simplest crude device to design and construct and the most likely one to produce a powerful nuclear explosion, possibly with an explosive yield of up to the equivalent of that of several thousand tons of TNT. But it would be harder for a terrorist group to acquire highly-enriched uranium than plutonium.

2 *The implosion type, using a solid sphere of plutonium metal as the fissile material.* This is essentially a crude version of the atomic bomb which destroyed Nagasaki. It is the most difficult of the three to design and construct, but is within the capabilities of a significantly large terrorist group. It would, however, be difficult, although not impossible, to obtain with this design a nuclear explosion with an explosive yield greater than that equivalent to the explosion of a few thousand tons of TNT.

3 *The implosion-type device using plutonium oxide as the fissile material.* This is perhaps the most likely nuclear device to be constructed by terrorists because of the increasing and widespread availability of plutonium oxide. It may also be the most attractive of the three designs because of the threat of the widespread dispersion of large amounts of

plutonium even if the device produces no nuclear explosion. It is very likely, however, that the device would produce a nuclear explosion equivalent in explosive yield to that of tens, or even hundreds, of tons of TNT.

Terrorist use of highly-enriched uranium

A terrorist group would find it easier to fabricate a nuclear device using highly-enriched uranium (HEU) than plutonium, even weapons-grade plutonium. This is because:

> the neutron source from spontaneous fission in such material is smaller than in even the best grades of plutonium by a factor of more than a thousand. In the relatively slow-moving gun-type device one might wish to assemble a couple of critical masses or so, which would imply bringing together something like 50 kilogrammes of 94 per cent U-235, since the critical mass with a reflector can be about half the bare critical mass of 52 kilogrammes.[2]

Luis Alvarez, a nuclear-weapons physicist, has emphasized the ease of constructing a nuclear explosive with HEU:

> With modern weapons-grade uranium, the background neutron rate is so low that terrorists, if they have such material, would have a good chance of setting off a high-yield explosion simply by dropping one half of the material onto the other half. Most people seem unaware that if separated HEU is at hand it's a trivial job to set off a nuclear explosion... even a high school kid could make a bomb in short order.[3]

In a nuclear weapon using HEU in a gun-type assembly, a mass of HEU, less than the critical mass, is fired down a cylinder into another less-than-critical mass of HEU placed at the end of the cylinder. When the two masses come together they form a super-critical mass and a nuclear explosion takes place.

A primitive gun-type weapon could use a thick-walled cylindrical 'barrel', with an inner diameter of about 8 centimetres and a length of about 50 centimetres. A cylindrical mass of HEU, enriched to, for example, 90 per cent in uranium-235 and weighing about 15 kilograms, would be placed at the top of the barrel. The larger mass of uranium, weighing about 40 kilograms, would be placed at the bottom of the barrel. This mass would have hollowed out of it a cylinder of the same size as the smaller uranium mass which thus would fit in it snugly. A high-explosive charge would be placed at the top of the barrel, behind the smaller mass of uranium. This charge could be fired from a distance by a remote-control device operated by an electronic signal. The total length of the nuclear explosive device is likely to be no more than about one metre and about 25 centimetres in diametre. It should weigh no more than 300 or so kilograms. It could easily be transported by, and detonated in, an ordinary van.

A crude nuclear weapon using highly-enriched uranium should explode with an explosive power equivalent to that of a few hundred tons of TNT.

Terrorist use of plutonium

Now and in the near future, a terrorist group may find it easier to acquire civil plutonium than HEU because the amount of plutonium available from civil reprocessing plants will rapidly increase as more reprocessing capacity becomes operational. Then increased amounts of plutonium separated from spent nuclear-power reactor fuel will be stored in a number of countries and it will become easier to obtain plutonium illegally. The storage normally takes place as plutonium oxide (PuO_2). If plutonium is stolen from a reprocessing plant it is, therefore, likely to be in the oxide form.

A nuclear device could be constructed using plutonium either in metal form or as the oxide. Whereas the design using HEU, described above, would have a high probability of producing an explosion equivalent to that of a few thousand tons of TNT, a primitive nuclear explosive using plutonium would only yield an explosion of this magnitude if the plutonium was in metal form, using a design similar to that of the Nagasaki bomb. But to convert the oxide into plutonium metal is a straightforward chemical process.

A small group of people with appropriate skills could design and fabricate such a crude weapon. All the physics data needed by a competent nuclear physicist to design a crude nuclear device have been published in the scientific journal *Nature*.[4] The group would need access to machine-shop facilities, which could be hired.

A sub-national group would probably use an amount of plutonium close to the critical mass – say, about eight kilograms of plutonium metal. Because this mass is close to the critical mass, it would not be necessary to use shaped charges to compress the plutonium to produce a super-critical mass. It would be sufficient to stack conventional high explosives around the plutonium.

A number of detonators would be positioned in the high explosive. If a large number of detonators, say, 50 or 60, is used, the shock wave is likely to be symmetrical enough to compress the plutonium satisfactorily. The detonators should be fired as simultaneously as possible. This can be done using an electronic circuit which generates a high-voltage square wave. The detonators could be fired by remote control.

The construction of a nuclear-explosive device using plutonium oxide would be much simpler than one using plutonium metal. The oxide is much simpler and safer to handle. Plutonium metal may, for example, burst into flames in air, as sodium may do; also, a sub-national group is likely to want to avoid the stage of conversion from the oxide to the metal.

The disadvantage with plutonium oxide is that the critical mass is much higher than that of the metal, about 35 kilograms. The radius of this sphere of plutonium oxide would be about 9 centimetres. In a crude nuclear-explosive device, the plutonium oxide could be contained in a spherical vessel placed in the centre of a large mass of a conventional high explosive. A number of detonators would be used to set off the explosive, probably by remote control. The shock wave from the explosion could compress the plutonium enough to produce some energy from nuclear fission.

The size of the nuclear explosion from such a crude device is impossible to predict. But even if it were only equivalent to the explosion of a few tens of tonnes of TNT it would completely devastate the centre of a large city. There would, however, be an excellent chance of an explosion equivalent to at least a hundred tons of TNT.

The explosive power of the device will depend mainly on how close to critical is the mass of the plutonium oxide. This, in turn, will depend on the risk the people making the device are prepared to take. If they get close to criticality they may be exposed to a strong burst of neutrons, a major health hazard.

A crude nuclear device constructed by a terrorist group could be contained in a vehicle such as a van. The van could be positioned so that, even if the device, when detonated, did not produce a significant nuclear explosion, the explosion of the chemical high explosives would widely disperse the plutonium. If incendiary materials were mixed with the high explosives, the explosion would be accompanied by a fierce fire.

The plutonium would burn in the fire, producing small particles. These would be taken up into the atmosphere in the fire-ball and scattered far and wide downwind. A large fraction of the particles would be small enough to be inhaled into the lungs. These particles would become embedded in the lungs and would irradiate the surrounding tissue with alpha-particles, emitted when plutonium nuclei underwent radioactive decay. Irradiation by alpha-particles is very likely to cause lung cancer.

The threat of dispersion makes a crude nuclear explosive device using plutonium a particularly attractive weapon for nuclear terrorists. The dispersal of many kilograms of plutonium over an area of a city would make the area uninhabitable until it was decontaminated, a procedure which could take many months. The great fear of radioactivity harboured by the general population considerably enhances the threat.

The threat of dispersion is perhaps the most serious danger that would arise from the acquisition of plutonium by a terrorist group. In fact, this danger is so great that the mere possession of significant quantities of plutonium by a terrorist group is a threat in itself. If a terrorist group proved to a government that it had plutonium in its possession it could effectively blackmail the government.

The government would not need to be convinced that the group had the expertise to design and construct an effective nuclear explosive device. It would know that even an ineffective nuclear device would scatter plutonium over a large area. And this would be threat enough for the terrorists' purposes.

Could a terrorist group make a nuclear explosive?

This question has been addressed by the scientists at the Office of Technology Assessment (OTA) of the US Congress. The OTA's conclusion is that:

> a small group of people, none of whom have ever had access to the classified literature, could possibly design and build a crude nuclear explosive device. They would not necessarily require a great deal of technological equipment or have to undertake any experiments. Only modest machine-shop facilities that could be contracted for without arousing suspicion would be required. The financial resources for the acquisition of necessary equipment on open markets need not exceed a fraction of a million dollars. The group would have to include at a minimum, a person capable of researching and understanding the literature in several fields and a jack-of-all-trades technician. There is a clear possibility that a clever and competent group could design and construct a device which would produce a significant nuclear yield (i.e., a yield much greater than the yield of an equal mass of high explosive).[5]

Similar conclusions were drawn by a group of American nuclear-weapons designers. They pointed out that there are some potential hazards in constructing a crude nuclear explosive device, including:

those arising in the handling of a high explosive; the possibility of inadvertently inducing a critical configuration of the fissile material at some stage in the procedure; and the chemical toxicity or radiological hazards inherent in the materials used.[6]

Lovins argues that the hazards should not be exaggerated. He shows that the radiation dose rates from plutonium, including reactor-grade plutonium oxide, are such that they would not deter a person from handling it. And he concludes that, given sensible precautions against achieving criticality accidentally, a terrorist group constructing a nuclear explosive would not face serious radiological hazards. In any case, such a group would probably be prepared to take some risks to achieve its purposes.[7]

The explosive yield of a crude nuclear device using reactor-grade plutonium as the fissile material would be unpredictable. But this is not likely to bother a terrorist group. It is likely to be satisfied with any yield above the equivalent of ten tons or so of TNT. And because such a device would disperse plutonium, even if there was no nuclear explosion, unpredictability is not an issue.

The consequences of the use of a nuclear explosive by a terrorist group

The largest conventional bombs used in warfare so far had explosive powers equivalent to about 10 tons of TNT. The largest terrorist explosion so far has been equivalent to about 5 tons of TNT (the bomb used to attack the US Marines' barracks in Beirut). A nuclear explosion equivalent to that of 100 tons of TNT in an urban area would be a catastrophic event, with which the emergency services would be totally unable to cope effectively.

Exploded on or near the ground, such a nuclear explosive would produce a crater, in dry soil or dry soft rock, about 30 metres across. For small nuclear explosions, with explosive powers less than a few kilotons, the lethal action of radiation covers a larger area than that affected by blast and heat. The area of lethal damage from the blast produced by a 100-ton nuclear explosion would be roughly 0.4 square kilometres; the lethal area for heat would be about 0.1 square kilometres; and that for radiation would be roughly 1.2 square kilometres.

Persons in the open within 600 metres of such an explosion would very probably be killed by the direct effects of radiation, blast or heat.[8] Many other deaths would occur, particularly from indirect blast effects: from the collapse of buildings, from being thrown into objects or from falling debris. And a large number of people would be seriously injured by blast, heat and radiation effects. Heat and blast will cause fires, from broken gas pipes, petrol in cars and so on. The area and extent of damage from fires may well exceed those from the direct effects of heat.

A nuclear explosion at or near ground level will produce a relatively large amount of early radioactive fallout. Heat from fires will cause the radioactive particles to rise into the air; they will then be blown downwind, eventually falling to the ground under gravity at rates and distances depending on the velocity of the wind and the weather conditions. The area significantly contaminated with radioactive fallout will be uninhabitable until decontaminated. The area concerned may be several square kilometres and it is likely to take a long time to decontaminate it to a level sufficiently free of radioactivity to be acceptable to the public.

An explosion of this size, involving many hundreds of deaths and injuries, would paralyse the emergency services. They would find it difficult even to deal effectively with the dead. Many, if not most, of the seriously injured would die from lack of medical care. In the UK, for example, there are only a few hundred burn beds in the whole National Health Service. There would be considerable delays in releasing injured people trapped in buildings. And, even for those not trapped, it would take a significant time to get ambulances through to them and then to transport them to hospital. Therefore, a high proportion of the seriously injured would not get medical attention in time to save them. Experience shows that when large explosions occur in an urban area the panic that sets in also affects the trained emergency personnel. This would be considerably enhanced by the radioactive fallout accompanying a nuclear explosion.

Terrorist attacks on nuclear-power stations

A modern nuclear power reactor generates about 1000 million watts of electricity, enough to provide the annual electrical power needs of a city with a population of about a million people. The attractiveness to terrorists of attacking such a nuclear power reactor is obvious. A terrorist attack on a nuclear-power reactor could release radio-activity. From the accident at the Chernobyl nuclear power reactor in April 1986 we know that nuclear reactors can release huge amounts of radioactive isotopes which can be scattered over very large areas by the wind. The risk of extensive radioactive contamination considerably enhances the danger of a terrorist attack on a nuclear-power station.

In this context, it should be remembered that an increasing number of spent reactor-fuel elements are being stored at nuclear-power reactors. The storage area for these elements, each of which contains a huge amount of radioactivity, may be specifically attacked deliberately to release radioactivity.

Spent-fuel elements are stored at the nuclear plant, which may contain one or more reactors, in a pool filled with water, located either inside the vessel containing the reactor or outside the containment but close to it. At some nuclear power plants, there is an additional facility to store spent-fuel elements within the plant boundary but away from the reactors. Huge amounts of liquid high-level radioactive waste is stored in tanks at reprocessing plants. The sabotage of these tanks by terrorists could release a large amount of radioactivity.

There is much public fear of exposure to radiation from radioactive materials. These factors all increase the attractiveness of an attack on a nuclear power reactor for terrorists. An attack on a nuclear-power plant would attract a huge amount of media publicity. A major aim of terrorists is to maximize media coverage of their activities to publicize their cause, which again increases its attractiveness.

In a recent study of the risk of terrorist attacks on nuclear power plants, Gordon Thompson explains that although there has so far not been any terrorist attack on a nuclear-power plant severe enough to cause a release of radioactivity, there is a worrying history of lesser attacks. In March 1973, the guards at the nearly completed nuclear-power reactor at Lima, Argentina were overpowered in an attack by 15 armed men. In

December 1977, four Basque terrorists detonated bombs which damaged the reactor vessel and steam generator, killing two workmen, at a nuclear-power plant under construction at Arminza, Spain. In January 1982, four antitank rockets were fired at the Superphenix fast-breeder reactor at Creys-Malville, France, damaging the containment vessel of the nearly-completed reactor. In December 1982, African National Congress fighters detonated four bombs inside a nuclear-power reactor under construction at Melkbosstrand, the Cape, South Africa. Other examples could be given.[9]

Gordon Thompson describes a possible scenario for a terrorist attack on a nuclear-power plant. If the main objective is to make a dramatic threat or take the plant out of production, the attack could be focused on peripheral parts of the plant, such as the switchyard or the condenser cooling-water system (cooling towers, cooling water canals connecting the plant to a nearby body of water, etc.). Such an attack could challenge the plant's safety systems (e.g., the emergency diesel generators). Failure of those systems to respond appropriately would then lead to a plant accident.

If the main objective is to

> produce a radioactive release, the attackers will seek to interrupt cooling to the reactor core and/or the spent-fuel pool, either by draining the coolant or by interrupting the processes that remove heat from the coolant. At the same time, the attackers will presumably breach the reactor containment, to maximize the size of the radioactive release. The release could begin within minutes or hours after the cooling is interrupted, depending on the scenario. If the attackers have achieved complete control of the plant, they could arrange for the release to occur after they have left the plant. Some reactor types are susceptible to violent power excursions, as occurred at the Chernobyl plant in 1986.

As at Chernobyl, a large power excursion could cause the reactor core to melt, leading to the release of a huge amount of radioactivity. Terrorists could, therefore, initiate a massive nuclear disaster. This would have all the health consequences associated with the Chernobyl nuclear disaster.

Nuclear power reactors are more vulnerable than they need be because the possibility of a terrorist attack has not been taken into account in the planning process for nuclear power. Consequently, nuclear-power reactors have not been designed or located to withstand attacks by determined and effective terrorists. The reactors are, therefore, vulnerable to an attack which could result in the release of radioactivity in amounts similar to or greater than those released during the 1986 Chernobyl nuclear accident.

Conclusions

The main reason why the risk of nuclear terrorism is growing is the increasing amount of separated plutonium in the world. Increasing amounts of plutonium are being removed from nuclear weapons and stored under civilian control. More and more plutonium from civilian nuclear-power reactors is being chemically separated from spent reactor-fuel elements in commercial reprocessing plants and kept in civilian plutonium stores. The global stockpile of separated plutonium is now about 500 tons, about half of it civilian and half military. The civilian stock is increasing year by year. Only a few kilograms are needed to make a nuclear explosive.

There are no economically viable peaceful uses for plutonium at least until breeder reactors have been demonstrated to be able to generate electricity economically. This is unlikely to happen for several decades, if ever. Most plutonium will, therefore, have to be stored or permanently disposed of.

Permanent storage could be achieved by incorporating plutonium in glass (Purex) blocks, perhaps mixed with high-level radioactive waste to prevent its removal, and then burying the vitrified blocks in deep geological repositories. In the meantime, all commercial reprocessing plants should be closed down. Only then will the risk of nuclear terrorism be reduced to an acceptable level.

REFERENCES

1. Kellen, K. (1987), 'The Potential for Nuclear Terrorism; a discussion', in Leventhal, P. and Y. Alexander (eds), *Preventing Nuclear Terrorism*. Massachusetts: Lexington Books.
2. Mark, Carson J., Taylor, T., Eyster, E., Maraman, W. and J. Welchsler (1987), 'Can Terrorists Build Nuclear Weapons?'. In Leventhal, P. and Y. Alexander (eds), *Preventing Nuclear Terrorism*, Massachusetts: Lexington Books.
3. Alvarez, L. W. (1987), *Adventures of a Physicist*, p. 125.
4. Lovins, A. B. (1980), 'Nuclear Weapons and Power-Reactor Plutonium', *Nature*, 28 February, pp. 817–23 and typographical corrections, 13 March:. 190.
5. OTA. (1977), *Nuclear Proliferation and Safeguards*, Washington DC: US Congress, Office of Technology Assessment.
6. See n. 2 above.
7. See n. 4 above.
8. Rotblat, Joseph (1988), *Nuclear Radiation in Warfare*, London: Taylor and Francis, 1988.
9. Thompson, G. (1996), 'War, Terrorism and Nuclear Power Plants', February.

FURTHER READING

1. Hounam, P. and S. McQuillan (1995), *The Mini-Nuke Conspiracy*, London: Faber and Faber; Imai, R. (1994), *Plutonium*, No. 3, October.
2. Selden, R. W. (1976), *Reactor Plutonium and Nuclear Explosives*, California: Lawrence Livermore Laboratory.
3. US Department of Defense (1987), *World Commerce in Nuclear Materials*, Washington DC: US Department of Defense, November.
4. Blix, H. (1990), Letter to the Nuclear Control Institute. Washington DC.

Address for correspondence

Brandreth, Station Road, Chilbolton, Stockbridge, Hants S020 6AW, UK

15 NON-LETHAL WEAPONS

NICK LEWER

Non-lethal weapons (NLWs) have been used throughout history, but rapid advances in technology are making available a range of weapons which offer enhanced opportunities before having to resort to lethal force, and have the potential of qualitatively influencing both military operations (especially peace support operations) and civil law enforcement. Chapter 15 will define NLWs, review the main non-lethal technologies and their operational applications, look at potential health dangers and implications for international arms control and disarmament conventions and declarations, and point to future concerns surrounding NLWs.

Meeting contemporary security challenges

During the last few decades of the 20th century the world experienced an increasing number of intrastate wars such as those in Bosnia, Croatia, Somalia, Afghanistan, Cambodia, Rwanda, Burundi, Zaire, Sri Lanka, Burma, East Timor and Sudan, which are violent, messy and dirty. These have been characterized by indiscriminate killing and genocide, the majority of the victims being civilians and non-combatants. In these conflicts the rule of government is often non-existent, international humanitarian law is ignored and gross abuse of fundamental human rights is a regular occurrence.

International reaction to these humanitarian crises has demanded intervention, and that 'something must be done'. In some instances, such as Bosnia and Somalia, this has led to the dispatch of UN peacekeeping, peace enforcement or peace support missions. These military missions, which fall into the category of Operations Other Than War (OOTW), have asked combat-trained troops to perform tasks often more akin to policing and observer roles within the constraints of increasing pressure from public opinion for 'bloodless' and less-lethal warfare, and under the watchful eye of the global media (the 'CNN' factor).

To help them do this, a range of non-lethal weapons (NLWs) has become available which give military force commanders more options to resolve situations before having to resort to lethal methods, so that the force applied is proportional to the threat. These specific non-lethal technologies, in association with other developments in the areas of precision targeting, delivery platforms, command and control systems, intelligence gathering, miniaturization and portable power supply units, can offer credible alternatives to lethal force in certain situations.

NLWs, which may be used as stand-alone systems or as force multipliers, can help to: reduce the risk of excessive military force against armed and unarmed opponents, promote international political support for peace support operations, and minimize infrastructure destruction and environmental degradation. These factors should contribute to, and enhance, post-conflict reconstruction and conflict resolution, and proponents claim that NLWs offer the prospect that war can be fought, and violence contained and controlled, in a more benign and humane manner.[1]

What are non-lethal weapons?

Non-Lethal Weapons (NLWs) can be described in terms of their 'ideal' design and intent characteristics which include:

- they should only incapacitate people or disable equipment, with minimal collateral damage to buildings and the environment;
- they should be discriminate and not cause unnecessary suffering;
- their effects should be temporary and reversible;
- they should provide alternatives to, or raise the threshold for, use of lethal force.

The very term non-lethal, however, has been subject to criticism as both a euphemism and an oxymoron. Other phrases which have been suggested that are said to reflect the real nature of NLWs include: 'less than lethal', 'pre-lethal', 'system disabling', 'non-injurious immobilizers', 'strategic immobilizers' 'denial of service concepts', 'soft-kill solutions', 'adjustable lethality' and 'weapons which do not cross the death barrier'.

The concept of non-lethality is not new[2] and there already exist NLWs, such as plastic and rubber bullets, incapacitating gases, electric stun guns, smoke and obscurants, and materials which disrupt power supplies. However, rapid advances in technology are making available a new generation of NLWs which will qualitatively affect the application of NLWs in military operational situations. NLWs have also found wide application with civil law-enforcement agencies in the arrest of violent criminals, personal protection for police officers, stopping vehicles, riot control and hostage rescue.

Non-lethal technologies

NLWs can be identified across widely-disparate technologies and may be loosely classified into antipersonnel and antimateriel weapons, although of course weapons designed for antimateriel purposes could also affect personnel. Those technologies which show

Table 15.1: Non-lethal technologies

Non-lethal technology	description
Ammunition	dual purpose lethal/non-lethal ammunition – conventional bullets encased inside a plastic sabot. At low muzzle velocities the sabot does not peel off the bullet resulting in a blunt, less-than-lethal munitions. At higher velocities the sabot peels off giving lethal effect
Anti-traction	water soluble polymers to produce 'super-slippery' surfaces
Biotechnology and genetic engineering	selective genetic/racial characteristics could form the basis for such NLWs; agents which degrade petroleum products
Carbon fibres	ultra-fine fibres to short out power supplies and disrupt electrical and electronic equipment
Chemical (anti-personnel)	incapacitants and inflammatories such as CS and Oleoresin Capsicum (OC) sprays; calmative agents which lower aggression and/or cause sleepiness
Combustion inhibitors	cut out vehicle engines using electrical or chemical methods
Computer viruses	disrupt, corrupt or destroy computer programmes
Defoliants	destroy vegetation thus denying food and cover to an enemy
Distraction devices	light and sound effects, which can be combined with irritants and dyes
Electrical	high voltage (as high as 300,000 volts) stun guns and 'Taser' weapons; blunt projectile ammunition which will stick to the target using a glue or small barbs and then deliver a short high-voltage pulse
Embrittlements	change the molecular structure of metals so they crack easily
Entanglement Nets	sensor guided nets (which may also be adhesive coated or electrified) to trap people or, for example, to entangle the rotor blades of helicopters
Environmental	climate control -rain making, fog dispersing
Foams	(1) sticky foams – barrier and capture systems (2) aqueous foams – high expansion foams deployed as visual and aural obscurants, and can make floor slippery. May be combined with irritant or inflammatory chemicals such as CS or oleoresin capsicum (OC)
High power microwaves (HPM)	destroy electronic systems. Can be produced by airborne nuclear explosions – which also causes a huge electromagnetic pulses (EMP) – and conventional explosives; disable personnel
Infra/ultra sound	directed acoustic pressure waves which can cause physical destruction.
Kinetic energy (KE)	wooden baton rounds, rubber bullets, rubber stingballs and pellets, plastic bullets, sponge grenades, beanbags, JellyBaton
Lasers	(1) low energy which can either temporarily or permanently blind; laser batons to distract and disorientate; (2) high energy laser can cause extensive burning
Loud noise/sound	acoustic generators to incapacitate or disorientate people
Odour	malodorous liquids ('skunk shots')
Optical	flash/explosive devices which dazzle or cause temporary blindness, strobe lights which confuse and disorientate
Soil destabilizers	alters properties of soil causing it to slide. Prevents passage of vehicles.
Sonic beam	shock waves or directed blast devices and ultrasonic beam weapons
Subliminal suggestion and holographic projection	subconscious dissemination of propaganda and information, and projection of spatial images
Super adhesives	prevent movement of vehicles and personnel
Super caustics/ corrosives	corrode/ degrade structural materials in buildings - damage irreversible
Vomiting agents	causes nausea (such as DN gas)
Water cannon	high pressure jets which may be marked with a dye to enable identification of targets, and also electrified

potential for dual-use applications (in civil and military sectors) have received increased research and development resources. NLWs can be delivered from a variety of platforms including unmanned aerial vehicles (UAVs), handheld launchers and dispersers, land vehicles and ship and piloted aircraft-based delivery systems. Table 15.1 gives examples of non-lethal technologies that are either under development or in production (this is by no means an exhaustive list).

In some countries 'self-defence' and 'personal-security' NLWs can easily be purchased by the general public, and they are now being extensively marketed via the Internet. These include electronic stun guns (capable of delivering 300,000 volts), incapacitating and inflammatory sprays (oleoresin capsicum (OC) Pepper and CS), and ultrasonic weapons.

Dangers to health

There are serious risks and dangers associated with NLWs. Kinetic-energy (KE) weapons such as rubber and plastic bullets can cause serious blunt trauma damage, the head, neck and sternal area in the chest being particularly vulnerable. Organs at risk are the heart, liver and spleen. In research carried out by Cuadros, he found that damage ranged from contusion of the heart to rupture of the heart muscles and the severing of arteries in the target organs, the latter leading to fatal bleeding if untreated.[3] New designs for KE weapons have attempted to minimize these problems. For example, high-density plastic bullets with a foam-rubber nose (sponge grenades), and the Jelly Baton which has a rubber core and plastic casing (causing it to expand momentarily on impact), have been developed.

To be effective in combat or violent riot situations chemical NLWs must act almost instantaneously, so high doses must be used. The effect of these on civilians (especially children) or soldiers of small stature or poor physical health may be terminal; a safe dose for one person is not necessarily a safe dose for another. Aerosol and gas NLWs are dependent upon the prevailing weather conditions such as humidity, temperature and wind direction. Variations in these can cause collateral damage to innocent bystanders. Chemical adhesives and foams have the potential to cause asphyxiation.

Optical NLWs such as high-intensity strobe lights, which are designed to cause disorientation, are particularly dangerous to people who suffer from epilepsy since they can induce seizures. Portable microwave weapons could, if calibrated wrongly, cook the internal organs of a victim, and lasers designed to destroy a weapon's sighting and optical systems could explode a soldier's eyeball if they got in the way. Electronic devices, like the Taser Gun, which shoot out long fine barb-tipped wires can cause skin contusions and, more seriously, eye damage. Other electronic high-voltage weapons have been sold to buyers who are known to use them for torture.

In the civilian arena there are fears that police and prison officers may be more vindictive and less accountable when armed with NLWs. There is a temptation, especially with some electronic devices, not only to use them when arresting criminals or controlling prisoners during trial or transfer, but also for punishment and interrogation. An example of such a device is the stun belt which can be activated from a distance, delivering a large shock capable of knocking the prisoner down, and causing loss of bladder and bowel control. Amnesty International has condemned these belts as 'cruel, inhuman and degrading'.

In adition to these physical effects, there is a danger of psychological damage as a result of the use of NLWs.

Operational aspects

As the list of non-lethal technologies above indicates, NLWs, which have offensive and defensive capabilities, have application across a wide variety of military and civil scenarios.

The military see a major role for NLWs in politically sensitive low-intensity conflicts, such as peace support operations, where use of lethal force must be avoided and collateral damage minimized.[4] The key missions for NLWs will be: (i) antipersonnel – control of riots and crowds, enforcing no-go areas, barriers, anti-sniper; (ii) antimateriel – inhibiting or stopping movement or mechanical functioning; and (iii) deterrence and warning. Their use has also been considered as force multipliers for lethal weapons: for example, vehicles or personnel could be 'glued up', and then destroyed more easily by lethal conventional weapons. Other plans propose using NLWs to adjust a target situation, that is to segregate the target from collateral objects, and then attack it with lethal weapons. The AGARD study identified 15 real-world target situations which represented desired missions in former Yugoslavia which could not be carried out because of danger of unacceptable collateral damage. These included: preventing hostile civilian crowds from harassing UN convoys on the road; preventing use of bridges without damaging the infrastructure; and preventing the use of helicopters without damaging surrounding buildings and people. The objective of missions may be to prevent the operation of a target for some time, rather than to destroy it, and to prevent death and injury to civilians who are often intermingled with targets. The use of precision-directed NLWs is vital here. Helicopters will have a particularly useful role in, for example: the spraying of aqueous and sticky foams and irritants; the carrying of acoustic weapons; applying entanglement nets; and spraying roads with tyre-degrading chemicals and Teflon-type surfaces, which will be useful in helping to enforce sanctions. The unmanned aerial vehicles (UAV) technology will play an increasing role as a NLW-delivery platform.

Conventions, treaties and the laws of war

Do NLWs contravene arms control and disarmament conventions and declarations? NLWs must be judged against well-established concepts:

(1) *Proportionality* accepts that all weapons can cause suffering, but states that any suffering must be balanced against military necessity, and combatants and non-combatants should not be subjected to unnecessary suffering or superfluous injury. Such terms are open to wide interpretation.

(2) *Discrimination* prohibits the use of methods or means of warfare which cannot be directed against a specific military target and thus may strike combatants and non-combatants without distinction. Whilst all weapons can be used indiscriminately some, such as many bacteriological and chemical weapons, are incapable of being directed at military targets alone.

(3) *The provisions of the Martens Clause* state that because a significant part of the law of war is in the form of customary principles, the rights of parties in conflict to use any means of injuring the enemy are not unlimited. This provision is of particular relevance to weapons which were not in existence at the time when conventions were drawn up and relates to issues of public conscience.

During the mid-1990s, when the UN 'Inhumane' Weapons Convention was under review, there was much controversy and debate surrounding blinding laser weapons. Organizations such as the ICRC and Human Rights Watch Arms Project argued that such weapons specifically designed to blind did cause unnecessary suffering and could be indiscriminate because a laser beam could be used to scan a battlefield, and that this potential for scanning makes indiscriminate use more likely and tempting than with conventional rifles. Whilst opponents of blinding laser regarded them as 'worse than lethal', there were also those who argued that it was better to be blind than dead.

Problems also exist with chemical NLWs which may be incompatible with the 1993 Chemical Weapons Convention (CWC). Because of the imprecise terminology of parts of the CWC there was uncertainty about the situations in which incapacitating gases may be used. According to the US, whilst the use of riot-control gases is restricted in the conduct of warfare (where it is feared they could mask the use of more lethal agents), they can be used by the military in situations such as peacekeeping and antiterrorist missions, and in controlling prisoners of war in rear-echelon areas. There is a danger of the distinction between a policing and control-action operation blurring with a war-fighting operation. Some critics of the CWC say it would be a tragic irony if nations used lethal means against combatants because non-lethal means were banned by international convention.

Discussion

The debate surrounding NLWs has been vigorous and controversial, involving, amongst others, military and security analysts, political scientists, technologists, the weapons' manufacturing industry, human rights campaigners, arms control experts and conspiracy theorists. Some soldiers claim that an increasing lethal/non-lethal option in operations is leading to a position where politicians and civil interest groups will interfere in command decisions as to the use of lethal violence – that is, when and under what conditions it can be used. This obstruction in emergency situations could endanger their lives, and a reliance on NLWs coupled with this interference will undermine how an enemy perceives the commitment behind deterrent threats:

> Military deterrence is an exercise in negative reinforcement for unacceptable behaviour, i.e., 'if you do this, we will kill you'. By advertising the use of and reliance on NLWs we are saying, in

effect, 'If you do this, you will be inconvenienced and maybe have to take a good bath'. This does not have the same deterrent ring to it somehow.[5]

Others have expressed the view that the availability of NLWs would tempt politicians to authorize military intervention earlier than they might otherwise do so, thus increasing the danger of becoming embroiled in a conflict from which it is difficult to exit. Non-lethal capabilities could be used pre-emptively before the start of open hostilities, hampering military movements and thus allowing more time for negotiation.[6]

Some research in the US has questioned the general consensus in law enforcement circles that NLWs are effective in reducing police–citizen killings, and one analysis produced no evidence that police killing rates were affected by the availability of less-than-lethal weapons.[7] Bailey's research called for more work in this area, and also as to whether ready access to NLWs affected the number of firearm discharges and citizen woundings.

The 1990s saw a surge of interest in NLWs and it could be argued that this reflected a move by weapons research laboratories, especially those with large nuclear projects who had experienced a decline in their programmes, as a way of maintaining their research teams and infrastructure. Thus it was a case, in some instances, of technology pushing new developments rather than operational requirements demanding them. But, as we have already noted, it was recognized that there were real uses for non-lethal technologies particularly in the areas of peace support operations and civil law enforcement.

The bottom line is that NLWs are not a panacea or a technological fix for the complex violent situations encountered by military forces and civil law enforcement officers, and it is impossible to guarantee that a NLW will never have fatal consequences. The ultimate threat and deterrent will remain lethal, but NLWs will increasingly offer more options before having to resort to lethal force. Western public opinion expects peacekeepers and police officers to keep the use of lethal force to an absolute minimum when carrying out their mandated duties in violent situations, and if NLWs provide such opportunities then their development and deployment should be encouraged.

However, as for any system there is wide scope for abuse, and human rights and civil liberties experts point out many dangers associated with NLWs. These include their use as political control technologies, their potential and actual use as instruments of torture and, the danger they pose to international arms control and disarmament treaties. The most sinister aspects of NLWs and other new weapons developments are yet to be seen, especially in the rapidly advancing fields of neurochemistry and biogenetic engineering, where sophisticated and subtle mind altering drugs can be targeted at specific groups, identified for example, by racial characteristics. Some would go further and express concern that such chemicals will offer tempting means for large scale social control by unscrupulous governments.

REFERENCES

1. Council for Foreign Relations (1995), *Non-Lethal Technologies: Military Options and Implications*. Report of an Independent Task Force, Washington DC: Council for Foreign Relations; Training and

Doctrine Command (TRADOC) (1996), *Military Operations: Concepts For Non-Lethal Capabilities in Army Operations.* TRADOC, Fort Munroe, Virginia 23651-5000, US: TRADOC, September; Lewer, N and S. Schofield (1997), *Non-Lethal Weapons: A Fatal Attraction? Military Strategies and technologies for 21st century conflict,* London: Zed Books.

2. Coates, J.F. (1970), *Non-Lethal and Nondestructive Combat in Cities Overseas,* Arlington, VA: Institute for Defence Analysis, Science and Technology Division, May.

3. Cuadros, J. (1997), 'Definition of Lethality Thresholds for KE Less-Lethal Projectiles', International Society for Optical Engineering (*SPIE*) 2934: 20–26; and Millar, R. *et al.* (1975), 'Injuries Caused by Rubber Bullets: a report on 90 patients', *British Journal of Surgery* 62: 480–86.

4. Advisory Group For Aerospace Research and Development (AGARD) (1997), *Minimizing Collateral Damage During Peace Support Operations,* AGARD Advisory Report 347 (May), Neuilly-Sur-Seine, France: AGARD.

5. Stanton, M. (1996), 'Nonlethal Weapons: Can of Worms', *Proceedings,* November: 58–60.

6. See TRADOC (1996), n. 1 above.

7. Bailey, W. (1996), 'Less-than-Lethal Weapons and Police–Citizen Killings in US Urban Areas', *Crime and Delinquency* 42, 4 (October): 535–52.

Further Reading

Alexander, J. (1999), *Future War. Non-lethal weapons in 21st century warfare,* New York: St Martin's Press.

Coupland, R. (1997), *Criteria for Judging Excessively Harmful Weapons Which Cause 'Superfluous Injury and Unnecessary Suffering',* Geneva: SinUS Project, Health Division, ICRC, April.

Dando, M. (1996), *A New Form of Warfare. The rise of non-lethal weapons,* London: Brassey's.

Institute for Foreign Policy Analysis (IFPA) (1996), *Non-Lethal Weapons: Emerging Requirements for Security Strategy,* Washington: IFPA, May.

International Committee of the Red Cross (ICRC) (1994), *Expert Meeting on Certain Weapon Systems and on Implementation Mechanisms in International Law. Report of meeting, Geneva 30 May–1 June 1994,* Geneva: ICRC, July.

Address for correspondence

Centre for Conflict Resolution, Department of Peace Studies, University of Bradford, West Yorkshire, BD7 1DP, U.K.
Tel: + 44 (0)1274 384192 (office) + 44 (0) 1274 384197 (answerphone); Fax: + 44 (0) 1274 384197;
E-mail: N.Lewer@bradford.ac.uk

HEALTH AND SOCIAL EFFECTS
OF WARFARE

Gas mask
Oliver Whitehead

16 MORBIDITY AND MORTALITY AMONG SOLDIERS AND CIVILIANS

DOUGLAS HOLDSTOCK

Non-combatants, including women and children, have been as much the victims of war as combatants. This chapter examines some of the statistics of the morbidity and mortality of war among soldiers and civilians, with an emphasis on the many uncertainties involved. Changes in the proportion of combatants and non-combatants affected by war are considered in light of the changing social background and technology of war over the centuries; it is suggested that up to the First World War (WW I) advances in technology (explosives, mechanisation, transportation) and professionalism raised both the relative and absolute mortality in the military. The advent of total war in the Second World War (WW II), with massive air attacks on cities, and in subsequent years the so-called low-intensity conflicts involving deliberate attacks on domestic targets, including health care facilities, have greatly increased the proportion of civilian, (including child) casualties. Some specific examples, including aspects of urban terrorism, are discussed. Possible remedies are considered, but it is concluded that only an end to war can provide reliable protection for non-combatants.

War and violence have been a feature of human life since before recorded history. In the earliest literate societies in the Middle East and Egypt, inscriptions record the triumphs, though rarely the failures, of national armies, and even further back, into prehistory, burials contain weapons, and bones show signs of wounds which must often have been the cause of death. In the historical period, very few years have been free of war somewhere in the world. This chapter considers the toll of war on both combatants and non-combatants, but with an emphasis on the latter. It examines apparent trends in the proportion of civilians killed in war and the underlying causes, and looks at fears and hopes for the future. Some aspects are considered in greater detail.

The toll of war

There are many difficulties and uncertainties in this undertaking. The further back in time one goes, the more unreliable the statistics. Both victors and vanquished have different motives for exaggerating or playing down their numbers of dead and injured, and even today figures can be grossly distorted for propaganda purposes: to mislead, to reassure or to alarm the home audience, the enemy or the wider world. In the developing world today, circumstances make reliable figures unattainable. Even the definition of a combatant and what constitutes a conflict in today's developing world, is imprecise; there is no clear-cut separation between regular soldiers at one end of the spectrum, through armed militias, more or less reluctant conscripts, freedom fighters, terrorists and their supporters to totally innocent and uninvolved civilians, including neutrals, at the other.

What constitutes a war-related death is particularly difficult to decide in the case of civilians. There can be little doubt when a city is subjected to mass bombing, or when soldiers go on the rampage in a captured city, though numbers will be very uncertain. But a clear division cannot be made between deaths directly and indirectly due to combat. Death due to starvation in a besieged town is presumably war-related, but what of deaths among refugees in Sudan or Rwanda, some of whom are frail or elderly and would have died, not necessarily prematurely, in any case? The 'Spanish 'flu' epidemic of 1918–19 killed more people than WW I; how many of the deaths can be attributed to the disruption of society, with effects ranging from malnutrition to war-weariness, resulting from the war?

The effects of war do not, of course, end with the last shot. As Shakespeare put it 'the evil that men do lives after them'. The 1618–48 Thirty Years' War left Central Europe devastated. Today's conflicts in the developing world will retard the progress of the countries concerned for decades, though the toll of ill-health and premature death will be unquantifiable; not all of it will be ascribed to war when the history is written and the statistics accumulated.

Last but not least, the definition of a war or conflict differs in the various more-or-less comprehensive historical studies, and this in turn has an effect on whether or not its victims enter the statistics. A common definition is 1000 or more violent deaths, but one criterion for major conflict is the involvement of more than 50,000 troops, and others exclude 'domestic violence' (in other words, civil war), which would exclude the recent genocide in Rwanda. Whatever the criteria adopted, the picture is horrifying. There may have been no more than 290 years of peace since 3600BC, with only 52 years since 1480AD free of major wars. During this time there have been, worldwide, over 13,000 episodes of major international and domestic violence, with around a billion battle deaths. In Europe alone, over 5800 wars resulted in nearly 800 million deaths before WW II. The indirect mortality, including civilians, may be far greater.[1] A breakdown of figures from 1500 to 1990, some of which are discussed in more detail below, gives a total of nearly 142 million war and war-related deaths, 64 million military and 76 million civilian.[2] From 1945 to 1992, there have been some 23 million deaths, two-thirds civilian and one-third military.[3]

The conduct of war

A principal factor influencing the morbidity of war, affecting both the military and the populace, is its changing technology. For much of recorded history this underwent little or no change, but over the last five hundred years there has been a series of developments with profound impact. This process culminates in the nuclear weapons of the last fifty years, but during the same period the changes in the waging of war have allowed conflict to persist and even intensify in countries unable to afford modern high-technology warfare.

Ancient and medieval

There was little change in the conduct of war from the time of Alexander of Macedon or Julius Caesar of Rome to Henry V of England. Men fought, except for arrows, hand-to-hand, and battles seldom lasted more than a day between armies of not more than a few thousand men.[4] Campaigns, in Europe at any rate, were seasonal; the climate made warfare more or less impossible in winter, and in any case the armies largely dispersed in the autumn to return home for the harvest. Only the occasional siege lasted more than a few months. Mortality among combatants would have been very variable; in addition to immediate deaths, many must have died from wounds and wound infections in the days to months after a campaign. Civilian morbidity and mortality would have been partly indirect from the social after-effects of conflict – no one to run the farm if the man did not return – but sometimes direct and massive if disease broke out in a besieged city. When a city fell at the end of a siege, the men and boys would often be put to the sword and women and girls sold into slavery. In Euripides' *Women of Troy*, Hector's widow, Andromache, gives vent to feelings which must be echoed today in many parts of the world:

> To be dead is the same as never to have been born,
> And better far than living on in wretchedness.
> The dead feel nothing; evil then can cause no pain.
> But one who falls from happiness to unhappiness
> Wanders bewildered in a strange and hostile world.[5]

War and technology

With the discovery of gunpowder by Roger Bacon (1220–92) came firearms, first the cannon (perhaps first used at Crecy in 1346) and later the musket, leading to a steady increase in battle deaths. Standing armies, with professional soldiers whose behaviour was notorious for its brutality, slowly became the norm. As communications slowly improved, armies could be kept in the field for longer periods, though with dire results for the regions fought over: during the Thirty Years' War (1618–48) large parts of Germany and Eastern France were devastated, with populations falling by a third or more, and taking many decades to recover.[6]

Over the next 250 years technological changes made war ever more destructive: railways and steamships increased the mobility of armies; advances in metallurgy increased the killing power of weapons. Up to the end of WW I the military themselves were the principal victims, and Europe the site of the majority of deaths (Table 16.1).[7] Dr William Eckhardt of the Lentz Peace Research Laboratory has given detailed figures of wars and war-related deaths from 1500 onwards. He defines war as an armed conflict involving one or more governments and causing a thousand or more deaths per year. For example, he estimates 2 million military and 2 million civil deaths in the Thirty Years' War, and 2 million civil and nearly 3 million military deaths in the 23 years of the French revolutionary and Napoleonic wars. In the US Civil War 620,000 out of 820,000 deaths in four years were military, in the Franco-Prussian War of 1870–71, 188,000 out of a quarter of a million.[8] This process reached its acme of destruction in the First World War (see below).

Table 16.1 War-related deaths, 1500 – 1990, by major geographical region

Region	Military	Civilian	Total
North America	1,288,000	204,000	1,532,000
Latin America	1,088,000	1,932,000	3,239,000
Europe	44,119,000	48,935,000	93,450,000
Middle East (inc. Egypt)	709,000	464,000	1,235,000
South Asia	1,171,000	2,302,000	3,610,000
Far East	13,398,000	16,513,000*	31,185,000
Oceania	137,000	50,000	187,000
Sub-Saharan Africa	1,597,000	1,806,000	6,625,000
Other Africa	202,000	442,000	837,000
Totals	63,709,000+	75,649,000+	141,901,000+

Source: William Eckhardt, Lentz Peace Research Institute, in: R.L. Sivard (1991), pp. 22–25 (see note 2). Full figures for individual countries and wars in the original.
* See note to Table 16.2; the figure quoted there for China would still leave Europe as the place with the highest death rate.
+ Incomplete. Individual and total figures and breakdown into military and civilian deaths not available in all cases: overall totals do not add up for these reasons and owing to rounding-up.

The twentieth century

The death-rate of war reached unprecedented levels in the twentieth century (see Figure 16.1). This increase is far out of proportion to the rise in population, and there is only a small increase in the number of wars. Yet the proportion of civil to military deaths in the two world wars is very different (Table 16.2). The huge number of military deaths in WW I is mainly attributable to the machine-gun, the resulting stalemate of trench warfare and the attempts of the higher commands on both sides to break the impasse at almost any cost in human lives. Civilian deaths in the Second World War in the study cited in Table 16.2 include 20 million in China, presumably reflecting both the effects of the Sino-Japanese war and the continuing civil war within China itself. Other estimates are appreciably smaller, presumably depending on whether deaths from famine are included. But WW II also saw for the first time total war with mass bombings of cities, first by Nazi Germany (Rotterdam, Coventry), later by the Allies, including the fire-bombing of Hamburg and Dresden, and finally the US attack on Japan. This ended

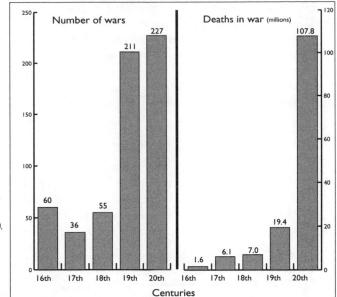

Figure 16.1 Wars and war deaths 1500–1990

Source: R.L. Sivard (1991), p. 20, (see n. 2), © World Priorities, Box 25140, Washington DC 20007, USA.
* covers only wars with estimated deaths of 1000 or more.

Table 16.2 Deaths : selected major participants, World Wars I and II

Country	Military	Civilian	Total
World War I			
Austria-Hungary	1,200,000	180,000	1,380,000
France	1,363,000	150,000	1,513,000
Germany	1,774,000	225,000	1,999,000
British Empire	908,000	9,000	917,000
Italy	460,000	300,000	760,000
Russia	1,700,000	na	1,700,000+
United States	126,000	na	126,000
Total (all participants)	8,418,000	1,374,000+	9,792,000+
World War II			
Britain	557,000	61,000	618,000
China	2,220,000	20,000,000	22,220,000
France	202,000	108,000	310,000
Germany	3,250,000	500,000	3,750,000
Italy	149,000	783,000	932,000
Japan	1,507,000	672,000	2,179,000
Poland	64,000	2,000,000	2,064,000
USSR	7,500,000	7,500,000	15,000,000
United States	292,000	Nil	292,000
Total (all participants)	16,933,000	34,305,000	51,208,000

n.a.: not available; nil: less than 1000.
Source: F.A. Beer (1981), pp. 37 and 38 (see n. 1). See also D. Wood (1968), *Conflict in the Twentieth Century*, London: Institute for Strategic Studies; and Q. Wright (1965), *A Study of War*, Chicago: University of Chicago Press, 1965. (This source gives a very much greater figure for civilian war deaths for WW II in China than that used for Table 16.1.)

with the atomic bombings of Hiroshima and Nagasaki, though in fact more died in the fire-bombing of Tokyo. By far the majority of deaths in all these cities were civilian.

Estimates of war-related deaths in Europe in WW II would also include the victims of the Nazi Holocaust, again almost all civilians and amounting to about six million. As many or more probably died in the then-Soviet Union, in purges and labour camps and from malnutrition. These are not strictly counted as war-related deaths, but are surely equally the result of the social unrest in twentieth-century Europe which lay behind both world wars.

Post-1945

The 50 years since WW II have not been years of peace. From 1945 to 1992 there were some 23 million deaths in 149 wars, 29 of them still in progress in 1992, the highest number ever in a single year.[9] The peaks in death rates shown in Figure 16.2 represent the Korean and Vietnam wars. Extending the chart to later years would produce a third peak; since 1992 a further 120,000 deaths have occurred in former Yugoslavia, and from half to one million in Rwanda.

The character of these wars has varied considerably. The first Gulf War (Iran–Iraq) resembled WW I, with prolonged periods of trench warfare and a high proportion of military to civilian casualties (450,000 : 50,000). In the second Gulf War there was an intensive high-tech bombing assault on Iraq, which although allegedly aimed at military targets and power and communications facilities also caused significant damage to residential areas. In combination with sanctions, damage to power, water and sanitation contributed to a high proportion of civilian casualties (about 100,000, roughly the same as military casualties).[10]

Apart from the Greek civil war and the recent wars in

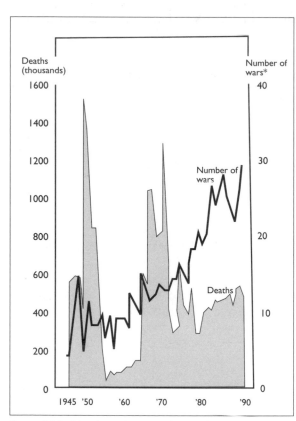

Figure 16.2   Number of wars and war-related deaths 1945–92.
Source: R.L. Sivard (1993), p. 20 (see n. 3), © World Priorities, Box 25140, Washington DC 20007, USA

former Yugoslavia, Europe has been almost free of war in this time. The US and the former Soviet Union have supplied much of the weaponry used in conflicts elsewhere. The principal sufferers in this period have been the Far East and sub-Saharan Africa (Table 16.3). Here the proportion of civilian deaths has once again been high, but for a different reason than in WW II and the second Gulf War; most of the conflicts have been protracted wars based on the theories of Mao Zedong, involving the use of guerrilla tactics to bring about the frustration and exhaustion of a stronger enemy. These were successfully employed by Mao himself in the overthrow of the Kuomintang government in China; by the Vietnamese against France and later the US; and in colonial wars in Africa. But these methods have led to a particularly high casualty rate among civilians. Sometimes these have been due to the intervention of western powers as in Vietnam and Cambodia, but local forces have massacred villages or even whole populations in Africa, and have deliberately targeted health care facilities in Latin America and sub-Saharan Africa. This type of war leaves behind physically and mentally crippled bodies, in lands with disrupted health care, and imposes a toll of epidemic disease and malnutrition, particularly in children and refugees, which makes nonsense of conventional statistics.

Table 16.3 War-related deaths, 1945–92, by major geographical region

Region	Number of deaths		
	Military	Civilian	Total
Latin America	234,000	471,000	714,000
Europe and USSR	11,000	11,000	367,000*
Middle East	666,000	494,000	1,329,000
South Asia	1,049,000	2,358,000	3,412,000
Far East	4,058,000	6,559,000	10,691,000
Sub-Saharan Africa	1,515,000	4,505,000	6,503,000
Other African	19,000	107,000	126,000
Totals	7,552,000*	14,505,000*	23,142,000*

Source: R.L. Sivard (1993), p. 21 (see n. 3). Full figures for individual countries and wars in the original.
* Incomplete. Individual and total figures and breakdown into military and civilian deaths not available in all cases: overall totals do not add up for this reason and owing to rounding-up. Figures were compiled before most of the deaths in Chechnya, Rwanda and former Yugoslavia.

How civilians come to harm

Non-combatants can suffer from war in many ways. Some are direct and obvious, from the systematic bombing of cities by both sides in WW II to the sniping and mortar-bombing of Sarajevo. Others are indirect, as in the case of the victims of lack of health care in Angola or Guatemala. Between these extremes, women, children and the elderly suffer in ways which are real enough to the victims but do not always figure in statistics or attract the notice of the news media. Some of these are discussed fully elsewhere in this book but are briefly mentioned here for completeness.

Women and children

Women have inevitably been drawn into twentieth-century total war. This has been mainly in non-combatant roles, for example as nurses (often close to the fighting) or as munition workers (resulting in ill-health from handling toxic chemicals and danger from explosions). In recent years women have taken up more active combat roles, particularly in the US services; whether this is a desirable spin-off of women's lib is perhaps not for a male to discuss.

Women though, have always been victims of the deprivations of war. Sometimes this has been in a spirit of self-sacrifice to feed their children and the fighting men, but they have also been used as sex objects, as hinted at in the passage from Euripides' *The Women of Troy* quoted above. In the Middle Ages armies which had overrun cities were traditionally allowed three days of pillage and rape; after the fall of Constantinople to the Turks in 1453 the scenes were so horrifying that the carnage was stopped after only one day. Christians could be as bad to one another, as when the Catholic Fourth Crusade sacked Eastern Orthodox Constantinople in 1204.[11] Not the least-disgusting aspect of the war in former Yugoslavia has been the institutionalizing of rape, mainly by Bosnian Serbs, to systematically dehumanize the population of whole towns.

Children have in the past also been mainly indirect victims of war but, particularly in sub-Saharan Africa in recent years, young teenagers have been violently conscripted into guerrilla armies, often being compelled to inflict serious violence on their own families and communities by way of an induction. This is of course a gross breach of the conventions governing war and of the UN Convention on the Rights of the Child, and as such a war crime, but given the difficulty of preparing evidence it seems unlikely that more than a tiny minority of those responsible will ever be brought to justice. Article 38 of the Convention on the Rights of the Child currently states that: 'persons who have not attained the age of fifteen years [should] not take a direct part in hostilities'. In 1999, the UN General Assembly approved an Optional Protocol from the UN High Commission on Human Rights that the minimum age for recruitment should be eighteen. Some developed countries, which would regard themselves as civilized and respectful of human rights, wish to retain the option of voluntary recruitment of young people under this age: the UK at 16 years and the USA at 17 years.

Scenes of conflict can psychologically scar child soldiers for life, and only time will show how much harm this will cause as attempts are made to reintegrate them into their communities, or whether indeed they will be accepted back. Their rehabilitation will be long and difficult and will have to take into account many local cultural factors.

Children are particular victims of millions of landmines, and new casualties will appear years after the end of the hostilities, given the difficulty in locating modern plastic mines. Many victims have to undergo amputations; in countries where most work is physical and agricultural, the burden of amputees on already-impoverished societies will be immense, and the inadequacy those individuals feel will be a major psychological burden throughout their lives.

Refugees

Statistically, by far the most common effect of today's wars on civilians is to render them homeless, and in absolute numbers those so afflicted must be the highest ever. As always, women, children and the elderly are disproportionately affected. Sub-Saharan Africa has been worst affected, Angola, Ethiopia, Mozambique, Rwanda and Sudan all having attracted notice at different times. Afghanistan and Cambodia could have provided similar scenes but were less accessible to western camera crews. Most refugee health problems stem from living in crowded and ill-equipped camps: cholera, dysentery, typhoid and respiratory illnesses are common, superimposed on chronic malnutrition.

If resettlement is difficult to achieve, refugee camps acquire a quasi-permanent status, as in the Israeli-occupied territories of the Middle East. Ill-health then arises from a complex of economic, political and social factors – poverty, poor housing, unemployment and the like – leading, for example, to tuberculosis and increased morbidity and mortality in babies and young children from a variety of infectious diseases. In older children and young adults this in turn leads to political unrest which can readily turn violent, as in the Palestinian *intifada* (uprising). Deaths, injury and repression then cause a further twist of the vicious spiral.

Urban terrorism

As already noted, definitions of what constitutes a war are arbitrary. For example, in former Yugoslavia, the clash between Croatia and Serbia would count as an interstate war because the former had been recognized as a sovereign state, the fighting in Bosnia as a civil war with more or less overt intervention from Croatia and Serbia. The line between civil war and violent civil unrest due to urban terrorism is even less clear-cut, though the consequences are equally apparent to the victims. Urban terrorism can also cross national frontiers, with some incidents causing hundreds of deaths or injuries. The terrorist regards himself, and his supporters see him, as a freedom fighter but others, especially his victims, experience him as a violent criminal.

This form of violence can persist for many years: more than 25 in the case of Northern Ireland. Some terrorist groups target security and military forces but many are totally indiscriminate (unless attacking civilian sympathizers of the other side is regarded as acceptable). Urban terrorism in turn merges into organized and then into indiscriminate violent crime. It may put Northern Ireland into perspective, or on the other hand may reflect on the social problems of the United States, to note that the death rate from criminal violence in New York has always exceeded that from the troubles in Northern Ireland.

Religious and ethnic differences

Several of the examples cited highlight the role of religious divisions as a cause of conflict: Arab and Jew in the Middle East, but also Sunni and Shia Muslims; Catholic and Protestant Christians in Northern Ireland; Catholic and Orthodox Christians and Muslims in former Yugoslavia. Religious differences shade into ethnic, as in the Muslim provinces of the former USSR, the conflict between Tamils and Sinhalese in Sri Lanka, and that between the Kurds and the ruling regimes in Iran, Iraq and Turkey. Islamic fundamentalism, expressed as terrorist violence of which civilians are the principal victims, currently threatens the stability of Algeria, Egypt and much of central Asia.

Epidemics

Before the antibiotic era, war-related infections probably killed more people, both soldiers and civilians, than war itself. Secondary infection of war wounds led to amputation or even death. Overcrowding, poor sanitation and pests such as lice and rodents often led to epidemics in besieged cities or army camps and frequently changed the course of wars. As noted above, epidemics still threaten refugees in Third World countries. War itself has contributed to the spread of epidemics, by refugees or by soldiers returning from overseas campaigns. Some such episodes are worth individual mention.

'Plague' in Athens

The first history of a war, Thucydides' *History of the Peloponnesian War*, includes a vivid account of the outbreak of an epidemic in Athens.[12] The Greek word is conventionally translated 'plague', though the very clear description sounds more like bacillary dysentery, typhoid or typhus. Many similar episodes must have occcured in later wars up to our own time. The Spartans were ravaging Attica, so that the Athenians were confined within their city walls, and the overcrowding was made worse by refugees from the surrounding countryside. According to Thucydides, some sufferers plunged into the water-tanks to try to relieve an unquenchable thirst; if the illness was water-borne, the report gives an irony of which he could not have been aware to his comment that 'the doctors were quite incapable of treating the disease because of their ignorance of the right methods'. It is not surprising that 'mortality among the doctors was the highest of all'; nor is the demoralization and breakdown of law and order so graphically reported elsewhere. Although 'the plague' came early in the war, some historians believe that Athens never really recovered from it.

Black Death

The arrival of true plague, infection with *Yersinia pestis*, in Europe in the mid-fourteenth century may have followed an act of war. The subsequent epidemic, the Black Death, halved the population of parts of Europe, and the economic aftermath of the disease lasted for decades.[13] The epidemiology of plague is even now not clearly understood. The infection is endemic among a variety of rodents in Central Asia, with sporadic human cases mainly transmitted from the black rat via fleas, but from time to time epidemic spread to humans occurs, perhaps related to a change in climate. One such outbreak reached the Tartars north of the Black Sea in the 1340s, and affected a Tartar army besieging the Genoese stronghold of Caffa, now Feodosia, in the Crimea. As a parting gesture before abandoning the siege because of the severity of the outbreak, the Tartars lobbed the bodies of some of their dead over the walls. Despite the best efforts of the Genoese to dispose of the corpses, plague was soon raging within the walls. Some of the inhabitants took to their galleys; by early in 1348 the plague was established in Sicily and Italy. The disruption of the Hundred Years' War may have contributed to its subsequent spread through France and England.

We shall never know whether the epidemic would have reached Europe without this episode. There was enough trade by this time between Europe and Asia to make it quite likely that the disease would have spread in any case, but the outcome of one siege could nevertheless have altered the course of history.

Trade, war and disease

In medieval Europe the roles of explorer, soldier and trader were more or less interchangeable. What is not in doubt is that armed Europeans sailing round Africa to Asia, and across the Atlantic, took their diseases with them and brought back new diseases on their return. In the Americas in particular, native mortality from influenza, measles, smallpox and tuberculosis was appalling, and in return Columbus and his crew may have brought syphilis to Europe. Europeans also took firearms to other continents; when they acquired them, the natives used the arms to attack the intruders but also turned them on one another. The mortality in the 17th and 18th centuries from the export of European arms and diseases will never be known.

'Spanish flu'

As already noted, some 18 million died in or of WW I, but more are thought to have died in the influenza epidemic that immediately followed the war. The influenza virus is genetically very labile, and mutants to which immunity is low appear regularly and cause epidemics. The 1918–19 pandemic would presumably have arisen in any case but it is hard not to imagine that the malnutrition, homelessness and psychological morbidity left by the war worsened the mortality from the epidemic.

Future threats

While war continues, the life and health of non-combatants will remain at risk. The precise nature of the threat will depend upon the form taken by any individual conflict. Some possibilities may not yet be foreseeable; the ingenuity of the military scientist may not yet be at an end. Some which present a particular threat to civilians are worth individual comment.

Nuclear weapons and nuclear winter

As described in other chapters, nuclear weapons are uniquely destructive; the majority of victims in Hiroshima and Nagasaki were civilians, including doctors, nurses and their patients.[14] At the time of writing, following the end of the Cold War, the threat of a nuclear exchange may be less than for many years, but will remain as long as the missiles exist. In particular, the use of a significant proportion of the arsenals could, by producing a vast amount of smoke and dust, significantly lower global temperatures for several years, which in turn could drastically affect agriculture worldwide and cause mass starvation. The most apocalyptic projections are of four *billion* deaths globally, with scope for inevitable inaccuracies allowing a range of possibilities: this justifies Carl Sagan's chilling warning that nuclear war could extinguish humankind (by definition, predominantly non-combatants).[15] Even the reduced arsenals of the superpowers when the reduction under the current START treaties is fully implemented could still be enough to produce a nuclear winter.

Nuclear terrorism

The dismantling of nuclear weapons after the end of the Cold War, and the economic collapse of the former Soviet Union, with insecurity among staff at nuclear-weapons' facilities, has led to fears of fissile materials or even nuclear warheads reaching the hands of rogue governments or even terrorist groups. Either might be more likely to threaten, or even use, these against cities and their populations in developed countries rather than against military targets. Even a crude weapon scattering plutonium by using conventional explosions could cause many cases of cancer and render a city uninhabitable, and the threat alone could cause panic and many deaths in an emergency evacuation.

Urban terrorism and chemical and biological weapons

A threat which has already been realized once is the use of chemical agents; the urban terrorist group, Aum Shinrikyo released the nerve gas sarin in Tokyo underground railway system early in 1995 and caused several deaths. It appears that Aum Shinrikyo had built a plant which could produce up to 70 tons of sarin, enough to kill hundreds of thousands, and were synthesising mustard gas, phosgene, LSD and other consciousness-altering drugs. The cult had recruited several scientists and at least one doctor. The chemistry required to produce the nerve or irritant gases is not difficult, although clearly not without risk to the operator, and similar episodes could well occur elsewhere.

Aum Shinrikyo were also experimenting with anthrax and botulism, and may have attempted to acquire the Ebola virus. Wealthy cults such as Aum Shrinrikyo, and ruthless governments such as that of Saddam Hussein, are capable of using modern biotechnology to produce bacteria and viruses for which no preventive measures or treatment are available.

Benefits

What can be said to relieve the gloom and doom which has constituted this chapter so far? Civilians have undoubtedly benefited greatly from the spin-off of war medicine. Modern nursing arose from the experience of Florence Nightingale in the Crimean War, and the Red Cross out of Henri Dunant's attempts to relieve suffering after the battle of Solferino in 1859. Advances in blood transfusion were stimulated by WW I, the development of penicillin and hence the antibiotic era by WW II. The experiences of the US forces in Vietnam led to considerable progress in the surgery of major trauma, and the need for the military to function in foreign climates has promoted knowledge of the treatment and prevention of tropical diseases.

Much more could obviously be said about all of these, but even so the cynic will note that this is the shortest section of this chapter. In fact, all the medical advances listed above could have come about without the urge to mitigate the effects of war. No doubt all would have taken place sooner or later, but surely our motives and priorities are at fault, and our allocation of resources to meet them?

Remedies

The immense scale of the morbidity and mortality discussed above clearly implies that medical measures can at best be palliative: no surgeon on earth can help the soldier shot through the heart, and children who tread on landmines die without receiving medical help or, at best, end up as amputees. The problem is, then, one of prevention. The prevention of war-related deaths among both soldiers and civilians clearly requires the prevention of war itself.

Sanctions

In *An Agenda for Peace* UN Secretary-General Boutros Boutros-Ghali discussed several options for preventing disputes escalating into war, such as preventative diplomacy and UN peacekeeping forces.[16] The UN Security Council can call for trade sanctions. The effectiveness of sanctions will clearly depend upon the degree to which they can be enforced. Deliberate evasion is common and profitable to the evader, and even without it the effect of sanctions is slow, but there can be little doubt that they contributed to the eventual ending of apartheid in South Africa. It is claimed that sanctions selectively harm the poorest in the targeted country, and experience in Iraq certainly supports this claim. Ten years after the second Gulf War the incidence of several infectious diseases has doubled, child malnutrition has increased and immunization rates decreased. The World Health Organization claims that over half a million children may have died as a result of sanctions, and sanctions may well have delayed restoration of health care facilities. Then again, the intransigence of Saddam Hussein himself must have been a contributory factor.

The arms trade

The great majority of wars since 1945 have been fought in developing countries with weapons manufactured in developed countries. An end to the arms trade would very considerably reduce, as existing weapons and ammunition are used up, the capability for making war both between and within nations.[17] Ending the arms trade will not be easy, though; it provides employment in and political influence for the arms manufacturing countries, lowers the unit cost for arms for national militaries of the producing nations, and enables an assessment of the effectiveness of the weapons.[18] Multinational agreement for phased reductions in arms production and transfers will be needed, and a draft convention for this to be achieved has been drawn up by a group including the International Association of Lawyers Against Nuclear Arms.

Meanwhile, the weapons already made and exported are very much in existence. Preventive diplomacy and other peacekeeping measures through the UN and regional organizations are therefore vital. Sadly, an attempt at the UN in July 2001 to curb the illicit trade in small arms was watered down by the United States.

Landmines

Many millions of landmines are scattered around the world's present and recent trouble-spots. Most of these will remain active for years, and many are deposited across - agricultural land in poor countries where this is a prime resource. Farmers are then faced with the choice of leaving the land unused or risking their, and their children's, lives and limbs.

The 1997 Ottawa Treaty bans the production, sale, stockpiling and use of anti-personnel landmines. It entered into force in 1999, and over 100 countries have signed or ratified it. Now the convention must become universal – some key states, including China, Russia and the United States have not signed it. Work to clear existing minefields, and the medical, psychological and social rehabilitation of victims, will be needed for many years.[19]

Automatic rifles

Over 500 million automatic rifles have been made and sold since WW II, and most of these are still in use.[20] They are often, particularly among African countries, passed on from one conflict to another, as from Ethiopia to Somalia and Sudan. This is much cheaper than through the 'legitimate' arms trade. With so many weapons already in circulation, curbs on official sales of small arms may sadly have little impact. More effective could be buying back weapons from their holders at just above the black-market rate, perhaps as part of a resettlement deal offering the soldiers a stable future in, for example, farming.

Conclusion

Non-combatants have always been the victims of war as much as the combatants. In recent years the proportion of civilian casualties has steadily increased and may have reached over 80 per cent of the total in some conflicts; it is suggested that this may be a return to the earlier situation before the mechanization of war greatly increased the mortality of troops in battle.

Whether or not this is the case, it is clear that medical care can at best palliate the effects of war, and that prevention is the only option. War is a cultural institution; its prevention requires adequate solutions to the social and environmental problems of the world and a stable system of world governance.[21] In the words of the 1995 Nobel Peace Laureate, Professor Joseph Rotblat, we must no longer think of ourselves as citizens of one nation, but as citizens of the world.[22]

REFERENCES

1. Beer, F.A. (1981), *Peace Against War*, San Francisco: W.H. Freeman, pp. 20–70.
2. Sivard, R.L. (1991), *World Military and Social Expenditures 1991,* Washington DC: World Priorities, pp. 20–5.
3. Sivard, R.L. (1993), *World Military and Social Expenditures 1993,* Washington, DC: World Priorities, pp. 20–1.
4. Tromp, H. (1995), 'On the Nature of War and Militarism', in R.A. Hinde and H.E. Watson (eds), *War: A Cruel Necessity? The Bases of Institutionalized Violence*, London: IB Tauris, pp. 118–31.
5. Euripides (1973), *The Women of Troy*, trans. P. Vellacott, Harmondsworth: Penguin, p. 111, lines 637–41.
6. Roberts, J.M. (1993), *History of the World*, London: Helicon, p. 469.
7. See n. 1 above.
8. See n. 2 above.
9. See n. 3 above.
10. Ibid.
11. Norwich, J.J. (1995), *Byzantium : the Decline and Fall*, London: Viking, 178–80.
12. Thucydides (1972), *History of the Peloponnesian War*, trans. R. Warner, Harmondsworth: Penguin, pp. 151–56.
13. Ziegler, P. (1991), *The Black Death*, London: Guild Publishing, pp. 5–7.
14. Hersey, J. (1986), *Hiroshima*, 2nd ed., Harmondsworth: Penguin.
15. Turco, R.P., Toon, O.B., Ackerman, T.P., Pollack, J.B. and C. Sagan (1983), 'Nuclear Winter : global consequences of multiple nuclear explosions', *Science* 222: 1283–92; and Harwell, M.A. and T.C. Hutchinson (1985), *Environmental Consequences of Nuclear War. Vol II : ecological and agricultural effects*, Chichester: John Wiley.
16. Boutros-Ghali, B. (1992) *An Agenda for Peace: preventive diplomacy, peace-making and peace-keeping*, New York: United Nations.
17. Sidel, V.W. (1995), 'The International Arms Trade and its Impact on Health'. *BMJ* 311: 1677–80.
18 Brozoska, M. (1995), 'The Arms Trade', in R.A Hinde and H.E. Watson (eds), *War: A Cruel Necessity? The Bases of Institutionalized Violence*. London: IB Tauris, pp. 224–37.
19. Goose, S. *Landmines: A Deadly Legacy*. Boston and New York: Physicians for Human Rights and Human Rights Watch, 1993.
20. See n. 18, p. 234, above.
21. Hinde, R.A. and H.E. Watson (eds) (1995), *War: A Cruel Necessity? The Bases of Institutionalized Violence*, London: IB Tauris, p. 1.
22. Rotblat, J. (1996), 'Remember Your Humanity', *Bulletin of Atomic Scientists* 52 (2): 24–8.

Address for correspondence

MEDACT, 601 Holloway Road, London N19 4DJ, UK.
Tel.: +44-(0)20-7272-2020; Fax: +44-(0)20-7281-5717; email: info@medact.org

17 THE EFFECTS OF WARS ON POPULATION

ANNA SILLANPÄÄ

Chapter 17 is based on the book *Wars and Populations* (Voini i Narodonacelenie) by the Soviet Latvian demographist Boris Urlanis (1906–81), originally published in the 1960s and translated into English in 1971. The book soon became a classic in its field and although the text is not novel, we feel that the basics of this book and Boris Urlanis's theories are still valid. *War and Populations* concentrates on Europe, but has scarce data on the former Soviet Union itself. There are some figures on victims of the Second World War, but nothing on the effects of Stalin's terror or the famines caused by civil war and forced collectivization.

The Holocaust and other Nazi atrocities, on the other hand, are presented in great detail. The figures on the former Soviet Union are nowadays available, and were probably known to Urlanis in the 1960s, but it is clear that Urlanis was not permitted to publish anything of the sort at the time or even later. This, of course, makes his book somewhat one-sided, but it does not diminish the validity of his methodology, theories and especially the vast amount of analysed data he presents on the effects of wars on population. (Editorial Board)

Boris Urlanis, a Latvian demographer, considered war as the scourge of human society. In the course of history there have been different reasons for waging wars: seizing new slaves in antiquity; seizing land and power for the ruling upper class in the Middle Ages; and accumulating capital and expanding markets, acquiring sources of raw materials and spheres of influence after the industrial revolution.

In his book *Wars and Populations* (1971) Urlanis studies the influence of wars on population from different angles: (i) quantitatively, by determining the size of population losses during a war; (ii) by changes in the composition of the population: wars significantly alter sex, age and family make-up; (iii) physical development and a population's ability to work; and (iv) morbidity and cultural level.

The effects of war on population

Natural disasters

All changes in population size during a war cannot be attributed only to the conflict. There can be co-existing natural disasters like floods, earthquakes and drought which are not caused by war. But war aggravates the effect of such natural calamities on a population by making it more vulnerable. Urlanis has an example of this. The 1943 famine in India was the result of unfavourable weather conditions, but was considerably exacerbated by the war which blocked the shipment of rice from Burma. A large proportion of the casualties should be counted as war victims. The same applies to the famine immediately after hostilities in Soviet Russia in 1921, when drought destroyed the crop in the Volga region. The crop failure as such was caused by climatic factors, but without the six years of war Russia would have been able to deal with it much better. There would have been some emergency stocks of grain, the transport system would not have been in such a chaotic condition and food could have been delivered to the drought-stricken areas.

Epidemics

During wartime epidemics commonly occur among soldiers and spread fast to the civilian population, but there are epidemics that are not connected to war in any way. The problem is to what extent wartime epidemics are the consequences of the conflict. The solution can be found by studying the origins of the epidemics, but that is not always possible. According to Urlanis most wartime epidemics are due to the war because wartime conditions favour both their start and their spread. The situation is more complicated when epidemics break out immediately after the cessation of hostilities, which was the case with the influenza pandemic ('Spanish flu') which swept over Europe shortly after the First World War (WW I). The outbreak of the pandemic cannot be associated with the war, but it is clear that the numbers of people affected and the case fatality rate were greater because of the four years of warfare that had made the population vulnerable.

Duration of the war and war effort

In Urlanis's opinion the effect of a war on a population depends largely on the duration of the war and the strain it imposes on the country involved. A short war like the Spanish–American war of 1898 did not require great effort from either the USA or Spain and did not noticeably affect the size of their populations. On the other hand, during the 20th century's two world wars living conditions, especially in Europe, were so severely affected that all changes in the size and composition of the populations can be counted as due to these events. In the United States everyday life was not noticeably changed and the losses of the civil population remained small, but in Germany the war affected everything and the losses were great both among civilians and soldiers.

Estimating human losses

Population size

The effect of war on a population can be estimated by comparing the actual size of the population with that expected. The actual population means the population of a country after a war and the expected population is the population the country would have had if there had not been a war. The difference between these is the shrinkage of population caused by the war. (Figure 17.1). The most common mistake in estimating population loss due to war is comparing the population after the war with the one before it. This gives only the population decline during the war but not the reduction in birthrate. A population shrinkage can happen even if the population has grown during the war.

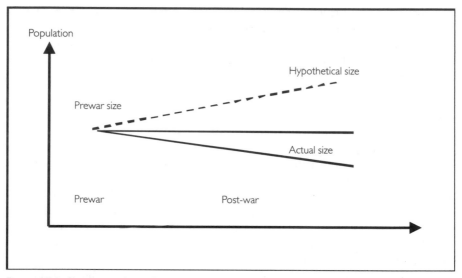

Figure 17.1 Shrinkage of population
Source: Boris Urlanis (1971), *Wars and Populations* (trans. Leo Lempert), Moscow: Progress Publishers.

Using Urlanis's methods expected population size can be extrapolated from the birth- and deathrates of three to five prewar years. To avoid mistakes one must also consider the changes of birthrate and mortality. The longer the war the more noticeable the error will be.

Estimating population shrinkage after a war is difficult: (i) population censuses are not carried out immediately after the cessation of hostilities; (ii) borders often change after a war, making it hard to compare pre- and postwar data; and (iii) emigration may often occur after a war and it is impossible to separate this from actual war losses.

Females

The excess of females (the difference between the numbers of women and men in a population) can be counted. According to Urlanis it represents the number of men deceased in the war, with some exceptions: (i) there could have been more women in the population even before the war; (ii) there are usually more men than women among emigrants; and (iii) the number and therefore the mortality of old women is greater than that of old men. Thus if the number of casualties among civilians has been great, the calculation underestimates the number of deaths among soldiers.

Population shrinkage

The difference between the expected and the actual size of the population tells us nothing about the concrete causes of population loss. It makes a difference whether the reduction occurred as a result of a sharp drop in births, higher general mortality or battle casualties.

Urlanis divides population shrinkage into four main categories: (i) soldiers dying at the front; (ii) civilians who died as a direct result of the enemy's war efforts or the indirect effects of war, like famines and epidemics; (iii) a drop in the birthrate and the resulting decline in the number of infants; and (iv) losses resulting from emigration.

The population of Poland, 1939–45

Poland is a good example of the factors just described. In 1946 the country had 23.9 million inhabitants. In 1939 there were 32.9 million people living in the same area. Poland's population declined by 8.4 million. The expected population in 1946 would have been 35 million; the population shrinkage calculated from this is 11.1 million. The shrinkage is the combined result of the Nazi Holocaust, high mortality due to hunger and epidemics, the drop in the birthrate and the eviction of Germans from the western part of Poland.

War and population dynamics

Birthrate

When estimating the impact of war on the birthrate, the number of births should be compared to the probable birthrate if there had been no war. The difference between these two tells us the effect of the war. After a war, the birthrate often rises higher than it was before the outbreak of hostilities. The exceptionally high number of postwar births should be distinguished from the wartime drop in birthrate when estimating the population shrinkage caused by conflict (Figure 17.2).

Before 1900. In the 17th century, during the Thirty Years' War, the birthrate dropped to half of its prewar rate and returned to its previous level only 20 years after the war had ended. The effect of Napoleon's wars on the birthrate was not as great as one would expect. In Russia, the birthrate in 1813 was 10 per cent smaller than two years previously. After the end of the war it began to rise and in 1816 it was 40 per cent higher than at its lowest point. In France the effects on the birthrate were even smaller, the wartime rate being 6 to 7 per cent lower than before the war. These low figures may reflect the fact that the birthrate was generally lower in Napoleon's time than in previous centuries. The later wars of the 19th century had even less effect on birthrate because the numbers of men participating in hostilities were smaller.

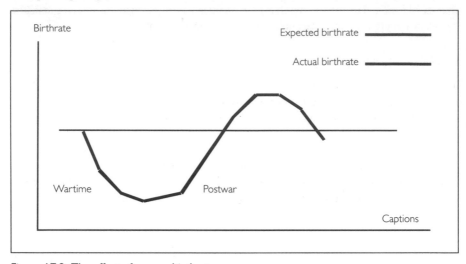

Figure 17.2 The effect of war on birthrate
Source: Boris Urlanis (1971), *Wars and Populations* (trans. Leo Lempert), Moscow: Progress Publishers.

1914–18. During WW I a large part of the male population of all countries involved was recruited to the front. Because a large number of families were torn apart and fewer new marriages took place, WW I had a greater effect on birthrate than any war before it. The rate dropped in all participating countries, although the magnitude of decrease varied significantly from country to country. The larges declines were seen in Hungary, Czechoslovakia and Bulgaria, where the rate was less than half of its pre-war figure. In Germany, Russia, France, Belgium, Austria and Italy birthrate dropped almost by a half, in England by only 25 per cent and in the United States by 10 per cent.

The greatest reduction in birthrate in the different countries took place at different times. In 1917, the rate began to rise in France when more holidays were given to soldiers; at the same time it was at its lowest in Russia where the casualties had been exceptionally high in 1916. Even some neutral countries seem to have suffered a drop in birthrate; for example in Switzerland the expected rate dropped from 23.2 to 18.5 in 1917.

After the war, the rate rose in all countries. However, in the countries that had lost the war it failed to reach prewar levels, while on the winning side it was higher in 1920 than in 1914 – in France by 25 per cent! On the whole it can be estimated that in western Europe population shrinkage during WW I was 14 million.

1939–45. WW II had a different kind of effect on birthrate than did WW I. A clear correlation exists between the war effort and the birthrate. The rate in Germany was not affected by the German attacks on Poland and western Europe, whereas the war against the Soviet Union in 1942 caused a decline in the German birthrate of one-fifth over the previous year, and in 1945 the rate was only 40 per cent of the 1940 level. In Italy, the rate declined throughout the war but less than in Germany. In 1945, it was 20 per cent lower than in 1939. In Japan the rate remained almost constant during the entire war; a decrease was seen as late as 1945, when the rate was 20 per cent lower than in 1944.

In France the birthrate in 1941 was 11 per cent less than before the war, but in 1942 it started to grow again. This might have resulted from the fact that after surrendering to Germany in 1940 France (apart from the underground movement) did not take part in military battles. In 1946, the birthrate was almost 50 per cent higher than before the war. In England, the rate dropped at the beginning of the war by about 5 per cent but after the greatest military activity had moved to the eastern frontier it grew significantly. In 1945 it dropped again, associated with the allies' attack on the western front. In Yugoslavia, the rate decreased througout the war: it was at its lowest in 1945, when it was one-third less than in 1939. In the USA, the rate rose at first, then dropped a little in 1944–45; it started to rise again at the end of the war. In the Soviet Union the rate decreased strongly even after the war. Altogether the growth of the birthrate after the war was twice as high among the winning parties than among the losers (see Table 17.1). The reduced birthrate during WW II is estimated to have caused a population shrinkage of over 20 million people.

Table 17.1 The growth of the birthrate after the Second World War (1945–46)

Winning countries	Growth of birthrate (%)
France	26
England	20
Belgium	17
The Netherlands	34
The United States	20
Canada	13
Mean	22
Losing countries	
Germany	4
Italy	26
Austria	7
Finland	10
Hungary	0
Romania	22
Japan	9
Mean	10

Source: Boris Urlanis (1971), *Wars and Populations* (trans. Leo Lempert), Moscow: Progress Publishers.

Civilian mortality

War affects civilian mortality primarily by increasing the mortality of children, the elderly and the sick. According to Urlanis, the increasing number of accidents at work, the shortage and poor quality of food, and the increased workload may also lead to premature death of healthy adults. It is, however, hard to determine the 'excess mortality' due to war. The decreased birthrate naturally results in a decreased number of infants, which in turn decreases the number of infant deaths and its proportion of total mortality. This may sometimes appear as decreased civilian mortality during a war.

Before 1900. In 1789, during the Russian–Swedish war, the deathrate in Sweden was 30 per cent higher than in prewar years. This could not have resulted from lack of food, because the harvest was normal. During the Austro-Prussian war in 1866, the mortality of the Austrian civil population was one-third higher than in 1865, but this was due to a cholera epidemic which had no direct connection with hostilities. In the Franco-Prussian war, the high mortality of civilians resulted mainly from the siege of Paris. Before the siege approximately 1000 people a week died in Paris; during the siege this figure rose to about 2800 deaths. In Prussia, the same war caused 200,000 civilian deaths in 1871–72. Half of these people perished from a smallpox epidemic carried to Prussia by French prisoners of war.

1913–18. WW I had a much bigger effect on deathrates than any war before it. Under-nourishment and a sudden worsening of living conditions sharply increased deaths among civilians; in the war zone, civilians were also threatened by sieges and air raids. It was in this war that aeroplanes and air raids were first introduced yet the number of civilian casualties from air raids (5000) was small compared to the figures for WW II.

In the European countries (apart from Turkey, where reliable data for the population is lacking) there were about 6 million more civilian deaths than would have been expected had there been no war. Mortality was extremely high in 1918, when the 'Spanish flu' epidemic spread over Europe. If there hadn't been a war, an epidemic this large would not have occurred and its effects would have been less devastating.

The victims of terrorism are direct casualties of war. During WW I, for example, the Germans incited the Turks to kill 1.5 million Armenians.

1939–45. WW II had an especially large effect on the population of Greece. The Italian–German invaders destroyed the country´s economy and forced the population to live near starvation and extinction. The fascists blocked the shipment of food from neutral countries, for example, by sinking Red Cross charity ships. In August 1941, the daily ration of bread was 60 grams per person; this was cut to 40 grams in October of the same year. Diptheria, typhus, dysentery and cholera raged all over the country. In Athens, 90 out of 100 newborn infants died. As the result of starvation and epidemics over a half a million civilians died in Greece. Other Nazi-occupied countries such as Norway also suffered from hunger.

In non-European allied countries there was no rise in civilian mortality. The population of the USA, Canada, Australia and New Zealand didn't suffer the horrors of war and civilian casualties were limited to those drowned when their ships sank in the Atlantic.

At the onset of WW II, as long as the Nazis were advancing, the civilian mortality remained quite small. Even in 1943, after the battle of Stalingrad, the deathrate among civilians remained at its normal level in Germany and Austria. In 1944 living conditions worsened rapidly, but there are no data available for Germany for 1944–45. Judging by Berlin, however, civilian mortality rose rapidly: at the beginning of the war, about 60,000 people died annually in Berlin, while in 1945 the number of deaths reached 161,000, including both direct and indirect victims of the hostilities.

A vast number of civilians died in air raids, most of them German and Japanese. At the outset of the war German losses were small; they started to increase in 1943. By the end of 1944, 14,000 Germans a month were being killed in air raids. The total number killed in this way was about half a million.

Altogether 320,000 civilians perished in Japan during WW II. The biggest numbers (95,000) were killed in the air raids of Tokyo, but Hiroshima and Nagasaki suffered the biggest losses in relation to their populations. The casualties of the atom bombs dropped on Hiroshima and Nagasaki are hard to estimate, because the number of victims continues to grow. The bomb dropped on Hiroshima is estimated to have killed 64,000 people in three months, which is one quarter of the inhabitants of the city. The Nagasaki bomb killed 39,000 people. The aftermath of these atomic bombs still leads to the death of people exposed.

On the allies' side, the casualties of air raids remained smaller because of better anti-aircraft defence and a stronger air force. In England 60,000 civilians died in air raids, out of which 24,000 were women and 7000 children. The biggest losses were suffered by the population of London in September and October 1940. After the Germans attacked the Soviet Union, the casualties in England were smaller. In the air raids on France, about 50,000 people were killed. The population of the Netherlands also suffered great losses. In Rotterdam, for example, the German air raids destroyed 80,000 homes and killed 30,000 people. Altogether, 1.5 million people were killed in air raids in WW II, which is 300 times more than in WW I.

The inhabitants of European countries sustained huge losses as a result of Nazi terror during WW II. The Nazis systematically murdered 11–12 million people whom they considered to be of inferior race. Special concentration camps were built and, according to the evidence put forward in the Nuremberg Trial, seven million people were killed in the biggest six camps. Special attention was paid to Jews, six million of whom were killed, which is three-quarters of the whole European Jewish population. The people of Poland, Yugoslavia and the Soviet Union were also severely affected.

The siege of Leningrad (1941–43) resulted in big losses among the civilian inhabitants. According to L.N. Smirnov, a Soviet prosecutor at the Nuremberg Trial, 632,253 people died in the besieged city of hunger alone.

Demographic consequences

As previously noted, the end of a war does not end its effects on population dynamics. The bigger the damage inflicted on a population, the longer that population takes to recover. WW II caused a population shrinkage of 45.2 million in the Soviet Union. The

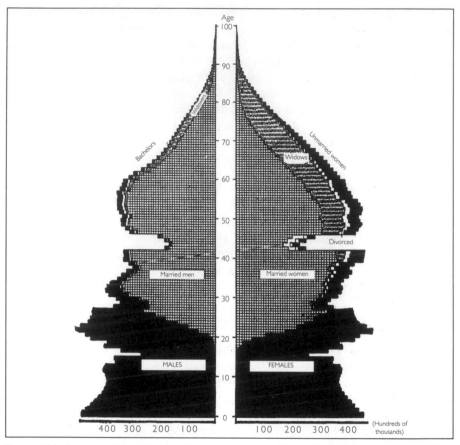

Figure 17.3 Age pyramid of the population of the Federal Republic of Germany, 1 June 1961

population rose to its prewar level only in 1956; that is to say the recovery period was two and a half times the length of the war. It was as late as 1963 before the population was as big as it probably would have been in 1950 if there had not been a war. In Germany, the population grew even slower: it took four times the duration of the war to return to its prewar level in 1965. In other countries involved in WW II, the losses were covered quite fast. Overall WW II had a significant impact on the population dynamics only in a few countries, whose proportion of the world's population is rather small.

The composition of the German population, for example, has been very uneven. This can be seen in the age pyramid of the population of the then Federal Republic of Germany in June 1961 (Figure 17.3). The lower dent represents the decrease in birthrate in the last years of WW II; the upper dent is in the 40–45-year age group, which represents the decrease in births during WW I. The excess of women is shown in the over-35 age group, due to the number of men who died in the war. These losses are also reflected in the number of widows, which is considerable in age groups over forty-five years. The number of unmarried women is also notable: women whose potential husbands were killed in the war.

The after effects of war on a population can be seen decades after the event. In the Soviet Union, the birthrate dropped in the 1960s, partly because of WW II. The number of young people of an age to start a family was relatively small because of the decrease in births in the 1940s. The same was also seen in the 1980s, only on a smaller scale.

Urlanis points out that in the immediate postwar years the number of boys born is higher than in peacetime. In Leningrad in 1940, 4.4 per cent more boys than girls were born; in 1945 the difference was 9.5 per cent. The same phenomenon was seen in other countries but on a smaller scale (Table 17.2). The increases in the relative number of newborn boys obviously helps to restore the balance between males and females. The biological mechanism producing their difference is unknown; it may be that in postwar years marriages increase markedly and so does the share of first-borns, that is to say, births by young mothers in good health.

Table 17.2   The number of newborn boys per 1000 girls in the Federal Republic of Germany

Prewar years		Postwar years	
Year	Number of boys	Year	Number of boys
1928	1062	1946	1079
1929	1062	1947	1075
1930	1061	1948	1078
1931	1062	1949	1076
1932	1063	1950	1072
1933	1065	1951	1066
1934	1069	1952	1071
1935	1067		

Source: Boris Urlanis (1971), Wars and Populations (trans. Leo Lempert), Moscow: Progress Publishers.

Conclusion

The effect of a war on population depends upon many factors, most importantly the length of the conflict and the toll it takes on the population: the greater the effect of war on a country's inhabitants, the longer it takes for that population to recover. The general ability of peoples to cope with difficulties such as epidemics and famine can also make a difference: richer countries with good health care and stable economies can handle the temporarily worsened living conditions better, but in the developing countries even a relatively minor conflict can result in a disaster.

REFERENCE

Urlanis, Boris (1971), *Wars and Populations*, Progress Publishers, Moscow.

Address for correspondence

Humppakuja 2 A 17, 40520 Jyväskylä, Finland. Tel: +358-40-550 4721

18 THE HEALTH AND SOCIAL CONSEQUENCES OF DIVERSION OF ECONOMIC RESOURCES TO WAR AND PREPARATION FOR WAR

VICTOR W. SIDEL and BARRY S. LEVY

Since the beginning of recorded history many societies have devoted major resources to war and preparation for war. Homer describes the 'hollow ships' of the Greeks on the beach outside Troy's walls and the profligate use of arms and supplies by the Greeks, the Trojans and their allies. Over the past three millennia the diversion of resources from the civilian economy to war has on many occasions sharply increased, with disastrous consequences to the people of the nations concerned. This has been especially evident during the period of the Cold War, and only in the past few years has there been a world-wide decline in the diversion of resources. In some countries, however, the economic costs of war and of preparation for war have not declined significantly and have even continued to increase.

Human costs of war

The most important costs of war are its human costs: the killing, maiming and displacement of people. These effects are largely covered in other chapters, but it must be noted here that during the twentieth century there were more than 100 million war-related deaths.[1] During this period, the percentage of civilian casualties in war increased from 10 to 90 per cent of all casualties (see Chapter 17).[2] In addition, many millions of civilians have died from hunger and disease caused by the destruction by war of infrastructure and agricultural capacity and from injury and disease while being forced to flee their homes. The numbers of refugees and displaced persons caused by war have grown alarmingly.[3]

Almost all the wars since 1945 have been fought in developing countries, often as surrogate conflicts between the US and the former Soviet Union. More recently, civil wars, whether in opposition to oppressive governments or arising from historic ethnic enmities or artificial geographic aggregations created by the colonial powers, have

Table 18.1 Military trends: world, industrialized, and developing countries, 1960–94

	1960	1970	1980	1990	1994
Public military expenditures (1987 US$ billion)					
World	324	458	535	667	567
Industrialized countries	274	352	366	473	416
Developing countries	25	55	95	117	110
Public military expenditures (per cent of GNP)					
World	5.7	4.8	4.3	3.8	3.0
Industrialized countries	5.8	4.8	4.2	3.7	2.8
Developing countries	3.7	4.6	4.6	3.9	3.0
Public expenditures (1987 US$ per capita)					
World	114	129	123	128	102
Industrialized countries	445	516	495	602	506
Developing countries	13	22	29	29	25
Armed forces (in millions)					
World	18.6	21.5	25.1	26.8	22.9
Industrialized countries	10.2	10.4	10.2	10.0	4.4
Developing countries	8.4	11.1	14.9	16.8	14.7
Arms exports (1987 US$ billion)					
World	9.2	16.5	49.5	43.6	17.6
Industrialized countries	5.3	10.9	20.8	26.6	15.0
Developing countries	0.3	0.6	1.5	2.0	1.1
Arms imports (1987 US$ billion)					
World	9.1	16.7	50.1	42.0	16.5
Industrialized countries	3.3	4.5	7.4	9.7	4.6
Developing countries	3.9	10.4	36.8	29.9	11.6

Source: Barry S. Levy and Victor W. Sidel (1997), War and Public Health, Oxford: Oxford University Press. Used with permission from Oxford University Press.

produced the greatest number of casualties. The United Nations Children's Fund (UNICEF) has estimated that during the decade from 1985 the terrible toll among children was as follows: 2 million killed; 4 to 5 million disabled; 12 million left homeless; more than 1 million orphaned or separated from their parents; and 10 million psychologically traumatized.[4]

In industrialized countries the direct costs of war include over 50,000 deaths and over 300,000 wounded among US troops in the Vietnam War and many casualties among Soviet and then Russian troops in areas such as Afghanistan and Chechnya. In addition, refugees have come, sometimes in large numbers, to industrialized countries and often place great strains on public health, education and other human services.

In addition to this direct human price of war, other costs not discussed in this chapter include the environmental pollution caused by the production, testing, stockpiling, use and even demilitarization of arms (see Part V, this volume). Chapter 18 will concentrate instead on the destructive economic costs of war and its preparation. We will use the term militarism to represent actual hostilities and military preparations as well as the social, economic and psychological effects they create.

The economic costs of militarism in developing countries

Military spending

From 1960 to 1994, several trends can be observed in military spending and the size of the armed forces in developing countries (Table 18.1). Public military expenditures (in constant dollars) increased more than four-fold in developing countries through 1990 although as a percentage of GNP these expenditures remained fairly constant. After 1990 these expenditures, both in constant dollars and as a percentage of GNP, began to fall. On a per capita basis public military expenditures (in constant dollars) in developing countries doubled throughout the 1990s despite rapid population growth, but since then have begun to decrease; likewise, the size of the armed forces.

Overall, although developing countries spend less than developed ones (when measured in equivalent currency) on arms (Figure 18.1), they spend much more when measured in human hours of productivity (Figure 18.2). The resources spent on arms pose a greater burden to many developing nations than they do for even heavily-spending industrialized countries. As summarized in the report of the 1987 United Nations International Conference on the Relationship between Disarmament and Development: 'The continuing global arms race and development compete for the same finite resources at both the national and international levels'.[5]

International arms trade

Most modern weapons of war are manufactured in industrialized nations, many of these are then sold or given to developing countries. Willingness to purchase or accept these weapons is in part due to the view in many postcolonial countries that possession of large arsenals is essential to being recognized as a developed nation. The arms are often used to keep military dictators in power. They may also fall into the hands of those who use them for private vendettas or private gain, or even into the hands of children. In addition, some industrialized countries, including the US, use their foreign aid as a method of transferring funds to their military industries, requiring the recipient governments to use the aid they receive to purchase arms from private industries in the donor country.

Annual arms imports (in constant $US) almost tripled from 1960 to 1980, but have since been declining . Estimates of the amount of arms traded depend on the definitions used and on the adequacy of reporting, but it is clear that over 90 per cent of arms transferred to other countries are supplied by the five permanent members of the UN Security Council (China, France, Russia, the United Kingdom and the US) and Germany, often termed the Big Six. A 1988 UN study estimated arms transfers between countries at US$14 billion annually in the early 1960s.[6] In 1994, the total rose to over US$35 billion. The US Arms Control and Disarmament Agency estimated that the US negotiated 47 per cent of the dollar value of all new arms sales agreements in 1993; the

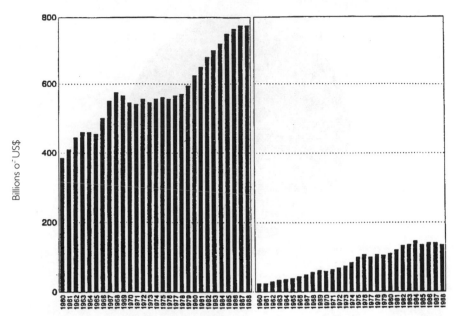

Figure 18.1 Burden of military expenditures in 1987 US$ in industrialized (developed countries (left) and developing countries (right)
Source: R.L. Sivard (1991), World Military and Social Expenditures, 1991, 14th edition, Washington DC: World Priorities, p. 11).

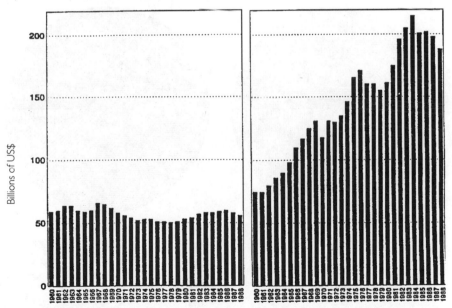

Figure 18.2 Burden of military expenditures in equivalent human-years of income in industrialized (developed) countries (left) and developing countries (right)
Source: R.L. Sivard (1991), World Military and Social Expenditures, 1991, 14th edition, Washington DC: World Priorities, p 11).

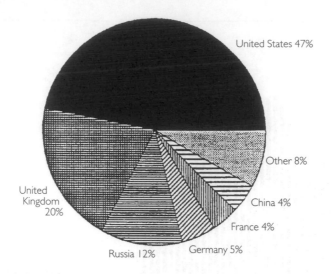

Figure 18.3 Distribution of new arms agreements (1993 US$ value)

Source: US Arms Control and Disarmament Agency estimate, reprinted from British Medical Journal, 23–30 December 1995, p. 1679.

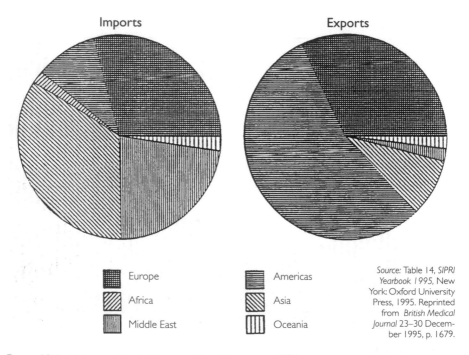

Source: Table 14, SIPRI Yearbook 1995, New York: Oxford University Press, 1995. Reprinted from British Medical Journal 23–30 December 1995, p. 1679.

Figure 18.4 Volume of trade in conventional weapons, 1994

Note: Among the imports, 58 per cent are to the developing and 42 per cent to the industrialized world; among the exports, 93 per cent are from the industrialized and 7 per cent from the developing countries.

UK 20 per cent; Russia 12 per cent; Germany 5 per cent; France 4 per cent; and China 4 per cent (Figure 18.3).

The continents on which the exporting and importing countries were located in 1994 are indicated in Figure 18.4. Of the imports, 58 per cent were into the developing and 42 per cent into the industrialized world; of the exports, 93 per cent were from the industrialized and 7 per cent from the developing countries.

In the 1980s, the US sold more than $134 billion in weapons and military services to more than 160 nations and political movements. US sales increased further during the 1990s. In 1993, the US controlled nearly 73 per cent of the weapons trade to the Third World.[8] An estimated 85 per cent of US arms exports went to non-democratic and often brutal regimes; in Panama, Iraq, and Somalia, such arms were turned against American forces. US arms also fuel conflicts and increase regional tensions. The Clinton administration did little to curb the proliferation of arms sales and the results of the 1994 congressional elections dampened efforts by some members of Congress to reduce them.

The UK is a major participant in the international arms trade and, by some estimates, has moved beyond Russia into second place. In 1993, approximately £2000 million worth of military equipment was shipped overseas and during that year new orders totalling some £6000 million were signed. Former colonial countries, with enormous development problems, such as India, are among Britain's largest customers. Britain, like the US, sells military equipment to countries that violate the human rights of their citizens, such as Indonesia, South Africa in the period before the end of apartheid, Uganda under Idi Amin, and Nigeria with its military government and recent political executions.

France also appears to be increasing its involvement in the international arms trade. In 1994, it negotiated US$11.4 billion in new arms sales agreements with Third World nations, while the US negotiated agreements totalling US$6.1 billion.[9] This comparison is misleading because the bulk of France's sales came from three exceptional multibillion dollar sales of a kind that are not likely to be repeated, and because the figures fail to reflect a number of deals negotiated directly by US industry with foreign purchasers.

Social and health consequences

The damage to health and human services and to economic development by the economic costs of militarism are also extremely well-documented. Developing countries are the most severely affected, suffering delay or reversal of economic development and deprivation of essential nutrition, housing, education, and health services (Box 18.1).[10]

Militarism has other impacts on developing nations: economic embargoes, a form of economic warfare, cause great hardships particularly to civilian populations; while despotic governments use large military forces to maintain themselves in office.

The Report of the 1987 UN Conference on Disarmament and Development summarized the issue for developing countries and for other nations:

> The world can either continue to pursue the arms race with characteristic vigour or move consciously and with deliberate speed towards a more stable and balanced social and economic development within a more sustainable international economic and political order; it cannot do both.[11]

18.1

Human Development: Cost of Arms Imports

Many countries continue to import expensive arms, even though they have a long list of more essential needs. This is clear from the arms deliveries and orders in the categories covered by the UN arms register. Some of the choices by developing countries in 1992 were as follows:

- China purchased 26 combat aircraft from Russia in a deal whose total cost could have provided safe water for one year to 140 million of the 200 million people now without.

- India ordered 20 MiG-29 fighter aircraft from Russia at a cost that could have provided basic education to all 15 million girls out of school.

- Iran bought two submarines from Russia at a cost that could have provided essential medicines to the whole country many times over (13 per cent of Iran's population has no access to health care).

- Republic of Korea ordered 28 missiles from the United States for a sum that could have immunized all the 120,000 unimmunized children and provided safe water for three years to the 3.5 million people without.

- Malaysia ordered two warships from the United Kingdom at a cost that could have provided safe water for nearly a quarter-century to the 5 million people without.

- Nigeria purchased 80 battle tanks from the United Kingdom at a cost that could have immunized all of the two million unimmunized children and provided family planning services to nearly 17 million of the more than 20 million couples who lack such services.

- Pakistan ordered 40 Mirage 2000E fighters and three Tripartite aircraft from France at a cost that could have provided safe water for two years to all 55 million people who lack safe water, family planning services for the estimated 20 million couples in need of such services, essential medicines for the nearly 13 million people without access to health care, and basic education for the 12 million children out of primary school.

Source: United Nations Development Programme (1994), *Human Development Report. 1994,* New York: Oxford University Press.

Economic costs of militarism in industrialized countries

While militarism has had its most dramatic impact on developing countries, it has also had an enormous economic impact in a number of industrialized nations. In industrialized countries the greater impact on civilian populations has been caused by preparations for war rather than by war itself. Huge amounts of financial and human resources are spent on arms instead of improving the quality of life and health of people. New and more devastating weapons have been developed, produced, tested, stockpiled and transferred to other countries. People have been led to believe in the resolution of conflicts by violent means, thereby contributing to increasing violence in their own

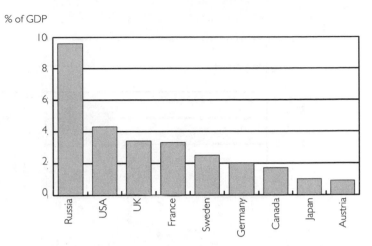

Figure 18.5 Military expenditures as a percentage of gross domestic product, 1994
Source: United Nations Development Programme (1996), *Human Development Report 1996*, New York: Oxford University Press.

countries, especially in urban areas. Individuals in disproportionate numbers from minority communities, particularly in the US, have been seduced into military services, with the diversion of many of the best and brightest individuals from positive roles they could play in civilian life.

Diversion of resources

Many industrialized nations have squandered their financial and human resources on destructiveness, and furthermore, most of them have not paid the bills, leaving an enormous debt to their children. This diversion has had a major adverse effect on the availability of resources for constructive purposes, including health and human services.

Military Spending in Industrialized Countries. From 1960 to 1990 public military expenditures (in constant US$) increased sharply, almost doubling their level (see Table 18.1). Since gross national product (GNP) also rose rapidly over the same period, after an initial rise weapons spending decreased as a percentage of GNP. Since 1990 there has also been a fall in constant US$ as well as a percentage of GNP. Per capita public military expenditures (in constant US$) in industrialized countries increased up to 1990 and have been declining since. Annual arms exports increased five-fold to 1990 but have since declined (Figure 18.5).

US military spending. During the 1980s, annual military spending in the US increased dramatically. During the eight years of the Reagan administration the total amount of military spending (in current $US) was about US$2 trillion, equivalent to about US$20,000 for each US family. The US share of world military spending increased annually from 1979 (approximately 22 per cent) to 1989 (almost 30 per cent). Meanwhile, the US federal budget deficit increased four-fold during the Reagan and Bush administrations to US$4 trillion.[12]

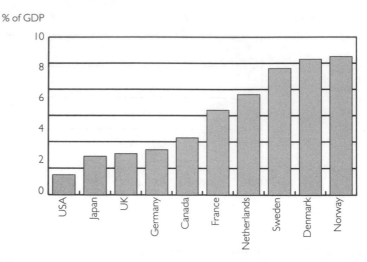

Figure 18.6 Official development assistance as a percentage of gross domestic product, 1994
Source: United Nations Development Programme (1996), *Human Development Report 1996,* New York: Oxford University Press.

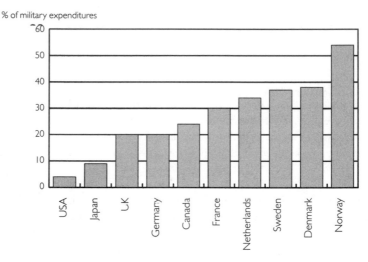

Figure 18.7 Official development assistance as a percentage of gross domestic product, 1994
Source: United Nations Development Programme (1996), *Human Development Report 1996,* New York: Oxford University Press.

Impact of military spending in the former Soviet Union. The impact of military spending in the former Soviet Union was even greater than in the US during the years of the Cold War. Although the two countries spent about the same amounts of money on arms from 1960 to 1981, the Soviet Union, because of its lower GNP, spent a substantially higher percentage of its GNP on arms, an estimated 11.5 per cent as compared with 6.2 per cent of GNP by the US Such enormous expenditures had major adverse effects on the economy and on health and human services.[13]

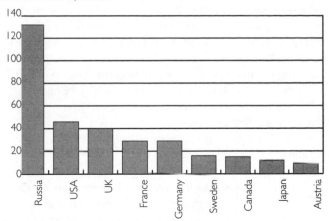

Figure 18.8 Military expenditure as a percentage of combined education and health expenditures, 1990–91
Source: United Nations Development Programme (1996), *Human Development Report 1996*, New York: Oxford University Press.

Military spending compared with development assistance. The amount that industrialized countries spend for military purposes indicates that they spend proportionately less on development assistance to developing countries. In 1989 the Scandinavian countries allocated around 1.0 per cent of their GNP for official development assistance, as compared to 0.2 per cent by the United States (Figure 18.6). Scandinavian countries and Japan allocated for official development assistance monies that ranged from 45 to 70 per cent of their military expenditures, as compared to 3 per cent for the United States (Figure 18.7).

Emphasis on military research. The spending of approximately three-fourths of the US federal research and development funds on the military has meant that less money is available for research that might have improved the quality of life. In fiscal year 1987, for example, military programmes consumed 71 per cent of the total federal research and development budget. In three years in the mid-1980s, military research and development increased by 28 per cent while health and human services research and development decreased by 5 per cent. This focus on military research has resulted in a brain drain that has drawn bright scientists away from performing research in non-military areas that could contribute to an improved standard of living. World expenditures on weapons research exceed the combined spending on developing new energy technologies, improving human health, raising agricultural productivity and controlling pollutants.

Inadequate funds for social development and human services. The huge amounts of tax revenues spent on arms divert monies from health and other human services (Figure 18.8). After correcting for inflation, the US increased its military spending during the 1980s by 46 per cent, while non-military spending decreased: by 19 per cent for child nutrition, 33 per cent for mass transit, 48 per cent for employment and training, 70 per cent for education and 77 per cent for housing. According to the National League of Cities, direct federal aid to US cities fell from almost $25 billion in 1981 to less than $10 billion in 1991 (in 1982 dollars). And during this period an increasing number of people lived below the poverty line: 29 million people in 1980, 33 million in 1985 and approximately 40 million in 1994. Over 40 million people in the US lack health insurance and risk being turned away from receiving health care if they are unable to pay. The US emphasis on achieving military supremacy in the world has had costs in its social development.

Impact on the domestic economy

These high levels of military spending have had profound adverse effects on the domestic economy.[14]

Diminished productivity. One result of massive arms investment is the diversion of capital away from productivity expansion in the civilian economy. Industrialized countries that spent far less on arms, such as Japan, the former Federal Republic of Germany (West Germany), Denmark, Italy and Sweden, surpassed the US and the former Soviet Union in the rate of growth of manufacturing productivity. Money invested in non-military products, services and technologies broaden the overall economic base and potential for further expansion. Although short-term deficit spending has benefited the rich, the resultant overwhelming debt will inevitably diminish the scope of future advancement. Adequate public support for health care and other human services depends on an expanding economic pie. The inevitable contraction based on excessive military spending is likely to restrict publicly-funded services for middle- and low-income families.

Inflation. Military spending exerts inflationary pressure by pumping money into the economy without increasing the supply of purchasable goods and services. Military procurement diminishes resources that would otherwise be used for the production of consumer goods.

Unemployment. The inflationary pressure of military spending generates anti-inflationary responses; in order to diminish the upward spiral of costs, the government tolerates an unacceptably high level of unemployment. Despite assertions to the contrary, military spending creates far fewer jobs than would expenditure for many civilian services. For example, US$1 billion spent on military contracts and personnel in 1992 created 24,000 jobs; the same amount of money spent on mass transit created 28,000 jobs; on housing, 34,000 jobs; on health care 38,000 jobs; and on education 40,000 jobs.[15]

Maintaining or increasing US military spending

According to the International Institute for Strategic Studies, in 1993 the US outspent the next 10 countries combined: US$277.1 billion as compared with US$240.1 billion. Analyses by the Center for Defense Information before the 1994 US Congressional elections, for example, indicated that proposed military spending outlays by the Clinton administration would remain at Cold War levels (in the range of US$257 billion a year). Maintaining this level of expenditure while most other countries of the world reduced theirs, would mean that the US share of global military spending would move from its level of 20–30 per cent in the 1980s to 45 per cent in 1997. The driving forces for this maintenance or increase in military spending include not only perceptions of national security needs but the desire for profits and for jobs. In 1995, the US Senate voted to maintain the level of expenditure while US Congressional leaders proposed an increase, inspite of that the US military budget could be reduced annually by at least US$40 billion with no increased threat to national security (see Figure 18.5).[16]

The US military–industrial complex and those of other arms-producing nations wield considerable power and influence. Major industries involved include aerospace, communications, electronics, computing and transportation. The incestuous relationship between the Pentagon and military contractors has created the opportunity for enormous profits (as a percentage of investment). Such sums of money and the political patronage produced lead to a military agenda (with) little relevance to any external military threat. Cost overruns, deception and fraud become the norm.

Influence on community and domestic violence

International and civil war, and preparation for war, influence community and domestic violence in a number of ways: they promote the idea that violence is an acceptable method of resolving conflicts; they make human lives appear cheaper; they make lethal weapons, including military assault weapons, readily available at the community and domestic levels; and they make local violence a little easier to accept. Social conditions help to cause both war and violence. In the US and other industrialized countries, the quality of life is lower and rates of tuberculosis, HIV infection and murder are higher in low-income areas than in high-income ones.

Disproportionate impact on minority communities in the US

In the US, individuals from minority communities comprise a disproportionate fraction of those serving in the military; in the process, many of the best and the brightest from these communities are taken away from roles that they might directly play in improving education, political action, health and hope.

In addition, militarism and war glorify violence, a fact that may be especially relevant to minority communities in which living conditions lead to frequent conflict that may escalate into violence. Limited possibilities for the future contribute to pessimism in these communities. Young African-Americans perceive from their personal experience that the community is a dangerous place to be, and a place where there are woefully inadequate social supports and limited access to health care and other services.

In this context, the military can look like a very attractive environment, especially as it is portrayed in television commercials: come join the military; get scholarships for school; work in a place where your employer is committed to promoting your health and well-being – smoking cessation, stress control, exercise programmes, good nutrition and universal access to health care.

In addition, there is a perception that the military is one of the few meritocracies in the US. It is an educator, a teacher of skills and a place for positive behaviour reinforcement by peers. And for those in the military reserves, including many black hospital workers, it offers a reasonable income supplement for fairly interesting and job-enhancing work. As a result, African-Americans, who comprise 12 per cent of the US population, make up approximately 22 per cent of the recent active-duty recruits into the US army. In the Persian Gulf War, approximately 30 per cent of US army personnel and approximately 25 per cent of the combat troops were African-American. Interestingly, the percentage of high school graduates among new African-American recruits exceeded the percentage of high school graduates among new white recruits. In fact, the US Army is the only educational institution in the US where African-Americans are consistently more highly educated than whites.

Yet, the primary goals for which many African-Americans joined the military are often unrealized. Almost one-third of recruits leave the military before completing their initial tours; the education benefits are not nearly as great as the television commercials make them seem; and individuals have to forego some pay in order to achieve some of these benefits, while little of the on-the-job training in the military is directly applicable to employment in the civilian workforce.[17]

Conclusion

The public-health consequences of military activities, in both industrialized and developing countries, go far beyond the direct casualties caused by weapons of war. The consequences of preparation for war and of militarism require the attention of public-health professionals, who can play an important role in their prevention.

ACKNOWLEDGEMENTS

Parts of Chapter 18 were adapted and updated in 1998 from the authors' 'Impact of Military Activity on Civilian Populations' in *War and Public Health*, edited by the authors (New York: Oxford University Press, 1997).

REFERENCES

1. Homer
2. Sivard, R.L. (1996), *World Military and Social Expenditures 1996*, 16th ed., Washington DC: World Priorities.
3. Bellamy, C. (1996), *The State of the World's Children 1996*, Oxford: Oxford University Press; and Astrom, C. (1991), *Casualties of Conflict: Report for the World Campaign for the Protection of Victims of War*. Department of Peace and Conflict Research, Uppsala, pp. 8, 19.
4. United Nations Development Programme (1994), *Human Development Report 1994*, New York: Oxford University Press (1994).
5. See n. 2 above.
6. United Nations (1987), Report of the International Conference on the Relationship Between Disarmament and Development., A/Conf. 130/39, New York: United Nations.
7. United Nations (1994), *Disarmament: responding to new realities in disarmament*, Sales No.E. 94.IX.8, New York: United Nations.
8. US Arms Control and Disarmament Agency (1995), *World Militia Expenditures and Arms Transfers, 1993–1994*, Washington DC: US Government Printing Office.

9. Hartung, W.D. (1994), *And Weapons For All*, New York: Harper Collins Publishers.
10. Congressional Research Service (1995), *Conventional Arms Transfers to Developing Nations 1987–1994*, Washington DC: Congressional Research Service.
11. See n. 3 above; Brauer, J. and M. Chatterji (eds) (1993), *Economic Issues of Disarmament*, London: Macmillan Press Ltd; Sidel, V.W. (1988), 'The Arms Race as a Threat to Health', *Lancet* 2: 442–4; Woolhandler, S. and D.U. Himmelstein (1985), 'Militarism and Mortality. An international analysis of arms spending and infant death rates', *Lancet* 1: 1375–8; Stott, R. (1994), 'The Third World Debt as a Symptom of the Global Crisis', *Medicine and Global Survival* 1: 92–8.
12. See n. 6 above.
13. 'Two Trillion Dollars in Seven Years' (1987), *The Defense Monitor* 16 (7).
14. Sivard, R.L. (1989), *World Military and Social Expenditures 1989*, Washington DC: World Priorities.
15. Dumas, W. (1986), *The Overburdened Economy: uncovering the causes of chronic unemployment, inflation and national decline*, Berkeley CA: University of California Press; and Dumas, L.J. (1993), 'Policy Dimensions of Economic Conversion: separating the wheat from the chaff', in J. Brauer and M. Chatterji (eds), *Economic Issues of Disarmament*, London: Macmillan Press, pp. 137–51.
16. Anderson, M., Bischak, G. and M. Oden (1991), *Converting the American Economy*, Lansing MI: Employment Research Associates.
17. Korb, W. (1995), 'Our Overstuffed Armed Forces', *Foreign Affairs* 74 (6): 22–34, November; and O'Hanlon, M. (1995) *Defense Planning for the Late 1990s: beyond the Desert Storm framework*, Washington DC: Brookings Institute.
18. Tuckson, R. (1991), *The Impact of War and Militarism on Minority Communities in the US*, Presentation, American Public Health Association Annual Meeting, Atlanta.

Address for correspondence
Victor W. Sidel, MD, Professor of Social Medicine, Montefiore Medical Center, 111 East 210th Street, Bronx, NY 10467 USA; email: Vsidel@igc.org
Barry S. Levy, MD, MPH, P.O. Box 1230, Sherborn, MA 01770 USA, email: Blevy@igc.org

19 HEALTH AND WAR IN MOZAMBIQUE

ABDUL RAZAK NOORMAHOMED AND
JULIE CLIFF

From 1980 to 1992, Mozambique suffered a devastating war of destabilization. Backed by the apartheid regime in South Africa, the Mozambique National Resistance (Renamo) waged war against the Mozambican government of the ruling party, Frelimo. The war ended with the signing of a peace accord in 1992, followed by the election of a Frelimo government in 1994.

During the war between 3 and 6 million of the population of about 16 million were internally displaced, about 1,500,000 sought refuge in neighbouring countries, and about 250,000 children were abandoned, orphaned or separated from their parents. Between 30 and 50 per cent of health units were destroyed or forced to close. The war caused about a million deaths, high rates of childhood malnutrition and epidemics of diseases such as measles and cholera. Landmine victims numbered about 10,000. Children were used as soldiers and were victims of violence. Responses to the war included special programmes for children. Postwar physical reconstruction of the health services has been rapid. Improving quality is proving more difficult, as low wages have led to low morale among health workers.

From 1980 to 1992, Mozambique suffered a devastating war of destabilization. Backed by the apartheid regime in South Africa, guerrillas of the Mozambique National Resistance (Renamo) waged war in the countryside against the Mozambican government of the ruling party, Frelimo.

Mozambique gained independence from Portugal in 1975, after a ten-year liberation struggle. The new Frelimo government provided support to the Zimbabwean movements fighting against the colonialist Rhodesian regime. The Rhodesians created a guerrilla movement, Renamo, as part of their counterinsurgency tactics. Renamo actions were smallscale during the time of Rhodesian support. When the Rhodesian regime fell in 1980, South Africa took over support of Renamo. From 1982 onwards, after a build-up period, destabilization intensified. Internationally, Frelimo was aligned with the socialist bloc, including the Soviet Union and China, which had provided support during the liberation war.

With the end of apartheid and the Cold War, the logic of the Mozambican war collapsed. A peace accord was signed in October 1992. After a two-year period during which UN troops were stationed in the country, general elections in 1994 led to the election of a Frelimo government. Most of the 92,000 soldiers in both armies were demobilized and a small new army of 12,000 created from both sides' volunteers.

Mozambique is now hailed as a successful example of a peace process. Not least among the successes has been the re-establishment of the health services and programmes for the treatment of child victims of war. The after-effects of the war are, however, profound, and reconstruction is an incomplete and ongoing process.

Chapter 19 looks at the impact of the 1980–92 war on people's health. We will also briefly describe psychological and social-rehabilitation programmes for children, and postwar responses by the Mozambican health service and the international aid community.

Impact of the war

We cannot easily measure the direct impact of the hostilities on health. Prewar baseline data are scarce, and the collection of reliable information during the conflict was difficult; reconstruction of the health services was a greater postwar priority than documenting the war's impact. Nonetheless, some studies were carried out and the health information system continued to function. We will present the available data on the direct impact on people's health but first we will look at the indirect impact of worsening socio-economic conditions and a deterioration in health services.

Socioeconomic

Somewhere between three and six million of Mozambique's population of about 16 million were internally displaced by the war; another 1,500,000 left to become refugees in neighbouring countries; and 250,000 children were abandoned, orphaned or separated from their parents.

The United Nations Children's Fund (UNICEF) estimated that by 1986 Mozambique's gross domestic product (GDP) was only half of what it would have been without the war. War losses from 1975 to 1988 totalled US$15 billion (at 1988 prices) or more than four times the 1988 GDP.[1] Extrapolation to 1992 gives a total cost of more than US$20 billion. GDP per capita fell from US$185 in 1980 to US$87 in 1992, making Mozambique one of the poorest countries in the world.[2]

Deterioration in health services

Renamo targeted health services during the war as they were a visible sign of government success in the rural areas. The already-existing bias toward urban health care therefore increased. Between 30 and 50 per cent of some 1000 health posts together with 200 health centres existing in the early 1980s were destroyed or forced to close.

The quality of the health services declined during the war years as supply and supervision became more difficult. Health workers' morale fell, both because of their difficult working conditions, and because of steadily declining real wages. The introduction of an economic structural adjustment package at the height of the war in 1987 further reduced real wages.

Government spending on the health sector fell by nearly 40 per cent in real terms between 1980 and 1991, leading to a dependence on external aid. This aid accounted for 68 per cent of expenditure in 1991 compared with 29 per cent in 1986. Donor dependence had many negative consequences: (i) instead of an integrated national health service, vertical disease control programmes were strengthened; (ii) the Ministry of Health had to shift its focus from managing the health service to dealing with donors and crisis management; (iii) some donors set up their own management and supply systems, thus weakening the national system; and (iv) though many international nongovernmental organizations (NGOs) arrived to provide relief in the rural areas, providing a valuable service and filling a vacuum, these were costly and unsustainable.

Mortality

In 1989, UNICEF made rough estimates of war-related mortality, dividing causes of death into three categories: (i) direct military action – 100,000 (based on the US State Department's Gersony report); (ii) the war-related famine of 1983–84 – another 100,000 civilians; and (iii) the largest category, excess infant and child deaths caused by increased malnutrition and disease and the breakdown of rural health services – 494,000 between 1980 and 1988.[3] Extrapolation of these figures to the end of the war in 1992 gives a rough estimate of one million war-related deaths.[4]

Other sources of information on war-related mortality are census data and mortality studies. In 1980, a national census estimated that Mozambique had a low life expectancy of 43.5 years and a high infant mortality rate of 159 (per 1000 live births). A limited national demographic survey was carried out in 1991. Life expectancy remained almost stationary at 44.4 years and the infant mortality rate fell slightly to 140. With peace, life expectancy should have risen and infant mortality fallen throughout the decade. Mozambique's infant mortality rate was the highest in the region; during the 1980s other countries showed falls of about 50 per cent. In 1997, a national Demographic and Health Survey (DHS) concluded that childhood mortality levels were about the same as those at the time of independence in 1975: levels fell both post-independence and post-war. But wartime infant and child mortality rates rose from 136 to 161 and 78 to 93 respectively.

In the cities, to where many people fled and where health service coverage increased, the census and surveys suggest that mortality fell during the 1980s. In Maputo City, infant mortality fell from 100 in 1980 to 73 in 1991. In Beira City, child mortality, expressed as the probability of dying before age five, fell from 246 in 1977–78 to 212 in 1988–89.[5] Sporadic and limited surveys in war-affected rural areas showed very high mortality rates in children, with mortality rates at ages 1–4 ranging from 69 to 125.[6]

Nutrition

Mozambique is a fertile country that could feed itself. Although periodic droughts occur in some areas, food production in other areas should make up for the shortfalls. The war made Mozambique dependent on food aid. By 1992, following a severe drought, the country was 90 per cent dependent on marketed and relief grain. In 1991, USAID ranked Mozambique as the 'hungriest' of 91 surveyed nations around the world, with a daily per capita food consumption of 1605 calories. Between 1983 and 1989, the proportion of land under cultivation fell from 10 to 4 per cent. Famines occurred several times during the war, always associated with drought.[7]

The Ministry of Health and NGOs carried out many anthropometric surveys in different parts of Mozambique during the war. The most comprehensive showed that 53 per cent of children under five were stunted (height for age below the third percentile) and 7 per cent were wasted (weight for height below the third percentile). Many studies showed high rates of acute malnutrition in displaced populations.[8]

Disease

Disease epidemics increased in severity and frequency both during and after the war, owing to overcrowded living conditions, population movements, poor hygiene, malnutrition and low vaccination coverage; at the same time, control measures were severely hampered.

Measles epidemics increased, as vaccination rates fell in the rural areas. In 1989, 23036 measles cases were notified, the highest number since 1980. Epidemics with high case-fatality rates were seen among displaced populations in rural areas. Two major cholera epidemics lasted for several years. In 1983, the peak year of the first epidemic, 10,745 cases and 447 deaths were notified. The second epidemic was more severe, with 23,577 cases and 631 deaths notified in 1992 alone. Both cases and deaths were under-notified, owing to the difficulty of confirming the diagnosis of cholera in rural areas.

In 1994, a plague outbreak, with 216 notified cases, occurred in Mutarara District in Tete Province. The return of about 85,000 refugees from Malawi combined with drought upset the ecological equilibrium, leading to an increase in the rat population around dwellings. Plague is endemic in the wild rodent population of Mutarara.

In 1992 and 1993, epidemics of konzo, a permanent spastic paraparesis associated with cyanide intoxication from eating bitter cassava, occurred in Mogincual District in Nampula Province. More than 300 cases were notified. During the war, populations turned to bitter cassava because it was highly productive and less likely to be stolen by monkeys. Bitter cassava must be processed to remove cyanide. In 1992, when fighting intensified in the period leading up to the peace accord, dependence on bitter cassava increased and people did not have time to process it adequately. Likewise, following the Peace Accord, displaced people returned home and had to plant and harvest bitter cassava early without adequate time for processing.

Other war-related epidemics included glomerulonephritis and scabies in Maputo City and meningococcal meningitis in military barracks and surrounding communities. The war probably had two opposing effects on HIV transmission: displacement and family separation increased transmission, while the cutting of transport links probably delayed the epidemic. More than 1,000,000 million refugees have now returned from neighbouring countries with high seroprevalence rates. HIV transmission is increasing rapidly: in the border provincial capitals of Manica and Tete, seroprevalence rates in antenatal screening increased from 10.4 to 19.2 per cent and 18.0 to 21.4 per cent, respectively, between 1994 and 1996.

Physical trauma

The total number of people wounded and maimed in the war is not known. One detailed study of trauma in a rural health centre in the south of the country registered 454 cases of war-injured in an eight-month period: 379 (84 per cent) were civilians and 89 (20 per cent) were children under 15 years of age. The study gives grim testimony to the brutality of the war. Of 22 amputations in men, 13 were of the penis, 2 of the ears, 2 of the eyes, 2 of the legs, 1 of the lips, 1 of the nose, and 1 of the hand.[9] Renamo guerillas systematically mutilated civilians in order to intimidate, particularly in the centre and south. There are also reports of mutilations by government troops.[10]

Landmines continue to kill and injure, as clearance is proceeding slowly. The Halo Trust found 3400 cases of death or injury from landmines in a retrospective study of health-facility records from 1980 to 1993. Records are, however, incomplete and many victims do not reach a hospital. They therefore estimated that the total number of mine victims between 1980 and 1993 was about 7000, a rate of about 0.5 per 1000. In 1994, two community household surveys in mined areas showed that the impact of landmines was possibly higher than originally thought. Casualty ratios were 8.1 and 16.7 per 1000 living people and amputee prevalence rates were 3.2 and 2.3 per 1000. The case fatality rate was 48 per cent. Most (68 per cent) of the victims were civilians. Eighty-one per cent of the injuries came from antipersonnel landmines. Sixteen per cent were women and 7 per cent were under 15 years of age.[11] In 1994, the Human Rights Watch Arms Project estimated that the total number of landmine casualties in Mozambique was between 10,000 and 15,000.[12]

Psychological

During the war, children witnessed, committed, or suffered violence and experienced danger, flight, hunger, separation and bereavement. Most at risk were child soldiers, unaccompanied children living in institutions or with foster parents, disabled children and street children.

Many studies have documented the psychological impact of the war on children. Despite differences in methodology, they have all shown high rates of abuse and consequent psychological reactions. For example, a careful study of 50 randomly-selected displaced children found that 24 per cent of children were markedly affected by their experiences of war.[13] In 1988, Boothby and his colleagues interviewed 504 children aged 6–15, all with direct experience of war. They came from 49 districts and covered a broad geographical range. Seventy-seven per cent and 88 per cent had witnessed killings and physical abuse or torture, respectively; 51 per cent had themselves been physically abused or tortured, with 7 per cent suffering permanent physical injury; 63 per cent had witnessed rape or sexual abuse and 16 per cent admitted to being raped; 64 per cent had been abducted from their families; 28 per cent of the abducted boys had been trained for combat, and 9 per cent of the abducted admitted to killing.[14]

Child soldiers were press-ganged or kidnapped and recruited into the armies of both sides. When the armies were demobilized, of a total of 92,881 soldiers, 25,498 stated that they had been recruited under the age of 18 years of age; of these, 11,507 were under 16. Twenty-three per cent of government and 41 per cent of Renamo troops had been recruited as children under eighteen. The lives of children captured by Renamo have been well documented. While some boys were integrated into auxiliary tasks, others were trained for combat. This training often included an induction experience such as forcing the child to kill.[15]

Street children appeared in the cities in large numbers for the first time during the war; about 3500 lived on the streets of Maputo and Beira. Immediately postwar, children suffered an additional indignity. The use of girl prostitutes between 12 and 18 years by UN soldiers in the provincial town of Chimoio became a scandal. The offending soldiers were sent home after a commission of enquiry.[16]

Women were also victims of the war.[17] Girls and women in Renamo bases were assigned to men as servants and wives, a form of enslavement or forced concubinage. Studies among displaced and refugee women have shown high rates of direct violence and stress, including torture, rape and separation from their children.

Chemical weapons

The Mozambican government reported that chemical weapons may have been used in an attack near the South African border in 1992. A projectile fired from the direction of the border had exploded in mid-air, releasing a dense cloud of black smoke that provoked generalized heat, vomiting and chest pains. Five soldiers were killed and ten injured. An eyewitness claimed that Renamo paratroops in the area were using gas masks. Later the same year, a report commissioned by the South African government alleged that the Seventh Medical Battalion had been involved in a chemical bomb attack in Mozambique. Further corroboration of the development of a chemical and biological warfare programme by the South African government has come from the hearings of the Truth and Reconciliation Commission.

Responses

Programmes for children

Many programmes have been developed for child victims of the war. International attention was first focused on 42 boys liberated from Renamo control by government troops in 1987. The adverse effect of media attention and the harmful effects of institutionalization on these boys soon became apparent. The experience strengthened the Mozambican government's policy on non-institutionalization. All but one of the boys were placed in families (12 with parents, 21 with extended family and 8 with neighbours). All showed a high potential for readaptation and only two (among the most troubled) had to be removed from their families.[18]

The Secretariat of State for Social Action coordinated a national family tracing and reunification programme with the strong support of national organizations and international NGOs. This programme consisted of identification of separated children, documentation of the child's personal details, tracing of family members and reunification. From 1988 up to 1995, about 20,000 children had been documented, of whom about half had been reunited with their families. These statistics underestimate the numbers of reunited, as much family tracing and reunification took place spontaneously once the war ended. Of those not reunited, most were living in substitute families. About 600 were living in government residential homes, and a further 300–400 in homes run by foreign NGOs or religious organizations. The consistency of government policy contributed to this low level of institutionalization.[19]

Programmes for child victims of the war have recognized that individual trauma counselling is both inappropriate and unfeasible. External assistance is unsustainable and may destroy rather than reinforce indigenous coping mechanisms. In Mozambique, families arrange the culturally appropriate acceptance or purification ceremonies to mark the return of their children. These ceremonies may be both traditional and religious. Children are then integrated into ongoing community reconstruction work.[20]

In the late 1980s, the Ministry of Education set up a special education programme for schoolchild war victims. The programme was unfortunately not sustained. Its manuals – 'Helping Children in Difficult Circumstances' and 'Communicating with Children' – have, however, been widely used.

Mozambican and international NGOs run a variety of other projects, mostly with limited coverage. An example is Healing through Play, a programme of the Mozambican Red Cross that trains village women to organize play groups.

Post-conflict transition (1992–94)

After the 1992 peace accord, refugees and displaced people returned home en masse, mostly spontaneously. This return put an enormous strain on the health services: about 5 million people needed services in new locations. Those returning to rural areas were often suddenly deprived of health care.

This period was chaotic. Many agencies began reconstructing peripheral health units without coordination. Some NGOs which had played an important role in relief during the war found it hard to adapt to the transition to peace. In the rush to reconstruct, they sometimes did not adhere to national standards. For example, they used poor quality building materials. In addition, they did not consider staff and equipment needs. Much reconstruction was unplanned, without the involvement of the Ministry of Health, which was supposed to assume the recurrent costs. However, given budgetary constraints, this was impossible. The Ministry of Health was also subject to wage caps imposed by the International Monetary Fund (IMF). Consequently, the number and type of new health personnel that could be employed were severely limited. The ministry could not hire or train sufficient personnel to staff reopened units. In 1996, about 100 health centres and posts were still closed or operating below acceptable standards.

Reconstruction also sometimes exacerbated existing inequalities. For example, in Zambezia Province, the health network was restored to almost prewar levels in three years. This rehabilitation perpetuated and worsened pre-existing inequalities, however, favouring easily-accessible districts.

Refugees returning from neighbouring countries were fortunate to have a powerful advocate in the United Nations High Commission for Refugees (UNHCR). The internally displaced within Mozambique had no such body. Thus, high priority was given to providing health services to returnees from neighbouring countries. Many refugees had previously benefited from higher quality health services than those available to the internally displaced. Through Quick Impact Projects, UNHCR rehabilitated or constructed more than 130 health units, of which 30 were in ex-Renamo areas. This reconstruction was mostly carried out in partnership with international NGOs and provided a bridge between returnee aid and longer-term development assistance.

The separate Frelimo and Renamo health services also had to be integrated. As many Renamo health workers did not meet formal government training criteria, special upgrading courses were organized and are still ongoing. Reintegration of the separate health services has been completed.

Postwar reconstruction and development (1995–97)

Foreseeing peace, Ministry of Health policymakers developed postwar reconstruction plans in the early 1990s. These have, however, been hampered by shortfalls in donor funding. Since 1993, the money available for the health services has been declining. Although the Mozambican government allocation has increased, it is insufficient to cover reconstruction and recurrent costs, and will be for the foreseeable future.

In this period of reconstruction, bilateral donors have played an increasing role. Many major donors such as the European Union, France, and Finland have reduced the proportion of their aid channelled through NGOs. They have increased support to Ministry of Health programmes and provincial health services.

The Ministry of Health plans gave high priority to expanding and re-establishing the primary health-care network. Impressive progress has been made, with at least 75 per cent of the network restored. Coverage and service consumption are expanding, with indicators such as consultations per head and vaccine coverage improving.

The poor quality of the health service, however, remains a major concern. Low wages are an important cause of low quality; health workers' wages fell steadily to 1996. For example, the monthly wage of a nurse fell from the equivalent of US$140 in 1991 to US$40 in 1996. Reconstructing a good quality service for the poor, who suffered the brunt of the country's war, remains a challenge for the health service and the international community.

ACKNOWLEDGMENTS

Thanks to the many ministry of health departments which provided information, and to Helen

Charnley, Sandro Colombo, Frieda Overvest, Enrico Pavignani and Terezinha da Silva for generously giving additional material.

REFERENCES

1. United Nations Children's Fund (1989), *Children on the Front Line. The impact of apartheid, destabilization and warfare on children in southern and South Africa.* UNICEF: New York, 1989.
2. Hanlon, J. (1996), *Peace without Profit. How the IMF blocks rebuilding in Mozambique*, Oxford: Irish Mozambique Solidarity, International African Institute and James Currey; Portsmouth NH: Heinemann.
3. See n. 1 above.
4. See n. 2 above.
5. Cutts, F., Santos, C. dos, Novoa, A., David, P., Macassa, G. and A.C. Soares (1996), 'Child and Maternal Mortality during a Period of Conflict in Beira City, Mozambique', *International Journal of Epidemiology* 25: 349–56.
6. Cliff, J. and A.R. Noormahomed (1993), 'The Impact of War on Children's Health in Mozambique', *Social Science and Medicine* 36: 843–8.
7. Human Rights Watch (1992), *Conspicuous Destruction. War, famine and the reform process in Mozambique*, New York: Human Rights Watch.
8. See n. 4 above.
9. Gaensly, R. (1990), 'Perfil epidemiologico dos feridos de guerra no Centro de Saúde Rural do Distrito de Massinga, Provincia de Inhambane, de Setembro de 1989 a Abril de 1990', paper presented at the Jornadas de Saude, Quelimane.
10 See n. 7 above.
11. Ascherio, A., Biellik, R., Epstein, A., Snetro, G., Gloyd, S., Ayotte, B. and P. Epstein (1995), 'Deaths and Injuries Caused by Landmines in Mozambique', *Lancet* 346: 721–24.
12. Human Rights Watch Arms Project (1994), *Landmines in Mozambique*, New York: Human Rights Watch.
13. See n. 6 above.
14. Boothby, N. (????), 'Children of War: survival as a collective act', in M. McCallin (ed.) *The Psychological Well-being of Refugee Children. Research practice and policy issues.* Geneva: International Catholic Child Bureau.
15. Ibid.
16. United Nations (1996), 'Impact of Armed Conflict on Children'. Report of the expert of the Secretary-General, Ms Graça Machel, submitted pursuant to the General Assembly resolution 48/157, A/51/306, New York: United Nations.
17. Cliff, J. (1991), 'The War on Women in Mozambique: health consequences of South African destabilization, economic crisis, and structural adjustment', in M. Turshen (ed.) *Women and Health in Africa.* New Jersey: Africa World Press.
18. See n. 14 above.
19. Charnley, H. (1995), 'Review of SCF's early experience of family tracing, reunification and community based care in Africa', in M. Brown, H. Charnley and C. Petty (eds) *Children Separated by War: family tracing and reunification*, London: Save the Children Fund.
20. Gibbs, S. (1994), 'Post-war Social Reconstruction in Mozambique: re-framing children's experience of trauma and healing', *Disasters* 18: 268–76.

Address for correspondence

Abdul Razak Noormahomed, Ministry of Health, CP 264, Maputo, Mozambique, Tel: 258 1 426740; Fax: 258 1 427133 Email: misau@gbvm.uem.mz

Julie Cliff, CP 257, Maputo, Mozambique, Tel: 258 1 424910; Fax: 258 1 425255; Email: jcliff@med1.uem.mz

20 POSTWAR HEALTH AND HEALTH CARE IN BOSNIA AND HERZEGOVINA

MAUNO KONTTINEN

In the early 1990s, after the gradual breakdown of the Socialist Federal Republic of Yugoslavia, Bosnia and Herzegovina launched a comprehensive national reform programme, including the rearrangement of health insurance and health-care delivery systems. The 1992–95 war completely foiled these plans, however.

The postwar public health-care system is essentially the same as before the conflict. Primary health care services are provided by small health stations, (*ambulantas*), and by bigger, more specialized health centres (*dom zdravljas*). General hospitals, mental hospitals and three university-level clinical centres form the network of secondary and tertiary care providers. Even though many health care facilities were destroyed or damaged during the war, present health-service delivery generally covers the basic needs of the population. Reconstruction work and the supply of medicines and other consumables are, however, still largely dependent on the generosity of the international community.

The most prominent current problems in the country are the general lack of money and industrial production and trade, the lack of mutual collaboration between the major ethnic population groups and the lack of common visions towards a prosperous and sustainable development. In the field of health care, the lack of financial resources to run and develop the service system is glaring. Another serious problem is the shortage of skilled medical staff, due to the massive emigration of professionals during the war. The third problem is how to re-educate and remotivate existing health care personnel in the changing and challenging situation of reform and reconstruction.

Chapter 20 presents the general postwar situation of public health and the health care system in Bosnia and Herzegovina, its previous achievements and deficiencies, the effects of the war and current problems deriving from these. The tools to achieve real, sustainable improvements are also discussed.

The country and the prewar health-care system

Bosnia and Herzegovina (BiH) is located in the middle of the Balkan peninsula, bordering Croatia in the north, west and south and the Federal Republic of Yugoslavia in

Note: White area: Federation of Bosnia and Herzegovina; shaded area: Republika Srpska

Figure 20.1 Bosnia and Herzegovina

the east and south (Figure 20.1). At the end of the Second World War, Bosnia-Herzegovina became a Constitutional State within the Socialist Federal Republic of Yugoslavia, together with five other republics: Croatia, Macedonia, Montenegro, Serbia and Slovenia. Following the elections in 1991, the Republic of Bosnia and Herzegovina became independent at the beginning of 1992. A few months later, in April 1992, the war broke out, with terrible consequences for the country, its population and economy. November 1995 finally marked the end of the conflict and the beginning of a reconstruction period.

At present, Bosnia and Herzegovina comprises two entities, recognized by the Dayton Accord of December 1995: the Federation of Bosnia and Herzegovina (FBiH) and Republika Srpska (RS). The two entities are distinguished by the Inter-Entity

Boundary Line (IEBL), which in effect follows the last frontier line before peace was concluded. Free movement of the people across the IEBL was guaranteed by the Dayton Accord. To this day this promise remains unfulfilled, however. Other violations of human rights are still common-place as well. The total area of the country is 51,129 km^2 (FBiH 26,076 km^2, RS 25,053 km^2). The capital of the FBiH is Sarajevo, the capital of the RS is Banja Luka. The Federation of BiH is divided into ten cantons, the Republika Srpska into four major regions.

According to the United Nations High Commissioner for Refugees (UNHCR), the total population of the country in October 1996 was about 4 million (FBiH 2,536,000, RS 1,452,000). The population can be divided into three ethnic groups, with the same eastern Slavic genetic origin. The Roman Catholic Croats inhabit the northern and western parts of the territory, most Muslim Bosnians live in the centre of the country, and Orthodox Serbs in the north-east and in the south-east. The accurate numerical distribution of the groups remains obscure at the moment. More than one million persons living in the country were displaced during the war, that is to say they moved voluntarily or were forced to move inside the country. In the federation, the share of the 639,000 displaced persons is 25 per cent of the total population, in the Republika Srpska the corresponding figures are 464,000 and 32 per cent. In 1997, more than 20,000 persons were still living in so-called collective centres, often in unacceptable conditions. In addition, the total number of refugees outside Bosnia-Herzegovina is approximately one million: 320,000 in other former Yugoslavian countries, 640,000 elsewhere. The return of the refugees has been slow due to unstable living and other conditions. In January 1998, there were still about 20,000 persons missing, most of them probably buried as victims of brutal massacres.

Prior to the conflict, the morbidity patterns in the whole of BiH paralleled those in other parts of Europe, with a growing proportion of chronic diseases. The percentage of all deaths caused by diseases of the circulatory system, neoplasms and external causes of death was comparable to that in most OECD countries. Acute myocardial infarction and cerebrovascular diseases had become the leading causes of death. Of deaths caused by neoplasms, lung cancer was the leading cause for men, breast cancer for women. In 1989, life expectancy at birth was 69.2 years for males and 74.6 years for females. Infant mortality rates had steadily decreased to 14.5 deaths per 1000 live births in 1991, still high for the European average of 9.3 per 1000. The rate increased during the war to 24.7 per 1000 live births, but seems to have declined again. Some estimates give the rate of 13.9 per 1000 in 1995 and 13.6 in 1996.

At the time BiH became independent, the country inherited a socialist health-care system with a legacy of accomplishments, for example well-trained clinicians, successful efforts against infectious diseases and easy access to health care services. The health care system was quite well staffed with 7032 medical doctors, 1408 dentists and 18,257 nurses for the population of 4.39 million. However, the legacy also held unresolved problems, like the duplication, waste and compartmentalization of services, emphasis on specialist and institutional care, long in-hospital stays, overstaffing patterns and high running costs due to non-competitive funding. One prominent feature has been the weak role of primary health care and the position of primary care physicians suffering from low salaries and poor societal status.

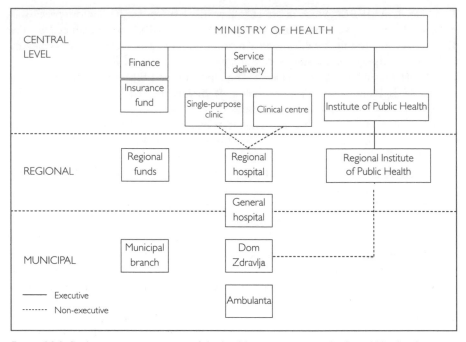

Figure 20.2 Preliminary organization of the health-care system in the Republika Srpska

Health-care delivery system

The present health-care system in Bosnia and Herzegovina is basically the same as before the war, that is to say it is organized on three levels. The first level, primary health care, is represented by the *ambulantas*, small health centres staffed by a general practitioner (GP) and a few nurses providing basic primary care to a population of usually between 2000 and 10,000 inhabitants. The *ambulantas* are accountable to the *dom zdravljas* (DZs), primary health-care centres providing ambulatory services and usually covering one commune or municipality of 20,000–50,000 inhabitants. In principle, the core of a DZ consists of a team of general practitioners and specialists, office nurses and visiting nurses who provide the principal primary health-care services: general medicine, occupational medicine, preschool paediatrics, school medicine, women's health care, tuberculosis surveillance, dentistry and epidemiology. In practice, however, services in the DZs are mainly provided by hospital specialists. Some DZs are physically located in a common complex with an *ambulanta* or a hospital, and several DZs also have beds for emergency cases and/or for closer observation of certain patients. The second level of care consists of 20 public general and regional hospitals, and at the top of the medical referral system there are three tertiary-level University Clinical Centres: in Sarajevo (FBiH), in Tuzla (FBiH) and in Banja Luka (RS). Other institutions include one private general hospital, four mental hospitals and eight rehabilitation centres with bed facilities.

The present health-care system is managed by the ministries of health in both entities. In FBiH, the regional decision-making power lies with ten cantonal ministries of health, whereas in RS the system is more centralized without the regional administration level (Figure 20.2).

Postwar health-care facilities and personnel

In 1991, before the war, the total number of hospital beds in BiH was 20,120, that is to say 458 beds per 100,000 inhabitants. According to the postwar survey performed by WHO in January–February 1997, there were 16,152 hospital beds in the country: 9260 in FBiH and 6892 in RS. This represents a rate of 404 beds per 100,000 inhabitants, clearly below the European 1990 average of 1020 per 100,000. The ratio is more favourable in Republika Srpska with 475 per 100,000, whereas in the federation the ratio is only 365 beds per 100,000 inhabitants. The distribution of the hospital beds is as follows:

	Somatic beds	DZ beds	Psychiatric beds	Rehabilitation beds
Federation of BiH	7404	456	500	900
Republika Srpska	5105	248	779	760
Total	12,509	704	1279	1660

It is impossible, however, to evaluate the true functional capacity of the hospital beds due to the lack of reliable hospital performance statistics. More generally, the number of hospital beds illustrates the space available for overnight care rather than the true output of institutional care. Many hospital beds are still closed because of the war damage or reconstruction work. The equipment is often deficient or out of condition, and the purchase of everyday consumables is still largely dependent on international generosity. Many modern short-stay medical technologies have not yet been adopted. Another major difficulty is the lack of funds to cover the running costs of the facilities.

As mentioned before, the prewar health-care system was reasonably well staffed. By October 1996, after the end of the conflict, there was a total of 4170 medical doctors in the country (2540 in FBiH, 1630 in RS). About 40 per cent of the profession left the country during the war. The present figure represents a density of 104 doctors per 100,000 inhabitants, far below the 1993 European average of 333 physicians per 100,000. Regarding the number of dentists, a total of 528 is even less favourable with only 13 professionals per 100,000 inhabitants (1990 European average 52 per 100,000). Only 37.5 per cent of the prewar profession has stayed in the country. Before the war, the number of nurses was 18,257, in 1997 only 12,814, that is to say 30 per cent of the nursing staff has emigrated. The present amount equals 320 nurses per 100,000 inhabitants, which is clearly lower than the 1989 European average of 559 per 100,000. Undoubtedly, there are numerous top-class professors and scientists, brilliant clinicians and other remarkable experts among the emigrated medical staff. This brain leakage means serious damage to the whole health-care institution, including the fields of science and education.

Population postwar health status

After the war, no major epidemics of communicable diseases have been reported. The four most frequently reported diseases are influenza (common cold), enterocolitis, chickenpox and scabies. Some minor outbreaks of various types of hepatitis, dysentery and trichinosis have been reported. The worst problem in this field is, however, the rapid increase of tuberculosis incidence (number of new cases during a given time). In 1996, the annual incidence rate was 57.4 per 100,000 inhabitants in FBiH and 43.1 per 100,000 in RS. Both figures were alarmingly high compared with the 1994 European average of 29.97 cases per 100,000.

Vaccination coverage dropped dramatically during the war. It has been estimated that today the proportion of fully immunized (complete vaccination programme) children under 5 years of age is 60–70 per cent. A national immunization day dedicated to poliomyelitis vaccination was organized by UNICEF and WHO in December 1996, due to the recent outbreak of the disease in the neighbouring countries. The result was excellent: 90–95 per cent coverage was achieved.

The prevalence and incidence of mental health disorders remains obscure. Attempts to establish reliable registers in this field have not been successful. It is apparent, however, that the situation of mental health patients has become worse during and after the conflict, and the number of persons suffering from postwar stress syndrome must be extremely high.

Physical disabilities and rehabilitation

In a survey performed by the ministries of health and WHO in December 1995, 12,296 disabled persons were registered. The distribution of the disabled between the two entities remains obscure. The estimates of persons requiring physical rehabilitation due to war injuries ranged from 40,000 to 70,000. The major injuries were bullet and shrapnel wounds resulting in 3000–5000 extremity amputations, 750 spinal cord injuries, 3000 peripheral nerve injuries, 1200 cranio-cerebral injuries and an unspecified number of fractures and soft-tissue injuries. The country is still infested with millions of landmines causing weekly accidental deaths and injuries (Figure 20.3).

Several organizations have provided supplies and services for the rehabilitation of war victims. A community-based rehabilitation (CBR) approach has been introduced in FBiH through contacts with local professionals, social workers, associations of persons with physical disabilities, governmental and local authorities, non-governmental organizations and WHO. More than 30 CBR units have been planned to cover the essential needs of the country. Many of them are already in active operation and the remainder are in the process of being established. There are seven prosthetic workshops in the country: five in FBiH, two in RS. The lack of specific education and training, the lack of suitable materials and components and the low productivity of the workshops are still the major problems in prosthetic services.

Postwar mines and unexploded deadly weapons in FBiH
(Posllijeratne mine i neeksplodirana ubojita sredstva u FBiH

Type and structure of injuries caused by mines and unexploded deadly weapons in FBiH,
1.01.1996– 31.03.1997

Injuries type (vrste povreda)	Total/Ukupno	Index per cent
Head injuries with skullbrain and maxilofacial fracture	17	7.4
Neck injuries with fracture	6	2.6
Thorax injuries with rib, sternum and chest spine fracture	14	6.1
Lumbar area abdomen and lumbar spine injuries	14	6.1
Upper limb injuries with fracture	15	6.6
Lower limb traumatic amputation	6	2.6
Lower limb injuries with fracture	106	46.3
Lower limb traumatic amputation	51	22.3
Total	229	100.0

* Data related to cantons Zeničko-Dobojski, Tuzlansko Podrinjski i Sarajevo. (*Podaci se odnose na Zeničko-Dobojski, Tuzlansko-Podrinjski i Sarajevo Kanton.*)
During this period 18 persons are registered as killed with mines and unexploded deadly weapons. (U ovum periodu 18 osoba je smrtno stradalo od zaostalih mina i neeksplodiranih ubojitih sredstava.)
Note: the data concern only 3/10 cantons.

Figure 20.3 Example of postwar mine injuries
Source: Bulletin No. 263, Federal Institute of Public Health, Sarajevo, April 1997.

Towards health-care reform

Unfortunately, the process of establishing a modern state health-insurance system in BiH was interrupted by the war. During the past 5–6 years, less than one-third of the inhabitants have paid for health insurance and, as health services have usually been provided free for all, only 20 per cent of health care costs have been covered by insurance funds. Co-payments represented some 2–3 per cent of the costs, while international humanitarian assistance covered some 30–40 per cent, mainly in kind. At this point, thorough reconsideration of the funding sources is essential because of the extremely high unemployment rate and the shortage of functioning enterprises.

Since 1996, the ministries of both entities (the Ministry of Health in BiH and the Ministry of Health and Social Affairs in RS) have prepared new strategic plans for health system reform and reconstruction and new legislation concerning health care, health insurance and privatization. Many general principles and trends are similar in both entities; for example, WHO's 'Health for All by the Year 2000' document is the basis of health policy in both FBiH and RS.

However, the reform process is sluggish. The political situation in the country is still unstable, unanimity between all ethnic groups is difficult to reach, and the re-establishment of regional and municipal administrative structures is partly unfinished.

Problems and challenges

The political division of the country enables the two entities to establish their own structures separately, in spite of the Dayton Accord. Even establishing common infrastructures, such as communication technologies and railroad networks seems a difficult, sometimes overwhelming task. The same applies to the creation of a common health-care system. In addition, many unresolved problems inside the federation await the unanimity of Bosnians and Croats. The lack of both human and financial resources is flagrant. The health ministries, other administrative institutions and all service providers suffer from the general lack of money and the relative lack of a skilled work-force to implement the renovations and to run everyday service-delivery and related tasks. The health-care staff in general urgently needs re-education and training to update its knowledge and skills and to enhance its motivation. This concerns especially the primary care doctors (the general practitioners), that is to say the future family doctors, whose motivation urgently needs improving by salary increases and enhanced societal appreciation. The basic medical education should be developed by updating the present curricula of the medical faculties and by renovating all medical libraries, equipping them with modern information and communication technologies. The availability of competent teachers should be ensured. The educated medical staff living abroad should be inveigled back into the country. This will be extremely difficult, of course, because of uncertain living and other conditions and insufficient salary levels, compared with the living standards many of them have reached in foreign countries.

International activities are often uncoordinated and overlapping, while some fields are inadequately covered. The health ministries are defeated by the overwhelming number of programmes and projects initiated by various international organizations and other actors. The insufficient functional capacity of the national authorities weakens the possibility of proper needs' assessment and priority setting, and many international activities have been planned and begun without close collaboration with local civil servants. In this respect, the current situation is still incoherent.

Any body that finds wise and durable solutions to the above problems and challenges will undoubtedly promote both the peace and reconciliation process and sustainable development in this torn and tattered country.

FURTHER READING

Physicians for Human Rights (1996), *Medicine Under Siege in the Former Yugoslavia 1991–95*, Boston.

The World Bank (1997), *Bosnia and Herzegovina. From recovery to sustainable growth*, Washington DC.

Ministry of Health, Federation of Bosnia and Herzegovina (1996), *Federation Health Programme: Health reform and reconstruction programme of the Federation of Bosnia and Herzegovina,* Sarajevo.

Ministry of Health and Social Affairs of the Republika Srpska (1997), *Republika Srpska: strategic plan for health system reform and reconstruction 1997–2000*, draft, Pale.

Procupet, Adriana, Konttinen, Mauno, Husic, Azra and Alexandra Mikulic (1997), *Federation of Bosnia and Herzegovina: public health and health care – a general overview*, Sarajevo: WHO Office for Bosnia and Herzegovina.

Procupet, Adriana, Konttinen, Mauno, Husic, Azra and Mikulic, Alexandra (1997), *Republika Srpska: public health and health care: a general overview*, Sarajevo: WHO Office for Bosnia and Herzegovina.

Carballo, M., Simic, S. and D. Zeric (1996), 'Health in Countries Torn by Conflict: lessons from Sarajevo', *Lancet* 348: 872–4.

Berckmans, Patrick, Dawans, Veronique, Schmets, Gerard, Vandenbergh, Daniel and Autier, Philippe (1997), 'Inappropriate Drug-Donation Practices in Bosnia and Herzegovina, 1992 to 1996', *The New England Journal of Medicine* 337: 1842–5.

— (1998), 'Inappropriate Drug-Donation Practices in Bosnia and Herzegovina', *The New England Journal of Medicine* 338: 1472–3.

The Economist (1998), 'A Ghost of a Chance. A survey of the Balkans', 24–30 January.

Acheson, Sir Donald (1999), 'Conflict in Bosnia 1992–3', *British Medical Journal* 319: 1472–3 and 1639–42.

Address for correspondence

National Research and Development Centre for Welfare and Health Stakes, Siltasaarenkatu 18 A, 00530 Helsinki, Finland, Tel:+358 9 3967 2027, Fax: +358 9 3967 2417; E-mail: mauno.konttinen@stakes.fi

21 WARFARE AND HEALTH
The Case of West Africa

KOLAWOLE T. RAHEEM

and KINGSLEY K. AKINROYE

Chapter 21 is based on the travels, interviews, discussions and observations of one of the authors during a study visit to Ghana, Nigeria, Benin Republic, Côte d'Ivoire and Danani (the border town between Liberia and Côte d' Ivoire) between March and May 1998. The Nigerian visit was sponsored by UNICEF's Lagos office as part of a vulnerability study. The target groups for informal interview and discussion were non-governmental organization employees, physicians and nurses working with war-affected people, refugees and returnees and those not directly affected by armed conflict.

Many West African countries are rich in mineral and solid resources which generate more than enough funds to provide adequate health services, but violent conflicts and corruption stand in the way of achieving this goal.

An outside picture, of the havoc being wrought by warfare can never convey the real situation as a visit to refugee camps and war-torn communities in West Africa would make clear. The destruction of the health sector, and of the health of refugees, returnees and internally displaced persons by war cannot be fully understood by statistics (for example, population per physician or nurses) alone.

We shall therefore use figures only sparingly in delineating the relationship between health and war in the region. Our main objective is to make Chapter 21 accessible to all concerned with finding solutions to the health problems created by war, and also to prevent them from reoccurring.

Destruction of cities and villages can cause uncontrolled movement of refugees, with rapid spread of preventable diseases becoming a major cause of morbidity. The effects of war on the physical and mental health of people in the sub-region have not been fully studied but casual observation shows that the health sector in war-torn countries, and in countries where there is political and economic instability, is poor. For example, life-expectancy is low in these areas: the more war-torn a country, the greater the likelihood that this is the case. It is likely, therefore, that the physical and mental health of people in the region is below normal. In many countries in the sub-region more money is spent on arms than on providing food or education; instead of going to school children are recruited to wage war and kill people. Over one-fourth of child soldiers are likely to have serious health defects and be in urgent need of medical care.

War in West Africa is a major cause of a rapidly increasing number of refugees and consequently of increases in poverty, armed robbery and insecurity. The sudden movement of people across borders is also an uncontrolled movement of disease from one country to the other. The receiving countries in the region are poor and have inadequate health services for their own citizens; the addition of thousands of refugees to the host populations makes the situation worse.

War or warfare in West Africa is rampant even though not usually or regularly reported in the international media. Many of the conflicts in countries since political independence from colonial rule have been inter- or intra-tribal in nature. They are so localized that they have failed to attract outside attention. Some have been highly intensive and turned to civil war. Since the Nigerian civil war (1967–70) many other wars have taken place but none, even though more brutal, seems to have claimed as many victims as in Nigeria. Despite the brutality and atrocities, the region's wars have received little coverage in the western media. This suggests that the international community is not fully aware of the serious damage being done to the well-being of people in the area. The consequences of these wars could eventually create problems for the west.

The civil wars in Liberia claimed hundreds of thousand of lives, while the ongoing war in Sierra Leone has also claimed thousands of victims and rendered many more homeless. The magnitude of the appalling condition of health services because of the conflicts cannot be overstated. Warfare is an effective facilitating agent of poverty and deadly diseases that travel beyond the borders of countries where wars are being waged. Preventable diseases become non-preventable because of the depletion of the health services by the burden of war. For example, instead of using available funds to prevent malaria, polio and the high rate of maternal and infant mortality, money is used to buy drugs for injured soldiers. The medical attention given to combatants in the region is usually much better than that given in public hospitals. This is a probable consequence of a colonial health-policy legacy inherited by the unstable governments in the sub-region.

In many countries the ravages of war and hostilitiess are visible, and stories told by eyewitnesses and refugees tell of the seriousness of these unreported conflicts. Devastating wars are continuing in Sierra Leone, Senegal and Guinea-Bissau. Our observations suggest that warfare may be the most potent factor preventing the development of the health sector in the sub-region. We hope that Chapter 21 will stimulate more discussion and further research on these issues. There is a need to sensitize the world about the strong correlation between war, conflicts and the very poor health sector in the area.

The West African Region and Warfare

West Africa (Figure 21.1) consists of 18 countries with more than 200 million people. It is an area of consistent warfare. Until the early 1960s the region was divided mainly

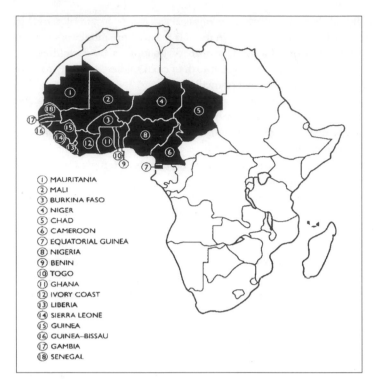

① MAURITANIA
② MALI
③ BURKINA FASO
④ NIGER
⑤ CHAD
⑥ CAMEROON
⑦ EQUATORIAL GUINEA
⑧ NIGERIA
⑨ BENIN
⑩ TOGO
⑪ GHANA
⑫ IVORY COAST
⑬ LIBERIA
⑭ SIERRA LEONE
⑮ GUINEA
⑯ GUINEA-BISSAU
⑰ GAMBIA
⑱ SENEGAL

Figure 21.1
West Africa and
Sahel

between the British and French. The ongoing warfare in the sub-region has many of its roots in the colonial partition of the area. For example, the conflict between Cameroon and Nigeria for the ownership of the Bakassi peninsula, a rich oil area, is a legacy of the agreements made by the British during the colonial period. But the wars also have a strong relationship with the tribal and ethnic mistrusts of the political and ruling élite.

For the past decade only a few of the countries have been relatively peaceful. Because of the constant violent conflicts governments have continued to increase their military budgets to the disadvantage of other sectors, like health.

The health sector and military spending

Military expenditure in the region continues to grow rapidly to the detriment of other sectors of the economy; health and education are the main victims. In reality, the trade in small arms is so enormous and disjointed that official statistics on arms imports do not tell the facts; military expenditure is likely to be much higher than that recorded. Tables 21.1–4 show the situation of the health sector in the majority of the the region's countries.

Niger and Sierra Leone are ranked number one and two respectively by the United Nations Children's Fund (UNICEF) as the countries having the highest rate of under-five mortality in the world.[1] The health indicators show that the sub-region is in need of urgent attention to improve the low level of health care services that are compounded by ongoing wars or conflicts. The UNICEF statistics also suggest that there is a probable correlation between wars and the high rate of disease and mortality.

Primary health care in the region has always been poor even without violent conflicts, which have aggravated the health problems and undermined the health service systems. Akinroye,[2] for example, described the hospitals in Nigeria as a 'veritable source of traps' that intensify instead of relieving pain, and spread diseases instead of providing cures. Hospital waste is a possible source of infection. The waste ends up untreated in dumping sites or rivers and has become a transmitter of deadly diseases like HIV.

The sub-region's basic health-care services are bedevilled by a lack of funds because a large part of these countries' income is spent on the military and in corruption. Diarrhoea, for example, is still one of the most common sources of morbidity and mortality in the area.

Table 21.1 Military expenditure in selected West African countries (as % of GNP in 1996)[3]

Burkina Faso	30	Cameroon	48	Chad	74
Côte d'Ivoire	14	Ghana	12	Guinea	37
Liberia	47+	Mali	53	Niger	11
Nigeria	33	Senegal	33	Sierra Leone	23+
Togo	39				

Table 21.2 Selected indicators[4]

	U5MR/1000	IMR/1000	Adult illiteracy %	Access to water %	Access to health %
Burkina F.	81.6	56	41	175	99
Cameroon	45.9	50	41	113	71
Chad	-	-	30	206	121
Côte d'Ivoire	46.2	76	30	128	89
Ghana	39.7	52	60	170	103
Guinea	76	55	80	226	133
Liberia	60.5	50	39	217	145
Mali	68	41	-	217	120
Niger	71.6	59	32	320	191
Nigeria	49.3	36	66	191	114
Senegal	61.7	48	40	120	63
Sierra Leone	79.3	37	38	320	164
Togo	56.7	60	61	135	84

Table 21.3 Sanitation coverage as percentage of the population[5]

1. Togo	4	5. Chad	21	9. Nigeria	34
2. Sierra Leone	11	6. Guinea	21	10. Ghana	43
3. Niger	16	7. Liberia	21	11. Côte d'Ivoire	46
4. Burkina F.	18	8. Mali	23	12. Senegal	56

Table 21.4 Other health indicators in selected West African countries (rate per 100,000 population)[6]

	Physicians	Nurses	Midwives
Burkina Faso	3	10	3
Cameroon	8	–	–
Chad	3	2	1
Côte d'Ivoire	9	31	13
Ghana	4	27	12
Guinea	13	–	–
Liberia	–	–	–
Mali	5	17	4
Niger	2	26	6
Nigeria	17	61	50
Senegal	–	–	–
SierraLeone	–	–	–
Togo	9	33	6

The health sector and warfare

The negative relationship between warfare and health cannot be overstated. The West African scenario, as one of the violent conflict areas in the world, suggests that the health sector cannot prosper when there is war. War-induced diseases or wounds put more pressure on the health budget. Because of war-related casualties the health sector will take even longer to recover after the cessation of hostilities.

A major casualty of warfare is the health sector. In many cases hospitals are destroyed and health workers killed. Funds that could have been used to promote health care or improve the health sector are diverted to military matters. The main concern of official health policy in the region's warring states is the health of combatants to the disadvantage of public and preventive health care. In some cases maimed civilians, if they are lucky, get their prosthesis paid for by the non-governmental organizations. Much energy and money are spent on making artificial limbs for amputees.

The region's health sector is generally very poor. Average life expectancy at birth is around 42 years, and between 37 and 40 years in war-torn countries like Liberia and Sierra Leone. Warfare is a significant factor in these low figures, given the destruction of the health infrastructure and the inability of people to get medical attention.

The negative effects of warfare on health in the sub-region have to be carefully studied to get an objective picture of the situation. Based on the interviews and observations made, we shall focus on three main issues that we think important:

(1) the extent of possible damage done to both traditional and orthodox health-care systems;

(2) the transborder spread of diseases and fast degradation of the environment; and

)(3 the mental health of war-affected people which up till now has generally been neglected; what we are suggesting is that the mental health of the people may be seriously damaged even after the war because of the inability to cope with the destructive postwar reality.

Traditional and orthodox health-care systems

Many people are nowadays dying of simple and preventable diseases because there are no hospitals or orthodox medicine. The traditional medicine is also hard to get because many of those who knew the art have died during the war and others are refugees somewhere. A large majority of those who practise medicine at the moment are quack or fake doctors.

This statement was made by one of the Liberian returnees. It is an expression of how badly damaged the health sector in Liberia is at the moment. I had discussions and interviews with six Liberians. Two were living as refugees in Accra, Ghana and two were returning home after many years as refugees in Nigeria. They had visited their country twice since the 1997 postwar elections. I also met two Liberians in Abidjan, Côte d'Ivoire; they shuttle between the two countries as merchants; they were neither refugees nor returnees. According to them, 'we stay in two countries'. The only functioning hospital, according to the Liberians interviewed, is in Monrovia.

In the hospitals there may be only one nurse, in many cases working for more than 18 hours a day, to attend the numerous wards with more than 40 patients. As can be expected, a large number of physicians, nurses and other hospital personnel have been forced to leave the country. The remaining health workers are under the mental or physical strain of living with war, which has rapidly increased the number of hospital patients who, unfortunately, cannot be treated because of lack of medicines. Only skeletal services are provided, where this is possible; the voluntary international medical agencies offer emergency support.

The destruction of the health care system has also increased the rate of fake medicine being sold or prescribed to those desperate for a cure. This is common even in peacetime; even surgery is performed by quacks who capitalize on the unavailability of proper government health policies, the inadequate number of qualified hospital personnel and lack of basic services. This situation worsens with war. Some physicians have remarked that: 'the destruction of the health care system as well as the shortage of food and medical supplies results in poor obstetrical care with increased numbers of spontaneous abortions and miscarriages. It also increases maternal and infant mortality'. Traditional medicine is affected when the war gets to the level of destroying villages and farms. The explosions and lead used in waging wars could harm the plants and water by polluting them. Consequently the medicinal effects of the plants may be drastically reduced.

Above all, food itself is the most basic and important medicine. When the environment is degraded because of destruction by military weapons and the forced movement of large numbers of people, food production becomes meagre and malnutrition increases. The ecological imbalance caused by refugees and returnees in West Africa has not been studied seriously. However, one can safely assume that the mass movement of people and sudden establishment of crowded camps will have negative effects on the environment. Refugee camps and returnee transit stations in the sub-region have poor hygiene standards. These usually overcrowded camps are in isolated places without proper drainage. Household wastes from the camps are carelessly dumped in nearby forest to decompose, leading to the possible pollution of the soil, plants and groundwater. It is easy to observe the filthy atmosphere in the camps in Nigeria, Ghana and Côte d'Ivoire. Preventable diseases like helminthiasis, cholera, dysentery and typhoid are common.

Transborder spread of diseases

Communicable diseases like meningitis, polio, malaria, HIV and helminthiasis (worm infection) are easy to carry across borders with the sudden mass movements of people. The refugee-receiving countries have no capacity to offer health services to the refugees.

The UNHCR, Red Cross and other voluntary agencies usually handle the influx of refugees in the host countries. However, these agencies are not able to carry out thorough medical screening of the refugees before they cross the border. The medical concern at the point of entry is first aid or the treatment of the very sick. The refugee camps are also places where disease spreads easily. Contaminated foods are given as gifts to the refugees; food rations are stored in unsafe places; because of the lack of refrigeration food deteriorates rapidly in the hot and humid conditions. Conditions and the way of life in the camps make careless sexual intercourse easy, leading in many cases to sexually-transmitted diseases; there are frequent reports of girls being raped. The nurses I met reported that many camp dwellers refuse medical check-ups.

Soldiers and rebels are also a significant source of venereal disease transmission. Rape is common in towns captured by either side. These armed combatants do not practise safe sex, and nobody is interested in advising them to go for a medical check-up. If they are mercenaries or peace-enforcement agents, and already infected with venereal diseases or HIV, it is almost 100 per cent certain that they will transmit the diseases across the borders, and that women may give birth to children infected by HIV or other diseases. It is, for example, suggested that about 15,000 children were born from sexual contact between the ECOMOG troops (the military body formed by West African governments to help enforce or keep peace in the region) and Liberian women during and immediately after the war. These children are now fatherless and displaced inside the country. It is probable that the same will happen in Sierra Leone where the same troops are actively supporting the government and involved in the war against the rebels.

Refugees are easy prey for pimps. The desperate conditions in which they find themselves lead very easily to prostitution. Many prostitutes in Accra and Lagos are said to be refugees. Prostitution is a source of disease transmission, especially in those countries where the health care systems are very inadequate.

Mental health and hypertension

The mental health of the refugees or displaced people in West Africa has not been a concern for the UNHCR or other support organizations. Even on their arrival, no organization has so far been keen to deal with their trauma – of rape, loss of parents or family members, of property. A refugee camp of about 2000 to 4000 people may have a health post. This is usually staffed by only one nurse, and a physician may visit the place once a week. The health post itself does not attract a nurse or physician to work there. As already mentioned, refugee camps are isolated from the towns and lack basic facilities like clean water, electricity and sanitation. The risk of malaria is high because the surroundings are waterlogged.

In the war zones those who are not able to migrate face the daily trauma of living with war and fear. Children are the worst affected. According to the BBC World Service, mental health workers estimate that war experiences can devastate minors. Many children have seen their parents murdered and some have been abducted and used as child soldiers (these children were usually drugged by their captors and might become addicts after the cessation of hostilities). The effects of such experiences have not been addressed. Armed robbery is prevalent in many West African countries, in many cases carried out by 14- to 20-year-olds. Those who have worked as child soldiers are those most likely to become couriers of hard drugs and small arms.

It is probable that hypertension (high blood pressure) may be rampant among refugees and the displaced because of the trauma of rape, maiming and murder or the mental torture of displacement and dependence on charity for food and shelter. Many refugees have seen family members die while fleeing to safety; the so-called refuge is itself mental torture. Permanent refugee shelters in West Africa take the form of camps poorly maintained by the UNHCR or the relevant local government organization. In many cases this low level of care is compounded by harassment from the officials in host countries.

Conclusion

Wars in West Africa have wrecked both traditional and orthodox health-care systems. They have had enormous and catastrophic effects on people's health and well-being. The human and material costs of war are a big drain on the health sector; while increasing sums of money are being used to prosecute wars, less is being spent on health.

The effects of war on the sub-region's health can be easily observed in the hospitals, in refugee camps and among the internally displaced. The negative effects are more obvious in countries where war is being waged on or has only recently ended. Investment in modern small arms is increasing in the region, making it easy for many people, especially the young, to get hold of them.

A major civil war is still raging in Sierra Leone. The conflict is one of the most brutal in the world. Other small wars that could be termed violent conflicts have become an almost everyday occurrence. In Nigeria, for example, localized violent clashes claim an average of about 50 lives a month. These conflicts have many causes: for example, an unacceptable new traditional chief, king or emir; oil pollution; the location of local government headquarters; religious demands; or minority groups struggling for political recognition.

The wars in West Africa have produced a situation in which medical services available to those affected have to be reconsidered:

(1) Refugees and displaced people live in poor areas and unhygienic environments. The sudden mass-migration of people facilitates general environmental degradation, leading to deforestation, soil pollution and ecological disturbance.

(2) Refugees are susceptible to sexual abuse and use as cheap labour. With no access to work it is more likely that they will live in impoverished conditions.

(3) Refugee children are likely to be uneducated and end up on the streets.

(4) The spread of disease is facilitated by the conflicts. There is need to evolve methods of preventing and treating such spread. At the same time refugees or the internally displaced should not become scapegoats and victims of those who want to promote xenophobia.

(5) The mental health of refugees and the displaced should be taken seriously. Rates of hypertension may be high. Many, especially children and women, have been traumatized by the loss of parents, rape and abuse. The numbers of amputees and other disabled also need to be considered.

All these factors have implications for the region's health sector. Reconstruction of the health care infrastructure will require large budgetary increases. Health-care systems will need to care both for war victims and for the basic health needs of the whole population. The effects of warfare in the region are likely to delay the improvement of the health sector and other socio-economic developments for some time to come.

REFERENCES

1. UNICEF (1999), *The State of the World's Children*, New York: UNICEF.
2. Akinroye, K. K. (1998),'Nigeria's Health in the Twenties', unpublished paper, 1998.
3. Mugane, P. (1997), *Material Vulnerabilities: National Indicators*, Lagos: UNDP.
4. Ibid.
5. Ibid.
6. WHO (1999),*World Health Statistics* (annual), Geneva: World Health Organization.

ADDITIONAL READING

Allukian, M.J.R. and P. L. Atwood (1997), 'Public Health and the Vietnam War', in B. S. Levy and V. W. Sidel, *War and Public Health*, Oxford: Oxford University Press.

Akinroye, K. K. (1998) 'Maternal and Child Health Disease in Nigeria', *Medilag Journal,* Vol. 2.

Laakso, L. and R. Lauhonen (1997), *Building Peace in Africa*, Helsinki: KATU.

Levy, B. S. and V. W. Sidel (1997), *War and Public Health*, Oxford: Oxford University Press.

Nnoli, O. (1998), 'Management of Community-based Conflicts: towards a futuristic perspective', paper written for the Yakubu Gowon Centre's National Conference on Enduring Peace and Sustainable National Development, Port Harcourt, Nigeria, 18–21 May.

Nur, I. M. (1997), 'Extent of Disasters in Africa', Addis Ababa: OAU.

Raheem, K. (1998), 'Armed Conflict in Africa and its Environmental Implications', paper presented at the Conference on Armed Conflicts in Africa, Red Cross Building, Lagos.

UNICEF (1998), 'Vulnerability Analysis in Nigeria', study carried out for UNICEF, Lagos.

'African Refugees' Survival Activities and Environmental Degradation: accelerating environmental disaster?', paper written for the LASU/AREF conference on 'The African Refugee Phenomenon: implications for socio-economic development in the 21st century', Lagos State University, 8–10 July 1997.

22 CHILDREN AND WAR

VAPPU TAIPALE

The written history of childhood is a very short part of the history of humankind. Children are an integral part of families and societies; they are born, die and grow up amongst people. But childhood used to be simply an unimportant phase of which there was no need to keep any special record. Infant mortality was high enough to prevent children from being considered too precious and important. The general feeling was that one had several children in order to have just a few survive. Children themselves are flexible, durable and extremely hardy in any circumstances; were they not so, humankind would have vanished at its very beginning.

Children have been part of labour forces everywhere, they were and in some places still are needed in fields and in factories. They have worked hard at taking care of their siblings or of livestock from their earliest years on. Children have always been, as a part of human societies, influenced by famines, illnesses, conflicts and occupations, witnessing human violence and participating in many ways in crises and warfare. The Children's Crusade of 1212 could be viewed as a phase of the paramilitary activities of children.

The promotion of the concept of childhood is a late phenomenon. We can see children and childrearing emerge in the discourse of philosophers like Jean Jacques Rousseau, but mostly historians place the birth of the modern concept of childhood at around the end of the 19th century. The whole idea that children need special attention and protection was developed slowly. It eventually led to the entrance into political discussion of the concept of popular education – every child has an ability to learn, and also a right to learn. Childhood criminality was another topic to be explored; children were taken to institutions for special education, not to jails any more.

At the start of the 20th century it was called the century of children by some enthusiastic scholars and politicians. A growing number of professions began to work with childhood issues, including, for example, teachers, kindergarten teachers and psychologists. Our understanding and knowledge of childhood grew exponentially during that period. But at the same time our ability to take responsibility for children has not shown too much improvement. The situation of children in our post-modern world is challenged by many persistent threats: poverty, child trafficking, both physical and mental exploitation and increasing risk of mental disturbances.

Towards international recognition of children's special needs

The legal protection of children was first introduced into international humanitarian law after the Second World War (WW II) (see Chapter 44), although the slow process had begun much earlier in the century. In the years leading up to the First World War, Europe was shaken by the Balkan Wars. In 1913, the British Macedonian Relief Fund negotiated help for refugees, and the vision of some sort of an agreement on the rights of the child was born. In 1919 the Save the Children Fund was founded and the first draft of the Declaration of the Rights of the Child was negotiated between nations, the International Committee of the Red Cross and emerging NGOs. The first Declaration with five articles was adopted in 1924 by the League of Nations. It says that 'the child must be the first to receive relief in times of distress'.

Experiences during WW II pointed at the urgent need to draw up a stronger instrument of public international law for protecting civilian populations, especially children, in wartime. The results led to the adoption of the 1949 Fourth Geneva Convention relative to the protection of civilian persons in time of war. From that time on children as members of the civilian population were entitled to benefit from the application of that convention. The first international legal regulations concerning armed conflicts not of an international character were also drawn up at the 1949 Diplomatic Conference, applying to children in the same way as to all persons who take no active part in the hostilities. In 1959, after long discussions and preparations, the Declaration of the Rights of the Child was adopted by the United Nations. Furthermore, a diplomatic conference was held from 1974 to 1977, resulting in the adoption of the two protocols additional to the Geneva Convention. The new provisions gave children the aid and protection they need, and forbade the recruitment of young people under 15 years of age.

In 1984, the Geneva International Peace Research Institute (GIPRI), the International Peace Bureau (IPB) and the Peace Union in Finland organized a conference on 'Children and War'. This was the first time that researchers and politicians met in order to cover the topic as thoroughly as possible. The issues explored included children as soldiers, children living in conflict areas, child evacuations, children's experiences in Hiroshima as well as in Kampuchea and Northern Ireland, and children's images of war and peace. The conference introduced the issues to international discussion, and the publication prepared for the conference is the most comprehensive volume on the topic, with the most detailed list of references then available.[1]

It was only in 1989 that the International Convention on the Rights of the Child was adopted by the 44th UN General Assembly. This convention describes the need of the child through three capital Ps: Protection, Provision, Participation. All are needed when it comes to the question posed by this book, war or health. As a baby and a toddler a child needs special protection, as all children do in times of crisis or conflict. But in order to grow up as a healthy human being, protection is not enough. Children need their part of the welfare of societies, their just provision, which is not materializing too clearly even in the most affluent countries. Children also need participatory rights: they need to have a say, and to be treated as important members of human societies. In the richest parts of the world children are easily treated separately in their own world, in kindergartens and at school, as if they didn't belong to adult society at all. In other parts of the world material circumstances may be so scarce that children lack the prerequisites for participation.

The Convention on the Rights of the Child compels all the nations which have ratified it to provide a report every fifth year to the Commission on the Rights of the Child. The second round of reports has recently taken place, and many of the countries take this responsibility very seriously. One most important step to further the cause of children was the work done by Ms Gracha Machel under the auspices of the United Nations.[2] The 1996 report entitled 'Impact of Armed Conflict on Children', discussed in the UN General Assembly, focused the world's attention on the situation of children. The report was developed through an interactive, consultative process that included six regional consultations, several field visits and workshops. The recommendations form a solid basis for worldwide action. Machel also calls on the international community to ensure that actions are carefully targeted and do not undermine the basic social services that are everywhere essential to the well-being of children.

The situation of children in reality

Since WW II, the international community has witnessed new kinds of conflicts. Methods and means of warfare have become increasingly sophisticated. Conflicts between regular armed forces and irregular combatants are more frequent. In modern warfare civilian losses are much more severe, and seem to be growing in severity all the time. The changing character of warfare has been elaborated elsewhere in this book (see Chapter 5).

It is not just that families and children find themselves abandoned within battlefields or get caught in the crossfire; they are also likely to be specific targets. Civilian areas, like hospitals and children's day-care centres, schools and market places are targeted by the armed forces in ethnic or other conflicts, and real protection of children is becoming more and more difficult. Also, the issue of children and war has become more and more complicated; it cannot easily be solved by simple and straightforward international action.

As estimated by UNICEF, the child victim figures for the 1990s include
- 2 million killed
- 4–5 million disabled
- 12 million left homeless
- more than 1 million orphaned or separated from their parents and
- some 10 million psychologically traumatized.

Although these are rough estimates, the numbers show that world development, with its globalized markets and information societies, has not provided a more secure environment for children.[3]

Not only wars and conflicts, but also poverty and environmental degradation affect children. Poverty is a major threat to the development of humankind. One of the great achievements of the 20th century, however, has been the reduction of poverty.[4] Income poverty has fallen, and the number of people deprived in other aspects of life has been reduced to 1–2 billion from 2–3 billion people three decades ago. Infant mortality has been cut by nearly three-fifths. More than three-fourths of the population in the developing countries now can expect to survive to age forty. Yet 800 million people lack access to health services, and more than 1.2 billion lack access to safe water. More than half a billion people are chronically malnourished, most of them children. The whole of this progress has been marked by gender inequality, and by disparities among regions both globally and within countries.

Over the course of this century there have been dramatic reductions in mortality in all industrialized countries, particularly for infants and children. However, this overall improvement masks less favourable trends: there are systematic differences in health across populations within all countries. There is an uneven distribution of health and disease that favours those in socially advantaged positions, regardless of whether socioeconomic status is measured in terms of income, education, occupation or other variables.

Child soldiers

Child soldiers were not a rare phenomenon in the past; on the contrary, minors have always been included in armies and there have been many teenaged military heroes in the history of most countries, starting from Alexander the Great and the Prophet Mohammed.[5] Many poems and songs tell about child soldiers and their courage, and even praise the opportunity to die young. In the Swedish army in 1655, during the reign of King Carl Gustav, a total of 302 boys were registered in the service of the Livonian regiment. The youngest ones, some even under five years of age, received pay and served as drummers and pipers. The older ones were paid as ordinary soldiers.

There are and have been institutional solutions to ensure the availability of new generations of soldiers. Besides the systematic means that nations have developed to draft soldiers, such as conscription or forcing landed proprietors to provide a man and a horse for warfare, people have developed a variety of other solutions. The orphaned boys of fallen soldiers were raised in special children's homes, soldier orphanages, to become soldiers when they reached 15 years of age. In the region of Sweden between the 16th and 18th centuries there was the institution of 'soldier boys' – an early form of child trafficking. The landed proprietors bought young boys, and if the state levied for military troops these young 'soldier boys' were offered up instead of the proprietor's sons.

In the period from the French revolution to the 20th century wars were waged somewhat more in accordance with international rules on sparing the civilian population and conscripting only boys of a certain age and physical condition. After that, child soldiers were first seen as a problem during modern warfare, after the awareness of children's need for protection grew stronger, and the character of wars changed.

The last decades of the 20th century saw more and more information emerging about children being used as soldiers, children voluntarily enlisting as soldiers, children being forced to become soldiers and kill their own family members, children being used as the first trespassers in minefields and children being given military training to be accustomed to extreme sadism and cruelty. The studies and research articles today are numerous and originate in several countries all over the world.[6] There is documentation on the state of affairs in Afghanistan, Burma, Cambodia, El Salvador, Lebanon, Mozambique, Nicaragua, Peru, the Philippines, the Russian federation (Chechnya), Rwanda, as well as in Northern Ireland and the former Yugoslavia.

The world has to admit that recruiting children to wage war is a crime in itself. Many of the international organizations and experts are now fighting for a higher age limit for recruiting. (The international negotiations intend to set the age of 18 as an international standard.)

Meeting the rehabilitation needs of child soldiers has become imperative in many countries where war has ceased, as in Mozambique. The practical needs presented by such a situation have brought to attention many important issues. Child soldiers are not a homogeneous group; their experiences have not all been the same. Many times children have not been involved in armed combat but have performed supportive tasks for armed groups, as children did in the ancient past. In a military culture the children themselves tend to exaggerate their bloody experiences in order to become part of a privileged elite amongst their peers. Some of the children have had really deeply traumatizing experiences and their psyches have been profoundly affected by hate and fear. Not attending school during their time in the battlefields, their peacetime options may be very limited. It is likely that the most productive solution the outside world can provide for these young veterans is not to separate them into child soldier programmes, but to enhance their education opportunities.

Children taking part in hostilities

In modern warfare, the civilians and combatants are often mixed. Children may grow up in circumstances where hostilities are deeply rooted in the minds of the civilian population and aggressive behaviour is supported. Young children are taught to throw stones or openly to show their disgust or hate, more grown-up children can use more sophisticated means to express their feelings and thoughts. Children are often also more continuously involved in hostilities, which can extend from indirectly helping combatants to actually participating in the fighting.[7] No international convention can categorically prevent children from taking part in hostilities, but what it can do is ensure that if children under 15 are captured they continue to benefit from the special protection to which a child is entitled.

There has been scientific discussion on the involvement of children in hostile actions. Many researchers had found that children who actively took part in actions had fewer psychosocial problems and adapted better to their living conditions. For instance, during the *intifada* of the Palestine Liberation Organization many children actively participated in activities and in arranging demonstrations. Against these findings, however, later it was shown that participation itself was not really a protective element for those children's development. Almost 90 per cent of them were exposed to one or more traumatic events, including arrest, house demolition, beatings, shootings and death in the family.

Even years later, traumatic experiences sustained during the *intifada* were still found to have left their mark: 23 per cent of the children showed at least some neurotic symptoms. The researchers concluded that the most decisive protective factor was communication with the parents.[8]

Repression of children

Militarism means the subordination of all values of the society to the needs of war and to preparation for war. There are different forms of militarism. Militarism can be structural; it can be targeted to the people's minds or their behaviour. Children are often living in circumstances of low-intensity warfare, where the adversaries tend to destroy the infrastructure of the targeted country without a show of open aggression.[9] There are a number of analyses, carried out by different human rights organizations, of the living situation of children in several countries in Latin America. The earlier political situation of South Africa is also documented as having led to largely oppressive actions and illegal violence against children.[10]

Children's minds are easily captured by strong, charismatic adults. Education for war has traditions that are longstanding compared to those of peacetime education. It has been said that in countries not exposed to conflict or warfare, the militarization of children's minds aims not so much at the potential military use of children but rather at the construction of the legitimacy of warfare and national defence.

Evacuation of children – protected zones

The idea of evacuating children from war zones to more protective surroundings was taken up in discussions on children's welfare at the beginning of the century. Actually, after WW I there were several such evacuations.[11]

The Swedish Red Cross was very active in asking many countries to send their 9–14-year-old children to Sweden to be cared for by ordinary Swedish families. Many countries such as Poland, France and Belgium refused, but others such as the Baltic countries and Austria responded very positively. As a result, the number of foreign evacuees reached 14,000 in the year 1920.

It was hoped that through these efforts malnourished children could be provided with better food and a better start for their lives. This was the result in most cases, but many children were also adopted in Sweden. Until recently there were not many critical reports on the results of the evacuations but for instance in Denmark the situation in some camps for German children was later explored by journalists. Some results suggest that many of the children died of hunger and malnutrition because the food rations were too small for survival.

During the Spanish Civil War children were evacuated to Sweden, and from England to the USA during WW II. The British evacuations ceased abruptly after the bombardment and sinking of one ship. In 1939, many nations worked hard at the international level to achieve some kind of agreement about protected zones for children. Great

Britain especially was active in these negotiations. The aim was to move children to special zones where there were no targets of military interest, mostly in the countryside, and to thus give children a more protected life. These negotiations didn't lead anywhere, mostly because of the intense opposition of the German representatives. However, children were evacuated from London to the countryside. One pioneer in child psychiatry, Anna Freud, together with Dorothy T. Burlingham, wrote a book in 1943 called *Children and War* that described their own experiences in Hampstead Children's home. The child psychiatrists became convinced that children need regular visits from their mothers; without keeping contact the separation was more stressful than the air-raids and horrors of war.

After WW II children caught up in the Greek Civil War were transferred to the socialist countries. The most massive evacuations of children during the war were, however, in Finland. Altogether 70,000 children, 8 per cent of children under 18 years of age, were evacuated to Sweden and Denmark, with many of them being evacuated twice because of the war sequelae. Most of them spent years in these neighbouring countries, forgetting their mother tongue and adapting to the far better living standards. This period in the lives of Finnish children was first explored by researchers in the 1980s. Although for many of the children the multiple separations were most traumatic, as a group the war children didn't differ from the control group which experienced both the war in Finland and the times of poverty and hunger thereafter. It is interesting to note that recently the former Finnish war children have founded an organization and a magazine of their own in order to explore their experiences, to record their memories and to get in contact with others with the same background.

The discourse on protected zones has recently come up in the discussions and negotiations that have followed the Convention of the Rights of the Child. UNICEF has recently started to develop the idea of peace zones – in warlike and conflict situations there could be declared a zone of peace for children to live in – and intends to pursue the possibility that zones of peace could be raised as a tenet of international humanitarian law.

Physical disability of children due to warfare

The biggest risk that warfare poses for children is landmines, but children are also exposed to battlefields and snipers. The landmine problem is described elsewhere in this book in more detail. There are at least 25 countries that are heavily mined, and Afghanistan, Cambodia, Angola and parts of Iraq and Somalia are facing what is practically a catastrophe. Children mostly play in places where adults do not work, and they are not sophisticated enough to remember all the dangerous places. There have been occasional rumours that adversaries lay out mines that look like toys, but so far there has been no verification that this cruelty actually takes place. In any case, many children have been injured as a result of playing with mines.

Disability resulting from war is a personal tragedy for a child. In many societies there are not enough rehabilitation opportunities for adult people, and it is estimated that disabled children receive rehabilitation in less than one out of five cases. A growing child with a prosthesis will need several of them during the early years of his or her life, but for many such children there may not even be the opportunity to get the first one. The child's education may suffer, and the societal attitudes are not always positive or supportive of people who have disabilities.

Since disability is a relationship between a person and his/her environment, in a crisis this relationship becomes even more inclement: everyone is affected by a crisis but the impact on disabled people is disproportionate. When the infrastructure of a society breaks down, people become increasingly dependent on their own physical abilities for survival. Even flight from danger is difficult for the caregiver of a disabled child. Therefore it is important to ensure that children with disabilities are involved in and not excluded from any societal or foreign aid programmes, and that the helping procedures do not further disadvantage and marginalize them.[12]

Displaced and unaccompanied children

In every crisis, conflict and war there are situations where families become dispersed. Catastrophes leave behind displaced children who cannot relocate their families. This has been evident in long-lasting civil wars like the one in Mozambique, as well as in shorter but sudden conflicts as in Rwanda and Burundi. When international organizations started to explore the phenomenon in the 1980s, they found that the number of children separated from families during emergencies was substantially higher than ever assumed. They realized also that the aid organizations didn't share their management skills in such cases and new projects always started from the very beginning.[13] Many of the children proved to be orphaned, but there were abandoned and runaway children as well. In many emergencies the majority of unaccompanied children are boys over 12 years, not infants as in the popular perception.

During wartime, adequate means of communication are seldom available, and even afterwards it is very complicated to reach families. The care and placement of displaced children often becomes entangled in legal, political and ideological complications, as the rights and interests of the child, the family, agencies and governments may compete.

In Mozambique, the families are reached through simple posters with a picture of the child. The name of the child is included if the child is old enough to give it, as well as any reasonable information about the situation under which the child lost his/her parents. These posters are spread around the region, and many happy reunions have resulted since the members of extended families strongly wish to keep their families intact and the authorities would rather support families in their reunion efforts than run orphanages.

Mental consequences of war

The psychological consequences of wars and conflicts for the minds of children were first a topic of discussion in the scientific world some decades ago. Initially there were individual case reports on traumatized children, and then some questionnaire and interview studies were conducted on the attitudes and emotions of survivor children.[14]

Nowadays there is an ample set of standardized questionnaires and scales to measure the inner world of children, and a rich array of studies from all around the world.[15]

The fact is that under conditions of war children are exposed to crude, violent, fearful and shocking experiences. They react in many ways, both immediately and years later, that range from autistic or psychotic reactions to bed-wetting and nightmares. Children are vulnerable to psychological stress.[16] A growing body of evidence shows that children's psychosocial development can be damaged by war experiences. There is not, however, accurate evidence enough to help the adults to anticipate the possible mental disturbances. There is a great variation of the timing, severity, frequency and nature of violent experiences that affect the development of children. Differences in exposure can be great, and stresses such as loss or bombing are too broad as categories to be used as a basis for generalizations. There are many discrepancies in the studies, reflecting the differences between war situations as well as in the living situations of children and the support they receive from their families and communities.

When the world became convinced of the mental needs of child survivors of war, different treatment and rehabilitation programmes were built up. When emergencies happen, it is typical that there are several, even hundreds of different organizations offering help, but mostly the scale of their activities is limited. The need for coordination is clear yet difficult to achieve. Important international organizations like UNICEF have contributed markedly to the coordination of mental support activities for children in war.[17] But there remains a debate whether the help and therapy provided is adequate at all, and whether psychosocial programmes focused on post-traumatic stress disorder that use a western medical model are appropriate for child survivors of war. Some criticism has been made that the programmes do not recognize the local cultural values enough, and the therapists do not master the language spoken. Sometimes it is said that western values are too insistent and the medical concept of therapy too formal for the reality of the situation. To solve any scientific discrepancies much more evidence-based research is needed, but to solve the problems of today's children in their everyday lives is much more urgent. So, as Joanna Santa Barbara states, the diversion of resources into psychosocial projects may not be in balance in comparison with the needs for community development, income generation and infrastructure rebuilding.[18]

Resilience is a relatively new concept in child psychology. It arose from observations that some children seemed to emerge relatively unscathed from even the most adverse social situations. There are factors that can help a child's positive development, and most of them, now recognized, are of a simple and general nature. Children need a sense of belonging, they need some positive experiences of their own skills and ability to manage challenging situations, they need some interactive skills, and they need a friend or several of them. This information may be helpful in planning rehabilitation activities for children.

Children have also themselves been active in describing their experiences by the ways and means which are natural to them. So there are collections of children's drawings from the Spanish Civil War as well as from the Hiroshima and Nagasaki atomic bomb catastrophes. Children's inner world is, however, more closely described in Chapter 23 of this volume.

REFERENCES

1. Kahnert, M., Pitt, D. and I. Taipale (1983), *Children and War*, Proceedings of symposium at Siuntio Baths, Finland, 1983, Jyväskylä: GIPRI, IPB, Peace Union of Finland.
2. Machel, G. (1996), *Impact of Armed Conflict on Children*. Report of the expert of the secretary-general, Ms Gracha Machel, submitted pursuant to General Assembly Resolution 48/157, New York: UN Department of Public Information, Development and Human Rights Section.
3. UNICEF (1998), *The Progress of Nations. The nations of the world ranked according to their achievements in fulfilment of child rights and progress for women*, New York: United Nations; and UNICEF (2000), *The State of the World's Children 2000*, Oxford: Oxford University Press.
4. UNDP (1997), *Human Development Report 1997*, New York: UNDP.
5. Kosonen, A. (1987), *The Special Protection of Children and Child Soldiers. A principle and its application*, Helsinki: Publications of the Institute of Public Law at the University of Helsinki, C:22.
6. Brett, R., and M. McCallin (1996), *Children: The Invisible Soldiers*, Växjö: Rädda Barnen; Human Rights Watch (1995), *Child Soldiers in Liberia*, New York: Human Rights Watch/Africa, Childrens' Rights Project; Human Rights Watch (1995), *Children of Sudan. Slaves, street children and child soldiers*, New York: Human Rights Watch/Africa, Children's Rights Project; and Dodge, C. P. and M. Raundalen (eds) (1987), *War, Violence, and Children in Uganda*, Oslo: Norwegian University Press.
7. Harbison, J. (ed.) (1983), *Children of the Troubles. Children in Northern Ireland*, Belfast: Learning Resources Unit, Stranmillis College.
8. Barnett, L. (1999), 'Children and War', *Medicine, Conflict and Survival* 15: 315–27.
9. Rister, A. (1989), 'Low Intensity Warfare', in *Kinder und krieg in Lateinamerika*, s 22–27, Göttingen: Lamuv Verlag.
10. Lawyers Committee for Human Rights (1986), *The War against Children: South Africa's youngest victims*, New York: Lawyers Committee for Human Rights; Brittain, V. and S.A. Minty (1988), *Children of Resistance. On children, repression and the law in apartheid South Africa*, London: Kliptown Books Ltd.
11. Kavén, Pertti (1985), *70,000 pientä kohtaloa. Suomen sotalapset* (70,000 small destinies, the evacuated Finnish children during the Second World War). Helsinki: Otava.
12. Hastie, R. (1997), *Disabled Children in a Society at War. A Casebook from Bosnia*, UK and Ireland: Oxfam.
13. Ressler, E. M. (1984), 'Unaccompanied Children in Emergencies', in *Child Victims of Armed Conflicts*, s 9–14, Stockholm: Rädda Barnen.
14. Herzka, H. S., von Schumacher, A. and S. Tyrangiel (1989), 'Die Kinder der Verfolgten. Die nachkommen der Naziopfer und flüchtlingskinder heute', *Verl. für Med. Psychologie im Verl. Vandenhoeck u. Ruprecht*.
15. 'Children and Conflict: Rights and Realities' (1999), *Medicine Conflict and Survival* 15 (4).
16. Muhumuza, R. (1995), *Gulu: Children of War. A Report from a UK–ODA Assisted Programme in Uganda*. Uganda/UK: World Vision.
17. Lundequist, B., Lööf, L., Berglund, T. P., Penaloza, C. and G. Ringsby (1995), *Barn, Krig, Psykoterapi* (Children, War, Psychotherapy), Växjö: Rädda Barnen.
18. Santa Barbara, J. (1999), 'Helping Children Affected by War: Introduction', *Medicine, Conflict and Survival* 15: 352–4.

Address for correspondence
National Research and Development Centre for Welfare and Health (STAKES)
Siltasaarenkatu 18
P.O. Box 220, 00531 Helsinki, Finland

23 CHILDREN'S RESPONSES TO THE THREAT OF NUCLEAR WAR

TYTTI SOLANTAUS

War and military conflicts are realities in our world today, for children as well as adults. Even those children who live in well-to-do industrialized countries away from the actual conflict areas are exposed to war and violence through the mass media. The development of mass media since the Second World War (WW II) has changed the world of children dramatically. That world used to reach to the garden gate or a nearby town, but now extends to the remotest areas of the world. Children learn about wars and conflicts in everyday news reports. Even a full war can be televised and watched by small children, as happened during the Persian Gulf War in 1991. The expansion of the child's world has happened gradually and, by and large, the adult world has not paid much attention to what it might mean to children.

Research on child development has focused mainly on personal relationships as the formative context for development. There are also studies on the impact of day care and school, but the larger society has mostly gone unappreciated. In spite of Bronfenbrenner's theory and arguments on the interplay of different levels of environmental systems in child development, there are very few studies which look into how global issues affect child and adolescent development.[1] The research on children and the threat of nuclear war forms a notable exception, and represents the first attempt in child psychology and psychiatry to study the meaning of the global environment to children.

Chapter 23 reviews studies of the impact of the threat of nuclear war on children and adolescents living in countries not directly involved in armed hostilities and conflict. Most studies were carried out in the early 1980s when the world faced an escalation in international tension and the threat of nuclear war.

Historical perspective

Children's fears reflect their outer and inner realities. They give us a window to children's experience and understanding of their life and environment. Fears of children living in the western world have been studied since the 1930s. A historical analysis reveals a change in the nature of these fears over the years. From the 1930s to the 1950s, fears concerning personal safety, animals, supernatural phenomena, darkness and lightning dominated.[2] After WWII, fears of war entered children's minds even in peacetime. Angelino, Dollins and Mech seem to have been the first ones to document political fears (war and communist take-over) in children.[3] These were first expressed by older children and then, a little later, also by younger ones.[4] By 1973 a threat of war dominated children's fears even among 8-year-olds.[5]

The fear-research documents a decline in supernatural and a rise in political fears. The decline in supernatural fears probably reflects the emphasis on scientific explanations in the modern postwar society. The rise in fears of war was most likely brought about by the development of the mass media and the portrayal of news related to war and conflict. Historically, it seems that children in the western world had become aware of the threat of large-scale war by the 1970s.

Worry and fear of nuclear war

The bombing of Hiroshima and Nagasaki during WWII started the nuclear age. Nuclear weapons are capable of mass destruction and they carry a threat of a global war. There has been a threat of nuclear war twice since Hiroshima and Nagasaki, first during the Cuban and Berlin crises in the early 1960s and then during the Euro missile crises in the early 1980s. In both periods of crisis, the high tension in the international arena gripped the public through the mass media.

Schwebel and Escalona, among others, studied children's reactions in the 1960s.[6] The studies revealed a surprisingly extensive awareness of the threat of war in children. They also showed that children connected the situation with their own lives and futures. In Escalona's study, over 70 per cent of the 10–17-year-olds referred to war and peace issues when discussing their own futures, and in Schwebel's study, about half of the children expected a war to break out.[7]

After the early 1960s, Cold War turned to *détente* and the threat of nuclear war subsided in the public awareness. Research on the psychological impact of nuclear weapons ceased after its peak in the 1960s. Opinion books also reached their peak in 1959–64 and fell away rapidly after that. Technical books, however, had a rising trend all through the period.[8] This reflects the actual situation: the public lived in the spirit of *détente*, but the development of nuclear armaments went on unhalted.

The late 1970s and early 1980s saw a further rise in international tension, and the threat of nuclear war became evident. Research on children's psychological responses boomed. The American Psychiatric Association set up a task force to study how children were affected.[9] This marked the beginning of extensive research on the psychological impact of nuclear threat on children.

In their first stage, the studies mapped the extent of children's and adolescents' fears and worries about nuclear war. The findings of the 1960s studies were quickly repeated: children were extensively aware of the world situation. In Finland, about 80 per cent of young people mentioned war as their top worry in a nationwide epidemiological survey of 12–18-year-olds.[10] The youngest age group, 12-year-olds, expressed more concern (90 per cent) than the oldest (50 per cent). Similar findings were repeated in several countries, although there were some cultural differences.[11] The level of worry was highest in the Nordic countries and the Soviet Union. However, even with the variations, nuclear war seemed to be one of the top worries of young people throughout the industrialized world during those years. This was especially true of pre-adolescents and adolescents, but Davies showed that even in children as young as seven, the main concern about the future was the outbreak of war.[12]

The level of worry seemed to rise through childhood years to early adolescence and then subside with increasing age. The rise in nuclear worries during the school years might be attributed to children's increasing access to television and newspapers. Younger children might not read and listen to news reports as much as preadolescents and adolescents.

The decline of nuclear fears after early adolescence has been discussed from several viewpoints. For one, the decline might be due to the development of cognitive capacities. With more understanding of societal issues, young people might understand that a global war is not going to break out without precipitating events and processes, and hence the threat is not felt as imminent as in the younger age group. The decline of fears in later adolescence might also be due to the development of compartmentalization of private and societal issues in one's mind. Developmental task theory has also been advocated here. In later adolescence, young people have to make important decisions about their lives, schooling, love relationships, family, and these might take precedence over societal problems. Overall, these studies leave no doubt that children and young people became aware of the threat of nuclear war in the early 1980s. The next question was how salient these worries and fears were, and how they affected children's lives.

Extent

The extent of the worry is reflected in children's affective reactions, preoccupations and anxieties. In Finland about 30 per cent of young people reported thinking about war at least weekly, including the 10 per cent who thought about it almost every day.[13] Almost 40 per cent of girls and 15 per cent of boys reported that they experienced intense fear or anxiety about war; about 10 per cent reported nightmares about war. Only about ten per cent said they did not think of war. These findings were repeated by Goldberg et al. in Canada.[14]

Girls reacted more strongly than boys: they were more preoccupied with thoughts, anxiety and nightmares about war. Thoughts about war were associated with higher anxiety in girls than in boys.[15] These gender differences in responses can be understood in the light of boys' and girls' different developmental processes with regard both to emotional development in general and to war and peace issues in particular. Girls tend to experience more fears and anxieties in general than do boys and they are also more willing than boys to express them.[16] This might explain part of the female preponderance.

On the other hand, war and military developments are very gendered issues. The military, technological and political knowledge and praxis reside in the male tradition. This might give men an image of mastery of war, including activity and heroism. Boys also play more video and computer war games, which might also give them a sense of mastery of war.

In the female tradition, there is no mastery of warfare; rather, women are victimized by war. Their activity is directed towards preserving life on the home front, tending the wounded, and burying the dead. Indeed, boys and girls seem to have different images of war. For boys, war means adventures and heroic elements, while for girls the image of war is one of plague and suffering.[17] This might contribute to girls' stronger emotional reaction to the threat of war.

Knowledge and understanding of war

Children learn about the world from the mass media, television being the most important of these. This was documented in the 1970s in relation to the Vietnam War[18] and it has continued unchanged.[19] School and parents come only after the mass media. Sommers *et al.* report that during the early 1980s, 75 per cent of Canadian adolescents received their information of nuclear issues from television, 39 per cent from teachers and only 31 per cent from parents.[20] Studies from other countries supported these findings.[21]

Despite their great anxiety, young people seemed very ill-informed about the nuclear issue in the 1980s. Their level of knowledge and understanding was low in spite of extensive mass media exposure.[22] It seems fair to say that the mass media informs, but does not educate.

One can distinguish two different sets of knowledge regarding war. One is factual knowledge about the technology of the weapons and the other is knowledge and understanding about the societal processes behind war. The former is easier to gain and, not surprisingly, boys seem to be superior to girls in knowledge about technical facts about nuclear weapons. Boys' higher involvement with war games and war comics might contribute to this.

Children's understanding of what war is about is dependent on the level of their cognitive development. Monaco and Gaier studied children at different developmental levels as to their understanding of the Gulf War.[23] Children under school age used their everyday experience to understand the situation; for example, when asked where Iraq was, an answer might have been 'Beyond Disney World'. Children often confused time, distance, cause and effect. They used concrete characterizations of good and bad. They often used terms about which they had no understanding, and there were many misunderstandings. One five-year-old boy wondered why 'we were at war with a rock' (Iraq). Children confused fantasy and reality and used material from fairy tales in trying to understand what was going on. They were highly sensitive to seeing and responding to other people's reactions regarding the war in their effort to make sense of the situation. Children often discussed the frightening images seen on television.

School-age children were better able to distinguish different aspects of war including the different nations involved. They were also capable of noting degrees of right and wrong and some children were able to ponder about whether the war was 'worth it'. School-aged children were more interested in factual details about missiles than younger children. Boys talked about 'heroes' and some wanted to serve in the military. School-age children often wanted to send caring messages to the soldiers, for example 'We are thinking of you'. They stressed that the soldiers were fulfilling their obligation.

Adolescent youngsters raised many of the same issues as school-age children did. In addition, they were more explicit about their own feelings and anxieties. They were also able to talk about the moral and humanitarian issues concerning war.

Many children in the Monaco and Gaier study had family members involved in the war. These children displayed more knowledge about the geography of the Gulf area, names of military leaders and details about weapons, but their cognitive reasoning about war was similar to that of the other children at the same developmental level.

The Monaco and Gaier study displays a clear developmental trend from undifferentiated, concrete thinking towards more defined and abstract ways of thought. It also reveals, once again, how even small children extract information from the environment and try to make sense of the world. It seems clear that children need adults' help and education to develop an understanding of war.

There are no studies concerning the impact of the level of knowledge on children's fears and worries about war. However, it has been postulated that a low level of understanding of the societal processes behind war might be linked to the image of war as a natural, uncontrollable catastophe, which was found in Engeström's study to dominate children's images of war.[24] This might make children more fearful. Accordingly in the early 1980s, Beardslee, Mack and Tizard reported that many children thought that war can break out at 'any time'.[25] The Monaco and Gaier study shows how vulnerable small children might be to developing immanent fears as they confuse time, distance and concepts.

The role of adults

Parents did not seem aware of their children's worries and preoccupations in the early 1980s. Although 80 per cent of Finnish young people reported worry about war, only about one-third said they discussed the issue at home.[26] The lack of sharing at home was especially noteworthy as about twice as many of these young people talked about war with their peers. The same seemed to be true in other countries as well.

Children attributed the lack of discussion at home to parents' not caring about the issue. In Holmborg's and Bergström's study of Swedish youngsters, 55 per cent perceived adults as very little concerned about or totally indifferent to the issue of nuclear weapons. However, at the same time polls showed that the worry about war was expressed by 80 per cent of the adult population in Sweden.[27]

A strange picture emerges. Both the parents and the children were worried about the war, but they did not talk about their worries with each other. Why so? Parents might not have been aware that children knew about the issue. Also, they might have actively avoided the topic with children, because they believed that by doing so they could protect children from worry about war. It is also not customary in our culture to talk with children about war and death. Children, on the other hand, might have interpreted their parents' silence as indifference to the threat of war, as was documented by Holmborg and Bergström.[28] It also has to be recognized that parents are not very well aware of their children's fears in general, and that children don't often talk about them to their parents.[29]

Discussing a worrisome issue with parents is a means for children to obtain emotional and social support. It is interesting, therefore, to see how this was associated with children's responses to nuclear threat. The studies showed that discussing the nuclear issue with parents was related to both higher anxiety and a stronger sense of mastery and more optimism about the future.[30] This seemingly contradictory finding is a most important one.

The relationship between anxiety and discussion is understandably a two-way street. Anxiety about war might make children discuss it, while discussion might arouse more awareness and anxiety. On the other hand, discussions with parents might increase children's understanding of the nuclear issue and make it seem more controllable by human effort. This might give children the higher sense of mastery and optimism detected in the studies. These results have implications for peace education.

Impact on mental health

Concern about children's mental health was a major consideration among child psychologists and psychiatrists in the early 1980s. They were worried that the level of worry and anxiety might be too much for children. The studies showed that children reacted to the threat of war with preoccupation, nightmares, anxieties and fears. However, in a great majority, these reactions were not associated with signs of poor mental health, maybe even to the contrary. Those who were worried were better socially adjusted, better educated and had more interests in societal life than those who were not. Neither were they any more anxiety-prone than the other young people. Worry about war seemed to be linked more with awareness and interest in global issues than with a debilitating, pathological anxiety.

However, a group of young people, about 4–5 per cent,[31] expressed high anxiety about war coupled with hopelessness, fatalism and alienation from the society. They presented a general picture of depression. Nuclear worries were not causative to their state, but a contributing factor. This group of young people underline for us that societal issues and the threat of war can be an additional strain for those who already feel alienated and hopeless in their lives.

Future challenges

In our times, children learn about the world, its threats and developments. They react to them affectively and connect them with their own lives. The threat of nuclear war in the early 1960s and 1980s caused suffering to children in terms of fears, anxieties and preoccupation. The nuclear threat studies show further that even small children try to make sense of the world and that without adult guidance they are left alone with their cognitive limitations and magical thinking. To effectively cope with the threat of war, children need education by and participation with the adult community, their parents and teachers. Mass media inform but do not educate. Only with the help of the adults in their lives can children reach an understanding of what is happening and gain a sense of mastery and optimism about the future.

The lack of education and participation might lead to compartmentalization of global and societal issues in later adolescence. This means that societal issues are separated from private aspects of life and compartmentalized in one's mind, possibly leading to unresponsiveness to and lack of responsibility for global issues. We know very little about these processes.

There seem to be two opposing trends in our society. One is the privatization of people's lives and the other the globalization of societal problems. Privatization leads to focusing one's attention on oneself and one's own family. Psychologically it seems to be based on compartmentalization of societal and private issues. On the other hand, global underdevelopment, environmental problems, poverty, war and conflicts tie the world to a common fate, affecting the lives of even the most private people. The development of global responsibility in people is one of the challenges of our time and of utmost importance to the fate of humankind. Children's awareness and interests concerning global issues offer a momentum for education and a starting-point for the development of global understanding and responsibility.

REFERENCES

1. Bronfenbrenner, U. (1979), *The Ecology of Human Development*, Cambridge: Harvard University Press.
2. Winker, J.B. (1949), 'Age and Sex Trends in the Wishes, Identifications, Activities and Fears of Children', *Child Development* 20: 191–200; and Lapouse, R. and M. Monk (1959), 'Fears and Worries in a Representative Sample of Children', *American Journal of Orthopsychiatry* 29: 803–18.
3. Angelino, H., Dollins, J. and E.V. Mech (1956), 'Trends in the Fears and Worries of School Children as Related to Socio-economic Status and Age', *Journal of Genetic Psychology* 89: 263–76.
4. Croake, J.W. (1969), 'Fears of Children', *Human Development* 12: 239–47; and Croake, J.W. and F.H. Knox (1973), 'The Changing Nature of Children's Fears', *Child Study Journal* 3: 91–105.
5. See Croake and Knox, n. 4 above.
6. Schwebel, M. (1965), 'Effects of the Nuclear Threat on Children and Teenagers. Implications for professionals', *American Journal of Orthopsychiatry* 52: 608–18; Escalona, S. (1963), 'Children's Responses to the Nuclear War Threat', *Children* 10: 137–42; and Solantaus, T. (1991), 'Young People and the Threat of Nuclear War: 'Out there is a world I belong to', *Medicine and War, International Medical Concerns on War and Other Social Violence*, Supplement 1, Volume 7.
7. See Schwebel and Escalona, n. 6 above.
8. Lowther, M.P. (1973), 'The Decline of Public Concern over the Atom Bomb', *Kansas Journal of Sociology* 9: 77–88.
9. Beardslee, W.R. and J. Mack (1982), 'The Impact on Children and Adolescents of Nuclear Developments', in *Psychosocial Aspects of Nuclear Developments*, Task Force Report No. 20, Washington DC: American Psychiatric Association.
10. Solantaus, T., Rimpelä, M. and V. Taipale (1984), 'The Threat of War in the Minds of 12–18-Year-Olds in Finland', *Lancet* 8: 784–5.
11. See Solantaus, n. 6 above.
12. Davies, R. (1987), *Hopes and Fears. Children's Attitudes to Nuclear War*, Occasional Paper No. 11, St Martin College, Lancaster: Centre for Peace Studies.
13. Solantaus, T., Rimpelä, M. and O. Rahkonen (19??), 'Social Epidemiology of the Experience of Threat of War among Finnish Youth', *Social Science and Medicine* 21: 145–51.

14. Goldberg, S., LaCombe, S., Levinson, D., Ross, P. K., Ross C. and F. Sommers (1985), 'Thinking about the Nuclear War: relevance to mental health', *American Journal of Orthopsychiatry* 55: 503–12.

15. See n. 13 above.

16. See Lapouse and Monk in n. 2 above.

17. Engeström, Y. (1979), *Koululaisen mielikuvitus ja käyttäytyminen rauhankasvatuksen kannalta tarkasteltuna* (Imagination and Behaviour of School Children from the Point of View of Peace Education), Tutkimuksia 19: Rauhan- ja konfliktintutkimuslaitos.

18. Tolley, H. (1973), *Children and War. Political Socialization in International Conflict*, New York: Teachers' College Press.

19. Sommers, F.G., Goldberg, S., Levinson S., Ross, C. and S. LaCombe (1985), 'Children's Mental Health and the Threat of Nuclear War', in T. Solantaus, E. Chivian, M. Vartanyan and S. Chivian (eds), *Impact of the Threat of Nuclear War on Children and Adolescents*, Boston: International Physicians for the Prevention of Nuclear War, pp. 61–93; and Patten, D. (1987), *The Psychological Impact of the Threat of Nuclear War on Adolescents in New Zealand*, paper presented at the Seventh Congress, International Physicians for the Prevention of Nuclear War, Moscow.

20. See Sommers *et al.*, n. 19 above.

21. See Solantaus, n. 6 above.

22. Zweigenhaft, R.L. (1984), 'What Do Americans Know about Nuclear Weapons?', *Bulletin of Atomic Scientists* 40: 48–50; and Zweigenhaft, R.L. (1985), 'Students Surveyed about Nuclear War', *Bulletin of Atomic Scientists* 41: 26–7.

23. Monaco, N.M. and E.L. Gaier (1992), 'Developmental Level and Children's Understanding of the Gulf War', *Early Child Development and Care* 79: 29–38.

24. Engeström, Y. (1985), 'Multiple Levels of Nuclear Reality in the Cognition, Fantasy and Activity of School-aged Children', in T. Solantaus, E. Chivian, M. Vartanyan and S. Chivian (eds), *Impact of the Threat of Nuclear War on Children and Adolescents,* Boston: International Physicians for the Prevention of Nuclear War, pp. 39–52.

25. See n. 9 above and also Tizard, B. (1986), 'The Impact of the Nuclear Threat on Children's Development', in M. Richards and P. Light (eds), *Children of Social Worlds*, Cambridge: Polity Press.

26. See n. 13 above.

27. Holmborg, P.O. and A. Bergström (1984), 'How Swedish Children Think and Feel Concerning the Nuclear Threat', in T. Solantaus, E. Chivian, M. Vartanyan and S. Chivian (eds), *Impact of the Threat of Nuclear War on Children and Adolescents*, Boston: International Physicians for the Prevention of Nuclear War, pp. 170–80.

28. Ibid.

29. See Lapouse and Monk, n. 2 above.

30. See ns 13 and 14 above.

31. Diamond, G. and J. Bachman (1986), 'High-school Seniors and the Nuclear Threat 1975–1984: political and mental implications for concern and despair', *International Journal of Mental Health* 15: 210–41.

Address for correspondence

National Research and Development Centre for Welfare and Health, P.O. Box 220, 00531 Helsinki, Finland
Email: tytti..solantaus@stakes.fi

24 CROATIA

PAUL STUBBS

Chapter 24 looks at some aspects of the impact on health of the war which began in the Republic of Croatia in 1991 and which did not end formally until the reintegration of eastern Slavonia in January 1998. It is certainly the case that the war in Bosnia-Herzegovina, discussed elsewhere in this book, had a much greater impact in terms just of numbers of victims, but the issues in Croatia should not be underestimated. The author focuses particularly on: children's health; the psychosocial impact of war; and the extent of post-traumatic stress disorder (PTSD). The chapter outlines some particular features of the war with significant health implications and seeks to address the impact on health of the conjunction of war with large-scale forced migration and the post-socialist economic transition. A tentative final section considers war as a stimulus to changes in service provision and notes, in particular, the rise of certain local non-governmental organizations (NGOs), suggesting that these may have the greatest long-term impact on service delivery.

Country profile, contours of war

Croatia, with a population of some 4.5 million people, was formerly one of the more developed republics in the Yugoslav Federation, reaching a per capita gross domestic product (GDP) before the onset of war of approximately US$5000 . Perhaps of greatest significance is the fact that health and welfare services were highly developed and, on most of the major indices of health, Croatia reached what are usually seen as western standards. By 1990, infant mortality, at 10.7 per 1000 live births, was only slightly higher than that of Greece, having been reduced from a 1983 figure of 18.7. The life expectancy at birth was 73.5 years. Whilst war had only a limited effect on these health indices it did produce a considerable economic deterioration: per capita GDP more than halved by 1992; income from tourism declined to near zero; there was a sharp rise in unemployment, and a vast increase in the proportion of GDP spent on non-production including, of course, defence expenditure. In addition, the Croatian population is an ageing one, with only 1.7 employed persons for every pensioner by 1997. In the longer term, this socio-economic deterioration may have a more lasting impact on health.

Following Croatia's declaration of independence in 1990 in the wake of democratic elections, full-scale war broke out in 1991. Some strands of the ethnic Serb community, which overall accounted for some 12 per cent of the population at the 1981 census, particularly in areas where they formed the largest single ethnic group, joined forces with the Serb-dominated Yugoslav People's Army. The shelling from the sea of the southern city of Dubrovnik, and the siege and subsequent fall of the eastern city of Vukovar, focused the world's attention on Croatia in late 1991. Under the Vance–Owen peace plan, early in 1992 the country became divided between regions controlled by the Croatian government and those controlled by rebels which became the self-styled Republic of Serbian Krajina (RSK). The plan created four United Nations Protected Areas (UNPA zones) corresponding broadly with these regions: (i) sector east, in eastern Slavonia including Vukovar; (ii) sector west, in western Slavonia bordering Bosnia, including Okucani and parts of Pakrac; (iii) sector north, the northern part of the old *vojska krajina* (military frontier), west of Karlovac; and (iv) sector south, also part of the old *krajina*, a large sweep of territory including the RSK capital Knin.

As a result of Croatian military action in May and August 1995, in Western Slavonia and in the *krajina* respectively, three of the four UNPA zones were returned to Croatian control, leading to the exodus of more than 210,000 ethnic Serbs. Eastern Slavonia was peacefully reintegrated into Croatia in a process which was completed in January 1998, although this also led to a new migration of Serbs from Croatia, so that the total Serbian population is now estimated to be less than 3 per cent and demographically very different from previously. The war created a large number of internally displaced persons, mainly from rebel-controlled areas, who still face huge problems, with many unable to return home because of the massive damage to infrastructure, including housing, and the poor economic prospects in much of the reintegrated regions.

Overall, the government estimates that some 9000 people were killed in the war, over 27,000 wounded and almost 3000 declared missing. When the war in Bosnia began, Croatia became the major host country for its refugees so that, at its peak in late 1992, some 350,000 Bosnian refugees, together with some 265,000 internally displaced persons, produced a situation where more than 15 per cent of the Croatian population consisted of forced migrants, who were accommodated in a range of locations from purpose-built collective centres through tourist facilities to private homes. Conditions in many collective centres and other improvised accommodation, whilst physically adequate, were not conducive to long-term optimum health, although major epidemics did not occur. In some places, tensions ran high, particularly during the 1993–94 conflict between ethnic Croats and Muslims in Bosnia.

Children's health: frontline towns

Nature of the conflict

A number of features of the conflict are important in understanding its health impact:

(1) The war was geographically very uneven, with over two-thirds of the country facing

little direct war consequences, other than a general decline in living standards, but with other areas facing high levels of destruction, with many parts of these areas changing hands several times. Slavonski Brod, on the border with Serb-controlled Bosnia, was shelled without interruption for over seven months, and nearby Zupanja was under general alert for over 300 days in 1995, for example. Croatian government estimates suggest that direct war damages amounted to over US$20 billion.

(2) The highly complex and shifting nature of the conflict over a long period of time meant that many frontline towns and cities experienced a prolonged 'no war, no peace' situation in which periods of relative calm would be interrupted by unexpected shelling.

(3) The threats against Croatian government territory came from diverse forces, from Croatian Serbs, Bosnian Serbs, and in the early part of the war the Yugoslav army and paramilitary units. As in the war in Bosnia-Herzegovina, there was specific targeting of civilian populations and so-called ethnic cleansing as particular war aims.

(4) Refugees and displaced persons were often accommodated in or near frontline towns and cities, which became very overcrowded whilst surrounded by underpopulated rural areas. Figures which suggest that some half a million people were forced to leave their homes, if only briefly, during the height of the conflict in Croatia, between October and December 1991, and that over one-third of this number were children under 14 years of age, indicate the extent of disruption to ordinary lives.

Effects on children's health

The effects of the war on children are of particular concern. In the period to September 1995: 265 children were killed; 957 wounded, including 86 who were permanently disabled; 4273 lost one parent; and 54 lost both parents. Most children were killed in the first six months of the war, particularly in eastern Slavonia. Infrastructural damage was also severe, with 528 educational, 29 children's health and 16 child-welfare institutions destroyed or damaged. Over 20 per cent of refugees and displaced persons were aged 14 years or younger, and in 1994 over 4000 refugee and displaced children were unaccompanied and 800 were orphans. The United Nations Children's Fund (UNICEF) estimated that, by 1995, some 400,000 children in Croatia were living in exceptionally difficult circumstances.

Of particular note is the psychological impact of the conflict on children. Research for UNICEF, carried out in 28 schools in 1992 and 1993, shows the extensive exposure of children to traumatic events. The children were divided into four groups: (i) from low-crisis areas; (ii) from crisis areas; (iii) displaced children; and (iv) refugee children (see Table 24.1).

A number of other health-related factors should be noted in terms of the increased risks faced by children and young people in the frontline areas, including: the presence of landmines and other unexploded devices and weapons in the home; a rise in self-harm and attempted suicide; a rise in family violence and child abuse; and a marked decline in immunizations and preventive health checks. In many ways, these and other more normal health-related problems, including drug misuse, crime and delinquency, may be longer-lasting war-related health and welfare problems, together with a rise in a culture of violence and intolerance towards any group perceived as different.

Table 24.1 Exposure to traumatic events among children in Croatia (per cent)

	Low crisis areas	Crisis areas	Displaced	Refugees
Close experience of shelling and bombing	18	77	60	52
Witnessing someone being wounded	not given	16	24	26
Witnessing someone being killed	not given	6	11	15

Source: Stuvland, R. (1994), 'School-age Children Affected By War: the UNICEF programme in former Yugoslavia', in L. Arcel (ed.), *War Victims, Trauma and Psycho-Social Care*, Zagreb: ECTF, pp. 111–26.

Needs and resources

Above all, the frontline towns and cities faced a chronic imbalance between increased needs and decreased resources and capacity to meet those needs. The reduced ability of health, education and welfare services to respond to needs was also exacerbated by a number of factors which are rarely addressed because they are much less spectacular or notable than the direct war effects. One issue is professional flight and stress whereby, in a cumulative process, many health and welfare professionals leave the frontline areas and cannot be replaced, leaving those who stay to face increasing pressure in situations where their own lives, and those of their families, remain insecure. In addition, many health and welfare buildings were destroyed in the war, damaged beyond use or by being cold or damp, for example.

The war may well have contributed to an increase in geographical variations in health in Croatia which has become, in many ways, a highly centralized society with major health resources being concentrated in the capital, Zagreb, where one quarter of the total population lives, and in the other big cities. Rural areas and, in particular, the former frontline areas, have continued to suffer from poorer services and reductions in access to health care. The work of a range of international agencies, including the World Health Organization (WHO) and UNICEF, has been important in seeking to provide emergency relief and promote longer-term, sustainable health and welfare structures. Overall, however, the Croatian health system remains affected by the impoverishment associated with war and its aftermath, combined with a declining donor interest because of the fact that there is no longer a full-scale emergency.

Psychosocial programmes

Why psychosocial?

A highly significant feature of the health response to the war in Croatia was the recognition, from an early stage, of the need for a range of psychosocial assistance to vulnerable groups and, in particular, the large numbers of people traumatized by war. The nature of the war itself and the exposure of large numbers of civilians to acts of brutality, directly or as witnesses, were important factors in this recognition. Violence was often experienced not from an anonymous enemy, shelling from a distance, but within communities themselves, sometimes perpetrated by people known to the victims, even by friends and neighbours. Rape as a weapon of terror within the war has been well-documented. The hostilities directly affected a high proportion of the population, especially in some localities with the most damage to social support structures. The violence was also largely unpredictable and rapid in its onset. The fact that this was a war in Europe, in a developed society, may also have contributed to the psychosocial response, together with the common ground which Croatian psychologists found with other European counterparts working for international agencies.

Extent of suffering

A WHO study in late 1994 estimated that some 154,000 people in Croatia, including the UNPA zones, had severe trauma reactions which would require urgent and qualified professional help, with a similar number estimated as suffering from trauma reactions which, under peace conditions, would also qualify for professional help. For almost the first time in a major complex political emergency, then, psychosocial interventions came to be seen as a crucial complement to political peacekeeping and peace-building, and to physical survival interventions. A range of programmes was supported by UNICEF, WHO, the European Community Task Force (ECTF), and other donors and international agencies. ECTF, in particular, pioneered programmes of psychosocial support through member state NGOs working directly and/or in partnership with local organizations. Activities ranged from emotional and social survival interventions, through task-oriented and more psychologically-oriented groupwork, to traditional counselling and intensive psychotherapy. In part because of problems of continued conflict in Bosnia-Herzegovina, there were far more psychosocial interventions in Croatia, in the big cities, near the frontline areas and in the collective centres.

The debate

A debate ensued about the assumptions upon which these interventions were based and the effects of psychosocial approaches in broader terms of social development and human rights approaches. The assumption of a direct, unmediated, link between experiencing particular events, manifesting trauma symptoms, being labelled as having PTSD and actually needing professional help, was questioned by some commentators. Indeed, in retrospect, some of the more cautious and nuanced approaches to questions of psychological hurt tended to be swept aside in a headlong rush to do something in the face of what was obviously large-scale need. This may have resulted in a strengthening of medical models at the expense of a concern with the wider social context. Many international NGO interventions were of a relatively short-term nature as the amount of funding for trauma work decreased and was replaced by other issues. Critiques suggesting that psychosocial work on trauma tends to reflect the dominance of western approaches to health and illness (which may be less appropriate in other cultural contexts) were also aired in Croatia, particularly with regard to refugees and displaced persons from rural settings. In the end, perhaps all that can be said is that the attempt to place psychosocial needs at the centre of an emergency response was a major innovation, with both positive and negative effects, whose long-term impact can only be measured through equally long-term, sophisticated, evaluative research.

Innovation in health: the role of local NGOs

Context

What cannot be denied is the contribution of a range of local initiatives, including those of local NGOs, in pioneering innovative approaches to health care in Croatia, including psychosocial care. It should be remembered that, as a state socialist system, the country did not have a mix of health services prewar: there was no private provision and only a small non-governmental sector, itself largely ignored and consisting of a few initiatives in the capital, Zagreb. In addition, medical models, supported by state subsidies and enhancing the power of an élite of medical professionals, tended to dominate. The war was, in itself, a stimulus to a range of initiatives which produced a widening of definitions of health to include more preventive and educative concerns, and focused attention on what might be termed 'newly discovered social problems', in particular child abuse and violence against women. Often, NGO services were perceived as less stigmatizing than mainstream state services and did not imply a labelling of a person as sick in some way. A range of helplines on all manner of health issues sprang up and stimulated greater open public debate about health questions.

Women's health

It is perhaps in the sphere of women's health that some of the most important NGO initiatives occurred, with organizations such as the Centre for Women War Victims concerned to link specific support for women's health needs with wider lobbying, and a concern with general questions of human rights. Inevitably, as activists in women's rights networked in global arenas, a wider range of possibilities emerged, including more positive definitions of health, challenging medical models and supporting self-help and community development. There has been a great deal of concern that women's rights have, in many ways, been a major victim of the postwar political settlement, which contains within it many authoritarian and even nationalist strands so that, for example, reproductive rights remain a major area of conflict. In addition, the health needs of minorities, including a largely ignored and impoverished Roma community, can be marginalized by mainstream services.

NGOs and government

In more general terms, the government has tended not to support the wide range of local NGOs, perceiving many of them as politically motivated and externally supported. Legislation on associations of citizens is seen, by many commentators, as one of the least progressive in the whole of central and eastern Europe. The efforts of activists do seem, however, to be producing some changes, with governmental and private funding beginning to be channelled to NGOs in the sphere of health. Many local NGOs themselves suffer from a continued reliance on decreasing international funding. In addition, most of the leading NGOs tend to be dominated by professionals and there are, as yet, few influential organizations representing consumers of health services, except for those groups representing war veterans.

Conclusions

In many ways, the conjunction of war, large-scale forced migration, and post-socialist transition has made the process of health reform highly complex in Croatia, with heightened expectations coexisting alongside shrinking resources. The possibility of a longer-term restructuring so that services are more equitable, based on a mix of public and private provision, preventive rather than curative, empowering rather than patronizing, and affordable, still seems remote, despite some positive movements in recent times. Above all, the contribution of health to wider peace-building and to a culture of non-violence, tolerance and respect for diversity, will be a slow process likely to be led by activists in local communities rather than by the government. Even so, the change in the composition of the government following the elections of January 2000 represented an important change in the context in which such initiatives must work.

Address for correspondence
Henrija Dunanta 2, 10090 Zagreb, Croatia. Tel. and Fax: +385 1 34 50 751; email: pstubbs@zamir.net

25 WOMEN AS VICTIMS

EVA ISAKSSON

With the continuing rise in civilian casualties in modern war, women form a significant group among those affected. However, the numbers of their specific experiences have been mostly neglected by research, by healthcare professionals and by military and civilian policymakers. Available information suggests that these experiences and women's subsequent problems differ from men's in many ways that need to be taken into account when treating female victims of war. Putting women on the agenda and taking their traumatic experiences seriously is a necessary first step.

Women's war experiences gradually became a topic of scholarly discussion only as recently as the second half of the 20th century. Until then, women were generally seen as that part of the population that didn't have to face actual warfare, and which was in fact perceived as being protected by the men from battles and from the enemy.

Current statistics defy this traditional view of women as a safe group. We know that increasing numbers of civilians are affected by warfare: according to one estimate, Second World War (WW II) civilian casualties represented 50 per cent, a figure which has since then often exceeded 80 per cent. *The State of the War and Peace Atlas* estimates that: 'There were about five and a half million war deaths in the first half of the 1990s. Three-quarters of them were civilians, including a million children'.[1]

It is difficult to find reliable statistics about the effects of warfare on civilians and, consequently, on women – how many are killed, wounded, raped or otherwise hurt. One reason for this scarcity of information is that 'figures for war deaths are at best unreliable. Most people killed in war are civilians, but in most wars there is no agency responsible for counting civilian war deaths. Casualty figures are routinely manipulated for propaganda purposes'.[2] Women are very seldom mentioned as a specific group but instead lumped together with the rest of the civilian population as in 'women, children, and the elderly'. What is the rationale in choosing to focus on women as victims of war in this chapter? One reason is the large number of female victims, steadily on the increase, which should be justification enough. Also, we have until now had relatively little information about how women are affected, and how their war experiences differ from those of men. What, then, are these differences, similarities and specifics?

Women and war: a brief historical overview

From early prehistoric times, warfare has been a male occupation. As it developed from a tribal, mostly ritualistic phenomenon into an activity aimed at acquiring more economic and political power, women started playing ever less decisive roles in societies, in which being a soldier mattered most. With time, warfare gained in scale and destructivity. Old Assyrian texts from c.1300BC describe annihilation of whole cities so that rivers and fields were running red with blood. In ancient warfare, women were either killed or taken as slaves or as wives, becoming property of the victors.

In societies where all soldiers were men and women were their property, the latter ended up contributing to the infrastructure of war. By the time that mass armies were formed, women played vital roles as camp followers to the plundering armies (16th–18th centuries). Besides soldiers, those armies consisted of large numbers of women and their children. Their numbers, indeed, were often significantly larger than the number of soldiers for whom they were working. These women were never far away from warfare; neither were those who stayed at home but lost their male family members to war, or who were alone at home when enemy troops advanced to kill, rape and plunder.

Industrialization and military reorganization ended the era of female camp followers in the nineteenth century. They were replaced by nurses and later by female support staff and female soldiers trained to do the work of male soldiers in positions that were considered suitable for women, so that more men would be available for combat. In reality, these women were often serving quite near front lines. Many of them were killed or wounded. Even those women who stayed behind in the two world wars and in other wars of the 20th century were not enjoying much safety in the era of weapons of mass destruction. Women who worked in munitions factories and in areas of conflict were targets for enemy bombing, as were civilians in all countries where fighting was taking place.

During the last century, more women have been affected by war than ever before. They have served as soldiers, support personnel, nurses, freedom fighters, factory workers, wives, military prostitutes and so on. Women have been under fire, they have fled their homes as war refugees, suffered from hunger and lack of resources; they have been killed, raped, wounded, widowed and deprived of education, decent housing, work and much more.

How war affects women

A woman's welfare and status is often very closely tied to her role as a wife and a mother. When male family members go to war, women are left to feed the elderly and the children during times when food and supplies have become scarce or unobtainable.

A large group of war victims consists of refugees. Often their flight from areas of conflict and violence is futile: they might suffer from violence during the flight, in refugee camps and even in societies where they try to settle. According to UNCHR, women and girls constitute at least 80 per cent of all refugees. Far from all of them reach some semblance of safety. Many women spend their lives in refugee camps not far from the warfare, facing constant danger, lack of nutrition and the daily threat of violence at the mercy of others.[3]

Christina Doctare from the Swedish organisation Läkare i världen stresses the differences in how women and men experience warfare: 'Men are ordered into a military system, and they follow orders given to them. Women are not surrounded by a comparable ordered existence – instead, they live in chaos'.[4]

This sense of chaos and inability to affect one's own situation is well expressed in a letter written by a woman from Yugoslavia to a friend in Uzbekistan:

> I am desperate, in fear, in horror, in the expectation of something still more terrible. I am afraid for my children. I am afraid for their future. Who has the right to deprive them of their childhood? Who has the right to deprive them of a future? Who has the right to wage war in my name?[5]

In war-ravaged conditions like those in former Yugoslavia, women on all sides have been subjected to sexual violence and rape, sometimes by troops on their own side. The civil war in Liberia (1989–94) produced large numbers of refugees and displaced people; almost half of the 2.5 million population had to flee their homes at least once. A study of women's experiences in the war indicated that in a random sample as many as 49 per cent reported acts of sexual or physical violence from soldiers or fighters.[6]

The prevalence of rape in war is discussed by Ruth Seifert in Chapter 26 of this volume. Often war rapes are presented in the media as an illustration of the cruelty of one side against another, women's vulnerability becoming a symbol of suffering and subjugation. This view is not very helpful for the women who have been raped.

According to Christina Doctare, these women's experiences are doubly traumatic:

> Men and women react quite differently to a violent situation. Men react with their sympathetic nervous system, by actively fighting back. Women react with their parasympathetic nervous system: their blood pressure sinks, their pulse slows down, their muscle tension becomes less, body temperature is lowered, a woman freezes, so to say. In such a situation, one becomes immobilized, does not fight back or try to flee. It is a very primitive reaction.[7]

Women who have been unable to defend themselves in a violent situation have to deal first with their own reaction, then with the reactions from others, hence the double trauma: first they are threatened with the loss of life and subjected to humiliation and shame; afterwards they are subjected to more shame caused by their inability to defend themselves. Later, these women tend to shut their traumatic experiences inside themselves, becoming insecure and depressed. Traumatic stress reactions can cause somatic symptoms that cannot be treated simply as a pharmacological problem to be solved by medication. According to Doctare, men's reactions to shocking events tend to be more straightforward, for example in the form of cardiac infarcts.

Sandra Raskovic, a Serbian psychotherapist, describes these women's traumatized identity, as they become dominated by feelings of victimization, shame, and guilt:

During the year 1992/1993 thirty patients were received in the Belgrade Psychiatric Hospital, Dr Laza Lazarevic. They all claimed to have been raped. After the psychotic phase was alleviated, some of them withdrew the initial claim; they seemed fearful of the environment's reaction, especially that of their husbands. The environment tended to forget their sufferings quite rapidly; these women and girls were, therefore, first exposed to shortlived interest, and then to distrust and openly-poisonous ambiguous comments. This applies particularly to the husbands of the victims who, feeling 'dishonoured', often felt that they had to react with harshness and accusations against their wives. For the victims this meant the continuation of hell.[8]

A Swedish study of female war refugees from Bosnia compared the self-rated quality of life in a random sample of refugees living in Sweden with a control group consisting of Swedish women.[9] They concluded that Bosnian women, irrespective of their health status, had poorer quality of life and more symptoms than Swedish women. The former had lower mean rankings in such variables as appetite, memory, leisure time, energy, patience, sleep, mood and health. This and many other studies tell a clear tale of large numbers of civilian women, on all sides, dealing with severe and long-term post traumatic symptoms caused by war.

Nurses and female soldiers

Civilian women certainly did not choose to live in conditions in which anyone could become the target of sudden and unpredictable violence. How about those women serving in the military and as nurses, who have chosen war or its possibility to be a part of their profession?

Before the end of twentieth century, military nursing used to be a rarely-discussed topic. Yet trained nurses had been working at the front since the 19th century, dealing with soldiers wounded in action, tending to the severely wounded and dying. These women were in close contact with the realities of warfare, but whatever stress it caused them was seldom if ever mentioned.[10]

The American military entry into the Vietnam War started slow changes. As the war continued, there was a growing demand for nurses. Ultimately, the unpopularity of the war in Vietnam had an effect on the long-term personnel policies of the US military. Women were no longer recruited only to free men for combat, but also to replace men in large numbers, as fewer men than before chose to join the army. Those American women who served in Vietnam often faced ridicule from civilians, their own families included, upon returning home. Most of these nurses had nowhere to turn to talk about their stressful war experiences and received little support for post-traumatic symptoms originating from their time at the front.

As the percentage of women in the very large US military forces rose to around ten per cent of the total in the 1980s, women's presence in the armed forces gained more visibility. Women's access to combat-related functions were debated in public, despite the relatively small number of women who actually held such positions. The great majority of female military personnel were in support positions traditionally reserved for women.

Fontana and Rosencheck studied a group of US women veterans who were being treated for stress disorders.[11] Of the 327 women in their study, about a half served in overseas positions, and 12 per cent had been exposed to enemy fire. However, as many as 63 per cent of these women told that they had experienced physical sexual harassment while in military service, and 43 per cent of the women reported having been either raped or subjected to attempted rape. In this study, so-called sexual stress was found to be almost four times as influential as a cause of post-traumatic stress disorder as duty-related stress. Other studies confirm that women working in the military are exposed to higher levels of stress because of the hostility and harassment directed to them because they are women than has been believed.

Some steps toward healing

Despite the lack of focus on women as a group affected by war, it is evident from the available information that women suffer from war in many specific ways and on a large scale. What is to be done about their situation? How does one try to start to heal women who might be physically unharmed, but who are 'manifesting withdrawal, avoidance of contacts, anxiety which grows into panic, depressive and sub-depressive moods'?[12]

Christina Doctare and others stress the importance of motivation. If a person has lost not only her human dignity and self-respect, but also all her trust in a better future, she is at risk of no longer caring what will happen to her and whether she will heal.

> These women need compassion and empathy.... The patient needs time, she needs to be listened to so that these diverse symptoms can be seen in a context. This does not exclude the application of modern medical knowledge as well.[13]

Defining rape as a war crime has in itself been helpful for those women who have been subjected to it. The study of violence experienced by women in the Liberian civil war helped the affected women by putting the violence also under the domain of health, and thus legitimizing it as something needing attention and action.[14] Acknowledging the existence of a human rights and health problem is a necessary start towards treating it.

Another area that needs more visibility is the fact that warfare will always cause suffering to the civilian population. Despite the image of, for example, the Gulf War as neatly restricted to military targets, in reality the war caused huge suffering to women in Iraq as the life-sustaining civilian infrastructure was largely destroyed. The sanctions following the war limited the distribution of food, medicine and all kinds of necessities. The effects of war were also manifested more concretely in the decline in women's access to basic gynaecological care and contraception while they were expected to give birth to as many children as possible. Even if medicines have been exempt from sanctions, inflation in a war-ravaged country has made women's needs a low priority when choosing what to import. Have the effects of warfare on women (and on children, the elderly and the disabled) been much if at all taken into account when military strategy and international political sanctions have been designed? If not, what does this tell about the priorities of those involved in decisionmaking?

The first step towards helping female victims of war, then, is putting them on the agenda, listening to their specific experiences and needs, and taking them seriously. Also, we need to let go of the assumption that war and the military serve somehow to protect women as a group, when quite the contrary is true.

REFERENCES

1. Smith, Dan (1997), *The State of the War and Peace Atlas* (3rd rev. ed.) London: Penguin.
2. Ibid.
3. Vickers, Jeanne (1993), *Women and War,* London: Zed Books.
4. Doctare, Christina (1998), 'Terveys ja ihmisoikeudet kulkevat käsi kädessä' (Health and human rights go hand in hand), interview, *Suomen lääkärilehti* (Finland) 32. 3706–8.
5. Raskovic, Sandra (1994), 'Serbian Women Victims of War', Toronto: Association of Serbian Women, http://suc.suc.org/politics/rape/raskovic.
6. Smith, Shana, *et al.* (1998), 'Violence Against Women during the Liberian Civil Conflict', *JAMA* 279: 625–9.
7. See n. 4 above.
8. See n. 5 above.
9. Sundquist, J., Behmen-Vincevic, A. and S.E. Johansson (1998), 'Poor Quality of Life and Health in Young to Middle-Aged Bosnian Female War Refugees: a population-based study', *Public Health* (UK) 112: 21–6.
10. Boyle, Joyceen S. and Sheila M. Bunting (1998), 'Horsemen of the Apocalypse: lessons from the Gulf War', *Advances in Nursing Science* 21: 30–41.
11. Fontana, A. and R. Rosenheck (1998), 'Duty-related and Sexual Stress in the Etiology of PTSD among Women Veterans who Seek Treatment', *Psychiatric Services* (USA) 49: 658–62.
12. See n. 5 above.
13. See n.4 above.
14. See n. 6 above.

See also E. Isaksson (ed.) (1988), *Women and the Military System,* New York: Harvester Wheatsheaf (including an annotated bibliography).

Address for correspondence
Observatory, PO Box 14, 00014 University of Helsinki, Finland.
Fax: +358-9-1912952; email: Eva.Isaksson@Helsinki.Fi

26 RAPE: THE FEMALE BODY AS A SYMBOL AND A SIGN

Gender-Specific Violence
and the Cultural Construction of War

RUTH SEIFERT

Chapter 26 discusses the symbolic meanings of the female body in the cultural construction of war. While the soldier's body is seen, and treated, as a sign of the political nation, the female body in many cultures is perceived (and treated) as a representation of the 'body of the nation'. Rapes in wars are not the result of male instincts gone wild, but can be decodified within the gendered construction of war and fulfil functions that by destroying women are aimed at destroying the culture of a nation. Thus, it is necessary to tackle the problem within cultural mechanisms, including the system of international law. Gender-specific violence in wars is deeply embedded in our gendered cultures and is also a deeply political act. It is not a private act (as claimed by many countries that do not recognize rape as grounds for political asylum) but must be considered a war crime and a crime against humanity and treated as such by the international community.

Why rape?

Mass rapes and the sexual torture of women in times of war and crisis are nothing new. But it was not until it became known in late 1992 that the Serbian army was establishing rape camps on the territory of the former Yugoslavia that the question of how these events should be interpreted became widely discussed. In most cases, it was assumed that there is a continuum between civilian and wartime rapes. In order to answer the question of the reasons for wartime rape, the question of the reasons for rape in general was also raised.

Sex drive

The explanations offered for rape are manifold. One explanation, which does not stand the test of scientific consideration but which nonetheless has immense ideological power, is the argument of the so-called sex drive. It was resurrected once more in the attempt to explain the systematic sexual torture of women in the former Yugoslavia. Referring to the war atrocities in the Balkans, the Bremen ethnologist Duerr offered a 'civilization critique' in which he called Man (sic!) the 'eternal animal' who by his nature has an inclination towards atrocities and cruelties. This also includes the 'misuse of women'. According to Duerr, even centuries of occidental cultivation did not change this fact.[1]

Duerr's theories fit into a series of attempts which in varying ways aim at linking cruelty and sexual violence with human and/or male nature. In the ultimate analysis, Susan Brownmiller, who prepared the ground for a scientific perspective of this phenomenon with her pioneering work on rape, also pursues an ahistorical approach.[2] On the one hand, she clearly characterizes rape as a social act: rape is a process of intimidation, by which all men keep all women in a state of anxiety. On the other hand, she assumes that the capability of raping is reason enough for the existence of the phenomenon and the development of male rape ideologies. While in this concept the sex drive does not lead to rape, the biological equipment is considered to be a sufficient explanation for the fact that men manifest their social power by means of rape. Male lust for power *vis-à-vis* women, combined with specific biological equipment, thus makes rape a transhistoric and universal phenomenon.

An act of violence

However, these theses of the aggressive male sex drive hardly stand the test of scientific scrutiny. Arguments against this theory have recently been provided from all fields of science. With unusual unanimity, psychological and sociopsychological studies are coming to the conclusion that rape is not a sexual act but an act of violence. That means that it does not fulfil any sexual functions in the mind of the offender. What is a source of satisfaction for the offender is, however, the humiliation and degradation of the victim and the feeling of power and supremacy over a woman. Offenders hardly ever talk about a sexual experience. They do talk, however, about the satisfaction they got from the feeling of supremacy over the victim.[3]

Ethnological research shows that rape is not equally common in all societies. There are rape-free and rape-prone societies. In rape-free cultures the status of male predominance is to a great extent secured. Ethnologists usually cite Islamic societies as an example. This does not mean that there is no structural violence against women in these societies.[4] Societies in which women enjoy a respected status, in which femininity is held in high esteem and in which the gender difference is not dramatized and staged, are also rape-free. This means that the difference does not play a prominent role in the political organization of these societies. Examples of this sort of rape-free culture can only be found in smaller tribal communities, that is to say where common western judgement expects to find a closer proximity to 'nature' or to 'uncivilized' behaviour. In contrast, societies in which the gender difference is strongly dramatized and/or in which women have a subordinate status and femininity is held in lower esteem than masculinity, are considered to be rape-prone. All western societies are considered to be rape-prone.[5]

Finally, there are a number of more recent papers by historians, in particular from the Anglo-Saxon countries, on the history of rape and sexual violence. Initially they discussed

Edward Shorter's thesis that, historically, sexual violence ought to be considered a libidinal outlet. In line with older sex drive-theory approaches, Shorter considers rape to be a result of male sexual frustration in pre-industrial societies with strongly regimented sexuality. In this context, male sexuality is established as an ahistoric constant and understood to follow the theory of a steam boiler: if no other adequate possibilities for sexual activity are provided, the tension discharges, and may do so, after all, in a violent manner.

This 'hydraulic reductionism' was countered with a number of arguments.[6] These challenged both the thesis of the ahistoricality of a sex drive and of sexual violence pervading history. After examination of available references, Porter comes to the conclusion that there is no reason for the assumption that rapes would have occurred particularly frequently in pre-industrial societies. Moreover, the historical demography shows that eras which were characterized by late marriage age by no means showed an increase in extramarital births but that, on the contrary, this rate was rather lower.

A sociocultural phenomenon

Thus, instead of superimposing an ultramechanistic behaviour model on history, it appears more useful to deal with the cultural construction of male sexuality. The sexual expectations based on varying constructions obviously seem to be subject to strong historical variations and resist all attempts to assume a biological or mental universalism.[7]

Based on an evaluation of historical papers on the issue of 'sexual violence', D'Cruze also comes to the conclusion that sex drive-theory approaches do not provide an adequate explanation for sexual violence.[8] D'Cruze discusses in detail Rossiaud's paper on gender relations in pre-Reformation Dijon in the 15th century. In this context, prostitution was a widespread and legalized practice. A sex market was available for all strata of the male population. Nevertheless, rape was a frequent phenomenon.

According to Rossiaud's estimates, 50 per cent of the male population of Dijon participated in a rape at least once during the study period. Usually, a woman was kidnapped from her house by several young men and raped within the group. The city council did next to nothing to prevent these events. Rossiaud concludes that the gang rapes represented a veritable initiation rite for juvenile males. Moreover, a status struggle between older and younger men in the city was fought through the rapes, that is to say through the violence inflicted on female bodies. However, this struggle never threatened the patriarchal system, for a common interest united the men across the boundaries of age and of class: the preservation of a supremacy relationship between the genders. On the one hand, the rapes were a means of communication between older and younger men but, on the other hand, they were also a symbolic expression of the subjugation of women in which well-established men were interested as well. D'Cruze concludes that sexual violence represented an aspect of the preservation of patriarchal power and was functional for the preservation of a specific gender order. Thus, when looking for the motivation of a rapist, a psychological search for clues is not enough; essentially, it must also be located in the sociocultural context of the gender arrangement.[9]

Rape in war

If anthropologizing approaches are not suitable for explaining civilian rapes, what does this tell us with regard to wartime rapes? Similar to civilian rapes, they were also located for a long time in the domain of an inscrutable 'nature' and were not analysed as to their historical and political importance. If one considers the material available, it can be concluded that we are facing a phenomenon which is taken into account only very inadequately by the formula of the 'temporary blackouts of hordes gone crazy'. In particular the sex-drive argument is hardly suitable in this context. Thus, a member of the (US) Supreme Military court in Washington stated that rapes in war regions do not depend on whether female bodies are otherwise available, for example in brothels, thereby allowing for a so-called satisfaction of the sex drive. In the void of war, rape is often simply preferred.[10]

The thesis that rape in war is a regrettable secondary phenomenon which is beyond the actual logic of war will be contrasted with a few figures. These figures should be considered only as examples and fragments, since war atrocities against women have never been collected as such nor systematically recorded.

The record begins in 1937 in the Chinese city of Nanking, which was occupied by the Japanese Army. During the first month of occupation, at least 20,000 women were raped and in many cases killed. Foreign missionaries independently of each other reported that they observed about ten gang rapes per day. The press subsequently kept referring to the 'rape of Nanking'.[11]

In 1943, the then-French residual army invaded Italy. Before the invasion, the French commander had guaranteed explicitly the right to pillage and rape in the territories that were taken. What followed were mass rapes of Italian women and numerous pregnancies. After the war, the Italian government reacted in a manner that was not emulated in any other country. It awarded the women a modest pension as war victims.[12]

Similar events took place in the course of the seizure of southwest Germany at the end of the war. Here, as well, the French commander explicitly promised that pillaging and raping would be allowed once Freudenstadt was taken, and here, also, extensive mass raping took place. During the following decades, the knowledge of these events was suppressed in the interest of German–French friendship.[13]

According to more recent research by Sander and Johr, the number of women raped by soldiers of the Red Army in the Greater Berlin area must be distinctly corrected upwards. Until recently it has been assumed that 120,000 women had been raped, whereas nowadays a number of several hundred thousands appears to be realistic. Another rape capital was the region of east Prussia.

At the Nuremberg War Crimes Trials, evidence was presented that the German Army Command established a brothel in Smolensk to which Russian women were deported. Similar to the situation in the former Yugoslavia today, rape and forced prostitution were often a pre-stage of systematic genocide in the eastern territories. The French prosecutor presented evidence which proved that the Wehrmacht had used rapes as a means of retaliation against the French resistance movement, that is to say as a politico-military weapon.

Susan Brownmiller's research on the Vietnam War suggests that in this war as well rapes of the enemy women by American soldiers were common practice. A few acts were reported by soldiers who did not want to participate in the rapes. During the court-martial trials, the rapers typically questioned the masculinity of the informant. In a case that became well-known, a soldier who had refused to rape was derided by his mission commander as being a gay and a sissy.[14]

In 1971, 200,000 women were raped during the war in Bangladesh. Many of these women were expelled from their families. They roamed aimlessly across the country, which caused the government to establish reception camps. Since these camps were not provided even with the bare necessities, they rapidly developed into slums. Women still live there today.

Even at the time, an Indian writer was convinced that this must have been a planned crime. The rapes had been conducted so systematically and extensively that deliberate military tactics must have been behind them. He suspected that this was intended to destroy Bengali national consciousness.[15]

Reports on the occupation of Kuwait by Iraqi troops record 5000 raped and sexually-tortured women.[16]

The former Yugoslavia is the latest example. According to investigations conducted by a fact-finding committee of the European Community in 1993, there are at least 20,000 raped and sexually-tortured women. The Bosnian government gives a number of 60,000. The committee stated that the mass raping and torture of women in Bosnia-Herzegovina must be considered to be a systematic and deliberate action. There were sufficient testimonies of witnesses to prove that rapes were a significant element of the Serbian warfare strategy.

Given the above numbers, it seems absurd to assume that rape is a marginal phenomenon of war. So far, the widely-quoted Geneva Convention to which most of the states of the world are signatories, has not done much about that. The Economic and Social Council of the United Nations complained as early as 1972, 'with the expression of deepest concern', that there was no slackening of war brutalities, in particular against women. However, its simultaneous appeal to member nations to observe the humanitarian statutory regulations for the protection of women and children, went unheard and produced no major changes: rapes are not acts of individual hordes gone crazy; rather they are an integral element of war.

Given the massive occurrence of wartime rape and the ineffectiveness of international arrangements, the question arises as to what purpose rape actually serves in war. Since rape involves historical, political, cultural, psychological and/or psychoanalytical aspects, it must be assumed that rape has to be discussed at different levels. Any monocausal explanation would be too shortsighted. The following section concentrates on symbolic and political functions which may provide explanations for continuing war atrocities against women.

Symbolic and political functions

The male soldier

The suggested interpretation of the massive sexual attacks on women in wars as being a political act on the scene of the gender arrangement seems to be too shortsighted. For it is not only the cultural construction of gender that plays a role here; we are also moving within the scope of the cultural construction of war. Obviously, in the interior of wars, a routine and systematic attack on the female body takes place, independently of the potential causes of the war; however, there is also a systematic attack on the male body as well as on objects.

The fact that in war human bodies are systematically and massively wounded, maimed and killed usually appears to us to be self-evident and so remains unquestioned. In a brilliant analysis, Elaine Scarry has demonstrated that the wounding of bodies in wars is by no means self-evident but definitely needs to be analysed.[17] Scarry does not consider violence, as generally presumed, as a means that is used because it has the power of self-enforcement. She delineates, instead, a scenario in which the symbolic dimensions of violence become evident. Within the symbolic construction of war, the violence against bodies has specific meanings. In this context, specific, symbolic meanings are inherent to the body of the soldier, who as a rule is male.[18] It does not only have functional significance within the scope of the technology of war; essentially, it acts as the cultural representation of the state.

The soldier who agrees to kill and die for his country implicitly performs several acts. He puts himself beyond the rules which apply to the way of dealing with other people's bodies. Thus, on the one hand he decivilizes himself in the sense that he detaches himself from the general rules of civilizational interaction; on the other hand, he also decivilizes himself by rescinding his personal physical and cultural learning processes and by lifting the killing inhibitions. Moreover, he offers his own body for disintegration for his country or for the ideas and the interests which his civilization represents. This means that his body functions as a cultural sign in the symbolic construction of war and invests the ideas or interests represented with the attribute of physical reality.

The killing and wounding in war not only serve the purpose of reaching a decision; they also offer the opportunity of charging immaterial convictions and positions with the power and the force of the material world. Thus ideas, such as that of the nation, are virtually substantiated. The extreme mouldings of body and culture and of body and politics meet in the figure of the soldier, 'for instance, when a fellow soldier finds the dead in the bushes, kneels down next to him, looks for evidence of his affiliation and finally tells the bystanders: he is American'.[19] Thus, the function of the attack on the body of the soldier is not only to bring about a decision which nobody will be able to avoid since the result seems to be incontestable.

The attack has additional functions. On the one hand, by killing and wounding the bodies the representation of the state or the nation in these bodies is destroyed. The significance of this fact becomes evident in the differing perception of the deaths of soldiers or civilian auxiliary personnel in war and crisis areas. Whereas death and wounding among the latter is noted with greater or less outrage, the death and the wounding of soldiers is apt to provoke political reactions and to mobilize national emotions. For the other side as well, the death of soldiers has a different meaning. Whereas attacks on civilians are likely to be denied, casualties among the enemy soldiers reinforce confidence. Their death is seen as a positive attribute to their own cause and interests. Here as well, the death of the enemy soldier has a substantiating effect: the killed and wounded bodies of the other side invest the opposing positions with reality.

They make the result a material reality because it is linked with the human body. The physical damage inflicted provides the material basis for the position of the victor and invests it with physical reality.

The female body

If this is the way in which the attack on the body of the male soldier is incorporated into the cultural construction of war, what then is the meaning of the attack on the female body? First of all, the following can be stated: the female body also functions as a cultural sign. It comprises, however, different aspects of meaning. It is not a representation of the state; nevertheless, in many cultures a symbolic meaning, which links body and nation, is attributed to it. At least in western cultures, the female body functions as the symbolic representation of the body of the nation. This is made evident by numerous representations of art of national symbols. To mention a few, there are the French Marianne as the symbol of France, the Statue of Liberty as the symbol of the United States, and the Bavarian Bavaria.[20] This also means, however, that the violence committed against women is aimed at the integrity of the group concerned.

The rape of women of a community, culture or nation can therefore be considered to be a symbolic rape of the body of the nation. This is also the conclusion drawn by the Vienna sociologists Benard and Schlaffer who did intensive research on rape victims from the former Yugoslavia and who, based on their immediate experience, advocate the following thesis: 'Somehow the woman seems to personify in a particularly archaic manner her people, her group; whoever destroys her collectively destroys the enemy'.[21]

On the same line is the idea that war rapes are designed to defile and soil the women of the other group or nation, and, so, simultaneously the other nation as a whole. This function plays a particular role in cultures which attach considerable value to female sexual innocence. In these cultural contexts, rapes are perceived as tarnishing the woman's honour.

In cultures which are rife with biological racism a defilement of the blood is also insinuated. Obviously this version plays a role in Serbian thinking, and it becomes evident by the bragging that little Chetniks are being fathered. According to this logic, the mere genetic outfit of the rapist – which is defined nationalistically, that is to say as being Serbian – brings about the subversion and soilage of the Bosnian population. Racist ideas of this kind were also part of National Socialist ideology and even influenced the treatment of rape victims after the breakdown of the regime at the end of WW II. For women who had been impregnated by Russians, it was far easier, as compared to the women raped by western allies, to get an abortion. According to a decree of 14 March 1945, unbureaucratic abortions were to be facilitated for women who had been raped by rapists of inferior race, in particular Russians. Women who had been raped by Germans or by western allies were to bear the child to full term.[22]

The construction of the female body as the symbol of a group, community or nation has another aspect. The cultural construction of gender comprises the construction of the female body as being susceptible to injury, that is as being always penetrable in general and exposed to the risk of being raped. In this context, the possibility of raping or being raped is treated as a basic anthropological fact. The oddity of this assumption, which is deeply rooted in common thinking, will be illustrated by way of an analogy. One could assume with the same right that, for anatomical reasons, men have always been castratable, so that there is a biologically-caused male susceptibility to injury. This potential possibility obviously does not find any expression in cultural life, however. Castrations do not have any cultural or social significance that would be comparable with the significance of rape.

Femininity is construed as being assailable and penetrable in general whereas masculinity, in contrast, is considered to be unassailable. As Wobbe showed, this gender construction is significant for the symbolic generation of community because, as it were, the female sex represents an unstable moment of the community, since the entire group can be potentially threatened through the female vulnerability to injury. This is reflected by collective imaginary fears such as the image of the 'Jewish seducer' as a threat figure in anti-Semitic concepts, or the image of the 'black rapist' in racist discourses.

In a specifically ethnic or national context, the violence inflicted on women of another group must be considered to be identical with the crossing of a border which marks an attack on the other group. In a way, the female body is a social territory, so that gender-specific acts of violence serve 'to both mark the social Us and to bring about, to defend and to expand the territorial occupation of the social sphere'.[23]

Examples from the former Yugoslavia are appropriate to illustrate the relevance of these symbolical correlations. As early as in the late 1980s, during the conflict between Serbs and Albanians in the Kosovo region, the women on both sides were represented as being particularly threatened. This was done to generate a feeling of national threat. This feeling of threat escalated when the Serbs stated that Serbian women had been raped by Albanians. In the Serbian press, the rapes were described as an attack on the property of the national collective and as a violation of the holy borders of the Serbian nation. The rapes symbolized a border crossing on to the adversary's territory and marked an attack on the physical integrity of the nation.[24]

Another observation which supports the thesis of the symbolic meaning of rape in the national context is provided by Mladen Loncar who studied the mass rapes in Bosnia-Herzegovina on behalf of the Croatian Ministry of Health. He argues that the mass rapes were designed to create a kind of Serbian solidarity and to destroy all ties of friendship which existed between Serbs, Croats and Bosnians. In other words: violence against women of the other ethnic group was intended to mark the forcible exclusion of the 'other' and to contribute to the establishment of a group of Us. The violence which is committed against women is a potential to inflict injury which affects not only the physical and personal integrity of the women involved; it also marks the limits of communities. The strong intertwinement of rapes and national and/or ethnical eruptions in the region of the former Yugoslavia may serve as an empirical illustration of Wobbe's thesis, acccording to which in our sociocultural interpretation system the female gender designates a group, and in the person, body and life of this group the construction of community is consummated and created.[25]

Against this background, it is possible to seek an explanation for the exceptions from the rule of rape in wars. One of these exceptions is reported from the Vietnam War. While the Vietcong exercised terror (also against the civilian population) their repertoire did not include rapes.[26] The American Civil War is cited as another exception. In this war hardly any rapes of white women are reported to have been committed by the armies of the north or the south.[27] Thus while in an ethnic or national context rape has a symbolic meaning (the creation of community and/or the exclusion of the other), in specific conflicts it is dysfunctional: when, as in the American Civil War, a society remains committed to integration into a common territory of states, or when, as in the case of the Vietcong, a common nation already exists, and war is intended to confirm this (albeit under changed circumstances).

It becomes evident that war rapes can be considered to be a cultural script which comprises a variety of messages. An element of this script is its war-strategic dimension. Beck attaches particular value to this aspect, assuming that rapes take place primarily because killing and raping is functional for military actions. In this context, the term strategy is something of a problem. In military usage strategy describes the planned and purposeful provision and the coordinated deployment of armed forces. This, in turn, means that armed forces are employed deliberately and in a specific manner in order to achieve a predetermined goal.

Military planning and rape

So far it is not entirely clear to what extent deliberate military planning played a role in war rape. But even if there is still a need for research on this question, one has to agree with the thesis of rape's war-strategic effect. On the one hand, it can be assumed that the military command would intervene massively against incidents which from their point of view were dysfunctional. On the other hand, rapes were used deliberately and systematically, at least in the former Yugoslavia. Amnesty International, Helsinki Watch and the World Council of Churches as well as the United Nations Commission on Human Rights report that Serbian government officials were aware of the rapes and approved them – in some cases even participated in rapes themselves – and that orders to rape were issued.[28]

One of the war-strategic functions evoked in this context lies in the effects which rape has on the male enemy. It generally results in humiliation and demasculization of the adversary. The rape of women of the adversary's population bears a message. The information goes from man to man that the opposing men are not capable of protecting their women. This is a compromising blow against their manhood. This communication function becomes evident in the former Yugoslavia when buses with women in the sixth or seventh month or pregnancy were sent back across the enemy lines, in most cases with cynical remarks written on the buses which refer to the unborn children. The women concerned are humiliated, but so is the male enemy. The communication from man to man is performed through the bodies of the injured women. The interviews with raped women in the greater Berlin area which were conducted by Sander and Johr also revealed this effect: in many cases, the partners and fathers of the attacked women felt more humiliated than the women themselves. A lot of men left their wives because of the rapes. The fear of the men's reaction on the one hand and the wish to spare their feelings on the other were also reasons why many women hid for decades the fact that they had been raped as well as the traumas they had suffered in consequence.[29]

The male reaction to rapes shows that rape is also designed to establish hierarchies among men. This function can also be found in civilian contexts of power and dominance. In the racist society of the American south, only raping a white woman was a punishable act. The rape of a white woman by a black man was liable to capital punishment; in most cases it was even punished by lynching. The rape of a black woman was, however, not considered a punishable offence no matter whether it was committed by a white or a black man. Making the attack on a woman a punishable offence also served to confirm the hierarchy among black and white men – the violation of white women was punished by white men, the violation of black women had to be tolerated by black women – and men. By way of the injury inflicted on the bodies of black women, black men were also made aware of the inferiority of their manhood.[30]

The demoralization of the enemy

War rape also includes a politico-military purpose in using rapes for the demoralization and demasculization of the (male) adversary. Rapes in war can be considered to be the highest symbolic expression of humiliation of the male adversary. They can undermine the morale of the troops. There are, for example, reports from the Israeli Six Day War stating that many Palestinians failed to offer any resistance to Israeli troops, fleeing instead because they were afraid of losing their honour by the rape of women.

In Bosnia, mass rapes were often performed as a public spectacle, for instance on the village square. The men were forced to attend the women's sexual torture. The bodies of Bosnian women were used as a film in which all Bosnian women and men were to be shown their worthlessness, their inferiority and their powerlessness. At the same time it was a campaign of destruction against the personal and ethnic identity and the self-esteem of the Bosnian population.[31]

In this context, an explanation can be developed for the silence about rapes and gender-specific violence in wars that can be observed again and again. If one considers collective violence committed against men and women, it becomes evident that in the cultural memory female war experiences and suffering are dealt with completely differently from the fate of soldiers: 'The victims of rape are not included in the public rite of mourning about the lost war; they are not venerated as heroines, and they are not awarded any compensations'.[32] This makes sense in so far as the commemoration of female war victims would pass on the violation of manhood into peacetime. This would be a continuous reminder that the 'national manhood' had been humiliated by the enemy. What is chosen instead is the mechanism of repression which works at the individual-psychological and collective-national levels.[33]

Women and war

The thesis of the destruction of culture by rape was also supported by a research project which for the first time inquired into the position of women in wars. The situation of women in the civil-war regions of Mozambique and Sri Lanka was studied. From the perspective of the women concerned, the war was anything but a matter of men or soldiers. The analysis showed that often it was not soldiers but civilian women who were at the centre of the conflicts. At times, indeed, they were explicitly the tactical objectives of the operations. The violence committed against women was apt to destroy the culture of the country. That was the purpose of the attack on women.

In times of war, women are those who keep the family and the community together. Due to their cultural position and their position within the family structure, they are a central objective of attack if one wants to hit a culture at its core. Their destruction aims at the annihilation of social and cultural stability; it affects cultural coherence. Consequently, in individual cases it can be considered to be an important war strategy.[34]

This finding is confirmed by the way the Serbians acted in the former Yugoslavia. It is reported that after the invasion of a region or a town there were specific phases to their behaviour: (i) the destruction of cultural monuments; and (ii) the imprisonment and, in most cases, the killing of intellectuals. For instance, a survivor of the Omarska concentration camp reported that: 'They killed the judges, the teachers, the chairman of the court, company directors – all the prominent personalities of Omarska'.[35] These two phases of destruction are also known from the German campaign in Poland, during WW II. First the cultural monuments were destroyed and then the Polish intelligentsia, that is to say the main representatives of Polish culture, were killed.[36] In the Serbian strategy, a third step consisted in the establishment of rape camps, this procedure being by no means unsystematic: in many cases, the Serbs appeared with rape lists and selected, first of all, intellectual women and the wives of well-known and well-respected personalities.

In conclusion, the following can be stated: the destruction of culture is performed by means of the destruction of material culture and immaterial culture and of human bodies. In this context, a specific value is attached to the ruination of female bodies. In particular, sexual violence against women fulfils several cultural functions in one single act. In this context, the assessment of a Zagreb observer appears to be only partially adequate: 'Rape saves bombs. By means of rape ethnic cleansing is achieved more effectively, at a lower cost. Rape is an economy of war'. However, as an analysis of the depth dimension of gender-specific war atrocities reveals, the point is not only to exchange an expensive means of war for a cheap one; it is to wage a cultural and symbolic destruction campaign that couldn't be conducted with bombs in a comparable manner.

Comparing once more the position of the soldier and the position of the rape victim in war, there is a decisive difference. Like soldiers, women who are involved in wars and become victims of sexual atrocities serve as cultural signs. Unlike the former, however, they never agreed, in any way, to put their bodies at stake in a process intended to settle national, ethnic or class conflicts.

This does not mean that women do not participate in wars, are not interested in wars and could not be questioned as to their responsibility. What this does mean is that women are not assigned an official position in the symbolic construction of war. This often has disastrous consequences for the expectations of women. Women from the former Yugoslavia reported that they felt completely secure in their cultural environment until the madness overtook them. In many cases they raised white flags on the assumption that they, as female civilians, were situated beyond the actual fighting. In individual cases, this naïve calculation proved right; in most cases, however, women had to realize that as unarmed civilians they were particularly exposed to the brutalities.[37]

This means also that whereas the conflict between male soldiers is construed as a subject–subject conflict, the attack on women is laid out as a subject–object conflict. Unlike the attack on the body of the soldier, the attack on the female body is not perceived culturally as a political act. Therefore, women are not provided with the possibility of systematic defence. A conflict is fought on female bodies in which women do not have any active, immediate political part. Whereas in national conflicts the female body, through its symbolic significance, serves as strategic territory, at the same time the hierarchical restrictions on women in peacetime are reproduced and confirmed in a manner that exposes women defencelessly to the enemy's attacks. Unlike supposedly conscious soldiers, rape victims are not aware of any cultural arrangement within the scope of which their bodies and their ordeals are to be used in combat, and that they are employed to substantiate, with their bodies, the power of a regime or an ideology.

Violence towards women and torture

Against this background, war atrocities committed against women seem to be more closely related to torture than to acts of war. This thesis can be examined in more detail against the background of an analysis of torture.[38] For a long time it was assumed that the purpose of torture was to force people to speak in order to extort information and confessions from them. A more detailed analysis has revealed that exactly the opposite applies. It is not to make people speak. The purpose of torture is to silence people. Exposing them to extreme pain obliterates their language and, thus, eliminates everything these people possess in terms of convictions, experience and connections to their environment. The pain is a means of disintegrating the substance of awareness and the capability of perception and of destroying a person's capacity of expressing him-/herself. In other words, torture fulfils the function of destroying the culture in a person. This is achieved by reducing this person entirely to his or her body and by attempting to obliterate everything that made him/her the person he/she is.

Another characteristic of torture is the fact that the suffering of the victim is transformed into a convincing demonstration of power, for the torturer and for the regime he personifies. As the victim is reduced to the hurting, helpless body and loses his/her self-determination, the torturer feels that he extends his territory and his power accordingly. The regime shows that it has the power to torment this body despite the resistance which the victim offers to the regime, the form of government and its ideology. In so doing, it shows that its power is more real than the resistance of the victim. The indisputable reality of the tormented body serves the regime as a sign of power. The regime engraves its reality into the reality of the tormented bodies. Similar to the suffering body in the course of war, the tormented body during torture gives material presence to an idea and/or a fiction which does not (yet) have any reality. So the change that occurs by wounding, tormenting and destroying the bodies has a vivid and compelling reality, 'since it is located in the human body, the original location of reality, and since it is an 'extreme' as well as a 'permanent' change'.[39]

The characteristics of rape fit into these features of torture. For what happens during rape, that is the forcible penetration of the interior of a human body or the forcible manipulation of his/her body, is generally a characteristic of severe torture. Amnesty International has found out that a diminution of torture can be observed with the increasing consolidation of power. This was the case, for instance, in Chile where the extent of torture decreased when the Pinochet dictatorship consolidated. In that case, the power then no longer had to be documented indisputably for everybody in the body of the tortured persons. This motive also applies to rape. As already stated, those very societies in which men no longer have women at their complete disposal and where women are gaining ground are particularly rape-prone. Analogously, rape is intended visibly to demonstrate male power for all women and men and to celebrate it on the female body.

The undeniable reality of the raped body also serves as a sign of male power. However, the female body is subject to a dual logic of violence: within the gender order, rape serves the preservation of a relationship of power and supremacy between the genders and, as the historical examples suggest, the establishment of a hierarchy among men. Moreover, within the scope of the symbolic construction of war, rapes are used to exclude the other person, destroy the culture of the other group, and to establish a hierarchy among male wartime enemies.

Conclusion

If violence is seen, as it were, as an anthropological basic capacity of the male which does not allow any further theoretical deliberation, then it has been understood only inadequately. Violence can be understood as being a script, a language which conveys meanings that can be decoded. Violence in general, and gender-specific violence in particular, are languages which make specific sense in specific cultural contexts.[40] The script of rape can be decoded against the background of the prevailing gender order and the symbolism of armed action.[41] This also means that sexual atrocities against women are by no means acts of unreasonable brutality which are owed to the male as Duerr's 'eternal animal'.[42] They are rather quite 'reasonable' acts which fulfil functions. These functions are deeply embedded in our symbolic systems. Rapes and/or sexual torture in the context of wars are culture-destroying acts with a strategic purpose. This strategy is exercised on the bodies of the women concerned, with their physical and mental existence in many cases being destroyed.

To make female vulnerability and/or propensity to injury the basis of the analysis, that is to treat them as an anthropological constant, would mean naturalizing cultural constructions, thereby withdrawing them from further investigation. This would not only result in marginalizing female suffering in wars, but also in an inadequate under-standing of the entire symbolic construction of war.

REFERENCES

1. *Der Spiegel*, 14 June 1993.
2. Brownmiller, Susan (1978), *Gegen unseren Willen. Vergewaltigung und Männerherrschaft*, Frankfurt-on-Main.
3. Heinrichs, Juergen (ed.) (1986), *Vergewaltigung. Die Opfer und die Täter*, Braunschweig.

4. Here, however, it should be objected that, while in Islamic societies there is no public rape, matrimonial rape seems to occur on a regular basis.

5. Sanday Reeves, Peggy (1986), 'Rape and the Silencing of the Feminine', in Sylvana Tomaselli and Roy Porter (eds), *Rape*, London.

6. Porter, Roy (1986), 'Rape – does it have a historical meaning?' in Sylvana Tomaselli and Roy Porter (eds), *Rape*, London.

7. *Ibid.*

8. D'Cruze, Shani (1993), 'Approaching the History of Rape and Sexual Violence: notes towards research', in *Women's History Review* 1 (3).

9. *Ibid.*

10. See n. 2 above.

11. *Ibid.*

12. Walzer, Michael (1977), *Just and Unjust Wars. A moral argument with historical illustrations*, New York.

13. Sander, Helke and Barbara Johr, *BeFreier und Befreite. Krieg, Vergewaltigung, Kinder*, Munich.

14. See n. 2 above.

15. *Ibid.*

16. Sasson, Jean P. (1991), *The Rape of Kuwait*, New York.

17. Scarry, Elaine (1992), *Der Körper im Schmerz. Die Chiffren der Verletzlichkeit und die Erfindung der Kultur*, Frankfurt-on-Main.

18. The significance of the fact that in most of the nation states the soldier is constructed almost exclusively as being male cannot be discussed here.

19. Seifert, Ruth (1995), 'Destruktive Konstruktionen. Ein Beitrag zur Dekonstruktion des Verhältnisses von Militär, Nation und Geschlecht', in Erika Haas (ed.), *Dekonstruktion und Feminismus*, Muenchen.

20. In a recent study on the depiction of Hungary in satirical journals from 1919 until 1938, Haslinger states that most representations of her identity immmediately after WW I are characterized by a surprising polarization. On the one side, there is Hungary represented as a defenceless, noble female exposed to brute force; on the other, there is the representation of the foreigner (Czechs, Romanians, Serbs) as the uncivilized soldierly attitude.

21. Benard, Cheryl and Edit Schlaffer (1993), *Vor unseren Augen. Der Krieg in Bosnien – und die Welt schaut weg*, Munich.

22. Poutrus, Kirsten (1995), 'Die Frau ist der Feind. Vergewaltigungen in Berlin bei Kriegsende 1945', in *Freitag. Die Ost-West-Wochenzeitung*, 19 May.

23. Wobbe, Theresa (1992), 'Rechtsradikalismus – nur eine Männersache? Anmerkungen zur Wobbe'; (1993), 'Die Grenzen des Geschelchts. Konstruktionen von Gemeinschaft und Rassismus', in: *Mitteilungen des Instituts fuer Sozialforschung.* No. 2, Frankfurt, Februar.

24. Milic, Andjelka (1993), *Women and Nationalism in the Former Yugoslavia*, in: Nanette Punk and Magda Mueller (eds).

25. Wobbe, Theresa (1993), 'Die Grenzen des Geschlechts. Konstruktionen von Gemeinschaft und Rassismus', in *Mitteilungen des Instituts fuer Sozialforschung* 2, Frankfurt, February.

26. See n. 2 above.

27. Fellman, Michael (1992), 'At the Nihilist Edge: Reflections on Guerrilla Warfare during the American Civil War', paper presented at the conference 'On the Road to Total War: the American Civil War and the German Wars of Unification', unpubl. manuscript, Washington: German Historical Institute.

28. PETWW (People for the Ethical Treatment of Women Worldwide), *Stop the Rape and the Genocide*, Iowa City: University of Iowa, College of Law.

29. See n. 13 above.

30. Wing, Adrien Katherine and Sylke Merchan (1994), *Rape, Ethnicity and Culture: spirit injury from Bosnia to Black America*, unpubl. manuscript, University of Iowa.

31. *Ibid.* and Guth, S. (1987), *Liebe und Männesehre*, Berlin.

32. Schmidt-Harzbach, Ingrid (1992), 'Eine Woche im Mai', in Helke Sander and Barbara Johr, *Befreier und Befreite*, Munich.

33. From an historical perspective, Linda Kerber advocates the thesis that the collective reaction to sexual voilence is almost always characterized by an unwillingness to name and interrogate the

victim and the offender.

34. Nordstrom, Carolyn (1991), 'Women and War. observations from the field', in *Minerva* 9 (1), Quarterly Report on Women and the Military.
35. Gutman, Roy (1993), *A Witness to Genocide*, New York.
36. Broszat, Martin (1963), *Zweihundert Jahre deutsche Polenpolitik*, Munich.
37. See n. 21 above.
38. See n. 17 above.
39. *Ibid.*
40. Shy, John (1993), 'The Cultural Approach to the History of War', in *The Journal of Military History* 57 (5).
41. As culture-analytical approaches to the history of war show, the symbolism features have different characteristics in different cultural contexts. For instance, Weighley postulates that there is a specific American way of warfare and of conducting military operations (see Weighley, Russell F. (1973), *The American Way of War*, New York).
42. See n. 1 above.

Address for correspondence

Albrechstrasse 47, 80636 München, Germany.
Tel: 089- 181487   Email: seifert.zimmermann@planet-interkom.de

27 FRONT LINES OF MENTAL HEALTH UNDER WAR CONDITIONS

The Example of Former Yugoslavia

SØREN BUUS JENSEN

Appropriate intervention strategies in the mental health field under war conditions in the countries of former Yugoslavia required a comprehensive evaluation of the specific needs of the traumatized population combined with an assessment of available resources for mental health assistance.

War-related traumatization was analysed in order to identify the stressor factors and the mental health problems provoked. Systematic needs assessments identified the main target groups for mental health interventions. Co-ordination is crucial for the overall efficacy of the operations in avoiding duplication of effort and identifying gaps. A comprehensive large-scale public mental-health approach should address, as a core issue, the treatment and prevention of traumatic stress and its consequences.

Emergency interventions must from the outset be coordinated with mid- and long-term strategies of rehabilitation and reconstruction. Humanitarian assistance may insist on a technical neutrality, for example working on both sides of the front lines, addressing those in most need of help. The organizations must also take a stand of ethical non-neutrality, opposing human rights violations by all parties. To do so may give the organizations future credibility to impact on the peace process and general postwar mental health development.

War conditions in the countries of former Yugoslavia forced the international community to set up humanitarian aid programmes. During this war, the first large-scale psychosocial/mental health intervention under war conditions was implemented.

In 1995 WHO estimated that about 1 million people in the countries of the former Yugoslavia were suffering severe emotional distress to an extent which in peacetime would have led to the offer of immediate and urgent professional assistance.[1] The massive increase of people in need of assistance was constituted by the victims of war, who suffered primarily from the consequences of war-related traumatic experiences due to violations of human rights rather than traditional mental-health problems.

No country has a mental health system or a sufficient number of professionals prepared for such a disaster. A calculation of the helping capacity estimated that the local professionals were able to cover only a small percentage of those who needed help. This provided the background for the international humanitarian missions.

In this chapter we focus first on the conceptual parameters of traumatization under war conditions: stressor and protective factors; the target objects; and the traumatic events, traumatization and traumatic reactions. We will then discuss issues of needs and resource assessments during periods of active warfare and its aftermath, and explore the main mental health-care problems in the emergency humanitarian assistance phase. Based on this, elements of the overall intervention strategies are outlined.

Traumatization: conceptual parameters

Psychological trauma concerns injury or damage to different aspects of intrapsychic and psychosocial functioning. The trauma (or wound) is caused by the experience of traumatic events. The degree of experienced traumatization varies with the balance between the stressor and the protective factors and is reflected in the symptomatic traumatic reactions.

Stressor factors

The stressor factors causing the most critical traumatic events contain elements of threat, injury, exposure to death, destruction, chaos and human suffering.[2] The war-related experiences, which have a significant impact on the self, are illustrated in Table 27.1.

Table 27.1 War-related traumatic stressor factors: direct or indirect experiences and impact on the self

i	Threat or injury to self, personality, identity, physical integrity or health
ii	Threat or injury to others that is witnessed directly or indirectly
iii	Threat or injury to the built or modified environment, which is experienced directly; witnessed as a bystander; or afterwards at or near the location
iv	Threat, traumatic bereavement/loss or injury to personal relationships, attachments and social networks of personal significance

Source: Adapted from Wilson and Lindy, see n. 2.

Target objects

The target object may be a person, a family, a group or even a society. The target object may be traumatized on many system levels: biological, cultural, social, interpersonal and personal.

Traumatic events

In a traumatic event the target object is exposed to stressor factor(s). Wilson and Lindy classify traumatic events into 12 different groups based on the category of stressor factors.[3] All of these may appear under war conditions, although some for obvious reasons are more relevant than others (see Table 27.2).

Table 27.2   Typology of traumatic events

A.	Types of traumatic events which significantly increase under war conditions:
i.	War trauma and civil violence
ii.	Political oppression, torture, internment
iii.	Mass genocide/ethnic cleansing
iv.	Traumatic loss, bereavement
v.	Physical injury, deterioration of chronic illness
vi.	Duty-related trauma
b.	Types of traumatic events which may increase under war conditions:
vii.	Domestic and family violence
viii.	Childhood abuse
c.	Types of traumatic events which may or may not increase under war conditions:
ix.	Occupational, work place trauma
x.	Technological, industrial and toxic disasters
xi.	Natural disasters
xii.	Anomalous traumas

Source: This typology is adapted from Wilson and Lindy (see n. 2) with special focus on traumatic events under war conditions.

Traumatization

The degree of traumatization caused by the experience of the same traumatic event varies among different individuals. The severity of the traumatization results from the balance between the critical dimension of the stressor factor(s) (see Table 27.1) and the presence of psycho-social protective factors.

The protective factors are related to individual coping abilities, family unity and strength, strength of social networks, and the individual ideological, political or religious consciousness.[4]

The traumatization can be classified further according to: the distance (physical, psychological, social) of the traumatic event from the target object; the frequency of the traumatic events experienced; and the context in which the traumatic events take place.

The distance to the stressors
- In primary traumatization the victim is the direct target object for the traumatic event: the tortured, the imprisoned, the raped, the exiled (refugee or displaced).
- In secondary traumatization the stressor factor is the primary traumatization of another victim. The secondary traumatized victim has a close relationship to the primary traumatized either emotionally or socially. For example: the wife and children of the murdered, disappeared or tortured man, the husband of the raped woman, the family or close friends of the refugees and displaced persons.
- In tertiary traumatization the stressor factor is the primary or secondary traumatization of others. The victim is not closely related to the target object but gets in contact with the primary or secondary traumatized for other reasons (e.g. witness to atrocities, neighbour of those expelled, member of a persecuted ethnic group, humanitarian aid workers or therapists helping victims of war).

Frequency and context. Under war conditions, the frequency of traumatic events is characterized by a repetitive impact of stressor factors. These are experienced by the victims in a context of threat, where fundamental human rights are violated systematically and deliberately.

This classification, however, says little about the degree or severity of the experienced traumatization (except from direct physical elimination of the victim). In order to elect priority groups for psychosocial and mental health interventions under war conditions, levels of traumatization must be considered. When nearly everyone is exposed to powerful stressor factors, an understanding of levels of traumatization is required so that emergency interventions are offered to the most vulnerable, who may be the least visible.

The traumatic reactions and sequelae. The traumatic reactions are the symptoms of traumatic stress and may lead to serious mental health complications (sequelae). The experience of the same traumatic event may cause post-traumatic stress disorder (PTSD) in some, while others may not develop these symptoms. The symptomatology of traumatic stress disorders, however, is quite similar on the individual level no matter the kind of traumatic event.

The traumatic sequelae may develop as a consequence of attention to the immediate traumatic reactions.

Impact on individuals and society

In order to plan psychosocial and mental health strategies of interventions and assessments we need the best possible answers to the following questions about potential target groups of war:

- How many are they?
- Who are they?
- Where are they located?
- What is the helping capacity of the local professionals?

These questions are addressed in the following section with special focus on the situation during the war in former Yugoslavia.

How many are they?

Due to the war situation no firm data exist on the frequency of war-related mental health problems, but a rough estimate of the magnitude of war-related traumatic stress disorders can be calculated on the following assumptions:

(1) *In peacetime*: 10 per cent of the population would experience a major traumatic event per year. Ten per cent of those (i.e., 1 per cent of the total population) may need professional help, which goes beyond immediate critical-incident debriefing.

(2) *In wartime*: people continue to have non-war related traumas, while everybody living in the war zone and all refugees and displaced people may experience at least one major trauma per year. Due to the severity of trauma, we may estimate that a minimum of 20 per cent may be in need of emergency assistance. Based on these assumptions, which could all be questioned, the guesstimate adds up to about 5 per cent of the total population.[5]

Who are they?

Based on needs assessments the target groups to be given priority in psychosocial emergency assistance are the people who are most vulnerable to war traumatization. These groups can be listed as follows:

People exposed to direct *war trauma.* People may develop mental problems due to war violence (direct war trauma). This group includes all refugees and displaced people. Some groups are especially vulnerable:

- *Children and adolescents* who are orphans or have been in concentration camps; children and adolescents whose families have disintegrated (e.g., fathers have been killed or have disappeared in the war, or their parents have been separated or divorced because they lived in (ethnically) mixed marriages; children and adolescents whose education has been disrupted after they became refugees and displaced.
- *Women* who have been tortured (e.g., raped or abused in other ways), or whose families have disintegrated (e.g., loss of husband, children, home); women living in mixed marriages.
- *Men* who have been imprisoned in concentration camps or who have witnessed or committed war atrocities; men in mixed marriages.
- *Elderly* who have been abused, raped or terrorized; elderly who are without support from their family and/or from the social and medical welfare system (see also Chapter 31).

People exposed to indirect *war trauma.* Another group which is especially vulnerable to war trauma is composed of those people who before the war had special need for assistance from the social welfare system, the health system and the educational system. This group is composed as follows:

- *Economically and socially marginalized populations* from before the war (e.g., jobless mothers living alone with their children; people with alcohol and drug problems; the chronically jobless).
- *People with chronic somatic illnesses and physical handicaps* (e.g., children who need special educational support; people who need specialized medical assistance).
- *Psychiatric patients and mentally retarded persons* whose health status has deteriorated due to the breakdown of the health system, damage to the hospitals, lack of medicine, food and general care and the dissolution of family and social networks.

The deterioration of the economy and the physical destruction of schools, hospitals and other governmental buildings has a general impact on social, educational and health structures. In consequence, these institutions are no longer able to take care of war-traumatized people.

Care of these vulnerable groups is also affected by the direct and indirect traumatization of the staff, including teachers, social workers, therapists and doctors. It may also be that their institution is destroyed and they no longer have a place to work. Because of the deterioration of the economy, many receive no salary, or only the barest minimum. Some may have to work in offices which are protected from shelling by sandbags and frequently have to take their patients, or the children in their classes, to the bomb shelter. Many become traumatized themselves and have little experience or training in how to deal with this new situation in which they are as their patients, clients or students. Many have to deal with ongoing trauma as well as the adverse consequences of post-traumatic effects. Nobody is outside the situation. This is an unusual and specific condition of countries under war conditions.

Where are they located?

The relative need for help was most significant in the direct war zones, for example in Bosnia-Herzegovina and in Croatia (in the former UN Protected Areas, including eastern Slavonia). The frequency of problems was expectedly higher in areas where heavy fighting took place: in towns and pockets of the country where the population lived for years under siege and constant threat (Sarajevo, Gorazde and Bihac) and in areas hosting large populations of refugees or people displaced from war zones (like Tuzla).

In Croatia refugees and displaced persons made up the biggest group of war-traumatized. In the Federal Republic of Yugoslavia, in the former Yugoslav republic of Macedonia and in Slovenia most problems of the war-traumatized were to be found among refugees.

What is the helping capacity?

An estimate of the frequency of the people in need of help has to be compared with estimates of the available helping capacity. Such a calculation can be set up, based on a series of assumptions; the resulting estimate is that if all trained professionals were doing nothing else than attending the most severely affected war victims, they would cover less than 5–8 per cent of acute needs.

Traumatic reactions and sequelae: special considerations

Traumatic reactions: the problem of a diagnostic approach towards human rights violation and problematic issues for professionals

The traumatic reactions or symptoms (e.g. the stress response syndromes) are caused by exposure to the critical traumatic events and mirror the degree of traumatization. Lack of attention to traumatic reactions may lead to secondary symptomatic complications: for example, the traumatic sequelae in all of their various forms and complexities. Before we discuss these reactions in detail, let us address the current debate among mental health professionals about the use of psychiatric diagnoses in situations of war, organized violence, genocide and atrocities.

On the one hand it is not reasonable to attach such diagnoses to whole populations, as they lose their value as working tools if applied indiscriminately. Moreover refugees and displaced do not appreciate further stigmatization through such labelling. They are not insane, but are suffering from the war. The careless use of psychiatric diagnoses can lead to the individualization of problems that are basically political. Indeed we have noticed several examples of this practice. More importantly, the over-reliance and inappropriate use of psychiatric diagnoses may obscure more profound issues to be addressed, or be a form of counter-transference reaction.

On the other hand, underdiagnosing by not recognizing symptoms or their significance may lead to overlooking the suffering of large numbers of people. The same problem arises from the use of traditional diagnoses (e.g. depression, neurosis) and treatment to label these reactions. These failures may enhance the risk of long-term chronic reactions. The most appropriate method of deepening one's understanding of trauma responses is to talk with those who have experienced the trauma. In this situation one should look for the symptoms which intrude involuntarily into the consciousness (e.g. flashbacks, nightmares, preoccupation with thoughts about the traumatic event). Other signs to watch for are a numbness of reaction or at the other end of the continuum, extreme reactions to trauma symbolic stimuli (e.g., the sound of a car backfiring). The above reactions lead people to fear that they are going crazy. A good clinician can recognize both the symptoms and the fear, and reassure the victims that they are not losing their minds but rather reacting in a normal and even adaptive way to extreme events, especially under conditions of prolonged civil warfare and genocide.

Traumatic stress disorders: the diagnoses

Given these reservations and a general clinical approach let us then address the diagnoses in use to classify traumatic reactions. These include the following:

(1) Acute stress disorder (ASD) is defined by symptoms lasting for at least two days and a maximum of four weeks. Persistence of symptoms would result in a PTSD diagnosis (see below). Both ASD and PTSD are considered to be normal, expected reactions to abnormal stressors.

(2) Post-traumatic stress disorder (PTSD) is the most common stress response in severe traumatization (primary, secondary or tertiary). The core symptoms are various forms of re-experiencing the trauma (like flashbacks and nightmares); various forms of avoidance, detachment, memory loss, psychic and emotional numbing and behavioural changes; and manifestations of increased arousal of the autonomic nervous system. The symptoms may vary significantly in terms of duration, frequency and severity. Irrespective of the diagnostic criteria, many patients manifest several other symptoms, like anxiety, depression, dissociative phenomena, personality changes, self-destructive behaviour, guilt, complicity, anger and fantasies of revenge and retaliation.

(3) Complex PTSD and 'Disorders of Extreme Stress Not Otherwise Specified' (DESNOS). The concept was introduced by Herman based on a review of the literature on prolonged or repeated trauma.[6] The victims may develop adaptive and defensive patterns of coping, which include forms of dissociation, somatization, self-destructive behaviours and characterological changes in personality functioning, ego-identity, structure of the self and ideological beliefs and values. In the context of war both extreme and repetitive traumatization is a constant risk through the continuous presence of critical traumatic events.

Sequelae from traumatic stress disorders: core issues for assessment and intervention

Patients with stress disorders may often present themselves to the health system with these problems. To recognize the underlying stress response syndrome is important for a relevant treatment approach. The most common sequelae to traumatic stress disorders are:

(1) *Self-medication with the risk of alcoholism and/or drug addiction.* Alcohol and/or minor tranquilizers are the most commonly used drugs in the attempt to reduce the anxiety. A massive increase of alcohol and drug addiction is to be expected, when the helping capacity directed at the underlying traumas is insufficient. A specially vulnerable group is soldiers/ex-soldiers, where massive abuse has been documented, for example within the rehabilitation institutions for physically wounded men. The abuse of alcohol and medicines is often connected to increased frequencies of both suicides/suicidal attempts and homicides. In some war zones local data support a five-fold increase in the suicidal rate and a twenty-fold increase in homicides (killings without direct motive, related to alcohol intake and easy access to weapons).

(2) *Psychosomatic complaints.* Since many people do not find the traditional mental-health institutions appropriate for them, many trauma patients primarily ask for help in the primary health-care system. Here the medical tradition in the countries of the former Yugoslavia favours an approach based on the prescription of medicines. Focus is then

more on the somatic aspects of the stress symptoms, and not the underlying traumatic experiences. Despite good intent, the primary care system is not able or prepared to deal with the psychological bases of somatic problems.

(3) *Explosive reactions to minor stimuli (trauma-like or trauma-symbolic situations).* The unresolved traumatization is often experienced and observed through explosive reactions, when the individual is exposed to trauma-like or trauma-symbolic situations. The emotional response exceeds what both the individual himself and an observer may find appropriate in relation to the character of the stimuli. It is often combined with an experience of a fear of going crazy because such acts are alien to their personality and nature. The combination of these reactions and alcohol may at least partly explain the increased involvement in violence (criminal and domestic). A special problem faces soldiers. Due to the specific war situation many soldiers are living in their homes and go to work in the war. The combination of alcohol, traumatic reactions related to witnessing or committing war atrocities and subsequent explosive reactions seem to be a dangerous cocktail for the whole family.[7]

(4) *Reactive psychotic behaviour.* In several psychiatric departments in the war zones an increase of trauma-related traumatic reactive psychosis was observed (Bihac, Sarajevo). Clinical observations suggest that these conditions are mainly seen when the patients are still living in the war zone, while the psychotic reactions are relatively rare among refugees and displaced persons living under more safe conditions.

(5) *Transgenerational impact of traumatic stress.* Traumatic stress studies of the children and grandchildren of Holocaust survivors and children of Vietnam veterans have illustrated an increased presence of traumatic stress disorders in the next generations. The perception of the children and maybe even grandchildren is coloured by the family memory of the traumatic experiences of the parents and maybe even grandparents (see also Chapter 31). Transgenerational aspects related to emotional responses of the victims of war in the countries of former Yugoslavia were clinically significant. Further studies from this perspective may contribute to a new understanding of both the development of conflicts and possible conflict resolution under war conditions.

Treatment of traumatic reactions: special considerations for war trauma and political oppression

The treatment of traumatic reactions may be curative and preventative. Assistance may be offered on different levels of intervention.

Critical-incident debriefing

Critical-incident debriefing strategies are well known in peacetime (for example, after single traumatic events like a ferry disaster, a terror attack or hostage-taking). The target population includes all individuals who experienced and shared a specific traumatic event. The traumatic event is reconstructed into a collective narrative where each participant contributes with his experiences of both what really happened and the emotions related to the events. Such brief interventions are often sufficient for a relatively large fraction of the participants. During the debriefing work, individuals in need of more extensive assistance may be singled out.

Due to the overwhelming number of traumatic events, these appropriate interventions are often not carried out under war conditions. We may expect, however, that such strategies could be very supportive, when carried out in a context of relative peace. Such periods exist, for example, when the war activities decrease during a ceasefire. It is a sad fact that even during the ceasefire shelling may occur as more or less single events. In such situations critical-incident debriefing interventions are appropriate to prevent further increase in the collective fear of a besieged city.

Survivors' groups

Special survivors' groups were developed as part of the resistance against the dictatorships in Latin America.[8] Within the framework of the human rights movement traumatized people and/or their families created a network of grassroot groups, where the participants shared the same kind of trauma (for example, families of the detained and disappeared, the ex-political prisoners). The group offered non-professional psychological support to individual members; the connection to the human rights movement added an overall meaning to the work. Often the survivors' groups were also connected to mental health professionals working in the non-government institutions within the human rights movement. There are only a few examples of this kind of work in the countries of former Yugoslavia. Some women's centres and human rights groups have created such contexts.

Counselling and therapy

The last decade has seen an explosive increase within the field of post-traumatic stress and post-traumatic counselling. Several different methods have been developed, although only a minority of these are aimed at interventions under war conditions. Most studies are based on the work with Vietnam veterans, refugees and natural as well as human-related disasters. A detailed discussion of these methods is, however, outside the scope of this presentation.

Deterioration of psychiatric disease through war-related traumatization or breakdown of health care

The health of patients with mental illness or handicap may directly deteriorate through the development of co-morbidity of the original condition and the war-related traumatic reactions. Clearly, the scientific literature has demonstrated the deleterious and long-term consequences of prolonged stress. The condition of these patients may also deteriorate indirectly through war-related lack of drugs, essentials and sufficient professional care, as commonly experienced during the war in former Yugoslavia. As a consequence, an increase of aggressive or psychotic behaviour, violence and diseases due to infections and bad living conditions are experienced in the institutions. The breakdown of the social network further reduces possibilities for a life outside the mental health institutions.

The mental health-care system: resources, programme development and implementation

The psychosocial projects

In her 1995 report, Agger reviews 185 ongoing psychosocial projects in Croatia and Bosnia-Herzegovina.[9] These were projects carried out in collaboration between national and international non-government institutions and international organizations. She gives an operational definition of psychosocial projects:

> The overall purpose of psychosocial emergency assistance is to promote mental health and human rights by strategies that enhance the already existing psychosocial protective factors and decrease the psychosocial stressor factors at different levels of intervention.

The overall purpose of psychosocial projects overlaps with the aims of the general mental-health system. However, most of these projects were run by non-governmental institutions and international aid organizations. Only a minority of the psychosocial projects were within or coordinated with the existing health system. An important task was to bridge this gap and stimulate collaboration and coordination to avoid the introduction of an alternative health care system, although the political situation in a war situation reveals clear differences of interests.

The traditional mental health institutions

WHO reports analysed the present state of mental health institutions and services in the countries of former Yugoslavia.[10] Information about the number of beds and the professional staffing were analysed to present the damage to the mental health system and to what extent resources were available. Due to the destruction of institutions many psychiatric patients ended up as refugees. In 1996, 15–20 per cent of psychiatric patients in both Croatia and Bosnia-Herzegovina were defined as refugees or displaced.[11] No convincing data exist on how many psychiatric patients have died or been physically injured due to war atrocities.

Some main problems in the mental health-care systems in the countries of former Yugoslavia under war conditions

The identification of these problems was needed to set up both preventive and treatment strategies. Some main themes identified were:[12]

Mental health was a prewar low priority area

The mental health-care system was suffering from years of low economic priority, with the focus directed more on institutional psychiatry and less on the development of community-based psychosocial structures. Damage to several mental-health institutions led in consequence to overload and overcrowdedness in many functioning institutions. Unequal distribution of mental health services developed due to border changes and the migration of the population. A breakdown of family network and social support structures tended to keep the focus on institutional mental-health care.

A lack of epidemiological information and coordination structures for service

A breakdown of prewar epidemiological tools and the lack of access to some regions due to ongoing war activities led to a lack of information about real mental-health needs. A similar lack of overall information about the resources within the mental health system (for example, the functioning institutions and the number of available professionals) reduced the possibilities of optimally utilizing the existing structures. A lack of information about the special mental-health needs among the refugees and displaced persons and other vulnerable target groups reduced the planning of comprehensive interventions. A lack of overall coordination of mental-health interventions already offered by governmental, non-governmental and international structures increased the risk of duplication and gaps.

A massive increase of patients in need of mental health care

The number of individuals who were not traditional mental-health patients but in need of help due to war-related traumatization increased dramatically. These were people with psychological sequelae to physical injuries and with psychological damage due to traumatic experiences: primary traumatization, (e.g., rape victims), secondary traumatization (e.g., the families of the disappeared persons) and tertiary traumatization (e.g., humanitarian aid workers and health care personnel). Accurate assessments of these populations in need of care was an urgent although difficult task.

A lack of drugs and medical essentials

A lack of psychotropic medicines and medical essentials was obvious in many areas and institutions. A lack of systematic needs' assessments as a basis for emergency supplies created uncertainty for a comprehensive distribution of the assistance. The differences in psychiatric traditions for the use of psychotropic drugs created requests for very expensive and specific drugs which were not available or did not respect the necessary priorities of the limited resources. A lack of state-of-the-art knowledge about efficacious drug treatment for PTSD and related conditions led to overwhelming requests for minor tranquillizers, which often ended up on the black market.

Staff education, training, supervision and care-taking

The new situation called for a series of staff-related activities such as:
- training opportunities for the general health and mental health professionals for mental health care in general and especially under war conditions;
- structures and opportunities for supervision of professional work;

- structures to take care of the care-takers (national and international staff) exposed to primary, secondary or tertiary traumatization; and
- academic exchange of knowledge and specialized training programmes with the international community

General public mental-health interventions

A lack of informative, attitude-challenging and educational material aimed at the public with focus on mental health issues in general and during wartime in particular led to a privatization and individualization of common and general mental-health problems. A lack of understanding of the relation between human rights violations and the mental health status of the population led to a medicalization and individualization of the diagnostic and therapeutic procedures.

Preliminary outlines for intervention strategies

A comprehensive implementation of the intervention strategies depends on a combination of economic resources, systematic needs assessment, the coordination structures to strengthen the efficacy of efforts, a sufficient number of professionals with the relevant skills and systematic monitoring and quality assurance of the activities.

Under war conditions, resources for mental health and psychosocial activities are reduced significantly. As a traditional low-priority area, mental health and poverty was a well-known combination even before the war. Just a slight reduction in the economic conditions of the mental hospitals was a threat to the basic living conditions of the patients. When the whole population lived under the stress of war, the resources to care for these patients were limited. So any intervention strategy in the mental health area had to address this group of severely-ill and care-dependent patients. Besides the traditional patients in the mental health system, we have already addressed the massive number of people who have confronted traumatic events and subsequent post-traumatic emotional reactions.[13] Among them many were in need of psychosocial interventions even in the emergency phase. At the same time, and not always without reason, most of the population did not consider the traditional mental health institutions to be the natural site to seek assistance. There was a lack of tradition for ordinary people to ask for help to overcome emotional distress and a corresponding lack of response from the health care system. The emotional symptoms were often presented as somatic complaints and treated as medical problems. Self-medication with alcohol or drugs was a risky alternative, at many levels of socio-economic consideration.

The tradition of psychosocially-oriented humanitarian aid in the emergency phase is still limited. For many reasons supply of food and shelter for basic survival has the overall priority. On the other hand, it has been observed in this war that the aid agencies channelled some of their support into psychosocial activities. The 185 psychosocial projects reported by Agger in January 1995 in Croatia and Bosnia-Herzegovina seemed, however, to cover only a small percentage of the needs.[14] The assistance to Bosnia-Herzegovina was relatively limited compared to that of Croatia (without saying that the assistance to Croatia was sufficient).[15]

Interventions in the psychosocial and mental health field

It is not possible to implement all proposals at once. It was, however, important to develop a main strategy as a framework for optimal work within a continuum of emergency interventions, mid- and long-term interventions and preventive strategies. Under war conditions we are not working in an ideal world. All initiatives had to adapt to the current and often changing situation, so the main strategies developed as a consequence of the problems identified above.

Needs and resource assessments: establishment of an epidemiology

In collaboration with national authorities, non-governmental institutions and international organizations we had to establish:

- an overview of the actual mental health needs based on geography, type of trauma, traumatic reactions as well as age and gender, with special focus on war zones, refugees and displaced and other vulnerable target groups;
- an overview of the actual mental health resources within the governmental health systems, the NGO psychosocial projects and international activities; and
- a continuous monitoring of mental health needs and resources as a basis for future interventions.

Due to the lack of functional epidemiological structures (health information systems) the main means of creating an overview was field missions, where international and national professionals tried to collect local and regional data based on a compilation of available information from the different institutions, organizations and direct observations. On 18 October 1994 we succeeded in having a first census, when we recorded the number of patients in 14 different institutions in 3 countries on this day.[16]

Later, a more systematic approach to the collection of data was developed within the WHO regional models. A series of overviews and analyses of the psychosocial projects was created. These overviews became a significant tool for the ongoing coordination of new initiatives.

Coordination structures

Regional level.   In each region (3–400,000 inhabitants) a regional coordination structure for psychosocial/ mental health interventions was introduced as part of the WHO regional model.[17] In this structure representatives from the governmental mental-health system met on a regular basis with representatives from the IGOs and NGOs running projects in the region. The aim was to coordinate efforts based on identified needs and resources and to establish mutual training and supervision programmes.

National level.   An international and national advisory board was planned to coordinate and develop guidelines for optimal intervention strategies in the emergency phase and relate these activities to mid-term and long-term plans. It was, however, difficult for political reasons to implement such a structure. After the peace agreement the coordinators of the structures that WHO had implemented in each region of the Bosnian Federation established themselves as a national (federational) coordination group with support from WHO.[18] Thus the WHO field operation with offices in each region showed that it was more appropriate to work from the regional towards a national perspective than vice versa.

Training, supervision and self-care programmes aimed at local professionals

No country has a sufficient number of professionals skilled to handle the massive trauma-tization of its population due to war conditions. In consequence it was important to set up training programmes aimed at the self-empowerment of different professionals. Typical target groups in each region were psychotherapists (psychiatrists and psychologists) to be trained in post-traumatic therapy; counsellors (nurses, social workers, medical doctors) to be trained in post-traumatic counselling; teachers to be trained in preventive activities with children and adolescents; and primary health-care providers to be trained in recognition and preliminary care of traumatic reactions in general practice.

All courses included elements of training, case supervision and self-care. The programmes were, whenever possible, connected to and acknowledged by the existing local academic institutions. This was to secure the recognition of the professionals by their own authorities after as well as during the war.

Reorientation of the mental health-care system

In the former Yugoslavia, several mental health institutions were damaged or destroyed. The prewar system was primarily based on institutional psychiatry. In the aftermath of war, it was to be decided if these institutions were to be reconstructed or if this was an opportunity to reorientate the mental health system towards a more community-based approach. It was an opportunity not just to rebuild the huge old prewar institutions. The postwar economy probably demands a reduction in health-care expenditure. Conse-quently a community-based mental health approach seems to be a less costly as well as more important and more appropriate way to meet the needs. This opened up the way for the long-term integration of the many emergency counselling centres funded by IGOs and NGOs into community-based mental-health centres. Developing a commu-nity-based mental health approach is, however, only possible if it is combined with the creation of training programmes to establish such a tradition.

Even if a community-based mental-health system is given priority, some of the mental hospitals and psychiatric departments have to be reorganized. A reduction in overloading and overcrowding is needed if basic human conditions are to be provided for patients. The present number of beds per 10,000 inhabitants is not as low as might be expected compared to European standards, but these figures need to be revised given that many of these beds are located in overcrowded wards.

A new drugs policy

A new drugs policy in the mental health field had to be introduced in collaboration with national experts. For use in the emergency phase, WHO has developed a mental hospital kit (MH-kit). It includes a limited number of essential psychotropic drugs aimed at the medical treatment of 50 in-patients a month. The MH-kit principle offers an opportunity to institute a specific drug policy. The distribution of the kits was not, but should be, combined with relevant treatment manuals and professional state-of-the-art seminars under war conditions. In the emergency phase, the kit principle also offers the opportunity to respond adequately to needs' assessment. The content of the MH-kit has to be evaluated through systematic monitoring. The kit approach has to be adapted, however, to the fact that the profile of mental health problems in European countries under war conditions is different from that in the developing countries, the traditional receivers of such aids.

Special attention needs to be paid to the mental and social rehabilitation of individuals who have suffered physical injuries as a result of war atrocities (amputees, traumatic brain injuries and spinal cord injuries).

Prevention and public mental-health information

This includes initiatives to elaborate and/or distribute relevant information and educational material aimed at health care under war conditions through pamphlets, newspapers, the mass media and international agencies. A special priority is the setting up of educational strategies which focus on human rights. The UN organizations may take the stand of technical neutrality, that is, working with both sides of the conflict; they may also take the stand of ethical non-neutrality by systematically defending human rights and counteracting all human rights' violations on all sides.[19] Such a position offers a point of departure, establishing a postwar dialogue to facilitate reconciliation and justice as part of the overall mental health status of the countries, regions and people.

In 1996 the European University Centre for Mental Health and Human Rights was established as a new structure retrospectively to document the mental health consequences of wartime human rights' violations and to monitor future mental-health consequences.[20] The project also aims at transferring knowledge gained during the war to other countries.

REFERENCES

1. WHO (1995), *WHO Mission in the Former Yugoslavia,* WHO Annual Report 1994, Zagreb: WHO Regional Office for Europe, Zagreb Area Office .
2. Wilson, J.P. and J.D. Lindy (1994), *Counter-transference in the Treatment of PTSD,* New York: Guilford Press.
3. Ibid.
4. Ager, A. (1993), *Mental Health Issues in Refugee Populations: a review,* Harvard: Harvard Medical School, Department of Social Medicine, working paper of the Harvard Center for the Study of Culture and Medicine.
5. Jensen, S.B. (1999), *Mental Health and Human Rights under War Conditions in the Countries of Former Yugoslavia,* Copenhagen: WHO/EURO; and Jensen, S.B. (1996), 'Mental Health under War Conditions during the 1991–95 Yugoslavian War', Geneva: *WHO Quart. Stat.* 49: 213–17.
6. Herman, J.L. (1992), *Trauma and Recovery,* New York: Basic Books.
7. See n. 5 above.

8. Agger, I. and S.B. Jensen (1996), *Trauma and Healing under State Terrorism*, London: Zed Books.

9. Agger, I. (1995), *Theory and Practice of Psycho-social Projects under War Conditions in Croatia and Bosnia-Herzegovina*, Zagreb: European Community Task Force (ECTF)/ECHO.

10. Wig, N.N. (1993), *The Present State of Mental Health Institutions and Services in the Countries of the Former Yugoslavia*, Geneva & Copenhagen: WHO; and Jensen, S. B. (1996), *The Present State of Mental Health Systems in the Countries of Former Yugoslavia*, Zagreb: WHO Mental Health Unit.

11. See Jensen (1999), n. 5 above.

12. *Ibid.*

13. See Jensen (1996), n. 5 above.

14. See n. 9 above.

15. Agger, I., Jensen, S.B. and M. Jacobs (1995), *Under War Conditions: What Defines a Psychosocial Project? Emergency needs and interventions for victims of war*, in I. Agger (ed.), *Theory and Practice of Psycho-social Projects under War Conditions in Croatia and Bosnia-Herzegovina*, Zagreb and Bruxelles: ECHO/ECTF.

16. See Jensen (1996), n. 5 above.

17. See Jensen (1999), n. 5 above.

18. Ibid.

19. See Jensen (1999), n. 5 above; and n. 8.

20. See Jensen (1999), n. 5 above; and Agger, I. and J. Mimica (1996), *Psychosocial Assistance to Victims of War in Bosnia-Herzegovina and Croatia: an evaluation*, Bruxelles: ECHO.

Address for correspondence

TPO Africa, Postbox 21646 Kampala, Uganda
Email: sbjensen@infocom.co.ug

28 THE UNDERPRIVILEGED, ELDERLY, MENTALLY ILL AND HANDICAPPED IN WAR

KLAUS DÖRNER

War is the conflict between two groups of strong people over the domination of a territory and the weaker people living in it. The weaker ones have a range of characteristics: age (children, elderly), gender (women), economic status (poor), handicap (bodily, mental, psychical) or cultural marginality (immigrants, refugees, asylum seekers, ethnic minorities). War has always been waged at the expense of the weaker population, with the underprivileged, elderly, mentally ill and handicapped suffering through, for example, destruction of their homes, deportation, hunger and epidemics, hostage seizing or ethnic cleansing.

The modern age

Notwithstanding this, around 1800 the modern age began with the attempt by human beings to liberate themselves from 'self-inflicted incompetence' (*die selbsverschuldete Unmündigkeit* – Immanuel Kant), to replace foreign domination with self-determination and to base all interpersonal relations on reason alone. Everything non-rational, all ambiguities and uncertainties, all disturbing, unproductive, indecent, inappropriate alien people should be annihilated, be it through exclusion, education, therapy, institutionalization or killing. Accordingly the nation should consist of rational, healthy, strong, good and social individuals only; this is the way the ideal of a society without suffering should be realized. This was the project of the Enlightenment. In the workings of this project all non-rational persons were perceived as alien, necessitating that the outer aliens be distinguished from the inner aliens – the strange, non-conforming people. Among the latter group the mentally ill were perceived as especially and extremely foreign because of their proverbially erratic and non-rational behaviour. This differentiation is significant especially from the aspect of war. With the advent of the modern age and the formation of nation states all members of another nation were perceived as outer aliens, so that a war against another nation is also waged against all its members, both strong and weak. One could even claim that since the advent of the modern age a permanent civil war has been waged against the inner aliens of a nation, in so far as the strong have been constantly trying various methods of changing the weak (non-rational): either making them strong through education and therapy; or excluding them, making them invisible in institutions; or abolishing them, even killing them. Therefore the beginning of the modern age is characterized by a process through which the previously-existing unity of manufacturing and social activities was split. The change-over to a market economy and industrialization created an extensive network of factories and offices for the productive strong, on the one hand. On the other hand, it led to the creation of an extensive network of social institutions like lunatic asylums, facilities for the mentally handicapped, cripple homes, prisons, workhouses, orphanages, kindergartens, old people's homes and nursing homes for the unproductive weak. With the help of these social institutions the strong try to rationalize the weak, although with only moderate success.

Naturally there were during the 19th century attempts to oppose the injustices of this process: whether in the cosmopolitan view that we are all citizens of one world, or from the philanthropic-romantic perspective that the people of a nation, although differing in productive capacities, can claim equal status based on their dignity. However, throughout the history of mankind the rationalization processes have always become active in a relatively short time-frame, whilst a longer period is required before a new and reasonable ethics is able to catch up with technical progress. Accordingly, opposition movements could not become widely effective during the 19th century.

Despite this, by 1900 a dangerous polarization had emerged in most European countries and the United States of America. This was underpinned by the fact that part of the classically poor accomplished their integration as a proletariat into bourgeois society through industrialization, the development of self-help organizations and, especially, through keeping the sub-proletariat at a distance, thus distinguishing all those whose productivity could not keep up with that of the others. This led inescapably to increasing discrimination against the underprivileged, elderly, mentally ill and handicapped. In Germany from the beginning of the 20th century these groups were referred to as the 'inferiors' (*Untermenschen*) and no action was taken against them. But then the race-hygienic forces gained a foothold in all political groups. These were no longer content with the institutionalization of the weak, but demanded their abolition, at first through compulsory sterilization to save on social expenses and from a sense of 'deadly pity' to save such weak, non-rational persons from a perceived desolate existence.[1] Simultaneously a newer, no longer only religious, but scientific anti-Semitism found acceptance among the general public, paving the way for violence against inner and outer aliens.

The First World War (WWI) signified an escalation in the synchronization of the war against outer and inner aliens. In Germany alone 70,000 institutionalized individuals died of hunger and subsequent infections. Yet the historical working-through of this process has not yet been accomplished. There are indications that the directors of the social institutions of the time believed it their patriotic duty to ensure that a sufficient number of institute inmates died so that the heroic death of so many strong persons in the war against the outer aliens would not lead to a further racial deterioration of the

German people. Some institute directors seem simply to have calculated that they could achieve ten times as high a death rate among inmates as amongst the free-living population by providing them with the same food rations, which inmates had no means of supplementing. This war experience of the fight of the strong against the weak was expressed in the title of their book by the liberal lawyer Binding and the psychiatrist Hoche: 'The Release through Annihilation of Life not Worth Living'.[2]

The way was paved for the next escalation in the synchronization of the war against the outer and inner aliens which was realized in Germany with the take-over by the National Socialists. The National Socialists' view of the modern project was to prove to the world that a nation, once it has found the brutality to rid itself of its social ballast, is economically and militarily invincible and can realize the dream of the Enlightenment without suffering. In 1933, immediately on taking power, the Nazis made the 'genetic health law' (*Erbgesundheitsgesetz*) their basic principle. They compulsorily sterilized at least 350,000 people using all those rationalizing measures in the civil war against the weak they could risk at a time of outer peace under the eyes of the world. And were admired and applauded by many other countries.

It was now evident that the Nazis would dare the next escalation with the beginning of the outer war. The historical truth is that on 1 September 1939 the war of annihilation began in Germany not only externally, but internally. Crucially, 17 October 1939 represents the most severely repressed date, best hidden even from international research. The Nazis, who had planned to exterminate major parts of the Polish population, had already started to murder the inmates of Polish psychiatric hospitals through shooting. Very quickly they noticed, however, that compared with the quantitative size of their murder plans, killing through shooting was not only technically but also ethically useless; because the shooting of one person by another always remains an interpersonal relationship. Therefore on 17 October 1939 the Nazis made airtight a bunker at Fort Number VII of the Poznan (Posen) fortification plants, ordered that gas from the state criminal department in Berlin be sent to Poznan, and administered to a group of mentally ill people from the adjacent Polish psychiatric hospital. This was the first time in the history of mankind, and in the context of the permanent civil war of the strong against the weak, that the handicraft of murder was replaced by industrial annihilation. The crossing of this threshold should not have been easy even for the Nazis. They needed not only the protection provided by the external war, but the combination of the hate against outer and inner aliens, because this first group consisted of Poles (Polish *Untermenschen*) as well as of the mentally ill ('inferior'). It was not until recently that documentation of these events became available.

After this it was no longer difficult to apply this industrial method of killing in Germany. Here an excess of 70,000 mentally-ill 'incurable' cases was estimated and by the middle of 1941 they had been murdered in five gassing plants. The programme was extended: (i) to mentally-ill and mentally-handicapped children and adolescents; (ii) to no-longer efficient inmates of concentration camps; (iii) from 1941 to the mentally ill in the Soviet Union; and (iv) after the notorious Wannsee Conference, as the 'final solution of the social question', the 'final solution of the Jewish question'. The gassing plants and trained service teams were transported to Poland, where they formed the core of the annihilation camps for Jews, Gypsies and parts of the Polish and Soviet-Russian population. In Germany, the directors of the mental hospitals were encouraged after 1941 to incorporate the now-normalized and individualized killing through drugs or food deprivation into their everyday treatment repertoire, in fact against each new prospective incurable case. The judicial culmination of this modern civil war of the strong against the weak was laid by the Nazis with the 1944 'aliens-to-the-community law' (*Gemeinschaftsfremdengesetz*). According to it each person diagnosed as not adequately rational, healthy, productive or decent could be exposed firstly to the method of re-education; if determined educationally unalterable, he/she was exposed to compulsory labour, which still offered a chance of probation. If this also failed, the system of medical administration set in train procedures that ended with clinical killing and negation of the judicial process.

The postwar era has until the present day been characterized by two contrary tendencies. The trend of further modernization and rationalization is still proceeding, especially in the border areas of medical progress at any given time, from prenatal diagnostics to gene therapy to the desire to kill handicapped neonates or practise active euthanasia. Moreover there are many documents giving evidence of the continued effectiveness of the modern rationalizing *Zeitgeist*, the general trend of the time. The author Wolf Wolfensberger calculates on the basis of extensive data that in the USA alone every year 200,000 handicapped persons are put to death through the activities of the health and social services.[4] Wolfensberger argues that the concept 'genocide' is well-founded because this number is higher than the number killed annually by the Nazis. Corresponding to this trend are the numerous wars of the postwar era, which are predominantly connected with the fight for the formation of nation states and national autonomy.

Since 1945, however, this trend has been opposed by another which has been stable and proceeding until the present day: this includes overcoming the nation-state idea, especially in Europe, and the gradual evolution of the awareness that we are all citizens of one world and that we have to become organized globally. Since 1945 all developed societies of the world have taken stock of themselves, as if they had suddenly realized that the Nazi terror was only the consistent extension of the 150-year-old history of institutionalization. These countries have begun to replace institutionalization with de-institutionalization and to encourage integration and proximity between the strong and the weak. Simultaneously the previously excluded weak population groups have gradually joined together in self-help organizations and are taking control of their own lives. This process at first involved the physically disabled and asocial adolescents, then the mentally handicapped, whose parents joined together, and finally, during the last 15 years, the mentally ill and their relatives. We are now getting along with fewer institutions every year, with the consequence that the average citizen has a somewhat bigger chance of encountering people who were excluded during the classical period of the modern age.

There is a symbolic starting-point for this trend which has now been proceeding for decades, although slowly. It is an incident which I know from a report by a certain Kabanov, the director of the Bechterew Institute in St. Petersburg/Leningrad. During the Second World War and the lengthy siege of Leningrad by the Nazis, in the winter of 1942–43 the icebound lake enabled bigger groups of the city's starving population to be evacuated and brought to safety, yet it was decided that the inmates of the psychiatric hospitals and the old people's homes would be saved first, because they were threatened most by the starvation. To the extent that we succeed in transferring this attitude to our everyday activities, we can ensure that, despite all adversities as for example in Yugoslavia, the permanent modern civil war of the strong against the weak – with and without the protection of wars against external aliens – will be stopped. We could thereby learn that social relationships between human beings are, in principle, always relationships between the stronger and the weaker.

REFERENCES

1. Dörner, K. (1992), *Tödliches Mitleid*, Gütersloh: Verlag Jacob van Hoddis.
2. Binding, K. and Hoche, A. (1920), *Die Freigabe der Vernichtung lebensunwerten Lebens*, Munich: Lehman.
3. Jaroszewski, Z. (1993), *Die Ermordung der Geisteskranken in Polen 1939 bis 1945*, Gütersloh: Verlag Jacob van Hoddis.
4. Wolfensberger, Wolf (1989), *Der neue Genozid an den Benachteiligten, Alten und Behinderten* (The new genocide of the underprivileged, elderly and handicapped), Gütersloh: Verlag Jacob van Hoddis.

29 WAR-INJURED VETERANS GETTING OLD

LEO JARHO

War injuries are often multiple, physical as well as mental. Special attention has been paid in recent years to those mental disturbances which stem from severe war experiences, such as torture and concentration camp internment. These can leave permanent psychological scars, especially when untreated (post-traumatic stress disorders – PTSD). The physical and mental consequences of war injuries and disease can be divided roughly as follows:

- traumatic war injuries: (i) brain; (ii) amputations; (iii) sensory organs – blindness and deafness; (iv) spinal cord; (v) burns, facial injuries, cosmetic late-effects; and (vi) other multiple damage;
- diseases, infections and starvation;
- mental trauma; and
- injury/disease combinations.

The degree of a disability depends upon the severity of the original trauma; social and individual factors will also determine how a disabled veteran gets along in life. A moderate to severe disability has great influence as a stress factor in the veteran's everyday life. Certain after-effects of injuries can also cause their own special disorders, for example, brain injuries, amputations, blindness. Under the exceptional wartime conditions, many injuries may not have originally received enough medial attention or treatment. Several years afterwards it may be difficult to analyse the consequential symptoms of war injuries. These symptoms could be hidden when wounded persons are young and have the strength to cope with them, but with aging this tolerance will decrease and the disability will become a new burden upon the veteran's state of health. For this reason it is important that a medical examination and follow-up carried out at a late date should be thorough; the results of the examination may guarantee the disabled veteran his right to compensation and after-care.

Injuries and aging

War veterans are usually young when they are injured. One should remember, however, that for many their life-span as disabled persons could continue for 50 years or more. Immediately after the injury, the prognosis is often good and rehabilitation tends to yield encouraging results. Even in the case of serious injury the prognosis may seem favourable. As young persons the injured have a great capacity to compensate for their disabilities, but during the decades to come they will change both physically and mentally. Along with aging, biological, psychological and social factors reduce their physical and mental capacity to cope. The more serious the injuries, the sooner the veteran's ability to compensate for the consequences of trauma will decrease. From the outset the seriously injured have great difficulties with their health balance. In the years that follow the health and coping strength of disabled veterans are influenced by the following:

- Long-lasting physical and psychosocial consequences of injuries, worsening after-effects and associated diseases.
- Normal aging, with decreasing mental and physical strength to cope with disabilities.
- Affliction by new diseases not actually related to a war injury, for example mental disorders, depression, psycho-organic changes, stroke. These will cause a new disability and helplessness.
- Judged by medical criteria, these different factors have in combination a strong worsening influence on the veteran's health, resulting in exceptionally grave disabilities which will have great need of medical and social services.

The health of an aging disabled veteran depends on the late symptoms of his war injury and on general geriatric diseases and other gerontological changes. In many countries there is adequate information about the physical and mental state and morbidity of their own-aged normal population, especially about those health disorders which cause serious handicaps. Available knowledge concerning the basic geriatric problems should also be applied to the aged-disabled war veterans, so that their needs for after-care can be evaluated.

Medical after-care

Medical after-care should aim to provide good mental, physical and social welfare for the disabled. Their quality of life is at stake. When the health of an elderly seriously injured veteran deteriorates, he must be helped as a whole person. In after-care the health problems of an injured veteran should not be separated into those caused by war service and those having no connection. Because of their grave disability, the veterans need extra medical services compared with the ordinary population.

Home care

The best place, even for the seriously-handicapped elderly veteran is generally his own home. This presupposes, however, that his general health is relatively good and that the possibility to receive adequate help exists. In addition, a veteran and his/her spouse should be mentally harmonious and prepared for home care. If the condition of the veteran with moderate or severe injury deteriorates and he needs help and observation round-the-clock, home care is usually too exhausting for relatives. The deterioration may be temporary, but recovery may be delayed. For this reason he/she needs regular medical follow-up, with a high standard of medical examination and treatment. Other possibilities for receiving help are rehabilitation as an outpatient or in an institution, day-hospital treatment and periodic or long-term institutional care. It is very important to perform comprehensive medical and social assessment to improve the diagnosis, treatment and placement. We should also examine the state of health and social situation of spouses, who have perhaps had a heavy burden through many years of taking care of their disabled spouse; they should also be given medical services, like rehabilitation.

Rehabilitation

The aim of rehabilitation is to improve the state of health and in a preventive context to keep it at an optimal level. Rehabilitation may be administered at an outpatient or institutional level. The former has more limited objectives, for example physio- or speech therapy.

The institutional rehabilitation period of, for example, 3–4 weeks consists of various measures including thorough medical examination and treatment, the checking of medicines previously prescribed, and therapy programmes according to the results of the examinations. Furthermore, an estimate should be made of social conditions and security at home, contacts with domiciliary care, possible stressful factors connected with the patient's absence from home, and the role of the institution in providing social activation and therapeutic atmosphere. The results of such treatment during a rehabilitation period can be dependent upon a number of factors, and the objective measuring of the treatment effects is difficult. Nevertheless, it has been documented that a high percentage, up to 50 per cent, of seriously injured veterans have felt great benefits from their rehabilitation period. Also the attending relatives could relax and renew themselves during the veteran's stay in rehabilitation.

Periodic and long-term institutional care

The aim of periodical institutional care is to supplement domiciliary care when the condition of the disabled deteriorates and he needs medical treatment and rehabilitation for a certain time. Long-term institutional care has to be of a high medial and social standard. The rehabilitating atmosphere is of great significance, and there must be individual social activation of the veteran. Attention should be paid to the training of institutional personnel so as to make them aware of the special nature of war injuries and the traumatic effects of war on an individual.

Summary

Disabled veterans may live up to 50 or more years as a disabled person. In different phases of their lives their medical and psychosocial requirements, to which they have to adjust, vary. At a young age they usually have enough capacity to get along in life. However, helplessness can only be compensated for by effort. When a veteran has a moderate or serious disability, his possibilities of coping with disorders decrease with aging. Many factors are influential here: normal aging, especially when over 75–80 years of age, brings about physical and mental deterioration and diseases with new disability in addition to war-health problems. This leads to large-scale helplessness and an increased need for receiving medical and psychosocial care: Measures to be considered should be:

- follow-up of general health state , high-standard medical diagnostics and treatment,
- follow-up of war injuries, high-standard diagnostics of their consequences and assessment of associated diseases. Special attention should be paid to problematic disorders, such as psychiatric disturbances and brain injuries.
- a veteran having moderate or severe disability needs to be treated as a whole, especially when he/she is burdened with new health problems in old age; medical and social care should be rendered on the basis of the veteran's condition irrespective of the connection with war injuries.

Implementation of rehabilitation-oriented medical and social after-care has created an even better quality of care for veterans suffering from a wide range of disabling conditions. This may help many older injured veterans to live as independently as possible in the community and maintain a good quality of life.

Propositions

Research

(1) Each country should carry out an epidemiological study among its disabled war veterans, providing data on number, age structure and their changes during the following years, and distribution according to such things as medical impairment and special injury groups.
(2) The consequences and associated diseases of war injuries should be examined and treated with high-standard modern medical methods and follow-up, with special emphasis on disorders that may have previously been hidden, even years after the initial war injury.
(3) The different countries should support the exchange of experiences and results of their scientific researches pertaining to long-term physical and mental health disorders of the war injured. The organization with the coordinating and activating role at an international level could be the World Veterans Federation.

Services

(1) Because the severely injured and aged veterans have increased needs for medical care, these needs should be met by developing medical and social services, such as domiciliary care, rehabilitation, periodic and long-term institutional care. The medical after-care needs of moderately and severely injured veterans should be seen as whole

and a service programme should be implemented pursuant to military laws.

(2) Governments should cooperate with the organizations representing disabled veterans and heed their advice when developing medical and social after-care for this group, since the disabled themselves know their needs best.

(3) Besides the improvement of medical services for the aging disabled veterans, economic and other social benefits should also be developed and not be subject to cuts. This socio-economic development should not, of course, be a substitute for their increasing need of medical and social services.

(4) Generally in domicilary care the wife has been responsible for attending to her severely injured husband over decades. This is an exceptionally heavy social duty. These spouses, who may later become widows, also grow old, with decreasing capacities and a worsening state of health. They should also have the right to receive free medical and social services.

REFERENCE

WISMIC News (1989)1(2): 10–11.

Address for correspondence
Kauniala Hospital for War-Injured Veterans, Kylpyläntie 19, FIN-02700 Kauniainen, Finland

30 WAR VETERANS

RISTO HYVÄRINEN

War veterans have always formed an importart part of a nation's population. The veterans have defended their society against other hostile nations or have in some instances acted as mercenaries fighting the wars of others. Wars have been waged for a variety of reasons yet, generally speaking, the soldiers involved in modern warfare fight because they believe that they are defending their own country or nation. When the war ends the former soldiers turns into veterans (if they have managed to survive); they may actually fight again in new wars and thus become veterans of several wars.

Members of resistance movements have often been treated as war veterans. It was typical of the Second World War (WW II) that many countries suffered enemy occupation and consequently developed resistance organizations within their own borders, producing great numbers of resistance veterans.

The veterans may be classified in many ways. An important distinction has always been between those who have served at the front line and others; a past as a fearless frontline fighter has always elevated the status of a veteran.

Victims of war who have not been in active service as soldiers are usually not included among veterans. Modern wars produce innumerable civilian casualties, for example: victims of bombings of all ages and war widows. Such groups usually form their own organizations and spheres of activity, as the social problems faced by them after a war are considerable.

Social context

Warfare has always been an important factor in social intercourse. The social class of knights and noblemen was an outcome of frequent hostilities and gradually developed into a hereditary division of labour. The task of the knights and noblemen was always clear and undisputed: to provide an armed defence for the society. The duty of other social groups during war was not at all as clear, although they could end up as victims as well as soldiers. Their fate was, however, a result of external circumstances, not of social class.

Since the time of the French Revolution warfare has developed increasingly towards total, industrialized war. This has led to a situation where all social groups are drawn as much as possible into the war effort. The actual battles still belong to the soldiers but the line grows increasingly difficult to draw.

The last two centuries have seen continuous attempts to define by means of international law some area within which warfare could be regulated but most have been in vain, and the difficulties will continue to increase. This fact is well illustrated by the many recent instances of complex ethnic warfare both in Europe and elsewhere. Some of the problems faced by veterans are directly related to such scenarios. International legislation will have to deal with them.

Wars fought by veterans naturally happen against a back-drop of politics as war constitutes the last resort in a drive to control an adversary. This holds true in regard to both international warfare and civil war. So far, the use of arms has been estimated as giving the best results in an open conflict situation, hopefully as a last resort.

Soldiers follow leaders, which means that the aims for which they have taken up arms have been set by the politicians or national governments. This is obvious if we look at the emergence and characteristics of nationalism, which has provided millions of soldiers in many wars with something to believe in as an excuse for warfare and as a powerful incentive to fight. This is true even today and especially where ethnic elements serve to strengthen nationalistic, religious, political or even paranoid feelings. The main emphasis is in all cases on the demand to follow the leader; where the soldiers refuse to obey orders from above the entire political character of a war changes.

The fact that the soldiers have served in extremely difficult and, indeed, life-threatening circumstances influences the immediate postwar atmosphere. It is a fundamentally traumatic experience to have fought in a war and to have survived, and the homecoming veterans are a large group. They continue, however, to follow their leaders. The outcome of the war may, of course, to some extent influence their outlook. After a defeat former leaders sometimes become targets of severe criticism, whereas the victorious ones may be elevated to priviledged positions in peacetime society: von Hindenburg, Eisenhower, de Gaulle, Mao Zedong. Veterans usually support the policies of the government. There are, however, some notable exceptions: for instance, during the 1917 Russian revolution large numbers joined the revolutionary army.

The veterans are a group within a society and they function within its bounds and culture, which in turn exert a strong influence upon the way they are treated. There are great cultural differences in this respect between various countries, which are also reflected in the armed forces as a whole; strategies, tactics and battle techniques may vary a great deal. Conversely, war is a great equalizer, and with the spread of modern warfare the armed forces everywhere are growing more and more alike.

Outright unnecessary cruelty is an aspect of war usually condemned by civilians. Efforts have been made to reduce in some respects the effects of violence connected with warfare. With the industrialization of modern warfare, the idea of war has come to be regarded in a negative light; the word itself in the western world has acquired a negative connotation. International law is now undergoing a development aimed at eliminating the most cruel aspects of armed hostilities, yet very little has actually been achieved. The veterans, however, are apt to believe in old ways of conflict resolution, that is to say coercion, especially if they have implemented them in their own wars. So great tensions exist but regrettably are not often brought out into open discussion.

There are, as might be expected, great differences of opinion as to which norms should govern armed conflict. According to the so-called western mind the Asian nations are historically, socially and genetically prone to exert extreme cruelty in war. Conversely, the Asian view of criminality is actually completely foreign to the western mind. In the aftermath of WW II the behaviour of the Japanese invaders was severely criticized in the West. Obviously, the memories of and reactions to cruelties performed during a war are only slowly forgotten and tend to remain highly controversial. On the other hand it is a fact that the actual war veterans, that is to say the former soldiers (many of them in the front line) have calmed down and many are now able to take a reasonably realistic view of the wars in which they were involved. There is also nowadays a great deal of communication between veterans' associations of different nations, even former enemy countries.

The special duties of soldiers have been the basis of the social status of the veterans. It is they who carry the heaviest burden in wartime. They face death and may die in battle. We praise the soldiers who have died heroically and who have managed to kill as many of the enemy as possible. Combatants have, so to speak, a licence to kill and war is largely legalized killing. In this function (killing) the armed forces stand very much apart and alone in society. As former soldiers veterans therefore occupy a highly visible social position. This is true in all countries except those that for some reason have no veterans, that is to say have not become veteran-conscious.

Compensation

The so-called fighting spirit is to a great extent dependent on the rewards to be expected after a successful battle. In modern times such rewards have consisted, for example, in donations of land, loot, money, powerful social positions, medals and badges of honour. As long as the war continues such promises of rewards are usually upheld, but soon forgotten when peace is signed. To put it more accurately, in a postwar economy badly weakened by war it becomes difficult to fulfil such promises. The demobilized veterans, however, do not as a rule forget.

The unique social position of the veterans, who after all have risked their lives in the service of their country, is, however, so strong that some kind of compensation has to be offered. This influences both the overall economy of the country and its domestic policy.

Rewards given to veterans may be seen by some groups as assets stolen from the rest of the population. This way of thinking does not necessarily create a conflict, especially when the number of veterans is small; even with larger groups of veterans it is generally felt that there are extremely good motives for special postwar treatment. When, however, the veterans are present in very large numbers both absolutely and relatively speaking, a conflict situation may arise between former soldiers and others.

Thus, the image of the veterans depends very much on their numbers. A detachment of the Finnish Guard (1000 men), took part in the 1877–78 Balkan War and were active as veterans after it without attracting problems in any way. On the contrary, they were regarded with the greatest admiration. But when the Finnish Armed Forces were demobilized after WW II and more than 600,000 soldiers were at one stroke transformed into veterans demanding all the privileges they felt belonged to them, the situation became highly problematic for a nation of less than four million.

The economic and social impact of the veterans is obviously dependent on postwar conditions in society. Continental Europe suffered grave damage during WW II as the armies rolled back and forth over it; many of its cities were bombed to the brink of total destruction, and the returning veterans faced a massive task of reconstruction that actually activated them as a group.

A rather different situation was faced by the United States. Postwar, public interest was now finally focused on global problems and on the demobilization and activation of the veterans who had fought on the European scene. Simultaneously the US grew more conscious of its international responsibility. The armed forces were actually given many international tasks.

In countries where the returning veterans were numerous, they formed a significant part of the older age-groups. As years passed, with peace prevailing, the question arose whether veterans' privileges should be extended to other elderly age-groups. The social respect afforded those who had participated in the war diminished as time passed and the postwar period receded.

How to meet the veterans' demands for various privileges promised them is an important issue of economic policy and its handling may well affect the future electoral prospects of the governing parties. If the war has ended in defeat it may be difficult to get general support for veterans' privileges. This was the case in many WW II countries, while such privileges were awarded in the victorious countries more than elsewhere; the United States, for example, has looked after its veterans in a praiseworthy manner.

Finland deserves special mention in connection with WW II. The country's domestic and foreign affairs are clearly reflected in matters relating to veterans. After a lost war the postwar period was grim and fraught with economic and social problems. As to the returning veterans, a large group were awarded so called veterans' building lots, medical and other care was arranged for invalids, while some groups went without special compensation. The wishes of the victors had to be met. Thus, regular veterans' associations were slow to be formed and only after about two decades did they gain a foothold and start to grow. By then, veterans had begun to claim compensation for their long years in the armed forces during WW II and for the suffering endured. Immediately after the war they received very little support for their claims, but as the political scene grew more stable and predictable in the 1980s and 1990s they profited from the change in atmosphere and received somewhat better economic support. The privileges of Finnish war veterans are at this moment comparatively very high level.

Veterans may have been hurt or unhurt physically and mentally but they are, above all, survivors. They could be named non-casualties, that is to say missed targets of the hostilities. Many of them are disabled: it has been estimated that about two-thirds of the casualties are lightly or seriously wounded. The maximum strength of the Finnish

Armed Forces during WW II exceeded 600,000, out of which the wounded comprised about 200,000; the total number of dead was over 90,000.

Disabled war veterans almost without exception receive special treatment. In addition to medical care they are helped and supported in many other ways. They receive an annuity dependent on the seriousness of their disability. In Finland the annuity is not very large, but is a proof of society´s respect, and valued as such. This is also the case in other European countries.

Veterans' associations

Veterans have many common interests. It seems therefore quite natural that sooner or later they should have begun to form associations. The first were founded in England after the Napoleonic wars; later in the 19th century similar associations were set up in Germany where they even began to assume some political significance.

During the following century and more especially after WW I interest in forming such associations grew worldwide. The American Legion was founded in the United States, Stahlhelm in Germany, the British Legion in England and Associazione Nazionale Combattenti in Italy, to mention just a few. The activity of the veterans' associations focused on political and economic issues. The veterans seemed generally to be inclined to support militaristic strivings, which may seem understandable in that period.

WW II gave rise to very strong emotions of various kinds. The veterans' associations were also involved in this turmoil of hate, envy and mutual accusations. This atmosphere led to a catastrophic situation which slowed down the peaceful development of the associations. This should be kept in mind when the work of the World Federation of Veterans is evaluated. The federation was founded soon after WW II by the veterans of the winning side. German and Japanese veterans and veterans from their allied countries were not invited to the first meeting of the federation in Paris 1950. The founding group was restricted, as the socialist countries as a whole did not join, irrespective of their affiliation during the war. NATO had been founded the previous year, in 1949.

The World Federation of Veterans (Federation Mondiale des Anciens Combattants) embarked upon a more global development during the 1950s. It acquired in the UN the so-called consultative status that may be extended to non-governmental organizations. The federation is not made up of government representatives, yet nevertheless separate governments have a great deal of influence over it. Its members are its member associations worldwide. There may be several member associations for any one country. Finland at the moment has four such bodies. Voting in the federation takes place according to countries, that is to say each member country has one vote. Its use has to be decided among the membership associations of the country as an entity.

Our contemporary history is reflected in the history of the federation. The influence of the UN is evident. The victorious western powers of WW II have also put their stamp on the activity of the federation. Many resistance movements joined. Holland was much involved in supporting the organization. By and by new forms of activity were added to the agenda as the Cold War subsided and new patterns formed on the international scene.

Among new members during the 1970s were many organizations having their roots in fairly recent armed conflicts. The leading position of the western industrialized countries was gradually weakened as Third World veterans marched into the limelight. The status of the socialist countries grew. The World Federation of Veterans began increasingly to resemble the UN.

In principle the federation works to support all matters relating to veterans' privileges, such as health care, rehabilitation, international law and military courts. Other lines of action can also be discerned as considerations of domestic policy give rise to rather strange suggestions. Leading posts in the organization are seen as desirable for many reasons, of which influence on the distribution of funds is not the least. The Third World, for instance, is often in need of economic support.

The question of language has assumed some importance within the federation although it is seldom referred to officially. France and the French-speaking nations are in a very strong position. This is partly an outcome of tradition, as the federation was founded in Paris 1950, where its headquarters remain today. The fact that the French chairman of the federation, Serge Wourgaft, was also its Secretary-General has made the French influence felt throughout the organization. In december 2000 the Federation elected a new chairman, Mr Abdul Ibrahim of Malaysia.

The federation has about 150 member organizations from 79 member countries. This makes for a very great number of individual members: no fewer than 27 million. Nowadays the federation may correctly be called global, or at least nearly global. It is to be remembered that only countries that have veterans are eligible. There are two important exceptions to this rule: the People's Republic of China and the Democratic Republic of Korea. The number of veterans there number many millions but have yet to organize themselves and reach the point where they will be able to send a membership application to the world body. It is possible that the already-existing membership of the Republic of China (= Taiwan) and Korea (South Korea) have been a hindrance.

Veterans' associations may also exist in countries which have taken part in wars or other kinds of armed conflict but nevertheless do not belong to the world federation. The relationships between various associations within one country may take different forms. There are usually not one but several such associations. In former eastern Europe there are usually three types of veterans' associations: one for veterans who fought for the Soviet Union; one for those who fought on the German side; and, additionally, other organizations. To reconcile their conflicting interests has not been an easy task.

Alongside the above-mentioned, there have at times emerged what could be called traditional associations in which the veterans have joined. They usually represent old values and goals that used to be embraced by the veterans. It is often difficult to fit them into the day-to-day activities of the veterans' associations, which are streamlined to further mainly the interests of the frontline veterans.

Heroes of war – after death

Some soldiers are killed in battles. Others survive to die later of so-called natural causes. The respect of society towards the fallen soldiers is clearly reflected in the burial rites accorded to them. The customs of the country as such also influence such burial rites: cremation is generally practised by nations of the Far East, whereas the Christian countries show a variety of burial customs.

The graves of the heroes of war often turn into political instruments. It is worth pointing out some factors influencing the choice of graveyards. Finland sent her war heroes all the way home if possible. On the other hand, countries that fought their wars far away from home had, for practical reasons, to bury their dead fairly close to the battleground. The procedure in such cases was usually to build a beautiful and large cemetery in some suitable place adorned with a big memorial stone into which the names of the dead heroes were carved.

The number of men killed in great wars is always enormous. Graveyards and monuments commemorating soldiers killed in WW II abound all over Europe: it is estimated that there are 2.2 million dead Germans buried inside the areas of the former Soviet Union; Germany has more than 250,000 war cemeteries in the area of former military operations; in the former Soviet Union the military graveyards are now being concentrated into 50 very large burial grounds (such a concentration of cemeteries has already taken place in France), and in Finland there are altogether about 70 monuments to Russian and Soviet war heroes.

Most countries try to keep alive the memory of their war heroes. In the German town of Kassel this task is fulfilled by a great centre sponsored by various civic organizations with hundreds of employees. In Italy and France such duties are taken care of by the ministries concerned. In Russia civic organizations such as Memorial and Obelisk work together with official authorities to maintain the dignity of and respect for the memories of those killed in the war. Veterans' associations in all countries are working in the same way and for the same goals.

Address for correspondence
Sarfsalö 14 C, 07780 Härpe, Finland

31 | PAST TRAUMA PERSISTING IN THE PRESENT

The Survivors of Earlier Wartime Trauma in Old Age

LINDA HUNT

The range of difficulties experienced by older survivors is described and the evidence of the extent of problems persisting decades after the end of war is summarized. It is suggested that a conspiracy of silence has prevailed in both social and political discourse. This reinforces the difficulties for survivors since it is clear that it is essential for those experiencing symptoms of post-traumatic stress disorder over the long term to confront and work through what has happened to them if they are to achieve a calmer, more satisfactory phase of life. This process of consciously thinking things through can be a painful and difficult experience, in which people usually require skilled professional help.

That the destructive consequences of war persist long after the treaties have been signed and the bomb craters have been filled in is very clear. They are apparent and problematic in the political, economic and environmental spheres. At the individual and family levels too, the awful, life-long, consequences for many people are visible and obvious, because of the physical injuries they have sustained. The long-term crippling psychological damage of traumatic experience of war is not so easy to see and has received much less attention. This chapter aims to show the significance for many elderly people of the damage and disruption from which they continue to suffer as a result of the personal, psychological traumas that they experienced as children and young adults, civilians and combatants, during wars which were fought decades ago. Reference will also be made to the fact that this damage and disruption can also have a negative impact on the children born, after the war is ended, to the victims of trauma.

The immediate impact of wartime trauma is beginning to be better understood and sound working definitions of what constitutes trauma and the associated post traumatic stress disorder (PTSD) have been formulated (see Chapter 27). Treatment services that help people in the immediate aftermath of traumatic experiences are now more readily available, particularly in the western world, for example to military personnel and aid workers. Recent conflicts, for example in Bosnia, Kosova and Rwanda, have also forced a more general acknowledgement that adult civilians and children can be victims of traumatizing experiences as a result of bombing, imprisonment, persecution or evacuation (see Chapter 27). However, it is only slowly beginning to be accepted that the impact of traumatic experience may not be transitory or even short-term. It is emerging, little by little, that severe symptoms of PTSD may persist over a number of years and that for some people who have apparently made good recoveries, the symptoms return many years later and in a most severe form.

It was not until 1965, 20 years after the end of the Second World War (WW II) that an article was published which acknowledged that what had been thought to be transitory problems experienced by some former WW II armed forces personnel were, in fact, proving to be persistent.[1] In the years that have followed, little research has been undertaken and many victims of trauma from that war have continued to suffer in silence, the cause of their problems and, frequently, the problems themselves, remaining hidden. However, clinical and anecdotal evidence increasingly point to a significant level of problems among elderly people who, many years ago (as children or young adults), had traumatic experience of war. In late life Bruno Bettelheim and Primo Levi both noted that, although they had written books in which they worked through some of their own Second World War concentration camp experiences, they were still burdened in old age by the after-effects of their war traumas.[2] Thirty years after his experience of persecution Levi wrote that 'memory of the offence persists, as though carved in stone, prevailing over all previous or subsequent experiences'.

It is not always easy to understand the implications of wartime trauma. This is especially the case for those of us whose life experience is distant in time, culture or social structure from that of a society involved in war. Novels can help to fill the gap, providing a vivid insight into the long-term effects of the trauma. One remarkable recent publication gives a moving account of the life of one person who was a child victim of war time trauma and of another man deeply affected by the trauma experienced by his parents before his birth.[3] This book illustrates with great clarity just how long-lasting and how destructive the effects of such traumas can be.

The nature and significance of past war trauma in old age

The following examples are typical of the sorts of situation with which people who are now elderly have been living for decades.

Example 1

To survive mentally is sometimes more difficult than to survive physically. Survivors are people apart, burdened by memories and past trauma. For us survivors there is no escape from the memories ...

This comment was made in 1998 by a 73-year-old man, reflecting on his situation more than 53 years after his release from Auschwitz. This man continues to have nightmares and flashback incidents in which he re-experiences events to which he was subjected while he was imprisoned in that camp in 1944 and 1945. He says that there are times when:

I am literally afraid to close my eyes because of the images that will flash before me if I do; waking is full of fear, too, because it is sometimes accompanied by a most dreadful feeling of emptiness, heaviness and sickness.

Example 2

A woman in her early seventies was referred to a psycho-geriatrician in 1995 with symptoms of depression and anxiety; in middle and earlier old age she had attempted suicide on three occasions and she was again expressing suicidal thoughts. In interview it emerged that as a young woman, living with her two small children while her soldier husband was away at the front with his regiment, her house was damaged during an enemy bombing raid. With the raid continuing she ran from the house in panic, only realizing that she had left her children inside when she was a little distance from the building. The children died and she was left with an overwhelming burden of guilt and remorse. She had never been able to come to terms with her behaviour, but although it was constantly in her mind, up until this point, 53 years later, she had told no one the true story of what had happened that night. She had not even been able to tell her husband of the events which had so dominated the rest of their lives and that of their family.

Example 3

A 61-year-old man, referred to a psychiatrist in 1996, described nightmares which he has two or three times every week. These are detailed re-enactments of actual events that he experienced 48 years earlier, as a young conscript soldier. In one recurring nightmare he is driving through the jungle with three other soldiers, one of whom is his close friend. They are caught in an ambush and his three companions are all shot dead. He jumps from the vehicle and crawls under it, where he remains hidden all night. When he wakes from this nightmare he is lying on the floor under his bed, drenched in sweat, terrified and with his heart pounding. If his wife is nearby he often shouts to her to 'get under cover'. When he wakes from a nightmare it always takes him some minutes to regain his sense of present reality.

Example 4

A woman, now 60, with the support of her counsellor, began to talk, for the very first time, of the pain and distress that had been locked within her for the 50 years since her parents disappeared. She was ten when they were taken away, while she crouched nearby, in the cupboard in which they had hidden her. She never saw her parents again, years later discovering that they had been imprisoned and then killed. She was taken in by other people and kept hidden in a cellar for the rest of the war. She was given adequate food, but otherwise was left alone there for months. After the war she made a life for herself, married and had children, but felt she must never speak about her traumatic experiences or the way in which they continued to haunt her waking life. A family crisis which reactivated feelings of anxiety and helplessness in a frightening situation that was not of her own making acted as the trigger which prompted her to seek to talk for the first time.

These four examples illustrate the variety of sources of wartime trauma and of situations in which older people continue to struggle with the consequences of their traumatic experience. They demonstrate features which are typical of older people still living with the presence of their trauma decades after their particular war is over. The two men described frequently re-experience events. That is to say, they are not simply recalling painful memories, but in their nightmares perceive themselves to be involved in the events all over again. The same events are regularly re-experienced in a remarkably unchanged form for years and all the physical responses to danger, fear and anxiety usually continue to be present. On waking, the current environment is perceived in terms of the re-experienced event, thus in example 3 the man, at home in his bedroom, instructs his wife to protect herself from enemy forces. These phenomena are common, but are frequently not recognized as related to earlier trauma. Indeed they are often misunderstood or thought to be indicators of mental confusion in elderly people.

All of the examples illustrate that these elderly people have been living with persistent cripplingly-painful emotions associated with horrifying earlier experiences, yet they have also had the courage to get on with their lives– to marry, develop careers and bring up families. When a war is over the urgent need, at both individual and societal levels, is to find ways of making ends meet, to rebuild communities and to reconstruct family life. There is little time or energy to attend to the internal turmoil and distress that are consequences of traumatic wartime experience. The two women in the examples had actually kept their suffering hidden, and this, too, is a common feature. It is particularly unhelpful that this should be so, as research has shown that keeping silent is associated with severe persistent problems.[4] The obverse of this point is also true: clinical experience indicates that opportunities to talk about the traumatic events and their consequences are an essential element in coming to terms with events and overcoming any associated problems.

There are several factors that interact together to keep victims of trauma silent. First, they have usually been given the strong message by their own relatives and friends that they should put their experience behind them rather than focus on it through talking about it. The people around them make it clear that they do not want to hear 'upsetting' stories.

People in positions of authority have tended to reinforce this kind of message. For example, in Britain, at the end of WW II, civilians and members of the armed forces were frequently advised to forget about what had happened to them and told by those in authority (for example, health-care professionals, armed services advisers) not to talk about their bad experiences. In Britain, and in other countries affected by the Second World War and the Nazi-inspired Holocaust which accompanied it, it was expected that people would 'pull themselves together'. The impression was given that exhibiting distress, anxiety or other behavioural symptoms was not socially acceptable. To some extent this orientation has persisted down the years and it may be that governments and the military have some interest in the maintenance of this sort of culture, since a greater general awareness of the horrific experiences to which many people have been exposed in war and the extent to which their subsequent lives (and those of their children) are damaged by these experiences may create an unwelcome necessity to acknowledge the extent of wartime trauma and the significance of its consequences. In passing, it should be noted that it could be important to monitor whether the more open approach adopted by those in authority in South Africa, through the Truth and Reconciliation Commission, serves not only to heal divisions between communities but also to help individuals, both victims and perpetrators, to overcome or lessen the long-term problems associated with past trauma that are described in this chapter.

In the face of the social pressures described above, victims of trauma quickly learn to keep their problems to themselves. Indeed, they often become afraid they may harm other people, including those who might be able to offer support or help, if they speak about their war experience and the continuing distress it is causing them. For many survivors this fear is exacerbated by a sense that they are only just managing to hold themselves together in the face of their internal turmoil and distress and that if they allow any of their inner feelings to burst out, they may actually disintegrate. Earlier chapters in this volume describe the disjunction between past, present and future that follows wartime trauma and the internal confusion that this causes the person affected. The kinds of extreme experience that are traumatizing overturn morality; innocence is lost; and moral and cultural frameworks and expectations are thrown into disarray. In the face of such situations, people may survive by denial: by redefining the unacceptable as acceptable; the abnormal as normal. To be struggling with all this year after year, to feel you have overcome the confusion and pain of war trauma, only to find it all resurgent in old age, are the disabling, damaging facts of life for many survivors. It is not at all surprising that they become frightened of what might happen if they begin to tell their story or that they keep it hidden, even although doing this increases their sense of isolation from friends and family and reduces the possibility of working towards the resolution of their difficulties.

Another factor constraining many survivors is the guilt they feel because they have survived when others did not. In youth and mid-life this is much less of a factor, because of the sense of triumph people have about having come out alive and because of their hopes for the future. But in old age, when people are faced with new losses – the death of those close to them; retirement from work; deteriorating health – and begin to realize that their life will also be coming to an end, there is little of triumph left. It is common then for thoughts to focus on the chance factors that enabled them to survive; on their own sense of unworthiness, in comparison with what they think of as the greater worth of others who did not survive; on what they feel was their failure to do enough to help save others, even when the reality is that they did all that it was possible to do. For some people, their preoccupation becomes the fact that during the war they committed acts which they now regard as immoral and which caused unnecessary injury or death for others. Older survivors who were children at the time of war and part of whose trauma is related to their forced separation from their parents, the reasons for which they could not possibly understand at the time, may still be struggling with the painful feeling that somehow they did something wrong themselves which actually made the separation, and all that followed, happen. As a result, confused feelings of guilt and unworthiness may pervade their lives, alongside anger and confusion about what happened to them.

Another group of older survivors for whom guilt is an especially powerful factor are women who have been subjected to sexual abuse at the hands of soldiers of the opposing army (see also Chapter 26). For example, it is not unusual for Dutch survivors who, as young women prisoners, were used as prostitutes or subjected to serial rape by the soldiers acting as guards in prison camps in Indonesia during WW II to be so burdened by guilt and shame that more than 50 years after release from the camps they have told no one of their experience or of the ways in which it has continued to affect their sexual/marital and other relationships down the intervening years. The intensity of guilt and shame often experienced by older survivors makes many feel that they have no right to relief from the consequences of their traumatic experience of war, that they should not talk about them or seek any help with lightening the emotional load that burdens them.

In summary, the situation of many of the older people who are still living with the consequences of earlier wartime traumas and dominated by the struggle to make sense of what has happened to them is one of distressing flashbacks and of crippling guilt and anxiety. It is also a situation in which they are often particularly isolated with their inner turmoil; in some significant way cut off, even from their closest friends and family.

A common problem?

Clearly, living with the burden of these difficulties over several decades and into old age has a profound influence on the quality of the lives of the people directly affected. The impact on the lives of their spouses and children is also serious, since the struggle to survive the trauma affects the survivors' capacity for open, intimate relationships and thus, their capacity to be 'good enough' partners and parents. The question of how many people suffer wartime experience that is so extreme as to be traumatic, with the consequent elements of PTSD persisting into, or re-emerging in, old age is, then, an important one. There is also a second important question to consider – to what extent are the children of victims of war trauma also damaged?

The research that would allow the provision of clearcut answers to these questions has not been carried out. Much of the work that has been done relates to WW II and can only act as an indicator of the total situation. This war was brought to an end in 1945 (more than 55 years ago), which means that all those directly affected are either already in the elderly age group or rapidly moving into it. The advantage of drawing on work which relates to this particular war is, therefore, that it should be possible to elicit a fairly complete picture of the position of older survivors.

In many countries in Europe and the Far East, whole populations were affected by this war and vulnerable to traumatic experiences, the emotional costs of which had to be paid throughout their subsequent lives. Civilian populations were vulnerable in occupied countries and in those still free to mobilize their military forces; members of armed forces were vulnerable both as combatants and as prisoners of war.

One country (the Netherlands) that was occupied from 1941 until 1945 has produced some useful research data.[5] There, it has been estimated that about one million people born before 1945 and still living in 1995 have been exposed to wartime violence. This means that 15 per cent of the population born before 1945 in that country can be described as 'war victims', although it cannot be assumed that all were traumatized by their war experience. A further Dutch study has shown that in 1995 approximately 10 per cent of a more or less representative sample of the Dutch population aged 60–72 years was still frequently affected by distressing memories of war (in this instance relating either to WW II or to the Dutch colonial war in Indonesia, 1947–49) and 5 per cent still met the criteria for a diagnosis of PTSD.[6] Of the remainder of the sample, a further 24 per cent regularly took action to avoid reminders of the war, indicating some continuing problems associated with their wartime experience. The large majority of people still suffering the after-effects of war in the Netherlands are civilians. They include people who were prisoners in camps in Indonesia and in the Netherlands, people in hiding and members of the civilian resistance, and ordinary civilians subjected to abuse, privation or bombing.

In some other countries significant proportions of the older male population have had experience of combat as members of the armed forces involved in WW II. In the USA, in 1994, it was estimated that 25 per cent of the men over the age of 55 had served in combat.[7] In Britain, and some other countries, the proportion must be higher than this. Among armed forces personnel the incidence of wartime trauma and PTSD are positively associated with the severity of combat experience and this also seems to be true for those still struggling with that trauma decades later. Small-scale studies carried out in recent years consistently indicate a high level of distress among veterans of this war and suggest that 40 and more years after the war had ended as many as 16–18 per cent of former combatants still met the diagnostic criteria for PTSD.[8]

Members of the armed forces who were also prisoners of war are rather more likely to meet these criteria, even at this distance in time. Recent literature, such as the account by Lomax of his personal struggle, over nearly 50 years, to confront and overcome the damage caused by his traumatic experience of imprisonment and torture in Singapore and along the Burma railway, makes vividly clear the severity of the problems faced by former prisoners of war.[9] Studies that have been reported in recent years suggest that 30 per cent or more of former prisoners of war are likely to have difficulties severe enough still to meet the criteria for a diagnosis of PTSD.[10] Again, it is suggested that these most persistent, severe problems are positively correlated with greater severity of physical and psychological hardship, but also with lower military rank.

Another group of people who survived traumatizing imprisonment of the most severe kind during WW II are those who have survived experience of Nazi concentration camps. The evidence of continuing severe distress is very clear and it has been estimated that something like 52 per cent of these survivors still met the criteria for a diagnosis of PTSD in 1992.[11] Some understanding of the degree of the contamination of present life by past experience of these concentration camps can be gained from personal accounts. Such accounts can movingly demonstrate the individual struggles pursued down the decades in an effort to overcome the damage to the sense of identity, to emotional health and to the capacity to make relationships that are the consequences of brutal separations of parents from children and husband from wife, of extreme hunger and privation, of imprisonment and of torture. For younger people and for those who have little knowledge of the historical and social circumstances of wartime trauma, this kind of literature is perhaps critical in enabling a real understanding of the situations with which so many older survivors of wartime trauma are still having to struggle.

While the evidence is incomplete, the case is incontrovertibly made. It is clear that significant numbers of older people are now, 55 years after the end of WW II, still living their lives under its dark shadow. Their postwar children have been born and brought up under that same shadow. There is now growing clinical evidence that they, too, have been damaged by that experience. For example, at the national centre for the treatment of victims of war trauma in the Netherlands (Centrum 45), already, by 1992, 10 per cent of the people coming for help were born after the end of WW II to parents who had been victims of horrifying wartime experience. By 1997, this figure had jumped to 24 per cent. Other agencies in Europe providing specialist services to survivors of wartime trauma are reporting increasing need of help among this second generation, too. The needs of this group are likely to go on increasing for some time, as the individuals reach middle and old age themselves and the urgency to solve old problems increases.

Of course, WW II is only one of a large number of wars fought over the last half century or so. There is every reason to believe that all of these wars will have resulted in similar long-term damage as a consequence of the traumatic experiences to which people have been subjected. Indeed, there is some evidence that experience in the Vietnam War is leading to long-term distress of the kind described in this chapter. There have been other fearsome experiences of violence, bombing and evacuation in many parts of the world, but rather little is known of their impact. For example, the violence, migration and destruction of communities that took place at the time that the two states of Pakistan and India were created in 1947 deeply affected many people. Little is known of the extent to which these were traumatizing experiences or of the continuing emotional and social difficulties of the people affected, most of whom will now be elderly. Right across the world, many more examples could be identified of war and violent terrorism that have left people struggling with the awful consequences of their traumatic experiences. We can only make informed guesses as to the number of the courageous older people there are who have contributed to the rebuilding of families and communities, while struggling year after year with the distress caused by their earlier wartime traumas.

Old age: a time of difficulty and opportunity

This chapter has emphasized the crippling nature of the distress many people have lived with for decades and the factors that reinforce the difficulties of breaking through the unhelpful conspiracy of silence that prevents people from talking through what has been happening to them. It has also highlighted the fact that in old age it is common to experience a resurgence of the emotional turmoil that was the earlier consequence of wartime trauma. This resurgence is often associated with other difficult life events, such as the death of family members, loss of employment or a serious illness.

Old age is a time of change and review. It is a phase of life during which people review their experience, their achievements and failures, opportunities taken and missed.[12] It is the time, too, when people recognize their own mortality and seek to move towards a good ending for their lives. Inevitably, for those people who have not yet found a way to come to terms with their earlier traumatic experience of war, whose lives are dominated by their own continuing post-traumatic stress, or who have not been able to understand or deal with aspects of their lives because of the pressures of growing up the child of parents traumatized by their war experience, the normal change and review process is made much more difficult and painful. The consequent stress and turmoil may be acute and extreme. 'We must not allow ourselves to become locked in with our memories. If we keep them inside we will choke on them'. This is the view of the 73-year-old man quoted in example 1, above. He found it ironic and quite unexpected when he discovered, rather accidentally, that if he talked about and consciously thought through some of his terrifying wartime experiences, the nightmares reduced in frequency. As he put it: 'The process of making things conscious prevents me re-experiencing them through nightmares'. He describes himself as 'proof, beyond doubt' that stress-reduction and healing comes through talking about the past; through sharing the terrible experiences.

His view, that consciously confronting and talking through experience of war trauma is an essential element of the process of lessening the long-term consequences, is consistently confirmed in clinical practice. It seems that healing is dependent on a degree of conceptual integration of the traumatic experiences. This means achieving a sense of connection between the past and the present and a feeling that it is possible to move on and to develop. The treatment approaches that demonstrate most promise of helping focus on working towards the integration of the person's understanding of the trauma with the current situation and their life as a whole. This process is much more than simply abreacting. It requires the individual to confront and reprocess the emotions associated with the trauma and, by so doing, to reconstruct their life story. Engaging in this process is emotionally difficult, but once the trauma story can be told, the way is open for changing earlier interpretations of events and of reducing feelings of hopelessness and helplessness. Decades after trauma, finding that it is possible to tell the story without falling apart can be a liberating experience.

Just because life review is a normal aspect of aging, older people are particularly well-motivated to work on the problems associated with their traumatic experiences. Contrary to popular myth, older people can make very good use of skilled professional help which will enable them to confront the painful issues and work through distressing feelings. In other words they have the capacity to make the difficult journey from being a victim of wartime trauma to becoming the survivor of it. Professional practice with this group of elderly people is only now being developed but some promising approaches have now been described.[13] While further research is needed, it is already very clear that in old age, decades after the original war trauma, people can be helped with coming to terms with their earlier experience and with reaching a new, calmer, constructive phase of their lives.

Working towards a better future

There are still very few treatment services that are especially designed to help older people who have experience of trauma from long-ago wars. The Netherlands seems to have been one of the first countries in which the need for such provision was recognized. Centrum 45 was founded there 25 years ago and is one of the best developed specialist treatment facilities. It provides a range of specialist resources and offers outpatient, day and inpatient facilities. It manages to increase the number of people offered service year on year, but continues to have a long waiting list. Little by little, the average age of first referrals is rising too, even though the numbers of people born postwar, to parents who were victims of war, is rising sharply.

Treatment facilities in other countries are seldom developed in as coherent a form as at Centrum 45 and for many people in many places there are no specialist services and few health and social-care professionals with skills or commitment to work with older people still struggling with earlier trauma. It is clear that if a larger proportion of the older people whose lives are still profoundly affected by the consequences of their wartime trauma are to be helped to achieve a less-distressed, more peaceful phase of life, then a much greater general recognition of the extent to which post-traumatic stress persists has to be achieved. If the long-term nature of the stress and the distress can be accepted at the political level and among the professional groups working in health and social care services, it will become possible to reach out to more people, and to finance more treatment services and the research that it is still necessary to carry out. General acceptance of the extent of the problem of persistent distress arising from wartime trauma will also help in the larger, long-term enterprise of discovering ways by which that trauma can be prevented.

General acknowledgement of the fact that wartime trauma has the potential not only to be such a persistent problem for those who have experienced it, but to extend its damage further, to the next generation, might also help to promote serious consideration of how far earlier war trauma can reach into society as a whole. To what extent is it possible for wartime trauma to be so extensive in its impact on a population that cultural attitudes and expectations are created and maintained which hold the abnormal to be normal; the unspeakably horrific to be commonplace – in short, to take the position that the world in which they live is so unstable and dangerous that they must have at the centre of their thinking the need to stave off the next attack from the 'enemy'? The answer to this question is not known but traumatic experience is, by its nature, unexpected, so if extensive experience of wartime trauma within a population did create such a culture, that culture might contain a high level of uncertainty about where the next attack would arise, and a tendency to anticipate ill-will on the part of any group seen as outsiders. As one wartime-trauma survivor has commented in conversation: 'After the end of hostilities there was a continuing fear of renewed persecution. This made it very difficult to find a way back into some kind of normal conventional life in a society that had already shown such hostility to us'. Could it be, for example, that after nearly 30 years of violence in Northern Ireland, people become locked into living their lives as if more horrifying experiences are inevitably imminent and so must be anticipated? Given the level of war and its associated violence that continually disrupted areas of the world in the half-century since the end of WW II, this is perhaps a question that should now be examined. Are there parts of the world where this culture and orientation could be the dominant feature of society? If this turned out to be the case, the urgency of providing help to enable war victims to become survivors, the need to consider the consequences of traumas on the children of victims, and the importance of addressing the extent to which older people are still struggling with the impact on them of their wartime traumas in their present lives, become very much greater at a societal level as well as at the level of the individuals and families directly affected.

ACKNOWLEDGEMENT

This chapter draws substantially on material contributed to the book *Past Trauma in Late Life* (1997), published by Jessica Kingsley Publications. I owe a debt of gratitude to all the contributors who worked with me on that book. Thanks are also due to the publisher.

REFERENCES

1. Archibald, H. and R. Tudenham (1965), 'Persistent Stress Reactions after Combat: a 20-year follow-up', *Archives of General Psychiatry* 12: 475–81.
2. Sutton, N. (1995), *Bruno Bettelheim: the other side of madness*, London: Gerald Duckworth & Co. Ltd; and Levi, Primo (1986), *Moments of Reprieve,*. London: Michael Joseph Ltd.
3. Michaels, A. (1997), *Fugitive Pieces*, London: Bloomsbury Publishing Plc.
4. Bramsen, I. (1995), *The Long-Term Adjustment of World War II Survivors in the Netherlands*, Delft: Eburon Press.
5. Centraal Bureau voor de Statistiek (1990), *Statistical Year Book 1990*, Den Haag: CBS.
6. See n. 4 above.
7. Spiro, A., Schnurr, P. and C. Aldwin (1994), 'Combat Related Post Traumatic Symptoms in Older Men', *Psychol. Ageing* 9 (1): 17–26.
8. See, for example, Blake, D., Keane, T., Wine, P., Mora, C., Taylor, K. and J. Lyons (1990), 'Prevalence of PTSD Symptoms in Combat Veterans Seeking Medical Treatment', *Journal of Traumatic Stress,* 3 (1): 15–27.
9. Lomax, E. (1995), *The Railway Man*, London: Vintage.
10. Speed, N., Engdahl, B., Schwartz J. and R. Eberly (1989), 'Post-traumatic Stress Disorder as a Consequence of POW Experience', *Journal of Nervous and Mental Diseases* 177 (3): 147–53.
11. See, for example, Kuch, K. and B. Cox (1992), 'Symptoms of PTSD in 124 Survivors of the Holocaust', *American Journal of Psychiatry* 149 (3): 337–40.
12. Butler, R. (1963), 'The Life Review: an interpretation of reminiscence in old age', *Psychiatry* 26: 65–76.
13. Hunt, L., Marshall, M. and C. Rowlings (eds) (1997), *Past Trauma in Late Life*, London: Jessica Kingsley Publications.

Address for correspondence
7 West Castle Road, Edinburgh EH10 5AT, United Kingdom
Tel: 00-44-131-229 6151; email: wetse002@wxs.nl

IV SOCIAL STRUCTURES IN CONNECTION WITH WARS

'Land mine victim'
Oliver Whitehead

32 ARMS TRADE AND PERCEPTIONS OF SECURITY

THOMAS A. CARDAMONE, JR

As we enter the 21st century, and the bipolar struggles of the Cold War slip further into history, states must re-examine their traditional conceptions of security. While a strong military is a necessity in today's world, threats from within can be just as destabilizing as those from outside a country's borders. Especially in the case of developing nations, which purchase the bulk of the world's conventional weapons each year, fiscal decisions weighing expenditures on guns or butter are gaining in importance. Analysts, government planners and international institutions are beginning to understand the importance of health care, schooling and stable economies as a function of security. This chapter utilizes statistics from two recent studies: a USA report on the global arms trade; and UN-country rankings based on development levels, to demonstrate that, for many countries, breaking the old habit of equating guns with security has yet to be achieved.

It could be argued that the old maxim 'peace through strength' actually worked for the United States. The US won the Cold War essentially by out-spending the Soviet Union on military technology while simultaneously maintaining a high standard of living. Stealth bombers, advanced attack jets and a vast array of nuclear weapons were developed and produced while Americans enjoyed the benefits, relative to the USSR, of a vibrant economy. For developing nations, however, with investment capital at a minimum and a plethora of chronic social problems to contend with, such dual-track spending is not an option. Nevertheless, the traditional equation of weapons-equals-strength continues to dominate the thinking of security planners the world over.

But as we enter the 21st century, new measurements are being used to determine which countries are secure and which are not. Growing global economic competition is beginning to supplant the notion of achieving strength solely through military means. The need to keep expenditures on military equipment in balance with domestic spending is slowly being seen as the mark of a strong nation. Other factors, primarily economic in nature, are also recognized as vitally important to national power. Issues of employment, inflation and trade, as well as access to health services, schools and clean water, will be the superstructure upon which strong nations are built in the coming decades.

Some analysts have begun to examine the traditional definition of security viewed through the prism of current events and conclude that focusing on well-protected territorial borders is not the only valid determinant of security. Professor Michael Klare of Hampshire College in Massachusetts believes that economic and social stresses can cripple the stability of a nation. Writing in *Current History*, Klare notes that 'many of the most severe and persistent threats to global peace and stability are arising not from conflicts between major political entities but from increased discord within states'.[1] Klare points to poor economic, social and environmental factors as being the catalyst for internal dissent.

Some governments are also beginning to use new criteria to judge security levels. As Jessica Mathews, a senior fellow at the Council on Foreign Relations, wrote in *Foreign Affairs*, the governmental concept of what constitutes security appeared to be changing, or was beginning to catch up with social changes as the 20th century came to a close. The idea of 'human security', she notes, 'is creeping around the edges of official thinking, suggesting that security be viewed as emerging from the conditions of daily life – food, shelter, employment, health, public safety – rather than flowing downward from a country's foreign relations and military strength.[2]

This shifting of official thinking may stem in part from a 1995 study conducted under the auspices of the USA Central Intelligence Agency (CIA). Titled the 'State Failure Task Force', researchers were tasked with identifying the underlying factors associated with the failure of national stability. One aim of the process was to determine if certain factors, or a combination of factors, could be seen to lead to instability, so that security planners might be better able to predict which governments were in the preliminary stages of crisis.

After more than 600 variables were examined in 113 cases of government collapse over a 50-year period, four measures – societal, economic, environmental and political – emerged as 'most likely to correlate with state failure,' according to the task force report.[3] Measurements such as high infant mortality rates, fluctuating inflation levels, little access to safe water and arable land, and undemocratic rule were key components of internal instability. While the report was quick to add that the models used in the study cannot predict state failure with certainty, there is value for policymakers in understanding the elements of failure so that policies might be implemented to prevent its occurrence. For instance, the report noted that 'broader measures aimed at raising general living standards associated with infant mortality. . . could play a significant role in reducing the risks of state failure'.[4] This point deserves to be underlined: the health status of the most vulnerable and least-represented group – children – can have an impact on the stability of an entire nation.

Additionally, international lending institutions have begun to examine the connection between military spending, economic development and stability. In August 1997, the International Monetary Fund (IMF) urged the Romanian government to scrap plans to spend US$1 billion on US-made Cobra attack helicopters because of the likelihood such spending would impede economic reforms. According to a report on the IMF's action in the *New York Times*, the fund believed spending on health and education to be more important to Romania's development.[5] Two months earlier the IMF also urged the US 'to administer their policies on military sales to developing and transition economy countries in a way that avoids encouraging unproductive expenditures and heightening security tensions'.[6]

Although analysts, some larger governments and international lending institutions have begun to reformulate their equations to determine security, how does this translate into actions by the governments most prone to internal collapse? Is spending on conventional arms beginning to wane? Is the concept of security beginning to change in developing nations? Studies show that while the level of the arms trade is down, that does not automatically translate to greater social development.

The arms trade today

Given the trend towards a growing recognition that national security is based in no small part on internal stability, the expectation is that a significant shift in governmental investment towards health or educational programmes would occur. But while the global levels of conventional arms sales have plummeted since the end of the Cold War (from US$54 billion in 1989 to just below US$32 billion in 1996) this drop cannot be attributed to social investment. The 40 per cent decline in the arms trade was driven primarily by economics, not policy. During the Cold War the Soviet Union (then the world's leading arms supplier) delivered billions of dollars in arms each year to its clients around the world at extremely favourable rates. This practice ended, and the value of worldwide arms exports dropped, when the Soviet Union collapsed and Moscow began to demand hard currency payments for its weaponry.

Coinciding with the drop in Soviet sales, the United States rose to be the world's predominant weapons supplier. After averaging approximately US$9 billion in sales in the last years of the Cold War, from 1990 to 1996 the US sold an average of US$16 billion in arms annually (see Table 32.1). This occurred during a time in which the threat of a superpower confrontation significantly diminished and politicians began to expound on the notion of a 'peace dividend', that is to say the reduction of military budgets with an increase in domestic spending.

According to William Keller, the deputy director of the Center for International Trade Strategy, the spread of weaponry actually accelerated in the 1990s. In the absence of a regional security justification, Keller writes in his book *Arm in Arm*, western nations have undergone a 'fundamental shift in the rationale for exporting powerful conventional weapons. Whereas arms exports once served to oppose Soviet power in the developing world, they are now necessary, at least according to their proponents in the United States, to provide jobs for Americans and to maintain the US military-industrial base'.[7] In effect, advanced weaponry is now seen as a legitimate commodity to be traded like any other.

Despite the great drop in global arms sales, developing nations continue to purchase the largest share of advanced conventional military equipment. According to the US

Table 32.1 Arms transfer agreements with the world, 1989–96 (in millions of 1996 dollars)

Country	1989	1990	1991	1992	1993	1994	1995	1996	TOTAL
United States	11715	23877	17896	23715	23928	13456	9230	11280	135095
Russia	18729	13615	6951	1979	2562	3859	8386	4600	60683
France	1812	3521	3812	7038	5338	9075	2761	3100	36458
UK	2296	2582	1233	2529	3523	1147	1023	4800	19134
China	1692	2582	673	550	641	834	205	500	7676
Germany	7129	2347	1906	1649	1068	1252	1943	200	17494
Italy	725	587	448	660	427	313	1125	400	4685
All other Eur.	5558	1995	2018	1869	961	2190	1636	1800	18029
All others	4350	3169	2242	2199	2242	1565	3886	5100	24754
Total	54006	54276	37180	42188	40691	33691	30195	31780	324007

Source: Richard F. Grimmett (1997), 'Conventional Arms Transfers to Developing Nations, 1989–1996', *CRS Report for Congress*, 13 August 1997, p. 79.

TABLE 32.2 Arms transfer agreements of developing nations in 1996 (in millions of 1996 dollars)

Rank	Recipient	Value
1	India	2500
2	Egypt	2400
3	Saudi Arabia	1900
4	South Korea	1200
5	Indonesia	1000
6	UAE	900
7	Qatar	800
8	Peru	800
9	Israel	800
10	Pakistan	700

Source: Richard F. Grimmett, 'Conventional Arms Transfers to Developing Nations, 1989–1996', *CRS Report for Congress*, 13 August 1997, p. 55.

Congressional Research Service, from 1993 to 1996, more than 63 per cent of all arms transferred were delivered to developing nations.[8] Therefore, the nations that presumably have the most difficulty in achieving the 'human security' levels described earlier are purchasing the greatest amount of weaponry. And, the CIA's 'State Failure Task Force' report notwithstanding, approximately 65 per cent of all US arms sales in 1996 went to developing countries.

An additional source of instability affiliated with the arms trade may also be emerging. According to a September 1997 report by the US government, the value of Military and Technical Assistance licences approved by the State Department totalled US$10 billion in fiscal year 1996. According to the Congressionally-mandated 655 Report, licences to sell design, engineering and manufacturing data for weapons systems were approved for Angola, Indonesia, Pakistan, Sri Lanka and some 60 other nations that year. While not every licence will necessarily result in a sale, such a potentially large transfer of weapons-related intellectual capital to developing nations can create an arms industry where none now exists and will limit the US government's ability to monitor how the technology is eventually used.

Internal security

Given the findings of the CIA's 'State Failure Task Force' report, and the fact that developing nations buy the greatest percentage of conventional weapons each year, an examination of the largest arms buyers' poverty rankings provide an illustrative look at some nations that could face internal security problems in the coming years.[9] Of the top ten arms purchasers among developing countries in 1996 (Table 32.2) two, India and Pakistan, are ranked by the United Nations Development Programme (UNDP) as having low human development.[10] Four nations, including Saudi Arabia, Peru, Indonesia and Egypt, were all ranked as having medium levels of development. The remaining four largest arms-buying nations, Israel, South Korea, the UAE and Qatar, were among nations with high development levels. The top ten developing nations listed in the Congressional Research Service weapons report purchased arms valued at US$13 billion, or 40 per cent, of all military equipment sold in 1996.

India led all developing nations in arms purchases from the US in 1996 with acquisitions valued at $2.5 billion. At the same time, the UN ranked India as 138 out of 175 nations in human development terms. According to the UNDP figures, of every 100,000 live births in India in 1990, 570 mothers died – a figure seldom seen outside the African continent. Other examples of general health levels showed that in 1995 more than 3.6 million Indian children perished before reaching their first birthday and, from 1990 to 1996, more than half the children under age five were reported as underweight.

Egypt was second in weapons purchases from the US in 1996, with US$2.4 billion in arms deals, and stood at 109 in the human development rankings. While the country's maternal mortality rate was somewhat better than that of India (170 per 100,000 births) and infant mortality in 1995 was 206,000, another indicator of human poverty, illiteracy, was quite high. Almost half of the Egyptian adult population cannot read and one-fifth of the population does not have access to safe drinking water, the UN reported.

TABLE 32.3 Human poverty profile of leading arms-buying countries

Human dev. rank	Country	Pop. w/out access to safe water (in % 1990–96)	Adult illiteracy rate (in % 1995)	Children not reaching grade 5 (in %, 1990–95)
23	Israel	n/a	n/a.	0
32	South Korea	7	2.0	0
44	UAE	5	20.8	1
55	Qatar	n/a	20.6	2
73	Saudi Arabia	5	37.2	6
89	Peru	28	11.3	n/a
99	Indonesia	38	16.2	8
109	Egypt	21	48.6	2
138	India	19	48.0	38
139	Pakistan	26	62.2	52

Poverty profile of women and children in leading arms-buying countries

Human dev. rank	Country	Maternal mortality rate per 100,000 live births (1990)	Children dying before age 1 (in 000s, 1995)	Underweight children under age 5 (in %, 1990–96)
23	Israel	7	2	n/a
32	South Korea	130	14	n/a
44	UAE	26	1	n/a
55	Qatar	n/a	0	n/a
73	Saudi Arabia	130	33	n/a
89	Peru	280	62	11
99	Indonesia	650	500	35
109	Egypt	170	206	9
138	India	570	3671	53
139	Pakistan	340	819	38

Key: n/a = data not available.
Note: The author selected column headings from UNDP charts.
Source: *Human Development Report 1997*, United Nations Development Programme, pp. 53–9.

Other leading arms buyers had similarly disturbing statistics. Thirty-five per cent of Indonesian children under age five are underweight and 38 per cent of the population does not have access to clean water. The Jakarta government was the fifth-largest arms buyer in 1996, with US$1 billion in acquisitions. Peru, which ranked tenth among arms buyers, spent US$800 million on military equipment while 56 per cent of the people there don't have access to health services. Even among nations with high development rankings, some states had weak showings in at least one category. Both the UAE and Qatar, for instance, both had adult illiteracy rates of more than 20 per cent (Table 32.3).

It should be noted that while the above illustrations used 1996 arms rankings, statistics indicate that half of the countries on the acquisitions list have been large arms buyers for years. For example, seven of the top ten buyers in 1996 were also in the top ten rankings for the 1993 to 1996 time period (Table 32.4). Further, five of the largest buyers last year have, since 1989, been among the leading recipients. Two countries that have spent large sums on weapons during that eight-year period (Egypt and India) were in the lower two-fifths of the UNDP's development rankings.

Table 32.4 Arms transfer agreements of selected developing nations, 1993–96 (in millions of current US dollars)

Rank	Country	Value
1	Saudi Arabia	20300
4	UAE	5200
5	Egypt	4900
6	Israel	4200
7	India	3400
8	South Korea	3300
9	Pakistan	2700

Note: All data rounded to nearest US$100 million.
Source: Richard F. Grimmett (1997), 'Conventional Arms Transfers to Developing Nations, 1989–1996', CRS Report for Congress, 13 August 1997, p. 54.

Compounding the detrimental effects of illiteracy or poor health care in developing countries, a shrinking supply of grain will also put pressure on these nations – especially those that spend vast amounts on military equipment. From 1950 to 1984 worldwide grain harvests grew 3 per cent per year. Since that time, however, grain production has grown only 1 per cent annually and is not keeping up with demand. At a consumption rate of 5 million tons per day, experts estimate current reserves would last less than eight weeks. While widespread hunger is not a current prediction, the Worldwatch Institute believes rising grain prices 'would hit people in developing countries the hardest', according to a *Washington Post* article.[11]

But while several nations in the Middle East and Asia have been large arms buyers for a number of years, recent developments in the southern cone of Latin America may foreshadow the next region to see a significant rise in military spending at the expense of domestic development. Chile has stated its intention to spend up to US$1 billion to purchase advanced attack aircraft, which is likely to spur other nations to follow suit. Several factors, including military parity in the region, improving relationships and economies and the lack of a security threat, demonstrate that the region has little need for this type of advanced military equipment. Yet calls for the acquisition of supersonic attack jets persist, based largely on the traditional thinking that aging equipment must be replaced to ensure a nation's security.

However, the challenges that plague the region, such as rampant drug trafficking, nagging guerrilla movements and narco-terrorists, non-existent or dilapidated infrastructure and continuing economic inequality create problems for which advanced fighter jets are not the answer. For example, a 1996 World Bank report found that Latin America could spend up to US$1 billion per week to maintain and upgrade communication, water and transportation systems. Further, just days after the Peruvian government announced its purchase of 15 MiG-29 fighters, at a cost of US$200 million, from Belarus in December 1996, the Japanese embassy in Lima was occupied by Tupac Amaru rebels. The siege, which lasted months, demonstrated that despite huge capital outlays Peru was still susceptible to serious internal threats.

After decades of military dictatorship and economic neglect, the social fabric of many nations in Latin America is still in the process of being restored. To sustain the progress towards democratic reforms, improving human rights records and recovering economies while helping ensure their nations' security, the governments in the region should be committing themselves to development. By providing the building blocks of human security, governments can help create national security from the bottom upward rather than by imposing it with the traditional use of a smothering police and military presence. Large arms buys at this juncture will only divert scarce economic resources and undermine attempts to improve the standard of living.

Regional security

Large arms buys can also have a detrimental effect on regional security. By training, military planners prepare for the worst-case scenario. Weapons acquisitions by one nation will be seen as a potential threat by its neighbours – which then leads to a purchase in response. For example, Ecuador purchased fighter jets in January 1996 which were followed less that a year later by Peru's MiG acquisition (after fighting a two-month border war in 1995 against Ecuador, Peru could not be expected to do less). These buys in turn reinforce the Chilean military's perception that they need their own advanced attack jets.

Such reactive arms acquisitions can create what has been dubbed the 'security dilemma'.[12] In his book on the global arms trade Professor Frederic S. Pearson, of Wayne State University, described the phenomenon this way:

> Weapons can … diminish security and relative power by threatening opponents so that they arm in return, leading both sides to feel more vulnerable and more caught in a vicious armament spiral. The costs of such arms races mount in terms of resources expended and benefits foregone.

In effect, while the intent of buying advanced equipment is to ensure a nation's security, that acquisition can actually increase the likelihood security will be diminished.

In addition, Keith Krause, the author of *Arms Imports, Arms Production, and the Quest for Security in the Third World*, writes that the security dilemma can 'lead to an upward spiral of armaments and military spending, the exacerbation of conflicts by worst-case thinking, and a concomitant decline in interstate security'. This very scenario occurred in Latin

America in the 1960s when countries beefed up their air squadrons with supersonic combat jets. Krause notes that

> Peru was the first state to acquire such planes; by 1975 Argentina, Brazil, Chile, and Venezuela had all followed suit. No war broke out, none was intended, and all states were forced to spend more than they would have wanted on national defense.[13]

This effect can be seen in other regions as well. NATO partners, and long-time antagonists, Greece and Turkey have participated in an arms race for years in an effort to back up political rhetoric with military power. Traditionally these two countries have been among the United States' largest arms customers: from 1992 to 1996 the USA sold Turkey US$5.6 billion in arms and supplied Greece with over US$3 billion in weaponry. But even with high levels of sophisticated weapons, and possibly as a result of the advanced nature of the equipment, in January 1996 the two countries came close to a military confrontation over an uninhabited island in the Aegean. The USA was then forced to rush a diplomatic team to the region to prevent a conflict. Had the diplomatic effort been unsuccessful, there was a distinct possibility that American-designed F-16 aircraft, flying under the Greek and Turkish flags, could have clashed against one another in Europe. More recent events, such as the temporary deployment of Greek and Turkish F-16s to the island of Cyprus in June 1998, only serve to underscore that high-technology weapons greatly improve the power projection capability of nations while simultaneously reducing the opportunity for diplomacy.

The protracted dispute between India and Pakistan over Kashmir is another example of how more weapons does not necessarily equate to additional security. Indeed, the mutual feelings of insecurity were induced by years of extensive arms acquisition on both sides of the border. A result of India's large advantage in conventional arms was the genesis of Pakistan's nuclear bomb programme, and the means to deliver such a weapon. Both nations' arsenals contain not only bomber aircraft but ballistic missiles, with steadily increasing range, as well. But for all the sophisticated weaponry, security remains elusive. A spate of nuclear weapons tests by both sides in May 1998 demonstrated the precarious nature of the peace in the region. As one Pakistani expert has noted, the Islamabad government's decision to pursue the nuclear option has actually made the country less secure because, 'should a war start due to India's insecurity, it would be total'.[14]

Outlook

There are rays of hope for the future, however. The IMF call for the Romanian government to halt the US$1 billion Cobra helicopter sale demonstrates that arguments by international players – institutions with tremendous political clout – can and are being made to help prevent unwise arms deals. While the IMF had some leverage over the Bucharest government due to the fact that Romania needed development aid, the fund's broad interpretation of its own good governance provisions is heartening. The next steps, then, are to prevent any backsliding by the lending institutions in this area and to urge them to apply the same standards to other nations as well.

Another example of a large international organization moving beyond its traditional roles, by taking a bold step into arms control issues, was seen in February 1998 when the UNDP cosponsored a disarmament conference in Oslo, Norway. At the meeting of government leaders, including many representing the Economic Community of West African States, an agreement was reached to implement a three-year moratorium on the import, export and production of seven categories of small arms and ammunition in West Africa. According to UNDP representative Ivor Fung, reducing the influx of new weapons is now considered a necessary first step by many organizations to pave the way for future economic and social development programmes. This approach, Fung said, 'brings another dimension to development efforts ... [because] there can be no development in an insecure environment'.[15]

Such efforts will gain significant support from endeavours such as those being made by Nobel Laureate Oscar Arias and others promoting a global disarmament campaign, which encourages nations to reorient priorities towards social requirements and human security. Arias, during the inauguration of the campaign in December 1995, explained human security as 'a disease that did not spread, an ethnic tension that did not explode, a dissident who was not silenced'.[16] An example of what could be accomplished by a redistribution of assets, Arias noted, was a 50 per cent gain in literacy with just a four per cent cut in military spending by developing nations.

Further, a multinational effort by non-governmental organizations is underway to institute a code of conduct on arms transfers by the major weapons-exporting nations, primarily UN Security Council members. Such a code would create criteria that potential purchasing governments have to abide by to be eligible to receive weaponry. While the criteria vary slightly from one code proposal to the next, in general, governments buying arms must be democratically elected, cannot abuse human rights, cannot attack a neighbour and must participate in the UN Register of Conventional Arms.

Great progress on promoting a code among governments was seen in May 1998 when the foreign ministers of all 15 European Union countries, after much prodding by non-governmental groups, agreed upon a set of criteria to restrict the transfer of arms in an attempt to prevent the misuse of military equipment by the purchaser. Another beneficial aspect of the European Code, as it is commonly known, is that it includes a 'no undercut' consultation provision. Under such an arrangement, if one member state denies an arms export licence on Code of Conduct grounds, any other member state wishing to grant a similar licence within three years of the date of denial must first consult with the member state that issued the denial.

There are drawbacks to the European Code, however: (i) the arrangement is voluntary and governments are not legally bound to abide by its provisions; (ii) while the code stipulates annual reports on arms exports by European nations, these reports will not be made public, even to parliaments in the region, thus severely reducing transparency; and (iii) the United States, the world's leading weapons purveyor, has no similar restrictions on arms sales, which will put pressure on the European nations to continue their present export policies. In 1997, the US House of Representatives passed code legislation but the Senate made no similar effort to create restrictive weapons sales criteria. Despite these weaknesses, the European Code is a good first step toward slowing arms sales to unsavoury governments.

Additionally, some experts are moving even further toward so-called hard arms control by promoting numerical limitations on certain weapons systems and banning the use of other arms. At the conclusion of a conference at the Carter Center in Atlanta, Georgia, in March 1998, former presidents Jimmy Carter (USA), Oscar Arias (Costa Rica) and Gonzalo Sanchez (Bolivia) called on all 34 democratically-elected heads of state in the western hemisphere to promote these ideas for a Latin American arms control agreement. With Chile's purchase of up to 24 advanced fighters looming in the not-too-distant future, the three presidents wrote that:

> [a]n agreement on arms restraint could ban weapons that do not currently exist in the region, such as long-range missiles and certain fighter jets, as well as some that are in only a few countries, such as mid-air refueling aircraft. It could put numerical caps on other types of weapons and call for savings in military expenditures to be shifted to education.[17]

While these ideas are far ahead of what the Latin American governments are currently willing to do, there are several benefits if such limits are implemented: (i) modernization of equipment could take place in a measured, transparent manner; (ii) numerical limits in themselves are confidence-building measures because neighbouring countries will be secure in the knowledge no nation will spend wildly to attain military supremacy; (iii) technological limits create security-building because the likelihood of a bolt-from-the-blue attack is greatly reduced; and (iv) by setting limits on armament acquisitions, governments can shift investment to domestic concerns such as health services and infrastructure improvements.

Conclusion

With such large levels of weapons still being sought by, and sold to, developing nations, the outlook for significant additional gains against the social scourges of poor health and illiteracy is in doubt. Decades of political instability in India and Pakistan would suggest, for example, that leaders in those nations might attempt to curb military spending to build a social infrastructure and broaden their base of political power. However, nuclear tests by both countries in early 1998 demonstrated that the current governments are following a distinctly different path. In India and Pakistan, as well as many other nations, continued high levels of spending on the military puts the future of millions of people in peril.

Ultimately, any change in current arms sales trends must begin in the buyer states. As has been shown, the major suppliers now perceive military equipment much like other goods – to be traded where there is demand. While arms export restraint on the part of suppliers is helpful, often at least one nation is willing to make an arms deal thereby undermining efforts to curtail proliferation. Demand for weapons is something the developing nations can control. But instituting acquisition restraint will take a tremendous effort from numerous groups before governments will perceive the idea as mainstream.

The combined work of major international bodies, non-governmental groups working on global campaigns like the Code of Conduct and Arias's global disarmament campaign and, primarily, affected groups in the developing nations themselves will be required to promote change in this area. Without a determined effort to influence the way governments operate, bureaucratic institutions will fail to make the intellectual leap needed to create a strong social fabric.

REFERENCES

1. Klare, Michael T. (1996), 'The New Global Schisms', *Current History*, 1 November.
2. Matthews, Jessica (1997), 'Power Shift', *Foreign Affairs*, January/February , p. 51.
3. US Government (1995), *State Failure Task Force Report*, Central Intelligence Agency, 30 November, p. vii.
4. Ibid., p. ix.
5. Lewis, Paul (1997), '2 Global Lenders Use Leverage to Combat Corruption', *New York Times*, 11 August, p. 4.
6. Dodd, Senator Christopher (1997), 'Arms Sales to Latin America: recipe for disaster', *New London Day* (Connecticut), 10 August, p. 11.
7. Keller, William W. (1995), *Arm in Arm*, New York: Basic Books, p. ix.
8. Grimmett, Richard F. (1997), 'Conventional Arms Transfers to Developing Nations, 1989–1996', CRS Report for Congress, 13 August.
9. The term internal security is used here in reference to the CIA task-force report and its findings that certain social and economic measures can be indicators that states may face the possibility of collapse.
10. United Nations Development Programme (1997), *Human Development Report 1997*, Oxford: Oxford University Press, pp. 53–5. The UNDP uses many factors to rank a nation's development level, including lifespan, literacy and income level.
11. 'Era of Scarcity?' *Washington Post*, 23 August 1997, p. 14.
12. Pearson, Frederick S. (1994), *The Global Spread of Arms*, Westview Press, p. 2.
13. Krause, Keith (1992), *Arms Imports, Arms Production and the Quest for Security in the Third World*, ed. Brian L. Job, Boulder: Lynne Reinner, p. 127.
14. 'Kashmir: Weapons Fuel Indian–Pakistani Tension', *Arms Trade News*, August/September 1993, p. 2.
15. 'Moratorium Agreed to Limit Small Arms in West Africa', *Arms Trade News*, April 1998, p. 2.
16. 'Arias Outlines Demilitarization Campaign', *Arms Trade News*, December 1995/January 1996, p. 1.
17. Excerpt from a letter written by Oscar Arias, Jimmy Carter and Gonzalo Sanches de Lozada to 34 Heads of State in the Western Hemisphere, dated 6 April 1998.

Address for correspondence

Council For A Livable World Education Fund, 110 Maryland Avenue, NE,Suite 201, Washington, DC 20002
Tel: 202-546-0795, Fax: 202-546-5142; email: cardamone@clw.org

33 PSYCHOLOGICAL THEORIES OF AGGRESSIVE BEHAVIOUR

LAURA KAUPPINEN

Aggression is considered one of the most substantial social problems for many societies, and there have been many theories trying to explain the acquisition, maintenance, and control of aggressive behaviour. It has been viewed in terms of death instinct, frustration drive, biological capability and learned habit. Like any form of social behaviour, however, aggression is most likely to appear when numerous predicting factors are present simultaneously. Current views of aggression stress both the biological-genetic as well as situational-environmental factors. The leading framework may be considered to be the social information-processing model. It is able to describe the specific mechanism through which people produce their aggressive acts and to integrate the emotional processes, biological determinants and learning principles involved in it. The social information-processing model sees people as equipped with their unique biological and learning backgrounds starting to process in some particular manner the information they receive from a social situation. A maladaptive way of processing social information results in the employment of aggressive problem-solving strategies, which finally manifest themselves in aggressive behaviour in that situation.

Fighting in the street, bullying at school, defaming a fellow worker to incur the boss's hostility or abusing a family member at home are examples of aggressive behaviour that people may encounter in their everyday lives. Even though one may be neither the aggressor nor the victim, aggressive behaviour may have a negative influence. One may, for instance, be afraid in the dark streets, become unpopular at school if trying to help the victim of bullying, suffer because of a bad working climate or be traumatized after witnessing the beating of one's mother by one's father.

The many negative effects of aggression have caused this mode of behaviour to be considered one of the most substantial social problems of many societies. Such behaviour has inspired researchers to find ways to reduce it, and thus it has become one of the central topics of psychological investigation of the 20th century. Aggressive behaviour has been viewed as the result of a death instinct, a frustration drive, biological capability, learned habit or a maladaptive way of processing social information.

Chapter 33 outlines the theoretical perspectives and empirical findings explaining aggressive behaviour. These comprise: Freud's psychoanalytic theory, evolution theory, temperament and twin studies, and results concerning gender differences, the frustration-aggression hypothesis, social learning theory and social information-processing models. The genesis of military aggression and war is not the topic of this chapter. Nevertheless knowledge of the general psychological principles of aggressive behaviour at individual and group level can contribute to our understanding of the behaviour, thinking and feelings of people living in violent and war-torn societies.

What is aggression?

An unambiguous definition of aggressive behaviour is still lacking, but it may be considered to be a socially-determined label for acts that people judge to threaten or cause physical or psychological injury to the targets.[1] Behaviour is here judged in terms of community-defined norms and standards of appropriate social interactions. Behavioural characteristics have a strong influence on how behaviour is judged. For example, physical assaults and humiliation are generally described as aggressive; intensity in an act (e.g. a loud voice) and serious outcomes such as. strong pain also usually increase the likelihood that the behaviour will be considered aggressive. Unintentionality and the presence of provocation may serve as mitigating circumstances. The definition is also related to those who judge and to the aggressor. Characteristics such as sex, ethnic background, socio-economic level and educational and occupational status play important roles.[2] In war conditions people are said to be habituated to aggression. They may therefore define aggressive behaviour along similar lines to the above, but the intensity of acts perceived needs to be stronger and the outcomes more serious before the behaviour is perceived as aggressive.

Biology and aggression

The early years of aggression research depended heavily on explanations that emphasized the role of intrinsic drives. The dominating approach was Freud's psychoanalytic theory. This viewed aggression as caused by the biologically-determined psychic energy of the death instinct that had turned outwards.[3] Freud considered that aggression is not totally avoidable because the energy of the death instinct within the unconscious id builds up pressure that inevitably has to be relieved. He even proposed that this primary hostility of human beings was responsible for the destruction of civilized society, for example, of human suffering and war. He thought, however, that most of the tension that the death instinct produced is discharged indirectly in non-aggressive ways because of the psyche's controlling forces. The superego as an agency of mind that was seen to internalize the norms and rules of the external world was considered a moral control on aggression and the ego was expected to try to find indirect and more acceptable ways for destructive energy to be relieved. Aggressive impulses were said to be sublimated, for example, in work or sports.

Viewing aggression as an instinct, however, may mislead by implying that releasing the aggressive drive will decrease further motivation to behave aggressively.[4] On the contrary, it has been shown that behaving aggressively *increases* the possibility of further aggression.[5] This does not in any way mean that aggression may not have a biological basis. It is, in fact, nowadays a quite generally accepted opinion that aggression as a behavioural strategy is universally a part of human inborn capabilities, maybe because it has had evolutionary importance for survival and reproductive processes.[6] It also seems that, at least to some extent, individual differences in aggressive behaviour are biologically determined. It has been found that if a child inherits a difficult temperament from his or her parents – for example, a high level of activity, irritability and irregularity – the likelihood of later aggressiveness is increased.[7] The comparison of identical and fraternal twins (twin studies) has shown that the level of aggression among identical twins is more similar than among dizygotic ones.[8]

When discussing the biological determinants of aggression gender differences should also be considered. Examination of overt aggression such as hitting and kicking indicates that males are more aggressive than females. A causal relationship between the level of the male sex-hormone testosterone and aggressive behaviour has been proposed,[9] but a typical type of female behaviour, relational aggression, also emerges.[10] This is intended to cause harm in another person's social relationships, for example by gossiping or backbiting.

In explaining the gender differences of acquired overt and relational aggression among boys and girls biological variables have appeared to be insufficient and it has been suggested that traditional social roles assigned to men and women are significant.[11] Biological explanations of aggression have also been more generally criticized for underestimating the influence of environmental factors.

Frustration-aggression hypothesis

The frustration-aggression hypothesis presented by Dollard, Miller, Dood, Mowrer and Sears was the first aggression model that emphasized the central role of external stimuli.[12] The authors developed the Freudian concept of instinct-directed aggression, and proposed that if people became frustrated, that is to say if some external obstacle prevented them from getting the satisfaction they desired, an aggressive drive which finally caused aggressive behaviour was triggered. Aggressive acts were said to reduce further motivation to behave aggressively. The existence of frustration was always considered to lead to aggression and conversely, every aggressive act was seen to be caused by frustration. Differences in the intensity of frustration were presented as mirroring differences in the intensity of aggression. Minor frustration was thought not to cause aggression because of the fear of punishment.

The frustration-aggression hypothesis stimulated much research.[13] Findings partly supported the theory, but it was found that frustration does not always result in aggression: people may, for example, develop an alternative goal or a different way of reacting. It was demonstrated that there were other aversive experiences in addition to frustration that stimulated aggressive behaviour, for example pain. Large individual differences in frustration-tolerance and aggressive behaviour emerged. The need to investigate the complicated effects of social learning, the importance of which was underestimated in the frustration-aggression hypothesis, became evident.

Social learning theory of aggression

The influence of learning in the development of aggressive behaviour was especially emphasized by Bandura. He argued that much aggressive behaviour is instrumental, that is to say learned in order to be used as a means to obtain a non-aggressive goal. Instrumental aggression, for example, bullying at school in order to increase one's own social status among a violent gang, is clearly distinguishable from emotionally-based, hostile aggression in which the primary goal is to cause injury, like hitting when angry.[15]

The learning of aggressive behaviour, and the attitudes and values supporting it, occurs, according to Bandura, in the same way as any other form of social behaviour: (i) people learn a totally new behavioural pattern; and (ii) further learning strengthens or weakens the already-acquired pattern. Modelling, the observed behaviour of aggression in either real life or in a fictional situation, for example from television, is considered to be the main means of acquisition. The learning of aggressive behaviour was also expected to occur through direct experience, but this is not considered to be as efficient as modelling.

Bandura emphasized that modelling is not a passive receptive process in which people simply absorb the vast array of examples they encounter in daily life. Instead, modelling requires (i) an observer who pays attention to the aggressive models, usually ones that are frequently observed, high-profile and attractive to the observer; (ii) that the acquired behaviour pattern be stored in the long-term memory and be reproducible; and (iii) that motivation to behave aggressively, or reinforcement for aggression, exists.

Reinforcement is one of Bandura's most important concepts: if aggression is followed by positive consequences the likelihood of behaving aggressively increases. Much reinforcement is external. Aggressive behaviour may result in higher social status, tangible rewards such as praise from friends, or alleviation of aversive treatment. People may also be directly instructed to behave aggressively. Reinforcement does not, however, have to be direct. People observe the consequences that result from aggressive behaviour enacted by other people, and may also reinforce their aggressive behaviour themselves. Self-reinforcement stems from the fact that people do things that give them self-satisfaction and a feeling of self-worth, and refrain from behaviour that results in self-criticism and other self-devaluative consequences. Bandura also speaks of punishment. It seems that punishment, either external or vicarious, decreases the likelihood of aggressive behaviour, although it is also possible that the punisher serves as an aggressive model and thus increases the possibility of further aggression.

Much learning of aggression takes place within families and subcultural environments, for example in peer groups. There is considerable evidence that observing aggression at home and participating in violent gangs increase the likelihood of aggressive behaviour.[16] Preconditions of social learning theory are also relevant in war and political violence. Bandura argues that aggression is effectively learned in intensive military training.[17] Rookies are tested for obedience and firmly disciplined for non-compliance, but are also isolated from family, friends and normal community life. They adopt the attitudes that killing is patriotic and become free from the restraints of self-condemning consequences. Soldiers and war heroes are also typically highly admired, which makes the subsequent modelling of their aggressive behaviour effective.

All that people have learned is not, however, manifest in their behaviour. Social learning theory posits that aversive experiences such as physical assaults, verbal threats, frustration and the endangering of positive consequences such as getting a prize, in addition to the anticipated outcomes of those events, cause emotional arousal. This, in turn, may result in aggressive behaviour depending on such regulatory processes as situation, reinforcement and cognitive representation of the problem at hand. For example, a person may attack a passerby in a street if he or she is with his or her friends from a violent gang who are likely to reward such acts, but unlikely to attack if walking the street with his or her parents.

Social learning theory has inspired much research and Bandura's work was a crucial advancement in studies of aggression. Maybe most importantly it was acknowledged that aggression is not an instinct that must be relieved from time to time. Social learning theory has also drawn considerable criticism.[18] It clearly underestimated the importance of biological determinants of aggression, but it was also unable to describe the specific psychological mechanism through which individuals produced their aggressive acts in any particular situation.

Social information processing models

In the 1990s social information-processing models of aggression presented by Huesmann and Eron[19] and Crick and Dodge[20] were the main frameworks for studying

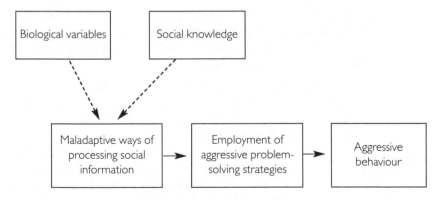

Figure 33.1 Social information-processing models: outline of the mechanisms underlying aggressive behaviour

aggressive behaviour. These models are able to describe the specific psychological mechanism through which people produce their aggressive acts, and to integrate emotional processes, biological determinants and learning principles involved in the development of aggressive behaviour.

Social information-processing models view each social situation as containing an array of social cues that people receive as an input when they come to the situation. Equipped with unique biological genotypes (determining, for example, one's temperament) and social knowledge, that is to say memories from past events (including, for instance, previous learning experiences) people start to process the information they have received in some particular manner through several information processing steps. Maladaptive ways of processing social information are considered to result in the employment of aggressive strategies to solve the social problems encountered, manifesting finally in aggressive behaviour in the social situation (Figure 33.1).

Processing steps

The processing of social information, it is suggested, includes five steps.

(1) A person encodes particular cues from a broad array of information concerning the external situation and his/her internal state, for example, people's tone of voice and his/her own heart rate. Crick and Dodge have suggested that a deficit in seeking those cues may risk socially adaptive behaviour.[21] For example, aggressive persons seek fewer situational facts, but pay more attention to aggressive environmental social interactions compared to their non-aggressive counterparts, which is likely to restrict their opportunities to make unbiased judgements.

(2) People use various processes to interpret the encoded cues. First, people make causal analyses of the events. For example, they evaluate whether the situation is a result of their own actions or of others' behaviour. A maladjusted way of processing information is to attribute positive outcomes to other people and negative ones to oneself. Second, people make inferences about the perspectives of others in the situation. In making these judgements aggressive individuals are more likely than their non-aggressive counterparts to perceive other people as intentionally seeking to harm them.[22] This phenomenon has been called hostile attributional bias, and is also applicable to the conditions of war and political violence when people tend to encode enemy behaviour as threatening and humiliating.

(3) The personal goal for the situation is formulated or clarified. A person orientates toward producing, or wanting to produce, particular states or outcomes. The goals may be internal such as feeling happy, or external such as making friends with the new neighbour. Relying on relationship-enhancing goals, like being friendly, decreases the probability of behaving aggressively, whereas adopting hostile goals is likely to increase that possibility, and the inability to coordinate individual and other people's goals predict aggressive behaviour. Crick and Dodge have suggested that coordinating and managing multiple goals simultaneously characterizes much socially skilful interaction.[23]

(4) The generation of social response alternatives, that is to say, one or more possible behavioural strategies. Strategies consist of individual ideas about possible behaviour in a specified social situation. Responses are accessed from long-term memory or, if the situation is novel, old information is used to construct new ones. As far as social adjustment is concerned the content of the strategies plays an essential role. It seems that social problem-solving strategies of the aggressive individual include more aggressive, and fewer friendly or effective means, such as help-seeking and compromising, compared to non-aggressive individuals. In order to behave with social skills, that is to say non-aggressively, it is also important that people have a number of different alternative strategies, or what one might call a large behavioural response repertoire. The likelihood of aggressive behaviour decreases if an individual is able to generate several possible outcomes for one situation. During war and political violence propaganda encourages narrow and aggressive conflict-resolution strategies. Huesmann and Eron have suggested that aggression is a quite direct and easy solution to retrieve from long-term memory, while less direct solutions are harder to generate, but often better.[24]

(5) Response evaluation. After individuals have found response alternatives for the particular social situation they have to select which one of the strategies is best, or if only one solution is produced they have to decide whether the response is acceptable. (i) On the basis of moral rules and values people evaluate the content of each response they have produced. Children may, for example, consider whether they approve the kicking of a classmate at school under peer provocation, or whether they disapprove of hitting for self-defensive purposes. If aggression is evaluated favourably the likelihood of behaving aggressively increases. (ii) People evaluate their ideas about the possible outcomes of the different behavioural alternatives: what would happen if I kick the classmate, or what would happen if I withdraw from the situation totally? People take into consideration both the quality and quantity of those outcome expectations. Anticipating few negative and many positive consequences for aggression increases the likelihood of behaving aggressively. Thus expecting that aggressive behaviour will increase self-esteem and produce tangible rewards (e.g., a child gets a desired toy) or reduce aversive treatment (stopping wrangling at home) increases the possibility of subsequent aggressive behaviour. In conditions of war and political violence people have to take a stance on their fear and the threat to their lives in evaluating the consequences of their own behaviour. Persons behaving aggressively may also think that victims deserve and do not suffer from aggression. Warfare and political violence are good examples of this. There is a general lack of empathy for enemy victims, and enemies are often considered to deserve aggression. (iii) People evaluate their degree of confidence to perform the behavioural response they select; aggressive persons indicate that aggression is easy and that aggressive impulses are difficult to inhibit.

When the processing has proceeded through the above-mentioned five steps a person will behaviourally enact the most positively evaluated problem-solving strategy.

His or her behavioural act will cause some changes in the external situation and internal state. That is when the processing of information in that new situation begins.

Crick and Dodge have emphasized, however, that the nature of social information processing is an on-line brain performance.[25] This means, that information processing from step to step includes a number of feedback loops. They can return before the end of processing to some earlier step and reconsider their inferences. People may also modify their way of processing information on the basis of the feedback that they receive from the external world. This ensures that people constantly learn how to process information. On-line processing also means that that several parallel processes are activated simultaneously. Life is not about encountering one social situation after another, but involvement in a number of social situations at the same time.

Social knowledge and biological variables

It is thought that every person processes information through the above-mentioned five steps by using the same innate information-processing mechanisms. Knowledge of earlier social information stored in long-term memory, for example, previous learning history and a person's genotype, related to his or her temperament, and a number of physiological variables explain individual differences in information processing and aggressive behaviour.[26]

The social knowledge of aggressive individuals is expected to be highly biased towards aggressive behaviour. From the point of view of social information-processing models, aggressively-biased social knowledge is considered to be acquired early in life, and maintained later through direct reinforcement, observational learning and practice. Direct reinforcement for aggressive behaviour is received mainly through adult instruction, especially from parents. Huesmann and Eron have suggested that in order to avoid social maladjustments like aggression, parents should moderate their children's social problem solving by help and advice about which strategies are realistic.[27] Direct reinforcement is also received through peer feedback. A person's environment may accept aggression, and behaving aggressively may, for example, increase a person's social status among friends who are involved in an aggressive gang. It is further possible that a person evaluates aggressive outcomes falsely. He or she may, for example, consider that the victims want to be in that particular role.

Learning aggressive ways of processing information through observation is likely to happen if a person has many opportunities to observe aggression, for example, fights between the parents at home, violence in the media or enemy threats in war. Parents should avoid serving as models and providers of opportunities for their children to observe and incorporate aggression into their own problem-solving strategies but instead act as models for the observation and incorporation of alternative strategies. Aggression is, however, learned through modelling only if the situation is particularly important, the scene is realistic, and a person can identify him- or herself with an aggressive actor. Being an object of aggression increases the likelihood of learning aggressively-biased cognitive programmes.

Practice is of prime importance in the process of maintaining aggressively-biased social knowledge. Repeated rehearsals of previously-learned aggressive problem-solving strategies by recall of the original scene, by fantasizing about it, and by play acting make those strategies more easily accessible from memory and aggressive behaviour more possible. In this way aggressive problem-solving strategies that have originally been learned as solutions for one particular social situation may be abstracted to a larger canvas.

Emotions

According to Crick and Dodge emotions play an important role in the processing of social information, influencing the final decision of whether to employ aggressive or non-aggressive problem-solving strategies resulting in aggressive or non-aggressive behaviour.[28] Crick and Dodge have suggested that other people's emotions may serve as cues to be encoded, for example perceiving two angry men in the street may cause that situation to be interpreted in a hostile way. In addition, emotions may serve as internal states influencing the whole processing sequence. (i) Emotions may affect the encoding and interpreting of cues. An angry person may, for example, search for hostile cues from the environment and emphasize their value. (ii) Feelings may enhance or inhibit the motivation to formulate a goal for one's behaviour; for example, anger may increase the likelihood of selecting an aggressive goal. (iii) Emotions may influence the search for response alternatives from memory. For instance, an angry person may quite easily generate aggressive solutions for the situation. (iv) Emotional states such as anger may serve as an excuse for enacting an aggressive response.

Interventions

The reasons for the breakthrough of social-cognitive information-processing models in aggression research are many, but among the most important was the need for effective intervention programmes for aggressive behaviour. Historically, intervention pro-grammes aimed at reducing aggressive behaviour have met with mixed success at best,[29] and a decrease in the individual level of aggressive behaviour is unlikely to occur spon-taneously.[30] In order to reduce the likelihood of behaving aggressively the mechanisms involved in the process of producing aggressive acts have to be understood. Interventions based on social-cognitive information-processing models have been promising.[31] Helping people to encode more social cues, to interpret those cues in a nonhostile way, to adopt nonaggressive goals and means to attain those goals, and to evaluate aggression as unfavourable has decreased the level of aggressive behaviour. Analogously, the model may be effective in peace education, allowing a detailed analysis of the processes that produce aggressive behaviour.

Conclusions

Many theories try to explain the acquisition, maintenance and control of aggressive behaviour. Current views, however, stress the social information-processing models that see aggressive behaviour as a result of maladaptive ways of solving social problems. These models recognize multiple reasons for adopting and employing aggressive problem-solving strategies leading to aggressive behaviour. They emphasize both biological-genetic and situational-environmental factors, because aggressive behaviour is most likely to appear when numerous predicting factors are present simultaneously.

ACKNOWLEDGEMENT

The author wishes to thank Dr Raija-Leena Punamäki for comments on this chapter.

REFERENCES

1. Parke, R.D and R.G. Slaby (1983), 'The Development of Aggression', in P.H. Mussen (series ed.) and E.M. Hetherington, *Handbook of Child Psychology*, Vol. IV, New York: Wiley, pp. 547–641.
2. Bandura, A. (1973), *Aggression. A social learning analysis*, New Jersey: Prentice-Hall.
3. Freud, S. (1920/1955), 'Beyond the pleasure principle', in J. Strachey (ed.), *The Standard Edition of the Complete Psychological Works of Sigmund Freud*, Vol. 18, London: The Hogarth Press; and Freud, S. (1923/1961), 'The ego and the id', in J. Strachey (ed.), *The Standard Edition of the Complete Psychological Works of Sigmund Freud*, Vol. 19, London: The Hogarth Press.
4. See n. 1 above.
5. See n. 2 above.
6. Lore, R.K., and L.A. Schultz (1993), 'Control of Human Aggression. A comparative perspective', *American Psychologist* 48: 16–25.
7. Prior, M. (1992), 'Childhood Temperament', *Journal of Child Psychology and Psychiatry* 33: 249–79.
8. Rushton, J.P., Fulker, D.W., Neale, M.C., Nias, D.K.B., and H.J. Eysenck (1986), 'Altruism and Aggression: The heritability of individual differences', *Journal of Personality and Social Psychology* 50: 1192–8.
9. Maccoby, E.E. and C.N. Jacklin (1974), *The Psychology of Sex Differences*, Stanford: Stanford University Press.
10. Crick, N.R. and J.K. Grotpeter (1995), 'Relational Aggression, Gender and Social-psychological Adjustment', *Child Development* 66: 710–22.
11. Eagly, A. H. and Steffen, V. J. (1986), 'Gender and Aggressive Behavior: A meta-analytic review of the social psychological literature. *Psychological Bulletin* 100: 309-330.
12. Dollard, J., Doob, L.W., Miller, N.E., Mowrer, O.H. and R.R. Sears (1939), *Frustration and Aggression*, New Haven, Conn.: Yale University Press.
13. Berkowitz, L. (1993), *Aggression. Its causes, consequences, and control*, New York: McGraw-Hill.
14. See n. 2 above.
15. See n. 13 above.
16. See n. 1 above.
17. See n. 2 above.
18. See n. 1 above.
19. Huesmann, L.R. and L.D. Eron (1989), 'Individual Differences and the Trait of Aggression', *European Journal of Personality* 3: 95–106.
20. Crick, N.R. and K.A. Dodge (1994), 'A Review and Reformulation of Social Information-Processing Mechanisms in Children's Social Adjustment', *Psychological Bulletin* 115: 74–101.
21. See n. 20 above.
22. See n. 20 above.
23. *Ibid.*
24. See n. 19 above.
25. See n. 20 above.

26. See ns 9 and 20 above.
27. See n. 19 above.
28. See n. 20 above.
29. Guerra, N.G. and R.G. Slaby (1990), 'Cognitive Mediators of Aggression in Adolescent Offenders: 2. Intervention', *Developmental Psychology* 26: 269–77.
30. Huesmann, L.R., Eron, L.D., Lefkowitz, M.M. and L.O. Walder (1984), 'The Stability of Aggression Over Time and Generations', *Developmental Psychology* 20: 1120–34.
31. See ns 19, 20 and 29 above.

Address for correspondence

Centre for Educational Assessment, PO Box 32, University of Helsinki, FIN-00014, Finland
Tel: -358-9-1914113; Fax: -358-9-1917043; email: laura.pakaslahti@helsinki.fi

34 LANGUAGE, COMMUNICATION AND DISCOURSE

PAUL A. CHILTON

Chapter 34 argues that violent conflict, while not caused by the many manifestations of language, is certainly closely linked to them. Four aspects of human language are considered: (i) as implicated in the conceptualization of war. The very notions of violence, conflict and war are defined in language use in particular societies, in particular historical circumstances. Destructive violence may not always be categorized as war in the conventionally-accepted sense. (ii) The construction of a national language involves force. National languages are the result of political processes that produce separate and potentially-conflicting sovereign entities. In the course of, and as a result of, linguistic homogenization states may use violence or may provoke it. (iii) Forms of communication play a part in the production and prevention of conflict. The channels and fora of communication, and the nature of communication itself, can be implicated in internal repressive measures and in the external waging of war. Given cultural and linguistic diversity among states, communicative channels and fora are required to overcome the potential for miscomprehension and misrepresentation. (iv) The complexities of discourse enter into the construction, promotion, motivation and justification of violent conflict. Discourse is the means by which underlying conceptualizations of peoples, communities and states are made concrete and promoted. In general, these four dimensions interact with economic, technological and social factors in the production of warfare, however defined.

Why bother with language?

Of all the structures that can be said to be involved in the causation and maintenance of war language is the most diffuse and the most difficult to define. This is because language is profoundly implicated in all human social activity and cannot be isolated as a specific causal factor in violent conflicts. None the less, it is clear that language and communication do play some role in war-fighting. For example:

- The decision to mobilize military force can only be executed through the verbal activity of political élites who possess the legitimacy to issue mobilization orders. A declaration of war is a linguistic act.
- Military operations themselves can only be set in motion and continued by verbal activity. Both these instances are cases of what linguists call speech acts, verbal activity that actually constitutes action. Such acts are both facilitated by, and reproduce, institutional structures. As La Boétie argued in the 16th century, everyone says 'yes' in such systems of command, no one dares or imagines the possibility of saying no.
- The above cases can only exist as part of a wider political, social and cultural structure which give them legitimacy. Indeed, what constitutes a legitimate concept of war can only be established in linguistic activity. Political structures are themselves constituted and instituted by forms of language and communication. Social and cultural forms include both cognitive and affective dimensions that support notions of legitimacy, permissible violence, patriotism, patriarchy, and so forth, and these too are dependent on, and in turn support, language and communication.
- Special cases of the above are historical instances of war justification and propaganda. Warfare, whether between sovereign states or civil war, is underpinned by the legitimate concept of war, but particular wars have to have particular propaganda to justify human and economic sacrifice.

Without these factors wars cannot be prosecuted; all the factors are constituted in language and communication. That is to say, wars would not be wars, in the sense in which late twentieth-century humans understand the term, unless certain verbal practices constituted the institution of war. From this follows an even more fundamental point concerning the relevance of language to war, or, rather, to the study of the problem of war:

> From the perspective of the constituting function of language, what is considered war is a product of history – a product of the beliefs, formal and informal laws, and customs of a particular period. This emphasizes the notion that war is a social invention, a fact created by an institution that takes certain actions and makes them a thing. The definition of war reflects the process by which the verbs to fight and to kill become nouns, the process by which the actions become an institutional fact.[1]

What this implies is that certain forms of violent conflict will not be conceptualized conventionally as war, for example: terrorist acts, low-intensity conflict, guerrilla warfare and civil war. Thus in spontaneous intuitive conceptualization not all wars will appear as equally good (or prototypical) cases of war. The point here is that wars are not defined and identified by objective criteria, the label 'war' is not simply stuck onto an objective correlate. Rather, what constitutes a 'war' is a function of prevailing conceptualizations realized in discourse, that is, in forms of interactive linguistic communication.

Another corollary is that the concept of war is in principle changeable, and thus the practice of 'war' is changeable. For those concerned with the effects of physical force on human bodies and minds, it is necessary to be aware of the possible narrowing effect of taking the concept of 'war' for granted. Language is able to stabilize concepts that may, over time, become irrelevant or in other ways dysfunctional. Two examples illustrate this point: the case of nuclear war, never fought, and difficult to imagine as 'war' at all, although it was, throughout the Cold War, imagined and spoken of in traditional war-fighting terms; and (ii) the changing nature of conflict in the post-Cold War period – the shift from total or absolute war to local wars, in which conflict is no longer primarily between the sovereign sealed entities we call states, but inside and across the boundaries of those entities. In practice, armed conflict now includes intervention, as in the case of UN forces sent to protect the Kurds inside Iraq in 1991, or in Bosnia in 1996. The conventional concept attached to the word war lags behind changes of this kind.

Such considerations suggest that certain forms of language and communication are necessary if not sufficient conditions in the initiation and maintaining of violent conflict. This chapter reviews in more detail some of the key ways in which language is implicated, but to do this it is necessary first to review what is understood by the term language itself, since, as will become apparent, this is part of the problem.

Language, languages and sovereign states

It is important to distinguish between a language (English, Finnish, Swahili, Urdu…) and language, which is the universal capacity of humans to acquire one or more languages. This distinction roughly corresponds to the French distinction between *langage* and *langue*. However, even this distinction can be misleading, since it gives the impression that a language (English, for example) is a uniform system throughout a territory. In fact what are conventionally referred to as languages show a great deal of variability in geographical and social space. Not only do different regions show greater or lesser degrees of variation in one or more levels of language structure (pronunciation, word-forms, syntax, vocabulary), but so also do different social strata, different ethnic groups, and possibly different gender groupings.

Furthermore, if one considers the language that people speak over a geographical area, one frequently finds one speech community shading gradually into another, without a sudden break. Such linguistic spaces are known as 'dialect continua'. In so far as it is possible to isolate distinct dialects in the linguistic flux, one can say that dialect X overlaps with dialect Y which overlaps with dialect Z… Adjacent dialects are mutually intelligible, though differences are perceived and may be exaggerated and associated with feelings of hostility, but between certain points along the chain mutual intelligibility decreases and ceases. An example of such a linguistic area is north-west Europe, where Germanic dialects shade into one another, overriding political boundaries. What is relevant about this kind of case is that differences between dialects (or varieties, to use a more neutral term) can be made socially and politically significant.

In the former Yugoslavia this was certainly the case for eastern and western varieties of Serbo-Croat used in Bosnia-Herzegovina. The varieties differ in relatively minor ways, and are certainly mutually intelligible. One key difference is salient: the use of the Cyrillic alphabet by Orthodox Serbs in the eastern regions, and the use of the Roman alphabet in the western regions. There are other differences on the level of pronunciation and morphology (the shape of words and their components), and to some extent the vocabulary itself differs slightly. A similar set of differences is found in, for instance,

American and British varieties of English. The differences in the Serbo-Croat dialect continuum were seized upon and politicized by nationalist movements during the disintegration of Yugoslavia that began in 1991. The pluralistic mixture and alternation of linguistic forms that had been the practice in education and the media in Bosnia-Herzegovina were abandoned as nationalistic discourses spiralled into conflict. Different nationalist discourses emphasized eastern or western variants, or words of Turkish origin, according to their perceived ethnic or religious allegiance, and according to an idea of linguistic 'cleansing'.[2]

This example is a clear case of linguistic difference being selected and given political significance specifically to create identity through difference. To this extent the activity of codifying what may be accidentally occurring differences contributes to cultural structures maintaining structures of hostility, violence, and warfare. This is largely the case because war, in its conventional understanding, is waged by sovereign states, and sovereign states also typically seek to establish a national language.

The role of language in the construction of states, though variable, is probably more crucial than many historians and political scientists acknowledge. From the linguistic point of view, Haugen distinguishes four phases of national language construction which historically have been part of state construction in Europe:[3] (i) a dominant élite selects a dialect; (ii) the social and political functions of the language are elaborated; (iii) dictionaries and grammars codify and prescribe the language and (iv) it is standardized through education and public media. It may be argued that such a process yields communicative and social benefits. Equally it can be argued that it leads to infringement of the rights of minorities and to conflict. Certainly, oppressive measures have been used within emergent nation states in order to impose linguistic uniformity and political adherence, for example, against the Celtic fringe in nineteenth-century Britain, and throughout France following the revolutionary zeal for the destruction of supposedly disloyal or backward 'patois'. Concentrating on war between sovereign states can obscure violence within states arising from the exploitation of linguistic and cultural differences, whether by established governments or by competing political groups.

Situations where such exploitation is possible arise as part of the territorial expansion and coalescence of states, invasions and colonial conquests. The result is the confrontation or overlaying of language pairs that are not immediately related and not mutually intelligible, although the languages involved in conflicts may be closely related pairs, as the Bosnian example shows. Clean demarcations between languages are only imaginable in a period when there are uninhabited spaces between distinct language communities. With the demographic and migratory expansion on the European land mass linguistic zones of conflict occur. Well-known fault lines, intimately bound up with conquest and invasion, occur in Alsace (French and German dialects), in the Low Countries (Dutch and French dialects) and in east–central Europe (German and Slav languages). These areas of merging and overlapping languages reflect the fringes of the Roman empire and the movement of Slavic and Germanic peoples in the fifth and sixth centuries. It would be absurd to claim that such linguistic cleavages actually cause war, but they are closely associated with other factors that can contribute to the justification of conflict and war, particularly if connected to discourses of nationalism, whether at the level of established governments or at the level of nationalist and potentially secessionist movements.

As noted above, linguistic cleavages result from population movement and invasion. A particular case of this is the nineteenth- and twentieth-century colonial expansion of the nation states of Europe, with their inherent tendency to self-definition through, amongst other things, linguistic distinctiveness. An extension of the linguistic unification of the territory of France was the imposition of French as the medium of colonial rule over Arabic and Berber in North Africa. In South Africa, two colonial languages – Dutch (developing as Afrikaans) and English – were dominant over indigenous African languages in different regions. Linguistic and political development in postcolonial situations can be unpredictable, however. It was Afrikaans that was associated with oppression from the standpoint of native Africans, less so English. The Soweto uprising of 1976 was triggered by a government decision to enforce rigidly regulations regarding the use of Afrikaans in schools.

The linguistic hierarchies of ex-colonies can reproduce themselves within the formerly colonizing state. France, as a result of immigration from its former colonies, inherits linguistic and cultural cleavages within the social structure that provide a potential for conflict. The United States, based on a mono-linguistic political culture, has two types of potential linguistic conflict, one between unrelated languages, and one between different social varieties of the same language that have become politicized. The first is the potential disaffection of the non-English speaking, and generally disadvantaged, Hispanic population. The second, reflecting America's past, is the emergence and recognition of a culturally distinct variety of English – Black Vernacular English. These two types are not in themselves sufficient causes of conflict, but they are available for political manipulation where other factors make conflict likely. It should be noted that Amerindian language and culture was perceived as so alien and threatening that its virtual annihilation was regarded as justifiable in the process of creating the United States during the 18th and 19th centuries.

Communication

The existence of a common language (for example, French or Serbo-Croat) within a territory, or straddling territories, does not guarantee that people talk to one another, or understand one another if they do. There are two additional, and related, dimensions to be considered under the rubric 'communication': let these dimensions be called C1 and C2. Communication of the first kind (C1) includes channels and fora which make communication among individuals and groups possible. Can people communicate face-to-face, by phone, photocopier, fax, email, TV, radio, letter, billboards and newspapers? This dimension is closely related to questions of censorship, freedom of speech, government control of media, and communicative empowerment. Communication of the second kind (C2) can be defined as the perception of some meaning as being intended by some agency, or the intention on the part of some agency that some such perception occur. Did so-and-so communicate what he or she meant? Did so-and-so 'get the message'? In this dimension things are not as simple as they might appear. A common assumption is that C2 is just a process of a sender packaging a message at one end of a line and a receiver decoding it at the other end. This notion seems natural to people because it is enshrined in everyday expressions like 'putting your meaning into words', 'getting the message through', 'extracting the meaning from the words'. This model may apply to C1 – it is possible physically to stop someone receiving phone calls or reading a particular newspaper – but it does not apply well to the process of C2, communication of the second kind. Linguists now understand communication, when it occurs, not in terms of the 'conduit' or 'message model' but in terms of an 'inference model'.[4] This model points out that people actively, though unconsciously, put together what they assume to be intended meanings, and do so not just by using the words they hear or see but by drawing on immediate contextual information and on background knowledge, including cultural knowledge. This is a much more helpful model in trying to understand how communicative processes can be involved in either fostering cooperation or in contributing to conflict.[5]

In the linguistic analysis of C2 two further technical ideas are useful: 'speech acts'[6] and the 'cooperative principle'.[7] Speech acts are acts in the sense that they alter the social relationships between people. Certain speech acts are only legitimate if they are uttered by certain authorized people, in certain circumstances. For instance, the declaration of war is a special kind of speech act performable only by legitimate authorities (for example, Congress in the United States), and the same is true for a military order, a threat of attack, a surrender and so forth. Some speech acts may not be permitted in a given society: challenging a superior's command, for instance, or uttering a disagreement with government policy. The existence and availability of speech acts in conflict or preconflict situations can suggest ways in which humans may or may not cooperate, may or may not fight.

The second technical notion, the 'cooperative principle', refers to the observation that people implicitly cooperate in order to make sense of what they are saying to one another. This does not mean that they do not lie and cheat – it would not be possible in fact to lie and cheat unless people assumed everyone was seeking to be both comprehensible and credible. The point is that people appear to share common assumptions in order to reach a minimum level of cooperation for communicative comprehension, principles such as relevance, saying no more and no more less than is needed at the time, not saying what is false and not being obscure . If a speaker appears to be flouting these assumptions, then people will look for some indirect implied meanings (implicatures). It is this relatively fluid framework of communication that yields the possibility of miscomprehension on the one hand and insinuation on the other.[8]

The role of communication is recognized in international relations, in theory and in practice. Both hostility and cooperation between states (or sub-state actors) are realized through communication. But certain forms of communication can forestall or resolve conflict, just as lack of certain forms of communication can contribute to the outbreak of violence.

The absence of C1 is crucial in what is known as 'prisoner's dilemma', one of the theoretical models that political scientists use to understand many problems in international relations. In this model, two individuals would be better off trusting one another not to grass, but cannot communicate in order to verify. In the circumstances it is rational for each to split on the other, but the payoff is less advantageous than if they had trusted one another and not spilled the beans. This analysis has been applied to arms races in the following way. Both sides would be better off cutting their arms buildup and devoting resources instead to domestic prosperity, but neither can rationally trust the other not to seek the strategic advantage. Another scenario that can be understood in terms of this dilemma is what is known as the 'tragedy of the commons', in which a collective good, for example common land, reaches a point of overuse and diminishing returns because it is rational for individuals, acting non-cooperatively and non-communicatively, to maximize their exploitation of it. Such a scenario potentially leads to conflict over the sought-after resource, for example, oil or fishing rights. In both these scenarios lack of trust is exacerbated by the absence of functional C1 and absence of appropriate C2. Numerous international institutions have been created in an attempt to fill what one might term the communication gap.

Many examples can be cited where C1 and C2 have made, or might have made a difference in a conflict or potential conflict. President Truman in the 1940s was faced with the question whether to develop the hydrogen bomb. Some advisers wanted America to be the sole possessor, but the Soviet Union also had the relevant know-how. So both would have been less exposed to risk if both disarmed, but, not having any prospect of an enforceable agreement (i.e. without appropriate C1 and C2), each side calculated they would be better off with the bomb, since neither could trust the other not to develop it. Historically, it can be argued that the Cold War years saw the development of an arms control regime that in effect set up forms of C1 (bilateral conferences, exchange of information, verification procedures) and C2 (negotiating strategies, cultural understanding) that limited the arms race. It is also arguable, however, that the C2 component was not adequate, that the communicative mode was geared to each bloc stabilizing its allies and clients rather than to disarmament itself. None the less, the Cold War did give rise to a web of C1 channels and fora: the Kennedy–Khruschchev hot line, the arms control agencies, summit meetings, Kissinger's shuttle diplomacy of the détente years, and the regular meetings of the Helsinki process that reinforced confidence and security-building measures.

Prisoner's dilemma hardly ever appears in its pure form in international relations, of course, since some form of communication nearly always exists. This is why the 'balance of terror' of nuclear deterrence never tipped over into global holocaust (though it had many other deleterious effects): each side knew enough about, and knew that the other side knew enough about, the consequences of choosing to attack. In crisis situations, such as the Cuban missile crisis of 1962, a variety of channels and back channels of C1 also contribute to the avoidance of war.[9]

Various things can go wrong in C2, even when C1 exists. There may be a lack of trust, lack of information, a shortfall of reliable inferences as to the other's meaning and intention, leading to over-reliance on what is known about the other's capability (that is, military resources). Thus even if, as was the case toward the end of the Cold War, both sides find that increasing armaments is costly and would prefer build-down, two sides that lack appropriate C1 and C2 may end up in what has been termed a 'perceptual dilemma'. This is really a communicative dilemma, as one summary makes clear:

> If it is hard to see what the other side is actually doing, if we have little contact with people from the other side, and thus little chance to judge their intentions at first hand, if they speak a

language that few of us understand and have a culture and ideology different from ours, then we may readily attribute hostile intentions to them and create the image of the 'enemy'.[10]

Such situations arise from the poverty of C1 and C2, but some well-known problems also arise from wrong assumptions about the very nature of C2. There is, for example, a tendency to assume that enemy states are unitary actors, that is, to oversimplify the C1 structure of a state regarded as hostile. Another tendency of decisionmakers is to underestimate how unclear their own communications are, failing to realize that their communications may not be understood in the way intended. This tendency probably arises from assuming the over-simple sender–receiver (or conduit) model of C2.

Channels and fora that may overcome the C1 and C2 problems have proliferated since the emergence of the European state system. Diplomacy is the earliest example, and its place in the emergence of international law is as a substitute for force. Embassies provide communicational lines between the decisionmaking bodies of states, and develop various modes of C2. While closely expressing a state's interests, these may be cooperative in function, as in the case of conflict resolution and negotiating techniques. A crucial aspect of both C1 and C2 in diplomacy is deciding who are the recognized interlocutors – who is to be admitted to talks and how rights to different speech acts are distributed. Thus Israel refused to recognize the PLO and vice versa for the purposes of negotiation until 1977, and the question of 'talking to terrorists' was a barrier in, for example, the conflict in Northern Ireland. More broadly, it can be argued that non-governmental actors should be included in citizen diplomacy.

International law provides a communicative framework in which expectations and norms make the interpretation of intentions more reliable. Numerous organizations provide fora in which officially recognized interlocutors can communicate within this framework. For instance, the existence of text on human rights provide a basis for inter-governmental and non-governmental organizations to intrude into what was once the closed domestic preserve of sovereign states. The most prominent IGO is the United Nations, whose agencies and publications function to increase C1 and C2 quantitatively and qualitatively. It must of course be recognized that all these channels, fora and modes of communication can be used not primarily cooperatively but also, or instead, in furtherance of a state's goals – for instance by using them for propaganda to influence third parties.

Policy decisions can be influenced by the power a particular individual or organization has, that is, by the power to have communicative access of a particular kind to the central decisionmakers. The communications of some individuals and organizations may be screened out, either physically blocked in the channels of C1 or socially and psychologically screened out in C2 if officials find it inconsistent with their own beliefs. An example is the filtering of feedback on the effectiveness of American military action in the Vietnam War: information opposing increased involvement was screened out at various bureaucratic and individual points or ignored when it did get through.[11] Another example is the apparently confused communication (both C1 and C2) that preceded Iraq's invasion of Kuwait in 1990, when statements by the American ambassador and other utterances seem to have resulted in lack of clarity concerning American willingness to defend Kuwait.

Increased communication may be unpredictable in its effects. While it is clear that the density of communication networks contributes to processes of social and political integration and economic interdependence, and thus to the elimination of conflict, increased communication also gives rise to increased perception of inequalities and thus to increased friction. Heightened contacts between societies of disparate culture or levels of development can heighten antagonism in the areas of trade, tourism and migration. Even more incalculable is the impact of the electronic communications revolution. Does the advent of rapid global communication support the Orwellian prediction of universal surveillance? Even if the answer is yes, it also empowers substate actors to resist governments, and also to create transnational cooperative networks. However, there is clearly a potential here for the increase of violence. Assuming that terrorism can be given an agreed interpretation, the Internet provides C1 for the exchange of information (bomb-making techniques, for example), the coordination of violent action, and the means of worldwide televisual propaganda and blackmail, and the disruption of electronic C1 and C2 (by the use of viruses, for example).

Discourse

Discourse is language and communication viewed in relation to their use within a particular culture or specific cultural setting. The term refers to the way words and phrases hang together, and to the characteristic way they interact linguistically. The latter aspect includes the kinds of conceptual framework people rely on and transmit, and the kinds of speech acts that characterize their social relationships. Discourse thus includes what are commonly called belief systems and ideologies (more or less coherently formulated belief systems). Discourses in this sense may be promoted to varying degrees by élites and state structures, though whether such promotion takes the form of propaganda and indoctrination or more subtle forms of influence depends on the form of the society.

War is a cultural institution and is sustained by discourse. One indication of the extent to which violent conflict is taken as natural in western culture is the prevalence of the metaphor 'argument is war' in everyday English expressions: undermine someone's argument, attack a position, shoot down someone's argument in flames, torpedo his theory, even nuke his argument. The possibilities are endless. These expressions are not just flights of rhetorical fancy but reflect a conceptual frame, a detailed knowledge of the conduct of war that is transposed onto the conceptual domain of argumentation. Indeed, it has been claimed that this conceptual structuring influences the way we actually do conduct debate.[12] The war frame also structures sport discourse. The fact that the 'sport is war' metaphor is reversible has considerable implications. It may for instance be that the 'war is sport' metaphor can motivate or justify conventional warfare, underpin the psychology of combatants and explain some apparently bizarre forms of atrocities.

Metaphorical forms of conceptualization can, then, be implicated in war discourse. More abstract forms of conceptualization, realized through language and discourse, are implicated in the ideologies and belief systems that first of all sustain the construction and maintenance of sovereign states and then sustain war between states. The most deeply embedded of such conceptualizations is the mental schema that represents states as bounded container-like entities. Such images of states are linked in the discourse of Realpolitik and realism with two other key concepts: 'the state is a unitary rational actor' and 'state containers necessarily seek to expand'. Such conceptualizations carry consequences for policy. If states are seen as rational actors then they are also seen as monoliths speaking with one voice, holding one view and seeking a specific goal, ignoring internal complexities, potential for change and other contingencies. If states are viewed as inevitably seeking to expand, it follows that they have to be contained by a policy of containment. This kind of thinking contributed to the whole edifice of the Cold War security state.[13]

Central to Cold War discourse, and logically dependent upon it, was the discourse of nuclear deterrence. The discourses of anti-communism and anti-capitalism provided the premises, together with the realist premise of the inevitable power-seeking nature of states. Nuclear weapons undermined the earlier conceptualization of war based on the Clausewitzian discourse, which viewed war as the use of force to achieve a political goal. Nuclear weapons could not be used; it was their non-use that became the keystone of a paradoxical discourse of war. Several discourses justified their development over 45 years. The technical discourse of professional strategists depended on game theory discourse, in particular on versions of the prisoner's dilemma scenario, and on the logic of first-strike and second-strike (retaliatory) force. As noted above, such discourse focused on military capability rather than intention, perhaps because of the inadequacy of communication, and this justified continued arms development. Such logics, fuelled by periodic (metaphorically expressed) misperceptions such as the 'missile gap' and the 'window of vulnerability', further served to justify continued weapons production. Since mutual knowledge about the annihilatory capacity of nuclear weapons should clearly inhibit rational actors, new elements of threat and uncertainty had constantly to be introduced. Although common knowledge of destructive power was in theory a part of deterrence discourse, the technical vocabulary tended to mask the nature and effects of weapons. In particular the physical effects on humans tended to be euphemized out of conscious reflection by terms such as 'collateral damage' and 'counter-city' targeting.

After the collapse of the Cold War-bloc system and of bipolar deterrence discourse, two broad, related features of conflict developed. On the one hand, there was increasing acceptance of intervention in conflicts that previously would have been categorized as 'internal'; on the other hand such internal conflicts were increasingly between sovereign entities (or would-be sovereign entities) and sub-state actors. The discourses that sustain such interventions and such conflicts acquired recognizable characteristics.

The 1991 Gulf War was the first major international conflict that required justification in a discourse other than that moulded by the Cold War framework. Popular support in the United States was carefully constructed by President Bush. A prominent part in the public debate was played by concepts and arguments drawn from 'just-war' theory. The theory of when it is just to wage war comes from the work of medieval Christian theologians and from the international law theorists, Grotius (1583–1645) and Pufendorf (1632–94), and may be thought of as a structured discourse in its own right. One idea used to justify the Gulf War was that it is just to go to war to defend a weaker state. The principle of sovereignty was implicit in this. Of course 'just cause' arguments of this type may involve many auxiliary discourses that are highly contestable. There may be 'positive' discourse, such as patriotic 'rally round the flag' discourse. Or, negatively, in order to mobilize popular opinion an 'enemy image' is often constructed. This may involve historical analogies and stereotypes. In the case of the conflict with Iraq, analogies between Saddam Hussein and Adolf Hitler were propagated. There was also a more indirect and diffuse propagation of enemy images based on western stereotypes of Arabs and Muslims, which had the potential to be applied to many other Middle East states. It can be argued that the more general discourse process activated here was the construction of an 'Other' which had the function of replacing the old Communist 'Other' and inducing a new western cohesion that extended to cooperation with the Soviet Union and its successors.

A second idea from just-war discourse is that war is just only when waged by a legitimate authority. In the past such an authority was taken to be a sovereign or sovereign state, but in 1990 it was the UN, or rather a force of nations willing to constitute a UN intervention force under American leadership. This in turn had to be legitimized. A key element in the auxiliary discourse was the notion of a new world order, an idea, which like the new enemy Other, filled a gap left by the loss of the Cold War order.

A third essential strand from just-war discourse involves proportionality (the proper degree of violence) and discrimination (who may and may not be violated in war). Here the public debate may be many-sided. In the UN–Iraq conflict the coalition governments were careful to stress that doctrines of proportionality and discrimination were being observed. Prominence was given to American high-technology (smart) weapons that could be precisely targeted (though one hit a civilian shelter), and to the known capacity of Iraq to use outlawed indiscriminate means such as gas and chemical weapons and the inaccurate Scud missiles. But it was argued by some observers that the UN allies themselves used disproportionate force on what was largely a conscript army. It was also argued that the impact of western methods was indiscriminate in the effects they had after the war both on the health of civilians, particularly children, and on the economic infrastructure and food-producing environment. An auxiliary factor was the reliance on the conceptualization of states as container-like entities, rather than as organic societies: viewed in this way, and with the media focus on Saddam, the internal damage to civilians became invisible.

The container model of the state may also contribute to explaining discourse surrounding other post-Cold War conflict situations. From the early 1990s new discourses of control, power and identity had to be found in the far-flung regions of the disintegrating USSR. It was not only the mechanisms for controlling C1 and thus innovative political activity that had collapsed, but also the discourses that supported those mechanisms, legitimized the actions of state agencies and provided a framework for social and political allegiance. The discourses of nationalism and ethnic identity, together with some auxiliary discourses, fulfilled these needs.

What discourse analysis can make clear is that 'nations' and 'ethnic identity' are not natural or universal phenomena that have simply resurfaced after being suppressed. They have to be constructed and promoted through talk and text. Any feature of difference (e.g. language, custom, religion, colour) may serve the underlying conceptual model. This model may be seen in terms of homogeneism, the assumption in political discourse that the homogeneity of a population is normal and natural.[14] This notion can in turn be related to the underlying image schema that views ideal communities as containers, with demarcated insides, outsides and boundaries. In the logic of such images, sovereign states have clear-cut borders defining those who 'belong' and those who do not. They are also linked to images of the human body and of course countries are commonly talked about as if they were persons.

There are further ramifications that emerge in discourse and action in situations such as the break-up of the former Yugoslavia. If a group is imagined as a container-like body (a 'body politic'), then linked notions will appear in discourse, and may be mirrored in physical behaviour. Thus, the containing boundaries of the body must be absolute and exclude alien elements, which are often conceptualized as infections or contagions that damage the society's health. These disease metaphors are linked to ideas of purity and impurity (cultural, ethnic, etc.) and thus to ideas of adulteration and the unclean. Ideally, containers should in this discourse prevent mixing and contamination. This nexus of concepts is the frame for ethnic cleansing, and explains the power of the concept. Further, in these conceptualizations of the body politic, what is feared for oneself, and what is threatened against others, is penetration of the body's boundaries. It is not implausible to think that these unconscious schemas underpinning homogeneist discourse are acted out in some way in the atrocities of rape and mutilation that are peculiarly characteristic of this type of conflict, and which do indeed in some of the reports appear to have a ritualistic communal element. Discourse analysts have noted that gender-based discourse is also involved, specifically fear of the loss of virility and the desire to prove it through acts of penetration. Masculinist discourse is not of course confined to such situations, any more than is the container-based concept of the state or the community. President Bush went to war against Saddam Hussein after being called a wimp (an insult to his manhood) by domestic political opponents.[15]

It is arguable that it was the prevalence of certain discourses in western societies that both facilitated the emergence of nationalist discourse and blocked the western will to intervene in the Balkans in the 1990s. After all, the notion of the homogeneous nation state, with a hard defensive shell, and the doctrine of self-determination, are deeply embedded in western political culture. Blommaert and Verschueren have argued that certain forms of multicultural policy espoused by some elected governments (policies that involve the separation of populations along language lines, for instance) can be seen as 'non-violent ethnic cleansing'.[16] Such underlying notions are of course more overt in the policies of the extreme-right opposition parties that have increased in Europe. If the patterns of western thinking about diversity are similar to those underlying the violent pursuit of homogeneity, then it is not surprising that intervention to prevent 'ethnic cleansing' could not be decisively formulated. The container concept, moreover, made it easy to regard the conflicts in the former Yugoslavia as an internal matter, a matter of civil war. (It should be noted that this inhibitory conceptualization had been overcome following the Gulf War in order to create safe havens for the Kurds of northern Iraq, when Kurds were about to transgress Turkish borders and perhaps destabilize the Turkish state.) It is also not surprising that western proposals for stopping the fighting in

Bosnia were predicated upon neat partition, despite the complex overlapping and nesting of human groups.

It is important to note that homogeneist discourse and the body politic metaphor are the basis for a reversible logic. On the one hand, as we have seen, this logic says that if the state is (or ought to be) a homogeneous body, then it is necessary to expel or exterminate foreign bodies (the Holocaust, ethnic cleansing in the Balkans, Hutu and Tutsi massacres in Rwanda and Burundi). This is the ethnic cleansing or purging model. On the other hand, the mirror image of this train of thought is also sanctioned by the image of the homogeneous body. If the state is a homogeneous body, then it has certain integral parts, without which it cannot be whole. This is the logic that can be mobilized to legitimize internal violence against groups that want to secede (Chechnya, the Kurds), or nationalist violence and warfare seeking to re-incorporate territories and inhabitants that allegedly belong to some supposed body politic (for example, Hitler's claim on Poland and the Sudetenland, the notion of Greater Serbia). The logic of such discourse does not of course in itself tell us anything at all about the rights or wrongs of a particular case. The point is that such images and their logic can be a powerful constituent in the discourses that lead to violence, whether in the form of what is conventionally regarded as war or in the form of civil conflict or in the form of terrorism.

REFERENCES

1. Vasquez, John A. (1993), *The War Puzzle*, Cambridge: Cambridge University Press, pp. 18–19.
2. Levinger, Jasna in Chilton, P.A., Mey, J. and M. Ilyin (eds) (DATE?), *Political Discourse in Transition in Europe 1989–1991*, Amsterdam: John Benjamins.
3. Haugen, E., 'Dialect, Language, Nation', *American Anthropologist* 68: 922–35.
4. Reddy, M. (1979), 'The Conduit Metaphor', in A. O. Ortony (ed.), *Metaphor and Thought*, Cambridge, Cambridge University Press.
5. Akmajian, A., Demers, R.A., Farmer, A.K. and R.H. Harnish (1990), *Linguistics: an Introduction to Language and Communication* (3rd edn), Cambridge, MA: MIT Press, pp. 307–30.
6. Searle, J. (1966), *Speech Acts: an Essay in the Philosophy of Language*, Cambridge: Cambridge University Press.
7. Grice, P. (1989), *Studies in the Way of Words*, Cambridge, Mass.: Harvard University Press.
8. Ibid.
9. Bell, C. (1983), 'Communication Strategies: an analysis of international signalling patterns', discussion paper, Council for Arms Control, London.
10. Russett, B. and H. Starr (1996), *World Politics: the Menu for Choice* (5th edn), New York: W.H. Freeman, pp. 236, 282.
11. Ibid.
12. Lakoff, G. and M. Johnson (1980), *Metaphors We Live By*, Chicago: University of Chicago Press.
13. Chilton, P.A. (1996), *Security Metaphors: Cold War Discourse from Containment to Common House*, New York: Peter Lang.
14 Blommaert, J. and J. Verschueren (1998), *Debating Diversity. Analysing the discourse of tolerance*, London and New York: Routledge, Chapter 5, pp. 136–7.
15. Goldstein, J.S. (1996), *International Relations* (2nd edn), New York: Harper Collins, p. 113.
16. See n. 14 above.

Address for correspondence
School of Language, Linguistics and Translation Studies, University of East Anglia, Norwich, UK

35 THE MEDIA IN POSTMODERN WAR AND TERRORISM

TAPIO VARIS

'The battle for hearts and minds is being fought on the net', wrote Simon Rogers in *The Guardian* at the outbreak of the war in Kosovo on 26 March 1999.[1] He said that there had never been a war like it before. Even though there had been articles about cyberwar in the public media, the NATO attack on Yugoslavia in 1999 may have been the first war fought also on the Internet.

One of the peculiarities of modern wars since the late 1950s is that they are not declared to be wars by legitimate parliamentary bodies and often have the nature of an intervention in the internal conflicts of sovereign states. Consequently, it is difficult to define when it is a question of terrorism and when of war.

During the Cold War there was the fear that a large-scale nuclear war might break out even by accident. However, in a legal sense a war does not normally start without elaborate procedures of parliamentary or conciliar discussions, with the accompanying declarations, orders and proclamations dealing with its means, ends, modes and justifications.[2]

In any case, even the undeclared wars are always intentional in the sense that symbolic acts which imply or lead to hostilities and war and justify them have been carried out by some government. Even the clandestine preparations for large-scale war require major preparations in the climate of opinion in which the mass media and other new sources of information like the Internet become crucial.

The 1991 Gulf War broke out on television when it erupted on prime-time evening news bulletins in the United States on Wednesday 16 January 1961.[3] The ABC network took the viewers of its 18.30 evening programme *World News Tonight* to Baghdad for a telephone interview with reporter Gary Shephard. In Iraq it was just past 02.30 on a moonless night after the expiry of the United Nations' deadline for its government to withdraw from occupied Kuwait. Within minutes the reporter said: 'Something is definitely under way here, something is definitely going on … obviously an attack is under way of some sort'. Over ten minutes later, at 23.47 GMT, British viewers who had

379

settled down to watch ITV's recorded highlights of that evening's Rumbelow's League Cup soccer matches had the war introduced to them by sports commentator Nick Owen.[4]

In Yugoslavia in 1999, the CNN effect was eliminated from the beginning when Yugoslavia expelled western media journalists from its territory. Yugoslavia also has capable operators for cyberwar, as Iraq did not. In recent media history, the Vietnam War was the first television war, the Gulf War in 1991 showed the power of real-time news journalism, and Kosovo in 1999 proved the strength of the Internet and cyberwar in the field of information and propaganda.

In the 1990s the western vocabulary increasingly emphasized terrorism as the threat to security. Walter Laqueur writes that current definitions of terrorism fail to capture the magnitude of the problem worldwide. In his view the terrorist operations have changed somewhat so that terrorism is not the militants' only strategy any more. He warns that terrorists can order the poor man's nuclear bomb from a catalogue and that 20 hackers with US$1 billion might shut down America: 'Chances are that of 100 attempts at terrorist super violence, 99 would fail. But the single successful one could claim many more victims, do more material damage, and unleash far greater panic than anything the world has yet experienced'.[5]

The media and the United Nations

After the end of the Second World War (WW II) efforts were made to rationalize the international communications system by bringing various organizations under the aegis of the UN. Their treaties and conventions were to be adjudicated by the International Court of Justice. However, the court was given no official sanctions to impose on countries against which it ruled. It had to rely on world opinion or moral authority as the basis on which the states would abide by its decisions. As a consequence, this philosophy has not produced instruments to deal with the problems of world communications. Robert Fortner concludes that 'both countries and corporate interests continued to press for, or to maintain existing, monopolies of knowledge, struggling to impose their versions of history and methods of interpretation on the world' s peoples'.[6]

But in the modern world all political, economic and military operations from preventive diplomacy to peacekeeping must take into consideration the new media environment and world public opinion. In the United Nations, world communications are a prerequisite for the work of the General Assembly and the Security Council. The media are seen to reflect the world's public opinion and it is important that the world media are as independent and free as possible to reflect people's views and opinions as well as to maintain a critical reporting of the governments.

However, since US President George Bush declared the 'new world order' at the outbreak of the 1991 Gulf War, the United States and her allies, especially the UK in their attack against Iraq in 1998 and NATO in the aggression against Yugoslavia in 1999, have literally bypassed the existence of the United Nations as the only legitimate international organization for legitimizing war. Their concern has been to interfere internally for humanitarian reasons.

It is obvious that the media publicity will be increasingly important for the peace-related decisions. This is especially true of the UN-peacekeeping operations. In fact, one of the key elements in the international environment where all UN activities now take place is the international media. The increasing telecommunications capabilities result in increasingly detailed graphic, timely information being available to audiences worldwide.

A UNIDIR (United Nations Institute for Disarmament Research) research document concluded that in peace operations, national and international news media coverage plays a significant role in quickly framing public debate and shaping public opinion. It is likely that future peacekeeping operations will often be demanded and executed under the worst possible conditions. That means a situation when preventive diplomacy has failed; when impassioned calls for action submerge careful analysis in emotions and impatience; when frustration supplants caution and facts on the ground are judged primarily by the media coverage they receive. The report concludes that it is precisely for this type of environment that decisionmakers and peacekeepers should prepare themselves.[7]

The sensitivity of these issues for the success of the UN became very clear in the media coverage of the UN operations in Somalia and former Yugoslavia. The possible mistakes of the UN are given wide publicity by the world's news media, which tend to stress action and war-related issues in a conflict rather than diplomacy, which, after all, is the strength of the UN and its true métier.

The great challenge to communication research as well as to policymaking now is to find a new approach that is forward-looking and based on enough past knowledge but free from Cold War conceptual frames. Information and communication technology represent a continuity, which has a solid past but challenges many previous assumptions. The analysis of technological developments is useful in order to understand the need to create specialized agencies and to introduce normative thinking in this field:

(1) It is important to look at the technological changes that have been decisive for many other changes. Currently, they are creating an entirely new learning environment for all international activities.

(2) How the intellectual thinking on communication and education has developed in relation to conflicts and wars needs to be studied.

(3) It is important to understand that culture and communication skills are essential for the merging global information society.

(4) When the media turn violence and conflict into a permanent open learning environment a new challenge enters the concept of global learning. Do we really learn anything from wars and what role do the media have in this?

International communication has no precise origins but it has existed as long as there have been nations and states. As we know, as soon as groups establish their separateness, at least some members find the need to communicate with individuals in other groups. Of course, the media have developed from runners, drummers, pigeons, ships, and trains. But with the advent of the telegraph, a fundamental transformation began: as early as 1837 successful electric telegraph experiments began. The technological developments of telegraph, submarine cable, telephone, wireless and radio led to the need for international control of the technical means of communication. The objective has been to facilitate necessary international cooperation and avoid transnational interference in the operations of other countries.

During the 20th century, especially between 1933 and 1969, the field of international communication became a field of increasing politicization and propaganda.[8] Although politicization never really ended during the period after 1970, a newly complex environment emerged, the result of both the application of new communications technologies and the proliferation of new states with the breakup of Europe' s colonial empires.

Towards a global knowledge society

In recent years fundamental changes have occurred in technology, the political world order and population growth that have had a profound impact on world economic, political and human development. The rapid developments in telecommunications, microprocessors and biotechnology and the introduction of information super-highways are changing national and international economies and the world order. The development of national information infrastructures is planned; these in turn are or will be plugged into worldwide efforts to create global electronic information super-highways, which are expected to revolutionize economies as well as education and learning environments.

It has been estimated that the present decisions concerning telecommunications and electronic information highways will have a socio-economic impact similar to the building of canals, railroads and motor highways. It is believed that information highways will be the key to economic growth for national and international economies. The information infrastructure already is to the major economies of the 1990s what transport infrastructure was to the economy of the mid-20th century.

Some critical researchers point out, however, that if the future user requirements do not align with national information infrastructure-provisioning capabilities, lengthy periods of wasteful and uneconomic network underutilization will result. For instance, the mid-1980s unveiling of ISDN (Integrated Services of Digital Network) has yet to overcome initial subscriber scepticism. During the interim, resources will not have been put to their best possible use. These information superhighways have been compared to the building of interstate highways in the earlier period; certain elementary points in this comparison need to be observed. Highways function only if all roads are connected to them; in the field of information superhighways there are weak links that determine the outcome of the whole system.

In the global perspective, there is a threat that the information gap is increasing. Even in the technologically-advanced countries a great number of individual homes are without computer connections and very few home computers have modems. In fact, the first users of information superhighways will be those that have the necessary equipment. In the early stages of motor highways the first users were those who had cars and could benefit from the new infrastructure. Highways changed the whole culture, including small business and shopping centres. The shops were no longer built within walking distance of their users but near the highways. In the case of information super-highways we do not yet know how much they will serve individual citizens and how much enterprises, organizations and administration.

In the 1990s the central role of information and communication technology for social and economic development could be observed. Traditional industrial societies faced difficulties and even collapsed, particularly in cases where obsolete models of thinking had dominated management, but the number of economies that were able to utilize new communication and information resources were growing, for example in the Pacific region and also in North America.

In the light of the exponential growth of electronic communications, the role of telecommunications will grow rapidly in world affairs. Consequently, the International Telecommunication Network (ITU) has to deal more and more with issues that are not only technical in nature. For example, it has to define more clearly its role in relation to development. A significant move took place in 1984 when a report of the Independent Commission for Worldwide Telecommunications Development, 'The Missing Link', was published. It concluded, among other things, that 'all mankind could be brought within easy reach of a telephone by the early part of the 21st century'.[9]

In 1994 the ITU held the first World Telecommunications Development Conference in Buenos Aires, Argentina. A Declaration on Global Telecommunication Development for the 21st Century was approved. It recognizes that telecommunications are an essential component of political, economic, social and cultural development. It is important that the document refers to the principle of 'the right of connection' between countries. The telecommunications gap between vision and reality persists, at technical and political levels, and hopes of closing it are modest. More than two-thirds of all households worldwide still have no telephone. Less that 2 per cent of World Bank lending goes to telecom projects.

Media and peace education

International governmental efforts in the fields of education and communication have been carried out by the United Nations Educational, Scientific and Cultural Organization (UNESCO) and the League of Nations, which both reflected the intellectual and moral integrity of scholars of their time.

The role of international communication and the media was not perceived as central during the period of the League of Nations after WW II. The organization passed one resolution in 1925 on the collaboration of the press in the cause of peace. It referred to 'moral disarmament' which was understood to be a condition of material disarmament.

In 1936 the League approved an international convention concerning the use of broadcasting in the cause of peace. This lengthy convention came into existence after politicization and propaganda in radio and other forms of international communication in Europe. The convention, still in force today, speaks of the need to prohibit such transmissions, which are likely to damage good international understanding, but has probably had no impact on anything. Even the deliberate interference in other countries' transmissions (jamming), was started in Austria in the early 1930s.

The International Institute of Intellectual Cooperation of the League of Nations was important even though not enough was accomplished. It was a characteristic feature of the times that only 15 smaller and medium-sized states signed the 1937 Declaration Regarding the Teaching of History which none of the bigger powers accepted, albeit for different reasons: the British government did not feel entitled to interfere in the field of local educational authorities and the free expression of opinion; the United States refused to sign because the federal government had no control over education; France did not want to curb the independence of teachers and historians; while the Nazi government of Germany totally opposed the aims of the declaration.[10]

The UNESCO Constitution was approved in 1945 after the experiences of WW II. It states that peace must be founded, if it is not to fail, upon the intellectual and moral solidarity of mankind. The means of communication between peoples should be developed and increased and these should be employed 'for the purposes of mutual understanding and a truer and more perfect knowledge of each other's lives'. The doctrine of the 'free flow of information' was assumed to be obvious prerequisite for peace.[11] The free flow doctrine was always problematic in the light of the global economic structure and its impact on communications. Technological changes have made it even more problematic today.

The chairman of the committee that drafted the Preamble, the American poet and librarian Archibald MacLeish, was once asked if we can educate for world peace:

> Of course we can educate for world peace. I would be willing, for my own part, to say that there is no possible way of getting world peace except through education. Which means education of the peoples of the world. All you can do by arrangements between governments is to remove the causes of disagreement, which may become, in time, causes of war. But peace, as we are all beginning to realise, is something a great deal more than the absence of war. Peace is positive and not negative. Peace is a way of living together, which excludes war, rather than a period without war, in which peoples try to live together.[12]

Later history has shown us the difficulties of building truly international educational and communication systems. Much intellectual work has been carried out on the basic problems of peace. One clear finding is that the criterion of peace depends on the times and on who defines it. During the period of the League of Nations, peace research referred mostly to the causes and functions of war and necessary and sufficient conditions for abolishing it; more recently, it has been broadened to include human rights and the quality of life. Communication and education are key issues. Now education is changing into a life-long learning process where communication skills are central.

In general, communication research can be seen as part of peace education in the wider sense. While early peace research targeted the decisionmakers and diplomats, it was later discovered that in order to promote peaceful relations among nations, one had to increase the general level of awareness of what was at stake.

In principle, UNESCO is ideal for cultural, scientific and literary intellectuals to promote peace on the world stage. In the early years of UNESCO in the late 1940s, the time of Julian Huxley's involvement, the organizaion was still perceived as an agency uniting qualified individuals from different civilizations, representing the human mind rather than governmental spokespersons. The UNESCO Constitution was drafted by Archibald MacLeish and the British politician Clement Attlee. The Axis governments had demonstrated the power of the media to control events; UNESCO's founders now wrote into the organization's constitution a mandate to create a communication programme that would advance the understanding of peoples.

A dialogue between cultures

The UN philosophy and Charter is essentially a product of European civilization, clearly intended to reinvigorate contacts among peoples and nations with its humanistic principles and aspirations. None of the countries then under colonial rule by European powers made any contribution to its formulation.[13]

The UNESCO Constitution also reflects the spirit of the anti-fascist struggle:

> The great and terrible war which has now ended was a war made possible by the denial of the democratic principles of the dignity, equality and mutual respect of men, and by the propagation, in their place, through ignorance and prejudice, of the doctrine of the inequality of men and races... Believing in full and equal opportunities for education for all, in the unrestricted pursuit of objective truth and in the free exchange of ideas and knowledge, [UNESCO's founders] are agreed and determined to develop and to increase the means of communication between their peoples and to employ these means for the purpose of mutual understanding and a truer and more perfect knowledge of each other's lives. (UNESCO Constitution, 1945)

In other words, UNESCO's mandate is to contribute to the preservation of peace and security by promoting cooperation between nations through education, science, culture and communication. In the field of information and communication the purpose is 'to promote the free flow of ideas by word and images'.

The ideologies of racial superiority have their roots deep in different civilizations and were not limited to the Italian, German or Russian societies at that time. As observed by *The Economist*: 'the fighters for freedom and against fascism and racism in 1939–45 were rank hypocrites, since they were themselves running dictatorial empires in which racial superiority was a strong theme'. No wonder that Mahatma Gandhi, when asked what he thought of western civilization, replied that it would be a good idea.[14]

The scholarly views of communication at the time of the founding of UNESCO were well reflected by the report of an unofficial body, the Commission on Freedom of the Press, generally known as the Hutchins Commission, 'Peoples Speaking to Peoples'. Communication was seen to link 'all the habitable parts of the globe with abundant, cheap, significant, true information about the world from day to day, so that all men increasingly may have the opportunity to learn to know, and understand each other'. The Commission set three objectives concerning international communication: (i) to improve its physical facilities and operating mechanisms; (ii) the progressive removal of political barriers and the lessening of economic restrictions; and (iii) the improvement of the accuracy, representative character, and quality of the words and images transmitted in international communication.

The report also noted that the 'surest antidote for ignorance and deceit is the widest possible exchange of objectively realistic information – true information, not merely more information'. Many scholars have similarly questioned the success of a mere quantitative increase of information for international understanding. Llewellyn White and Robert Leigh, for example, pointed out very early that there is evidence that a mere quantitative increase in the flow of words and images across national borders may replace ignorance with prejudice and distortion rather than with understanding.[15]

In view of the 1999 war in Kosovo one might conclude with the catchphrase of the popular American writer, Francis Fukuyama, who writes of 'the end of history and the last man'.[16] One might add, though, that the new millennium seems to have begun with the emergence of techno-barbarism. In fact, Fukuyama warned against the danger of returning to being the first men, engaged in bloody and pointless prestige battles – only this time with modern weapons.

Many scholars have addressed the issues of war, peace and the media. Quincy Wright analysed the problem in his book *A Study of War*.[17] Wright observed that among the causes of war is the difficulty of making peace a more important symbol in world public opinion than particular symbols that may locally, temporarily or generally favour war. He noted that wars have always required propaganda for both their initiation and their conduct, and that the methods have long been elucidated: 'The objects of war propaganda are the unification of our side, the disunion of the enemy and the good will of neutrals'.[18]

Wright went on to note that efforts have also been made among both 'primitive and civilized' peoples to preserve peace by propaganda. Here, the problem is more difficult than the problem of war propaganda because, to be effective, peace propaganda must gain attention simultaneously within earshot of all potential belligerents, and yet peace, in Wright's view, is intrinsically less interesting to human beings than war.

Several peace researchers have outlined the requirements for peace-oriented media at times of conflict. Johan Galtung emphasizes, among other things, the importance of giving a voice to both or all parties in the conflict, trying to make explicit the intellectual frame of reference within which conflict is to be understood, and avoiding over-emphasis on élite nations in media reporting.[19]

In connection with the information warfare over Kosovo in 1999 Jan Oberg raises critical issues of media coverage. He asks, for example, whether there is a larger story behind what we see on the screen. Who are the victims of what? What is a military target, and how does it differ from a civilian target?[20]

It is always necessary to ask what are the sources of the information being disseminated by various parties to the conflict and who are the experts used in the media. The problem of violence is not necessarily problematized in the media but used to legitimize action. In some humanitarian crises like in Rwanda in the 1990s there were radio stations that openly urged people to kill. In the long run media education and critical communication skills and competencies are the only way to combat distorted information, media manipulation and war propaganda.

REFERENCES

1. Rogers, Simon (1999), 'The First Web War', *The Guardian*, 26 March.
2. Wright, Quincy (1965), *A Study of War* (2nd edn), Chicago and London: University of Chicago Press.
3. Taylor, Philip M. (1992), *War and the Media. Propaganda and persuasion in the Gulf War*, Manchester: Manchester University Press.
4. See n. 3 above.
5. Laqueur, Walter (1996), 'Postmodern Terrorism', *Foreign Affairs*, September/October: 24–36.
6. Fortner, Robert S. (1993) *International Communication. History, Conflict, and Control of the Global Metropolis*, Belmont, California: Wadsworth Publishing Company.
7. Raevsky, A. and I.N. Vorobév (1994), 'Russian Approaches to Peacekeeping Operations', UNIDIR Research Paper No. 28.
8. See n. 6 above.
9. ITU (1984), *The Missing Link*, Report of the Independent Commission for Worldwide Telecommunications Development, ITU .
10. Mertineit, Walter (1979), 'Strategies, Concepts and Methods of International History Textbook Revision: a German share in education for international understanding', *International Journal of Political Education* 2: 101–14.
11. Alger, Chadwick F. (1990), 'Telecommunications, Self-Determination, and World Peace', in Sven B. Lundstedt (ed.), *Telecommunications, Values and Public Interest*, Norwood, NJ: Ablex Publishing Corporation, pp. 36–51.
12. *The UNESCO Courier*, October 1985.
13. Jaipal Rikhi (1982), *The Military Mind*. Gandhi Marq, No. 38 and 39.
14. *The Economist*, 11 September 1999.
15. White, Llewellyn and Robert D. Leigh (1972), *Peoples Speaking to Peoples*, Report on International Communication from the Commission on Freedom of the Press, New York: Arno Press (reprinted edition).
16. Fukuyama, Francis (1992) *The End of History and the Last Man*, London: Hamish Hamilton.
17. see n. 2 above.
18. Ibid.
19. Galtung, Johan (1986) 'On the Role of the Media for World-Wide Security and Peace', in Tapio Varis (ed.) *Peace and Communication*, San Jose, Costa Rica: Universidad para la Paz.
20. Oberg, Jan: PressInfo #62: 'The Information Warfare about Kosovo', http://www.transnational.org 15.4.1999-04-27.

FURTHER READING

Boulding, Elise (1988), *Education for an Interdependent World: towards a global civic culture*, Columbia University: Teachers College.
Enzensberger, Hans Magnus (1994), *Civil War*, London: Granta.
Galtung, Johan (1992), 'The Emerging Conflict Formations', in Katharine Tehranian and Majid Tehranian (eds), *Restructuring for World Peace*, Cresskill, New Jersey: Hampton Press.
Huntington, Samuel P. (1993), 'The Clash of Civilizations?' *Foreign Affairs* 72: (3), Summer.
Katz, Elihu (1992), 'The End of Journalism? Notes on watching the war', *Journal of Communication* 42 (3), Summer.
Kennedy, Paul (1993), *Preparing for the Twenty-first Century*, London: Harper Collins Publishers.
Lewis, Peter (ed.) (1993), 'Alternative Media: linking global and local', New York: UNESCO Reports and Papers on Mass Communication, No. 107.
United States Institute of Peace (1994), *Preventive Diplomacy and American Foreign Policy. A guide for the post-Cold War era*, New York: United States Institute of Peace.
Tehranian, Majid (1992), 'Restructuring for Peace: a global perspective', in Katharine Tehranian and Majid Tehranian (eds), *Restructuring for World Peace*, Cresskill, New Jersey: Hampton Press.

UNESCO (1993), *Activities in the Matter of the Free Flow of Information and Freedom of Expression*, New York: UNESCO Communication Division, 5 April.

United Nations (1994), 'Development and International Economic Cooperation', General Assembly, A/48/935, New York: UN, 6 May.

Varis, Tapio (1982) 'Peace and Communication – an approach by flow studies', *Journal of Peace Research* 3.

Varis, Tapio (1992) (ed.) *The New Media. Cultural identity and integration in the new media*. Publications of the University of Industrial Arts B 28, Helsinki.

Varis, Tapio (1993) 'Culture, Communication and Dependency. A dialogue with William H. Melody on Harold Innis', *The Nordicom Review* 1.

36 WAR AND ALCOHOL

JUSSI SIMPURA

Research literature on alcohol and war is scattered, with two exceptions: studies on drinking as a part of health behaviour among armed forces in times of peace are many, as are public health studies where military conscripts have been used as a representative sample of the male general population. More important from the public health perspective are studies that concern the effects of war on the availability of alcohol, and the role of wartime experiences as a motive for increased drinking. In the former case, there is some evidence that war often leads to reduced availability, lower consumption and consequently to less alcohol-related harm. Two aspects of alcohol and war are rarely dealt with in research: (i) the effect of drinking on the military capacities of the population at large; and (ii) the effect of alcohol on the capacities of troops in action. From a public health perspective, the most important of these six aspects is the issue of changes in availability due to war.

Drinking can be connected to war in many different ways:

- from the point of view of public health, the most evident connection goes through the effects of war on alcohol consumption (this is mainly a question of supply of alcoholic beverages in wartime conditions);
- on the demand side, war can be seen to provoke drinking as a reaction to the hardships of the conflict, in particular among military troops but also among civilians.
- alcohol has debilitating effects on military capacities, both of the population at large and of troops in action;
- military personnel have often served as a research population for public-health studies on alcohol; and
- drinking is in many ways connected with specific aspects of military life in different countries, both in practices and in rituals, in everyday life and in celebrations.

36.1

Six perspectives on alcohol and war

War and availability of alcohol

Drinking as a reaction to wartime hardships

Alcohol and military capacities of the population

Alcohol and military capacities of troops in action

Armed forces as public health laboratories

Drinking and military life – past and present, myth and reality

In this brief review, we shall have a look at each of these six aspects. The emphasis will be on the public-health effects of war through changes in drinking, although research literature is most scarce at this very point. When compiling this chapter, the author was struck by the lack of general, systematic and extensive reviews of the interconnections of alcohol and war that would cover several of the six aspects and several different spheres of alcohol cultures. It is hoped that Chapter 36 will be a start, stimulating more comprehensive presentations of the subject.

Availability of alcohol

Evidently, the most striking effects of war on alcohol-related public health matters derive from changes in the availability of alcohol in wartime. In most cases, war diminishes the supply of alcoholic beverages, thereby reducing per capita alcohol consumption. Again in most cases, such changes are expected to have a positive effect on health, although research evidence is practically non-existent. However, in a country where a large proportion of the population would have to turn to abstinence in the absence of alcoholic beverages, some health losses could accrue because of the J-shaped risk curve between drinking and cardiovascular mortality.[1] On the other hand, diminishing availability of alcoholic beverages of good quality can also lead to aggravated alcohol-related harm, as homemade products and surrogates are consumed to substitute for better beverages. There is, however, no research literature on these potentially harmful public-health consequences of wartime changes in the availability of alcohol.

The scattered statistics on WW II alcohol consumption for Denmark and Norway support the view that war reduces drinking and thereby also drinking-related harm.[2] In some cases, wartime changes in availability of alcohol may have far-reaching consequences on drinking. The most notorious example is Denmark during WW I and thereafter.[3] In 1917 the Danish government decided to multiply taxes on distilled spirits, because of the lack of grain and in order to gather more tax revenues. As a consequence,

Denmark turned almost overnight from a typical Nordic spirits country into a Central European beer country. This sudden change was accompanied by a decrease in per capita alcohol consumption and alcohol-related harm. As an example, alcohol-related suicide rates showed a significant decline.[4] Historically, the event was important in shaping the later famous Danish liberal attitude towards drinking. At that time, the turn from spirits to beer was celebrated by the meagre Danish temperance movement, as beer was considered a healthy alternative to spirits, and a relatively non-intoxicating beverage.[5]

Wartime conditions may, however, have complicated effects on specific alcohol-related harm. Again, the best-known example comes from Denmark, this time from the years of WW II. Parallel to changes in alcohol consumption since the outbreak of WW II, liver cirrhosis mortality was slowly declining from 1920 to 1943, when it reached the level of 2.5 per 100 000. Then it rose dramatically in 1945 to 17.3, falling back again in 1947 to 4.4.[6] Mortality changes were very different for men and women. This peculiar variation certainly did not reflect changes in alcohol consumption, as might have been expected on the basis of respective changes in other times almost everywhere. Understandably, the Danish case puzzled alcohol researchers, as liver cirrhosis mortality is used as a rough standard indicator of overall level of alcohol-related harm in many sources.[7] The explanation for the peculiarity was found in an (also war-related) epidemic of hepatitis in 1944, without any link to changes in alcohol consumption.[8]

Although a wartime decline in alcohol consumption would basically have beneficial effects on public health, the link is not always easy to demonstrate. A study from Norway, for instance, concluded that 'in particular the decreased consumption during the Second World War failed to be echoed in the male excess mortality'.[9]

A specific aspect concerning the availability of alcohol in wartime was demonstrated during the Nazi occupation of eastern Europe in WW II. Many of the occupied countries and Poland in particular experienced a boom of illegal spirits' production (moonshining) that 'was actively supported and even approved of by the majority of the population'.[10] Illegal distillation became another symbol and means of civil resistance. But the Nazi occupiers also took advantage of the situation, introducing a system of exchange of agricultural products and other scarce commodities for spirits. Some sources even indicate that this policy had the design of weakening the occupied peoples by a rich supply of alcohol.[11]

Wartime and increased drinking

Turning to the demand-side effects of war on alcohol, two aspects can be discussed:

(1) Both among civilians and soldiers at the front, the hardships of war could be assumed to increase psychosocial stress. Higher levels of stress are associated with higher alcohol intake, and in several studies differences in stress have explained remarkable variations in alcohol consumption and alcohol-related harm. Understandably, there have not been any general population studies nor case-control studies of stress and drinking in wartime conditions. Evidently, however, the possible drinking-inducing effects of wartime stress have been far too small to compensate for the opposite effect of diminishing availability on the supply side.

(2) Specific traumatic wartime experiences may have a long-term effect on various behavioural and psychiatric traits, including problem drinking. Some studies suggest that such effects are at least of measurable size in extremely exposed populations, although the importance of such cases on the general population level has seldom been discussed.[12]

In addition to individual-level changes one could speculate on population-level cultural changes after the war. Drinking might have provided some relief in countries which had lost a war. The case of Japan could be considered here. In the post-Second World War decade, Japanese drinking habits clearly increased, although they retained and developed further many of their peculiar features.[13] Although the idea of alcohol as a postwar relief and escape could seem attractive, one should remember also more materialistic explanations. In the case of Japan, the effects of a forced cultural opening to the west should be considered. In most industrial countries, postwar was an era of increasing alcohol consumption. The explanation for this phenomenon, which typically did not occur in the years immediately after the war, has been sought in improved economic conditions and increasing urbanization.

A further, related explanation for wartime influences on drinking could be found in changes of behavioural patterns due to new habits learned or adopted at the front. In the case of smoking, for instance, there is clear evidence that soldiers of some countries may have turned into more frequent smokers during the war years and then retained that pattern in peacetime. No studies have reported such effects for alcohol.

Finally, wartime conditions are likely to weaken service provision to those suffering from problem drinking but no recent studies were available to review the results of this factor.

Alcohol and the military capacities of the population

From the military point of view, excessive drinking may in the extreme case damage the population's health to such an extent that it becomes increasingly difficult to recruit able-bodied soldiers. This aspect has not been mentioned explicitly in recent research literature. However, in older temperance-minded writings the issue was sometimes included in the lists of potential harmful effects of drinking. An illustrative example with reference to relevant older literature comes from the years of WW I.[14] More recently, according to mass media debates over the status of the Russian army, one of the problems in recruiting conscripts in the 1990s was cited as youngsters who were drunkards already, or whose bad physical condition could partly be attributed to growing up with a drunken parent or parents.

Drinking and active performance

There are also historical examples of alcohol being blamed for lack of success in certain military operations. In post-WW I Germany, temperance-minded circles maintained that the temptations of French wine and other alcoholic beverages was overwhelming for the

German troops at a decisive moment. Therefore, the answer to the question 'Why we lost the war' was to be found in alcohol.[15] A more recent example can be found, this time in the Chechnian war of the 1990s, where it was claimed that the performance of the Russian troops deteriorated because of overconsumption of vodka. It is of course difficult to evaluate the truthfulness of such claims. In general, studies on this aspect are too few to allow broader conclusions to be drawn.[16]

A public health research laboratory for alcohol issues

In countries with obligatory military service, armed forces have provided researchers with an opportunity to study drinking behaviour and the prevalence of drinking-related problems in representative samples of the general male population in their twenties.[17] In the Nordic countries, in particular, studies of army conscripts have been important in following changes in drinking patterns.[18] Smoking and the use of drugs have often been included in such studies. In some research, troops on active service and other military groups have been used as a study population on drinking-related issues.[19]

Armed forces have often provided the study population for research into treatment and research methods. Soldiers are easily available for follow-up of different treatment strategies and programmes.[20] They are also good material for developing methodology, for example in health-behaviour studies.[21] A third group in this category consists of studies in which the success or failure to complete military service is used as one of various outcome indicators of potentially risky lifestyles in respect of alcohol.[22] A fourth group of studies has focussed on changes in drinking during military service as a factor influencing later drinking behaviour and alcohol problems.[23]

Drinking and military life

Studies on the effects of military service on later drinking behaviour already refer to the specific conditions of military life that may produce peculiar patterns and problems. The military profession has often, but not always and not everywhere, ranked high in studies on the occupational risk of alcohol-related harm.[24] In many countries, alcoholic beverages occupy an important place in the traditions of everyday military life and especially in celebrations. The famous rum shots of the British navy or the importance of the supply of vodka in the WW II Red Army are well-known examples. Indeed, a sufficient supply of alcohol for the troops was an important issue in wartime conditions. There were also armies in which the supply of alcohol was consciously limited to a minimum or allowed at specific celebrations only. For instance, the Finnish army during WW II, coming from a background of low alcohol consumption, celebrated the 75th birthday of its commander-in-chief at the front with shots of liquor that became famous for generations thereafter.

Working conditions in the military may, of course, make drinking a particularly risky behaviour.[25] In the extreme case, drunken soldiers may by their misunderstandings and unregulated actions cause an unintended escalation of military conflicts. There are also examples of the opposite. The Finnish troops chasing the German army away from northern Finland in autumn 1944 had to stop the attack for a while when a regiment refused action – culpably, in the view of many – after having found the liquor stores the Germans had abandoned by mistake.

A particular aspect of military life and drinking is service in foreign countries. Cross-cultural contacts and new conditions may produce unexpected results. For instance, studies on the drinking habits of European soldiers serving in UN peacekeeping troops in the Middle East show that both internal discipline and local conditions have in these cases reduced drinking during the service period, compared with drinking before and after.[26] The strict limitations on alcohol availability in Saudi Arabia effectively reduced drinking among American soldiers during the Gulf War, and some alcohol-related harm, common among troops serving elsewhere, almost vanished.[27]

During the Gorbachev alcohol reform, the Soviet Army paid much attention to drinking among the armed forces.[28] Examples of prevention and treatment of alcohol problems in the armies of other countries were widely reported in Soviet military journals. Perhaps the armed forces also hoped to set an example for other branches of Soviet society. There are no research reports showing how successful these efforts actually were.

A number of studies have compared military drinking patterns and the prevalence of alcohol-related harm with respective results from other professions.[29] As already stated above, military personnel are not always a particularly heavy-drinking group. Many studies have shown a high prevalence of heavy drinking among army personnel, but others indicate that professional soldiers do not differ very much from contemporary males of the same age in the general population.

Conclusion

The links between alcohol and war are many, and the results of various studies show no simple set of effects of war-related phenomena on alcohol issues. From the public health perspective, the effects of war on alcohol consumption and alcohol-related harm are probably mostly positive. More negative effects may result from peacetime drinking among military troops.

Chapter 36 shows how scattered the information on war and alcohol is. Many potentially interesting research issues have remained untouched in the research literature. Although data on wartime alcohol-related conditions may be difficult to find, some of the issues raised could perhaps be addressed in retrospective studies.

The relative importance of alcohol among other war-related public health issues is hard to assess. If wars typically reduce alcohol consumption, then it is likely that, from a public health perspective, the role of alcohol is less emphasized during wars than in the years of peace. Even this important question remains open in the absence of reliable research.

REFERENCES

1. See, for example, G. Edwards *et al.* (1994), *Alcohol Policy and the Public Good*, Oxford: Oxford University Press.
2. Thorsen, T. (1988), 'Da Danmark Blev Aedrueligt', *Alkoholpolitik* 5(4): 209–19; and Skog, Ole-Jørgen (1993), 'Alcohol and Suicide in Denmark 1911–24 – experiences from a "natural experiment"'. *Addiction* 88: 1189–93.
3. Eriksen, S. (1993), 'Skabelsen af den Danske Liberale Drikkestil', *Nordisk alkoholtidsskrift* 10(1): 3–13.
4. See Skog, n. 2 above.
5. See Thorsen, n. 2 above; and Hindhede, M. (1923), *Den Danske Krigsrationerings Indflydelse paa Sundhedstilstanden. Med saerlig hensyn til alkoholindskraenkningens betydning:* Copenhagen: Afholdsfolkenes Oplysningskontor.
6. Petersen, J. and T. Thorsen (1985), 'Alkoholforbrug og Levercirrosdödelighed i Danmark 1920–1982', *Alkohol- og Narkotikarådets Skriftserie* 4, Copenhagen.
7. See n. 1 above.
8. See n. 6 above.
9. Skog, Ole-Jørgen (1987), 'Trends in Alcohol Consumption and Deaths from Diseases', *British Journal of Addiction* 82: 1033–41.
10. Moskalewicz, J. and A. Zieliski (1997), 'Poland', in D.B. Heath, *International Handbook on Alcohol and Culture*, Westport: Greenwood Press.
11. Moskalewicz, J. (1985), 'The Monopolization of the Alcohol Arena by the State', *Contemporary Drug Problems*, 117–28, Spring.
12. Goldberg, J., Eisen, S.A., True, W.R. and W.G. Henderson (1992), 'Health Effects of Military Service. Lessons learned from the Vietnam experience', *Annals of Epidemiology* 2 (6): 814–53; Labbate, L.A. and M.P. Snow (1992), 'Posttraumatic Stress Symptoms Among Soldiers Exposed to Combat in the Persian Gulf', *Hospital and Community Psychiatry* 43 (8): 831–3; and Boscarino, J.A. (1995), 'Post-traumatic Stress and Associated Disorders among Vietnam Veterans: the significance of combat exposure and social support', *Journal of Traumatic Stress* 8 (2): 317–36.
13. Shimizu, Shinji (1990), 'An Alcoholic Society: drinking culture and drinking behaviour in Japan', *Seisin Hoken Kenkyu (Journal of Mental Health)* 36: 85–100.
14. Brunzlow (first name n.a.) (1917), *Wehrkraft und Alkohol*, Berlin: Mässigkeits-Verlag.
15. Schmidt, Hans (1925), *Warum Haben Wir den Krieg Verloren?*, Hamburg: Neuland-Verlag; Schmidt, Hans (1925), *Unsere Niederlage im Weltkrieg*, Hamburg: Neuland-Verlag.
16. Bray, Robert M. *et al.* (1991), 'Drug and Alcohol Use in the Military Workplace: findings from the 1988 worldwide survey', in Gust, S.W. *et al.* (eds), *Drugs in the Workplace. Research and evaluation data,* Volume II, NIDA Research Monograph Series 100, Rockville, pp. 25–43; Holcomb, J. F. (1982), 'Alcohol and the Armed Forces', *Alcohol Health and Research World* 6 (2): 2–17 ; and Zadoo, V., Fengler, S. and M. Catterson (1993), 'Effects of Alcohol and Tobacco Use on Troop Readiness', *Military Medicine* 158 (7): 480–4.
17. Vittadini, C. *et al.* (1992), 'Studio Sulle Abitudini Alcoliche Personali e Familiari in Gruppi di Giovani alla Prima Visita di Leva', *Minerva Med.* 83 (7–8): 445–9; Seppälä, T., Aranko, K., Peitso, A., Korte, T. and K. Koskenvuo (1989), 'Psychoactive Drug Use among Young Men Entering Military Service in Finland in June 1987', in *Prevention and Control, Realities and Aspirations*, Proceedings of the 35th International Congress on Alcoholism and Drug Dependency, Oslo: National Directorate for the Prevention of Alcohol and Drug Problems, Vol.4, pp. 149–73; Martinsen, B. and H.-J. Stang (1985), 'Rusmiddelbruk under militaertjeneste', *Tidsskrift for den Norske Laegeforening* 105 (15): 1049–51; Benson, G. (1985), 'Course and Outcome of Drug Abuse in Military Conscripts', *Acta Psychiatrica Scandinavica* 71(1): 38–47; and Andreasson, S. and P. Allebeck (1991), 'Alcohol and Psychiatric Illness. Longitudinal study of psychiatric admissions in a cohort of Swedish conscripts', *International Journal of the Addictions* 26 (6): 713–28.
18. See n. 17 above; and Bovim, G., Aasland, O.G. and J.S. Tyssedal (1990), 'Endring i Bruk av Alkohol og Tobakk under Rekruttskolen', *Tidsskrif for Norske Laegeforening* 110 (13): 1705–6.

19. Fletcher, J.-D., Price, D.K. and C.C.H. Cook, 'Problem Drinking and Family History', *British Journal of Addiction* 86 (10): 1335–1441; and Centerwall, B.S. and C.D. Robinette (1989), 'Twin Concordance for Dishonorable Discharge from the Military. With a review of the genetics of antisocial behavior', *Comprehensive Psychiatry* 30(5): 442–6.

20. Salonen, J. T., Hämynen, H., Leino, U., Kostiainen, E. and T. Sahi (1985), 'Relation of Alcohol, Physical Activity, Dietary Fat and Smoking', *Scandinavian Journal of Social Medicine* 13 (3): 99–102; Burling, T.A., Seidner, A.L., Salvio, M.A. and G.D. Marshall (1994), 'Cognitive-behavioral Therapeutic Community for Substance Dependent and Homeless Veterans. Treatment outcome', *Addictive Behaviors* 19 (6): 621–9; Fisher, E.M. *et al.* (1995), 'Single Site Treatment Evaluation Study of a Military Outpatient Drug and Alcohol Program', *Alcoholism Treatment Quarterly* 12 (4): 89–95; and Baggaley, M.R., and D. Morgan-Jones (1993), 'Long-term Follow-up Study of Military Alcohol Treatment Programme Using Post-treatment Careers as an Outcome Measure', *Journal of the Royal Army Medical Corps* 139 (2): 46–8.

21. Arvers, P., Pibarot, A., Job, A. and J. Picard (1993), 'Evaluation des consommations de boissons alcolisées au cours du service national', *Annales Pharmaceutiques Francaises* 51 (4): 205–10; and Embree, B.G. and P.C. Whitehead (1993), 'Validity and Reliability of Self-reported Drinking Behavior. Dealing with the problem of response bias', *Journal of Studies on Alcohol* 54 (3): 334–44.

22. Embree *et al.*, n. 21 above.

23. Bray, n. 16 above; and Bovim *et al.*, n. 18 above.

24. Bray, n. 16 above; Bray, Robert M. *et al.* (1991), 'Standardized Comparisons of the Use of Alcohol, Drugs and Cigarettes among Military Personnel and Civilians', *American Journal of Public Health* 81(7): 865–9; and Hennessy, M. and R. Saltz (1990), 'Situational Riskiness of Alcoholic Beverages', *Journal of Studies on Alcohol*, 51(5): 422–7.

25. Bray *et al.*, n. 24 above.

26. Mellin-Olsen, J. (1988), 'Alkoholintakket blant Norske FN-soldater. Er det så stort som massmedia antyder?', *Tidsskrift for den Norske Laegeforenign* 108 (22): 1635–7; and Malone, J.M. (1986) 'Lebanon – Its Effect on Smoking and Drinking Habits among Irish United Nation Troops' *Irish Journal of Medical Sciences* 155(7), 229–231.

27. Gunby, Phil (1991), 'Service in Strict Islamic Nation Removes Alcohol, Other Drugs from Major Problem List', *Journal of the American Medical Association* 265 (5): 560–1.

28. Pakhomov, A.F., Dikusar, V.F. and V.M. Ianovskii (1986), 'Opyt Provedeniia Anti-alkogol'nykh Meropriiatii v Aviatsionnykh Chastiakh', *Voennii Medichinskii Zhurnal* (November) 11: 55–7; Kolupaev, G.P., Miroschnichenko, L.D. and I.G. Urakov (1987), 'Antialkogol'naia Politika v Vooruzhennykh Silakh Kapitalististicheskikh Stran', *Voennii Medichinskii Zhurnal* (September) 9: 75–8.

29. Bray, n. 16 above; and Embree *et al.*, n. 21 above.

Address for correspondence

National Research and Development Centre for Social Welfare and Health, PO Box 220, FIN-00531 Helsinki, Finland
Tel: +358-9-3967 2022; Fax +358-9-3967 2170; Email jussi.simpura@stakes.fi

37 EDUCATION FOR CONFLICT RESOLUTION

A Contribution to Peacekeeping
in the Republic of Macedonia

VIOLETA PETROSKA-BESKA

Since its declaration of independence and separation from former Yugoslavia in September 1991, the Republic of Macedonia has been constantly facing the problem of ethnic tension, especially between the Macedonian majority (mostly Christian Orthodox) and Albanian minority (mostly Muslim). This discontent among the population is one of the most serious threats to the stability of the country, as well as to the stability of the whole region. The high level of mutual mistrust has caused a lack of communication and almost complete separation between these two ethnic groups, which is manifested clearly in the area of education.

Many aspects of students' in-school and out-of-school activities promote ethnocentrism and radical nationalism, which is a serious potential source of ethnic conflicts in the country as a whole. In its effort to introduce a culture of constructive and peaceful conflict resolution, the Ethnic Conflict Resolution Project is engaged in several major activities aimed at reducing ethnic stereotypes and prejudices, fostering open communication among students of different ethnic backgrounds, developing their self-esteem and self-awareness, encouraging cooperation between them and building active tolerance.

Since its declaration of independence and after its separation from former Yugoslavia in September 1991, the Republic of Macedonia has faced the constant problem of ethnic tension. This discontent among the population is one of the most serious threats to the stability of the country, as well as to the whole region.

The emergence of ethnic tension may be seen as a consequence of both the present economic decline and the current political climate in the country and in the Balkans as a whole. Macedonia is bordered to the south by Greece, a neighbour that still prevents most of the international community from recognizing Macedonia by its constitutional name; to the east by Bulgaria, which has accepted the name Macedonia but rejected the existence of a Macedonian ethnicity; to the north by Serbia, a neighbour with which Macedonia has no officially delineated international border, and which has yet to resolve

Figure 37.1 Geographical position of the Republic of Macedonia

the status of Kosovo, a territory where over 90 per cent of the population are ethnic Albanians; and to the west by Albania, a country that has manifested a controversial degree of interest in the status of ethnic Albanians living in neighbouring countries (Figure 37.1).

Since starting the independence process, most political parties in the Republic of Macedonia have given priority to ethnic interests in their effort to gain popular support, contributing to the growing nationalism of almost all ethnic groups in the country. Most influential political parties can be divided into two opposing streams, according to the ethnic background of their members and followers. One stream involves parties representing the interests of the Macedonian majority, the other representing the interests of the Albanian minority.

Existing historical, social and religious differences between ethnic Macedonians and ethnic Albanians, together with the growing ethnic tension, have been a constant potential source of conflict escalation in the country. Ethnic Macedonians are the dominant group demographically as well as socially, politically and economically. As the second-largest ethnic group in the country (Figure 37.2), ethnic Albanians object that they are treated as second-class citizens and call for equal status with ethnic Macedonians. To overcome this situation, representatives of Albanian political parties demand recognition of Albanian as an official language, Albanian-language education at all levels, free use of Albanian national symbols, proportional representation in government and other concessions as a part of the recognition of Albanians as a constitutive nation in the Constitution of the Republic of Macedonia. At the same time, representatives of Macedonian political parties object to the Albanian demands because they find them dangerous for the integrity of the country. This situation is a constant source of ethnic tension.

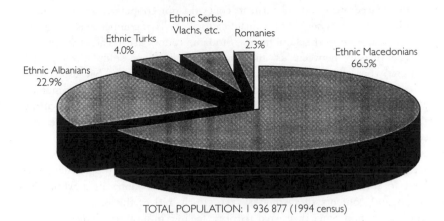

TOTAL POPULATION: 1 936 877 (1994 census)

Figure 37.2 Ethnic composition of the Republic of Macedonia

The existing intolerance between the Macedonian and Albanian ethnic groups is a result of the mutual mistrust that has its roots in the past, but which has been strongly encouraged by certain actions of contemporary political players. These conditions, further abetted by the significant influence of the mass media, have progressively widened the distance between ethnic groups and intensified ethnic intolerance. Existing mutual mistrust has become so strong that it has already caused ethnic Albanians and ethnic Macedonians to fear each other and to share the opinion of radical nationalists from their respective sides who claim that 'it has become obvious that living together with the "others" is no longer possible'. The average ethnic Albanian feels as threatened by the Macedonian ethnic group as the average ethnic Macedonian feels threatened by the Albanian minority.

Education as a source of ethnic tensions

The level of mutual mistrust has caused an almost complete separation between the two major ethnic groups. Most of the ethnic Albanians have retreated within their ethnic group, taking into consideration only their own interests. The same has happened to the ethnic Macedonians. As a consequence, communication between the two groups has deteriorated in many areas of everyday life.

This is clearly evident in the field of education. Using the opportunities offered by Macedonia's educational system, Albanian students attend separate classes at both elementary- and high-school levels, where they are taught in their mother tongue. Even in ethnically-mixed schools where Albanian students study under the same roof with Macedonians, separation and lack of communication are obvious during breaks, as well as during other extracurricular activities.

The same situation applies to teachers. Even when they are colleagues from the same school, most Macedonian and Albanian teachers do not cooperate. They frequently compete collectively over issues like job qualifications, levels of competence, administrative positions and even over school names. Students cannot escape an atmosphere in which a clear division between 'us' and 'them' prevails. They study surrounded by negative stereotypes and prejudices which can be easily exaggerated because students cannot challenge their authenticity: Macedonians and Albanians do not communicate directly, but learn about each other from the 'experiences' of other members of their own ethnic community. Any conflict between students, therefore, may come to be regarded as having an ethnic dimension.

In addition, most of the available textbooks at elementary- and high-school level contribute to students' exaggerated identification with their ethnic group, making them more loyal to their own ethnic community than to the country as a whole. The composition and contents of textbooks very clearly reflect the basic intention of ethnocentric education. Since they evoke patriotic feelings in support of an ethnic cause, most textbooks may easily be considered a potential source of radical nationalism.

The Pedagogical Faculty is regarded as a crucial case in inter-ethnic relations within the area of education. It began several years ago as a demand by Albanian university students studying to become pre-school and primary-school teachers. Since they would be teaching students in the Albanian language only, these students themselves wanted to have all their courses taught in Albanian (something they had experienced in the past but that had been discontinued). After futile attempts to negotiate and with backing from political players, Albanian students began boycotting courses offered only in Macedonian. Under pressure, the government eventually passed a law permitting the Pedagogical Faculty to provide the teaching of all courses for Albanian students in the Albanian language.

In reaction, Macedonian students from the Pedagogical Faculty, with political assistance, initiated a series of street marches against that law in an attempt 'to protect the constitution and the integrity of the country'. Besides a small number of Macedonian university students, a huge number of Macedonian high-school students joined the marches. A big proportion of these students came from ethnically-mixed schools, most of the time directly or indirectly supported by their teachers. Many of the banners carried in the demonstrations were highly anti-Albanian. Accusations that these high-school students were manipulated by radical political parties (because of their age, it was argued that these high-schoolers were not fully conscious of, or responsible for, the parts they played in such an event) contradicted what they had been taught about Macedonian history in school namely that, according to their textbooks, many of the country's national heroes had led national movements for peace and justice.) Their textbooks glorify numerous national heroes who were at the forefront of national movements for peace and justice.

It is not difficult to predict the consequences of these events. On one side, we have young ethnic Macedonians who are convinced that ethnic Albanians are their enemies, 'since they refuse to have anything to do with Macedonia'. On the other side we have ethnic Albanians who are full of bitterness for being exposed to heavy provocation and insults. Many of them, irrespective of ethnic community, will soon become teachers who will educate and raise future generations of young people in Macedonia.

This is an illustrative example of how education can be used as a potential peace breaker in a country balancing on the edge of universal conflict escalation. Nonetheless, education can be applied as a peacekeeping tool if one finds a proper way to use it for reducing ethnic tension.

Education for conflict resolution

Most conflicts contain a small core of truly incompatible goals surrounded by a larger exterior of misperceptions of the other's motives and goals. Closely connected to misperceptions, stereotypes and prejudices are both a result and a cause of ethnic tension. During a conflict, one side perceives the opposing group and its members as the 'other' who is strange, foreign, or alien. Held at psychological distance and regarded as fundamentally different, that other becomes a screen on which it is possible to project one's worst fears. Furthermore, this projection is usually a shared perception: what we see in 'them' tends to be what others see in us. One way to fight the negative impact of prejudices is to reduce the distance between us and them, which requires seeing them as more like 'us'.

This is difficult to accomplish when there is limited communication between the groups in conflict. In present-day schools, by going through primary and secondary education in separate classrooms, Macedonian and Albanian students have little chance to experience their similarities, and they have to rely on stories that exaggerate their differences. Education for conflict resolution can contribute to overcoming this obstacle.

By introducing the culture of constructive and peaceful conflict resolution in schools, people's understanding of conflicts can be expected to change; from looking at conflict as always being a destructive battle between incompatible interests to perceiving it as a possibility for mutual growth and for improvement in a relationship which, besides interests, also involves needs, feelings and values. In that sense, various activities can be undertaken to foster such a positive climate in schools.

- students can be encouraged to fight against stereotypes and prejudices by talking openly about existing preconceptions and the mechanisms involved in developing or maintaining but also in reducing them;

- Open communication can be fostered by teaching students, teachers, and parents active-listening skills, how to address their own needs and feelings, and how to respect the needs and feelings of others;

- Self-esteem and self-awareness can be strengthened in order to help students look for self-support instead of relying on collective affirmation from their ethnic group;

- Cooperation can be encouraged among students, and especially between Macedonian and Albanian teachers, who will then carry it over to their students;

- Active tolerance can be built by stimulating children's proactive interest in the communities that surround them.

Ethnic Conflict Resolution Project (ECRP) activities in education

The Ethnic Conflict Resolution Project (ECRP) is based at the Faculty of Philosophy, University of Saints Cyril and Methodius in Skopje. Since its activities have been developed and maintained with financial support from the international community, the ECRP has been acting as an independent entity. It was founded in January 1994 with the overall goal of helping the citizens of the Republic of Macedonia to take an active position towards the resolution of seemingly intractable conflicts rooted in ethnic and other differences.

ECRP acts upon two major assumptions:

• Conflicts with an ethnic dimension are an unavoidable part of people's lives in Macedonia and a source of high tension in the country. For that reason, ECRP works with people and for people from different ethnic communities, mainly of Macedonian and Albanian ethnic background.

• Most of the ethnic tension in the country has been created as an instrument to acquire political power. Therefore, ECRP makes efforts to introduce a culture of peaceful conflict resolution at the grassroots level, hoping that, in the long run, it might make people resistant to this kind of political influence.

So far, ECRP has been involved in four kinds of activities: training, research, developing literature, and consultations. For the time being, the ECRP's major area of interest has been the field of education. It was not chosen by chance, but out of necessity. Education was and still is regarded as a source of ethnic tension and consequently can be used as a battlefield for the reduction of tension. ECRP has developed four major educational programmes which have been carried out at the pre-, elementary-, and high-school levels, with the serious possibility that they will be institutionalized in the country's educational system. These ECRP programs are: Conflict Resolution Games, Conflict Awareness Seminars, Appreciating Differences, and Bilingual Macedonian–Albanian Kindergartens. In addition, the ECRP organizes camp activities, mostly with high-school students.

Conflict Resolution Games

The Conflict Resolution Games programme was designed to educate, motivate and challenge younger elementary school students (4th-graders, average age 10 years, whose language of instruction is either Macedonian or Albanian) to address complex issues of conflict and conflict resolution on a personal and group level and to apply this knowledge to creating positive and effective change in their own behaviour. The programme's main objectives are: (i) to develop critical-thinking skills to identify the causes of conflict, and strategies for cooperation and conflict resolution; (ii) to offer an opportunity to face and internalize an alternative approach to violence in responding to conflict situations; and (iii) to contribute to the development of a community in which children are capable of communication aimed at resolving all kinds of conflicts.

The programme consists of 27 sessions taught on a weekly basis, with students being actively involved in working out creative new approaches. Using cooperative games, role-playing, small-group discussions, creative problem solving and simulations, trainers challenge the students to think critically about the nature of conflicts, the impact of perceptions, communication and needs in conflicts, anger management and other issues related to the concept of conflict and conflict management. The project is supported by a Macedonian and an Albanian version of a specially-prepared training manual.

Conflict Awareness Seminars

The main objective of the Conflict Awareness Seminars is to work with elementary- and high-school students, their parents, school staff and university students in order to introduce the culture of constructive and peaceful conflict resolution as widely as possible. The scheme is organized as a six-hour training session of lectures, discussions and exercises on topics such as: the nature of conflicts; sources of conflicts and reactions in conflict situations; factors influencing conflicts (perception, stereotypes and prejudices); competitive versus collaborative negotiation; elements and phases of collaborative negotiation; and third-party intervention (mediation and arbitration). Two versions of the training manual (one for elementary-school students and one for high-school students and adults) have been prepared, one in Macedonian and one in Albanian, to support the training of trainers programme.

Appreciating Differences

The objectives of the Appreciating Differences programme are: (i) to foster self-awareness as a basis for accepting and not fearing differences; (ii) to look at differences as a stimulus for personal and group development; (iii) to realize that there are similarities between people of different cultural (ethnic and religious) backgrounds, just as there are differences among people of the same cultural background; and (iv) to learn how important it is to appreciate differences and tolerate diversity. So far, this is the only programme in the Republic of Macedonia intended for ethnically mixed groups of high-school students. It is organized in extracurricular workshops with discussions and exercises based on lectures and video materials.

Bilingual Macedonian–Albanian Kindergartens

Bilingual Macedonian–Albanian Kindergartens have been one of the most challenging ECRP enterprises. The main objectives are defined as: (i) fostering respect for one's self and others; (ii) building relationships and interdependence; (iii) learning the language of the other ethnic group; and (iv) understanding conflict and factors that influence conflicts, as well as developing skills for constructive and peaceful conflict resolution. Three pilot groups of about 20 children (ages: 3–6, representing both ethnic groups) are about to be established within existing public kindergartens. Kindergarten trainers are given special training on how to apply an interactive approach in the educational process and how to develop children's affirmative, communication, cooperative and conflict-resolution skills.

Camp Activities

Camp activities have been designed as extracurricular workshops for high-school students from different towns and from different ethnic backgrounds. They are usually carried out in a hotel, outside of students' home towns, in order (i) to develop mutual understanding and respect; (ii) to build active tolerance; (iii) to practice cooperation and freedom of expression; and (iv) to overcome existing ethnic, religious, and gender prejudices. The basic strategy for achieving these goals involves group-discussion sessions with many experiential exercises, and joint free-time activities with group entertainment.

Address for correspondence
Faculty of Philosophy, Bul. Krste Misirkov bb, 91000 Skopje, Republic of Macedonia

V WAR AND ENVIRONMENT

Sniper victim
Oliver Whitehead

38 CONVENTIONAL WARFARE AND THE HUMAN ENVIRONMENT

ARTHUR H. WESTING

Warfare is by its very nature deadly and destructive. This chapter outlines the extent of environmental disruption that can be associated with conventional warfare (that is to say warfare that does not involve nuclear or other weapons of mass destruction). Of particular concern here from the standpoints of both nature and human health and safety are the employment of: (i) environmental manipulations, especially those that release dangerous forces; (ii) forest-clearing chemicals and devices; and (iii) anti-personnel cluster bombs and landmines.

The adverse effects on nature and humans just alluded to are associated not only with the actual pursuit of conventional warfare, but to some extent also with the prewar and postwar periods. Thus a brief preliminary section is devoted to outlining this aspect of the problem.

Peacetime impact of the military sector[1]

Hundreds of wars were fought in the 20th century alone, several dozen of them always being in progress somewhere or other in the world. However, whether at war or peace, most nations maintain armed forces. Such armed forces are maintained by states for various reasons, among them: (i) to deter an attack from outside their borders or, failing that, to defend against such an attack; (ii) to threaten an attack on another state in support of some foreign-policy objective or, failing that, to carry out such an attack; and (iii) to deter or quell internal uprisings. In fact, most wars in recent decades have been internal ones, so-called civil wars fought between government and insurgent forces.

The social and environmental ramifications for states to maintain armed forces for any or all of the above reasons result from: (i) establishing military fortifications and other military facilities; (ii) equipping and supplying armed forces with weapons and other military needs, and in turn disposing of these once they become obsolete or otherwise unwanted; (iii) training armed forces and testing the weapons they use; and (iv) routine deployment of armed forces nationally, in other nations, and in areas beyond any national jurisdiction.

The social and environmental impacts of peacetime military activities are very roughly proportional to the fraction of gross domestic product (GDP) they represent in a nation, which is now of the order of 2 per cent or 3 per cent for both industrialized and non-industrialized countries. However, it must be recognized that were the military sector in a country made smaller, the human, material, financial and intellectual resources made available thereby would be shifted to the civil sector, presumably to carry out more socially useful activities, but the environmental impact would remain more or less comparable.

Environmental manipulations

Environmental manipulations in wartime can be (a) unintentional, (b) intentional, or (c) intentional for purposes of amplification through the release of so-called dangerous forces.

Unintentional manipulations [2]

Unintentional (ancillary, incidental, collateral) environmental manipulations in wartime can result from the often profligate employment of high-explosive munitions against enemy personnel and *matériel*. Another frequent source of such unintentional manipulations is the use of tanks and other heavy off-road vehicles. Both of these forms of ancillary environmental damage can be especially disruptive of local habitats and the creatures that depend upon them. The construction of base camps, fortifications and lines of communication can add to the environmental disruption. Battle-related activities can also lead to certain amounts of local air and water pollution. Further ancillary wartime environmental damage derives from the often heavy exploitation by armed forces in the field of timber, food and feed, both within the theatre of military operations and beyond.

Intentional manipulations [3]

The pursuit of war often involves the intentional destruction of field or forest as a specific means of denying to the enemy the benefits of such components of the environment. The benefits being denied to the enemy include access to water, food, feed and construction materials. Often even more important, the denied benefits include access to cover or sanctuary, as noted in the section below on forest clearing. The long-term environmental impacts of denial (or barrier) operations through the employment of mines is also discussed below.

A number of important rivers flow through more than one country, providing an opportunity for a nation upstream to divert or befoul the waters before they reach a downstream nation with which it is at war, a major calamity in an arid region.

The Gulf War of 1991 has gone down in history as the conflict providing the most spectacular example of intentional oil releases, by Iraq in Kuwait, for various hostile purposes. Some of the oil that was caused to escape remained in liquid form; some was or became ignited to produce dense clouds of dark soot-laden smoke. Some of the liquid oil was released on land and some into the Persian Gulf. The oil releases into the environment resulted primarily from the sabotaging of about 730 oil wells (of which around 630 were torched), of 20 or so collecting centres, and of 3 or more oil tankers; various storage tanks and pipelines were also breached. Numerous sabotaged oil wells continued to discharge oil for many months. The huge resulting releases ultimately amounted to perhaps 10 million cubic metres (60 million barrels). On land, some 200 small lakes of oil were created, leading to the death of much wildlife and to diverse other environmental problems, including the contamination of groundwater. Of the escaping oil, of the order of 1 million cubic metres (6 million barrels) was released into the Persian Gulf, severely contaminating Kuwaiti offshore waters and about 400 kilometres of coastline, primarily Saudi Arabian, thereby disrupting marine habitats and killing much migratory marine wildlife (avian, mammalian and reptilian). The huge amounts of smoke released into the atmosphere (soot plus various combustion gases) produced a pall that persisted for several months, leading particularly to adverse human health effects especially for those already suffering from respiratory ailments or who were otherwise in a frail condition.

Intentional manipulations to release dangerous forces[4]

Under certain conditions, it is possible to manipulate some component of the natural or built environment for hostile military purposes in a way that is intended to result in the release of dangerous pent-up forces. This sort of military effort, which is often referred to as environmental warfare, becomes especially tempting when the hostile manipulation involves a relatively modest expenditure of effort (i.e., of triggering energy) leading to the release of a substantially greater amount of directed destructive energy. Environmental manipulations of particular concern with reference to magnified destructive potential involve fresh-water impounds, nuclear power stations and, to a lesser extent, forest lands. Attacks upon certain industrial facilities could also release dangerous forces, in the form of toxic chemical clouds, over a considerable area.

Many hundreds of major dams have been constructed in recent decades throughout scores of countries that impound huge quantities of water. A significant fraction of those dams could be breached with relative ease, either through direct attack or sabotage, releasing the impounded water to cause immense levels of death and destruction. Hostile actions of this nature have been spectacularly successful in various past wars (notably so in such recent conflicts as WW II and the Korean War of 1950–53); and their social and environmental impacts can take many decades to recover from. Indeed, the most devastating example of a single adverse manipulation, military or otherwise, throughout history appears to have been the intentional release during the Sino-Japanese War of 1937–45 of Yellow River waters. In order to stop the Japanese advance, in June 1938 the Chinese dynamited the Huayuankow dike near Chengchow. Several thousand Japanese soldiers drowned, and the Japanese advance into China along this front was halted. However, in the process, the flood waters also ravaged major portions of Henan, Anhui, and Jiangsu provinces. Several million hectares of farmland were destroyed as were 4000 villages and 11 cities; at the same time several hundred thousand (and perhaps many more) Chinese drowned. The river was not brought back under control until 1947.

Almost 200 clusters of nuclear power stations have now become essentially permanent additions to the human environment, plus a number of additional nuclear reprocessing plants and nuclear waste repositories, distributed in over 30 countries. These sites are amenable to assault, again either through overt attack or sabotage, with the possible attendant release into a surrounding area measurable in thousands to millions of hectares of iodine-131, cesium-137, strontium-90 and other radioactive elements. The most heavily contaminated inner area would become life threatening, an outer zone of lesser contamination would become health threatening and a still greater zone would become agriculturally unusable. A radioactively polluted area such as this defies effective decontamination. Indeed, it is known especially from the Pacific islands used for testing in the 1940s and 1950s and from the Chernobyl accident of April 1986 that the health-threatening degradation of the land will take centuries to recover.

Under certain habitat and weather conditions, forest fires can be initiated that are subsequently self-propagating and enormously destructive of the forest resource itself, of human artifacts and of the enmeshed flora and fauna. In killing the vegetation of a forest ecosystem (its autotrophic component), such incendiary warfare leads to substantial damage to the wildlife (its heterotrophic component) as well as to the nutrient budget, the latter via soil erosion and nutrient dumping (the rapid loss of nutrients in solution). Substantial recovery from such unbalancing of a forest system must be measured in decades. Incendiary warfare in grassland (prairie) and tundra ecosystems could, under special conditions, be equally or even more damaging.

The quite widely adopted 1977 Protocols I and II on the Protection of Victims of Armed Conflicts (UNTS, nos 17512 and 17513) include some important specific constraints on the destruction of the environment as outlined above, whereas the less widely adopted 1977 Environmental Modification Convention (UNTS, no. 17119) provides some more or less ineffectual relevant constraints.

Forest clearing[5]

Forests are destroyed during wartime primarily to deny an enemy cover and concealment, and to a much lesser extent to deny the timber resource to the enemy. Forests can be devastated for hostile purposes over huge areas by various means, among them: (i) spraying with herbicides; (ii) the use of heavy tractors equipped with special forest-clearing blades; (iii) saturation bombing; and (iv) at certain times and places, by the setting of self-propagating wild fires.

Herbicides were employed on a dramatic scale for forest clearing by the USA in Indochina during the war of 1961–75 (some 72 million litres sprayed onto almost 2 million hectares), as were heavy tractors (clearing over 300 thousand hectares) and saturation bombing (totaling about 7 million tonnes). Although incendiary attacks are most common, and most successful, against urban and industrial targets, they are also occasionally attempted, with greater or lesser success, against rural grassland or forest targets.

The forest destruction carried out in order to deny the enemy cover and concealment can bring about great damage to upland forest ecosystems and can lead to utter destruction of coastal ones. In destroying the vegetation of a forest ecosystem, the wildlife is decimated concomitantly primarily owing to a loss of its natural habitat. At the same time, the soil and its nutrients are eroded and washed away, the more so the more rugged the terrain. Depending on the severity of attack, vegetational type and local site conditions, natural recovery of the assaulted forest ecosystem can take years or decades.

The use of chemical warfare agents, including herbicides, is prohibited by the widely-adopted 1925 Geneva Protocol on Chemical and Bacteriological Warfare (LNTS, no. 2138). Protocol III of the 1980 Inhumane Conventional Weapon Convention (UNTS, no. 22495) includes a modest restriction on the destruction of forests by fire. There are no specific restrictions in the laws of war on bombing or on the use of tractors for hostile purposes.

Cluster bombs and landmines[6]

This section considers the wartime use of landmines and other weapons with similar long-term effects, a gruesome and much-employed means of warfare that is often taken for granted, but for which at least a partial remedy is available.

To begin with, high-explosive landmines, both antipersonnel and antivehicle, are relatively inexpensive, easily employed and effective means of hindering, slowing down or channelling the movements of enemy forces as well as of sapping their morale. Landmines are thus widely and heavily employed by both regular armies and insurgent forces. They are usually constructed and emplaced so as to defy premeditated discovery, but are of course designed so as to detonate when inadvertently disturbed. Scatterable landmines, now widely employed by technically advanced armed forces, can be remotely delivered in great numbers by various means, including artillery, rocket and aircraft. The vast majority of all landmines used in warfare are, in fact, not set off by the combatants at which they were directed and, tragically, most of them remain ready to explode for many decades into the future.

Then there are the high-explosive munitions other than landmines – grenades, artillery shells, mortar rounds, bombs, sub-munitions (bomblets), rockets, and so forth – that are often expended in vastly greater numbers during warfare than are landmines. The increasingly popular explosive sub-munitions dispensed via air-dropped cluster bomb units (CBUs) are generally employed in staggeringly high numbers. Whereas most of these many sorts of high-explosive munitions explode as intended at the time of release, a significant fraction, the so-called duds (perhaps 10 per cent), malfunction. And, in turn, a significant fraction (perhaps 50 per cent) of these residual duds remain ready to explode when jolted at some future time. The long-term impact of high-explosive 'duds' is thus quite comparable to that of residual landmines.

The sub-munitions or bomblets are encased in a bomb-like cluster in groups of several dozen to several hundred or more. The resulting cluster bomb can be delivered to a target area by aircraft (fixed-wing or helicopter); or, if appropriately configured, by artillery, mortar tube or rocket launcher. The bomblets are of various sorts, but are typically charged with a high explosive and constructed for either antipersonnel or anti-tank purposes, or a combination of these. The bomblets can be equipped with a wide variety of fuses for above-ground, contact, or delayed detonation. Indeed, some fuses make bomblets difficult to distinguish from remotely delivered (scatterable) landmines.

For example, during the 1961–75 Indochina War cluster bombs were used by the USA as area-denial and antipersonnel weapons. Of the order of 1.5 million cluster bombs appear to have been expended during that conflict, roughly 7 per cent of the total number of bombs dropped. Those 1.5 million cluster bombs contained roughly 750 million bomblets, dropped onto portions of Viet Nam, Laos and Cambodia over a period of about a decade.

During the Persian Gulf War of 1991, the USA (and presumably other members of the United Nations Coalition Forces) used cluster bombs as antipersonnel and antitank weapons. Some 60,000 cluster bombs were expended by the USA alone during that conflict, more or less evenly divided between anti-personnel and anti-tank types, together representing about 30 per cent of the total number of bombs dropped. Those 60,000 cluster bombs contained almost 30 million bomblets, dropped onto portions of Kuwait and Iraq over a period of about a month.

The immensity of the overall problem of landmines and other unexploded remnants of warfare is difficult to grasp. At present, there are more than, perhaps many more than, 65 million functional landmines emplaced in some 56 countries around the world. Presumably even larger numbers of potentially still-explosive dud munitions are to be found additionally in those same and other countries. The records of the International Committee of the Red Cross (Geneva) reveal that these explosive remnants of warfare are now resulting in more than 800 human fatalities plus further thousands of maimings each month. In Cambodia alone explosive remnants have produced more than 36,000 amputees within the past decade or so; and in Somalia more than 23,000.

The problem of the explosive remnants of warfare exists in many parts of the world, but is perhaps most acute in Africa, where some 18 countries are seriously afflicted with them, including especially Angola, Eritrea, Ethiopia, Mozambique, Somalia and Sudan. In the Middle East the worst affected countries are Iran, Iraq, and Kuwait; in Asia: Afghanistan, Azerbaijan, Cambodia, Laos and Vietnam; in Latin America: El Salvador and Nicaragua; and in Europe: Bosnia-Herzegovina, Croatia and Serbia-Montenegro. In Poland, with its residuum of explosive WW II remnants, of which thousands are still being found and disposed of each year, several dozen individuals continue to be killed or maimed annually.

Human existence and well-being depend upon continuing access to huge rural areas throughout the world for agriculture, horticulture, grazing, forestry, hunting, fishing, mining, and pleasure. When a rural area being used like this by the local inhabitants becomes a battlefield, the effects of exploding munitions and other actions can be devastating. When that rural area has been a theatre of military operations that left a residuum of unexploded munitions, this will have severe consequences, both direct and indirect.

To begin with, remnant-clearing operations are themselves apt to be environmentally disruptive, sometimes very much so. Moreover, they are time-consuming, technically difficult, expensive (often prohibitively so), never fully successful and, above all, exceedingly dangerous.

In many rural areas throughout the world, the local population is forced by circumstances to continue to use the land upon which it has depended, with the result that there is an appalling frequency of fatalities and maimings, both human and livestock. Thus, in former battle zones farming, herding and forestry become hazardous pursuits. Wood destined for lumber becomes unsafe and troublesome with metal embedded in it. Other aspects of local development are equally hampered, including the construction of roads, power lines and irrigation systems. Income from tourism can be all but eliminated. Moreover, any material and financial resources diverted to clearing, or to remnant-generated medical, veterinary and other expenses, are lost to productive activities.

In short, the various familial and societal disruptions resulting from explosive-remnant deaths or permanent disabilities, losses of livestock and other property, reduced opportunities for subsistence food production and for income, forced migrations and so forth become a great impediment to the sustainable development of the local economy. To the extent that areas are deemed simply too dangerous to be exploited, the resulting refugees or migrants are likely to overburden both the natural and social resources of their sites of destination, whether rural or urban, which is likely, therefore, to lead to additional, off-site damage to the environment.

The presence of landmines and other explosive remnants makes recovery following armed conflict an extremely onerous matter, raising serious social and environmental concerns. Other than eliminating warfare itself, every effort must be made to minimize adverse postwar consequences on humans and nature. In the present context, international technical and financial cooperation is needed to help clear the unexploded remnants of past armed conflicts, something that has been unanimously urged recently by the United Nations General Assembly. Landmines and every other type of high-explosive munition that is apt to become an explosive remnant should without exception be designed to have a built-in, non-removable mechanism for becoming harmless in due course.

The long-term postwar problem of landmines and other unexploded ordnance is a singularly grave and intractable one. This is the case especially in view of several factors: (i) the great, and to a substantial extent successful, efforts in mine design and emplacement techniques to prevent their discovery by the enemy; (ii) the efforts to keep munitions functional in the face of extremely adverse environmental conditions (quite successful, to judge from their extraordinary longevity); (iii) the vast levels of wartime munition expenditures, exacerbated by such recent ordnance innovations as scatterable mines and sub-munitions (bomblets); and (iv) the emphasis in at least some types of warfare on large-scale area neutralization or area denial.

Existing constraints in international law on the use of landmines and other explosive remnants do not as yet provide adequate protection to civilians, either in time of armed conflict or after its cessation. Two multilateral instruments are of relevance here: (i) the 1980 Inhumane Conventional Weapon Convention (UNTS, no. 22495), Protocol II of which restricts the use of landmines (the convention has not as yet won many adherents despite its rather weak restrictions on landmines and none at all on other explosive remnants); and (ii) the 1997 Ottawa Mine Convention (UNTS, no. 35597) that simply outlaws the very possession of antipersonnel mines, which a slowly growing number of states is now joining.

It is manifestly clear that landmines and comparable weapons should be outlawed by all states, or at the very least their employment severely circumscribed. Protocol II of the 1980 Inhumane Weapon Convention could serve this purpose through (i) far wider adoption, and (ii) appropriate strengthening. if it were to become widely adopted, the 1997 Ottawa Convention, would of course be better yet.

Conclusion[7]

Conventional warfare can be devastating, both socially and environmentally. However, it is important to realize that the level of destruction does not in fact depend so much upon the modernity of the armed forces involved or upon the sophistication of the weapons available to them, but rather largely upon the objectives, the will and the tenacity of the parties to the conflict. Improvements in weaponry have followed one on the other throughout the long sweep of human history, but so far this has not led to any discernible increase in the damage brought about by warfare, only in the efficiency with which it is perpetrated. By way of example, one of the most socially and environmentally devastating wars in recent centuries was fought with quite primitive arms by the standards of today. In the Chinese Rebellion of 1850–64 the Tai Ping (Great Peace) movement was ultimately unsuccessful in its attempt to overthrow the ruling Manchu dynasty. The Tai Ping forces pursued their rebellion with continuing violence of a high order and with much pillaging. It was countered by the Manchu forces with equal or greater terror and violence. Among other means, the government forces employed large-scale scorched-earth tactics in order to starve the rebellious regions into submission. The final total number of war deaths is estimated to have been between 20 and 40 million, representing about 7 per cent of China's total population at the time. The population and countryside particularly of the lower Yangtze River region (Anhui province plus portions of the surrounding provinces) were devastated and had still not regained their prewar conditions a century later.

The global biosphere is being damaged ever more decisively by grossly expanding human numbers and needs with ultimately disastrous consequences for human and all other life on earth. It is now becoming even more true and more obvious that warfare is an outrageously frivolous human pastime. However if it is not to be avoided, at least the most perfidious acts and unintentional impacts of war must be minimized. Such restraints must occur for both social and environmental reasons, the latter not only because they have an important indirect effect on the health and safety of humans, but also to protect nature and its wild creatures in their own right.

REFERENCES

1. Westing, A.H. (1980), *Warfare in a Fragile World: military impact on the human environment*, London: Taylor and Francis.
2. Ibid.; Westing, A.H. (1976), *Ecological Consequences of the Second Indochina War*, Stockholm: Almqvist and Wiksell, and Westing, A.H. (1990), 'Environmental Hazards of War in an Industrializing World', in Westing, A.H. (ed.). *Environmental Hazards of War: releasing dangerous forces in an industrialized world*, London: Sage Publications, pp. 1–9.
3. Westing, A.H. (1980, 1990), n. 1 above and (1994a), 'Constraints on Environmental Disruption During the Gulf War', in J. O'Loughlin *et al.* (eds), *War and its Consequences: lessons from the Persian Gulf conflict*, New York: Harper Collins College Publishers, pp. 77–84.
4. Westing, A.H. (1990), n. 2 above; (1984a), 'Environmental Warfare: an overview', in A.H. Westing (ed.), *Environmental Warfare: a technical, legal and policy appraisal*, London: Taylor and Francis, pp. 3–12; (1984b), 'How Much Damage Can Modern War Create?', in F. Barnaby (ed.), *Future War: armed conflict in the next decade*, London: Michael Joseph, pp. 114–24; and (1997), 'Environmental Protection from Wartime Damage: the role of international law', in N.P Gleditsch (ed.), *Conflict and the Environment*, Dordrecht: Kluwer Academic Publishers, pp. 535–53.
5. Westing, A.H. (1980), n. 1 above; (1976), n. 2 above; (1989), 'Herbicides in Warfare: the case of Indochina', in P. Bourdeau, *et al.* (eds), *Ecotoxicology and Climate*, Chichester, UK: John Wiley, pp. 337–57; and (1997) n. 4 above.
6. Westing, A.H. (1997), n. 4 above; (1985), 'Explosive Remnants of War: an overview', in A.H. Westing, (ed.) *Explosive Remnants of War: mitigating the environmental effects*, London: Taylor and Francis, pp. 1–16; and (1994), 'Unexploded Sub-munitions (Bomblets) and the Environment', in ICRC (ed.), *Expert Meeting on Certain Weapon Systems and on Implementation Mechanisms in International Law*, Geneva: International Committee of the Red Cross, pp. 75–81.
7. Westing, A.H. (1980), n. 1 above; and (1984b), n. 4 above.

Address for correspondence
134 Fred Houghton Road, Putney, VT 05346, USA.
Email: westing@sover.net

39 MILITARY POLLUTION – NUCLEAR WASTE

Sailing Directions Classified

ALEKSANDER YEMELYANENKOV
and ANDREI ZOLOTKOV

At the end of the 1980s ecologists and journalists, supported by members of the then Soviet parliament, for the first time called public attention to the dumping of radioactive waste (RAW) in northern seas. The authorities would neither confirm nor deny those reports for quite a while. It was in October 1992 that President Yeltsin ordered a special inquiry led by his adviser Aleksei Yablokov. Its findings were presented to the president four months later.

The very fact that members of non-governmental organizations and independent experts were invited to participate in the project is significant. Reminiscences and testimonies by participants in dumping operations collected by our colleagues or published in the mass media were closely studied. In many cases such publications prompted additional requests addressed to ministries and agencies who, as in the old days, preferred to keep information locked away.

President Yeltsin, unlike his predecessors in the Kremlin, did not pretend that the problem of RAW in Russia did not exist. He studied the report, supported its conclusions and issued written instructions to Prime Minister Chernomyrdin, Foreign Minister Kozyrev and the chief of the presidential staff, Filatov, asking them to find sources of financing and to formulate comprehensive approaches to handling RAW. They were also asked to define Russia's official position in relation to foreign partners. In return, Russia pledged to submit to the International Atomic Energy Agency (IAEA) and to the secretariat of the London Convention official reports of all instances of radioactive waste dumped in the world ocean.

Where did the waste come from?

Radioactive dumps in Russian sea areas are as old as its nuclear-powered ships and their numbers have been growing for 30 years. There is documentary evidence that dumping in the seas began in 1959 with permission from the leaders of the former USSR, and continued up to 1992 in designated areas of the Baltic, Barents, White, Kara and Okhotsk seas and the Sea of Japan, as well as off the Novaya Zemlya archipelago and the Kamchatka peninsula.

In the Arctic (the Barents and Kara seas) there are 13 such areas, two for dumping liquid and eight for solid waste. Off Russia's far-eastern shores RAW was dumped at 10 sites. There are, furthermore, several recorded cases of the unauthorized sinking of ships carrying RAW on the way to the dumping sites, as well as instances of emergency dumping of liquid RAW at naval bases and combat training areas.

Experts have found that 22 of the 23 areas used fail to meet the basic requirements established by the London Convention, such as the depth of the sea at the dumping site, distance from the coast or geographical latitudes. The latter requirement would in fact prohibit the dumping of any RAW in the Barents, Kara or White seas. At consultative conferences of the London Convention Soviet officials repeatedly stated that the Soviet Union had never dumped RAW in the sea and did not plan to do so in the future.

How was secrecy maintained?

The routine dumping of liquid and solid RAW was carried out primarily by Russian naval ships and those of the Murmansk Shipping Company. Decisions to that effect were made jointly by various agencies: the ministries of defence, atomic energy, merchant marine, and health. Particularly hazardous cases were taken to the government and even to the Politburo of the Communist Party's Central Committee. All decisions were classified, and experts involved in the operations sworn to secrecy.

What do the dumped wastes look like?

The wastes and repair cast-offs came from nuclear-powered submarines and surface ships of the Arctic and Pacific fleets, as well as of the nuclear-powered icebreakers and lighter carriers owned by the Murmansk Shipping Company. A considerable part of the waste also came from the shipyards of the former USSR Shipbuilding Industry Ministry.

Solid low- and medium-active RAW was as a rule dumped in metal containers, buried separately or inside ships to be sunk. In 1964 through 1991, 4900 containers with solid low- and medium-active RAW and 19 ships with 144 big-size objects were sunk in northern seas. Their total activity is estimated at 16,000 Curies (Ci) (592 TBq). Off Russia's east coast, 6868 containers with medium- and low-active solid waste, 38 ships and more than 100 other big objects are reported to have been dumped between 1986 and 1991. Their total activity measures 6200 Ci.

At the same time, the Baltic, Barents, White and Kara seas received about 100,000 cubic metres of liquid RAW with a total activity of 24,444 Ci (905 TBq); the Barents Sea accounts for 52 per cent and the Kara Sea for 47 per cent. Incomplete or lost archives have not permitted accurate estimation of the amount or parameters of liquid RAW dumped in the Far-Eastern seas, but the available accounts confirm a total of activity of 12,295 Ci (455 TBq).

The knowledge of hazardous dumps off the Novaya Zemlya islands available earlier has been updated with information about two reactors from Pacific Fleet submarines which have lain on the bottom of the Sea of Japan at a depth of 3000 metres since 1978. In 1989 the removable screen from a submarine reactor was dumped off the east coast of the Kamchatka peninsula. At the moment of dumping the activity of the three objects was estimated at 116.2 Ci (4.3 TBq).

Who monitors the situation in the areas of RAW dumps?

A system to monitor and control situations in the maritime areas where RAW has been dumped is non-existent, although there are quite a few research institutions whose direct or indirect job that would be. It was not before 1992 that the navy began to arrange for radio-ecological monitoring in the aforesaid areas. Before that, sporadic studies of radiation situations were held in areas 50–100 kilometres away from solid RAW dumps. No systematic control in the areas of nuclear dumps has been held.

Experts currently believe it will be impossible to tell for how much longer the protective casing of RAW will last or when, how quickly or in what amounts radio-nuclides will begin to escape into the sea water. The joint Russian-Norwegian expedition of 1992 failed to achieve the expected results, because it was not given permission to visit areas where the most dangerous RAW had been dumped.

What steps was the president advised to take?

A special section concerning maritime dumps was recommended to be included in the state programme for handling RAW. Special attention was paid to developing coastal infrastructures of the nuclear-powered fleet and advanced and reliable storages, introducing fundamentally new technologies to remove and dump RAW.

The first draft of the report contained the proposal for an immediate ban on dumping radioactive waste in the sea. However, most government commission members later voted that that demand was unrealistic. A compromise option was preferred: no more solid waste or spent nuclear fuel should be buried at sea and the dumping of liquid RAW should be reduced gradually, as coastal facilities for their processing are commissioned.

Moreover, the last section of the report was completed with a warning: a reduction, or overall ban, on the dumping of RAW at sea without a simultaneous solution to the problem of ground waste would inevitably increase waste on industrial premises and military bases, resulting in an aggravated radiation and general ecological situation and increased social tensions. It was soon to be seen how justified that fear was.

Caught red-handed?

The international scandal following the dumping of liquid RAW by Russian naval ships in the Sea of Japan in the early 1990s made it clear once again how damaging the retention of the old policies and practices is. As a matter of fact, the amount of waste dumped this time, as compared to previously, hardly matched the scale of the political scandal Greenpeace mounted in response. But it was not the exact number of Curies that really mattered, but the very instance of undeclared dumping, and in that sense the action of the Greens was appropriate.

Military and foreign ministry officials were quick to explain that Russia would be forced to dump RAW in the sea for a certain period of time, because all of its coastal storages are full, and the capacity of facilities to process and harden nuclear waste is catastrophically inadequate. This open-hearted confession came too late. The authors of the report were well aware that liquid radioactive waste accounts for no less than 90 per cent of the total amount of RAW resulting from the use of nuclear-powered submarines, surface ships, icebreakers, one lighter carrier and coastal repair and maintenance facilities. At the facilities of the Northern Fleet and the Murmansk Shipping Company alone 5000–5500 cubic metres of liquid RAW is formed annually, and only a little less at those of the Pacific Fleet.

The costly coastal complexes to process liquid waste and decontaminate reactor equipment, built in the Kola peninsula and near Vladivostok, have remained inoperative to this day. A similar unit aboard the sea-going transport ship, the *Amur*, has been idle and slowly but surely becoming unfit for use.

Who are we and where are we going?

It all began when a name for our organization, the Movement for Ecological Security to Novaya Zemlya, was being chosen. We were often asked why 'to Novaya Zemlya'? Our goal is to put an end to nuclear testing in Novaya Zemlya and worldwide. To Novaya Zemlya is a call for a renewed, safer world, for a new world order based on neighbour-liness and cooperation, ruling out the use of violence and military threat as a political argument.

The range of practical objectives includes: restoring the genuine picture of everything that has happened in Novaya Zemlya since a nuclear test site was opened there; finding out the effects of nuclear testing on people's health for subsequent medical and social rehabilitation; Novaya Zemlya's denuclearization; and the reclamation of its natural resources.

Three years ago our movement's Council of Experts developed several special-purpose projects, including one named *Lotsiya* (Sailing Directions). Its aim was to gather and classify all information about the dumping of RAW in the Arctic seas and to draw up a map with exact coordinates and a description of potentially dangerous areas in order to make it available to fishermen, ichthyologists, hydrographers and any concerned organizations. It is too early to say that all the goals formulated in that project have been achieved, but the ice has been broken. A second project, called *Lotsiya-2* (Sailing Directions-2) provides for the radio-ecological surveillance of superannuated dumps in order to establish the real risks they pose to humanity and to the environment. This is opening up many opportunities for cooperation and contacts.

40 NUCLEAR POLLUTION IN THE FORMER USSR

SERGEI KOLESNIKOV and ALEKSANDER YEMELYANENKOV

Daring and risky nuclear-fission experiments the United States launched half a century ago were promptly replicated by the Soviet Union. Pretty soon the nuclear race began to affect the environment and health of big groups of the population. The first nuclear programmes had a military thrust. Tight security and neglect of basic safety requirements were the inevitable side-effects. No information about radioactive contaminations in the former USSR or exposure of civilians or military personnel to radiation had appeared in the mass media until the Chernobyl nuclear-power plant disaster.

Under public pressure monopolistic government agencies had to admit that nuclear accidents, people's exposure to radiation and hazardous escapes into the environment had occurred more than once before Chernobyl.

Distress call from Muslumovo, on the Techa river

When in the late 1940s the envoys of the then Soviet security police chief Lavrenty Beriya's chose a site in the south Urals for a plutonium plant, nobody cared about the local people. The classified facility was built near the Muslumovo village on the Techa river, several dozen kilometres upstream.

Local people began to realize only ten years later what kind of a deadly neighbour had settled nearby. On 29 September 1957 a tank with radiochemical waste exploded at the plutonium production plant in Kyshtym (currently the Mayak industrial association). Two million Curies (Ci) of long-lived radionuclides escaped into the environment, forming the so-called east Urals radioactive trace, which covered 217 villages with a total population of 272,000. In two subsequent years 10,200 people were resettled. The trace from the 1957 explosion overlapped with the previous contamination of the basin of the

Techa and Iset rivers caused by many years of authorized discharge of radiochemical waste from the Kyshtym nuclear complex (Chelyabinsk-65). According to official sources in two years alone, 1950 and 1951, 2.7 million Curies (MCi) of waste were discharged into the Techa river. Radiation affected 124,000 people. By 1960 7500 residents had been resettled, primarily from small villages. The others continue living in the contaminated territory.

Muslumovo is not only a big village, but a railway station too. After a brief conference scientists held with the authorities it was decided to leave everything as it was. Resettling Muslumovo seemed too costly. Some precautions were taken, though. Several artesian wells were drilled and local people were advised not to use water from the river, not to let livestock graze on its banks; not to use hay from or plant potatoes on the flood-plains; and not to go fishing.

Those who could leave the village did so at once. However, most people stayed and ignored the taboos: they did go fishing, they did pasture cattle and they did stack hay for the long Ural winters, but many never lived to see the spring and died in the prime of their lives. Nearly all children born in that village suffer from anaemia and become invalids before beginning school.

The dress rehearsal

Some details of a little-known nuclear accident that took place eight months before Chernobyl are now outlined. A spontaneous chain reaction of fission of uranium nuclei occurred in a nuclear submarine at the ship repair yard of the USSR navy in the Maritime Territory (Chazhma harbour) on 10 August 1985. It happened as the reloading of reactors neared completion and the reactor's lid was tested for leaks. Violations of safety rules were the main reason.

The reactor's thermal explosion destroyed the control compartments and the protection system. One fuel element with a freshly-loaded active section was ejected from the reactor. Immediately after the explosion a fire started in the reactor compartment. It was localized four hours later. Products of combustion together with fission and activation products in the form of sludge and particles of unreacted fuel fell out within a range of 5 to 100 metres.

A radioactive trace was formed, crossed the Dunai peninsula northwestwards and approached the sea on the coast of Ussuri Bay. On the peninsula the trace was 5.5km long, and aerosol particles fell out on the sea as far as 30 km from the site of incident.

The radioactive agents released into the atmosphere (except for radioactive noble gases – RNB) totalled 185 TBq (5 MCi). The escape of RNB was estimated at 81,000 TBq (2 MCi). Submarines and special ships in the area of the accident, piers and the premises and facilities of the repair yard were seriously contaminated.

The accident formed a source of the radioactive contamination of Chazhma harbour. Currents have gradually moved radioactive contamination towards the mouth of Chazhma harbour. The radioactivity of bottom sediment is primarily due to cobalt-60 (96–99 per cent) and partially to caesium-137.

The radioactivity in the sea water in the areas is at background levels found elsewhere on the Pacific coast. All radioactivity is in the near-bottom silt and can be removed only with it or with the surface soil layer. This is, however, expected to have serious ecological effects because the total activity of radionuclides in the bottom sediment is relatively small (about 5 Ci), and the half-life period of the main radionuclide (cobalt-60) is 5.26 years.

At the time of the accident and in the course of efforts to minimize its effects 290 people were exposed to high doses of radiation. At the moment of the accident 10 people died instantly (8 officers and 2 enlisted men). Ten people developed acute radiation sickness, and 39 others milder forms of response to radiation.

What is to be done about the Soviet nuclear submarine sunk in the Norwegian sea? Take it or leave it?

A fire occurred in the after-part of the Komsomolets nuclear-powered submarine (NPS) on 7 April 1989. The submarine surfaced only to sink after several hours of futile attempts by the crew to keep it afloat. Forty-two crew members died. The disabled submarine bottomed at a depth of 1680 metres off Bear Island, 300 nautical miles away from the Norwegian cost.

The risk of a quick escape of radionuclides distinguishes this nuclear disaster from other such accidents, including those involving US submarines. The pressure hull of the Komsomolets submarine is made of titanium. The interaction in sea water of the titanium hull and steel parts with components of the reactor and other units of the NPS Komsomolets (made of various materials) noticeably increases the rate of corrosion.

Before the NPS sank the reactor was switched to a cool-down mode; that ensured nuclear safety at the time the submarine sank and afterwards. Since the moment the submarine sank the risk of a nuclear explosion has been ruled out by virtue of the design of the nuclear ammunition (NA). However, the problem of radio-ecological safety still remains.

According to experts who in their estimates relied on the energy output of the submarine's power plant, the active section of the reactor contains about 42kCi of strontium-90 and 55kCi of caesium-137. The warheads contain about 430 Ci of plutonium-239.

The first expedition to the site of the Komsomolets disaster took place in May 1989, when the research ship *Akademik Mstislav Keldysh* research ship conducted general surveillance. A full-scale research programme was effected by the second expedition, involving several ships, from April to September 1991. Two deep-sea navigable ships (DNSs) of the Mir type were equipped with standard radiation monitors and special radiometric instruments. Thirty-two samples of water and soil were taken during six divings by the DNSs in the immediate vicinity of the submarine's hull. By January 1992 analysis showed that although the first circuit of the reactor was not water-tight, the escape of radionuclides was very low (their concentration did not exceed 10pCi/l of caesium-137. Damage was found in the pressure hull in the upper part of the fore compartments. It turned out that torpedo tube-caps are half-open and sea water is in contact with the hulls of torpedo rockets. The hulls of nuclear warheads are no longer water-tight, either, and active materials are washed by sea water, too. The third expedition by two research ships lasted from 7 May till 18 June 1992. DNSs carried out six submersions around the Komsomolets NPS and the surfacing rescue chamber was found 399 metres away.

As had been originally expected and already confirmed for the first time in 1991, insignificant amounts of caesium-137 had escaped into the environment. The maximum concentration of caesium in the immediate vicinity of the NPS totalled 180 Bq/m^3, and the average concentration on the deck just above the reactor compartment 29.6 Bq/m^3 (the permissible concentration of caesium in drinking water is 550,000 Bq/m^3). Although according to the official account the analysis of samples of water and bottom sediments and of selective sorbents failed to register an escape of plutonium-239 from nuclear ammunition, other sources say several leaks have taken place already. They do not as yet constitute a hazard.

As the area around the Komsomolets NPS was studied, the distribution of natural and cultural nuclides in bottom sediments proved uneven. Areas with slightly higher, though not yet hazardous, concentrations of radionuclides measure tens of square kilometres and were spotted tens of kilometres away from the NPS. The complicated hydrological (a current of 1.5m/s) and geomorphological situation in the area make it impossible to attribute unequivocally the varying concentrations of cultural nuclides to escapes from the Komsomolets.

A major escape of the reactor radionuclides into the sea water in the near future is highly unlikely. The radio-ecological situation is far more serious. The first escapes of plutonium-239 from nuclear ammunition were expected as soon as 1995–96, but uncontrolled escapes of plutonium may be impulsive and take place over a period of several years. As a result the sea bottom around the NPS may be seriously contaminated with products of corrosion of plutonium-239, both highly active and chemically toxic.

The Polar Institute of Fishing and Oceanography (PINRO) has estimated likely economic damage from the contamination of sea products with plutonium-239: one can expect the contamination of marketable fish to be twice as high as the maximum permissible level. Apart from serious economic losses (up to 2.5 thousand million roubles in 1991 prices) an angry political reaction from the Scandinavian countries is inevitable.

The most drastic preventive measure would be to recover the NPS Komsomolets. Such an operation would cost more than US$250 million. At some point in the future the damage to the pressure hull and the continuing corrosion may make the submarine impossible to recover. Partial hermetic sealing may prevent an early and quick escape of radionuclides. One of the probable methods of such sealing implies pumping a gel containing 1–2 per cent of chitosan (an active sorbent of heavy-metal alkalis) into the submarine. In the presence of calcium contained in the sea water the gel would be polymerized to form a glass-like mass highly resistant to erosion even by strong currents and would practically prevent the escape of radionuclides into the environment for decades. Another likely solution of the problem would be to separate and recover only the fore part of the NPS with NA and to bury or destroy the nuclear ammunition later.

Conclusion

Disputes by the military, politicians, scientists and journalists over the sunken nuclear submarine continue. The focus of attention has now shifted from the causes of the disaster that has already occurred to a disaster that may still happen: is it true that the two torpedoes with plutonium warheads and the nuclear reactor are capable of poisoning the Norwegian sea? Or does it make sense to avoid over-dramatizing the situation, bearing in mind that before the Komsomolets disaster two American and two Soviet nuclear submarines had sunk with 7 reactors and no less than 50 nuclear warheads (both torpedoes and ballistic missiles) on board?

We are confident that this dispute has been counterproductive from the outset. A potential risk will remain a risk, even if it does not constitute a world threat. The duty of each genuine professional should be to eliminate or minimize that risk. So we choose to leave the evergreen question headlining the previous section unanswered for the time being.

Chernobyl in Siberia? Commentary on a 1993 emergency

The Siberian chemical plant (SCP) and Tomsk-7, the town nearby, are on the right bank of the River Tom, 15 kilometres north of Tomsk. The plant was built in 1953. Five channel-type graphite-moderated reactors were commissioned there to produce fissile materials. Three reactors have now been shut down, but the SCP has remained Russia's major source of plutonium, uranium and transuranic elements.

On 6 April 1993 gross abuse of processing parameters by plant personnel led to the destruction of a unit on the irradiated nuclear-fuel processing line. Before the explosion the unit contained $25m^3$ of a solution of 8773kg of uranium and 310g of plutonium. The activity of all nuclides totalled 559.3 Ci. A greater part of the radioactive solution, according to experts, remained in the unit and the canyon. Five per cent of beta- and gamma-activity escaped into the environment.

The accident was accompanied by a quick salvo-like discharge of radioactive agents into the processing room and thence into the environment through the ventilation system, blow-off communication lines and exhaust chimney, as well as through a breach in the wall at a height of 15 metres.

When the accident occurred there were 160 people in the building. At the moment of the explosion and during the fire-extinguishing operation on the roof there were no casualties. The highest individual-equivalent exposure dose of the personnel and those involved in eliminating the fire measured 0.6 rems (3 people), which is equivalent to 14 per cent of the annual permitted dose for the personnel who service the unit.

In the immediate vicinity of the destroyed unit the gamma-radiation dose was as high as 5 R/h, and outside the building, up to 3.4x10-3 R/h. The trace with levels of gamma-radiation above 60x10-6 R/h, was 15 kilometres long and 3 kilometres wide. The contaminated area totalled $123km^2$.

Considering the size of the trace and its location, as well as the radionuclide composition of the contamination, a government inquiry concluded that urgent measures to protect the population and environment from radiation were unnecessary. Independent experts disagreed.

What happened at the SCP on 6 April 1993 could have had far more serious consequences. It was a lucky coincidence that the radioactive cloud bypassed Tomsk, a regional centre with half a million residents. As was the case with Chernobyl, panic, the exodus of foreigners from nearby cities, unforeseen costs and losses, uncontrolled consumption of iodine, amongst other consequences, made themselves felt. A small lead tomb was constructed over the destroyed unit. In the Kemerovo region microroentgens were confused with milliroentgens and the river Chernaya, where the escape went, with the Bolshaya Chernaya river on the edge of the region, which caused great fears in neighbouring areas. Some officials planned to move civil defence units to 'fight the radiation'.

The row over the technological accident at the SCP was directly proportional to the level of secrecy still in effect at such facilities and inversely proportional to the scale of the event, which the mass media were quick to dub another Chernobyl.

Though the radio-ecological effects of these events were very different, the very response to the Tomsk-7 incident is indicative of the complicated social, political and economic situation in post-socialist Russia and the level of radiation and ecological security.

ACKNOWLEDGEMENT

Chapter 40 is based on the materials in the 2nd collection of the IPPNW-Russia information series: *Atom Declassified* and *Half a Century with the Bomb*, compiled and published by IPPNW-Russia.

41 MILITARY POLLUTION – CHEMICAL WASTE

Threats Posed by Chemical Weapons
in the Baltic and Other Seas

B.B. BONDARENKO, L.G. KASYANENKO, Ye N. ROSE
and O.N. SIMONOVA

Chemical weapons were invariably dumped in the Baltic and other seas amid tight security and there is still no free access to such information. Chapter 41 is based on official sources, press publications and testimonies by witnesses and participants. It is only the tip of the iceberg. The real scale of the hidden danger is yet to be assessed in full.

Data gathering and classification

The chemical weapons problem dates back to the Second World War (WW II). Nazi Germany had by 1943 increased the production of war gases (WGs) to 180,000 tonnes, including 20,000 tonnes of nerve gases. For a number of reasons chemical weapons were not used in WW II, and after the surrender of Germany the allies found 250,000 tonnes of chemical weapons, twice the reserves of Britain, the USSR and the United States.[1]

The occupation authorities of the victor nations established a special body to co-ordinate the dumping of chemical weapons. It was decided that each country would be responsible for dumping chemical weapons it would find in its zone of occupation.

At the end of 1945 and the beginning of 1946 chemical weapons found in the American and British occupation zones (about 200,000 tonnes) were collected and taken to the port cities of Kiel and Emden where they were put on seized German torpedo boats, mine-sweepers, outdated British warships and damaged passenger ships. The hulls of ships damaged by bombardments in Northern European ports, 50 transports in all, were also used.[2] Some were able to go to their last destination without assistance, others had to be towed. Controlled explosions and in some cases artillery fire were used to sink them. Apparently, that had to be done in bad weather conditions when the sea was rough and there was the risk that uncontrolled transports carrying deadly cargoes might be washed ashore.

As discovered only recently, in some cases chemical weapons stored aboard defunct ships were encased in concrete. In the strait of Skagerrak nine ships dumped by the British were found in 1990, lying at a depth of 200 metres. Their holds containing chemical weapons had been filled with concrete. How safe those dumps are is anyone's guess, however, large amounts of dead starfish found around the dump were evidence that certain leaks of war gases had taken place. (At this point it is worth recalling that a massive death of starfish and fish, whose tissues proved to contain high concentrations of toxic agents, was registered in the White Sea near Arkhangelsk in 1990.) In addition to the nine ships dumped in the Skagerrak area six other such sites are known. In two of these areas chemical weapons were dumped with permission from the Soviet command, and in the four others, with the agreement of the Americans and the British. A total of 302,875 tonnes of chemical weapons was dumped in the six areas.

The list of Anglo-American dumps includes those near Skagen (Denmark's northern extremity) and between Fyn Island (Denmark) and the mainland. There, in the area of the Little Belt strait, about 10,000 shells with mustard gas, tabun and soman, as well as phosphorus bombs, were dumped at a depth of about 30 metres. Tanks with nerve gases and several barges with other chemical-warfare agents are scattered over an area of 36 square kilometres.[3] Professor D. Woppel, of the German Hydrographic Institute, says that German hydrographers have studied that problem since 1970 and found bombs and shells in 11 places in the southern part of the Little Belt strait.

According to unconfirmed reports 120,000 tonnes of British chemical weapons are buried somewhere in the Atlantic, in the western part of the English Channel, near the Hebrides, in the Irish Sea and near the east coast of Canada.

Over the past few years a great deal has been clarified about Nazi chemical weapons dumped by the Soviet Union. In the second half of 1945 and in 1946 ship convoys brought chemical weapons from all parts of what was then east Germany to a special transit terminal in Wolgast, northern Germany. About 35,000 tonnes of them had been stored there by the end of 1946, including:

- mustard gas shells;
- 250-kilogram mustard bombs, 1.5-tonne containers with mustard gas;
- bombs with adamsite and diphenylchlorarsine;
- cyanides in thick rubber bags; and
- zyklon gas.

From May 1947 seven ships took turns to pick up chemical weapons in Wolgast and carry them to the chosen dumping site 70 miles west of the Latvian port of Liepaja and the same distance from the Swedish island of Gotland. Officers and men of the Red Army's chemical troops dressed in full protective gear dumped 5000 tonnes of chemical weapons at a depth of 105 metres. To lessen the risk of a leak in case of an accidental collision of chemical shells or containers, the ships moved slowly along a charted route in an area of 1500 km². On nautical charts that area is marked as an explosives dump. The same note about the explosives' dump (not mentioning chemicals) is found on the charts of another chemical dumping-ground, near Bornholm Island. What is it? Deliberate misinformation prompted by reasons of secrecy? Or was St Petersburg's deputy mayor, Rear-Admiral Shcherbakov right when he said on the radio that the Soviet command had no way out other than dumping explosives together with chemicals?[4] If so, the dumped chemical weapons would be far more difficult to recover and render harmless.

There is yet another version of these events. Lieutenant-Commander K.P. Terskov, a participant in the operation, says that the command at first decided the dumping area would be 56 miles south-west of Liepaja, where the sea is no less than 100 metres deep.[5] Bombs were dumped there from two mine-sweepers. Both the crews and loaders were German. If bombs remained afloat, they were shot at and sunk.

The site proved a bad choice. Shuttle voyages from Wolgast and back took too much time and the tight deadline set by the command, 1 January 1948, proved impossible to meet. Besides, as bombs were dumped from ships in a rough sea, several workers were affected by war gases. K.P. Terskov then found another site meeting the 100 metre-depth requirement five miles south of Christianso Island. He says that 40,000 to 45,000 tonnes of chemical weapons were dumped there. Nautical charts of that area are marked as either a dump for war gases or a dump for war gases and explosives. All these chart marks are north or east of Christianso Island, while K.P. Terskov says that dumping work was done to the south of the island. There is even a 103 metre-depth mark which, Terskov says, he used as a reference point. It is quite possible that the exact location was deliberately distorted. The origin of such marks is still a mystery. According to the Russian Defence Ministry's Central Map-Making Unit the original marks were copied from foreign nautical charts, although references were made to Soviet sources.

According to retired Captain N.M. Tataurov, who participated in the dumping operation near Christianso Island, a special sound buoy was placed at the dumping site to help sailors find their bearings in thick fog.[6] Tataurov's transport ship began to dump ammunition near the buoy and drifted for no more than one mile. That was done to minimize the dumping area. However, many bombs had positive or zero buoyancy and had to be sunk by heavy machine-guns or fast-fire artillery. Yet some were carried away, as far as the shores of Sweden.

Tataurov says that in addition to bombs and shells one-tonne containers and big rubber-coated bags with 'some chemicals' (probably cyanides) were dumped in the area within a radius of five miles. The dump's exact location is unlikely to be ever determined even if the log-books of mine-sweepers and transport ships involved in the operation are found, because the accuracy of navigation instruments in the 1940s and 1950s only allowed the computation of coordinates within an error margin of several miles.

Search for and localization of chemical-weapons dumps

Three main controversies remain in respect of chemical-weapons dumps: the exact location, the amount and nature of war gases and the dumping techniques used. Emphasis must now be placed on finding and localizing WG dumps using impartial, independent methods. This applies in particular to the Baltic Sea.

The available methods are geophysical, geochemical and medico-biological, and the best results can be expected from their combination. Geophysical methods make the search safe. This is very important, because chemical weapons and conventional explosives were often dumped side by side. The sophisticated navigation systems of research or hydrographic ships would make it possible to determine the location within ten metres.

When chemical dumps have been found, the localization and identification stage will begin, with hydrochemical methods playing the leading role. Chemical analysis of water and soil samples would be used extensively. The effectiveness of these methods depends on the solubility of WGs in water, the speed of their hydrolysis, surface and bottom currents and tides, and other hydrometeorological conditions.

Medical and biological methods of identifying the presence of WGs may be used alongside geophysical and hydrochemical ones. They may be required if the risk of various WGs affecting the participants in the search operation proves too great. Such methods are also important in assessing the long-term effects of WGs which may, in various ways (for instance, through food chains), affect the health of the population in coastal areas.

Medical and biological aspects

The conservation, recovery and elimination of chemical weapons dumped in the sea add up to a costly and risky business. Before any decisions are made a number of questions have to be answered:

(1) Is it necessary to recover WGs from the sea bottom at all?
(2) Have the chemical weapons dumped nearly five decades ago affected the medical and ecological situation and can they affect it in the future?
(3) Are chemical weapons dumped in the sea, including those in the Baltic, an ecological delayed-action mine?

To answer these and many other questions one has to know to what degree WGs leaking into the sea have affected or may affect the gene pool and immunity of the population in coastal areas. Detailed inquiries are still to be made, but it is already clear that even small doses of WGs (just like those of DDT or lead) may be harmful to the gene pool and the risk that they will affect the health of future generations is high. The already-studied delayed effects (including those through food chains) of small concentrations of WGs and products of their hydrolysis on the human body are an indication of this.

Diverse chronic effects of nerve gases (tabun, sarin and soman) may provoke vascular dystonia, toxic encephalopathy and hepatitis, polyneuritis and the akinesia of biliary tracts, affect the bronchial tree, upset humoral and cellular immunity, suppress unspecific resistance, bring about changes in the blood system, cause bias to allergic reactions and more frequent chromosomic aberrations in the lymphocytes of peripheral blood cells, upset menstrual cycles and spermatogenesis, provoke spontaneous abortions, still-births and innate disorders and result in the development retardation of newly-born babies. The chronic influence of blister WGs (mustard gas, lewisite) and irritants (diphenylchlorarsine, adamsite, arsene) affects the bronchi, lungs, eyes, skin, blood-production organs and the alimentary tract (see also Chapter 10 in this volume).

The risk of a direct influence of WGs on living sea organisms depends directly on leakage rates and the volume and speed of WG hydrolysis. The use of inadequate methods in the search for chemical weapons, often dumped in the same areas as explosives, may cause the latter to explode and provoke a prompt escape of large quantities of WGs into the water and the atmosphere. In this case the risk of serious effects of WGs on living organisms will be high.

Corrosion will increase the risk of WG leaks with every year. In that sense the hydrodynamic features of the given sea area are very important. In the Baltic Sea, which is icebound throughout the winter and where the circulation of water at that time of year is insignificant, leaking WGs are likely to mass up in the areas of dumps. In other seasons this is less probable. The Baltic Sea is shallow and heavy waves are frequent, making water circulation fast.

One must also remember that WGs and products of their hydrolysis may react with other organic and inorganic substances and compounds polluting the Baltic Sea every year. According to some sources, the Baltic Sea is polluted with three to four million tonnes of toxic agents, including 1 million tonnes of nitrogen and its compounds and 50,000 tonnes of phosphorus and its compounds.[7]

All this merely emphasizes the risks that chemical weapons dumped in various seas pose. Deplorably, the question of doing away with this threat has not been considered at an inter-state level since WW II, although this problem cannot but concern the eight Baltic sea countries and the costs of resolving it are too great to be borne by any one country. It would be natural for government organizations in the Baltic Sea nations with the financial and technical potential to pool their efforts. Particular attention should be paid to the joint control of finances, results and safety of such work, to be undertaken by independent non-governmental organizations in the countries concerned.

One way to realize this proposal would be to set up a special committee of representatives from independent organizations to draw up a programme, coordinate all work and control its results. Cooperation with the appropriate structures of the (1992) Helsinki convention for protecting the environment in the Baltic Sea area would certainly prove helpful in bringing this about.

REFERENCES

1. *Poisk* (1992), N. 19 (in Russian).
2. *Izvestiya*, 23 October 1990 (in Russian).
3. *Priroda i Chelovek* magazine, 1990, No. 2 (in Russian).
4. The statement was made on 14 March 1992.
5. *Izvestiya*, 25 January 1991; *Chas Pik*, 16 March 1992 (both in Russian).
6. *Chas Pik*, 23 March 1992 (in Russian).
7. Terva, V. (1992), *State of the Baltic Sea*, Helsinki, Finland: IPPNW First Around the Baltic Meeting, 27–30 August.

42 GULF WAR ILLNESSES
The role of chemical, radiological and biological exposures

GARTH L. NICOLSON, MARWAN NASRALLA,
JOERG HAIER and NANCY L. NICOLSON

Veterans who served in the Persian Gulf region during Operation Desert Storm have slowly presented with chronic illnesses that produce complex signs and symptoms, such as polyarthralgia, chronic fatigue, short-term memory loss, sleep difficulties, headaches, intermittent fevers, skin rashes, diarrhoea, vision problems, nausea, breathing and heart problems and other signs and symptoms that are collectively called Gulf War syndrome or Gulf War illnesses (GWI). Although there is not yet a case definition for GWI, the chronic signs and symptoms loosely fit the clinical criteria for chronic fatigue syndrome and/or fibromyalgia syndrome. Some patients have additionally what appears to be neurotoxicity and brainstem dysfunction that can result in autonomic, cranial and peripheral nerve demyelination, possibly due to complex chemical exposures. Often these patients have been diagnosed with multiple chemical sensitivity syndrome (MCS) or organophosphate-induced delayed neurotoxicity (OPIDN). Chemically-exposed patients can be treated by removal of offending chemicals from the patient's environment, depletion of chemicals from the patient's system and treatment of the neurotoxic signs and symptoms caused by chemical exposure(s). A rather large subset (40–45 per cent) of GWI patients have transmittable infections, including mycoplasmal and possibly other chronic bacterial infections, that have resulted in the appearance of GWI in immediate family members and civilians in the Gulf region. These infections can be treated with antibiotics, vitamin and nutritional supplementation, and in some cases oxidative therapy. It is likely that veterans of the Gulf War who are ill with GWI owe their illnesses to a variety of exposures: (i) chemical mixtures, primarily organophosphates, antinerve agents and possibly nerve agents; (ii) radiological sources, primarily depleted uranium and possibly fallout from destroyed nuclear reactors; and (iii) biological sources, primarily bacteria, viruses and toxins, before, during and after the conflict. Such exposures can result in poorly-defined chronic illnesses, but these illnesses can be treated if appropriate diagnoses are forthcoming.

Multifactorial illnesses of the Gulf War

Gulf War syndrome and Gulf War illnesses (GWI) are terms that have been used to describe a collection of chronic signs and symptoms reported by US, British, Canadian, Czech, Danish, Saudi, Egyptian, Syrian, Moroccan and other Coalition Armed Forces that were deployed to Operation Desert Storm (ODS) in 1991. Over 100,000 American veterans of Desert Storm/Shield (approximately 15 per cent of deployed US armed forces) returned from the Persian Gulf and slowly (6–24 months or more) presented with a variety of complex signs and symptoms characterized by disabling fatigue, intermittent fevers, night sweats, arthralgia, myalgia, impairments in short-term memory, headaches, skin rashes, intermittent diarrhoea, abdominal bloating, chronic bronchitis, photophobia, confusion, transient visual scotomata, irritability and depression and other signs and symptoms that until recently have defied appropriate diagnoses.[1] These symptoms are not localized to any one organ, and the signs and symptoms and routine laboratory test results are not consistent with a single, specific disease.[2]

The signs and symptoms of GWI have been reported by 27 out of the 28 Coalition Armed Forces that were deployed against Iraqi units in Kuwait and Southern Iraq. The only exception is France. This brief review will summarize some of the possible exposures that occurred, the types of illnesses that resulted from these exposures and some of the treatments that have been used on GWI patients. Because of space limitations, these topics cannot be discussed in detail. Instead, they are summarized along with a few references that should be useful.

The signs and symptoms of GWI

Most investigators who study Gulf War Syndrome or GWI do not believe that it is a separate, new syndrome.[3] However, there are unique characteristics of the illnesses. GWI has been called 'mucocutaneous-intestinal-rheumatic Desert Syndrome' by Murray-Leisure *et al.*, who reported illnesses in Desert Storm veterans that did not fit standard US Veterans' Administration diagnosis categories.[4] Murray-Leisure and her colleagues placed patients into three broad categories: (i) mucocutaneous lesions with pustular dermatitis; (ii) intestinal disorders with irritable bowels; and (iii) rheumatic complaints of large-joint polyarthralgias with night sweats. Minor criteria included: heartburn, rectal fissures, bleeding or hemorrhoids, lactose or meat intolerance, splenomegaly and splenic tenderness, weakness and/or chronic fatigue, headaches, muscle aches, polymyalgias, memory loss, hair loss, fevers of unknown origin, unexplained leukocytosis or neutropenia, nasal ulcers or sores, chronic sinus or nasal congestion, atypical chest pain, new-onset asthma or chronic bronchitis, ear infections or tinnitus and dental infections. In addition, Haley *et al.* found several different neurological diagnoses in GWI patients, indicating that simple disease categories for GWI patients may prove to be elusive.[5] Veterans of a US Navy Mobile Construction Reserve Battalion were analysed, and evidence of neurologic injury involving the central, peripheral and autonomic nervous systems in patients with GWI was found. Baumzweiger and Grove have described GWI as neuro-immune disorders that involve the central, peripheral and autonomous nervous

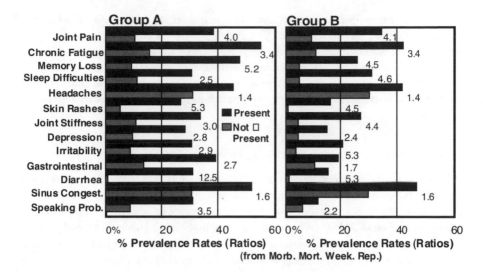

Figure 42.1 Case-cntrol study on Gulf War illnesses conducted by the CDC

The bars indicate the frequencies of common symptoms in deployed (solid bars) and non-deployed (stippled bars) members of Air National Guard (Unit A) and Air Force Reserve (Unit B) units where approximately equal numbers of airmen were deployed or not deployed to the Arabian Gulf region. The numbers by the solid bars indicate the ratio of prevalence (data from n. 11).

and immune systems.[6] They attribute a major source of illness to be brainstem damage due to central, peripheral and cranial nerve neuropathy with demyelination. Patients tend to have muscle spasms, memory deficits, attention deficits, Ataxia, and increased muscle tone, which are often seen in neurotoxin-induced brainstem dysfunction. GWI patients can also have chronic bacterial and viral infections that are an important source of morbidity.[7]

Although the chronic signs and symptoms of GWI usually do not result in illnesses that progress to cause death,[8] there are now thousands of US Desert Storm veterans dead from a variety of illnesses that may have been obtained from their service.[9] The possible reasons why these deaths have not been reported in official studies of the problem could be the limited size of study groups and time intervals used for analysis, the lack of information on veterans who have left the armed forces, and the primary use of military hospitals for the analysis.[10] In the US, estimates of between 8000 and 25,000 or more dead have been advanced but the exact figures may never be known. Although for years the US Department of Defense and the UK Ministry of Defence officially stated that there were no illnesses associated with deployment to Desert Shield/Storm, just the opposite has been found,[11] bringing into question whether official US or British government studies will ever acknowledge the problem.[12]

That veterans with GWI have chronic illnesses at higher rates than military personnel from the same units that were not deployed to the Persian Gulf was shown in a case-control study performed by the US Center for Disease Control.[13] In the reserve and national guard units studied, hundreds of soldiers or airmen that were deployed to the Persian Gulf region were compared to similar numbers of soldiers or airmen from the same units that were not deployed (Figure 42.1, two units are shown). In the four units that were studied, the deployed soldiers had a variety of chronic-illness signs and symptoms that were not present in the same frequencies in the non-deployed men and women.[14] For certain signs and symptoms, this difference was dramatic (for example, an over-13 times higher incidence of diarrhoea in deployed personnel). This study showed that deployment to the Kuwaiti Theatre of Operations (KTO) was an underlying risk for obtaining chronic illnesses.

Post-traumatic stress disorder: an unlikely diagnosis for GWI

Although it has been generally accepted that many Gulf War veterans have medical problems, as mentioned above, the signs and symptoms of GWI are not well-established as criteria for particular illnesses, and they do not readily fit into the common ICD-9 diagnosis categories used by military and veterans' hospitals.[15] This has resulted in many veterans receiving diagnoses described as an 'unknown' disorder, or GWI patients have been diagnosed with psychological problems, such as post-traumatic stress disorder (PTSD).[16] Most physicians and scientists that work on GWI do not accept that GWI can be easily explained by psychiatric or psychological diagnoses, nor can they be successfully treated as somatization disorders.[17] Unlike PTSD, GWI has a number of significant signs that are different, such as neuro-muscular problems, skin disorders, gastrointestinal problems, muscle and joint pain and temperature abnormalities (intermittent fevers). That many of the reported signs and symptoms do not fit the diagnosis of PTSD has not stopped military and veterans' hospitals from liberally using this diagnosis for GWI and treating GWI patients accordingly.[18]

Similarity of GWI to chronic fatigue syndrome and fibromyalgia syndrome

The variable incubation time of GWI, ranging from months to years after presumed exposure, the cyclic nature of the relapsing fevers and the other chronic signs and symptoms, and their appearance in immediate family members are consistent with an organic disease.[19] The syndromes most similar to GWI are chronic fatigue syndrome (CFS) (often termed myalgic encephalomyelitis) and fibromyalgia syndrome (FMS).[20] We have proposed that the signs and symptoms found in many GWI patients may be caused by chronic exposures to chemical mixtures and host responses to infectious agents, resulting in cytokine production and a variety of other responses that result in a CFS- or FMS-like disorder.[21] When the signs and symptoms of GWI were compared to the signs and symptoms of CFS, the similarity was striking (Figure 41.2).[22] CFS is primarily characterized by persistent or relapsing, debilitating fatigue or easy fatigability in a person who has no previous history of similar symptoms, that does not resolve with rest and is severe enough to reduce or impair average daily activity below 50 per cent of the patient's premorbid activity level. In addition to the absence of clinical conditions that could easily explain the symptoms, such as malignancies or auto-immune diseases, patients present with mild fever, sore throat, arthralgia, myalgia, generalized muscle weakness, headaches, painful lymph nodes, sleep difficulties, and neuropsychologic complaints such as memory loss, photophobia, confusion, transient visual scotomata,

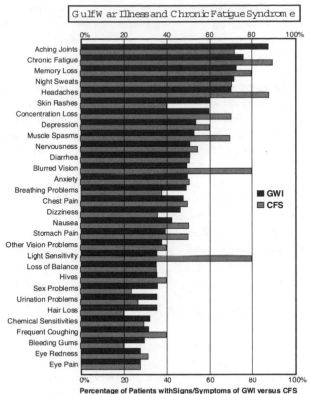

Figure 42.2
Prevalence of common signs and symptoms found in 650 patients with GWI compared to literature values for CFS
(data from Nicolson, G.L. and N. L, Nicolson (1995), n. 1)

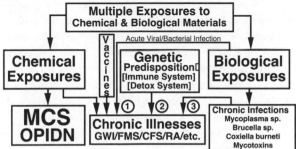

Figure 42.3 Multiple exposures (chemical, radiological, biological) or multifactorial causes that may have resulted in GWI in susceptible individuals (modified from Nicolson, G.L. and N.L. Nicolson (1998), n. 12)

irritability and depression. These signs and symptoms closely parallel those found in GWI (Figure 41.2).[23] This indicates that GWI is not a separate or new syndrome; it is a CFS-like disorder.[24] The signs and symptoms of GWI also overlap with FMS, a condition similar to CSF but one that has polymyalgia as its major sign/symptom and does not necessarily involve cognitive problems.

There are some differences between GWI and CFS/FMS that may be important in determining the various possible causes of GWI. Baumzweiger and Grove have stressed that, unlike CFS and FMS, GWI is associated with Ataxia and increased motor tone, symptomatic of brainstem dysfunction.[25] They have described three different forms of GWI: (i) 'simple' GWI is described as brainstem problems secondary to other disorders, such as infections; (ii) 'complex' GWI is similar to simple GWI but with brainstem, autonomic, cranial nerve and peripheral nerve demyelination occurring as well; and (iii) 'neurotoxic' GWI in which two or more specific neurotoxic, viral/microbial or physical traumatic 'hits' to the brainstem occur, resulting in severe brainstem inflammation, limbic system involvement and personality behavioural changes. These categories of GWI may prove useful in determining the role of various exposures in the progression of the condition.

Possible causes of GWI

Part of the confusion in diagnosing GWI is that the overlapping chronic signs and symptoms displayed by patients can be caused by quite different types of exposures. Veterans of the Gulf War could have been exposed to chemical, radiological and/or biological agents, or more likely combinations of these exposures (Figure 42.3).[26] Accurate diagnosis and successful treatment of GWI will depend on identifying the underlying exposures involved, because the illnesses caused by toxic exposures are treated differently according to their origins, whether chemical, radiological or biological.

Chemical exposures

Veterans of the Gulf War were exposed to a variety of chemicals, including insecticides such as the insect repellent N,N-dimethyl-m-toluamide and the insecticide permethrin, battlefield smoke and fumes and smoke from burning oil wells, use of the anti-nerve agent pyridostigmine bromide, solvents used to clean equipment and a variety of other chemicals, including in some cases possible exposures to low levels of chemical warfare (CW) agents.[27] Although contentious, this last source of chemical exposure (CW agents) may have occurred due to the destruction of CW stores in factories and storage bunkers during and after the war as well as possible offensive deployment of CW agents.[28]

Low-level exposures to mixtures of chemicals, particularly organophosphates with other chemicals, can result in chronic illnesses, including chronic neurotoxicity and immune supression, and these probably play an important role in many GWI cases (Figure 42.3).[29] Abou-Donia and Wilmarth found that combinations of pyridostigmine bromide, N,N-dimethyl-m-toluamide and permethrin produce neurotoxicity, diarrhoea, salivation, shortness of breath, locomotor dysfunctions, tremors and other impairments in healthy adult hens.[30] Multiple chemical sensitivity syndrome (MCS) and organo-phosphate-induced delayed neurotoxicity (OPIDN) are examples of chronic illnesses caused by multiple chemical exposures.[31] Patients with these syndromes can present with many of the signs and symptoms found in GWI patients, and in fact many GWI cases may eventually be explained by complex chemical exposures in the Gulf. In these patients, memory loss, headaches, cognitive problems, severe depression, loss of concentration, vision and balance problems, chemical sensitivities, among others, typify the types of signs and symptoms found in chronic chemically-exposed patients.[32]

For the most part, the GWI signs and symptoms began to present between 6 months to 2 years or more after the end of Operation Desert Storm. The slow onset of clinical signs and symptoms in chemically-exposed individuals is typical for OPIDN. Of particular concern was the possibility that low levels of CW agents were present in the Persian Gulf region from the bombing of CW factories in Iraq, from storage facilities (and their demo-lition after the war by engineering units) in Iraq and Kuwait, and from the offensive use of CW delivered by SCUD B (SS1) or FROG missiles, by aircraft or vehicles outfitted with CW sprayers, or by artillery shells and rockets, CW mines and other sources.[33]

Iraqi armed forces were known to have extensive stores of such weapons, and intelligence reports indicated that orders to use offensive CW agents against coalition forces were handed down to the battalion level during the conflict. In testimony to the US Congress, army CBW (chemical and biological warfare) officers indicated that over 14,000 CW alarms sounded during but not before or after the Gulf War air/ground offensive, and some soldiers were given medals for identifying the types of CW that were released in the KTO.[34] Extensive stockpiles of mustard (blister agent HN or HT), lewisite (blister agent L), sarin (nerve agent GB or GF), tabun (nerve agent GA) and other CW agents were present in the KTO, and extensive stores of these weapons were released into the atmosphere during the air campaign and by the destruction of Iraqi storage bunkers after the conflict.[35] Low-level exposure to nerve agents combined with other organophosphate exposures may have resulted in large numbers of delayed casualties and GWI.

Environmental hazards and non-transmittable biological exposures

Several possible environmental hazards were present in the KTO. In addition to the chemicals released by burning oil-well fires and ruptured petroleum pipelines, soldiers were exposed to fine, blowing sand. The small size of the sand particles (much less than 1mm) and the relatively constant winds in the region resulted in some inhalation of small silica particles. The presence of small sand particles deep in the lungs can produce a pulmonary inflammation or disorder that can progress to pneumonitis. This form of pneumonitis has been called Al-Eskan disease, and it usually presents as a pneumonia or flu-like condition that can eventually progress to more widespread signs and symptoms, including fibrosis, immunosuppression and opportunistic infections.[36] Although it is extremely doubtful that most GWI is Al-Eskan disease, the presence of silica-induced immune suppression in some soldiers could have resulted in the appearance of chronic infections in these patients.[37]

Parasites such as leishmaniasis and schistosomiasis and bacteria that cause malaria and cholera are endemic to the Middle East and could be the cause of illnesses in at least some of the veterans with GWI.[38] Characteristic signs and symptoms occur in these illnesses, and diagnostic tests are available for most of these agents; moreover, there have been no reports that they are the cause of illness in large numbers of patients with GWI. In some patients infections by *Leishmania tropica*, spread by the sandfly *Phlebotomus papatasi* may be involved. This type of infection can result in viscerotropic leishmaniasis and elevated temperature, lymphadenopathy and hepatosplenomegaly.[39] However, most of the common signs and symptoms of GWI do not fit with this explanation, and diagnosis of leishmaniasis is relatively uncommon (estimated at less than one hundred) in Gulf War veterans. Nonetheless, it is unclear how prevalent leishmaniasis infections are in GWI patients.

Biological toxins were also present in the KTO.[40] The Iraqi army had ample stores of aflatoxin (*Aspergillus flavus* toxin), ricin (from *Ricinus communis* beans), *Clostridium botulinum* toxin and possibly other toxic agents. Another type of toxin that is potentially dangerous is the tricothecene mycotoxins produced by various species of fungi. Mycotoxins act quickly by direct cutaneous contact and cause erythema accompanied by blisters, wheezing, pain and burning sensations. Some of these toxins can be fatal in very low doses (inhaled ricin in extremely small doses can cause inflammation of the respiratory mucosa with haemorrhage into the lungs or edema, haemorrhage of the GI tract and death within 8–72 hours) or cause delayed carcinogenic or immunosuppressive effects (aflatoxin exposure). The preferred method of delivery of these toxins was by biological warfare (BW) sprayer on to the sand or by aircraft.[41] Over 50 Italian-made BW sprayers were found fully deployed in southern Iraq and western Kuwait, and aircraft fitted with BW sprayers were captured by U S forces at airfields in southern Iraq.

Murray-Leisure *et al.* have described another aspect of GWI: its association (non-inhalation) with sand exposure.[42] This is most likely caused by a chronic transmittable infection found in sand that is endemic to the region. The risk for sand-associated illness appeared to be highest in the months of August, September or October. Although no infections were identified, the slow appearance of the same signs and symptoms in spouses and children of veterans with GWI suggested that a slow-growing micro-organism was being transferred by mucocutaneous, sexual or transplacemental mechanisms but probably not by causal contact (see pp. 439–441, below). Anthrax, caused by the Gram-positive *Bacillus anthracis*, a commonly used BW agent, is often found in soil. It can gain entrance through skin wounds but also by inhalation or ingestion. Anthrax infection does not result in a chronic illness, however, because its signs and symptoms, such as malaise, fever, fatigue, headache, respiratory distress and other more severe signs and symptoms, usually appear in 1–6 days of exposure.

Radiological exposures

An important contaminant of the battlefield environment in the Gulf War was depleted uranium (DU).[43] Depleted uranium, a byproduct of uranium processing for civilian and military use, was used in armour-penetrating ammunition and in protective armour on tanks and other vehicles because of its hardness and high density. Depleted uranium contains about 30 per cent of the normal amount of U-235, a dangerous radioisotope with a half-life of over 4 billion years.[44] When a DU-penetrator hits an armoured target, it disintegrates due to the resulting kinetic energy transfer that results in high temperatures. Depleted uranium rapidly oxidizes at high temperature, resulting in the formation of uranium-oxide particles. The particles that form from disintegration of DU-penetrators are usually small, and due to their high density they probably settled on damaged armoured vehicles, reinforced bunkers and on to the surrounding sand. Uranium-oxide particles can be easily inhaled along with smoke or fine sand. If even one small particle of less than 5 micrometres in diameter is trapped in the pulmonary system, the lungs and surrounding tissues can be exposed over a year to up to hundreds of times the annual whole body-radiation dosage permitted radiation workers by US regulations.[45] Fortunately, exposure can be monitored, and studies on the radiation exposures of Gulf War veterans should be initiated as soon as possible to determine the prevalence and extent of uranium-oxide exposure.

In addition to battlefield contamination with DU, civilian nuclear reactors in Iraq were destroyed during the air campaign. This may have resulted in the release of long half-life isotopes like Sr-90, U-235, Co-90 and others into the air. Similar to the bombing of CW and BW factories and storage facilities, this could have resulted in some blow-back onto coalition forces, since the prevailing winds in the region were generally from the Northwest to Southeast. Unfortunately, there appears to be no available assessment of the contamination to the region from the release of nuclear-reactor materials into the environment.

Transmittable biological exposures

There is some evidence for the presence of transmittable biological agents in GWI patients. In many cases, the veterans' immediate family members appear to have the same or similar signs and symptoms.[46] One estimate derived from inquiries from over 1200 GWI families indicated that approximately 77 per cent of spouses and 65 per cent of children born after the Gulf War now have the signs and symptoms of GWI.[47] When immediate family members presented with the same or similar illness, the onset of their GWI signs and symptoms usually occurred from six months to one year or more after the onset of the veteran's illness, and not every family member developed GWI signs and symptoms. Because of the apparent slow rate of transmission of GWI to immediate family members, the general public is probably not at high risk for contracting GWI from casual contact with GWI patients.[48] Veterans with transmittable biological exposures could have received these through natural means (e.g. soil, water), or they could have obtained their exposures from contaminated vaccines, Iraqi BW sprayers, BW warheads on SCUD or FROG missiles or artillery 'blow-back' contamination after the destruction of BW factories and storage bunkers or contaminated vaccines.[49]

In support of a biological hypothesis for a subset of patients with GWI, infectious agents have been found in GWI patients' urine[50] and blood.[51] Using a microscopic technique for determining bacterial infections in urine, Hyman has found that many Gulf War veterans show evidence of bacterial infections that can be successfully treated with several courses of broad spectrum antibiotics.[52] We found that most of the GWI symptoms can be explained by chronic pathogenic bacterial infections, such as mycoplasmal infections.[53] Mycoplasmal infections usually produce relatively benign diseases limited to particular tissue sites or organs, such as urinary tract or respiratory infections.[54] However, the types of mycoplasmas that we have detected in Desert Storm veterans, such as *Mycoplasma fermentans* (*M. fermentans*) that may be causing many of the chronic fatigue and other signs and symptoms of GWI, are very pathogenic, colonize a variety of organs and tissues, and are difficult to treat.[55] In studies of over 200 patients (including both US and British veterans) with GWI and their symptomatic family members, evidence of mycoplasmal infections has been found in about one-half (45 per cent) of the GWI patients' blood leukocyte samples.[56] The incidence of mycoplasmal infections in non-deployed, healthy subjects was found to be approximately 5 per cent.[57] The appearance of mycoplasmas in the leukocytes of some controls could indicate that these individuals are in a very early stage of the illness or that they are non-symptomatic carriers of the infection.

Since the group of mycoplasma-positive patients may be more symptomatic than the average GWI patient, it is likely that the final incidence of mycoplasmal infections in GWI will be lower than the incidence rate reported above.[58] In addition, not every Gulf War veteran had the same type of mycoplasma DNA sequences inside their white blood cells, although the most common infection found by far was *M. fermentans* in GWI patients. Interestingly, when civilian patients with CSF or FMS were examined for systemic mycoplasmal infections, high frequencies of these infections were also found (approximately 60 per cent), indicating another link between these disorders. The main difference was that in addition to *M. fermentans* several other species of mycoplasmas were found in civilians with CSF or FMS.[59]

Preliminary evidence suggests that the *M. fermentans* found inside white blood cells of GWI patients may have been modified to make it more pathogenic and more difficult to diagnose. Using the nucleoprotein gene tracking assay we have found unusual gene sequences associated with the same mycoplasma nucleoprotein fraction. For example, we have found HIV-1 *envelope* (*env*) gene sequences but not the other genes of the HIV-1 virus in equivalent nucleoprotein subfractions in a subset of GWI patients.[60] Although this preliminary result will require confirmation by sequencing the mycoplasma genome in the area of the putative inserted gene, the presence of the HIV-1 *env* gene could explain the unusual pathogenic properties of this mycoplasma and its ability to attach to and enter a variety of cells and tissues. Since the other genes of the HIV-1 virus were not detected in ODS veterans, these mycoplasma-positive GWI patients are not infected with the intact HIV-1 virus. Although GWI patients possess some of the signs and symptoms of an immunodeficiency syndrome, they do not progress to AIDS, nor do they generally test positive for intact HIV-1 virus in their serum or plasma (unpublished data). Some GWI patients, however, do test positive (false positive) in some AIDS tests that probe only the gp120 product of the HIV-1 *env* gene. In these patients additional testing for other HIV-1 gene products or enzymes has proved negative, suggesting support for the hypothesis that only the HIV-1 *env* gene and its encoded product are associated with *M. fermentans* infection of the type found in some GWI patients.

Other chronic infections have also been found in GWI patients. For example, some evidence for *Brucella* infections has been found by us in some GWI cases using forensic polymerase chain reaction (unpublished observations). This is in contrast to official reports by the Walter Reed Army Institute of Research.[61] Inhalation of *Brucella spp.* (*Brucella melitensis* strains predominantly) can cause the slow onset of brucellosis, a chronic illness that shares many but not all of the signs and symptoms of GWI. The prevalence of *Brucella spp.* infections has not been carefully determined in GWI patients.

Other possible infections (not limited to chronic agents) include Q fever, caused by *Coxiella burnetii,* anthrax caused by *Bacillus anthracis,* botulism caused by the botulinum toxin released from *Clostridium botulinum,* and other possible BW agents. A report has appeared on Q fever meningoencephalitis in a GWI patient.[62] Other possible transmittable diseases are those carried by zoonotic sources, such as plague-forming *Yersinia pestis*, a gram-negative, non-spore-forming bacillus obtained from the bite of insects (fleas), or malaria, caused by *P. falciparum* or *P. vivax* from the bite of infected Anopheline mosquitoes. Airborne virus-caused diseases, such as viral hepatitis caused by hepatitis viruses, might be a secondary problem in some GWI cases. Most of the signs and symptoms of these infections are more acute, however, than those found in GWI patients.

Treatment of GWI

Chemical exposures

The treatment of chemically-exposed patients usually involves removal of offending chemicals from the patient's environment, depletion of chemicals from the patient's system and treatment of the signs and symptoms caused by chemical exposure(s).[63] Chemically-exposed patients are often extremely sensitive to a variety of commonly encountered chemicals, including perfumes and air fresheners, petrochemical fumes, chlorine, cleaning solutions and solvents. They are also very sensitive to certain foods and special diets are often necessary, and in some cases direct skin contact with certain substances can cause strong cutaneous reactions. Therefore, an important part of treatment for chemical exposures requires limiting exposure to a variety of common chemicals and the gradual removal of toxic chemicals.[64]

Patients with MCS or OPIDN benefit from procedures that slowly remove chemicals from their bodies. We recommend dry saunas for help in chemical removal, as well as magnesium sulphate-hydrogen peroxide baths. Unfortunately, some GWI patients may have irreversible nerve damage due to low-level nerve agent exposure potentiated by the effects of the antinerve agent pyridostigmine bromide. Nonetheless, most chemical contamination can be reduced through a programme of heat depuration, physical therapy and nutritional supplementation in a specially-constructed less chemically-contaminated environment as described by Rea *et al.*[65] In this programme, patients receive up to 2 hours/day of heat (average 75 minutes/day, essentially dry saunas at 140–160°C) in divided doses with graded exercise (average 60 minutes/day) and massage (average 45 minutes/day). They also receive purified water, vitamins (initially intravenous vitamin C 15 g/day for 5–7 days, then 2–8 g/day oral vitamin C, 10,000–25,000 IU/day vitamin A and 400–800 IU/day vitamin E, plus others), minerals (1000 mg/day calcium, 500 mg/day magnesium, 30–60 mg/day zinc, 200 mcg/day selenium,

10 mg/day manganese, 500–1000 mg/day chromium and 2 mg/day copper, plus others) and antioxidants (3 x 75 mg/day reduced glutathione) and 600 mg/day ketoglutaric acid. Using this programme over 63 per cent of over 200 patients studied reduced their levels of toxic chemicals and showed improvements in chemical sensitivity.[66]

In addition to heat, exercise and diet, a variety of medications can alleviate some of the signs and symptoms of chemical exposures in GWI patients. Many patients have benefited from anti-anxiety, anti-depressant and anti-inflammatory drugs, but this may not be beneficial for some GWI patients.[67] Baumzweiger and Grove have recommended use of dihydropyridine calcium channel blockers in GWI patients to normalize the neurotoxic effects of chemical exposures.[68] After placing 111 GWI patients on dihydro-pyridine calcium channel blockers, they noted that neurological signs and symptoms improved. For example, heart-rate acceleration, blood-vessel irritability, neuro-psychiatric and neuro-immune status improved in patients on the calcium channel blockers Nimodipine, Amlodipine or Felodipine. Baumzweiger and Grove also recommend the psychoactive medications Bupropion (Wellbutrin) and Amantadine (Symmetrel) for cognitive deficits and the extra-pyramidal signs and symptoms, and Trazodone benzodiazepines for insomnia.[69]

Radiological exposures

The successful treatment of patients exposed to DU depends on the extent of exposure. Most patients would have been exposed to DU by inhalation of uranium-oxide particles. Such particles can remain inert in the lungs for extended periods of time, resulting primarily in local tissue alpha irradiation and the resulting radiation damage and immune suppression. Systemic U-235 can be removed by chelation therapy, usually with ethylenediaminetetraacetic acid (EDTA) or penacillamine. Using chelation therapy heavy metals can be removed from the circulation and tissues, and this procedure also aids in the breakdown of the plaques that line the arteries and cause arteriosclerosis. Successful chelation therapy requires slow intravenous infusion of the chelation agent (usually EDTA) in a course of 20–30 separate treatments. Although EDTA can be taken orally, only about 5 per cent or less is actually absorbed. Nutrients such as vitamin C, the amino acids L-cysteine and L-aspartic acid have been used to remove heavy metals but they only weakly chelate heavy metal ions, although they also protect against free radical and ionizing radiation damage.

Biological exposures

If infectious micro-organisms are identified in GWI patients, they can be treated with the appropriate antibiotics. Such treatment should result in improvement and even recovery in patients exposed to bacteria or mycoplasmas, such as *M. fermentans*.[70] This is what has been found with many GWI patients.[71] The recommended treatments for systemic mycoplasmal infections require long-term antibiotic therapy, usually multiple 6-week cycles of doxycycline (200–300 mg/day), ciprofloxacin (Cipro: 1,500 mg/day), azithromycin (Zithromax: 500 mg/day) or clarithromycin (Biaxin: 500–750 mg/day).[72] Multiple cycles are required, because few patients recover after only a few cycles, possibly because of the intracellular locations of mycoplasmas, the slow-growing nature of these micro-organisms and their inherent resistance to antibiotics. For example, 87 GWI patients that tested positive for mycoplasmal infections were treated with antibiotics.[73] All patients relapsed after the first 6-week cycle of therapy, but after up to 6 cycles of therapy 69 out of 87 patients recovered and returned to active duty.[74] Once patients recovered and were able to return to active duty or normal activity, mycoplasma gene sequences could no longer be detected in their blood leukocytes. The clinical responses that are seen are not due to placebo effects, because administration of some antibiotics that are not effective against mycoplasmal infections, such as penicillins, resulted in patients becoming more not less symptomatic, nor are they due to immuno-suppressive effects that can occur with some of the recommended antibiotics. Interestingly, CFS, FMS and GWI patients that slowly recover after several cycles of antibiotics are generally less environmentally sensitive, suggesting that their immune systems may be returning to pre-illness states. If such patients had illnesses that were caused by psychological or psychiatric problems or solely by chemical exposures, they should not respond to the recommended antibiotics and recover slowly. In addition, if such treatments were just reducing auto-immune responses, then patients should relapse after the treatments are discontinued.

Other suggestions

Patients with CFS, FMS or GWI usually have nutritional and vitamin deficiencies that must be corrected.[75] Also, use of antibiotics that deplete normal gut bacteria can result in the over-growth of less desirable flora, so *Lactobacillus acidophillus* supplementation is recommended.[76]

In general, GWI patients should practise avoidance of offending or irritating environments. Many such patients have been placed on anti-depressants and anti-anxiety medications without consideration of the source of their illness or other considerations, such as chemical and biological exposures. Although such medications can alleviate temporarily some of the signs and symptoms of GWI, they are unlikely to recover from their chronic illness on these drugs alone.

ACKNOWLEDGEMENT

The authors' studies were supported by a grant from the Rhodon Foundation for Biomedical Research, Inc. and private donations from the families of GWI patients.

REFERENCES

1. NIH Technology Assessment Workshop Panel (1994), 'The Persian Gulf Experience and Health', *JAMA* 272: 391–6; Nicolson, G. and N. Nicolson (1995), 'Chronic Fatigue Illness and Operation Desert Storm', *Journal of Occupational and Environmental Medicine* 38:14–17; and Haley, R.W., Kurt, T.L. and J. Hom (1997), 'Is There a Gulf War Syndrome? Searching for syndromes by factor analysis of symptoms', *JAMA* 277: 215–22.

2. See NIH, n. 1 above.

3. Nicolson and Nicolson, and Haley *et al.*, n. 1 above.

4. Murray-Leisure, K.A., Daniels, M.O., Sees, J., Zangwill, B., Suguitan, E., Bagheri, S., Brinser, E., Kimber, R., Kurban, R. and W. Green (1998), 'Mucocutaneous-, Intestinal-, Rheumatic Desert Syndrome (MIRDS): I. Definition histopathology, incubation period and clinical course', *Journal of Internal Medicine* 1: 47–72.

5. See Haley *et al.*, n. 1 above.

6. Baumzweiger, W.E. and R. Grove (1998), 'Brainstem-Limbic Immune Dysregulation in 111 Gulf War veterans: a clinical evaluation of its etiology, diagnosis and response to headache treatment', *Journal of Internal Medicine* 1: 129–43.

7. Nicolson, n. 1 above; Nicolson, G.L., Hyman, E., Korényi-Both, A., Lopez, D.A., Nicolson, N.L., Rea, W. and H. Urnovitz (1995), 'Progress on Persian Gulf War Illnesses: reality and hypotheses', *International Journal of Occupational Medicine and Toxicology* 4: 365–70; Nicolson, G.L. (1998), 'Chronic Infections as a Common Etiology for Many Patients with Chronic Fatigue Syndrome, Fibromyalgia Syndrome and Gulf War Illnesses', *Journal of Internal Medicine* 1: 42–46.

8. Writer, J.V., DeFraites, R.F. and J.F. Brundage (1996), 'Comparative Mortality Among US Military Personnel in the Persian Gulf Region and Worldwide during Operations Desert Shield and Desert Storm', *JAMA* 275: 118–21.

9. Nicolson *et al.* (1995), n. 7 above.

10. Murray-Leisure *et al.*, n. 4 above.

11. Kizer, K.W., Joseph, S. and J.T. Rankin (1995), 'Unexplained Illness among Persian Gulf War Veterans in an Air National Guard Unit: preliminary report, August 1990–March 1995', *MMWR Morbidity and Mortality Weekly Report* 44: 443–7.

12. Eddington, P.G. (1997), *Gassed in the Gulf*, Washington DC: Insignia Publishing; and Nicolson, G.L. and N.L. Nicolson (1998), 'Gulf War Illnesses: complex medical, scientific and political paradox', *Medicine, Conflict and Survival* 14: 74–83.

13. See n. 11 above.

14. Ibid.

15. See n. 1 above.

16. *NIH*, n. 1 above; and n. 12 above.

17. See ns 4 and 7 (Nicolson *et al.* 1995) above.

18. *NIH*, and Haley *et al.*, n. 1 above.

19. See ns 2, 3, 5 and 7 (Nicolson *et al.* 1995) above.

20. See ns 2 and 7 (Nicolson 1998) above.

21. See n. 2 above.

22. Ibid.

23. Ibid.

24. Ibid.

25. See n. 6 above.

26. see ns 6, 7 and 12 (Nicolson *et al.*) above.

27. See n. 12 above.

28. Ibid.

29. See ns 1 (Haley *et al.*) and 12 (Nicolson *et al.*) above; and Abou-Donia, M.B. and Wilmarth, K.R. (1996), 'Neurotoxicity Resulting from Coexposure to Pyridostigmine Bromide, DEET and Permethrin: implications of Gulf War exposures', *Journal of Toxicology and Environmental Health* 48: 35–56.

30. See Abou-Donia *et al.*, n. 29 above.

31. Ziem, G.E. (1992), 'Multiple Chemical Sensitivity: treatment and followup with avoidance and control of chemical exposures', *Toxicology and Industrial Health* 8: 73–86.

32. Ibid.

33. See n. 12 above.

34. See Eddington, n. 12 above.

35. See n. 12 above.

36. Korényi-Both, A.L., Molnar, A.C., Korényi-Bothm A.L. and R.F. Fidelus-Gort (1992), 'Al-Eskan

Disease: Desert Storm pneumonitis', *Military Medicine* 157: 452–62.

37. Ibid.

38. See n. 4 above.

39. Magill, A.J, Grogl, M., Fasser, R.A., Wellington, S. and C.N. Oster (1993), 'Viscerotropic Leishmaniasis Caused by *Leishmania tropica* in Soldiers Returning from Operation Desert Storm', *New England Journal of Medicine* 328: 1383–7.

40. See Eddington, n. 12 above.

41. See Nicolson *et al.*, n. 12 above.

42. See n. 4 above.

43. See Nicolson, Hyman *et al.*, n. 7 above.

44. Ibid.

45. Ibid.

46. See ns 4 and 7 (Nicolson 1988) above; Nicolson, G.L. and N.L. Nicolson (1996), 'Diagnosis and Treatment of MycoplasmalInfections in Persian Gulf War Illness-CFIDS patients', *International Journal of Occupational Medicine, Immunology and Toxicology* 5: 69–78; and Nicolson, G.L., Nicolson, N.L. and M. Nasralla (1998), 'Mycoplasmal Infections and Chronic Fatigue Illness (Gulf War Illness) Associated with Deployment to Operation Desert Storm', *Journal of Internal Medicine* 1: 80–92.

47. US Senate Committee on Banking, Housing and Urban Affairs (1994), 'US chemical and Biological Wwarfare-related Dual-Use Exports to Iraq and their Possible Impact on the Health Consequences of the Persian Gulf War' , Report, 103rd Congress, 2nd session,103–900, 25 May .

48. See ns 4 and 7 (Nicolson 1998) above.

49. See Nicolson, n. 12 above.

50. See Nicolson, Hyman *et al.*, n. 7 above.

51. See n. 46 above.

52. Hyman, E.S. (1994), 'A Urinary Marker for Systemic Coccal Disease', *Nephron* 68: 314–26.

53. Nicolson, G.L. and N.L. Nicolson (1995), 'Doxycycline Treatment and Desert Storm', *JAMA,* 273: 618–19.

54. See Nicolson and Nicolson (1995), n. 53 above.

55. See n. 46 above.

56. Ibid.

57. See Nicolson *et al.* (1998), n. 46 above.

58. See n. 46 above.

59. Nasralla, M., Haier, J. and Nicolson, G.L. (1999), 'Multiple mycoplasmal infections detected in blood of Chronic Fatigue and Fibromyalgia Syndrome patients', *European Journal of Clinical and Microbiological Infectious Diseases* 18: 859–865.

60. See Nicolson *et al.* (1998), n. 46 above.

61. DeFraites, R.F., Wanat, E.R., Norwood, A.E., Williams, S., Cowan, D. and T. Callahan (1992), 'Investigation of a Suspected Outbreak of an Unknown Disease among Veterans of Operation Desert Shield/Storm', 123rd Army Reserve Command, Fort Benjamin Harrison, Indiana, Report, Epidemiology Consultant Service (EPICON), Division of Preventive Medicine, Walter Reed Army Institute of Research, Washington, DC, April.

62. Ferrante, M.A. and M.J. Dolan (1993), 'Q Fever Meningoencephalitis in a Soldier Returning from the Persian Gulf War', *Clinical Infectious Diseases* 16: 489–96.

63. See n. 31 above; and Rea, W.J., Pan, Y., Johnson, A.R., Ross, G.H., Suyama, H. and E.J. Fenyves, E.J. (1996), 'Reduction of Chemical Sensitivity by Means of Heat Depuration, Physical Therapy and Nutritional Supplementation in a Controlled Environment', *Journal of Nutritional and Environmental Medicine* 6: 141–8.

64. Ibid.

65. See Rea *et al.* n. 63 above.

66. Ibid.

67. See n. 6 above.

68. Ibid.

69. Ibid.

70. See ns 53 and 59 above.

71. See Nicolson and Nicolson (1996) and Nicolson *et al.* (1998), n. 46 above.

72. Nicolson, G.L. (1998), 'Considerations when Undergoing Treatment for Chronic Infections Found in Chronic Fatigue Syndrome, Fibromyalgia Syndrome and Gulf War Illnesses' (Part 1), 'Antibiotics Recommended when Indicated for Treatment of Gulf War Illness/CFIDS/FMS' (Part 2), *Journal of Internal Medicine* 1: 115–17, 123–8.

73. See Nicolson *et al.* (1998), n. 46 above.

74. See Nicolson and Nicolson (1996) and Nicolson *et al.* (1998), n. 46 above.

75. See n. 72 above and Nicolson, G.L. (1999), 'The Role of Microorganism Infections in Chronic Illnesses: support for antibiotic regimens', *CFIDS Chronicle* 12 (3): 19–21.

76. See n. 72 above.

Addresses for correspondence

Prof Garth Nicholson, Dr Nancy Nicholson
Institute for Molecular Medicine, 15162 Triton Lane, Huntington Beach, California 92649-1041 USA
Email: gnicolson@immed.org   Website: www.immed.org

Dr M. Nasralla
International Molecular Diagnostics 15162 Triton Lane, Huntington Beach, California 92649-1041 USA
Email: mnasralla@imd-lab.com   Website: www.imd-lab.com

Dr J, Haier
Dept. of Surgery, Wilhelm-University , Walderstr. 1, Munster 48149, Germany
Email: haier@uni-muenster.de

43 KOSOVO WAR
First Environmental Impact Assessment

PEKKA HAAVISTO

Nowadays environmental impact assessments are made on everything: whether it's a new supermarket, motorway, harbour, or just a plan to cut trees from a forest, people want to know what are the real environmental and health consequences. But if you have started a war, nobody is interested in the environmental consequences. There are, of course, many other things to occupy people's minds: material damage, political games and human suffering, even if the human suffering is multiplied many times over by the destruction of the environment.

The war in Kosovo was a turning-point. United Nations Secretary-General Kofi Annan decided to send an Inter-Agency Needs Assessment Mission to the Federal Republic of Yugoslavia during the conflict. The mission was headed by the then-UN Under-Secretary General Sergio de Mello. His report stated that a 'detailed assessment of the full extent of the environmental impact is urgently required'.

Dr Klaus Töpfer, Executive Director of the UN Environmental Programme (UNEP), took the intiative by establishing in early May 1999 the joint UNEP/UNCHS (Habitat) Balkans Task Force with a mandate based on the recommendations of the Inter-Agency Needs Assessment Mission. Dr Töpfer invited me, as a former Minister of Environment and Development Cooperation of Finland, to chair the work of the Balkans Task Force from the UNEP European Regional Office in Geneva.

The (Habitat) Balkans Task Force

Our initial visits to the area showed clearly that the war had caused much damage, not only to human beings but also to the environment. Many environmental problems were linked to the River Danube, which is also a source of drinking water for the down-river countries Bulgaria and Romania. The task force, consisting of more than 60 international experts from six UN agencies, 19 countries and 26 scientific institutions and

NGOs, finally assessed the environmental damage to industrial sites, the River Danube and biological diversity in protected areas, the threat to human settlements and the risk from depleted uranium weapons

Industrial sites

Our first team of experts investigated industrial sites in Pancevo, Novi Sad, Kragujevac, Nis, Bor, Prahovo and Pristina in July 1999. We took samples, some of which were analysed immediately in our mobile field laboratories (provided by Denmark and Germany) while others were taken to Hungary and Germany for further analysis. In the politically-sensitive situation we were in, we didn't want to use local laboratories.

The River Danube

Another international expert team with nine scientists from eight countries and representatives from the World Wildlife Fund and Green Cross assessed the situation of the River Danube in close cooperation with the International Commission for the Protection of the Danube River. The experts took numerous water and sediment samples for examination by independent laboratories in various countries. The team visited four different sites along the Danube, including the Iron Gate Reservoir on the borders of Serbia, Romania and Bulgaria. The team examined the Lepenica and Morava rivers, both tributaries of the Danube, close to Kragujevac. There the scientific work focused not only on sampling river water, bottom and bank sediments but also on mussels and other invertebrates. For comparison, samples were taken upstream and downstream of the industrial areas.

Biological diversity

In September, a third group of experts travelled to the Balkans to assess the damage to biological-diversity sites, such as selected protected areas and national parks which were targeted during the war. The team visited Kosovo's Fruska Gora and Kopaonik national parks, Zlatibor in Serbia and Lake Skadar in Montenegro.

Depleted uranium

Our expert group on depleted uranium consisted of well-known scientists from the World Health Organization, the International Atomic Energy Agency, the EU Commission, the Swedish Radiation Protection Institute, the World Wildlife Fund and other organizations. The group looked into the risks to human health, as well as damage and pollution of soil and water. The preliminary assessment and a parallel desk study had to rely on available published information. We faced a strange situation, when NATO and its member states were not willing to give the UN assessment team any detailed information on the use of weapons with depleted uranium in the Kosovo conflict. Given these circumstances, and taking a precautionary approach to the issue, the experts recommended that at places where contamination had been confirmed, measures to prevent access should be taken; likewise, local authorities and people concerned should be informed of the possible risks and appropriate precautionary procedures.

One of our problems in the field was to distinguish between previous pollution and pollution caused by the bombings. Many of the industrial sites, such as the oil refinery in Novi Sad, plants in Pancevo, the Zastava car factory in Kragujevac or the mining town of Bor, showed signs of previous environmental pollution at alarming levels. In Pancevo our team was welcomed by some local representatives of NGOs. There certainly has been need for independent environmental assessment for quite some time. People have also suffered from different pollution-related diseases. For example, in Pancevo a special type of liver cancer (Pancevo cancer) was named as one of the work-related diseases in the petrochemical factory. From the environmental point of view it is of course irrelevant if the pollution is new or old, but for questions related to warfare we tried to make that distinction. Authorities who plan the clean-up process have to take care of both new and old environmental problems.

We are sure that even if words like 'ecocatastrophe' or 'ecocide' (the word used during the bombings by Yugoslavian authorities and referring to 'genocide') overestimate the consequences of the war, there are several environmental hot-spots in the area. I am especially concerned about the mercury released in Pancevo – altogether eight tonnes of metallic mercury – the probable dioxin problems in Pancevo and Kragujevac, as well as the overall risks to drinking water in many of the industrial towns, for example in Novi Sad.

Another concern was the electricity shortage in Serbia due to the war. We all know that especially in winter lack of electricity, oil and gasoline poses a humanitarian problem for the population. In some towns the district heating system was damaged. But lack of electricity causes additional environmental problems, preventing the proper use of fresh water and wastewater pumping-stations and processes. In the mining town of Bor sulphur-dioxide emissions into the air increased as a result of the electricity shortage.

Human settlements

One part of our team also worked in Kosovo, in Pristina, especially with the damaged human settlements and on land-property issues. Our experts proposed a quick impact project to the UN agency in charge in Kosovo (UNMIK), which helped to identify neighbourhood improvement projects and allowed contractors to obtain tools by contributing their expertise to needed reparations. Another quick project on organizing land-ownership records in various municipalities is being considered. We are also working on a project proposal on partnerships for local development. This is a programme of strategic and practical actions to develop sustainable urban governance in Kosovo. We convened a workshop with international experts from Bosnia-Herzegovina and other countries and discussed the modalities of establishing an independent claims commission on housing and property-rights matters under UNMIK. One of the most essential things before reconstruction is to know who owns what and under which legal framework. This is a huge task, especially in Kosovo.

In Serbia we can already see reconstruction work going on in the targeted industrial sites. This is causing an additional health risk to the workers, who are not aware of the environmental and health risks of mercury, dioxines, PCBs or asbestos. People are at risk if proper protection is not arranged. To avoid new serious helath consequences all toxic materials should be removed and the areas decontaminated before reconstruction starts.

Unfortunately, several months after the war many people are still suffering from its consequences and serious threats to human health call for immediate action. The human settlement problem consists not only of reconstructing houses and bridges but also of establishing administrative procedures to ensure property rights and ownership information systems. We now have the Kosovo Albanians back in Kosovo, but in Serbia the numbers of refugees have increased. Environmental problems caused by the stream of refugees into unprepared areas, with sanitation and drinking-water services under enormous pressure, are still an issue. Romania and Bulgaria fear the transboundary pollution from targeted industrial facilities.

The Balkans Task Force final report was given to UN Secretary-General Kofi Annan at the beginning of October 1999. The report acts as a reliable source of information for the affected population and provides a tool for the international community for humanitarian assistance. For the first time environmental consequences of the war have led to a recommendation to clean up the four most seriously damaged industrial hot-spots as part of the humanitarian assistance. While the Yugoslav government can deal with some of the priorities, it certainly requires outside help.

The recommendations of the report also include providing ongoing technical support to UNMIK in Kosovo in order to produce guidelines and procedures for municipal administration. Technical support should be given to develop a property ownership-information system, mentioned above, and to upgrade property registries and documentation.

The organization of the UNEP/UNCHS Balkans Task Force was an ad-hoc initiative. Voluntary funding for the work came from Austria, Belgium, Denmark, Finland, France, Germany, Italy, the Netherlands, Norway, Sweden and the United Kingdom. Additional support in kind was provided by Russia and Slovakia, and by NGOs including Greenpeace, the World Wildlife Fund (WWF), IUCN, the Green Cross and the WCMS.

Conclusions

What can we learn from the Kosovo crisis and its consequences for the environment and human health? I shall try to summarize:

(1) The crisis in the Balkans has had serious environmental impacts, and environmental hot-spots need to be cleaned up immediately to avoid further risks to human health.

(2) The response to emergency situations has to be seen as part of the humanitarian effort to protect the people of the area. Whatever the political situation, international action is needed to protect both people and nature.

(3) The conflict in the Balkans raises an interesting question about modern warfare and the targeting industrial facilities, with the risk of heavy pollution close to big cities. It is up to the international community to discuss and decide whether the rules of modern warfare are up-to-date when looking at the risks to human health and the environment.

(4) The international environmental impact assessment of war damage after the Kosovo conflict was the first of its kind. Several months after the cessation of hostilities many people were suffering from the consequences and the environment was at great risk. The international community should be given a clear responsibility to minimize the war-related health and environmental threats as soon as possible. In the Balkans time is being wasted, and people are facing the risks.

REFERENCES

The final report of the (habitat) Balkans Task Force and our mission reports, photographs, maps and other documents are available at our website http://www.grid.unep.ch/btf/.

Address for correspondence
International Environment House, 13, chemin des Anémones, room 513, CH-1219 Châtelaine-Geneva, Switzerland.
Tel:+41-22-917 8254; Fax: +41-22-917 8064; GSM +41-79-221 8072; Email: pekka.haavisto@unep.ch;
http://www.grid.unep.ch/btf/

VI | PREVENTION AND MANAGEMENT OF WARS

Land mines
Oliver Whitehead

44 THE LAWS OF GENEVA AND THE HAGUE

GUNNAR ROSÉN

The four Geneva Conventions of 12 August 1949 and their two Additional Protocols of 8 June 1977 make up the so-called Law of Geneva and are the main codification of present international rules for the protection of victims of war. In addition to the Law of Geneva, the 1907 Law of the Hague on the laws and customs of warfare itself, although technically outdated, is still in force as customary law. It has since its introduction been complemented with several international treaties which prohibit or limit the use of certain weapons and methods of warfare. Relevant to the Geneva and Hague laws are several other legal instruments, including the Charter of the United Nations, the so-called Nuremberg Principles and several conventions, UN resolutions and other agreements for the protection of refugees, child soldiers, cultural property and general human rights. Particularly after the adoption of the Additional Protocols to the Geneva conventions, the essence of the Hague conventions and some other, older international treaties and declarations have been included in the Law of Geneva, which now consists of:

(i) the convention for the protection of the wounded and sick in the field (land warfare);
(ii) the convention for the protection of the wounded, sick and shipwrecked at sea;
(iii) the convention for protection of prisoners of war;
(iv) the convention for the protection of civilians;
(v) Additional Protocol I relative to international armed conflicts; and
(vi) Additional Protocol II relative to non-international conflicts.

Without regard to the fact that there are some formal differences between states having become parties to the conventions (accessions, ratifications, reservations), the number of states that were parties to the main conventions was 188 in 1999 with around 150 Additional Protocols. At the same time the number of members of the United Nations was one hundred and eighty-five. By special resolutions the UN General Assembly has urged all states to become parties to the conventions and protocols. Even when the UN cannot itself be a formal party to them, it requires that all states providing troops to UN peacekeeping and other forces are parties to them and that the UN forces themselves strictly respect them. The Law of Geneva is legally binding on its parties and all their citizens. Grave breaches are crimes under international law which, if necessary, surpasses national laws. The conventions are binding on the parties even in cases in which the counterpart is not a party or does not respect them.

Central aims

By customary law civilians who did not actively participate in hostilities, as well as cities and localities which did not put up armed resistance or were not used for it, were protected as such. According to the St Petersburg Declaration of 1868 the right of the belligerents was limited to weakening of the military power of the enemy, avoiding even in warfare all unnecessary destruction and infliction of suffering. The later Geneva and Hague conventions were intended only to alleviate the fate of soldiers. As a result, the provisions protecting civilians in the 1907 Hague conventions are very vague and general. In fact, the most important is the famous Martens' clause presented in the introduction to the Fourth Hague Convention on land-warfare,

> that in case they are not included in the Regulations, the inhabitants and the belligerents remain under the protection and the rule of the principles of the law of nations, as they result from the usages established among civilized peoples, from the laws of humanity and the dictates of the public conscience.

The totalitarian warfare of the Second World War (WW II) and the enormous losses amongst the civilian population under the bombings and as the result of atrocities in occupied countries brought about a great change in the development of the law of war. For the first time the protection of civilians became a primary objective. Yet the 4th Geneva Convention of 1949 deals almost entirely with protection and treatment of civilians already under enemy control, not with bombings and other attacks against civilian enemy objectives. Only with the adoption of the Additional Protocols of 1977 were clear rules set for modern warfare, the central issue being the protection of civilians.

However, drastic changes in world affairs and the ways and means of conducting politics and hostilities since WW II and even after the adoption of 1977 protocols have jeopardized efforts to strengthen respect for international law. Regular wars between sovereign states have become rare and been replaced by a great variety of armed conflicts, which often are a mixture of international and civil wars, ethnic conflicts, guerrilla warfare, terrorism and mafia-war. Alarming and sad new phenomena are intentional and ruthless attacks against civilians, carried out by heavily-armed regular troops or militia in order to destroy or drive away unwanted ethnic groups. Consequently civilian losses are now much higher than those sustained by militaries. To a great extent the phenomenon is connected with the falling apart of many states and the weakness or even unwillingness of their governments to control the situation. Countermeasures by the international community, still fairly limited and too late, have been interventions by peacekeeping and similar forces, turning the principle of non-intervention in the affairs of formally sovereign states into a burning issue. A highly important step towards developing and strengthening the respect for international law has been the setting up of international courts, even if still in an embryonic phase, to judge crimes against peace, war crimes and genocide.

Prohibited means of warfare

The following provisions of International Law form the basis for instance for the Hague Tribunal when estimating the crimes committed in the former Yugoslavia. The right of the belligerents to injure the enemy with whatever means is not unlimited. Distinction must always be made between persons taking part in the hostilities and the civilian population and spare the latter as much as possible. Indiscriminate attacks and use of indiscriminate weapons are prohibited, including attacks not directed against specific military objectives, area bombardments of cities and localities without separating military and civilian targets, and the use of weapons whose effects cannot be limited to military objectives. Particular attention must be paid to spare specifically protected objectives and to avoid the use of methods that would cause excessive damage to installations and the environment necessary for the survival of the population (Protocol I).

In the Hague tradition the prohibitions on the use of particularly inhuman weapons have been updated with newer special treaties. The following are prohibited by older and newer agreements:

- the use in hand weapons of bullets expanding in the human body, poison and poisoned weapons; and the use of weapons, the fragments of which cannot be detected in the human body by X-rays;
- the use of poisonous gases and chemical or bacteriological weapons;
- the use of napalm and other incendiary weapons against civilians or in vicinity of civilian objectives;
- the use of booby-trap mines and anti-personnel land mines (the latter convention not yet adhered to by the military super-powers and several other states); and
- the use of methods of warfare which may cause serious and long-term damage to the natural environment.

Nuclear and other weapons of mass destruction are not yet prohibited as such, provided that their effects can be strictly limited to military objectives.

Protected objectives

Particularly protected objectives (provided that the said objectives are not used for military action or to shield military action) are:

- civilian and military hospitals and other medical units and transportations;
- duly marked hospital and safety zones;
- permanent and mobile civil defence units and rescue services;
- installations containing great dangerous forces, such as dams, dykes, nuclear power plants and chemical or bactcriological factories;
- installations, warehouses and transportations of the Red Cross and other authorized relief organizations;
- installations, warehouses and other objectives necessary for the survival of population; and
- churches, temples and cultural objectives.

Under the directives and permission of military or civilian authorities the protected objectives shall be marked with recognized international protective signs:

- the red cross or red crescent on white ground (in Israel unilaterally the red star of David, not internationally recognised);

- the sign of civil defence;
- the sign of cultural property; and
- the markings of installations containing dangerous forces.

It is strictly prohibited to attack objectives marked with protective signs. Their misuse leads automatically to the loss of protection.

Before any military action the commanders on all levels have to make a reconnaissance of the target area and note the concentrations of civilians and protected objectives. Attacks must be directed only against military objectives. Among tactical alternatives the means of combat shall be chosen so as to minimize civilian casualties and damage to civilian property.

Protected persons

Protected by the Geneva Conventions, provided that they do not participate in hostilities or in any hostile acts against the enemy, are the following persons:

- wounded, sick and shipwrecked soldiers, including also crews and passengers of military aircraft in distress and 'hors combat';
- surrendering enemy soldiers and prisoners of war;
- all medical personnel of the armed forces, including also army chaplains and other religious personnel;
- the entire civilian population, particularly the wounded and sick, mothers and children and the elderly;
- the civilian medical, sanitary and religious personnel;
- the civil defence and rescue service personnel;
- the personnel of the Red Cross and other relief organizations, if duly authorized; and
- authorized war correspondents, including foreigners

The so-called fundamental principles for the treatment of protected persons are presented in the famous Article 3 of all four conventions and completed in Article 75 of the first Additional Protocol. The physical and mental health and the integrity of persons who are in the power of the enemy party or interned or otherwise deprived of liberty in connection with an armed conflict shall be treated humanely without any adverse distinction founded on nationality, race, religion, faith, wealth or any other similar criteria. Particularly forbidden under all circumstances are:

- murder, torture and cruel treatment, including corporal punishments;
- the taking of hostages and collective punishments;
- humiliating and degrading treatment, including enforced prostitution;
- the passing of sentences and carrying out of executions without judgements by regularly constituted courts;
- omission to collect and care for the wounded and sick.

More detailed regulations and directives are given in several other articles in connection with provisions concerning the different branches of protection.

Combatants and non-combatants, prisoners of war

Distinction must always be made between combatants and non-combatants, in other words between the active members of armed forces and soldiers who have laid down their arms after having become wounded, sick or shipwrecked, or fallen into enemy hands. No longer a threat to the enemy, the latter are considered as individuals *hors de combat* (out of the fight) in need of protection and assistance like civilians.

Those defined as legal combatants and, in enemy power, entitled to the status of prisoners of war (POW) are as follows:

- members of the regular armed forces, including also members of militias and volunteer corps, if attached to the army;
- partisans and members of guerrilla units, if wearing their national uniform or a distinctive sign and carrying their arms openly;
- persons who accompany an army without actually belonging to the armed forces (technical personnel, members of labour units, transportation and logistics support personnel); and
- inhabitants of a non-occupied territory who at the approach of the enemy spontaneously take to arms, for instance in order to defend their village (in which case the protection of a civilian objective can be lost).

The status of a legal combatant or a prisoner of war is not enjoyed by irregular groups of fighters outside the control of military authorities, terrorists and mercenaries. Combatants using a false uniform are treated as spies.

Commanders are responsible to see that their subordinates are familiar with the laws and customs of war and respect them. Basic directives for common soldiers state:

- attack only military objectives and enemy soldiers;
- do not destroy more than what your mission requires;
- do not kill or hurt wounded or surrendering enemies. Disarm them and hand them over to your superiors;
- collect all wounded, also enemies, and care for them;
- treat humanely both enemy civilians and soldiers in your power. Cruelty is met only with harder resistance and revenge;
- respect the red cross and other international protective signs; and
- all looting, robbery and taking the law into your own hands is strictly forbidden.

The 3rd Geneva Convention on the protection and treatment of prisoners of war is the most detailed of the conventions. As prisoners are usually taken by all parties, the principle of reciprocity functions best, not counting civil wars and internal feuds in which blind hate and revenge easily take over.

One of the basic principles is that the POWs are not in the power of soldiers or units which have captured them, but are a direct responsibility of the government or high command of the detaining power. Regardless of their detention, the POWs have to be treated as individuals in full possession of their civil rights. The fundamental guarantees apply to them:

- They shall not be enforced to reveal more information than their name, rank, date of birth and the number of their identity disc or corresponding information;
- they must be protected against the dangers of the hostilities, including their use as shields against attacks of their own party;
- they cannot be compelled to do dangerous work, for instance to clear mines, or to participate in military activities against their own country;
- their quartering, food, medical care and general well-being must correspond to the level of the armed forces of the detaining power;
- they shall not be condemned to harder disciplinary or other punishments than the soldiers of the detaining power – on the contrary, the captivity and total dependence of the enemy should be considered as mitigating factors.

Female POWs and child soldiers enjoy special protection and privileges. Children under fifteen years of age shall not be recruited in armed forces.

In international armed conflicts, which include those in which 'peoples are fighting against colonial domination, alien occupation and against racist regimes in their right of self-determination', the parties appoint a neutral country or usually the International Committee of the Red Cross (ICRC) to act as a protecting power in order to safeguard the rights and interests of the POWs. Among the most important tasks of the ICRC is the registration of all POWs and the exchange of lists of them between the parties, the establishment of contact and correspondence between the prisoners and their relatives and the provision of assistance to them. The protecting power must always have access to the POW camps and other places of detention and to speak with the prisoners without witnesses in order to be able to supervise their treatment according to the conventions. The ICRC may already during the war organize exchanges of certain groups of prisoners and, after the end of the hostilities, the earliest possible exchange of them all.

The system of protecting powers is not included in Additional Protocol II on non-international conflicts. In principle measures against internal dissident forces are a matter for the jurisdiction of a sovereign state. The definition of an international armed conflict itself and the mixed character of modern conflicts, however, have given cause to question the validity of the principle. The ICRC has the right to offer its good offices in these situations and, through sheer diplomacy, has been able to extend its protective role, also to many internal conflicts, including registration of and assistance to political detainees.

Occupation

The 3rd Geneva Convention has its origins in the experiences of WW II and aims in the first place at protecting the civilians of occupied countries. The guiding principle is that the occupying power is only a temporary authority in the territory and holder of its public property without right to alter its constitution or the civil rights of the population. The occupant has the right to give orders related to the situation and particularly to his own safety, but at the same time he is fully responsible for the safety and livelihood of the population. The fundamental guarantees as stated in the Geneva conventions and protocols have to be respected under all circumstances.

The normal administration and institutions of the country have the right to continue their functions on the largest possible scale, even if controlled by the occupying power. The occupant has the right to use public property for its own war effort and confiscate supplies against quittance, collect taxes or comparable payments to be used solely for the needs of the population and to cover the costs of the occupation, but not to a degree which might endanger the life and health of the people.

The inhabitants of an occupied territory may be compelled to participate in public and other works, necessary for the needs of the society or the occupying forces, but to no greater degree than the citizens of the occupying power. The work has to take place in the territory; the enforced transfer of labour force to another country, still more the expulsion of people from their own country, is strictly prohibited. Likewise it is forbidden that the occupying power colonizes the territory with its own nationals before the final peace or other post- war settlement.

The occupying power may intern people it considers dangerous for its own safety. Crimes against the occupying forces are treated by their military courts, but the accused must have the right to defence and a fair trial according to international rules and customs. Persons under 18 years of age shall not be condemned to death. Detailed rules, comparable with the rules for the treatment of prisoners of war, concern the conditions of internment of civilians. The occupying power must accept the offer of the ICRC or a neutral state or organization to act as a protecting power with the right to visit the internees, register them and assist them according to rules very similar to the rules concerning prisoners of war.

Civil wars and internal armed conflicts

Additional Protocol II extends the basic humanitarian rules that are in force in international armed conflicts to non-international conflicts. As a minimum the states, parties to the conventions and protocols, have to respect the fundamental guarantees forbidding under all circumstances murder and torture, degrading treatment, the taking of hostages, collective punishments and acts of terror and pillage.

Additional Protocol II does not apply to riots or isolated acts of violence and terror which are treated under normal criminal law. At its full extent it applies first in situations in which organized dissident armed forces under responsible command exercise such control over a part of the territory that they are able to carry out concerted military operations and to reciprocally implement the protocol. However, even in cases where the dissidents have not declared their respect for the law of war or make themselves guilty of its breaches, the parties to the Geneva convention stay bound to respect the provisions of the protocol. Particularly detailed regulations concern the treatment of persons whose liberty has been restricted because of the conflict. Even when an official protecting power is not nominated in these situations, the ICRC and other Red Cross (Red Crescent) organizations and relief societies may offer their services.

Care of the wounded and sick

The Geneva conventions were originally intended to alleviate the sufferings of wounded and sick soldiers in the field and to protect military hospitals and medical units, often operating close to the battlefield. To some extent a distinction is still made between military and civilian medical and sanitary services, particularly in the use of the red cross (red crescent) emblem, but the general rules for both are about the same. The fundamental principle and basis for the protection of medical services is their absolute impartiality.

The modern definition of medical units is wide, covering all establishments and units, whether military or civilian, organized for the search, collection, transportation, diagnosis or treatment, including first-aid treatment, of the wounded, sick and shipwrecked, or for the prevention of disease. In addition to actual hospitals, medical stations and ambulance units, the term includes annexed or auxiliary services, such as laboratories, blood transfusion services and pharmaceutical units. 'Medical personnel' refers to all persons assigned to the said services, including administrative and logistics personnel, whether military or civilian. Their definition also covers the medical personnel of national Red Cross societies and other national voluntary aid bodies if duly authorized by a party to the conflict. The relevant provisions apply also to foreign medical units and their personnel, if duly authorized by a party to the conflict or by the UN or some other neutral intermediary. In an armed conflict religious personnel are comparable with medical personnel and have the right to carry their protective sign.

The regulations concerning the use of the distinctive red cross (red crescent) protective sign are different in peacetime and during an armed conflict. The army medical units and medical personnel have the right to use them at all times according to the internal rules set by the military authorities themselves. The original and official sign of military medical personnel is the white red cross armlet carried on the left arm and properly stamped. For better visibility it is today often used also on such things as helmets and vests. Hospitals and other medical installations, hospital ships, ambulance vehicles and air planes have to be marked with red-cross markings of great size, visible from a distance and from the air. Sometimes for military reasons, sometimes in order to avoid criminal attacks, the said objects are today also left unmarked, but then risk not being treated as protected targets.

Non-military medical services must have the authorization of the military or civilian high command to use the protective red crescent or red-cross emblem in war time. Its use without official permission is strictly forbidden. This also applies for the personnel and units of the national Red Cross societies and other voluntary organizations if not attached to the official medical services. Voluntary first-aid groups belonging to the Red Cross, civil defence and industrial rescue units can be granted a temporary right to use the emblem as long as their assignment continues, for instance during bombardments.

In peacetime, permission to use the red cross emblem outside the military services can be granted only by the national Red Cross society. This applies in particular to the markings of first-aid stations and ambulance vehicles.

No military activities, harmful to the enemy, are permitted under the protective emblem. Misuse leads automatically to the loss of protection. In addition to armed resistance this includes, for instance, the use of medical installations as observation posts and communication centres, hiding of armed fighters and the transportation of arms or other than wounded soldiers in ambulance vehicles. Medical personnel do not have a right to participate in hostilities except in immediate self-defence and in protection of their patients. For this purpose military medical personnel have the right to possess a handarm. Transport of the wounded can be protected by a military escort.

All the wounded and sick shall be collected and cared for without distinction based on the fighting party, nationality, race, religion, wealth or any similar grounds. Treatment priority must be decided only on medical grounds following the same standards for all. It is strictly forbidden to submit enemy patients to any experiments or methods of treatment which differ from those used on national patients. Voluntary blood donations are permitted, but all physical mutilations or removal of tissue or organs for transplantation even with the consent of the patients belonging to the adverse party, are strictly forbidden. The patient has the right to refuse amputation or any surgical operation. In such a case the medical personnel shall try to obtain a written statement to that effect.

Quartering, food and hygienic conditions have to be on the same level regardless of the party. Any wilful act or omission which endangers the health of a protected person is considered a grave breach of the conventions. Detailed records on all phases of the treatment shall be kept for the use of the protecting power. The dead shall be buried with dignity and their place of burial marked.

Nobody, including ordinary civilians, shall be punished for caring or assisting a wounded or sick person regardless of the party. Medical personnel cannot be forced to act against the ethics of their profession.

Medical personnel falling into the hands of the adverse party are not to be considered prisoners of war, but have as a minimum to receive the protection and benefits equal to the status of POWs. They have the right to continue to treat their own nationals and, if this is not required any more, they should be repatriated.

Misuse of the red cross (red crescent) protective emblem is a serious crime. Its respect is based on reciprocity. Misuse endangers the safety of the compatriots on both sides of the frontier.

War crimes

Parties to the Geneva conventions are under an obligation to disseminate them effectively among their armed forces and the entire population and to take any measures to prevent their breaches. Every commander is responsible for his subordinates' familiarity with the law of war and their respect for it.

According to the earlier view the only way to treat war crimes was under the jurisdiction and legislation of each country separately. At the Nuremberg trials after WW II a new concept was introduced, and the so-called Nuremberg Principles were later adopted by the United Nations as a part of international humanitarian law. A personal responsibility and liability to punishment under international law was declared to exist beside the national laws and, when necessary, above them. A category of criminals was thus established under international law regardless of the fact that they might not have been prosecuted under national law, claiming, for instance, to have acted under superior orders. At the same time three categories of grave violations of international law were defined:

(1) Crimes against peace, including preparation and initiation of a war of aggression in violation of international treaties.
(2) War crimes consisting of grave violations of laws and customs of war.
(3) Crimes against humanity, by which were meant murder, extermination, enslavement, deportation and other actions against civilian populations, as well as persecution on political, ethnic or other grounds, when committed in connection with crimes against peace or war crimes (genocide).

Any person who has committed a crime under international law is held personally responsible for his part in it whether he is a head of state or a common soldier. Acting under orders may be considered a mitigating factor, but does not relieve the individual of legal responsibility.

Criminals under international law are outlaws worldwide. Parties to the Geneva conventions and members of the United Nations are under obligation to assist each other in searching for persons alleged to have committed international crimes and to bring them before either national or international courts. There is no time limit. War criminals from WW II have been condemned in recent days.

The United Nations has for the first time set up in The Hague an international tribunal to examine and judge war crimes in former Yugoslavia. A system of permanent international courts is currently being planned.

FURTHER READING

1. *International Red Cross Handbook* (1994) (13th edn) Geneva: International Committee of the Red Cross/ Federation of Red Cross Societies.
2. *Krigets lagar. Folksrättliga konventioner gällande under krig, neutralitet och ockupation* (1996), version 2.1. Stockholm Försvarsdepartementet.
3. *Kansainvälisiä ihmisoikeusasiakirjoja II: Sodan oikeussäännöt* (1981), Helsinki: Ulkoasiainministeriön julkaisuja.
4. Collection of intenational instruments concerning refugees (1988), Geneva: Office of the United Nations High Commissioner for Refugees (UNHCR).
5. Sandoz, Swinarski and Zimmerman (eds) (1987), *Commentary on the Additional Protocols to the Geneva Conventions* Geneva: ICRC/Martinus Nijhoff Publishers.
6. de Mulinen, Frédéric (1987), *Handbook on the Law of War for Armed Forces*, Geneva: International Committee ofthe Red Cross.
7. Jakovljevic, Bosko (1982), *New International Status of Civil Defence*, The Hague, Boston, London: Henry Dunant Institute/Martinus Nijhoff Publishers.
8. Rosén, Gunnar (1993), *Sodan lait. Käsikirja*, Helsinki: Suomen Punainen Risti. 2 vols.
9. Rosas, Allan (1976), *The Legal Status of Prisoners of War,* Helsinki: Suomalainen Tiedeakatemia.
10. Kosonen, Arto (1987), *The Special Protection of Children and Child Soldiers*, Helsinki: University of Helsinki, Institute of Public Law.
11. Törnudd, Klaus (1986), *Finland and the Norms of Human Rights,* Dordrecht, Boston, Lancaster: Martinus Nijhoff Publishers.
12. Pentikäinen, Merja (ed.) (1994), *The Right to Refuse Military Orders*, Jyväskylä: IPB, Peace Union of Finland, Finnish Lawyers for Peace and Survival.
13. International Committee of the Red Cross (1987), *Bibliography of International Humanitarian Law Applicable in Armed Conflicts,* Geneva: International Committee of the Red Cross/Henry Dunant Institute.

45 FROM NUREMBERG TO THE INTERNATIONAL CRIMINAL COURT

MARTIN SCHEININ

Chapter 45 focuses on three areas where law is relevant for the medical profession in times of war: (i) a recapitulation of the lessons of the Nuremberg and Tokyo war crimes tribunals that were established after the Second World War to deal with some of the worst war criminals. Besides senior military leaders, Nazi doctors responsible for medical experiments on human beings were also put on trial; (ii) a stocktaking of legally binding post-WWII international treaties on human rights and humanitarian law, with special emphasis on prohibited forms of conduct that may involve the medical profession; and (iii) the establishment of an International Criminal Court through the Rome Statute, adopted in 1998 but not yet in force.

Lessons of the Nuremberg trials and the Nuremberg doctors' trial

In the aftermath of WW II, military trials were held in Nuremberg and Tokyo against some of the worst German and Japanese war criminals. Although these trials were not free of 'victors' justice', and although they were defective when analysed against the contemporary normative framework of international human-rights treaties in the area of fair-trial guarantees, they established certain principles that are important even today.

The first lesson of Nuremberg and Tokyo is the rule that the international community has jurisdiction over war crimes and crimes against humanity, even when such acts were lawful under the laws of the state where and at the time when they were committed. Existing universal and regional human-rights treaties recognize that the prohibition against retroactive criminal law does not extend to situations where the act in question was a blatant violation of fundamental internationally-recognized norms. For instance, in the International Covenant on Civil and Political Rights, one of the major human-rights treaties of today, the provision prohibiting retroactive criminal sanctions (Article 15, Paragraph 1) is followed by Paragraph 2 that reads:

Nothing in this article shall prejudice the trial and punishment of any person for any act or omission which, at the time when it was committed, was criminal according to the general principles of law recognized by the community of nations.[1]

A second lesson of post-WW II trials against German and Japanese war criminals is spelled out in Principle IV of the Nuremberg Principles, codified after the trials in 1950 by the International Law Commission:

The fact that a person acted pursuant to orders of his Government or of a superior does not relieve him from responsibility, provided a moral choice was in fact possible to him.[2]

The defence of a superior order does not affect the responsibility of each and every individual that participated in war crimes or crimes against humanity.

A third lesson is served by the Nuremberg Doctors' Trial. Twenty-three individuals were convicted for the atrocious medical experiments conducted by the Nazis, in grave violation of the integrity, dignity and rights of individuals subjected to these experiments. The principles on which the ruling by the Nuremberg Tribunal were based in the doctors' case have played a central role in all later discussions and codifications of the principles of medical ethics.[3] In Nazi Germany, medical experimentation on humans was conducted in almost every concentration camp. The range of experiments dealt with in the Nuremberg Doctors' Trial included the following:[4]

- limits of human endurance at high altitudes and under high and low pressure;
- effects of severe chilling and freezing;
- inducement of malaria and epidemic jaundice;
- exposure to mustard gas;
- effectiveness of sulphanilamide on spotted fever;
- experiments regarding bone, muscle and nerve regeneration, together with bone transplants from one person to another;
- experiments to render sea-water drinkable;
- speedy and mass sterilization, castration, and abortion by unorthodox methods; and
- the effects of poisons and pharmaceutical preparations on phosphorous burns.

Rules of legally-binding international treaties

Parallel to the elaboration of international standards for medical ethics, by and large adopted by the medical profession, the post-Nuremberg era has also meant a codification of international human rights in the form of legally binding international treaties between states.

The genocide convention

On 9 December 1948, one day before the approval of the Universal Declaration of Human Rights, the United Nations General Assembly adopted an international Convention on the Prevention and Punishment of the Crime of Genocide. After ratification by 20 states, the convention entered into force in 1951. The Genocide

Convention is based on the principle of individual criminal responsibility by political leaders, by civil servants and by individuals, as clearly prescribed in its article IV.

International humanitarian law conventions

Historically humanitarian law is based on the so-called law of war, legal norms applicable in wars between states. The protection of hospitals and medical personnel during warfare is an old and recurring theme in the laws of warfare.[5] After WW II, the so-called Geneva conventions were adopted in 1949 when an international diplomatic conference finalized its work on four Geneva Conventions on International Humanitarian Law. These conventions aim at securing the protection of vulnerable categories of persons during warfare: civilians, prisoners of war and the wounded, sick and shipwrecked. The conventions entered into force in 1950, and today almost all states of the world have ratified them.

The conventions single out a category of international crimes, so-called grave breaches, in relation to which they require all states parties to enact individual criminal responsibility for all those who commit those acts, as well as those in command. As the conventions direct themselves first and foremost to situations of war, it is manifest that the crimes in question are punishable when committed during warfare.

Besides provisions affording protection for hospitals and medical staff during war, the Geneva conventions include many provisions that are of direct relevance for the responsibilities of medical personnel. Torture, mutilation, biological experimentation on human beings, denial of medical treatment and deliberate exposure to contagious diseases are all prohibited in the conventions. All decisions to prioritize some patients must be based on compelling medical grounds. Medical personnel cannot waive any of their rights under the conventions.

In 1977 the four Geneva conventions were complemented with two additional protocols in order to strengthen the protection of civilian persons (Protocol I) and to extend the body of international humanitarian law to cover civil wars and other non-international armed conflicts (Protocol II). In particular, Protocol I includes provisions that express certain fundamental principles in relation to the work of medical personnel: Article 16 of Protocol I reads:

(1) Under no circumstances shall any person be punished for carrying out medical activities compatible with medical ethics, regardless of the person benefiting therefrom.
(2) Persons engaged in medical activities shall not be compelled to perform acts or to carry out work contrary to the rules of medical ethics or to other medical rules designed for the benefit of the wounded and sick or to the provisions of the Conventions or of this Protocol, or to refrain from performing acts or from carrying out work required by those rules and provisions.
(3) No person engaged in medical activities shall be compelled to give to anyone belonging either to an adverse Party, or to his own Party except as required by the law of the latter Party, any information concerning the wounded and sick who are, or who

have been, under his care, if such information would, in his opinion, prove harmful to the patients concerned or to their families. Regulations for the compulsory notification of communicable diseases shall, however, be respected.

Prohibition against torture and related acts in general human-rights treaties

Inspired by the experiences of Nuremberg, one of the most important universal human-rights treaties includes in its provision against torture and other forms of inhuman treatment a clause specifically addressed to those conducting medical experiments. Article 7 of the International Covenant on Civil and Political Rights (1966) states:

> No one shall be subjected to torture or to cruel, inhuman or degrading treatment or punishment. In particular, no one shall be subjected without his free consent to medical or scientific experimentation.

In addition to this provision, today ratified by 145 states, the prohibition against torture and related acts has been spelled out in the Convention against Torture and Cruel, Inhuman or Degrading Treatment or Punishment (1984) and in Article 3 of the European Convention on Human Rights (1950), Article 5 of the African Charter on Human and People's Rights (1981), Article 5 of the American Convention on Human Rights (1969) and in the Inter-American Convention to Prevent and Punish Torture (1985).

Towards an international criminal court

The tragic events of the 1990s, often taking the form of civil wars, other types of internal ethnic conflict, or of genocide, have been addressed by the international community through the development of international criminal law. Ad hoc criminal tribunals were established through two resolutions of the United Nations Security Council to deal with crimes committed in former Yugoslavia (1993) and Rwanda (1994). The establishment of an International criminal court is a further step that it is hoped will soon mean that appropriate legal machinery is in place right at the start of any new crisis.[6]

The Statute of the International Criminal Court (ICC) was adopted in Rome on 17 July 1998 and will require ratification by 60 states before its entry into force. The statute not only establishes international criminal liability for the crime of genocide, crimes against humanity, war crimes and the crime of aggression, but also specifies these crimes in great detail (except for the crime of aggression which will require a separate process of specification before this part of the statute becomes operative) and prescribes the penalties for those who commit the international crimes in question. It is noteworthy that non-ratification by a particular state does not fully protect its nationals from being subject to the jurisdiction of the ICC: it is sufficient that either this state or the state within the territory of which the crime was committed is a party to the statute.

In articles 6 to 8, defining the acts that constitute genocide, crimes against humanity or war crimes, there are several provisions that are of specific importance when doctors or medical personnel participate in serious violations of human rights. The following acts are, for instance, punishable as genocide:

- causing serious bodily or mental harm to members of a national, ethnic, racial or religious group; and
- imposing measures intended to prevent births within the group.

Under the ICC statute, crimes against humanity include the following acts:

- torture;
- rape, sexual slavery, enforced prostitution, forced pregnancy, enforced sterilization or any other form of sexual violence of comparable gravity; and
- other inhumane acts of a similar character intentionally causing great suffering, or serious injury to body or to mental or physical health.

Furthermore, the definition of war crimes includes, inter alia:

- torture or inhuman treatment, including biological experiments;
- wilfully causing great suffering, or serious injury to body or health;
- subjecting persons who are in the power of an adverse party to physical mutilation or to medical or scientific experiments of any kind which are neither justified by the medical, dental or hospital treatment of the person concerned nor carried out in his or her interest, and which cause death to or seriously endanger the health of such person or persons;
- committing outrages upon personal dignity, in particular humiliating and degrading treatment; and
- committing rape, sexual slavery, enforced prostitution, forced pregnancy, enforced sterilization or any other form of sexual violence also constituting a grave breach of the Geneva conventions.

The establishment of a permanent international criminal court is a logical step in the strengthening of international law in the field of war crimes and crimes against humanity. It should, however, be remembered that the ICC will only complement existing arrangements for criminal responsibility. The Geneva conventions and the Convention against Torture, for instance, explicitly require that states that have ratified these treaties exercise criminal jurisdiction over persons that commit crimes that fall under the provisions of the pertinent treaties. In most cases, states have implemented their obligations through provisions of criminal law that extend not only to their nationals and not only to crimes committed within their own territory but also to any person suspected of torture, war crimes or crimes against humanity that finds himself within the jurisdiction of the state in question. This principle of universal jurisdiction will in the future be complemented by the jurisdiction of the ICC which will have most relevance in cases where states fail to implement their existing obligations.

NOTES

1. The international treaties quoted or referred to in the text can be found in several collections, for instance: *Human Rights; a Compilation of International Human Rights Instruments*, United Nations, New York and Geneva (1994) (Volume I.1 and I.2) and 1997 (Volume II). Internet access is available at <http://www.unhchr.ch/html/intlinst.htm>.

2. The Nuremberg Principles, as codified by the International Law Commission, can be found in *The Yearbook of the International Law Commission* (1950), Vol. II, pp. 374–80.
3. The role of the World Medical Association and its general assemblies has been central in the codification and elaboration of standards for medical ethics. Reference can be made, for instance, to the Declaration of Geneva (1948, with subsequent amendments), the International Code of Medical Ethics (1949, with subsequent amendments), the Declaration of Helsinki (1964, with subsequent amendments) and the Declaration of Tokyo (1975). A part of the documents can be found at <http://www.wma.net/e/home.html>.
4. Green, Leslie C. (1999), 'War Law and the Medical Profession', in *Essays on the Modern Law of War* (2nd edn), Transnational Publishers. The list of medical experiments conducted by the Nazis, given at the end of the first subsection of the present chapter, is given by Green on p. 512.
5. Ibid.
6. The documentation related to the establishment of the International Criminal Court can be accessed through <http://www.un.org/icc/>. The International Law Page of this website includes links to the criminal tribunals for Former Yugoslavia and Rwanda.

ADDITIONAL READING

Pentikäinen, M. ed. (1994), *The Right to Refuse Military Orders*, Jyväskylä: Gummerus.

Address for correspondence

Åbo Akademi University, Institute for Human Rights, 20500 Turku, Finland.
Tel: +358-2-215 4322; Fax +358-2-215 4699; Email martin.scheinin@abo.fi

46 DEFENSIVE SECURITY

SAUL MENDLOVITZ and MERAV DATAN

If the rulers and officials and gentlemen of the world sincerely desire to promote what is beneficial to the world and to eliminate what is harmful, they should realize that offensive warfare is in fact a great harm to the world.

Mo Tzu, fifth century BC

The Contracting Parties, on a bilateral and multilateral basis, shall actively contribute ... to the further reduction of the armed forces and armaments to levels corresponding to their defence needs.

Treaty between Romania and Ukraine, 1997

Chapter 46 has a singular political objective. It is a contribution to a global political movement aimed at restructuring military organizations on the basis of the doctrine and practices of defensive security.

The framework for this discussion is a critique of the United Nations *Study on Defensive Security Concepts and Policies*.[1] The study stems from a 1990 General Assembly resolution requesting the Secretary-General 'with the assistance of qualified governmental experts and taking into account the views of Member States and other relevant information' to submit a report on this topic.[2] This essay provides a review of the key concepts of the study, examines their implications and applicability in today's political context, and considers requirements for furthering defensive security concepts and policies.

The chapter has four parts: part 1 sketches the political, policy, and research contexts for the study; part 2 highlights some of the ideas presented in the study within its self-imposed guidelines, namely, the United Nations Charter regime as it now operates; part 3 relaxes this restriction and considers the implications of defensive security, both collective and individual, if applied fully, consistently, and equitably; and part 4 then suggests an interpretation of recent developments that foreshadow greater receptivity for the principles of defensive security.

Politics, policy and research

The political impetus for the UN study is generally attributed to the government of President Gorbachev of the former Soviet Union.[3] Early in his administration President Gorbachev evinced an interest in altering Soviet armed forces so that they would be perceived to be defensive. In his report to the Communist Party of the Soviet Union Congress in February 1986 he declared that: 'in the military sphere we intend to act in such a way as to give nobody ground for fears, even imagined, about their security'. In April of that same year in a special session of the Congress he proposed deep cuts in conventional forces which were followed up on 11 June 1986 by an announcement of the Warsaw Pact known as the Budapest Appeal. That appeal had a major follow-up in an article which Gorbachev published jointly in *Pravda* and *Izvestija* on 17 September 1987. There he argued for 'reasonable sufficiency', which he defined as 'a structure in the military forces of countries that suffices for the prevention of possible aggression, but is insufficient for attack'.[4] In 1988 he declared that: 'in the interests of security in Europe and the whole world the military concepts and doctrines must be based on defensive principles'. And in President Gorbachev's major address to the 43rd Session (1988) of the United Nations General Assembly, he not only announced the reduction of Soviet armed forces by 500,000 personnel over two years 'and substantial reductions in conventional armaments', but declared that Soviet armed forces 'will become clearly defensive'.

The evolution of the public announcement of Soviet policy on these matters was influenced by the interaction of major military and political policy officials with a loose network of scholars. This network had been studying and promoting non-offensive defence[5] and similar concepts. A number of these scholars were also consulted by the group of experts who prepared the UN study.[6]

Defensive security is a term that had not been used prior to this study and is still not commonly employed. Nevertheless, we believe that there is good reason to concentrate on the study. This is the only authoritative formal document within the UN promoting the notion of structuring armed forces so that they are capable only of defence. As such, it provides an entry to continuing discussion of these matters within the UN system. Furthermore, the general assembly resolution, as well as the final paragraph of the study, calls for 'intensive dialogue amongst the member states about these matters'. The study also recommends that individual states ascertain to what extent it would be possible for each of them to structure their armed forces to fit within the doctrine of defensive security. Thus it provides a peg for interested individuals and groups to engage the political and military structures of governments and international organizations for furtherance of the establishment of a worldwide defensive security regime.

The study also makes clear that in using the terminology of defensive security, it comprehends the closely-related concepts of: non-offensive defence, non-provocative defence, defensive defence, confidence-building defence and the like. The study offers a new term but relies upon past and ongoing research and writing in this area.

There is one additional matter of political relevance. A fledgling and vigorous political project promoting this effort is already under way. It is being organized by a consortium of four transnational associations: the International Association of Lawyers

Against Nuclear Arms; International Physicians for the Prevention of Nuclear War; the International Peace Bureau; and the World Order Models Project. This consortium has worked together for some five years lobbying the World Health Organization and the UN General Assembly to seek an advisory opinion from the International Court of Justice on the legality of the threat or use of nuclear weapons. That opinion was given in July 1996.[7] It is noteworthy that these organizations have now turned their attention to dealing with the more general framework of military security. They have begun with educational programmes amongst their own membership. They are also approaching other citizens' groups, officials at the United Nations and policymakers around the world.

Defensive security and the UN Charter regime

The UN *Study on Defensive Security Concepts and Policies* is significant and commendable for a number of reasons: it was conducted by a transnational team of governmental experts, including military and political analysts and, as such, it reflects the importance ascribed to serious analysis of defensive security as a potential remedy for the instability and violence in today's political environment; and it identifies important issues relating to international peace and security and suggests strategies and measures to promote defensive security. Underlying the entire analysis is the notion that armed forces and military capacity should serve strictly defensive purposes.

The UN study defined defensive security as: (para. 12):[8]

a condition of peace and security attained step-by-step and sustained through effective and concrete measures in the political and military fields under which:
  (a) Friendly relations among states are established and maintained;
  (b) Disputes are settled in a peaceful and equitable manner and the resort to force is consequently excluded;
  (c) The capacity for launching a surprise attack and for initiating large-scale offensive action is eliminated through verifiable arms control and disarmament, confidence- and security-building measures and a restructuring of armed forces towards a defensive orientation.

The Secretary-General's foreword summarizes the difficulty of operationalizing defensive security and points to four problems:

Issues addressed in this connection include
  • the difficulty, if not impossibility, of distinguishing between offensive and defensive weapons systems;
  • the dilemma of maintaining effective counter-offensive capabilities while at the same time not projecting an offensive posture;
  • the implications of collective defence and joint commitment of states for defensive security; and
  • the applicability of defensive security at the bilateral, regional, and global levels.

In an attempt to deal with the difficulties pointed at in the Secretary-General's foreword, the study discusses a range of concepts which have been developed in this area. Among these are: 'reasonable sufficiency', 'defensive sufficiency', both of which appear in Soviet and Commonwealth of Independent States' doctrines, and 'non-offensive defence'. Reasonable sufficiency relates a state's level of forces to that possessed by a potential adversary (paras 84–5). Defensive sufficiency is defined as

> a posture of armed forces ... that is capable of preventing and containing aggression by a potential enemy, but does not enable the launching of large-scale offensive operations without additional deployments ... and other measures. (para. 86)

Non-offensive defence (NOD), 'a type of military force posture that emphasizes defensive capabilities and eschews offensive or provocative capabilities' (para. 87) receives the most thorough analysis among these concepts. The study notes that definitions of NOD vary, cites a few examples and underscores their emphasis on defensive orientation. Proponents of NOD share a belief that attack, and preparation for attack, as a form of defence, is inherently destabilizing (para. 89). The basic assumptions of NOD, as summarized in the study, are as follows (para. 92):

(a) Heavy armored forces, particularly if deployed in forward locations, are inherently offensive and provocative because they combine a high degree of mobility, firepower and protection;
(b) The vulnerability of crucial military assets invites pre-emption by the opponent;
(c) Military capabilities that threaten the territorial integrity of the opponent are provocative.

Another noteworthy observation contained in the study is the recognition that the perception of a threat, even independent of the intent of the state creating the perceived threat, is a significant and troubling element in international relations.

According to the study's author, the concept of defensive security goes beyond NOD and the other concepts discussed above in that it:

> encompasses both political and military elements aimed at ensuring that all States conduct their policies in conformity with the Charter of the United Nations and adopt a military posture and a level of forces that, while ensuring an effective defence, poses no threat to other States. (para. 96)

As noted above, the definition of defensive security consists of three elements, which may be represented as friendly relations, peaceful and equitable dispute settlement, and defensive orientation.[9] Combining military and political aspects of security in this manner is attractive in that it implicitly recognizes the interdependence of hard and soft security issues. Militarization, threat or use of force and armed conflict are ultimately inseparable from issues of development, human rights and justice. Achieving the conditions for friendly relations and peaceful dispute settlement would complement and catalyse the military restructuring required for defensive orientation.

Nevertheless, the study restricts the potential applicability of defensive security concepts by including friendly relations and peaceful dispute settlement in its definition. These requirements may be too global and demanding to suggest or even allow for the emergence of a focused agenda for a defensive security dialogue. Friendly relations and peaceful and equitable dispute settlement are broader and more amorphous concepts than NOD and defensive restructuring as presented in the study. It may very well be that the first two elements are necessary for defensive orientation to be fully and irreversibly achieved, but there is probably no reason to circumscribe the defensive security dialogue in this manner from the outset. One probably need not, that is, have friendly relations and peaceful and equitable dispute settlement to achieve a system in which 'a surprise attack and initiating large-scale offensive action' can be eliminated or drastically reduced. Self-interest might, for example, be a sufficient motivation for defensive restructuring despite sometimes tense relations or inequitable dispute settlement. Indeed, once an international security regime limited to defensive capability is achieved, even in part, it would likely facilitate the realization of friendly relations and peaceful and equitable dispute settlement.

Other issues brought to light in the UN study include the indivisibility of security among states and the obligation of self-restraint implicit in the UN Charter. The indivisibility of security refers to the notion that the security of every state is inseparably linked to that of others 'within a particular group or region' (paras 99–102). The study lists the following principles of 'common security': '(a) All States have a legitimate right to security; (b) Military force is not a legitimate instrument for resolving disputes between States; [and] (c) Restraint is necessary in expressions of national policy'.

The study further develops the final point relating to restraint in a variety of contexts. At the very outset, it affirms the security paradigm established by the UN Charter through the oft-cited articles on the prohibition of threat or use of force (Article 2(4)) and the exception for self-defence (Article 51).[10] In the words of the authors, 'Together, these provisions imply an obligation of self-restraint and an emphasis on defence in the development of military capabilities' (para. 10). The discussion of common security returns to this point through the following conclusion: 'Reductions of armaments have to be pursued in the context of common security, which would ensure the necessary conditions for trust and stability' (para. 99). In addition, the analysis of political considerations notes that

> to be truly credible, reassuring and stabilizing, political pronouncements of defensive intentions should find their material expression in the manner in which armed forces are composed, trained, equipped, organized and deployed. (para. 110)

raising the obligation of self-restraint from a statement of intention to a series of concrete measures.

It is precisely in the context of this recognition – that the right of self-defence as enshrined in the UN Charter carries with it an obligation of self-restraint – that the greatest strength and the greatest weakness of the UN study surface. Rights often suggest reciprocal duties, and implementation of the idea that the right of self-defence implies an obligation to reassure others of peaceful intentions would probably go a long way towards facilitating effective agreements on disarmament and arms control. Yet the authors of this study stop short of applying their conclusions universally. They do not hold collective security alliances to the same standards of restraint and reassurance to which they hold individual nation states, as we discuss below.

Application of defensive security to collective and individual self-defence

The UN *Study on Defensive Security Concepts and Policies* identifies important issues relating to international peace and security and suggests strategies and measures to promote defensive security. However, the framework for the analysis of defensive security does not sufficiently challenge the UN Charter system of collective security. Indeed, defensive security, according to the study, 'encompasses both political and military elements aimed at ensuring that all States conduct their policies in conformity with the Charter of the United Nations' (para. 96). The security system envisioned in the UN Charter, and the reasons for its failure, has been the subject of more analyses than one might care to count. In presenting defensive security as an element of the UN vision, the study does not appear to be offering anything new. Moreover, and of greater concern, the study seems to accept an interpretation of key Charter provisions that supports the policies of powerful states and military alliances.

But this study actually does offer more than another prescription for UN-style security. Although it never explicitly challenges the way that powerful states have interpreted the Charter – this is one of its greatest weaknesses – the study does lay the foundation for a critical review of the doctrines and policies of powerful states. It correctly recognizes that military buildup, regardless of intent, can create threat perceptions and arms races that lead to insecurity and instability; implicit in this, and explicit, in fact, in the study, is an obligation to reassure others and pursue reduction in armaments. The study also notes the indivisibility of security of states within a particular group or region and recognizes that offensive military capacity is in itself a threat to peace and security. As discussed above, the analysis of UN Charter articles 2(4) and 51 finds implicit 'an obligation of self-restraint and an emphasis on defence in the development of military capabilities' (para. 10). Yet it applies this obligation unevenly. In particular, the policy implications of defensive security, as identified in the study, are applied differently to individual and collective self-defence.

As noted above, the study reviews such concepts as 'reasonable sufficiency', 'defensive sufficiency', and 'non-offensive defence'. It observes that common security is based on a recognition that the security of every state is also linked to the security of other states. Reductions of armaments 'have to be pursued in the context of common security' (para. 99). According to the authors, it is therefore necessary to promote awareness of the indivisibility of the security of states and the importance of confidence-building measures and changes in military force postures (para. 100). Although the study never explicitly states that the right of self-defence carries with it a duty, it provides material for reframing self-defence in such a way. To suggest that self-defence as a right gives rise to certain obligations as well is an attractive concept. It can be used to explain the misapplications of self-defence which have generated arms races, threat perceptions and resort to force. These were instances in which self-defence as a right was invoked without proper regard for the duties it carries.

The study does not apply the concepts of restraint and related implicit obligations to collective defence alliances. In fact, it commends 'collective security, regional and other cooperative arrangements consistent with the Charter of the United Nations' (paras 158–67). There is no careful application of the notions of offensive capability, threat perceptions and resulting instability in the analysis of these collective arrangements. The critique is either quite general – applied to individual and collective self-defence as a single concept – or specific to state practice. Consider, for example, the following observation (para. 76):

Governments raise armies, build weapon systems and use armed forces all in the name of defence. Yet while two adversarial States are likely to justify their own military preparations in defensive terms, they will probably view each other's preparations as conveying aggressive or offensive intentions. How, in these circumstances, can one determine which military postures and activities are more defensive and which are more offensive in nature?

No parallel observation is made with respect to collective defence alliances, even though their military capability is likely to exceed that of individual states in quantity and force projection quality.[11] The doctrine of collective self-defence enshrined in the UN Charter has served as the basis for powerful military alliances and doctrines based on threat.[12] The study notes this point in observing that collective self-defence includes an ability to 'project military power' beyond state borders; it admits that 'such a capability by definition provides those states with a potential for an offensive action' which is inconsistent with the notion of possessing only the capability to defend one's own territory (para. 144). It briefly notes that a way to resolve this conflict might be through role specialization, whereby states in a collective defence arrangement would individually specialize in different force-projection roles.[13] But more generally, the study almost dismisses the concerns that collective-defence alliances might pose (para. 144):

> In those situations [of potential for an offensive action], the possession and eventual use of such capabilities should be for the sole purpose of implementing collective self-defence in accordance with the relevant provisions of the Charter of the United Nations and consequently should not be perceived as posing a threat to neighbouring states.

Contrast this to the standard suggested for states (para. 11):

> To be effective, the obligation of self-restraint and defensiveness in military affairs must be readily discernible in both the declarations and the actual military capabilities of states. In other words, it is necessary for states to give practical content to defensive security concepts by pursuing policies that are consistent with the defensive orientation of these concepts and their visible expression of corresponding force postures.

One of the strengths of this study is its acknowledgement that, despite defensive intent, offensive capability can create instability. Yet this awareness seems to disappear when collective defence is examined.

Moreover, it is recognized that these alliances are often formed in response to a 'common threat perception' (para. 145), yet there is no consideration of the common threat projection that such an alliance might present. Such a common threat projection might differ in nature and magnitude from the threat that a single state poses. Consider, for example, a situation between two adversarial states, only one of which belongs to a collective defence alliance. How would the state which does not belong to such an alliance perceive a potential threat posed by the alliance as a whole? It must be concerned not only about its adversary's capability, but about the collective capability of the alliance to which the adversary belongs.

A timely example is the expansion of the North Atlantic Treaty Organization (NATO). In the words of Alexei Arbatov, deputy chairman of the Defence Committee of the Russian Parliament:

> The enlargement of NATO, although still in the initial stage, has already revived some

traditional misunderstandings and created new misperceptions between Russia and the West.

There is a broad political consensus in Russia that the expansion of [NATO] not only runs counter to Russian security interests, but also violates some commonly-accepted rules on which the Cold War was ended.[14]

Although the new NATO members, Poland, Hungary and the Czech Republic, are not even adversaries of Russia, their proximity to that country and their new alliance with a formerly adversarial body could create threat perceptions within Russia that would undermine progress towards peace and security in the form of disarmament and arms-control measures. In the words of a US analyst, NATO expansion 'puts the entire post-Cold War settlement, in which the post-1987 arms agreements are embedded, in jeopard'.[15] Here we see an example of a collective security alliance posing a direct threat to the very principles the doctrine of defensive security wishes to promote.

Towards defensive security

In contrast, Europe also provides an example of a different kind of alliance in which defensive security concepts are pursued in a manner designed to reduce threat perceptions and power projection. The UN Study cites as a positive example of defensive security principles the 1990 Treaty on Conventional Armed Forces in Europe (CFE) (paras 33–4). Through the CFE treaty, members of NATO and the former Warsaw Pact have agreed to reduce their conventional armaments in five categories: tanks, artillery, armoured combat vehicles, combat aircraft and attack helicopters, regarded as essential for offensive military action. The CFE treaty also provides for information exchange and verification provisions, confidence-building measures generally considered important for the achievement of defensive security. As noted in the study, the preamble of the CFE underscores the objective (para. 34):

> of establishing a secure and stable balance of conventional armed forces in Europe at lower levels than heretofore, of eliminating disparities prejudicial to stability and security and of eliminating, as a matter of high priority, the capability for launching a surprise attack and for initiating large-scale offensive action in Europe.

Although the CFE treaty evolved and applies in a strictly European context, the principles on which it is based could in some form apply worldwide. Universal adaptation of these principles might in fact be essential for their preservation on a smaller scale. We see this if we consider one of the side-effects of the CFE treaty: the spread of surplus weapons eliminated in Europe to other regions of the world. Without an effort to coordinate regional defensive security initiatives on a global scale, through international dialogue and cooperation, the successes of one region might flood other regions with unwanted, cheap offensively-oriented armaments.

Other accomplishments in the field of disarmament and arms control suggest, perhaps foreshadow, the emergence of a new security paradigm based on defensive restructuring. According to a recent analysis:

> The military capabilities of the countries of Europe are ... less threatening now than in the past, and this has been accomplished by arms control. Specifically, it has been accomplished by the

remarkable series of accords that were signed beginning with the Intermediate-range Nuclear Forces (INF) agreement of December 1987, and culminating with the START II accord of January 1993. These arms control agreements are similar in appearance to those of the earlier part of the Cold War, but ... they differ in content in two truly revolutionary ways.

First, the *later series of arms reduction agreements is characterized by 'defence dominance'*. That is, they have reshaped military arsenals to make them more useful for defence than for offence in the case of conventional forces, and more useful for deterrence than for actual war fighting in the case of nuclear armaments. Country 'X' will be concerned, of course, about the capabilities if its neighbour, Country 'Y' no matter what 'Y' says about its own intentions. Country 'X' will be *least* concerned about Country 'Y' if Country 'Y' has no weapons at all. But the nations of Europe have not laid down their arms completely, and are unlikely to do so.

The next best circumstance, from the point of view of peace, is if Country 'X' does not feel threatened by the armaments of Country 'Y' because those armaments are suitable for self-defence and not for attack. That is now the status quo in Europe thanks to arms control.

The second revolutionary feature of the post-1987 arms agreements, both conventional and nuclear, is that they establish transparency.[16]

We find further evidence of a possible trend towards defensive restructuring in recent treaties between a number of east European countries. Romania and Hungary agreed, in 1996, that:

The Contracting Parties, in order to strengthen European peace and security, support the continuation of processes aimed at controlling and limiting European armed forces and armaments to the *level necessary for defence*. They will furthermore support the elaboration of new confidence-building and confidence-strengthening measures and will strive at making similar steps in their bilateral relations.[17]

Similar language appears in a treaty between Romania and the Ukraine:

The Contracting Parties, on a bilateral and multilateral basis, shall actively contribute to the process of disarmament in Europe, to the further reduction of the armed forces and armaments to *levels corresponding to their defence needs*.[18]

The CFE and friendship treaties discussed above suggest a shift in security policies and strategies. Admittedly, the level of military capacity necessary for self-defence is subject to self-serving interpretations. Self-defence, recognized under the UN Charter as the only lawful resort to force save for UN Security-Council action, has frequently been invoked by both sides to an armed conflict and by states acting in anticipatory (pre-emptive) or retaliatory self-defence. Nonetheless, and despite an ongoing debate among legal scholars as to the continuing validity of the UN Charter regime prohibiting the threat or use of force, there appears to be emerging an unprecedented reliance on strictly defensive needs as a basis for developing international security arrangements.

Diplomats, negotiators and analysts might reinforce this trend by reading the affirmative commitments to disarmament and arms control as binding obligations. In other words, rather than viewing the language of the UN Charter and treaties that call for disarmament and force reductions as aspirational, one might read these statements as positive commitments made in the face of and despite a shared history of resort to force and reliance on threat in the name of security.

Conclusion

The creation of a defensive security system would be a major paradigm shift for the world. Prevailing practice and normative understanding have tolerated individual and collective offensive-action capacity. The shift that would be involved in denying offensive capacity does not comprehend complete and general disarmament. The range of defensive structures might run from Costa Rica, a no-armed-forces state, to Switzerland, a porcupine defence. Neither of these states has the potential for aggression. One relies, however, on a policy of posing no threat while the other is prepared for formidable resistance to any attack. Downsizing and restructuring of armed forces toward defensive security will depend on and shape national and collective threat perceptions.

A defensive security regime would require progress in the political sphere as states restructure their armed forces unilaterally, bilaterally or multilaterally. There are several regions and sub-regions throughout the world where this might occur. A defensive security regime should also be enshrined in legal documents with binding commitments, affirming the United Nations Charter prohibition on the threat or use of force. The right of self-defence should not be invoked as justification for developing large-scale offensive capacity and military doctrines requiring force projection. Military and legal analysts can contribute to the paradigm shift necessary for defensive security by reminding policy-makers that self-defence in international law has a greater context: no threat or use of force.

The United Nations *Study on Defensive Security Concepts and Policies* is a welcome addition to debates on military and security matters. It offers a goal that we hope the readers of this volume will support and promote.

REFERENCES

1. UN Office for Disarmament Affairs (1993), *Study on Defensive Security Concepts and Policies*, Report of the Secretary-General, Study Series 26, UN Doc. A/47/394, UN Sales No. E.93.IX.12.
2. General Assembly Res. 45/58 O (1990).
3. The following historical sketch is derived from Bjorn Moller, *Dictionary of Alternative Defense* (Lynne Rienner, 1995) and personal conversations with Carl Conetta, *Project on Defense Alternatives*, Cambridge, MA.
4. The term was first used by Robert MacNamara and President Richard Nixon. See Moller, n. 3 above, p. 280.
5. A term coined in 1985 by Bjorn Moller and Anders Boserup.
6. One may think of the origin of support for defensive doctrine as having had four periods since the end of WW II: (i) in the early and mid-1950s three 'neutral' states (Austria, Switzerland and Finland) announced their defensive orientation. They were not considered seriously because they were seen as marginal to major geostrategic and geopolitical behaviour; (ii) in the late 1950s as the Germans began to be concerned about the possibility of their territory becoming a battleground between the superpowers (possibly including nuclear weapons) a number of German scholars and activists began to think about how to avoid this catastrophe; (iii) the deployment of the Pershing missile in 1979 provoked a good deal of thinking about defensive defence and by the early 1980s the Peace Research community in Europe was heavily involved in exploring the concept; And (iv) the Conventional Forces in Europe Treaty was, in a formal sense, a highlight of this movement.
7. *Legality of the Threat or Use of Nuclear Weapons* (1996), UN Doc. A/51/218 (1996).

8. All paragraphs in the study are numbered. Citations refer parenthetically to paragraph numbers.

9. This shorthand is not used in the study itself and does not pretend to encompass all the concepts involved.

10. Article 2(4) of the UN Charter provides that: 'All Members shall refrain in their international relations from the threat or use of force against the territorial integrity or political independence of any state, or in any other manner inconsistent with the Purposes of the United Nations'. Article 51 provides that: 'Nothing in the present Charter shall impair the inherent right of individual or collective self-defence if an armed attack occurs against a Member of the United Nations, until the Security Council has taken measures necessary to maintain international peace and security. Measures taken by Members in the exercise of this right of self-defence shall be immediately reported to the Security Council and shall not in any way affect the authority and responsibility of the Security Council under the present Charter to take at any time such action as it deems in order to maintain or restore international peace and security.' Under the UN Charter Article 42, the other exception to the prohibition on the threat or use of force, besides self-defence, is action by the Security Council to maintain or restore international peace and security.

11. NATO's 1991 strategic concept, for example, requires all allies to restructure their forces to increase force projection capability beyond national borders 'to fulfil collective defence commitments' among other reasons. Sloan, Stanley (1997), 'Transatlantic Relations: Stormy Weather on the Way to Enlargement?' *NATO Review* 5 (September–October).

12. The term 'collective self-defence' is used interchangeably with 'collective defence' in general and in this study.

13. The study mentions role specialization only twice: (i) in para. 149 it briefly explains the concept, 'which might pose serious practical problems for its implementation'; and (ii) in para. 268, towards the end of the report, it suggests further study of this concept. We support this suggestion.

14. Arbatov, Alexei (1997), 'As NATO Grows, Start 2 Shudders', *New York Times* (op-ed.), 26 August: A23.

15. Mandelbaum, Michael (1997), 'The Post-Cold War Settlement in Europe: a triumph of arms control', *Arms Control Today* (March): 6.

16. Ibid., p. 4 (emphasis added).

17. Treaty of Friendship, Cooperation, and Good Neigbourliness Between Romania and Hungary (1996), Article 2 (emphasis added).

18. Treaty between Romania and Ukraine (1997), Article 7, para. (a) (emphasis added).

Address for correspondence

IPPNW/PSR UN Office
777 United Nations Plaza, 6th Floor
New York, NY 10017, USA
Tel: +1-646-865-1883; Fax: +1-646-865-1884; email: mdatan@ippnw.org

47 ELIMINATION OF NUCLEAR WEAPONS

Strategies for overcoming the political deadlock

MERAV DATAN, BRIAN RAWSON
and LARS POHLMEIER

Achieving the complete elimination of nuclear weapons is largely a question of political will rather than technical problems. The authors identify the negotiation and conclusion of a treaty – a Nuclear Weapons Convention (NWC) – as an important tool to overcome the present political deadlock. A model of such an NWC has already become an official discussion document at the United Nations. It could resolve the disagreements of the governments on how to fulfil their legal obligations to eliminate nuclear weapons. The model Nuclear Weapons Convention demonstrates that complete nuclear disarmament is achievable, implementable, verifiable and maintainable. The model NWC is a compre-

hensive approach that includes all aspects of nuclear disarmament. Negotiation of an NWC could and should start immediately.

Nuclear disarmament would both require and reinforce a paradigm shift away from deterrence and military-based doctrines, and towards collective security. Non-governmental organizations (NGOs) have played an increasingly important role in this process. The drafting of the model NWC is only one example. Today there is substantial support for nuclear disarmament within governmental organizations. However, NGO input is vital if the elimination of nuclear weapons through a Nuclear Weapons Convention and true international security are to be achieved.

The post-Cold War window of opportunity for eliminating nuclear weapons is in jeopardy and the beginning of the 21st century appeared to be marked by political deadlock on nuclear disarmament. This is particularly ironic in the light of recent promising developments such as the advisory opinion of the International Court of Justice on the illegality of nuclear weapons, the opening for the signature of the Comprehensive Test Ban Treaty (CTBT), the Canberra Commission on the Elimination of Nuclear Weapons, and a variety of governmental and non-governmental organizations calling for complete nuclear disarmament. All governments state publicly that complete nuclear disarmament is a desirable goal, but there is total disagreement over how and when to achieve it. Although there are conventions for the elimination of biological and chemical weapons, there is not yet a similar convention for the elimination of nuclear weapons. The resulting standstill is allowing time for countries to further develop nuclear weapons and heighten their dependence on them.

The political deadlock is causing considerable strain in governmental fora. There is rising scepticism regarding the capacity of the governmental framework for disarmament negotiations to achieve genuine nuclear disarmament and maintain nuclear nonproliferation. There are rising doubts as to the good faith of some of the states with nuclear weapons that claim commitment to complete nuclear elimination.

The situation appears to be growing more volatile and unpredictable. Such volatility was demonstrated by the 1998 nuclear tests by India and Pakistan, the corrosion of the Russian nuclear infrastructure combined with its increased reliance on nuclear weapons, and increased US funding for the Star Wars space-based anti-ballistic missile defence system and the sophisticated testing of nuclear weapon components. *The Bulletin of Atomic Scientists*, which uses a clock icon to illustrate the nuclear threat, has once again moved the clock's hands closer to midnight.

At the same time, a rising chorale of voices, including experts from the fields of defence, science, law and policy, has called recently for complete elimination of nuclear weapons as the only viable solution for averting nuclear catastrophe. Furthermore, the International Court of Justice in its historic 1996 ruling declared nuclear weapons generally illegal, and unanimously affirmed a universal obligation to negotiate and conclude nuclear disarmament in all its aspects.

Overcoming the obstacles to the elimination of nuclear weapons is a matter of political will and vision. States with nuclear weapons lack the will to abandon their political and military dependence on those weapons. Such states are also limited by traditional deterrence thinking, which posits superior military power as an essential guarantor of national security and relies on the threat of 'mutually-assured destruction' to prevent resort to force in the event of conflict. This military approach to security can only result in arms races and the continuing pursuit of military dominance. In its place, a human rights- and justice-based concept of security, including collective and positive security assurances, would go a long way toward addressing the grievances and perpetual threat perceptions that fuel arms races and pursuit of military approaches to security. In short, a paradigm shift is required, from the current paradigm of military security to a paradigm of human security, the early signs of which are already visible in the activism of non-governmental organizations and the policies of states without nuclear weapons.

An active and growing legion of public citizens' groups seeks to bring about the changes in political will and vision necessary to progress toward the elimination of nuclear weapons. Among their efforts is the promotion of a model Nuclear Weapons Convention (NWC).[1] The NWC is a model treaty drafted by disarmament experts and advocates of the elimination of nuclear weapons which explores the legal assurances necessary for elimination. Another project is the Middle Powers Initiative (MPI), a small group of abolition advocates focusing on contact with friendly governments. The MPI seeks to fortify the pro-abolition coalition of countries of medium size and stature.[2] The Abolition 2000 network spreads communication and strategies for abolition among global grassroots' movements. This international network consists today of more than 1500 organizations.[3]

It remains to be seen whether public citizens' groups, sympathetic governments and advocates of nuclear disarmament can generate sufficient political and moral will to drive policymakers toward acceptance of increased cooperation for nuclear disarmament, or whether future nuclear scares will drive them instead toward an every-country-for-itself nuclear free-for-all.

Why pursue the complete elimination of nuclear weapons?

Slippery slope to Armageddon: the risks of inaction

Since the dissolution of the Soviet Union in 1991, public fears of a nuclear war have drastically subsided and the issue has faded from the media. The nuclear tests by India and Pakistan in 1998 provided a sobering wake-up call of nuclear danger. Not only did they raise the spectre of a tragic nuclear exchange between the two countries, they also demonstrated the vulnerability of the concept of non-proliferation and provided impetus for other countries to acquire nuclear weapons.

Less attention has been paid recently to the equally dangerous situation caused by existing nuclear stockpiles. The states with nuclear weapons maintain thousands of nuclear warheads with a combined explosive potential 200,000 times greater than that of the Hiroshima bomb. These weapons are on alert and are ready to be fired at a moment's notice.

France, the UK, the US and now also Russia maintain policies that permit first use of nuclear weapons; that is, they maintain the option to use nuclear weapons even when nuclear weapons are not used or threatened against them. This opens up the possibility that nuclear weapons could be used in a range of conflicts, not just those between nuclear states. In fact, the US has made implied threats to use nuclear weapons three times since the end of the Cold War: against Iraq, Libya and North Korea.

Nor is the nuclear arms race over. States with nuclear weapons are continuing to research, design, test, modernize and develop nuclear weapons. France, the US and Russia are conducting nuclear testing through a range of sophisticated technical means not specifically prohibited by the CTBT. These include sub-critical explosive tests, computer simulations, and fusion experiments. The US recently deployed a new nuclear weapon and continues to build Trident nuclear submarines; it is also about to recommence the production of tritium which is a key material for nuclear weapons production.

The failure of the states with nuclear weapons to abandon their nuclear policies and practices is linked intrinsically to the proliferation of nuclear weapons to other countries. The continuing existence of nuclear weapons and of unsafeguarded fissile material also creates a risk of acquisition or construction of a nuclear weapon by a terrorist organization, which may have fewer constraints than a government against its use. International Physicians for the Prevention of Nuclear War (IPPNW) reported on the increasing possibility of such a scenario.[4]

The implications of any use of nuclear weapons hardly need to be spelled out. The International Court of Justice (ICJ) warned in 1996 that any use even of a small tactical nuclear weapon would threaten escalation into a devastating nuclear exchange. The ICJ also noted the uniquely destructive aspects of nuclear weapons in both blast and radiation and stated that: 'The destructive power of nuclear weapons cannot be contained in either space or time'. In June 1998, the *Bulletin of Atomic Scientists* moved the hands of their doomsday clock forward from 14 minutes to 9 minutes to midnight. The editors noted that:

> The end of the Cold War gave the world a unique opportunity to control and reduce the threat of nuclear catastrophe. It is clear that much of that opportunity has been squandered... No nuclear state is moving significantly toward nuclear disarmament. Between them Russia and the United States still have upwards of 30,000 nuclear weapons – strategic and tactical – and 7000 warheads ready to be fired with less than 15 minutes notice.

Near-universal political will: the call for elimination of nuclear weapons

In 1970 the Nuclear Non-Proliferation Treaty (NPT) entered into force, and today has 187 states' parties, the largest membership of any disarmament treaty. The NPT aimed at preventing further acquisition of nuclear weapons beyond the five countries which possessed them at the time: the USA, USSR, France, UK and China. In exchange for the commitment of the states without nuclear weapons not to acquire them, Article VI of the NPT bound the states with nuclear weapons to complete nuclear disarmament: 'Each of the parties to the treaty undertakes to pursue negotiations in good faith on effective measures relating to cessation of the nuclear arms race at an early date and to nuclear disarmament'.

Three decades later, the United Nations General Assembly, responding to public advocacy, brought the issue of nuclear weapons before the International Court of Justice (ICJ). On 8 July 1996 the ICJ concluded unanimously that: 'There exists an obligation to pursue in good faith, and bring to a conclusion, negotiations leading to nuclear disarmament in all its aspects under strict and effective international control'.[5]

The significance of the ICJ decision is that it affirmed that there is an obligation to achieve the goal, not merely to postulate it. The goal is to achieve nuclear disarmament 'in all its aspects'. The elimination of nuclear weapons should occur under international control and, like any legal obligation, this obligation must be performed within an appropriate time-frame and cannot be postponed indefinitely.

While the ICJ opinion cited the NPT as an important indication of disarmament responsibility, it did not assert that the obligation is confined to states' parties to the NPT. ICJ President Bedjaoui, in his separate declaration, stated that the obligation has 'assumed customary force' and that 'it is the duty of all to seek to attain it more actively than ever'.[6]

The US and the UK argued at the ICJ that their nuclear disarmament obligation was linked to progress in conventional disarmament and in developing alternative security systems to the system of nuclear deterrence. The court did not accept this argument and, apart from the requirement for international control, made no mention of conditions that were required to move toward nuclear disarmament.

Thus the question to be asked is not why there should be a nuclear weapons convention, but why states with nuclear weapons have not yet agreed to start negotiating one. With this in mind, a group of disarmament experts and abolition advocates drafted a

47.1

Global support for nuclear weapons' abolition – by governments, experts and the public

- On 6 February 1985 the cities of Hiroshima and Nagasaki launched an appeal calling for the complete prohibition and elimination of nuclear weapons. The appeal has since been signed by more than 60 million people, making it the largest petition in the world.

- In November 1995, Abolition 2000, an international network calling for negotiations on a nuclear weapons convention, was established. More than 1500 organizations have now joined this network.

- In 1996, 1997 and 1998 the United Nations General Assembly adopted resolutions specifically calling for negotiations leading to the conclusion of a nuclear weapons convention prohibiting the development, testing, production, stockpiling, transfer, use, and threat of use of nuclear weapons and providing for their elimination. A number of other resolutions also supported the call for such negotiations.[7]

- On 14 August 1996 the Canberra Commission on the Elimination of Nuclear Weapons released its report calling for a programme for the complete elimination of nuclear weapons.[8]

- On 5 December 1996 the former US General Lee Butler and more than 50 other retired generals and admirals from 17 countries including Russia, the UK, France, India and Pakistan released a statement calling for the elimination of nuclear weapons.

- On 13 March 1997 the European Parliament called on all members to support negotiations leading to the conclusion of a convention for the abolition of nuclear weapons.

- On 17 June 1997 the US National Academy of Sciences released a report calling for a long-term strategy of complete elimination of nuclear weapons and intermediate steps including restricting the role of nuclear weapons to deterring nuclear threats.

- Public opinion polls conducted in 1997 and 1998 in Australia, Belgium, Canada, Germany, Holland, Japan, Norway, the UK and the US indicated overwhelming public support for a nuclear weapons convention.[9]

- On 2 February 1998, 117 civilian leaders, including 47 past or present heads of state, released a statement calling for the elimination of nuclear weapons.

- On 9 June 1998 the foreign ministers of Brazil, Egypt, Ireland, Mexico, New Zealand, Slovenia, South Africa and Sweden released a joint declaration calling for a new agenda for nuclear disarmament culminating in the elimination of nuclear weapons.

- On 18 June 1998, and again on 24 February 1999, US Representative Lynn Woolsey introduced resolutions to the US House of Representatives calling for negotiations leading to the conclusion of a nuclear weapons convention.[10]

- In October 1998, 50 US bishops released a statement, 'The Morality of Nuclear Deterrence', condemning nuclear deterrence and calling for nuclear abolition.

- In December 1998 the Canadian Standing Committee on Foreign Affairs and International Trade recommended that Canada take an active role in encouraging reform of the policies and postures of the states with nuclear weapons and of NATO, and also take an active role in the pursuit of complete nuclear disarmament.

model Nuclear Weapons Convention, which is now a formal UN discussion document, introduced by Costa Rica. There will be further discussion of this model convention below.

Global support for nuclear disarmament in general, including support for a nuclear weapons convention, is widening amongst the general public, the majority of national governments, numerous cities and panels of experts (see Box 47.1).

Resistance by states with nuclear weapons

The governments of states with nuclear weapons continue to resist any but the most minimal nuclear disarmament steps. The resistance is rooted in the continuing perception that nuclear weapons are useful militarily, politically and economically. The United Kingdom, for example, has argued that nuclear weapons are necessary in order to prevent 'subjection to conquest which may be of the most brutal and enslaving character'.[11] The US has argued that

> we believe the policy of nuclear deterrence has saved many millions of lives from the scourge of war during the past 50 years. In this special sense nuclear weapons have been used defensively every day for over half a century ... to preserve the peace.[12]

There is also evidence of an unspoken belief among the states with nuclear weapons states that nuclear status confers political power. In 1995 the Mexican Ambassador to the UN in Geneva noted that:

> What is at the heart of this debate is that it ... forces a rethinking of the whole cold war power structure... Look at France... The French government thinks that their legitimacy comes from having nuclear weapons. Take away their nukes and their Security Council veto, and what are they? A little more than Italy and less than Germany.[13]

The corporate and scientific interest in maintaining a robust nuclear weapons industry also constrains nuclear disarmament to limited steps. Claiming that thousands of jobs and careers depend on the production and maintenance of nuclear weapons, scientists, bureaucrats and corporations exercise considerable lobbying influence. Weapons laboratories in the US convinced the Clinton administration that congressional support for a Comprehensive Test Ban Treaty (CTBT) would require a guarantee of continued funding of nuclear weapons research and testing programmes of Cold War proportions.[14]

Limitations of the step-by-step approach

The states with nuclear weapons advocate a step-by-step, or incremental, nuclear disarmament process that has brought them no closer to nuclear disarmament now than when they accepted their obligation to disarm under the Non-Proliferation Treaty (NPT) more than 30 years ago. As a matter of numbers alone, there has been little net reduction from the stockpiles that existed when the NPT entered into force in 1970. At that time there were 39,000 nuclear weapons. Today there are still over 30,000. More important, the states with nuclear weapons have made no moves away from policies of threat or use. The UK, the US and France have been joined by Russia in refusing to rule out the first use of nuclear weapons and are collectively continuing to keep thousands of nuclear weapons on alert status. In addition, the threat of use, including even use in a pre-emptive first strike, has been extended to cover threats from chemical and biological weapons.

While the step-by-step process has delivered a number of limited disarmament and arms control treaties, including the Strategic Arms Reduction Treaties (START) and Intermediate-range Nuclear Forces agreement (INF), the Partial Test Ban Treaty (PTBT) and conclusion of negotiations on the CTBT, these have had little effect on the policies of the states with nuclear weapons, on their ability to inflict unimaginable damage on other states with their remaining weapons, or on their ability to design and develop new weapons and delivery vehicles.

Under START I, START II and the proposed START III treaties, the US and Russia are reducing their stockpiles of nuclear weapons but have no intention of going below numbers necessary to 'confront an enemy with risks of unacceptable damage and disproportionate loss'.[15] The PTBT, hailed as an important disarmament step, did not in fact halt nuclear testing, since the states with nuclear weapons merely shifted to underground tests. The CTBT has loopholes that allow some states with nuclear weapons to continue certain forms of testing, as discussed above; nor is its entry into force definite. The proposed Fissile Material Cut-Off Treaty (FMCT) would not effect the huge stockpiles of highly enriched uranium (HEU) and plutonium. Tritium is being exempted from the FMCT negotiations. The achievement of insignificant steps can actually have a detrimental effect on, and delay progress toward, elimination of nuclear weapons by giving an appearance of progress that can reduce the impetus for disarmament. In the 1961 negotiations on a nuclear test-ban treaty, for example, both the PTBT and a CTBT had been proposed. There was considerable public and political pressure for a CTBT, but the conclusion of the PTBT took the wind out of the sails of the CTBT campaign. When the CTBT was finally signed in 1996 (with ratification still pending), most states with nuclear weapons had developed the ability to conduct a range of non-explosive nuclear weapons tests. Thus, incremental, or step-by-step, progress on nuclear disarmament, while essential for focusing on the details, is insufficient to address all the various proliferation risks or to guarantee the comprehensive coordinated efforts necessary for complete nuclear disarmament.

What is currently missing in the policies of the states with nuclear weapons is a genuine commitment to complete nuclear disarmament, some attempt to envision this goal and any effort at a plan, however rough. A coordinated effort across states and institutions, in the framework of voluntary governmental and non-governmental participation, is necessary if there is to be a reversal of the nuclear threat. One element of such coordination will be a multilateral agreement to prohibit and eliminate nuclear weapons, a Nuclear Weapons Convention (NWC).

Paradigm shift from military security to human security?

Resistance to the elimination of nuclear weapons is not only a matter of persisting political interests tied to nuclear weapons, but also of failure to move toward new policy visions that depart from deterrence doctrine and the pursuit of national security based on military might rather than collective well-being.

Weapons of mass destruction represent the logical extension of traditional military thought, with its reliance on force and domination of armed conflict. An outgrowth of this security paradigm is the principle of deterrence, by which a military threatens overwhelming, even unthinkable, superior force on other states in order to protect its national interests. Proponents make two claims about deterrence: that the threat of nuclear weapons will prevent either a conventional or nuclear attack, and that the success of such deterrence will ensure that nuclear weapons will not be used (at least by rational states).

However, deterrence is inherently unstable and is bound to fail at some point:

(1) For deterrence to be effective it must be based on a willingness to use nuclear weapons, but that willingness itself can lead to its failure to prevent nuclear war. If in a conflict situation an enemy is not convinced that nuclear weapons will be used against them, they may decide to use force against the nuclear state. This situation has occurred already on a number of occasions since 1945, for example when Argentina invaded the Falkland Islands despite the British nuclear deterrent. Such failure of deterrence to prevent conventional attack could downgrade the deterrent value of nuclear weapons. Thus the desire to maintain the credibility of the nuclear deterrent threat would provide an incentive for the use of nuclear weapons.

(2) Nuclear war could also occur by accident or miscalculation. A number of accidents that could have resulted in an inadvertent nuclear exchange have already occurred.[16] If nuclear weapons are kept on alert status, probable failures or incorrect information transfers in military computers could have catastrophic results.[17]

(3) Nuclear deterrence stimulates other states to develop or acquire either nuclear weapons or other weapons of mass destruction in response.

(4) When deterrence fails, there is no fall-back plan, and the consequences might include nuclear holocaust.

(5) Nuclear weapons and deterrence logic do not fit into an emerging world where power structures are being transformed from state-based to more interlinked systems, including transnational and international corporations, a global market, international institutions, communications systems, environmental and social effects of policies and practices, civil society organizations and movements, and even a globalization of cultures and identities. A paradigm shift is afoot as the world moves away from self-contained nation-state systems to interstate interdependence combined with globalization. In the field of security policy, a corresponding shift is from deterrence policy to increased reliance on collective security measures. Whether the emergent paradigm will be capital-driven or human rights-driven depends largely on the concept of collective security that develops. A security model that takes into account global humanitarian needs, such as health, education, social and economic justice, ecological balance and human rights is scarcely compatible with a model that relies on the capacity for mass destruction as the cornerstone of security. The global elimination of nuclear weapons will necessarily involve the different elements of global society in its implementation and will generate new mechanisms for global cooperation. The blossoming support globally for a nuclear weapons convention is resulting partially from this paradigm shift in political, social, and economic systems and in consciousness.

Getting to zero: towards a nuclear weapons convention

A nuclear weapons convention provides a logical mechanism for satisfying the ICJ requirements that nuclear disarmament be negotiated and completed under strict and effective international control. It is also a logical way to achieve the elimination of nuclear weapons in a non-discriminatory manner that will incorporate the security concerns of states that currently possess nuclear weapons. In addition, it offers a logical way to reduce and to eliminate the threat from nuclear weapons, rather than partial steps that leave numbers of nuclear weapons in the arsenals of some states, even if the numbers are small.

When there is sufficient political will, negotiations can be concluded fairly quickly. The Partial Test Ban Treaty, for example, was concluded in ten days of determined negotiating in July 1963, after years of deadlock. Agreements on time-frames for negotiations can sometimes help facilitate the process. The parties to the Non-Proliferation Treaty in 1995 agreed to a time-frame for concluding negotiations on a Comprehensive Test Ban Treaty no later than 1996. Such a time-frame helped bring the negotiations to an early conclusion.

However, negotiations on an NWC are likely to be complex and may take some time. States with nuclear weapons will likely require a high level of confidence that there will be universal compliance with an NWC before they agree to eliminate their nuclear weapons. Moreover, the nuclear systems of the different states are asymmetrical, requiring fairly complicated disarmament formulas.

Political deadlock: when and how to eliminate nuclear weapons

Among the official and de facto nuclear-weapon states, the governments of the US, France, Russia, the UK, and Israel suggest that even thinking about an NWC is premature. They are unwilling to provide a time reference for beginning, let alone concluding, such a convention. The governments of India, China and Pakistan support the commencement of negotiations on an NWC, but give no indication of when such negotiations could or should be concluded. At the other end of the spectrum there are calls for comprehensive negotiations on the complete elimination of nuclear weapons under a time-bound framework. In August 1996, the Non Aligned Movement submitted a proposal to the UN Conference on Disarmament calling for the entry into force of an NWC by the year 2010 and the complete elimination of nuclear weapons by the year 2020. Abolition 2000, an international network for the abolition of nuclear weapons, called in April 1995 for the conclusion of an NWC within five years.

Proponents of a comprehensive approach argue that this is the only way to deal with the dramatically different levels, or asymmetries, in national nuclear arsenals and capabilities. The potential for the issue of asymmetries to undermine incremental treaties has been clearly demonstrated in the case of the CTBT. The CTBT was originally proposed by India, yet India rejected the CTBT when it was finally concluded, because by that time other states with nuclear weapons had developed the means for non-explosive testing while India had not. Thus, the resulting CTBT would be discriminatory, barring some countries from testing while others had advanced to a high-tech method of testing not explicitly barred under the treaty.

The model nuclear weapons convention

In response to ongoing political deadlock, public citizens' groups (civil society organizations) have sought to find creative ways to identify obstacles, raise political will and explore technical and legal questions pertinent to the elimination of nuclear weapons. Because political, legal and technical aspects of nuclear disarmament are interrelated, improvement in one area can stimulate the others. It is not necessary to wait for progress on political negotiations before working on the problems posed by the legal and technical complications. Therefore, citizens' organizations are working to make progress towards complete nuclear disarmament by engaging any and every relevant sector in practical questions of how to safely and securely disarm.

With this in mind, an international consortium of lawyers, scientists, physicians and disarmament specialists drafted a model Nuclear Weapons Convention, to address perceived obstacles to nuclear disarmament, such as technical issues and security doubts and concerns, and to stimulate the political will to begin negotiations on such a convention. The model NWC is intended to demonstrate that an agreement on the elimination of nuclear weapons is possible to achieve, to implement, to verify and to maintain.

Technical issues

The primary obstacle to complete nuclear disarmament today is political will, not technical capability. The scientific experience of many international and inter-governmental bodies will be useful, whether their current functions remain or change. These include:

- International Atomic Energy Agency;
- Nuclear weapons free-zone implementation agencies;
- Comprehensive Test Ban Treaty Organization;
- United Nations Special Commission (on Iraq); and
- the US and Russian disarmament and non-proliferation bodies, including:
  - Verification mechanisms for the START and INF treaties;
  - Cooperative Threat Reduction (CTR);
  - Material Protection Control and Accounting (MPC&A);
  - Nuclear Cities Initiative.

Some of these mechanisms and procedures developed in the implementation of incremental disarmament steps have provided a basis for the verification and implementation approaches proposed in the model NWC. In addition, the experience of negotiating and implementing the Chemical Weapons Convention (CWC) will offer valuable experience for the NWC. The CWC introduced intrusive challenge and routine inspections of facilities at a new level, and this experience will provide a measure of the degree to which declarations of existing stocks and continued monitoring can build trust and confidence. Similarly, recent developments of the International Atomic Energy Agency's 93+2 Programme, enhancing safeguards on nuclear facilities, will pave the way for verification of the NWC.

The nuclear weapons convention approach also provides a natural way to ease or reverse the opposition of nuclear weapons scientists and corporations to nuclear disarmament. The convention indicates that considerable scientific expertise and corporate involvement will be necessary for the destruction of nuclear weapons and for the verification of the nuclear weapons-free regime. The Cooperative Monitoring Center at Sandia National Laboratories in the US offers an example of an agency, established within the nuclear weapons infrastructure, which now researches and develops the technology essential for verification of nuclear disarmament. The resources, skills and talent that have contributed, knowingly and unknowingly, to the nuclear weapons industry are crucial for dismantling or converting this infrastructure. As on the political level, the key to reversing current technical and scientific trends is awareness of the global picture, commitment to nuclear disarmament and coordination of efforts.

Security doubts and concerns

Some policymakers in the states with nuclear weapons maintain that pursuit of complete nuclear disarmament would reduce their security. They claim further that the future international security system cannot be predicted in advance, and they see the demand for an NWC as an attempt to predict the future.

The concept of a nuclear weapons convention can be a tool in exploring these and other concerns that are sure to arise as the states with nuclear weapons consider moving away from a security policy that they know and with which they have lived for decades, albeit very dangerously and with many undesired consequences. The claim that nuclear disarmament would reduce the security of states with nuclear weapons relies on the policy of nuclear deterrence as the basis of national security. This position holds that nuclear deterrence has kept the nuclear powers from using nuclear weapons and concludes that nuclear weapons are therefore necessary to ensure that they are never used. Besides the inherent illogicality of this position, it assumes that nuclear deterrence, unlike every other human policy, is somehow entirely foolproof.

The greatest security risk faced by all nations today, in the sense of physical destruction, is in fact the use of nuclear weapons, and maintenance of these arsenals is no guarantee that they would not be used. The states with nuclear weapons are also in general the major military powers, and their reliance on nuclear weapons is an extension of their reliance on military superiority for their own security. In actuality, they face no threat from states without nuclear weapons on the scale of the threat they pose. Ironically, their own nuclear arsenals make them the targets of other states with nuclear weapons. Thus, abandoning dependence on nuclear weapons would increase their domestic as well as global security. However, entrenched military thinking and the distrust cultivated during the nuclear age do make it difficult for policymakers to see beyond the current set of policies and interstate relations. The NWC, by offering a long-term vision of a future where no state relies on nuclear weapons, is one tool for thinking beyond the current vicious circle of nuclear threat and counterthreat.

Moreover, lack of certainty about the future can provide an incentive rather than a disincentive to seek further answers, and need not prevent progress toward elimination of nuclear weapons by all who share this goal. Lack of certainty did not prevent large-scale planning to develop nuclear weapons in the mid-20th century, thereby shaping the international security regime for generations to come. Thus, a coordinated effort to envision a different security system, without nuclear weapons, can help to identify potential measures that could be taken today despite the absence of a universal commitment. Identifying and strengthening potential steps would help to shape a future security regime that does not depend on nuclear weapons.

The question of timing

One frequently-heard objection to the NWC is that it is impossible today to set dates for completion of the tasks of nuclear disarmament. Some proposals have sought to provide a time-bound framework that sets deadlines for the completion of particular disarmament objectives. This approach may have the advantage of applying political pressure, and therefore can contribute to nuclear disarmament. However, the approach adopted by the model Nuclear Weapons Convention does not suggest a time-bound framework for conclusion of the negotiations or fixed dates for the complete elimination of nuclear weapons. Rather, it calls for the immediate commencement of negotiations that ought to be concluded in a quick but comprehensive manner.

At some stage a time-frame for elimination of nuclear weapons will have to be negotiated. The model NWC suggests that this be done in phases, from entry into force. This is somewhat like incorporating a step-by-step incremental process into a comprehensive approach. The model NWC attempts to balance the need for a speedy elimination of nuclear arsenals with the concerns of safety, confidence and irreversibility.

An incremental-comprehensive approach has many advantages over a purely step-by-step one. It would ensure that negotiations would continue beyond the achievement of small steps and increase the momentum to complete the elimination by instilling greater confidence that the final goal is achievable. For example, the de-alerting of nuclear weapons, with appropriate verification, is one of the suggested steps of this approach. This would increase confidence on all sides that they would not be subject to a surprise attack, enabling a move away from a launch-on-warning posture as states would have advance warning of any moves to re-alert the opposing forces' weapons before they could be launched. An incremental-comprehensive approach would help overcome the problems of asymmetry in nuclear arsenals. Negotiating parties would be willing to accept temporary imbalances in forces or capabilities because they would be confident that such temporary imbalances would be rectified by subsequent measures that would be part of the negotiating programme. Ultimately, the only real balance will occur when no state possesses nuclear weapons. If they recognize a clear programme to reach that goal, states will more easily agree to the steps along the way.

There would be checks and resting-points along the way were confidence and security not sufficiently developed to advance to the next step. For example, the model NWC proposes a series of phases for reducing the numbers of nuclear weapons. Before commencing a phase of reductions, states would have the opportunity to affirm their confidence that other states have implemented their obligations under the previous phase. The question of the timing of the NWC has, therefore, many aspects: advocates argue that precisely because of the complexity of the various political, legal and technical questions, negotiations should commence immediately, at least as discussions regarding complete nuclear disarmament that might lead to a nuclear weapons convention, taking into account the incremental steps as they relate to comprehensive disarmament; on the other hand, the process of nuclear disarmament should emphasize safety, security and irreversibility over speed. The model NWC and responses to it have demonstrated that many questions deserve further attention before a satisfactory solution can be found, but that the urgency of these questions and the importance of safe, secure and irreversible disarmament all point to the need for greater governmental and non-governmental participation in preparation for a nuclear weapons convention.

Conclusion

Political stagnation in official nuclear-disarmament negotiations has not dissuaded non-governmental or civil society organizations from making progress on practical questions about the safety, security, and attainability of the elimination of nuclear weapons. Although Chapter 47 highlights the model NWC, a similar strain of innovative thinking by NGOs has bred a vast number of other initiatives to promote new policy approaches and political coalitions aimed at the abolition of nuclear weapons. The people power provided by NGOs delivers not only political pressure but also new political thinking.

The opening of some official intergovernmental nuclear disarmament sessions to a limited amount of NGO input suggests that a critical number of governments recognize the value of NGOs contribution. NGOs presented fresh data and arguments to delegates during the official proceedings of the series of annual preparatory conferences leading up to the NPT Review Conference of the year 2000. Perhaps it is exasperation with the slow pace of official negotiations that has compelled many governments to consult with NGOs.

In the current era NGOs are playing an increasingly visible role in advancing both nuclear and non-nuclear disarmament policies. Upon acceptance of the 1997 Nobel Peace Prize on behalf of the International Campaign to Ban Landmines (ICBL), a network of disarmament NGOs, Jody Williams made the optimistic statement that NGOs comprise the 'new superpower'. Faced with the slow pace of official negotiations on control of landmines, the ICBL, together with friendly governments, was able to depart from the established negotiations by way of an independent process hosted by the Canadian government . By this method, the ICBL and governments were able promptly to bring into effect a treaty signed by over 130 countries calling for a ban on production, transfer and use of landmines.

This is perhaps the most celebrated example of new diplomacy, that is to say the collaboration between governments and citizen groups of the non-governmental sector. But public pressure and advocacy has long played a crucial historical role in driving progressive political reform. With nuclear disarmament, the historic 1996 ICJ ruling on the illegality of nuclear weapons came only after an intensive, international NGO campaign urging the UN General Assembly to submit such a question to the court. NGOs organized a massive petition drive, with millions of petitions submitted before the court as evidence of overwhelming, global political support for the elimination of nuclear weapons.

Concerned citizens of many different societal sectors will continue to play a key role in disarmament efforts, whether inside or outside of official disarmament fora, and should by all means take a proactive role in urging nuclear disarmament. Increasing the political will for nuclear abolition is not a matter to be left only to experts. After all, the participation of numerous societal sectors will be necessary in enacting nuclear reductions, just as numerous sectors are involved in their production and in preparing responses to nuclear disaster. Further, the threat of such a disaster reaches every last living creature, and it is entirely logical for each person to take a role in protecting his or her health. To use a medical analogy: although the patient seeks counsel from medical experts, it is ultimately the patient who weighs the various options, their risks and benefits, and finally decides what course of action to take. It is now up to the public to declare a course of action toward total elimination of nuclear weapons.

ACKNOWLEDGEMENTS

The authors wish to thank Alyn Ware, Lawyers' Committee on Nuclear Policy for his invaluable editing assistance in the preparation of Chapter 47.

REFERENCES

1. International Physicians for the Prevention of Nuclear War (1999), *Security and Survival: the case for a Nuclear Weapons Convention; the model convention on the prohibition of the development, testing, production, stockpiling, transfer, use and threat of use of nuclear weapons and on their elimination.* International Association of Lawyers Against Nuclear Arms (IALANA), International Network of Engineers and Scientists Against Proliferation (INESAP), International Physicians for the Prevention of Nuclear War (Cambridge, MA: IPPNW).
2. Middle Powers Initiative (1999) *Fast Track Towards Zero Nuclear Weapons*, Cambridge, MA: IPPNW, 2nd edition.
3. Abolition 2000: Website http://www.abolition2000.org .
4. IPPNW (1996), *Crude Nuclear Weapons: proliferation and the terrorist threat*, Cambridge, MA: IPPNW.
5. International Court of Justice (1996), *Legality of the Threat or Use of Nuclear Weapons* (Advisory Opinion of the ICJ, 8 July), UN Doc. A51/218 (1996), reprinted in *International Legal Materials (ILM)* 35: 809 and 1343. The advisory opinion and separate declarations and opinions of judges are available on the website of IALANA: www.ddh.nl/org/ialana/opiniontable.html
6. Ibid., n. 7.
7. United Nation General Assembly (UNGA), Resolution (Res.) 51/45 M, 10 December 1996; UNGA Res. 52/38 O, 9 December 1997; UNGA Res. 53/77 W, 4 December; UNGA Res. 52/38 L adopted on 9 December 1997; UNGA Res. 52/39 C, adopted on 9 December, 1997; UNGA Res. 53/77 X adopted on 4 December 1998; UNGA Res. 53/78 D, adopted on 4 December 1998.
8. Canberra Commission on the Elimination of Nuclear Weapons, Canberra, Australia, 1996. Available at Canberra Commission homepage: www.dfat.gov.au/cc/cchome.html .
9. Melman Group Poll, 'Public Attitudes on Nuclear Weapons', commissioned by the Stimson Centre, interviews 10–15 September 1997.
10. House of Representatives: H.Res 479, 105th Congress, 2nd Session, 18 June 1998, H.Res.82, 106th Congress, 1st Session, 24 February 1999.
11. Sir Nicholas Lyell, UK Attorney General, Statement to the International Court of Justice, 15 November 1995.
12. John McNeill, Senior Deputy General Counsel for the Department of Defense. Statement to the

International Court of Justice, 15 November 1995.

13. 'Ban the Bomb?' *The Nation*, 9/16 January 1995.

14. Western States Legal Foundation (1998), 'A Faustian Bargain: why stockpile stewardship is fundamentally incompatible with the process of disarmament'.

15. US Doctrine for Joint Nuclear Operations, 15 December 1995.

16. See, e.g., 'Selected Accidents Involving Nuclear Weapons 1950–93', Greenpeace, March 1996, at http://www.greenpeace.org/~comms/nukes/ctbt/read3.html .

17. Forrow, Lachlan, Blair, Bruce, Helfand, Ira, Lewis, George, Postol, Theodore, Sidel, Victor W., Levy, Barry S., Abrams, Herbert and Christine Cassel (1998), 'Accidental Nuclear War: a post-Cold War assessment', *New England Journal of Medicine* 338: 1326–31.

Address for correspondence

Merav Datan and Brian Rawson
IPPNW/PSR UN Office
777 United Nations Plaza, 6th Floor
New York, NY 10017, USA
Tel: +1-646-865-1883; Fax: +1-646-865-1884; email: mdatan@ippnw.org and brawson@ippnw.org

Lars Pohlmeier
Burgdammer Kirchweg 1; 28717 Bremen, Germany
Tel: +49-421-631429; Fax: +49-421-6368004; email: LarsPohlm@aol.com

48 THE WORLD COURT PROJECT

KATE DEWES
and ROBERT D. GREEN

From 1986 to 1996, a worldwide network of peace activists, doctors and lawyers evolved the World Court Project (WCP). This was based on a simple premise: while the chemical and biological weapons conventions outlaw those weapons of mass destruction, there is no such specific prohibition on nuclear weapons. They succeeded in persuading the UN to ask the International Court of Justice (ICJ), or World Court, for two advisory opinions on the legal status of nuclear weapons. The court's historic decision in July 1996 confirmed that the threat or use of nuclear weapons would generally be illegal, and that there exists an obligation to pursue in good faith and bring to a conclusion negotiations leading to complete nuclear disarmament under strict and effective international control. In May 1993, the World Health Organization (WHO) adopted a resolution asking the court whether the use of nuclear weapons in war would violate international law in view of the weapon's health and environmental effects. A year later the UN General Assembly adopted a resolution asking whether the threat or use of nuclear weapons in any circumstance would be permitted under international law. Chapter 48 traces how the WHO resolution was a crucial precursor to the General Assembly success.

The path which led to the water-hole was narrow with a steep rock face on either side and one day the elephant sat down in the middle and would not budge. He faced the on-coming traffic of cattle, dogs, horses and hyenas with disdainful equanimity: a roar, a blast of the trumpet or a nudge with the tusks and they backed off smartly.

Then the Woolly-Haired Ox (WHO) remembered something. He went to the mouse-hole and called: 'Little mouse, little mouse (ICJ*), could you please tell the elephant to get out of the road?' – 'Moi?' asked the little mouse, 'He'll never listen to little me'. However, as soon as Jumbo saw mousie he let out a yell and trotted off in haste. (Itsy-bitsy Curly-tailed Jay-mouse = ICJ*)

Erich Geiringer 1992

Ever since the nuclear age began, there have been serious initiatives to outlaw nuclear weapons by a variety of states and citizen groups within the United Nations. These included calls for a Nuclear Weapons Convention, and attempts to include nuclear weapons in the 1949 Geneva conventions along with chemical and biological weapons. All were blocked by the states with nuclear weapons using their economic and political power, including their Security Council veto. A paradox exists where they now accept the illegality of chemical and biological weapons while insisting on their right to maintain their nuclear arsenals, thereby sustaining a discriminatory, immoral and destabilizing position.

Citizen groups in a number of countries, including Japan, Germany, the USA, UK, Canada and the Netherlands, attempted to challenge the legality of nuclear weapons at state level through local and national courts.[1] In 1973, Aotearoa/New Zealand (NZ)[2] and Australia took France to the World Court in a contentious case over the legality of its atmospheric nuclear tests in the South Pacific. In the early 1980s, International Peace Bureau (IPB) President Sean MacBride, the US Lawyers' Committee on Nuclear Policy (LCNP) and others suggested using the World Court advisory opinion route through the UN General Assembly.

However, the first concerted effort to convince governments to sponsor a UN resolution to request such an opinion did not begin until 1986, when retired New Zealand (NZ) magistrate Harold Evans initiated a campaign which became known as the World Court Project (WCP). In 1988 he addressed the NZ branch of the International Physicians for the Prevention of Nuclear War (IPPNW). Later that year IPPNW's World Congress adopted a NZ-sponsored resolution supporting his initiative. In 1993, IPPNW worked closely with two other co-sponsors of the WCP – the International Association of Lawyers Against Nuclear Arms (IALANA) and the IPB – plus 22 governments to persuade the World Health Organization (WHO) at its annual assembly (WHA) to request an advisory opinion from the court on the legality of the 'health and environmental effects of the use of nuclear weapons'. A year later the UN General Assembly adopted a more ambitious resolution asking for an opinion on the threat or use of nuclear weapons.

Early initiatives by physicians and the WHO

Prior to the early 1950s, few physicians had spoken out strongly against nuclear weapons, and the general public remained largely unaware of the ongoing health and environmental effects of nuclear testing. As doctors and scientists began disseminating information about the health effects of the 1954 US nuclear test at Bikini Atoll, worldwide protests grew rapidly.

In 1957, Nobel Laureate and famous physician Albert Schweitzer delivered a substantive Declaration of Conscience from Oslo, highlighting the effects of nuclear tests and calling for an end to them. It was broadcast from 150 transmitters, heard by millions throughout the world and reprinted widely in the press.[3] Within a year he broadcast another three appeals which were soon widely published in the booklet *Peace or Atomic War*. He also wrote to many of his influential friends, urging them to join the struggle for nuclear abolition:

The argument that these weapons are contrary to international law contains everything that we can reproach them with. It has the advantage of being a legal argument. If the battle is fought along these lines, it will achieve the desired results. No government can deny that these weapons violate international law ... and international law cannot be swept aside![4]

However, when he was asked by US physician Norman Cousins to sign an Appeal with the Pope to the World Court to outlaw nuclear tests in 1958 he declined, challenging lawyers 'to use and raise the argument that atomic weapons contradict the law of humanity'.[5] With the signing of the Partial Test Ban Treaty in 1963, public debate on nuclear issues subsided, especially in Europe.

Physicians continued to raise the nuclear issue within the WHO. From 1954 to 1979 the organization focussed principally on the 'biomedical and environmental aspects of ionizing radiation'. During the 1960s it passed various disarmament resolutions about the effects of radiation, especially in relation to nuclear testing, and called for states to accede to the 1925 Geneva Protocol against gas and germ warfare. In 1970 it called upon:

all medical associations and all medical workers to consider it their moral and professional duty to give every possible assistance to the international movement directed towards the complete prohibition of chemical and bacteriological means of waging war.[6]

In response to a 1981 resolution, the WHO appointed an International Committee of Experts to write a report on the 'effects of nuclear war on health and health services' which was presented to the 1983 World Health Assembly. Another resolution was then adopted which declared that 'nuclear weapons constitute the greatest immediate threat to the health and welfare of mankind' and 'prevention is the only answer to the risk of nuclear war'.[7] Immediately following IPPNW's establishment in 1981, Co-President Bernard Lown met the WHO director-general and other officials to explore how the two organizations could work together. In 1985 IPPNW was granted NGO status and in 1986 Swedish doctor Ann Marie Janson was appointed as the organization's WHO Liaison Officer. She later played a leading role in the World Court Project (WCP).

Evolution of the World Court Project: 1986–92

In 1986, following a visit to New Zealand by US Law Professor Richard Falk, Harold Evans sent a 100-page Open Letter to the prime ministers of Australia and NZ challenging them to sponsor a UN resolution to seek a World Court opinion on 'the legality or otherwise of nuclear weaponry'. Australia rejected the idea, but Prime Minister David Lange showed interest. Evans followed it up with appeals to all 71 UN member states with diplomatic representation in Canberra and Wellington. Some Non-Aligned Movement (NAM) states and the Soviet Union (with Gorbachev in power) indicated interest.

Within NZ a dialogue with government ministers and officials ensued, strongly backed by the newly-formed Public Advisory Committee on Disarmament and Arms Control, whose mandate was to monitor the implementation of the Nuclear Free Act. The Chair of IPPNW (NZ), Dr Robin Briant, was one of the eight members along with

Kate Dewes. In May 1988, Dewes was one of two citizen advisers in the NZ government delegation to the Third UN Special Session on Disarmament in New York. When addressing a UN Committee, she promoted the WCP and later discussed it with leading NGOs, and with diplomats from India, Mexico, Sweden and Australia.

Spurred on by Evans, the Public Advisory Committee and other leading citizens' groups, the NZ government began seriously considering the proposal. It would not, however, risk going it alone in the UN and directly challenging the fundamental defence policies of its western allies. NZ was already under intense pressure as a result of its 1987 nuclear free legislation. The realities of the Cold War mindset meant this type of initiative was probably doomed from the outset at that time. Government officials and politicians were wary of exacerbating already tense relationships by pursuing something which might fail, thereby 'damaging the credibility of the ICJ and the greater cause of nuclear disarmament'. Moreover, they were lobbying for a seat on the UN Security Council.

Although disappointed by the government's decision not to proceed in 1989, Evans and others were not deterred. They began mobilizing citizen support among a wide range of groups. Encouraged by the knowledge that others were working along similar lines, and advised by key NZ politicians to build up international support, they took their cause to Europe.

Evans attended the IPB's annual conference in the UK in September 1989, where his strategy was endorsed. A few weeks later his proposal was adopted at IALANA's inaugural World Congress in The Hague. On his way back, Evans met supportive doctors and lawyers in Malaysia during the Commonwealth Heads of Government Meeting there. He sent letters to six sympathetic Commonwealth leaders asking them to work together to sponsor a resolution.

In March 1991, New Zealander Alyn Ware was visiting New York, representing citizen groups worldwide opposing the Gulf War. He approached several UN missions and found strong support for the WCP idea. Parliamentarians for Global Action (PGA) gave helpful guidance, and Costa Rica began drafting a UN resolution with the intention of co-sponsoring it at the 1992 UN General Assembly. PGA promoted the WCP in its newsletters, which went to 600 members in over 40 countries.

Three months later Dewes and IPB Secretary-General Colin Archer found similar support in Geneva missions. The idea was seen as non-discriminatory and supportive of the UN Decade of International Law, it complemented moves for nuclear-free zones in Africa and the Middle East, and would strengthen efforts to secure a Convention on Prohibition of Use of Nuclear Weapons. However at least 50 states, including some neutral ones, would be needed as co-sponsors to withstand the severe pressure expected from the states with nuclear weapons.[8]

At the same time, IPB proposed hosting a WCP launch with IALANA and IPPNW during IPB's centenary in 1992. Encouraged by this growing support, Dewes then visited the UK to meet with a network coordinated by Keith Mothersson, who had pioneered a key aspect of the WCP's success: harnessing public conscience and the law. IPB published his ideas in a WCP primer, *From Hiroshima To The Hague*. He proposed invoking the Martens clause from the 1907 Hague Convention, which required the World Court to take account of the 'dictates of the public conscience' when deciding any legal question.[9]

Following its inaugural meeting, WCP(UK) set up a pilot scheme for the collection of individually-signed Declarations of Public Conscience to test public reaction – which was positive, even in a state with nuclear weapons. The idea quickly spread to countries with active anti-nuclear movements, including Australia, Canada, France, Germany, Ireland, Japan, the Netherlands, Norway, NZ , Sweden and the US. Declarations were translated into nearly 40 languages.

Article 96 of the UN Charter and Article 76 of the WHO Constitution state that, in addition to the General Assembly and Security Council, other UN organs and specialized agencies may also request advisory opinions of the court on legal questions arising within the scope of their activities. In late 1991, Wellington doctor Erich Geiringer of IPPNW(NZ) began encouraging IPPNW to spearhead a request to the WHO's annual assembly.

During 1991, with the Cold War over, initial support for the WCP had already been secured from several leading members of the 110-member Non-Aligned Movement (NAM). At the Geneva launch of the WCP in May 1992, Zimbabwe, as Chair of the NAM, became the first government to announce its support.

At this meeting, an International Steering Committee (ISC) was formed, and Alyn Ware returned to New York as a volunteer with the Lawyers' Committee on Nuclear Policy (LCNP), IALANA's US affiliate, to coordinate action on the project at the UN. He was later appointed LCNP's executive director.

The ISC helped mobilize international support for the WCP. It compiled an international list of endorsing organizations and prominent individuals. By 1994 over 700 bodies had endorsed it, including many city councils, Greenpeace International and the Anglican Communion of Primates. Over 200,000 individual Declarations of Conscience had been collected, plus letters of support from Mikhail Gorbachev and South African Archbishop Desmond Tutu.

World Health Assembly requests an advisory opinion: 1992–93

Just before the May 1992 WCP launch, IPPNW masterminded an attempt to table a resolution in the WHA. The draft resolution called upon the WHO Executive Board:

> to study and formulate a request for an advisory opinion from the International Court of Justice on the status in international law of the use of nuclear weapons in view of their serious effects on health and the environment.

The move failed due to lack of time to build up government support, and because the resolution was not formally on the agenda. Within weeks, however, IPPNW had attracted 14 co-sponsors for the resolution, and a significant number of health ministers indicated interest.

Following the 1992 WHA, IPPNW coordinated an intense and well-organized campaign in every country where it had members, visited health ministers and advisers in the four former Soviet states and Africa, made 'soundings' within the WHO bureaucracy, and visited over 20 diplomatic missions in Geneva to shore up support from the 1992 co-sponsors and others. This was complemented by the LCNP coordinating lobbying in New York and by the other co-sponsors visiting health and foreign ministers in their capitals.

They succeeded in attracting 22 co-sponsors from three key regions – Africa, Latin America and the South Pacific – led by the health ministers from Zambia, Mexico, Tonga and Vanuatu (some of whom were also IPPNW members). The resolution requested an advisory opinion from the World Court on the following question: in view of the health and environmental effects, would the use of nuclear weapons by a state in war or other armed conflict be a breach of its obligations under international law including under the WHO Constitution?

IPPNW organized a strong lobbying team for the effort, led by Ann Marie Janson and including George Salmond, a former NZ director-general of health. Over the years they had amassed insights into the WHO processes and knew many of the delegates. They coordinated meetings with the co-sponsoring countries, prepared comprehensive background papers, countered misinformation and answered questions as they were raised in committees. IPPNW also successfully lobbied the World Federation of Public Health Associations which unanimously supported the initiative.

Arguments by the NATO nuclear-weapon states and their allies that the WHO lacked the competence to ask the question were countered by the fact that the WHO had since 1981 been investigating the health and environmental effects of nuclear weapons. Hilda Lini, Vanuatu's Health Minister and WHO Regional Vice-President, proved a successful lobbyist on the inside. Her speech, a powerful mix of passion and facts delivered from the point of view of a South Pacific Island woman and mother, apparently had a significant impact on the (female) US surgeon-general. Despite intense lobbying by the western states to block it, countered by a successful ploy by the co-sponsors to invoke a secret ballot, the resolution was adopted on 14 May 1993 by 73 votes to 40, with 10 abstentions.

The question was finally received by the World Court in September 1993, which then invited states to make written submissions on the WHO question by September 1994. Of 35 submissions received, 22 argued that any nuclear weapon use would be illegal. The states with nuclear weapons (except China, which took no part) and some of their allies argued that the case was inadmissible, and/or that the use of nuclear weapons is not necessarily illegal. IALANA and IPPNW drafted model submissions which some states used in the preparation of their cases. Submitting states were then given until June 1995 to comment on submissions by other states.

The WHO resolution's impact

With hindsight, it is clear that the failure of the 1992 attempt was fortunate. The resolution's initial wording could have allowed the pro-nuclear lobby to derail it and neither the international movement nor the leading anti-nuclear states were ready to carry it through to the court. By May 1993, the WHA resolution had laid a solid foundation for the forthcoming General Assembly proposal. Its success paved the way for NAM to consider co-sponsorship, knowing it needed the backing of at least 111 states to withstand even greater pressure than that exerted at the WHA. On the other hand, the threats, bribes and other tactics of the pro-nuclear lobby had only served to reinforce NAM's resolve.

IPPNW's prominent involvement ensured that at least one case was brought before the court. No one country would have had the courage or incentive to incur the wrath of the nuclear powers. There were only a few economically secure states where public opinion was strong enough to bolster sympathetic politicians and ministry officials. But even those, like NZ and Sweden, were not prepared to go it alone, risking alienation from their friends, and NAM was not cohesive enough to withstand the pressure.

IPPNW had a long and respected history of working with the WHO and health ministries in many countries. Janson and Salmond were astute strategists who were also well-organized and, as already mentioned, knew the WHO processes intimately. Many delegates were friends and colleagues. They developed good relationships with many officials, typists and even ushers who often helped them by sharing vital information or handing documents to delegates on their behalf. IPPNW produced very readable and well-referenced papers and ensured that key delegates understood the arguments, giving them strong support during their presentations to committee meetings. Citizen groups were free to lobby delegates without being accused of being part of the traditional UN power-plays. Delegates understood that these protagonists were motivated by a desire to preserve the health and well-being of humanity. The fact that most of the IPPNW team were fellow health professionals added to their credibility.

According to IPPNW's Director Michael Christ, the WCP energized affiliates like no previous campaign. Members saw it as:

> a shining light that held the federation together through difficult times, because it was clear what the objective was and there was a time-frame. It was a project where a whole range of affiliates could participate in a whole lot of different ways, ranging from writing a letter to their minister of health to a full-blown campaign of public education with the media, collection of Declarations of Public Conscience, and face-to-face meetings with decision makers.[10]

Lessons learned at the two WHAs were also extremely valuable for the preparation for the UN General Assembly. As 1993 drew to a close, nearly a million Declarations of Public Conscience had been collected and the WCP had gained prominence in Japan, Australia and other influential western states. Citizen groups encouraged governments to put in a submission on the WHO question and vote in favour of the resolution. Unlike many other peace movement objectives, these were achievable goals within a set time-frame, and a growing number of groups in the international movement began to make it a priority.

UN General Assembly challenges nuclear deterrence: 1993–94

A major objection to the WHO resolution by western governments was that the General Assembly was the correct forum for the issue. Following the WHO success, Zimbabwe's foreign minister convinced NAM to table a more ambitious resolution at the 1993 UN disarmament session. This asked the World Court urgently to render its advisory opinion on the following question: is the threat or use of nuclear weapons in any circumstance permitted under international law? In broadening and strengthening the WHO question, NAM directly challenged the legality of nuclear deterrence doctrine and the privileged status of the nuclear powers as permanent members of the UN Security Council.

Ware coordinated the UN lobbying and helped in the preparation of legal submissions from New York. During the last week of October 1993 Zimbabwe, backed by a determined group of South Pacific states, lobbied hard within the First Committee. They were helped by a WCP team including Hilda Lini and Maori elder Pauline Tangiora. The presence of two indigenous women from the South Pacific had a powerful impact on the diplomats of small-island states, who treated both women with deep respect because of their senior positions within their tribes. They also knew of Lini's role at the WHA and of NZ's citizen leadership in the project.

After some crucial lobbying by Vanuatu and others, the resolution was introduced reluctantly by Indonesia as chair of NAM. Peggy Mason, Canada's Disarmament Ambassador, described the reaction: 'Hysteria is not too strong a word to describe the nuclear weapon states' point of view around here'.[11] The US, UK and France sent delegations to many NAM capitals threatening trade and aid if the resolution was not withdrawn. On 19 November, the NAM consensus cracked, and Indonesia announced that action had been deferred. Nonetheless, every UN member government probably now knew about the WCP, and how it threatened the privileged position of the states with nuclear weapons.

In June 1994, Zimbabwe again persuaded NAM foreign ministers not just to re-introduce the 1993 resolution, but put it to a vote. The NATO nuclear states continued their intense opposition to the resolution. The UK claimed that the resolution risked 'being seen as a deliberate attempt to exert pressure over the Court to prejudice its response [to the WHO question] ... [it] can do nothing to further global peace and security'.[12] The French showed signs of hysteria: 'It is a blatant violation of the UN Charter. It goes against the law. It goes against reason'.[13]

NAM was not deflected. On 18 November 1994 the resolution was adopted in the First Committee by 77 votes to 33, with 21 abstentions and 53 not voting. Despite it being the most radical resolution on the UN's disarmament agenda, China did not vote, Ukraine abstained and the normally compliant western caucus of non-nuclear states collapsed. By abstaining, Canada and Norway broke ranks with NATO; Japan and Australia with the US; and Ireland with the European Union along with two prospective neutral non-NATO members Sweden and Austria.

The most serious insubordination, however, was that NZ, then a Security Council member, voted in favour, the only western-allied state to do so. This undid at a stroke the progress made by the US in luring the one such state with nuclear-free legislation back under Washington's control. The NZ government had been under intense pressure from the peace movement and politicians from various parties to support the resolution. Despite several high-level visits by both US and UK military and diplomatic personnel, the government withstood the pressure to abstain.

The common theme in this breakdown in western cohesion was the strength of public support for the WCP. The work to collect signed Declarations of Public Conscience and other endorsements had borne fruit. A probably decisive factor, however, was a carefully-focused faxing campaign to capitals of supportive states. In the run-up to the vote, several hundred individual letter-writers worldwide faxed prime ministers personally with expressions of gratitude, and encouraged them to withstand any coercion by the nuclear states. In one instance, a South Pacific representative to the

UN who had received middle-level instructions to abstain was shown a letter from his prime minister replying to a WCP correspondent which stated that his government's support for the resolution would stand. On the basis of this the representative not only voted in favour but also spoke, encouraging other countries to support this resolution.

Resolutions adopted by the First Committee are normally confirmed by the General Assembly in a final plenary session, without any noticeable change in votes. However, a UK representative told Ware that NATO intended to 'kill' the resolution. The WCP launched a new faxing campaign, adjusted to capitals of supportive states which had abstained or not voted. In the plenary session on 15 December 1994, there was an attempt to pass a resolution calling for 'no action' and another trying to remove the word 'urgently', but both were defeated. Eventually, the resolution was adopted by 78 votes to 43, with 38 abstentions and 25 not voting, including China. William Epstein, a distinguished disarmament adviser at the UN, described it as 'the most exciting night in the UN for thirty years'.

Because of the word 'urgently', the World Court received the Assembly resolution within a few days. On 2 February 1995, the court called for new written submissions by June 1995, and written comments on other states' submissions by September 1995. Eight of the 28 submissions made were from states which had not responded to the WHO case. The court then decided to consider the WHO and General Assembly questions separately but simultaneously, with oral presentations, in The Hague during November.

Oral proceedings on advisory opinions: 1995

Before the court's public hearings began on 30 October 1995, another citizen delegation presented nearly 4 million more declarations, over 3 million of them from Japan. A team from IALANA offered on-the-spot legal advice to supportive government deputations. The hearings opened with WHO's legal counsel, who acknowledged that it was a 'delicate task' to represent a 'neutral' position. There was no consensus among the 190 member states and sometimes their views were 'diametrically opposed' on this issue.[14]

For the first time citizen witnesses addressed the court and confronted the judges with the horrific situation of the victims of nuclear weapons. After strong public pressure, the Japanese government allowed the Mayors of Hiroshima and Nagasaki to testify. Their presentation included huge photographs of the bombings, and was accompanied by the muted sobs of the *hibakusha* (surviving victims) present. Then Lijon Eknilang from the Marshall Islands described the intergenerational effects of the 1954 US tests. Women gave birth to 'jellyfish' babies: ... these ... are born with no bones in their bodies and with transparent skin. We can see their brains and hearts beating'. Dressed in white with a wreath of flowers in her hair, she held the court spellbound.

The WCP played an important part in promoting debate on these issues. It provided a forum for the non-nuclear majority of states to challenge the status quo that had threatened to persist with indefinite extension of the Non-Proliferation Treaty; also, governments of the western nuclear states were forced to defend the legality of their nuclear deterrence policies in a court. It also helped to revive public opinion against nuclear weapons after the end of the Cold War had initially eased people's concerns about them. Certain western non-nuclear states, especially NZ and Australia, publicly distanced themselves from their nuclear allies.

Through the WCP, a sound working relationship developed between citizen groups and anti-nuclear governments, which was to prove most valuable in the follow-up to the World Court decision. Most importantly, it led to an historic decision from the court which has had a considerable global impact.

The World Court's decision: 1996

The court lived up to its historic challenge by responsibly addressing the momentous question posed by the General Assembly about the legal status of a threat or use of nuclear weapons... As with other normative projects, such as the abolition of slavery and the repudiation of apartheid, perseverance, struggle and historical circumstance will shape the future with respect to nuclear weaponry, but this process has been pushed forward in a mainly beneficial direction by this milestone decision of the World Court.[15]

Professor Richard Falk

On 8 July 1996, the International Court of Justice delivered its findings on the two questions before it on the legal status of nuclear weapons. The court did not give an advisory opinion on the WHO question, because it judged that the question did not arise within the scope of WHO's responsibilities. It relied, however, upon WHO's evidence of the health and environmental effects of nuclear weapons for both questions. Moreover, WHO's request had prepared the ground for the broader and deeper General Assembly question.

On the latter question, it gave a 34-page main advisory opinion followed by over 200 pages of individual statements and dissenting opinions by the 14 judges (one died just before the oral proceedings began).

In a crucial subparagraph, the court decided that 'a threat or use of nuclear weapons would generally be contrary to the rules of international law applicable in armed conflict, and in particular the principles and rules of humanitarian law'. In doing so, it confirmed that the Nuremberg Principles apply to nuclear weapons.

It added a caveat:

However, in view of the current state of international law, and of the elements of fact at its disposal, the court cannot conclude definitively whether the threat or use of nuclear weapons would be lawful or unlawful in an extreme circumstance of self-defence, in which the very survival of a state would be at stake.

Nonetheless, even in such an extreme case, threat or use must comply with the principles and rules of humanitarian law. The court also treated threat and use as a single, indivisible concept.

Finally, the judges unanimously agreed that:

there exists an obligation to pursue in good faith and bring to a conclusion negotiations leading to nuclear disarmament in all its aspects under strict and effective international control.

For such an historic event, media coverage in western Europe and North America was suspiciously sparse, superficial and, at times, inaccurate. However, in NZ and Australia the event was reported extensively, reflecting the level of public interest. The positive responses from the two countries which Harold Evans had approached a decade earlier was in marked contrast to their opposition to the case until 1995. Australia's Foreign Minister Gareth Evans claimed the opinion would 'drive Australia's push to eliminate the world's nuclear arsenal' and 'help very much the role of the Canberra Commission'.[16] NZ's Prime Minister Bolger hailed it as a 'tremendous victory ... a watershed decision ... (which) vindicated the anti-nuclear crusade'.[17]

The advisory opinion has become an extremely useful tool for both governments and the peace movement. Following the decision, the UN General Assembly adopted a resolution calling for its implementation through the immediate commencement of negotiations leading to the conclusion of a Nuclear Weapons Convention (NWC), that is to say an internationally-verified agreement on the abolition of nuclear weapons. The European Parliament followed with a similar resolution in 1997. A model NWC was subsequently drafted by peace movement experts and has been published and circulated by the UN. The model NWC has been considered by a number of governments at the UN Conference on Disarmament, and submitted to the US Congress in a resolution calling for negotiations to achieve an NWC.

In western nuclear and allied states, anti-nuclear activists are using it in high-profile, ingenious civil-obedience campaigns to expose their governments and challenge them to comply with the law. This in turn has helped force debate amongst some NATO states and Japan about how the opinion affects their defence policies. A new coalition of influential middle-power states has referred to the court's decision in a new initiative at foreign minister level calling for the immediate start of serious negotiations to eliminate nuclear weapons and for the implementation of practical steps towards that goal.

Conclusions

The WCP provided the international peace movement with a unique opportunity to work together for a focussed goal with deadlines, using existing networks with access to key decision-makers. It built on earlier campaigns, drawing together many strands of activity from a wide range of countries, which included the perspectives of women and indigenous peoples.

Vigilant citizen groups based at the key nodes of the WHO, the UN General Assembly and the World Court helped to hold decision-makers accountable. The collection of declarations, endorsement by over 700 citizen groups worldwide and an impressive list of prominent supporters helped sympathetic politicians and diplomats withstand pressure from the nuclear states and their allies, and reminded the judges that the eyes of the world were on them. Draft submissions, books and papers prepared by lawyers and doctors were important tools for diplomats in countries where expertise in international law and the medical effects of nuclear weapons was lacking.

Grassroots activists also had a role in the collection of Declarations of Public Conscience, writing to politicians and newspapers, and faxing ambassadors. They frequently elicited responses from decision-makers which were used to apply pressure even in the highly formalized proceedings of the UN. The WCP gave hope to ordinary citizens that an ICJ opinion could succeed in breaking the logjam and inertia surrounding nuclear disarmament, and achieve real change. It also became a conduit for creating a more democratic United Nations, bringing nearer the realization of the original vision expressed in the opening words of the UN Charter: 'We the peoples ... determined to save succeeding generations from the scourge of war ...'.

The World Court opinion has underpinned many recent initiatives by both citizen groups and states calling for nuclear abolition. There has been a succession of authoritative reports, including the Canberra Commission on the Elimination of Nuclear Weapons and statements by 61 former generals and admirals and 117 civilian leaders. Public opinion polls in the United States and the United Kingdom show 87 per cent support for negotiating a Nuclear Weapons Convention and 92 per cent of Canadians and Norwegians and 72 per cent of Belgians want their governments to lead on this. Over 1600 citizen groups supported a Convention being signed by the end of the year 2000. For the first time in decades a growing number of governments are reviewing their policies in light of the World Court opinion, and seriously considering total elimination. There is a sense of urgency amongst citizens and governments as they work together to achieve a new millennium free from the threat of nuclear annihilation.

The World Court Project provided the international anti-nuclear movement with a way of raising the consciousness about the legality of nuclear weapons. Michael Christ describes how:

> We created a new political forum, a new political opportunity which didn't exist before until citizens' groups decided that this was going to happen and we created it out of nothing. It was an idea... it is WE ... it is not just lawyers, the doctors or the Peace Bureau ... it is no one group ... it has been like a thousand points of light.[18]

REFERENCES AND NOTES

1. Dewes, Kate and Robert D. Green (1998), 'The World Court Project: how a citizen network can influence the United Nations', in Ann Fagan Ginger (ed.), *Nuclear Weapons Are Illegal: the historic opinion of the World Court and how it will be enforced*, New York: Apex Press, pp. 473–95.
2. Aotearoa is the Maori name, New Zealand the European. Both are official.
3. Jack, Homer (ed.) (1988), *Albert Schweitzer on Nuclear War and Peace*, Illinois: Brethren Press, pp. 57–67, 96–7; Norman Cousins (1985), *Albert Schweitzer's Mission: Healing and Peace*, New York: Norton, pp. 173–5.
4. Letter from Schweitzer to Pablo Casals in Hans Walter Bahr (ed.) (1992), *Albert Schweitzer, Letters 1905–1965*, New York: Macmillan, pp. 279–80; Pauling, Linus (1958), *No More War!*, New York: Dodd, Mead and Co, pp. 255–67.
5. See Jack, p.182 and Cousins, pp. 213–14, n. 3 above.
6. Geiringer, Erich (1993), 'WHA Resolutions on Arms Control and Cognate Matters before 1992', WCP (NZ) Working Paper, February, 4 pp.
7. WHO Resolution 36.28, 1983.
8. Report of meetings with missions by Dewes and Colin Archer, July 1991.
9. Mothersson, Keith (1992), *From Hiroshima to the Hague*, Geneva: IPB, pp. 143–8.
10. Ibid. For more details of the 1992–93 WHAs, see Dewes, Kate (1998), 'The World Court Project: the evolution and impact of an effective citizens' movement', PhD thesis, Christchurch, pp. 190–235.

11. Schapiro, Mark (1993), 'Mutiny on the Nuclear Bounty', *The Nation*, 27 December .
12. UK Explanation of vote on Draft Resolution A/C.1/49/L.36 'Request for an Advisory Opinion from the ICJ on the Legality of Nuclear Weapons', Agenda Item 62, 18 November 1994.
13. Explanation of vote by France on Agenda Item 62, 18 November 1994.
14. Presentation by Claude-Henri Vignes, Legal Counsel of WHO, to the World Court, 30 October 1995.
15. Falk, Richard (1997), 'Nuclear Weapons, International Law and the World Court: a historic encounter', *The American Journal of International Law* 91 (1) (January).
16. Attwood, Alan (1996), 'Nuclear Arms Ruling Helps to Make World Safer, says Evans', *The Age*, 10 July; 'Australian Win in Fight to Ban Bomb', *West Australian*, 10 July.
17. Rentoul, Michael (1996), 'PM Hails World Court Decision: "tide turns" against N-weapons', *The Press*, 10 July; Simon Kilroy, 'Bolger Welcomes Nuclear Ruling', *The Dominion*, 9 July.
18. Interview with Michael Christ by Kate Dewes, 25 April 1995, New York (see n. 10 above).

Address for correspondence

Disarmament and Security Centre, P O Box 8390, Christchurch, Aotearoa/New Zealand
Tel/Fax: (+64) 3 348 1353; email: kate@chch.planet.org.nz, robwcpuk@chch.planet.org.nz
Website: www.disarmsecure.org

49 CONFLICT MONITORING

JENNIFER LEANING, JONATHAN FINE and RICHARD GARFIELD

During the 1990s 30 or more armed conflicts were under way at any one time. Under peaceful conditions, underdevelopment, natural disasters and social disintegration, poverty and the maldistribution of resources contribute to catastrophic outcomes. If there has been insufficient study of these phenomena, reports on war have been even more limited. Yet, war, with unbridled disregard for human welfare, multiplies the consequences of peacetime deficits.

Organized centres of learning have done little to promote the systematic monitoring and study of the consequences of conflict. Despite the existence of extraordinary information technology, intelligence and surveillance systems, epidemiological and biological methods and enhanced logistical support, made possible by growing cooperation between non-governmental and public sectors, monitoring to date has focussed almost exclusively on military targets and economic objectives.

What monitoring shows us to date

Warfare took an increasing toll on human populations in the twentieth century. Although fewer countries were engaged in wars and wars tended to be of shorter duration, those wars tended to result in more deaths (Table 49.1). The rise in deaths per year of warfare parallels an increase in both the potential killing power of projectiles and explosives on one hand, and the growing geographic range of the battlefield on the other hand (Table 49.2). The move from the arrow to the crossbow was the first major innovation to increase the range and destructive force of projectile weapons in the modern era. This was followed, in succession, by the development of simple firearms, rifles, machine guns and submachine guns. More bullets discharged, with greater range and accuracy, have led to a rapid multiplication in the number of projectiles that a combatant can hurl per minute. Thus, while the average number of bullets required to

Table 49.1 Estimated average annual military deaths in wars, worldwide, by century

Century	Average annual military deaths	World mid-century population (in millions)	Average annual military deaths per million population
17	9500	500	19.0
18	15 000	800	18.8
19	13 000	1200	10.8
20	458 000	2500	183.2

Source: German Red Cross (1993), 'War and Conflict Monitoring', Humanitares Volkerrecht, Vol. 1.

Table 49.2 Number of military deaths per year of warfare, by war (000s)

War	Duration	Military deaths per year
Thirty Years	1618–48	6
Spanish Succession	1701–13	18
Seven Years	1756–63	20
Revolutionary Wars in Europe	1792–1801	38
Napoleonic Wars	1805–15	51
US Civil War	1861–65	125
World War I	1914–18	2520
World War II	1939–45	5561
Korean	1950–53	666
Vietnam	1965–75	106

Source: German Red Cross (1993), 'War and Conflict Monitoring', Humanitares Volkerrecht, Vol. 1.

produce a casualty has grown rapidly, the number of casualties a solider can produce in a battle has risen even more rapidly. The data on which this information is based come from military information systems. Indeed, almost all information on morbidity and mortality from wars comes from military data bases, the fundamental purpose of which is to improve the killing power of their forces. We argue that more can be learned from these data sources, and independent monitoring oriented toward protecting the lives of those not engaged in combat is now needed.

The size of the field of combat has also expanded rapidly. Until the 1800s warfare among nation states was sited on a field of battle. Mobilization of mass numbers of citizen-soldiers in the Napoleonic wars created larger battle fields, but mobile warfare with rapidly moving positions in large geographic areas was born only later with the mechanization of war transport in the US Civil War. Subsequent development of motorized transport, tanks, submarines, bombing planes and laser-guided missiles created the possibility of a battlefield without geographic limits.

By the early decades of the 20th century, these remarkable technological advances in killing power had created almost limitless capacity for destruction between opposing armies. Indeed, the major limitation in killing capacity in the First and Second World Wars (WWI and II) was the limited capacity to produce and deliver materials of war, not the power to kill.

Personal protective devices, the occupational health equipment of the soldier, have not developed as rapidly as has killing power. Improvements in helmet construction and design, Teflon and flack jackets, and armoured vehicles have shifted the site and type of wounds but only slightly attenuated the rate of wounding. More important in reducing mortality among troops have been advances in medical techniques to reduce damage and speed recovery. Rapid evacuation, fluid expanders, shock attenuation and advanced theatre-definitive surgical treatments are associated with a great reduction in mortality from major groups of injuries. War is indeed credited as the incubator of many major surgical advances. These advances, again, are the product of monitoring morbidity and mortality among troops. But what of noncombatants and civilians? Very little monitoring and even less protection of these groups have been implemented to date.

The growing size of the battlefield and killing power of armaments has had an ominous effect on non-combatant populations. Non-combatant troops not on the front lines of battle and civilian populations located in the growing battle range have increasingly been exposed to risks of war-related morbidity and mortality which, until WW I, occurred only among frontline troops. As war has increasingly engulfed entire populations to produce and distribute the materials required for modern war, they and their economic systems have increasingly become military targets. This generalization of military objectives to the entire population and territory of the enemy characterizes the twentieth century concept of 'total war'. The result of this trend has been a rapid rise in the proportion of all mortality which is experienced by civilian populations, varying from a low of 14 per cent in WW I to a majority of all casualties in the wars of the 1990s.

Mass destruction of the enemy as a tactic of warfare has been attempted repeatedly throughout history. Laying under siege, laying waste to essential goods and services, poisoning water supplies or enslavement of a losing enemy often accompanied warfare in premodern times. Yet over thousands of years, warrior codes and rules of conduct guided most wars so as to limit destruction to economic systems and civilian populations. The production of biological, chemical and nuclear weapons and tactics of indiscriminate bombing with conventional explosives created unprecedented opportunities for mass destruction in the 20th century. Rules to limit the development and use of such tactics and weapons followed, starting with biological and chemical weapons early in the century, including the mid-century treatment of prisoners and people in occupied territories and limited access to nuclear weapons, landmines and blinding laser weapons late in the century. These rules, however, applied effectively only to nation states and multi-state coalitions interested and capable of asserting authority over combatants in their territories. With the end of the Cold War, some areas formerly controlled by nation states have devolved to independent or chaotic administration. Such areas no longer need to be affluent or well-organized to secure weapons of mass destruction. Landmines and some chemical and biological weapons, for example, can be secured in even the poorest parts of the world. The breakdown of nation states makes monitoring both more difficult and more important.

Problems with existing monitoring

Rapid and reliable indicators of health and well-being could improve relief efforts. Such indicators run a gamut from rumours (e.g. the Holocaust) to the calculation of attributable death rates from specific extra-legal causes (such as the effects of the embargo against Iraq). Yet the availability of information for emergency public-health assessment is usually impeded by the very events and circumstances whose impact is being assessed. Public health data lend an air of objectivity and legitimacy to the public arena. Such data are thus also often misused as a propaganda vehicle, as various political actors use the numbers to their perceived advantage.

The systems to collect routine population data are easily disrupted by violent events. Refugee movements can rapidly modify a population's demographic patterns and significantly alter denominators, while case registration of violence-related morbidity may occur across another border. These shifts make quantitative interpretation of incidence data problematic, unless special local studies or adjustments are made. Further, poor prior-reporting capacity in traditional morbidity/mortality outcome indicators is commonplace in much of the developing world. Where the adverse effects of conflict are indirect or diffused, as in refugee displacement or the effect of embargoes, there are the additional complications of determining the chain of events linking proximal and distal causes. The governmental apparatus responsible for collecting such data may be dismantled, abandoned or destroyed, cutting off information altogether.

Intelligence estimates of the consequences of wars are not generally made public. Confusion over casualty counts during the Vietnam War, following the 1989 invasion of Panama by the USA, in the Gulf and Balkan conflicts and in the Rwandan and Congo genocides raises concern over the lack of objectivity. Parties to conflict, whether governments, insurgents, or their allies, are important, but unreliable, sources of information on casualties and violations of standards for the protection of combatants and non-combatants.

Who monitors?

Systematic and sustained international monitoring of human rights abuses in situations of conflict continues to be beyond the capacity, and, until recently, the mandate, of existing international or non-governmental organization.[1] However, almost from their inception, some organizations within the human rights community, including Amnesty International (AI), Human Rights Watch (HRW) and Physicians for Human Rights (PHR) have dealt with violations of humanitarian law and the human and medical consequences of domestic and international conflicts.

Human Rights Watch and Amnesty International have taken steps to formalize and expand their work in situations of conflict. In 1993, HRW established The Arms Project to trace weapons manufacture, transfers and the effects of a variety of weapon systems. In 1995, AI broadened its mandate to include monitoring some of the indiscriminate consequences of armed conflict. PHR also expanded its commitment to forensic investigations in conflict zones, providing teams of specialists for the United Nations and the Hague Tribunal to document genocidal actions in the former Yugoslavia, Rwanda and Congo.

Reports from these international human rights organizations are of historic importance. Yet most of this reporting is improvised, intermittent and has dealt only with selected, though notable, aspects of conflicts. These include the indiscriminate use of force against civilians, casualty estimates, violations of the Geneva conventions and the use of chemical weapons. In some cases, field investigations have been made only after conflicts have either gone on for years or been terminated. Most aspects of most of the conflicts in the world today go unmonitored.

Landmines have received greater attention than most other weapon-systems effects, following a 1989 investigation and report on landmines in Cambodia by HRW and PHR. These two organizations, together with Medico International and the Vietnam Veterans of America Foundation, established the International Campaign to Ban Landmines. The latter, coordinated by the Vietnam Veterans foundation, has generated extensive documentation of the human and ecological consequences of landmines.

The International Committee of the Red Cross (ICRC) has led by formulating standards and proposals to restrict the use of weapons likely to cause unnecessary suffering in war or other situations of conflict. The Stockholm Peace Research Institute (SIPRI), along with several other research groups, have similarly carried out authoritative studies on weapon systems and their effects.

Media are essential elements in monitoring conflicts, but few are reported on and coverage has become increasingly superficial. The increased costs of maintaining correspondents in the field and the shift from global to regional and local armed hostilities have also discouraged coverage. Little reporting is done on the destruction of the social and economic infrastructure of societies at war. We learn next to nothing about job loss, inflation, capital flight and other measures of hardship and social disruption such as crime and lawlessness, the loss of educational opportunity and the impact of war on religious and cultural institutions. Mental health assessments among children, orphans, war-wounded and societies at large are rife with speculation. This area in particular is in need of systematic and rigorous study.

Opportunities to protect populations

Experience illustrates that humanitarian assistance and public health intervention can make an enormous difference to the well-being of populations. In Bosnia, access to NATO-supplied emergency food and fuel is estimated to have averted 100,000–200,000 deaths; in Somalia, food distributed during the height of the struggle averted an estimated 300,000 deaths; at Goma, Zaire, emergency food distribution, water supplies, and diarrhoea treatment are estimated to have prevented 150,000 deaths; sanctions against Iraq, on the other hand, are believed to be responsible for more than a three-fold increase in infant mortality. Yet in embargoed Cuba, despite a 45 per cent decline in economic activity and a 70 per cent decline in foreign currency available for health goods, careful distribution and use of essential goods is associated with a further decline in the already low rate of infant mortality. As was learned in Europe during WW I and II, material deprivation can be compensated for at the social level to maintain collective survival.

Recommendations for better monitoring

Recent wars in Rwanda and the former Yugoslavia produced massive increases in mortality rates for both combatant and non-combatant populations. Low-intensity conflicts in North Ireland or Beirut generated relatively small increases in mortality rates yet had a pervasive effect on the life of the entire nation. Mortality data thus have to be supplemented with appropriate indicators of morbidity in much larger populations. Many important events have psychological, social and physical effects which manifest themselves only later (e.g. rape in Bosnia, radiation in Hiroshima, amputations resulting from mine explosions in Cambodia). For those affected the impact must be measured for decades.

Innovations to improve monitoring

The collection of monitoring data in the midst of social disaster, while difficult, is often possible. Approaches include:

- taking convenience samples;
- collecting qualitative information from witnesses or survivors;
- combining data from all sides of a conflict, using both official and non-official sources;
- estimating indicator values by analogy with other disasters.

Measures of access to essential goods are also needed. These include essential medicines, minimal calorie levels, shelter and physical security. As essential goods become scarce, indicators of the relative equity in their distribution become increasingly important. Innovative approaches to the collection of such data are needed. Recent efforts include cluster samples, sentinel sites, data on goods shipped and market price surveys.

Existing survey instruments are of limited utility in monitoring armed conflicts. Most studies are handicapped by a lack of established and relevant protocols, questionnaires and field-tools suitable to conflict situations. The major exception is the research led by the Atomic Bomb Casualty Commission.

The kind of survey work undertaken in the instances cited above is affected by the nature of hostilities, the time and resources available for the study, but equally by the vision and technical skill of those responsible. The methods employed in each of these studies, and those enumerated elsewhere, merit careful review and analysis. The main point here is that for a variety of reasons relatively little attention has been given to the methodology of the study of conflicts.

Underlying all the technical limitations has been a lack of government and institutional interest in assuring careful documentation. Understandably, innovations in mediation and conflict prevention have attracted greater interest. But reliable information will be essential to improve the effectiveness of the great public campaigns to end conflicts, limit inhumane weapon systems, stop indiscriminate weapon use, help heal devastated societies and bring war criminals to justice.

Future direction

Systematic and sustained monitoring of conflicts is an urgent, humanitarian task. To achieve this goal, six fundamental components are needed:

- objectivity and impartiality in research, analysis and reporting;
- freestanding monitoring organizations, independent of governments and insurgents;
- the development of new assessment methodologies;
- new approaches to publicizing study results;
- facilities to train conflict-monitoring specialists; and
- resources adequate to the task of sustained and systematic monitoring of conflicts.

We will look briefly at each of these issues:

Objectivity and impartiality in research, analysis and reporting. For over a generation, the international human rights community has demonstrated the power, and efficacy, of independent monitoring. The global press has relied extensively on the findings of the leading groups, precisely because they have demonstrated that objectivity and impartiality are non-negotiable, fundamental attributes in their pursuit of violations of internationally guaranteed rights. These principles are the foundation on which future conflict monitoring must be based.

Freestanding, monitoring organizations, independent of governments and insurgents. Independent monitoring organizations are another essential prerequisite in the study of human rights violations. By and large, international human-rights organizations have proved their integrity and are widely accepted as the best source of reliable information and advocacy. Their early efforts in monitoring international and civil conflicts need to be expanded. Alone, however, these bodies are not able to provide for global monitoring. A freestanding international, non-governmental organization dedicated exclusively to conflict monitoring is required. In 1993, a group of international legal and human rights specialists met in Germany to study this need. The resulting Bochum Declaration calls for the creation of such an institution, War Witness International. We applaud this declaration as an historic document speaking to this need.

One or more institutions to develop new methodologies for use in situations of conflict. Clearly, the methods of monitoring armed conflicts will come from diverse sources, for example medical schools, schools of public health and veterinary medicine, departments of epidemiology and forensic sciences but also from other research institutes, public and private, such as the centres for disease control, military academies, the intelligence community and human-rights NGOs. A freestanding international NGO, such as War

Witness International, would play a large role in the development of new methodologies and will need a research division for this purpose.

New approaches to publicizing study results. No monitoring will accomplish much unless the institutional structure is in place to publicize and campaign against the worst violations of human rights and humanitarian law. Therefore, equal emphasis will have to be placed on building the institutional components to carry out global campaigns to inform, and mobilize, public opinion with the findings of the monitoring bodies.

Facilities to train conflict-monitoring specialists. The experience of recent decades illuminates a crucial deficit: a cadre of specialists trained for fact-finding in conflict situations. Little attention has been paid to this need. International human-rights NGOs have had to make do with highly-motivated and dedicated individuals, mostly trained on the job. With the possible exception of legal studies departments, universities have not to date recognized, nor been enlisted in, the training of human-rights and conflict investigators. This task logically will go hand in hand with the development of new methodologies and, therefore, it makes sense to see these functions sited at institutions with these dual facilities.

Resources adequate to the task of sustained and systematic monitoring of conflicts. The need for systematic, global conflict monitoring is self-evident. Early estimates of the costs of maintaining an international conflict-monitoring NGO, such as War Witness International, are US\$22–\$30 million a year. Though this sum is minuscule compared to the investment by nations in armaments, no consortium of funders is yet committed to this initiative.

Four operational considerations and immediate steps to be taken:

Observance of Geneva conventions. Irregular armed forces are generally ignorant of the Geneva conventions. Since their tactics often involve the deliberate targeting of civilians, they may not be interested in learning about these rules and thus efforts aimed simply at after-the-fact notification of guidelines inhering in the conventions are probably relatively useless. The consequences of this wanton ignorance are many and far-reaching: hospitals are not free from marauding soldiers; guns may be trained on doctors forcing improper treatment decisions; emergency ambulance transport is blocked; and hospitals and clinics are deliberately attacked.

The following are suggestions for improvement:

(1) Support campaigns throughout the world to teach all levels of society (children and adults, civilians as well as military) the essential values and actions described in the Geneva conventions. The ICRC is attempting to launch such efforts but needs more resources and other partners in order to do so.

(2) Institutionalize and generalize from the excellent example of what happened (albeit late in the war) in Mogadishu, when from December 1991 to January 1992 the relief agencies in the city banded together and gained the agreement from all warring

factions to ban the presence of armed soldiers within all hospital compounds. The groups involved were: MSF, ICRC, Save the Children and the International Medical Corps. By mid-January, incursions into the hospitals had effectively ceased and signs were posted on all entry gates and walls leading into all the hospital compounds.

Techniques for counting large and rapidly moving populations. We do not know how to estimate reliably or count in close approximation when huge numbers of people move quickly through forested areas or sweep across narrow border crossings. This inability then leads to many other deficiencies, particularly in assessing the food and water requirements of the population, and also contributes to serious political wrangling, for example, the UN vs US version of numbers of Rwandan Hutu refugees still unaccounted for in Congo. There are indications that the US military, possibly among others, has infrared and satellite technology that would permit good estimation of numbers. The following are suggestions for improvement:

(1) Identify and adopt best practices in military surveillance for counting large numbers of people in transit.
(2) To the extent the technology permits or could be improved upon to permit, use it to distinguish between men and women, and adults and children.

Procedures for establishment of refugee camps. In several recent complex emergencies vast refugee populations have encamped in crowded camps in unsuitable locations. The 1951 Convention on Refugees specifies distance for these camps from international borders but says nothing about environmental viability. We need to be anticipating that these large numbers of people forced into motion by widespread violence and human rights abuses will stay away from their country of origin for an indefinite, and probably indefinitely long, period of time. The first requirement of the camps, therefore, is that they are able to provide adequate water supplies and have the potential for sanitation arrangements that will sustain a given population and not contribute to its rapid slide into disease. (Goma is a negative case in point.) The following are suggestions for improvement:

(1) At the outbreak of a crisis likely to lead to a refugee exodus, send a team consisting of a civil engineer, water and sanitation specialist, agronomist and public-health expert, along with UNHCR officials and local leaders from the host areas to identify where suitable refugee camps might be sited. If and when the occasion arises, UNHCR and the host country should follow the recommendations of this team and direct the refugees to the designated sites.
(2) A similar team could be convened at the regional level, charged with the task of developing overall anticipatory guidance to the UN and the states of the region regarding suitable potential sites for refugee settlement and border areas for refugee transit in the event of an outbreak of crisis in the region. These site determinations would be based entirely on geography and environment, building on what we know about likely terrain for population passage and suitable terrain for population encampment. This identification could be accomplished without great risk of political embarrassment or injury if it were presented as a precautionary planning

move, a disaster plan, addressing all possible sites of exit, entry and settlement. The odds are that within the regions of Africa virtually all countries, under one scenario or another, could serve as either a host or originating country, and virtually all borders would see themselves crossed in either an entry or exit mode.

Build in support and training for local monitors. The following is a suggestion for improvement:

Have every medical and health team build in a training component for local staff and expand the staffing ratio for those deployed to include a senior person whose main responsibility will be the training and integration of local resources.

Conclusions

It is time to assess the effects of the technologies and strategies of warfare on civilians. Such monitoring should lead to the establishment of new standards for humanitarian intervention, specification of legitimate targets and methods for protecting the general population. Recent steps in this direction include the United Nations Convention on the Rights of Children (1992), signed by more countries than any previous human-rights convention. A subsequent 1996 UN study, *The Impact of Armed Conflict on Children*, extends the protection of civilians, recommending the prohibition of military conscription among those under 18, the banning of landmines, the establishment of non-militarized zones and assessment of the likely impact of economic embargoes on non-combatants.

It is becoming possible to identify crimes against humanity as they occur, begin prosecution for war crimes while the fighting continues and mobilize emergency responses to support survivors. The development of a new, blinding laser-weapons system was stopped in 1995 prior to field dissemination. Public-health assessments facilitated the identification of sex crimes as prosecutable in international courts. These advances must be recognized and celebrated if we are to prevent such horrors in the future.

REFERENCES

1. German Red Cross (1993), 'War and Conflict Monitoring', *Humanitares Volkerrecht*, Vol. 1.

Address for correspondence
Richard Garfield RN DrPH, Professor of Clinical International Nursing, Columbia University, 617 West 168th Street, New York, NY 10032
Tel: 212-305-3248; Fax: 212-305-6937

50 GLOBALIZATION
Expanded Opportunities to Prevent Regional and Global Conflict through Negotiation, Mediation and Preventive Diplomacy

WILLIAM W. MONNING

The art and science of principled negotiation and mediation practice as applied to regional and global conflicts in the past two decades has been instrumental in ending and averting violence. The use of third-party mediators and track-two negotiations to break through impasse and prevent or resolve violent conflict is becoming more accepted internationally (e.g. the Camp David Agreement, the Oslo Accord on the Middle East, and the Dayton Accord). The role of physicians, health-care workers and non-governmental organizations has been instrumental in promoting non-violent conflict resolution. With economic globalization and the emergence of regional and global trade agreements, non-traditional fora for the use of alternative dispute resolution (negotiation, mediation and arbitration) can be employed to address attendant social, environmental and economic disputes impacting trade and to address related core issues that can lead to violent conflict. Expanded training in principled negotiation and mediation techniques combined with a campaign to popularize the acceptance of mediation and preventive diplomacy before the resort to violence can be actively promoted by physicians, health-care workers and non-governmental organizations.

> The best general is the one who never fights
>
> Sun Tzu

Overview

Principled negotiation and mediation practice has been refined as an art and science in the past two decades. The role of third-party mediators and second-track or parallel negotiations has resulted in the resolution of regional conflicts and the diminution of the threat of nuclear war. Expanded forums for negotiation, mediation and arbitration (alternative dispute resolution – ADR) offer new avenues for governments, non-governmental organizations (NGOs) and citizen diplomats (e.g., physicians and health workers) to promote non-violent conflict resolution as an acceptable process preferred to violence and war.

Unfortunately, another common thread to the successful negotiation and mediation scenarios of the past two decades is that they only succeeded after protracted warfare, conflict or arms proliferation. The challenge of globalization is to promote and establish the acceptance of alternative dispute resolution methods as necessary and desirable alternatives to violence, conflict or war.

Chapter 50 is designed to identify the evolution of negotiated and mediated dispute resolution; recognize the role of NGOs, physicians and citizen diplomats in the process; and explore the need and opportunity for expanded training, promotion and acceptance of ADR techniques in this new era of globalization.

Definition of terms

Negotiation is any bilateral or multilateral communication among parties which seek to protect and advance the interests of their constituencies through discourse and dialogue with their adversaries or allies.

Mediation is the practice of relying upon a non-party to a particular negotiation or conflict to facilitate or help the parties reach a mutually-agreeable resolution. A mediator usually does not have decisionmaking authority and cannot impose her/his will on the parties. Mediation is usually a voluntary (non-binding), confidential process that allows the parties to abandon negotiation at any time to pursue other remedies.[1]

Arbitration is a process used by parties where decisionmaking authority is vested in a neutral arbitrator(s) by agreement of the parties (often contractual or by treaty agreement). The arbitration process: is more formal than mediation; can include the presentation of witnesses and evidence; and the decision rendered is most often binding on the parties.

Alternative Dispute Resolution (ADR) is the use of negotiation, mediation and/or arbitration to resolve conflict as opposed to the use of formal litigation which involves the utilization of court systems, trials and the decisionmaking authority of a judge or jury.

Second-track or parallel negotiation or mediation involves the development of a framework for non-principals (non-parties) to a dispute who are able to explore options for resolution in a manner that is not binding on the participants' government, business or other interest group. It provides a free opportunity to develop options that may eventually influence principal parties with decisionmaking authority.[2]

Preventive diplomacy and conflict intervention involve the assertion of third parties, United Nations representatives or others in anticipation of the escalation of a local, regional or international dispute with the intention of promoting peaceful conflict resolution before the outbreak of hostilities.

Principled negotiation and third-party mediation

Throughout human history, people have negotiated territorial rights, commercial agreements and the terms and conditions of ceasefires, treaties and peace accords to end war.

During the 1970s and 1980s, a virtual revolution took place in the study and application of the art and science of principled negotiation and mediation practice.

The advent of interest-based negotiation resulted in adversaries and partners learning to look beyond traditional positional bargaining to create a joint problem-solving atmosphere between and among parties. Rather than force a contest of wills, negotiators work to build constructive frameworks for principled dialogue which place a high premium on the participants' ability to brainstorm multiple options and to rely on fair and objective standards as criteria in formulating durable agreements. More traditional forms of negotiation resulted in a contest of wills rooted in emotionally-charged positional bargaining that often ended in stalemate and/or a resort to violence.[3]

In areas of violent regional conflict, international arms negotiations and high-risk hostage situations, principled negotiators and mediators have been able to use new skills and techniques in interest-based negotiations to bring opposing parties to the bargaining table. Consider the breakthroughs that were made possible by the use of principled negotiation and mediation in the following conflicts:

- Camp David Peace Agreement between Israel and Egypt with the US serving as mediator (1978);
- Oslo Declaration of Principles between Israel and the PLO, facilitated by third-party mediation of second-track negotiations (1993);
- SALT and START treaty agreements between the US and the USSR (1978–92);
- INF Treaty including the US, NATO and former Soviet Union (1987);
- Non-proliferation (NPT) and Comprehensive Test Ban (CTBT) treaties, both involving multinational parties with diverse interests and power (1963–1996);
- Zimbabwe: former Rhodesian government and ZAPU/ZANU with the British government as mediator (1979);[4]
- Mozambique: government and Renamo with mediation by the United Nations, Italy, Portugal, Zimbabwe, Botswana, South Africa and the Community of Sant' Egidio (religious) (1975–92);[5]
- South Africa: between former de Klerk government, Nelson Mandela and the African National Congress (ANC) (1991–93);
- El Salvador: Faribundo Marti National Liberation (FMLN) and Salvadoran government with the Secretary-General of the United Nations as third-party mediator (1992);
- Guatemala: Guatemalan government and Unidad Revolucionaria Nacional Guatemala (URNG) with the United Nations as third-party mediator (1996);
- Chiapas, Mexico: Zapatista National Liberation Army (EZLN) and the Mexican government with Bishop Ruiz as mediator (from 1994);
- Korean Peninsula: the US, China, North and South Korea with former US President Carter as non-official mediator; the US government, and the International Atomic Energy Agency (from 1994); and
- Bosnia-Herzogovina: Dayton, Ohio, Accord with the US and United Nations as mediators (1995).

There are other examples too numerous to list in this chapter. The common thread represented throughout these high-profile negotiations is the role of third-party mediation or effective bilateral and multilateral negotiators working to bring parties together to achieve peace where violence once prevailed, or to reduce the threat and risk of mass destruction as in the case of the nuclear arms agreements.

While these examples all represent positive outcomes or evolving resolutions of past conflict made possible by persistent negotiators and mediators, the challenge of the post Cold War era is to incorporate the use of alternative dispute resolution or preventive diplomacy before the outbreak of hostilities or the expenditure of precious resources on weapons proliferation.

The role of physicians, health workers and NGOs

The previous examples of successful mediation and conflict resolution involved primarily governmental interests, insurgent non-governmental parties and official diplomatic or religious-based mediators. What role, if any, can non-governmental, medical, health-worker or other peace-oriented individuals and organizations play in the negotiation and mediation of regional and international disputes? A review of the influence of the International Physicians for the Prevention of Nuclear War (IPPNW) and other NGOs demonstrates the influence that can be exercised in second-track or parallel negotiations and upon the conduct of principal governmental and official parties to conflict and negotiations.

The World Court Decision

One of the most impressive examples of the role of IPPNW working in concert with other international and national organizations to influence public policy and negotiations is represented by the 1996 declaration of the International Court of Justice (the World Court) at The Hague which condemned the first use of nuclear weapons as illegal under international law. (This case is discussed fully in Chapter 48.)

While not a direct party to the proceedings, IPPNW was able to exercise its influence in negotiations with the World Health Organization (WHO) and with member states to bring the case to hearing and to a decision. IPPNW also participated in a common campaign with other NGOs, including the International Alliance of Lawyers Against Nuclear Arms (IALANA).

The development of this international campaign necessitated inter- and intra-organizational negotiations to achieve a common strategy and tactics in the promotion of the World Court Project. For this model to be replicated in future, organizational representatives will have to be selected on the basis of their negotiating skills and experience. Many a noble effort has failed because of internal organizational divisiveness, conflict and the inability of group leaders to build consensus.

The Prato Declaration

In October 1990, on the eve of the Gulf War, IPPNW convened a regional conference in Prato, Italy to focus on the threat presented by the deployment of nuclear weapons and other weapons of mass destruction in the Mediterranean and the Middle East regions.

Physician and other organizational members of IPPNW affiliates in 13 countries were able to negotiate a second-track, non-governmental Declaration and Appeal calling for the establishment of a nuclear weapons' free zone in the Middle East region including: a ban on all weapons of mass destruction; respect for national sovereignty; and recognition of the legitimacy of the State of Israel, and the right of Palestine to achieve statehood. The Prato Declaration was delivered to the ambassadors at the US, Soviet and Iraqi embassies in Rome with copies delivered to the Israeli and other governments in the region.

The negotiation and mediation process which led to the achievement of the Prato Declaration mirrored the concerns, tensions and barriers to peace in the Middle East region. The ability and courage of physician members to identify common interests and to ignore the legal prohibitions of their home governments against consorting with the enemy made the negotiation of the Prato Declaration possible.

Although symbolic in nature, the Prato Declaration served to galvanize attention to the inherent risks of nuclear weapons use in the region and to approximate the potential medical and environmental damage that weapons of mass destruction might inflict. National and international reports on the Prato Declaration as news served, in some measure, to accommodate and legitimize subsequent peace accords in the area.

Among the important contributions of second-track or parallel negotiations are: testing public reaction to prospective terms and conditions of official agreements; sensitizing the public and official entities to the possibility of finding common ground; and introducing specific options to the official negotiators.

The Tapachula, Mexico declaration

In July 1989, IPPNW members from the US, Mexico, the Caribbean and Central and South America convened in Tapachula (Chiapas) Mexico to negotiate a model resolution addressing the convergence among nuclear weapons proliferation, the proliferation of conventional weapons, underdevelopment and drug trafficking. Under the leadership of Dr Manuel Velasco Suarez (Mexico), protracted negotiations resulted in the issuing of a public and widely-publicized declaration that was delivered to the heads of state of each national affiliate represented.

The negotiations among IPNNW affiliates were difficult and at times strained as a drafting committee composed of representatives of all affiliates worked through the night. But the final declaration served to strengthen the regional identity of the Mezo-American affiliates and increased IPPNW's regional and international visibility and credibilty. The Tapachula Declaration also served to project the voice and principles of IPPNW as part of the legitimate and continuing national and regional discourse on issues of war and peace.

The United Nations' Partial Test Ban Treaty Amendment Conference (1990–91)

On the eve of the Gulf War, an unprecedented campaign of citizen diplomacy and negoti-ations between NGOs and official state representatives to the United Nations took place in New York City. The Parliamentarians for Global Action (PGA) and IPPNW worked with Greenpeace International/USA, the US Citizens Campaign for a CTB, the Nevada–Semipalatinsk Movement and other grassroots and NGO organizations in an effort to convert the 1963 Partial Test Ban Treaty to a Comprehensive Test Ban Treaty (CTBT).[6]

The campaign seized on the language of the original treaty that empowered a majority of its signers to trigger an amendment conference to convert the partial treaty to a CTBT. Between 1963 and 1991, more than 1919 nuclear weapons tests were detonated by six nations.

The movement was driven by focussed advocacy and protracted negotiations with the official party representatives of more than 100 nations and other members of the UN Security Council. The final vote on the amendment proposal reflected a tremendous mobilization of support if not a total victory. The governments of the United States and the UK were isolated as the sole dissenting votes (exercising their veto power as members of the Security Council); 22 countries abstained from the vote, and 74 nations voted in favour of the proposed amendment.[7]

The potential for broad media coverage of the Amendment Conference was eclipsed by the commencement of the US and Allied forces' bombing campaign in Iraq on 16 January 1991. Nonetheless, the importance of the multiparty negotiations and the creation of the peaceful forum to register international support for a CTBT exerted a positive influence on the extension of the Non-Proliferation Treaty (NPT) in 1995 and the 1996 Comprehensive Test Ban Treaty (CTBT).

These examples of parallel negotiations and focussed advocacy campaigns each involved multiparty talks led by physicians through IPPNW and affiliate organizations, other NGOs and grassroots activists. The NGOs made significant contributions to government decisionmaking, the shaping of public opinion and the empowerment of citizens in the exercise of their democratic rights.

Another critical component of these campaigns was the ability of the organizational representatives to negotiate consensus among multiple interests, positions and agendas. In fact, the application of principled negotiation techniques and effective mediation skills is critical to building consensus in support of durable public and international campaigns.

In a broad sense these NGO and citizen initiatives constitute a form of preventive diplomacy or early intervention, designed to avert a nuclear catastrophe by the achievement of interim declarations, agreements and treaties leading to the ultimate abolition or neutralization of nuclear weapons and other weapons of mass destruction.

Globalization and new fora for alternative dispute resolution

Expanded utilization of ADR fora

Globalization has resulted in the creation of new international organizations and trade agreements that include new fora for alternative dispute resolution including expanded access to mediation and arbitration mechanisms. To ensure that these new ADR mechanisms can be extended to prevent regional and global conflict, the fora must not be limited to the resolution of narrowly-defined commercial disputes.

The world has entered an era of profound political, social and economic transformation. The 1990s marked the end of 45 years of ideological and military confrontation between the former Soviet Union and the west. This security transition coincided with an equally dramatic ideological and economic shift in North–South relations. The world is moving from trade policies of import substitution to export-driven growth based on open market principles.

Global trade, investment, technology, information and finance increasingly constitute the economic facts of life, as well as the building blocks for future international security. All countries acknowledge the need to forge a world trading system based on economic interdependence, and a widely-shared vision of broad participation, diffusion of benefits and international security.

There has been a veritable proliferation of global and regional trade agreements: the World Trade Organization (WTO), European Union (EU), North Atlantic Free Trade Association (NAFTA), Asia–Pacific Economic Cooperation (APEC), Free Trade Agreement of the Americas (FTAA), among many others. These new international organizations and rules serve to stabilize economic and political relations among states and at the same time address the global dimensions of economic activity.

International commercial diplomacy is a key in the transition to global interdependence. It can assist the former Soviet states in their struggles to become market economies, embracing more pluralistic and democratic forms of governance. Trade diplomacy is required to help China, the world's remaining communist power, accommodate its internal economic structure to global market forces.

The benefits of expanded economic interdependence are not as automatic or as certain as some might wish. The great promise of globalization is a rising tide of economic prosperity not only in the advanced industrial states but ever more deeply in the developing world. There is abundant evidence from East Asia to China, from the Middle East to the Americas that the promise of global economic expansion is far from empty.

There are challenges as well. Economic and political liberalization has left questions of social justice, ethnic and religious tensions, labour conditions and environmental protection to national authorities. They face conflicts arising from the relationship of their own domestic policies to established norms and rules required for participation in the emerging international system of trade and investment. Some may opt for lower standards to increase competitiveness.

This can result in environmental degradation, substandard working conditions, wage competition with low-wage jurisdictions, and increasing wage disparity, both within and among countries. Unless these inequities and imbalances are adequately understood and continuously addressed through constructive negotiating frameworks, the promise of increased peace and security may be undermined by the resultant antagonisms that may lead to regional and global conflict.[8]

Under the WTO's Dispute Settlement Body developed under the General Agreement on Tariffs and Trade (GATT), under NAFTA's Chapter 20 and through other regional trade agreements, ADR methods are both encouraged and required. With the expansion of these trade agreements to include previously underdeveloped or newly-trading nations, the opportunity arises for the education and training of governmental, business and academic leaders on the basic principles of ADR.[9]

To take full advantage of these new dispute-resolution forums, governmental, commercial, and NGO representatives must be exposed to the efficacy of ADR fora and the requisite negotiation, mediation and arbitration training necessary to function as effective international negotiators. As ADR is established as a preferred mechanism for dispute resolution and settlement, government and other leaders will be better-equipped to resolve conflicts whether of a commercial or non-commercial nature using the skills and techniques popularized by the expansion of ADR as a beneficial consequence of globalization.

Cross-cultural sensitization

In cross-cultural and multilingual negotiation and mediation settings, the parties must be well-versed in the history, culture, politics and negotiating style of their adversaries and negotiating partners. An effective negotiator or mediator in one culture may not be so in another cultural environment.[10]

Similarly, the role of qualified interpreters can be decisive in a negotiation and the negotiator's ability adequately to prepare the interpreters for the technical, historical or issue-specific language that may be used is critical. Monitoring the quality of interpretation is an important function of responsible and effective negotiators.

Students of international negotiation and diplomacy must consider the impact on the process, momentum and outcomes of fora dependent on simultaneous or consecutive interpretation. While larger, official fora (e.g. UN, WHO, WTO) provide highly-trained professional interpreters, smaller bodies that are used by NGOs and other parties may have to rely on interpreters with minimal formal training. A key responsibility of an effective negotiator or mediator is to determine the skill, subject-matter knowledge and accuracy of an interpreter.

Even where a common language is used, if that language is not the first language of a party to the negotiations the incidence of misunderstanding, confusion or failure is ever present. When possible, negotiators should reduce substantive and interim settlements to writing, in the form of interim agreements that can be reviewed, translated if necessary and brought back to the negotiating table for further refinement.

Globalization is a process that will continue to present new opportunities and serious challenges. Promoting the expanded use of ADR fora, cross-cultural and appropriate language training will enhance prospects for positive outcomes in conflicts where violence or war is all too often an option.

Physicians, health workers, and citizen diplomats as teachers and students

The art and science of negotiation and mediation can be learned.[11] There may be certain personalities who are more naturally able to play the role of an effective negotiator or mediator, but everyone can learn.

In my experience as an instructor in negotiation and mediation techniques for international students, I have observed that many people have poor negotiating instincts and habits. We either try to please our adversary to the detriment of our interests in order to preserve harmony or we try to overpower our adversary through threats, emotional outbursts and the exercise of raw power.

The use of negotiation and mediation simulations is of critical importance in training principled negotiators. A simulation exercise can be based on real negotiation scenarios or hypothetical factual situations. A student cannot incorporate and integrate negotiation skills simply through the reading of theory. As in a martial art or other discipline, a student of negotiation must learn to incorporate the art and science into their tool kit of professional skills. Practice, repetitive drilling, making mistakes and viewing videotaped simulations is how aspiring negotiators and mediators learn to perfect their command of the tools and techniques.[12]

One of the shortcomings of international diplomacy has been the selection of lead negotiators who may have years of service in representing a governmental bureaucracy but who have received no formal training in principled negotiation or mediation practice. As a result, government and other organizational representatives have learned to negotiate by trial and error or in an on-the-job apprenticeship where mistakes can be costly and failures may lead to war or violence.

The expanded opportunities and profound challenges of globalization require an increased commitment to educate a new breed of diplomat (official, military, NGO or commercial). He/she must be educated in the principles and techniques of principled negotiation and mediation practice and become knowledgeable about ADR options. Such training will ensure a greater likelihood that emergent disputes will be managed proactively, constructively and without the resort to violence.[13]

Conclusion

The historic capacity of the international physicians' movement and citizen diplomats positively to impact and influence governments, military leaders, commercial interests and public opinionmakers can be projected into the next century. A critical measure of success will be a function of our ability to promote the acceptance and use of alternative dispute-resolution systems as essential mechanisms for those in power at the local, regional, national and international levels to avert deadly and destructive conflict.

A worthy prescription for those seeking to end war and promote health would be to introduce principled negotiation, mediation and alternative dispute-resolution training at all levels of education, government, military and commerce so that our human potential to resolve conflict peacefully can be maximized and human suffering, including the resort to war and violence, diminished and eliminated.

REFERENCES

1. Moore, Christopher W. (1996), *The Mediation Process, Practical Strategies for Resolving Conflict*, San Francisco: Jossey-Bass Publishers.
2. Susskind, Lawrence E., Chayes, Abram and Janet Martinez (1996), 'Parallel Informal Negotiation: a new kind of international dialogue', *Negotiation Journal*, Vol. 12, No. 1, New York: Plenum Press (January).
3. Fisher, Roger, Ury, William and Bruce Patton (1991), *Getting To Yes, Negotiating Agreement Without Giving In* (2nd edn), New York: Penguin Books.

4. Rothchild, Donald (1996), 'Successful Mediation: Lord Carrington and the Rhodesian settlement', in Chester A. Crocker, Fen Osler Hampson and Paula Aall (eds), *Managing Global Chaos*, Washington DC: US Institute for Peace Press.

5. Hume, Cameron (1994), *Ending Mozambique's War: the role of mediation and good offices*, Washington DC: US Institute of Peace Press.

6. Schrag, Philip G. (1992), *Global Action: nuclear test ban diplomacy at the end of the Cold War*, San Francisco: Westview Press.

7. Ibid.

8. Monning, William, Keller, William and Geza Feketekuty (1997), 'Commercial Diplomacy and International Negotiations', Monterey Institute of International Studies, Center for Trade and Commercial Diplomacy Video Conference to Mexico, Central and South America and the Caribbean with San Diego State University's International Training Center, 12 June.

9. North American Free Trade Agreement (NAFTA) (1994), Chapter 20, subchapter B, Dispute Settlement.

10. Cohen, Raymond, (1995), *Negotiating Across Cultures: communication obstacles in international diplomacy*, Washington DC: US Institute of Peace Press.

11. Raiffa, Howard (1996), *The Art and Science of Negotiation: how to resolve conflicts and get the best out of bargaining*, Cambridge, MA: The Belknap Press of Harvard University Press; Kremenyuk, Victor (ed.) (1991), *International Negotiation: analysis, approaches, issues*, a publication of the Processes of International Negotiations (PIN) Project, San Francisco: Jossey-Bass Publishers; Fisher, Roger, Kopelman, Elizabeth and Andrea Kupfer Schneider (1994), *Beyond Machiavelli: tools for coping with conflict*, Harvard Negotiation Project, Cambridge: Harvard University Press; and Moore, Christopher, W. (1996), *The Mediation Process*, San Francisco: Jossey-Bass Publishers.

12. Winham, Gilbert R. (1991), 'Simulation for Teaching and Analysis', in Victor Kremenyuk (ed.), *International Negotiation*, Chapter 28, n. 11 above.

13. See n. 8 above.

Address for correspondence
Monterey Institute of International Studies, 425 Van Buren Street, Monterey, California, 93940, USA
Tel: (831) 647-6426; fax: (831)647-6435, email: bmonning@miis.edu

51 | THE ROLE OF INTERNATIONAL ORGANIZATIONS

Does the United Nations still matter?

MERI KOIVUSALO

International organizations work in maintaining peace, negotiating conflicts, responding to humanitarian crises (e.g. human rights violations, refugee crises, health consequences of warfare) and rebuilding of societies. The United Nations (UN) is the main global intergovernmental organization with responsibilities in these areas. In addition to the UN agencies some other organizations, especially humanitarian and relief organizations such as the Red Cross or Red Crescent, can be seen as traditional international actors in war, health and peace issues.

The number and role of humanitarian international organizations increased substantially during the last decades of the 20th century and other agencies also became involved in global activities on war and health. The scope and activities of non-governmental organizations (NGOs) are vastly different in terms of their number, resources and official legitimacy in the global politics of the early 21st century when compared to earlier periods.

In the aftermath of the Cold War the role of military and economic organizations such as the North Atlantic Treaty Organization (NATO) and the Organization of Economic Cooperation and Development (OECD) has been evolving towards a more global outlook in broader fields with significance for areas of health and development. The primary focus of Chapter 51 is on the role of UN bodies in war and health issues at global level and why these are important in spite of the UN's current limited support and resources.

The United Nations

The maintenance of international peace and security was one of the primary purposes for establishing the United Nations (UN), and a central part of its mandate. The traditional role of the UN is involvement in international conflicts through action by the

51.1

The purposes of the UN, as set forth in the Charter, are:

- To maintain international peace and security;

- To develop friendly relations among nations based on respect for the principle of equal rights and self-determination of peoples;

- To cooperate in solving international economic, social, cultural and humanitarian problems and in promoting respect for human rights and fundamental freedoms;

- To be a centre for harmonizing the actions of nations in attaining these common ends.

The United Nations acts in accordance with the following principles:

- It is based on the sovereign equality of all its members;

- All members are to fulfil in good faith their Charter obligations;

- They are to settle their international disputes by peaceful means and without endangering international peace and security, and justice;

- They are to refrain from the threat or use of force against any other state;

- They are to give the United Nations every assistance in any action it takes in accordance with the Charter, and shall not assist states against which the United Nations is taking preventive or enforcement action;

- Nothing in the Charter authorizes the United Nations to intervene in matters which are essentially within the domestic jurisdiction of any state.

Source: United Nations (1998).

Security Council. This basis for action has faced difficulties with the emergence of intra-state ethnic conflicts (Box 51.1).

The UN charter obligates member states to settle their disputes using peaceful means and in such a manner that international peace, security and justice are not endangered. According to the charter they are to refrain from the threat or use of force against any state, and may bring any dispute before the Security Council. The Security Council is the UN organ primarily responsible for maintaining peace and security. Under the UN Charter, member states are obliged to accept and carry out the Council's decisions. The Council is also empowered to enforce its decisions by imposing embargoes and economic sanctions or authorizing the use of force to ensure that mandates are fulfilled; it has also established international criminal tribunals to prosecute those accused of serious violations of international humanitarian laws.

The UN Charter also empowers the General Assembly to 'consider the general principles of cooperation in the maintenance of international peace and security' and 'make recommendations ... to the Member States, the Security Council or to both'. The Assembly provides a forum for finding consensus on difficult issues and the airing of grievances and diplomatic exchanges. The General Assembly considers peace and security issues in the First (Disarmament and International Security) and Fourth (Special Political and Decolonization) committees. Health issues are in principle dealt in the Third Committee (Social, Humanitarian and Cultural). However, health issues in the UN are primarily the responsibility of the special agencies, such as the World Health Organization or the International Labour Organization. These have their own separate assemblies to provide fora for debate on their subject matters.

The UN's role and responsibilities may also be viewed from the point of health concerns. Such an approach would focus attention more on the World Health Organization, the United Nations Children's Fund (UNICEF), the United Nations Development Programme (UNDP) and different immediate relief- and refugee-oriented measures. Chapter 51 examines United Nations organizations briefly in terms of this role in war in part to provide a short introduction to the UN's role in peacemaking, peacekeeping, peacebuilding and peace enforcement.

United Nations, war and peace*

The UN peacemaking activities refer to the use of diplomatic means to persuade parties which are in conflict to negotiate a peaceful settlement of their dispute. In this the Secretary-General has a traditional role in dispatching special envoys or missions for specific tasks, such as fact-finding or negotiation missions. In the use of preventive diplomacy the impartiality of the Secretary-General has been the one of the major assets of the United Nations. Envoys and special representatives of the Secretary-General are engaged in preventive diplomacy and mediation to help to reconcile conflicting parties. In many cases this work is undertaken in close cooperation with other international and regional organizations.

The UN's peacekeeping role was recognized signally in 1988, when the peacekeeping forces were awarded the Nobel Peace Prize. While peacekeeping forces were not specifically envisaged in the UN Charter, their role has expanded. The costs of peace-keeping operations were some US$1.2–1.4 billion in 1996–97. This might seem a large sum, but is effectively less than 0.2 percent of world military spending. Peacekeeping forces are authorized and deployed by the Security Council with the consent of the host government, and usually other parties as well; these may include military and police personnel, together with civilian staff. The soldiers of the forces have weapons, but in most situations can use them only in self-defence. The United Nations has no military force of its own, and member states provide the personnel, equipment and logistics required for operations, on a voluntary basis.

The enforcement measures of the United Nations are laid out in the United Nations Charter, which entitles the Security Council to apply a range of measures from economic sanctions to international military action. The enforcement of economic sanctions is allowed when peace is threatened and diplomatic efforts have failed. Economic sanctions have been applied in a number of situations, against the apartheid regime in South Africa in 1977 and most recently against Iraq, the former Yugoslavia and Libya.

*This part of Chapter 51 in part draws on *Basic Facts about the United Nations* (1998), United Nations Department of Public Information, New York: United Nations.

Military action has been authorized by the United Nations in Iraq (1991), Somalia (1992), Rwanda (1994), Haiti (1994) and Albania (1997). These actions were sanctioned by the Security Council but under the control of the participating states. They were not United Nations peacekeeping operations, which are established by the Security Council and directed by the Secretary-General.

The UN peace-building activities are important especially in the aftermath of a conflict. These measures are based on the apprehension that peace and security are not measured only in terms of the absence of conflict. Lasting peace requires economic development, social justice, environmental protection, democratization, disarmament and respect for human rights. The focus of these activities is to strengthen and consolidate peace, and they include such measures as election monitoring (these latter vary from technical assistance to the conducting of the actual electoral process). UN assistance can also be instrumental in building and consolidating democracy as was the case, for example, in helping armed opposition movements transform themselves into political parties in Mozambique, El Salvador and Guatemala.

Development assistance is also a central tool for the United Nations in the consolidation of peace. Many United Nations organizations play this role in the recovery stage. In the 1980s the UN addressed the problems of landmines and since 1993 the General Assembly has called for a moratorium on their export. Over time this has developed into an international convention banning their production, use and export. UN peacekeeping activities have included mine-clearance programmes and the organization also trains personnel in mine defusing and removal, and provides funding for national programmes.

Regarding disarmament, the basis of the UN's role is grounded in the Charter and subsequent decisions of the General Assembly. The Assembly has two subsidiary bodies dealing with disarmament issues: the Disarmament and International Security Committee (the First Committee) and the United Nations Disarmament Commission. The First Committee meets during the regular UN session and deals with all disarmament issues on the Assembly's agenda while the Disarmament Commission is a specialized body which focusses on specific issues. These can be, for example, the creation of nuclear weapon-free zones and guidelines for international arms transfers. The General Assembly held special sessions on disarmament in 1978, 1982 and 1988.

The UN Conference on Disarmament is the international community's only formal multilateral negotiating forum for disarmament agreements. It defines its own rules and develops its own agenda, but takes into account the recommendations of the Assembly and reports to it annually. The negotiations on the Chemical Weapons Convention (1993) and on the Comprehensive Nuclear Test Ban Treaty (1996) took place in the Conference on Disarmament.

A major form of promotion of disarmament has been through the negotiation of treaties regulating and limiting production, use and export of arms. The Chemical Weapons Convention (CWC) also established a body for the purpose of overseeing the implementation of the treaty (Organization for the Prohibition of Chemical Weapons). Other conventions include the Biological Weapons Convention and the Convention on the Prohibition of the Use, Stockpiling, Production and Transfer of Anti-personnel Landmines. Efforts have also been made to enhance the registering of conventional arms and in the control and reduction of small arms and light weapons, the primary weapons used in contemporary conflicts. The United Nations is also involved in debates concerning the use of outer space, which is based in the Committee on the Peaceful Uses of Outer Space, established by the General Assembly in 1959.

In the area of research and knowledge the General Assembly approved in 1980 the establishment of the University of Peace, which is a specialized international institute for studies, research and dissemination of knowledge on peace-related issues, situated in Costa Rica. The United Nations Institute for Disarmament Research (UNIDIR) is based in Geneva and undertakes research on disarmament and related problems, particularly international security. The International Atomic Energy Agency (IAEA) was established in 1957 to promise the peaceful use of atomic energy under a system of IAEA safeguards. IAEA was later given the task of verifying that nuclear material is not diverted for military purposes.

51.2

Human rights declarations, covenants and conventions

- The Universal Declaration of Human Rights (1948):
  Includes, e.g., the right to standard of living adequate for health and well-being; to social security; to take part in government; and of equal access to public services.

- The International Covenant on Economic, Social And Cultural Rights (1976):
  Include,s e.g., the right to social protection; to an adequate standard of living; and to the highest attainable standards of physical and mental well-being.

- The International Covenant on Civil and Political Rights and the First Optional Protocol (1976):
  includes rights dealing with, e.g., participation, freedom of movement and equality before the law as well as prohibition of measures and practices such as torture, cruel or degrading treatment, arbitrary arrest, war propaganda, and advocacy of racial or religious hatred.

- The Convention on the Prevention and Punishment of the Crime of Genocide (1948)

- The Convention Relating to the Status of Refugees (1951)

- The International Convention on the Elimination of All Forms of Racial Discrimination (1966)

- The Convention on the Elimination of All Forms of Discrimination against Women (1979)

- The Convention Against Torture and Other Inhuman or Degrading Treatment or Punishment (1984)

- The Convention on the Rights of the Child (1989)

- The International Convention on the Protection of the Rights of All Migrant Workers and Members of Their Families (1990)

Source: United Nations (1998).

Human rights

In addition to those functions directly related to war, peace and disarmament, the United Nations is also involved in the areas of human rights, humanitarian action, international law and decolonization. Since the adoption of the Universal Declaration of Human Rights (UDHR) in 1948, human rights have received an unprecedented level of global attention and support. Human rights commitments have also been extended further through General Assembly decisions. These have gradually established the universality and indivisibility of human rights and their interrelatedness to development and democratization.

The post of UN High Commissioner for Human Rights was created to strengthen and coordinate the work of the United Nations on the protection and promotion of all human rights of all persons worldwide. Human rights have also become a central theme in the recent reform efforts combining key areas of peace and security, on the one hand, and development and humanitarian assistance on the other. In addition to the UDHR other related declarations have been finalized, creating a structure of formalized global principles. (Box 51.2).

In the work of promoting and protecting human rights the work of the UN is based on several fronts: as a global conscience, lawmaker, monitor and nerve-centre responsible for the communication of violations of human rights, researcher, forum of appeal, fact-finder through special representatives and working groups and as a discreet diplomat through the activities of the Secretary-General. The 1993 World Conference on Human Rights in Vienna provided the first global review of human rights since the previous conference in 1968 in Teheran. The declaration adopted at Vienna proclaimed that 'democracy, development and respect for human rights and fundamental freedoms are interdependent and mutually reinforcable'.

Justice and law

The International Court of Justice (ICJ) also known as the World Court, is the primary UN organ for the settlement of disputes. Since the founding of the ICJ in 1946, states have submitted 75 cases and international organizations have requested 22 advisory opinions. The World Court has made scores of judgements on international disputes concerning economic rights, rights of passage, the non-use of force, non-interference in the internal affairs of states, diplomatic relations, hostage-taking, the right of asylum and nationality. The disputes on issues such as land frontiers, maritime boundaries and territorial sovereignty can be brought before the court by countries in search of an impartial solution to their differences and as an aid to preventing escalation of disputes. The Court has also given two opinions on request of the General Assembly and the World Health Organization concerning the legality of the threat or use of nuclear weapons.

The International Law Commission was established by the General Assembly to promote international law and other activities to enhance development of international legislation in other areas such as trade and environment. However, when the focus is on war and peace another important aspect of UN work is that of the development of international humanitarian law: the principles and rules regulating the means and methods of warfare as well as the humanitarian protection of the civilian population, of sick and wounded combatants and of prisoners of war. The UN has held international criminal tribunals on mass violations of humanitarian law for Rwanda and the former Yugoslavia. In 1998 the Rome Statute of the International Criminal Court (ICC) was adopted, calling for an establishment of a permanent International Criminal Court. The ICC would have the power to investigate and bring to justice individuals who commit the most serious international crimes, including genocide, crimes against humanity and war crimes.

Health

In the field of health the role of UN organizations becomes important especially when coordination and collaborative efforts are needed. Many international non-governmental relief organizations are larger in the magnitude of their operations than the equivalent UN agencies. While the Red Cross and Red Crescent societies have maintained their crucial role in immediate relief measures, there is a growing appreciation of the necessity and role of coordinated action. This is due especially to the increasing emergence of NGOs as key actors in providing for relief and rehabilitation in the 1980s and 1990s.

Various UN agencies that are mainly engaged in development and humanitarian work have also at times hosted the more diplomatic debates on peace and security. WHO has been influential in debates on the recognition of predominantly political issues within the international community, thanks to its position as the first UN body to hold an annual meeting. It has also been the site for discussions concerning nuclear and chemical war and safety, owing to its mandate as a normative UN body and specialized agency on health.

UNICEF's advocacy of the rights of children has been significant. This work culminated in the (1989) International Convention ratified by 191 states as of May 1998. UNICEF has also been important in more focussed efforts to draw attention to the fate of children in warfare, child soldiers and child victims of landmines. UNICEF's advocacy role has thus extended to those peacekeeping issues which may involve children and to the study of how warfare, sanctions and enforcement affect children. UNICEF has, for example, been a vocal campaigner on landmines, which kill and maim thousands of children every year. In 1997 the Secretary-General appointed a Special Representative for Children in Armed Conflict in order to strengthen the protection of children in conflict situations.

Humanitarian assistance

In the field of humanitarian assistance the Office of the UN High Commissioner for Refugees (UNHCR) provides international protection and assistance to refugees and displaced people, thus tackling one important aspect of conflicts and emergencies, and the World Food Programme (WFP) still delivers a substantial amount of the world's emergency food assistance. The Inter-Agency Standing Committee was established in 1991 to coordinate responses to humanitarian emergencies, with the UN Emergency

Relief Coordinator acting as the system's primary policy adviser. The Office of Coordination of Humanitarian Affairs also deals with governments and NGOs and serves to facilitate in complex emergency efforts. In the delivery of humanitarian assistance the UNDP, UNHCR, UNICEF and the WFP have the primary roles in delivering assistance.

The UNDP is the agency for operational activities especially in natural disasters. However, it has an essential role in terms of enhancing rebuilding, development and mitigating the causal roots of conflicts through development efforts. In addition, the increasing recognition of the relevance of long-term peace-building efforts and rehabilitation in the aftermath of conflicts highlight the role of the UNDP in the field.

The UNHCR mandate in the UN system is to provide international protection and assistance to refugees and internally displaced persons. In 1997 the Commissioner provided assistance to more than 22 million people. The UN also hosts a special agency, the United Nations Relief and Works Agency for Palestine Refugees in the Near East (UNRWA), set up in 1950 to provide relief and social services to Palestinian refugees. This organization has recently regained importance amidst renewed conflicts in the Middle East. In 1993, as part of the support to the peace process, the Agency started its Peace Implementation Programme to improve living conditions in refugee communities throughout its area of operations.

The World Food Programme provides supplies to the victims of war, ethnic conflict, political strife or natural or man-made disasters. According to the United Nations, a decade ago two out of three tons of the food aid provided by the WFP was used to help people become more self-reliant, while today 70 per cent of WFP resources go to victims of conflict.

WHO's Division of Emergency and Humanitarian Action coordinates the activities of the WHO in emergencies. WHO provides expert advice on epidemiological surveillance and the control of communicable diseases, and provides emergency drugs and supplies with the aim of reducing the adverse health consequences of emergencies. Health considerations have increased in emergencies, especially when mass movements of people have been linked to conflicts and warfare.

In addition to relief and rehabilitation work other UN agencies are involved with work on war-related human rights violations and the environmental implications of warfare. The United Nations Environmental Programme (UNEP), for example, is taking responsibility for assessing the environmental implications of the recent NATO bombings in Kosovo. It is important to note that non-violent UN interventions can also have adverse health implications. Such consequences have become the subject of public debate recently, particularly in relation to the trade sanctions against Iraq. The UN has maintained the mandate for sanctions, in spite of their implications for ordinary people and especially children.

War and health: do UN agencies matter?

In the 1990s the role of the UN agencies was challenged on all fronts. In the field of preventive diplomacy the G7 leaders or, at times, individuals with the support of their governments have emerged as the increasingly-favoured means for negotiating and dealing with preventive diplomacy. NGOs have also become more involved in conflict-resolution activities. In the field of enforcement NATO has become more important. In peace-building activities donor resources are now frequently channelled through NGOs working on emergency relief and operations.

It would, however, be shortsighted to overlook the role and relevance of the UN as the global forum and actor in the field of war and peace. While that role is comple-mented by different actors, the current trend of sidelining United Nations organizations may well be the wrong answer to the expressed problems of UN operations. The current emphasis on effectiveness, technical expedience and timeliness easily confuses the actual problems of representation and legitimacy of various actors and neglects the importance of jointly-accepted rules and practices, including the need to provide international legal architecture for rights and responsibilities at the global level.

It is paradoxical that in many cases the increasing role of NGOs and the plurality of actors in the field of emergencies has highlighted the need for coordinating bodies and guidelines for action. As many NGOs are as large, or even larger, than UN organizations and their programmes, the relevance of the UN bodies is no longer primarily in the scope of their programmes or of their immediate relief work but rather in their role as legitimate inter-governmental bodies. However, this is rarely perceived as a strength of the UN agencies and instead there is an emphasis on delivery where most of the resources are laid. In practice much of the work of agencies such as the UNDP and UNHCR is subcontracted to NGOs, which have better links or more experience in the specific country, area or issue.

The NGOization of UN agencies through subcontracting provides grounds for concern over the nature of rehabilitation work where this may indirectly increase the role of external actors and aid in national and local public structures. This is a problem as it creates long-term dependency and less self-reliance. On the other hand complementary and supportive roles between NGOs and the UN agencies are apparent in campaigning on common causes or on issues and in areas where inter-governmental agencies lack the necessary support and agility or face more hardship in operating at the frontline. These questions concern, for instance, the reporting of human rights violations by govern-ments or dealing with internal and ethnic conflicts in which population displacement takes place.

It is of importance to ensure that UN agencies do not end up in increasingly competi-tive relationships with NGOs, national aid agencies or commercial actors involved in the aid delivery business, or become sidelined by actors such as NATO, G7 or the OECD in terms of fora of debate, decisionmaking and role in the negotiation of global rules and the basis of action. Special attention has been drawn to the emerging encroachment of NATO on the UN mandate and functions during the Kosovo crisis.

It is clear that requests for further democratization of the UN and especially the transparency and accountability of the Security Council can, and should, be made. However, it is also necessary to recognize that there are no alternative organizations or structures which represent a more democratic basis in terms of global governance or for external interference in times of conflicts or human rights violation. It is therefore necessary that the UN reforms do not overemphasize technical effectiveness or cost cutting at the expense of diminishing the professional and knowledge base of UN bodies.

The UN budget is very small in comparison to the broad mandate of the organization. The regular budget has not grown, while unpaid arrears further hamper the effective work of the organization, providing fewer resources and more limited capacity to engage a professional work force. Globalization has increased the role of transnational corporate and commercial actors in policymaking. There is a danger that corporate sponsorship of the UN may also influence its actions and decisionmaking in ways which may further complicate accountability and global governance issues.

The UN system is important and its working capacities and conditions need to be ensured in an appropriate way. It is also important that any further reform activities do not weaken the capacities of UN bodies to work and their legitimacy as global actors, but serve instead to enhance the democratization, transparency and accountability of all UN organizations and the UN system as whole.

BACKGROUND LITERATURE

Baehr, P.B. and L. Gordenker (1999), *The United Nations at the end of the 1990s*, London: Macmillan.

Beigbeder, Y. (1997), *The Internal Management of United Nations Organizations. The long quest for reform*, London: Macmillan.

Bennis, P. (1996), *Calling the Shots. How Washington dominates today's United Nations*, New York: Interlink Publishing.

Childers E. (1994), *Challenges to the United Nations. Building a safer world*. London and New York: CIIR and St Martin's Press.

Childers E. and B. Urquhart (1994), 'Renewing the United Nations System', *Development Dialogue* 1.

Donini, A. (1995), 'The Bureaucracy and Free Spirits: stagnation and innovation in the relationship between the UN and the NGOs', *Third World Quarterly* 16: 421–39.

Gordenker, L. and T.G. Weiss (1995), 'NGO Participation in the International Policy Process', *Third World Quarterly* 16: 543–55.

Gordenker, L. and T.G. Weiss (1995), 'Pluralising Global Governance: analytical approaches and dimensions', *Third World Quarterly* 16: 357–87.

al Haq, M., Jolly, R., Streeten, P. and K. Haq (1995), *The UN and the Bretton Woods Institutions. New challenges for the twenty-first century*, London: Macmillan.

Koivusalo, M. and E. Ollila (1997), *Making a Healthy World. Agencies, actors and policies in international health*, London: Zed books.

Nordic UN Project (1991), *The United Nations. Issues and options*, Stockholm: Almqvist and Wiksell.

Siddiqi, J. (1995), *World Health and World Politics*, London: Hurst and Company.

Tessitore, J. and S. Woolfson (eds) (1998), *United Nations Association of the United States of America. A global agenda,* issues before the 53rd General Assembly of the United Nations, New York: Rowman and Littlefield Publishers.

United Nations (1998) *Basic Facts about the United Nations*, New York: United Nations.

United Nations Handbook (1998), Wellington: Ministry of Foreign Affairs and Trade.

Worldwide web

United Nations homepage: http://www/un.org. Links to individual UN agencies can be found from here.

International Peace Bureau homepage: http://ipb.org

Stockholm International Peace Research Institute (SIPRI): http://www.sipri.se

Human Rights Watch: http://www.hrw.org

Commission on Global Governance homepage: http://www.cgg.ch

People's Decade of Human Rights Education: http://www.pdhre.org

Global Policy Forum: http://www.globalpolicy.org/

Chomsky, N. *The Current Bombings*, ini http://www.globalpolicy.org/security/issues/chmsky99.htm

Paul, J.A. and S. Akhtar, *Sanctions: an Analysis*, in: http://www.globalpolicy.org/security/sanction/analysis2.htm

Global Policy Forum and World Federalist Movement, *Increasing the Transparency and Accountability of the Security Council*, in http://www.globalpolicy.org/security/ngowkrp/brief96.htm

Golub, P.S., *An International Community?* in: http://www.globalpolicy.org/globaliz/politics/intcomm2.htm

Address for correspondence

National Research and Development Centre for Welfare and Health (STAKES), Siltasaarenkatu 18, P.O.Box 220, 00531, Helsinki, Finland

52 THE INTERNATIONAL RED CROSS

JARI PIRJOLA AND PÄR STENBÄCK

The International Red Cross and Red Crescent movements have been providing assistance and protection, in war and peace, to millions of people for over 130 years. The Red Cross was born of a desire to bring assistance without discrimination to the victims wounded on the battlefield and to prevent and alleviate human suffering wherever it may be found. It aims at mobilizing the resources of civil society to the assistance of victims of war and natural disasters. Through its programmes and activities in almost every country of the world its different components provide humanitarian assistance, protect life and health and try to ensure the respect of the human being. The work of the Red Cross movement is based on seven principles: humanity, impartiality, neutrality, independence, voluntary service, unity and universality, which guide the conduct of the movement's components at all times.

The International Red Cross and Red Crescent movements consist of separate but complementary bodies: the International Federation of the Red Cross and Red Crescent (IFRC), the International Committee of the Red Cross (ICRC) and 175 national societies. The highest deliberative body of the movement is the International Conference of the Red Cross and Red Crescent. The conference generally meets every four years to discuss, adopt and modify the movements' governing rules. The conference brings together all the movements' bodies – IFRC, ICRC and the national societies – together with more than 180 states that are party to the Geneva conventions.

Before we examine the role and responsibility of the International Red Cross's different bodies it is useful to say a few words about the history of the movement.

The history of the International Red Cross

Henri Dunant, the founder of the Red Cross, writes in his memoires, *A Memory of Solferino*, that

It was the sight of the wounded at Solferino (in 1854) which gave me the idea, a vague one at first, of the urgency and feasibility of securing permanent inviolability for the wounded and for those caring for them. Although considered as utopian by those around me, that idea continued growing in my mind before the publication of my book, in which I was led providentially to proclaim that any wounded persons *hors de combat* should be regarded as sacred, whatever his nationality might be.

In these words Henry Dunant sets forth the humanitarian endeavour that some years later came into existence as the International Committee of the Red Cross. Unofficial delegates from 16 countries met in Geneva during 26–29 October 1863 and agreed to approve the Resolutions of the Geneva Committee, as the first body of the Red Cross was called at that time.

At that meeting it was decided that states would foster the creation of private Red Cross societies to complement the work of military medical services during armed conflict. To have a legal base for this humanitarian initiative, the first Geneva Convention was signed in 1864 by the representatives of twelve countries. The whole of Europe, including Russia and Turkey, acceded to the convention, and during the first ten years after its adoption 22 national societies were established.

Following the signing of the 1864 convention, the Red Cross was frequently called on to act in the field. It held regular conferences, which brought together not only representatives of states but also of the ICRC and national societies. These conferences were the first in the series of meetings with the purpose of adopting and developing international rules for assistance and humanitarian work, work that is still in progress.

During the First World War (WW I), Red Cross activities expanded significantly. All the Red Cross societies of the countries at war organized relief for the wounded, built hospitals and operated ambulances. The ICRC also assumed new activities, following the opening of the Central Tracing Agency in Geneva.

It was decided gradually that the Red Cross should play a more active role in peace-time: national societies should use their resources not only on behalf of war victims but also to promote health and organize relief for the victims of natural disasters. Peacetime humanitarian assistance entered the agenda of the movement. This resulted in the founding of the League of Red Cross Societies in 1919 with its headquarters in Geneva.

Components of the International Red Cross

International Federation of the Red Cross

The name of the League of the Red Cross Societies was changed to the International Federation of Red Cross and Red Crescent Societies (Federation) in 1991. The International Federation is composed of and represents 175 member national societies with an international secretariat in Geneva. According to the statutes of the movement, the general objective of the Federation is to

inspire, facilitate and promote at all times all forms of humanitarian activities by the national societies, with the view to preventing and alleviating human suffering and thereby contributing to the maintenance and promotion of peace in the world.

According to its principles the Red Cross provides assistance to the most vulnerable groups without discrimination as to nationality, race, religious beliefs, class or political opinion. Aid priorities are determined on the basis of need alone.

The Federation is active both at the international and local levels. At the international level it works to prevent and alleviate human suffering mainly in the event of natural or man-made disasters. Its role is to organize, coordinate and direct the international relief actions of the national societies. When the Federation is working with natural or techno-logical disasters, the ICRC is assisting the victims of armed conflict or disturbances.

The Federation also helps national societies to prepare for disasters and assists in planning long-term development programmes and other humanitarian activities including community-based health care programmes. It has a wide range of activities in the field of health services: for example, communicable-diseases alleviation and vaccination, health education and mobile clinics, are carried out together with local Red Cross societies.

One example of the Federation's health-related activities was its efforts, with the help of the local Russian Red Cross district in the Karelia Oblast, near the Finnish border, to prevent the spread of diphtheria among the homeless in the area, through social mobilization and a vaccination campaign. In the first two days of the campaign, more than 80 homeless people were vaccinated against the disease and screened for other ailments. As well as fighting the diphtheria epidemic the programme created awareness of communicable diseases among other local disadvantaged groups.

Another important field of activity for the Federation is its population movement programmes. There are over 35 million refugees and internally displaced persons in the world today. More than 60 per cent of the Federations' operations involve assistance to populations on the move. During the war in Rwanda, from where almost two million people fled into neighbouring countries, the IFRC set up an extensive food distribution network and carried out emergency medical, and water and sanitation programmes.

In Albania, with the support of the IFRC, the Albanian Red Cross provided assist-ance to the thousands of refugees seeking protection from the effects of war in Kosovo. The Red Cross distributed food, together with toiletries, blankets, medicine and mattresses. As the situation in Kosovo was considered an armed conflict the Inter-national Committee of the Red Cross had an especially important role to play.

International Committee of the Red Cross

The other important member of the International Red Cross Movement is the International Committee of the Red Cross (ICRC). ICRC is a private, independent humanitarian institution, with its headquarters based in Geneva. The ICRC aims mainly to protect and assist victims of armed conflicts. It takes action either on its own initiative according to its statutes or by virtue of the mandate received from the 1949 Geneva conventions and the 1977 additional Protocols.

The mandate of the ICRC covers both international and internal armed conflicts. For instance, in an often-cited and important article common to three of the four 1949 Geneva Conventions, covering conflicts not of an international character, it is stated that: 'An impartial humanitarian body, such as the International Committee of the Red Cross, may offer its services to the parties of the conflict'.

As most present-day conflicts are internal, fought in destructured, chaotic states like Somalia, Liberia or Sierra Leone and led by different warlords, it is crucial that international legal regulations be applicable to the internal conflicts and that the ICRC has a mandate to assist the victims.

Besides offering assistance to the military and civilian victims of armed conflict or internal strife, the ICRC works as a guardian and promoter of international humanitarian law (IHL). In keeping with the ICRC definition, humanitarian law refers to those rules, established by treaty or custom, which are specifically intended to solve humanitarian problems arising from both international and non-international armed conflict. The ICRC is not only protecting victims but also trying to prevent violations of humanitarian law through diplomacy and the dissemination of that law.

What other tasks is the ICRC entrusted with? According to its statutes its role is to maintain and disseminate the Fundamental Principles of the Red Cross movement and to recognize newly-established national societies which fulfil the conditions for recognition. The statutes also give the committee the role of training medical personnel and the preparation of medical equipment, in cooperation with the national societies and the military and civilian medical services and authorities.

The Geneva conventions give the ICRC the right to visit prisoners of war. Article 126 of the third Geneva Convention stipulates that the ICRC delegates shall have freedom to visit all places where prisoners of war may be held. When delegates are executing this function they have the right to discuss with the prisoners alone, without witnesses. The main aim of the visit is to monitor conditions of detention and the treatment of detainees; to protect detainees; and to ensure communication between them and their families. For example, during the war between Iraq and Iran ICRC delegates visited some 100,000 prisoners of war in the two countries.

Another prominent area of ICRC activity based on the Geneva conventions is the tracing of family members missing due to the armed conflict, sending personal messages to relatives and reuniting separated families. Article 74 of the First Additional Protocol to the 1949 conventions states that parties to the convention must facilitate the reunion of the dispersed families and encourage the work of the humanitarian organizations engaged in this task.

During the war in Bosnia-Herzegovina, the ICRC launched one of the biggest operations to restore family links since the Second World War. During the war over 18 million Red Cross messages were exchanged both within Bosnia and Herzegovina, Croatia and the Federal Republic of Yugoslavia. These messages are of paramount importance in time of war, as they are often the only means people have to exchange family news and to locate their relatives.

Health: some observations

It can be said that many activities of the Red Cross are directly or indirectly linked to health issues. Whether you are providing food, medicine or water to the war victims or fighting in peacetime against communicable diseases, the focus is on health. The Red Cross movement's work to ban antipersonnel landmines and raise general awareness of the landmine problem also has a clear link to health.

Reuniting families or finding the parents of a child separated from them during conflict is a crucial issues for the well-being of people. Health and a healthy environment is indeed a vital part of the International Red Cross's work. For war victims, as the ICRC *Handbook on Health and War* puts it, health most often means survival, which in turn depends on access to food, water and medical care.

Humanitarian organizations like the Red Cross may act directly on behalf of the victims, providing them with food, vaccination and medical care. In all circumstances, whether targeted for war victims or victims of natural or man-made disasters, humanitarian assistance should as far as possible be accompanied by appropriate rehabilitation of local services, for example agriculture, health services and water supply systems. We should not only heal wounds but also strengthen people in their ability to assist and care for themselves, so contributing to the long-term development processes, the impact of which will be more lasting than that of short-term emergency humanitarian operations.

Health, humanitarian law and the International Red Cross

In armed conflicts the application of IHL is a precondition for effective provision of health-related activities. An underlining principle that can be found in the Geneva conventions and their Additional Protocols is that the wounded and sick shall in all circumstances be treated humanely and receive the medical care and attention that is required by their medical condition. No other distinction between them, such as religion, nationality or race, is allowed. Besides the wounded and sick, the Geneva conventions and the Additional Protocols provide the same protection to medical personnel as is provided to the protected persons (see Chapter 44).

Protected persons and objects should be identified with the Red Cross emblem as strictly stipulated in both the conventions and in domestic legislation. According to international law the Red Cross emblem, a red cross or red crescent on a white ground, designates all persons, buildings and means of transport that are entitled to protection and respect. National societies may use the emblem to identify their own activities. In wartime, societies may use the big protective emblem and in peace time the small indicative emblem to show that the designated person or object belongs to the Red Cross. The ICRC and the Federation are also entitled to use the protective sign in the exercise of their duties.

Challenges and current issues

The Red Cross movement is a developing movement which tries to adapt its responses to changed circumstances and needs. One prominent forum for readjusting priorities and having a dialogue with national governments is the International Red Cross Conference. The conference, one of the biggest humanitarian fora in the world, can draw the attention of the international community to issues of humanitarian concern. For example, in the resolutions of the 1995 26th International Conference the vulnerability of children was stressed. The ICRC, the Federation and national societies were asked to intensify their efforts to locate unaccompanied children and reunite them with their families. Other issues raised were: antipersonnel landmines; the importance of water for the survival of civilian populations during armed conflict; and the safety of humanitarian personnel.

The effects on ordinary people of economic sanctions imposed by states to influence events in other countries have also been under discussion in the International Red Cross and were on the agenda of the last conference. The Federation has on many occasions stressed that the possible humanitarian consequences should always be taken into consideration before sanctions are designed or imposed. Whether or not sanctions should be used is a political question outside the mandate of the IFRC. The Federation wants to raise awareness about the effects of sanctions and remind states that they should, once sanctions are used, mitigate their unintended results.

The antipersonnel landmine problem has been a huge challenge to the International Red Cross movement. In 1995 the ICRC launched a campaign which called for a total and immediate ban on these weapons. The efforts of the movement, especially those of the ICRC, to achieve a ban on antipersonnel landmines were met with success with the adoption, in Oslo in September 1997, of a Convention on the Prohibition of the Use, Production, Stockpiling and Transfer of Antipersonnel Mines (the Ottawa Treaty) (see Chapter 9).

The ICRC, which is mainly working in war areas, has been increasingly concerned about the number of children that are recruited or voluntarily taking part in conflicts in different parts of the world. At least 300,000 children under age 18 are directly involved in such hostilities. Such children are subject to appalling psychological and physical dangers. One problem is that international or human rights law does not unambiguously prohibit the participation of children under 15 in international armed conflicts, even though states must take feasible measures to prevent their participation. The protection of children in internal conflicts is stronger as children under 15 shall be neither recruited nor allowed to take part in hostilities. The ICRC has been participating in the current efforts to raise the minimum age for the recruitment and participation of children from 15 to 18 by adopting a new optional protocol to the United Nations Convention on the Rights of the Child.

53 DEFENCE RESTRUCTURING AND CONVERSION

JUSSI S. JAUHIAINEN

Chapter 53 studies the regional outcomes of defence restructuring and conversion, especially as regards the defence industry and military bases.[1] Post-Cold War disarmament has created a downturn in the economy and in employment in defence-dependent localities in western Europe. European countries have until recently protected their military industries. Today capital and the defence industry are increasingly global. That makes it more difficult to exercise local influence. In eastern Europe, generally, military industries lost their market in the post-Cold War changes. Today higher production costs and a poorer technological level impair their international competitive-ness. Conversion of military bases to civilian activities is expensive, and direct conversion is not always useful, or even possible. In some regions, however, reconcentration of military activities has already taken place. The lack of investment in eastern Europe make conversion difficult, and abandonment has in many cases been the most feasible solution. The European Union gives financial aid for defence-dependent regions, but European regions with similar problems have nevertheless had different outcomes. No single model or solution can be found for regional problems of defence restructuring.

Background

Post-Cold War disarmament

Substantial reductions in world military spending were seen between the years 1985 and 1995. In 1985 world expenditure on armed forces was US$1331 billion; this figure had dropped by 35 per cent to US$865 billion in 1995. More than 8000 military bases were closed over the same period and millions of hectares of former military areas returned to the civilian sector.[2] The success of disarmament in Europe is significant.

Cuts in armament, reductions in military expenditure and demilitarization are generally considered positive developments. However, whereas the global outcomes are positive, the socio-economic outcomes in defence-dependent regions are negative. The closing of military bases and industries creates unemployment and a downturn in local economies. Hundreds of thousands of jobs have been lost. For example, in the United States the direct loss of civilian employment in 1990–95 was 245,000 and in Germany 129,000 jobs; in the European Union (EU) job cuts in the defence sector between 1990–97 were substantial: 1,334,000 soldiers, 255,000 civilian employees and 314,000 employees in the defence industry lost their jobs. Almost four-fifths of job cuts in the EU defence sector affected Germany.[3]

It is, however, important to remember that countrywide figures are a generalized picture of geographically concentrated problems in towns and regions. This is true for both unemployment and military sites. For example, in the German state of Lower Saxony the closed military sites covered 3120 hectares, but in its eastern neighbour state of Brandenburg they totalled 160,000 hectares. Defence is essentially a national question, but the outcomes of defence restructuring are felt most at regional and local level. The earlier economically successful defence-dependent regions have become declining areas in Europe. The rapidity of the change means that only a few of them are eligible to receive regionally specific financial aid from the EU. For this reason the EU has created additional programmes for defence-dependent areas.

Comparison between the west and the east

The spending on the defence sector uses national financial resources that could otherwise be used to foster local development. This was the case on both sides of the Iron Curtain. Nevertheless, there were substantial differences between western and eastern Europe in the local significance of armed forces during the Cold War period. In the west the military bases and industries had, at least partly, a positive effect on the local economy by creating direct and indirect civilian employment. Military personnel also established social contacts with local people. Officials, soldiers and workers used money in the localities where the defence industry plants and military bases were located. The closing of these activities has created serious problems in many west European and North American regions and towns.

In eastern Europe the situation was quite different. There were few if any contacts between the local people and military personnel; military bases and defence industrial plants did not even appear on maps. The effect of the defence sector on the local economy was in fact negative, since migration to these towns was restricted and the local labour force was used in activities that typically did not bring returns to the local economy. Some cities became completely closed. The environment in the military areas degraded badly, especially in the former Soviet air and missile bases. Later on, the environmental degradation had impaired possibilities for the reuse of these areas. These different backgrounds in the countries of western and eastern Europe have created differences in the short-term outcomes of defence restructuring, but similarities exist in the long-term possibilities. Everywhere the same question is posed: what to do with the former military areas?

Defence restructuring and conversion

From the macro-economic point of view, cuts in military expenditure create opportunities in the civilian sector: they bring more possibilities for economic investment, research and development. However, defence restructuring and conversion also involve cost losses in employment, production, and innovation. Restructuring and conversion are not new issues. They normally follow a period of war. For example, after the Second World War (WW II) economic growth and industrialization made conversion relatively easy and generally successful. The post-Cold War situation is different, coinciding as it does with the serious turbulence in global economic development. The conversion of military activities into civilian ones is always problematic and requires time and specific support from public-sector policies. An additional problem in the 1990s was that restructuring the defence industry coincided with the crisis in mass-production industries.

Regional aspects

The regional outcomes of restructuring and conversion are difficult to measure. This is not only due to the secrecy of the defence sector, but because all spatial levels from international to local are involved in the development: it includes direct military jobs and indirect and direct civilian jobs. One difficulty is in the concept of the region itself: whether it is defined on an administrative, economic or cultural basis. This problem is clearly seen in Europe, where some regions have legislative and budgetary powers, while others are like extended hands of the national government. A general trend in Europe, however, is that the regions are increasingly responsible for their development and have more administrative, political and economic clout.

Once it was said that natural resources and geographical location determined the success of a region. Today, in the post-Cold War period, it is difficult to ascribe the success of regions to defined factors. Scholars generally agree that innovativeness, entrepreneurship, networking and learning capacities ia population and the companies located on its territory are more important in explaining success than material resources and geography. When speaking of defence restructuring, the starting-point of regions may be similar, but the outcomes can be different, some areas and localities being more able to convert their problems into possibilities and use them. This also means that it is difficult to find a single answer for regions facing problems of restructuring and conversion.

Military bases and industrial plants can be used as an example to illustrate difficulties from the regional perspective. Military bases are normally located in the territory of a single municipality, but the effects of defence restructuring do not stay within the administrative boundaries: civilians from different towns and regions work in the bases and industries; and the cuts in activities and base closures influence other municipalities and sometimes other administrative regions. What, then, is an appropriate level at which to study the problems of restructuring: a municipality, an administrative region, an economic region or a country? This is a challenge both for research on restructuring and conversion and for efficient problem solving.

Decisionmaking regarding the development of military bases and industries is not made in the locality or in the administrative region, but usually at central government level. The headquarters of defence industries are seldom even located in the same country as the factory. This means that even regions with substantial administrative powers are weak in solving questions of restructuring and conversion, and the conversion problems are made even more difficult by the generally weak knowledge at higher levels about the specific problems of localities and regions.

Closure and conversion

Development of the defence industry is part of the larger industrial restructuring underway in the western world. During the period 1985–95 employment in the industry was reduced by 40 per cent in EU countries and by 48 per cent in North Atlantic Treaty Organization (NATO) countries. In eastern Europe the reduction was even greater; an average of 54 per cent, varying between 35 and 82 per cent between countries.[4] In 1990 there were 1,237,000 employees in the defence industry in the EU. Though their number was reduced to 923,000 in 1997, defence is still an important source of employment in Europe.

Transformation

The defence industry was previously national, vertically integrated and state protected. It seldom worked and competed with the same market-economy rules as enterprises in the civilian sector. Today defence industry enterprises are merging and are increasingly becoming joint ventures. The capital involved in these activities is, as a result, becoming more and more flexible. The enterprises are large and global, and the manufacture of defence products takes place through horizontal subcontracting. The outcome at a local level is that production sites and specific towns, regions and localities are less and less secure in the continuity of production at their factories. The specific location is no longer important for the producer. This is part of the new geographical division of labour in the defence industry, a picture that is similar to those in other fields of large-scale manufacturing.

There are substantial differences in defence industry development in the post-Cold War period between North America, western and eastern Europe. Several North American defence-production enterprises have merged; some of them are among the world's largest enterprises. There is a constant pressure to employ dual-use technology and the same enterprises produce goods for both the military and civilian sectors. Their production and markets have become global and they compete with other companies around the world. The picture in western Europe is different. Despite the general principles of the EU, European countries protect their defence industries. This is an exception (Article 223) that was allowed for the member states of the Treaty of Rome. Today this exception creates problems of scale for European defence enterprises. North American enterprises have reduced their production costs more efficiently and are able to invest more in research and development. This has allowed their penetration into Europe. It can be assumed that North American defence companies have less interest in specific production localities in Europe than their European counterparts; their dependence on national governments in Europe is also smaller, allowing them larger spatial flexibility which in turn creates insecurity for the localities where the industrial plants are situated.

In eastern Europe, the general pattern was that the defence industries were specialized and produced goods for all-Soviet use. In many cases the producers did not know where their products ended. In the post-Cold War climate the defence industries lost their traditional market. The reorganization of national armies required new products, but the countries in transition did not possess enough resources for the reorganization of their defence sectors. Without reorganization of the national defence industry the gap between international and national products became large. The admission of several eastern European countries to NATO has demonstrated that only a few national defence products fulfil NATO requirements.

Relocation of the labour force of the defence industry

One problem associated with defence restructuring is the re-employment of its staff. The general economic problems in the defence-dependent regions make it difficult to relocate people to other types of manufacturing. The labour force in the defence industry is generally made up of highly-skilled professionals with specialized knowledge. Research, development, technology and innovations are part of defence production. It is not easy, however, to convert the specific skills of defence workers into use in civilian enterprises. The civilian sector requires efficiency in time and production costs, offers no job security and demands risk-taking in development. These are not characteristics of defence production. The outcome is that defence-dependent regions suffer from structural unemployment. The special technological skills of overqualified and unemployed workers quickly become out-dated. This leads to their under-qualification and continued unemployment. However, a long tradition in defence sector production can create a specific regional milieu where high-quality output is appreciated. There are cases, for example in Hungary, where technological innovations, a qualified labour force and small and medium-sized enterprises have successfully emerged from defence restructuring.

Closing and re-use of military bases

A change in the security environment is the main reason for military base closures. The withdrawal of Soviet forces from eastern Europe began in 1989 in Hungary and was mostly completed in the Baltic states by 1994. The NATO countries in the West decreased their forces accordingly. The cessation of Cold-War hostilities released large areas of former military occupation for other uses: for example, in Germany 328,000, in the United States 212,000, and in Latvia, a small Baltic state, 104,000 hectares of land were returned to civilian production.[5] As we saw earlier, the areas were regionally concentrated, for example, to the western regions of Poland and the Czech Republic and to the coast of the Baltic states; in western Europe there was also regional concentration, but less directly towards the eastern part of the continent.

There are four principal possibilities for the reuse of former military areas: (i) remilitarization; (ii) direct conversion to similar civilian activities; (iii) redevelopment into new civilian schemes and (iv) land-use and abandonment. The options selected depend not only on the locality or region, but especially on the market and on the availability of resources.

Remilitarization

Remilitarization has occurred in some central areas where activities from peripheral military bases in the regions have been concentrated, for example, in the German state of Rhineland Palatinate. In all eastern European countries the former Soviet military areas exceed the need of national armies. Some bases have been remodelled for this use, but that is only a partial solution to the question of re-use. In the Baltic states the former military areas covered 1.7–2.0 per cent of the countries' territory, but today there is no need for such large military sites.

Direct conversion

Direct conversion is difficult, especially in eastern European countries where many military facilities were sited in isolated areas. Small infrastructures located in towns (for example, used for military housing and offices) have been successfully converted in both parts of Europe. The direct conversion of larger infrastructures, such as airports and harbours, requires specific measures: in the west several international and national programmes have facilitated technical and financial conversion and redevelopment but in eastern Europe, the quality of military objects has generally been inadequate for modern civilian uses and there are, for example, too many airports for successful conversion. Lack of documentation regarding the base infrastructure is a further problem.

Redevelopment

To a large extent market and demand dictate the viability of redevelopment and the possibilities of a change in the land-uses of former military areas. If the land is not a scarce resource, the costs of demolition and environmental clean-up make it more expensive to redevelop a former military site than to construct a completely new one, for example, for housing, offices, industries or leisure. On the other hand a good geographical location close to densely-populated areas or communication lines increase possibilities for redevelopment. The economic downturn in western Europe has slowed the redevelopment process, whereas in the east the transitory phase of a weaker economy has made the future of many projects uncertain.

Abandonment

Abandonment means a negative outcome because the former bases normally require maintenance costs. This has been the most common result for the former military areas in eastern Europe due to the lack of investment funds and new market opportunities.

Cleaning up the environment is expensive. For example, in 1994 the clean-up costs in Estonia were estimated to be over US$4000 million, seven times the country's annual budget. The most serious problems of environmental contamination were: leaked fuel that contaminated the groundwater; radioactive waste; unexploded ordnance; chemicals and other hazardous materials; and untreated organic waste.[6] The former Warsaw Pact Organization countries agreed with the Soviet Union/Russia that the infrastructure left in the military areas would compensate for the environmental damage created by the Soviet military forces during the Cold War period.

Solutions

Individual regions and localities normally do not have enough resources to tackle the problems of defence restructuring and conversion. For this purpose, regions, states and the EU have to develop financial and technical aid programmes. In 1989 the EU launched KONVER I to accelerate the diversification of economic activities in regions heavily dependent on the defence sector. The cost of the programme was 130 million euros; it was continued as KONVER II for 1994–99 at an additional cost of 744.3 million euros. Conversion was included in other EU programmes like PERIFRA I (year 1991, 21 million euros), PERIFRA II (year 1992, 31.4 million euros) and RECITE. Funds for conversion in eastern Europe and the former Soviet Union have been allocated through the ECOS-Ouverture, PHARE and TACIS programmes.[7]

The implementation of the programmes has not been easy and the results between countries variable. One problem in allocating financial resources has been the difficulty of identifying the spatial scale of the problems and the best authority to find solutions. The regionally specific financial aid has in some countries been allocated, as intended, to regions that suffered from defence restructuring, whereas in some other countries the regions selected did not suffer so much.

Experience in the United States suggests that in case of military-base closure it is useful to divide the re-use procedure into different phases. The first step is to form a local redevelopment authority consisting of representatives of the public and private sector together with local communities to provide leadership and build consensus for base reuse. This group then identifies the needs and goals, performs a feasibility study, for example, a SWOT-analysis, regarding re-use possibilities, and builds up a consensus regarding the future. This strategic and feasibility phase is then converted into operational planning and project implementation.[8] This is an ideal type of development and naturally there is normally some friction between the interest groups, market and resources. However, in many localities the decisionmaking regarding re-use is still done on an ad hoc basis without learning from other experiences.

Conclusions

The process of defence restructuring has both costs and benefits for the regions. The outcomes vary between western and eastern Europe and between regions in the

European countries. In most cases there are large short-term costs and uncertain long-term benefits. This is the reason why many former military areas remain without specific use. They present an obstacle rather than a real possibility for local economic development. The EU has launched several programmes to help defence-dependent regions, and certain regions have been better in using this additional funding. It is difficult to identify the reasons for regional success. In eastern Europe a general problem remains economic weakness. There have also been difficulties linking imported western know-how with the local practices. It should be noted, however, that in the 1990s there were some examples of reconcentration of defence industry and related activities that have benefited some regions. The variety of problems and regional differences means that it is not possible to find a simple and universally adaptable model for conversion.

REFERENCES

1. The writing of Chapter 53 was assisted by EU Marie Curie Training and Mobility of Researchers grant, No. ERB4001GT961028.
2. Bonn International Centre for Conversion (1996), see Suggested Reading, pp. 44–50.
3. Brömmelhörster, Jörn (1997), see Suggested Reading, pp. 9–11.
4. See n. 2 above, pp. 112–14.
5. Ibid., pp. 205–6.
6. Ibid., p. 38.
7. Brömmelhörster (1997), see Suggested Reading, p. 19.
8. Department of Defence (1995), see Suggested Reading, pp. 19–29.

SUGGESTED READING

Bonn International Centre for Conversion (1996), *Conversion Survey 1996. Global disarmament, demilitarization and demobilization*, Oxford: Oxford University Press. See also their world wide web site http://www.bicc.de/.

Bonn International Centre for Conversion (1997), *Conversion Survey 1997. Global disarmament and disposal of surplus weapons*, Oxford: Oxford University Press.

Bonn International Centre for Conversion (1998), *Conversion Survey 1998. Global disarmament, defence industry consolidation and conversion*, Oxford: Oxford University Press.

Brömmelhörster, Jörn (1997), 'Fostering of Conversion by the European Union', Report 9 Bonn: BICC.

Department of Defence (1995), *Community Guide to Base Reuse*, Arlington, VA: Office of Economic Adjustment. Also available on world wide web: http://www.acq.osd.mil/es/.

Jauhiainen, Jussi *et al.* (eds) (1999), *Post-Cold War Conversion in Europe. Defence restructuring in the 1990s and the regional dimension*. GRIP 3/99, Brussels.

Käkönen, Jyrki (ed.) (1994), *Green Security or Militarised Environment?* Aldershot: Dartmount.

Markusen, Ann, Peter Hall, Sabina Deitrick and Scott Campbell (1991), *The Rise of the Gunbelt*, New York: Oxford University Press.

Markusen, Ann and Joel Yudken (1992), *Dismantling the Cold War Economy*, New York: Basic Books.

Address for correspondence
Department of Geography, FIN-00014 University of Helsinki
Tel: +358-9-292 50776; Fax: +358-9-50760; email: jussi.jauhiainen@helsinki.fi

54 HUMANITARIAN ASSISTANCE TO COUNTRIES AT WAR

An exercise in futility?

HANNU VUORI

The meaningfulness, even ethical justification, of humanitarian assistance to a country at war has sometimes been questioned, suggesting that such assistance may just prolong the war and the suffering. Using the humanitarian assistance programme of the World Health Organization (WHO) in the former Yugoslavia as an example, Chapter 54 examines the validity of these claims. It begins with the big picture, the totality of the international response to the emergency. Bosnia in particular challenged the humanitarian community that, for the first time, faced a total collapse of an industrialized country. It became the UN's largest peacekeeping and humanitarian assistance operation ever. In addition, almost 300 governmental development agencies and non-governmental organizations operated in the region. WHO had a programme consisting of the distribution of drugs and medical supplies, health and nutrition monitoring, public health interventions, physical and psychosocial rehabilitation and health care reform. An analysis of the achievements of WHO's programme shows that in spite of war, humanitarian assistance can improve the technology of providing aid, maintain ethical principles, keep the health care system going, contain the deterioration of the health of the people, introduce health care reforms and, most importantly, help to maintain human dignity.

Almost 3 million refugees and displaced persons, at least one million persons with a psychological trauma, 200.000 dead, 400,000 wounded out of which around 30,000 were disabled or in need of rehabilitation – this was the ultimate human toll of the war in the former Yugoslavia by the time of the Dayton Accord in December 1995. Landmines are likely to add to these numbers for years to come. But this was not all. Hunger, cold, fear and uncertainty were the constant companions of millions of people. The health care system was a shambles: hospitals and health centres were destroyed; many health-care providers had fled; and the lack of drugs, consumables and spare parts rendered toothless whatever remained of the once-proud health-care system.

For the World Health Organization (WHO), this tragedy seemed a perfect justification for offering humanitarian assistance. So it seemed for many other UN organizations, governmental aid agencies and non-governmental organizations (NGOs) – close to 300 humanitarian bodies worked in the former Yugoslavia trying to alleviate suffering. We were surprised, therefore, when cynics and critics, including both WHO staff and representatives of our member states, asked: 'Are you sure you know what you are doing? Has WHO any legitimate business in the former Yugoslavia?'

Doubting Thomases

Like many of his agemates my then 16-year-old son Karri was a sceptic. With his older brother, Niko, he had seen the ugly face of the war in the former Yugoslavia from many angles and in many places. He visited Croatia, Serbia and Montenegro and Muslim, Croat and Serb-controlled parts of Bosnia. He saw the destruction of Mostar, the telltale signs of ethnic cleansing – houses without a roof but no bullet holes in the walls – in western Slavonia, refugee camps in Dalmatia, rusting tanks in the Brcko corridor, empty pharmacies in Serbia and desperate patients waiting for their turn on the only functioning dialysis machine in Montenegro.

He also saw the attempts of the UN and NGOs to help: the huge Ilyushin 74 cargo planes chartered by the UN for the Sarajevo air lift, the little Volkswagen Golfs of the UN military monitors trying to follow the tanks of the armies, the European Union (EU) monitors in their white uniforms overseeing respect (more often, disrespect) for the countless ceasefire agreements between the warring factions, the long convoys full of humanitarian aid donated by government agencies and NGOs negotiating the icy mountain roads on their way to Bosnia; the mountains of wheat flour unloaded from ships in the harbour of Ploce for the World Food Programme (WFP); the fitting of WHO prostheses for patients with amputated legs; and the ubiquitous plastic sheet with the logo of the UN High Commissioner for Refugees (UNHCR) covering broken windows and roofs all over Bosnia.

All this impressed him. He could see that the helpers were many and that their aid was abundant and covered most human needs. Yet his final analysis was:

> Does all this make sense? The war continues. The armies daily kill and wound both civilians and soldiers and destroy historical monuments, schools and hospitals without mercy; the hatred between the people increases. Your food, shelter and drugs do not solve anything; they do not bring any lasting relief. The warring parties do not even like you or appreciate your help. They question the appropriateness of your aid and obstruct its delivery. If they want to kill each other, why don't you let them do that? Come back with your aid when the war is over and it can have a lasting effect.'

Karri is not the only Doubting Thomas. The UN humanitarian agencies have found them in the parliaments, ministries, development agencies, media and general public of all countries they have approached for donations for the massive humanitarian assistance programme in the former Yugoslavia. In the case of WHO, their doubts crystallized in three questions: (i) Is WHO the right agency for humanitarian assistance (i.e., has WHO the organizational mandate, the requisite human and material resources and the needed experience and skills)? (ii) Will your help make any difference in a country at war? and (iii) Is it ethically correct to help the partners in a fratricidal war? The first two questions were easy to understand and relatively easy to answer. The third question took us by surprise.

Today Bosnia enjoys peace, albeit unstable, and the need for immediate humanitarian assistance has diminished although by no means ceased. Unfortunately, there will be other crises where the international community will be called upon to provide humanitarian assistance, and as soon as a humanitarian assistance programme starts, the sceptics will try to undermine it. The experiences of one organization (WHO) in one emergency (the war in the former Yugoslavia) in one field (health) cannot unequivocally answer a question as complex as: Does it make sense to give humanitarian assistance to a country at war? Yet I believe that WHO's work in the former Yugoslavia illustrates many important aspects of this issue. I try to answer the sceptics by looking first at the magnitude of the help given, then at WHO's mandate programme and finally at the impact of the aid. This will leave the thorny issue of the ethical justification of the programme till last.

A massive international effort

The big picture

WHO took part in a huge effort by the international community. The UN system carried out the first interagency assessment of humanitarian needs in the former Yugoslavia in August 1992. This assessment revealed a little over 2 million refugees and displaced persons. Their immediate, life-saving needs for shelter, food and health care amounted to US$500 million; their total needs to US$1000 million. Beginning with the first inter-agency mission, the UN Secretary-General and High Commissioner for Refugees appealed twice a year to the international donor community. The size of the appeal varied according to the number of refugees but was usually around US$500 million. Although the UN system never got the full amount, it was fairly easy to get donations, particularly food, in comparison with emergencies in developing countries. Probably the bad conscience of many European countries partly explains this relative success: they knew that they had not done enough politically to prevent the crisis; they were also afraid that a catastrophe so close to home might spread.

By the time of the Dayton Accord, UNHCR had distributed well over US$1000 million, the WFP over US$500 million, and WHO and UNICEF each about US$100 million. The former Yugoslavia was UN's most expensive peacekeeping and humanitarian assistance operation, carried out with the help of 45,000 soldiers and civilians from some 40 countries. Its most tangible and best-known part was the Sarajevo airlift. The Berlin airlift, the previous world recordholder, operated for 462 days, the Sarajevo airlift almost three times longer with, at times, over 20 sorties a day. The rest of Bosnia and the other republics got their supplies by road. The aid included WFP's food, WHO's drugs and medical supplies, UNICEF's vaccines and UNHCR's shelter material, fuel and explosives for mining coal.

Besides the UN agencies, almost 300 governmental and non-governmental humanitarian organizations operated in the former Yugoslavia, most of them in Croatia and Bosnia. Their gamut reached from the Saudi High Commissioner and Danish International Development Agency through Medécins sans Frontiers and Care to countless small, often religious groups. Their policies were as diverse as their backgrounds. The governmental agencies were driven not only by humanitarian motives. A key goal for them was to keep the refugees within the boundaries of the former Yugoslavia rather than letting them inundate the donor countries seeking asylum. The NGOs had most sympathy forraped women ; the Serbs in Croatia were pariahs. Children were at the top of the agenda; the elderly got much less attention. The supply of food and blankets was fair but there was always a lack of schoolbooks and heating oil. Many organizations gave drugs, but not always according to the priorities; in addition, some drugs had passed their expiry date. The UN agencies helped the needy, disregarding which warring faction they belonged to. According to its mandate, UNHCR helped refugees, and WHO the entire population. Many NGOs, particularly the religious ones, limited their help to a single parish or institution. Many were biased against those whom they considered the enemy.

Enter WHO

In June 1992, Dr Jo Asvall, WHO's Regional Director for Europe, asked Sir Donald Acheson, the recently-retired UK Chief Medical Officer to head WHO's humanitarian assistance programme for the former Yugoslavia. So began a project that grew to become WHO's largest-ever humanitarian assistance programme with an annual budget of almost US$50 million and 120 employees in 8 offices in 5 countries. WHO entered the scene over a year after the first shots of the war were fired in Slovenia in June 1991 and over half a year after the other UN humanitarian agencies had started their operations.

Why this delay? It relates to the first question of the doubting Thomases: 'Is WHO the right agency to provide health related humanitarian assistance?' The situation was completely new for WHO's European Regional Office. Yes, there had been earthquakes in Turkey and in Armenia and WHO had helped. But the nature and magnitude of the crisis in the former Yugoslavia was something completely different. It was in fact a great challenge for the entire international humanitarian community; called upon for the first time to provide large-scale humanitarian assistance to an industrialized country.

Both WHO's member states and Secretariat were at a loss: Did WHO have a constitutional mandate to get involved? Did the organization have the requisite infrastructure, personnel and know-how that would enable an effective and flexible response to a large, complex and politically-sensitive crisis? Even money was a problem. WHO's budget did not contain a penny for humanitarian assistance. We had to rely on voluntary donations but these were by no means assured. Was it right to tie the organization into something that it could not perhaps sustain? Many member states and members of the Secretariat were afraid that the programme would stretch WHO's meagre resources, already sorely needed in the former socialist countries, too thinly.

In spite of these doubts, WHO took the risk and launched a humanitarian assistance programme with the mission 'to protect the health of the population in the former Yugoslavia during the conflicts and prepare national health services for postwar development'. The organization was saying to the doubting Thomases:

> Yes, your first question is valid but after a careful analysis, we feel that WHO is the right organization. We also have a clear mandate. WHO's constitution requires us to act as a directing and coordinating authority on international health work, providing appropriate technical assistance and, in emergencies, necessary aid upon the request or acceptance of governments.

Judging from the continuous flow of donations, the member states seemed to buy this argument. It was now up to WHO to show that the programme made a difference.

WHO in the former Yugoslavia

From drugs to health-care reform

WHO started modestly with just two tasks: to act as a public health adviser to the UN lead agency, the UNHCR and to coordinate health-related assistance given by other humanitarian agencies. It soon became evident that this was not enough. To gain credibility in the eyes of the other agencies and, more importantly, to meet unmet humanitarian needs, we had to roll up our sleeves and get our hands dirty in hands-on operational activities. The first and most obvious of them was the distribution of drugs and other medical supplies. But to distribute supplies effectively, we needed to know what, where and how big the needs were. This led to our public health programme that consisted of health and nutrition monitoring programmes and public health interventions based on the findings of the monitoring.

In principle, we wanted to use data collected by the local health authorities. In Bosnia, however, the public health system had partly collapsed. The national level knew precious little of local level needs. We had to resort to our own data collection. Our health monitoring unit asked several health centres to act as sentinel sites and regularly send key information, particularly on communicable diseases. We also received information from the local health authorities and from the field staff of other UN agencies and NGOs.

During the first two winters (1992–93 and 1993–94), the media were predicting hundreds of thousands of deaths from hunger in Bosnia, particularly in Sarajevo and the Muslim enclaves. Rumours were abundant, facts scarce. WHO wanted to detect the impending catastrophe as early as possible to draw the world's attention to it and to direct the aid to the most vulnerable population groups. We organized nutrition monitoring. As agriculture continued in Bosnia throughout the war, the rural areas had at least some food. We focussed therefore on the largest cities, carrying out nutrition surveys among three samples at regular intervals: households living in their own home; households living in a collective shelter; and the elderly living alone. In addition to information on nutritional status, we collected data on food supply, breastfeeding practices and the immunization status of the children. We weighed, measured and examined children under five and their mothers for signs of clinical malnutrition and deficiency.

Health monitoring soon revealed specific problems that had to be addressed: for example, the delousing of refugees; supplies of medical oxygen and blood; health problems caused by hypothermia; patients needing prostheses; and psychological trauma. The last two problems led to WHO's rehabilitation programme. As part of our physical rehabilitation programme we fitted prostheses, supplied material for clean intermittent cathetrization of paraplegic patients and promoted the concepts of community-based rehabilitation and a friendly society for the handicapped. Our psychosocial rehabilitation programme trained local psychiatric and primary health-care personnel in the detection and treatment of post-traumatic stress disorder while our sister organization UNICEF trained parents and teachers.

Although WHO came to the former Yugoslavia to provide humanitarian assistance, we did not forget our traditional role and strength as the health policy adviser of the governments. The warring factions were interested in two applications of this expertise: the reconstruction of destroyed health facilities and the reform of the health-care system. As WHO is neither the European Reconstruction Bank nor an engineering company, we concentrated on our fourth main programme, health-care reform. All republics of the former Yugoslavia had already concluded before the war that they could no longer afford the top-heavy, hospital-, physician- and drug-oriented system they had inherited from the Socialist Federal Republic. With WHO's support, they wanted to create a more equitable, streamlined and cost-efficient health-care system. Figure 54.1 shows the five components, supported by coordination and public relations, of our programme.

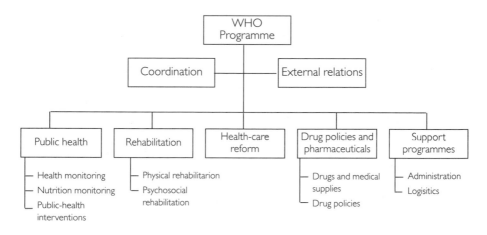

Figure 54.1 WHO's humanitarian assistance programme in the former Yugoslavia

What was accomplished?

That's what we did. What did we accomplish? Possible achievements fall into three categories: improvements in the delivery of humanitarian assistance; improvements in the functioning of the health-care system; and improvements in the health of the people.

Whatever the achievements, they do not belong to WHO's programme alone. They were the results of teamwork. Albeit not related directly to health, UNHCR's shelter programme, WFP's food aid and UNICEF's support for education helped also to maintain health. Many NGOs had good health programmes. None of these programmes would have been possible without the support of many donors such as the European Community Humanitarian Office and the American, British, Canadian, Danish, Dutch, Finnish, Italian, Norwegian and Swedish development agencies. Nor should one forget those countries that put their transport planes, road convoys and the courageous men and women operating them at the disposal of the UN system.

Improving the delivery was relatively easy. The improvements in the delivery of humanitarian assistance are the easiest ones to document. WHO feels that we improved both the delivery technology and the principles applied to the delivery. We introduced the large-scale use of kits for the delivery of medical supplies. Our experts estimated the average need of supplies for a given population for a given period of time. These supplies were prepackaged with standard labels and instructions, etc. Thus, a mental-health kit contained all the drugs 50 mental hospital patients needed for a month, a surgical kit contained the supplies needed for the postoperative treatment of 100 patients for 10 days. The kits were easy to procure, transport and store. During the conflict, we developed some 20 kits with prices ranging from US$15 (hygiene kit) to over US$12,000 (laboratory kit). We asked the end-users what they thought of our aid. The majority found kits better than bulk supplies. Many other humanitarian agencies seemed to agree; they began to order their supplies in kits and have continued this practice in other emergencies.

In the city of Mostar alone, the health authorities had to burn 300 tonnes of donated drugs – expired, of poor quality, badly labelled, etc. In Sarajevo, the health authorities asked WHO to check and approve all incoming shipments of drugs. We found that 35 per cent of unsolicited donations were of questionable quality. Such donations stole space from more useful aid and endangered the lives of the airlift pilots. We therefore developed guidelines for drug donations and distributed them to all donors, embassies, health authorities and humanitarian agencies in the former Yugoslavia. They were a great success. All major donors welcomed and used them. Some other humanitarian agencies adopted them as well and insisted that all donations given to them should meet our criteria. After minor revisions, they have become the standard for drug donations world wide.

Encouraged by this success, we ventured to write guidelines for visiting health professionals. Many health professionals laudably wanted to donate their experience and some of their time to help the victims of the war. Sarajevo was the most popular destination. Unfortunately, the help was often minimal. The visitors' usually had far too little time at their disposal to adapt to the local conditions and they often expected far too much from the local system (e.g., in terms of equipment and postoperative care). The Bosnian Ministry of Health asked us to screen all such prospective visitors. Saying no to people who felt that they were needed and had something to offer was not an easy or pleasant task but written guidelines that we could send in advance lessened the burden.

We feel that we influenced the principles of delivery. We also feel that as a big, inter-governmental organization with which many health authorities had been dealing already before the war, we were sometimes the only organization that could successfully defend these principles. The following are some examples:

(1) *Neutrality*: WHO supported the health care of all warring factions. By clearly demonstrating its neutrality, WHO was able to make realistic needs assessments and support the health care of minorities under particularly bad conditions (e.g., Muslim and Croat minorities in the infamous Banja Luka region);

(2) *Stress on needs*: When resources are singularly scarce as in a war, factors external to health (e.g., economic considerations) often guide their use. Waving the flag of health, WHO acted as a bad conscience reminding the authorities of the health needs in general and of the needs of vulnerable groups such as the elderly, physically handicapped and mental patients in particular. We also fought against earmarking the donations by the donors for too-specific purposes. Such earmarks often served more the political goals of the donor than the health of the people.

(3) *Stress on public health*: WHO prioritized public health at the expense of clinical medicine (although our medical supplies naturally buttressed clinical care). WHO feels that, together with UNICEF, we made a real contribution to keeping vaccination programmes alive and increasing breastfeeding in Bosnia during the war. We also managed to stop indiscriminate distribution of mother's-milk substitute by some health authorities and humanitarian agencies. We even tried to launch anti-smoking activities although they failed: for too many, smoking seemed the only pleasure left.

Improving the health-care system was more difficult. WHO was the main supplier of drugs in central Bosnia, the UN Protected Areas in Croatia, Serbia and Montenegro and one of the main suppliers in Sarajevo. But nobody supplied spare parts. When getting our surgical kit – our flagship kit – for the first time Professor Konjhodzic, Physician-in-Chief of Sarajevo's University Hospital, said: 'This kit is wonderful but useless. We cannot use it because we have no spare parts for our last anaesthesia machine'. In the beginning, the local hospital engineers did wonders by cannibalizing broken machines of the same type for the benefit of the remaining, functioning ones and by other ingenious ad hoc repairs. As time passed, they came to their wits' end. The lack of a simple spare part in a simple machine could stop a whole chain of activities. It took lots of work to identify the needs, order the parts, bring them to Bosnia and ensure that they reached the right machine in the right hospital. WHO was possibly the only humanitarian agency that could do that.

The war cut the international contacts of Bosnian health professionals and crushed their chances for continuing education. While the airlift primarily served Bosnian officials participating in the peace negotiations, we managed to send some physicians to meetings and training courses abroad. More important however, were, the numerous training activities we organized in all republics of the former Yugoslavia. Their subjects ranged from breastfeeding through surgery of peripheral nerves and treatment of post-traumatic stress syndrome to community-based rehabilitation. The courses were very popular and thousands of health professionals participated. They may have reduced the brain-drain that sapped health care in Bosnia, Serbia and Montenegro.

Many observers, including some WHO staff, were sceptical about our health-care reform programme: Isn't it foolish to try to change a system when you don't even know who is going to run that system tomorrow? How can you tackle something as big as the health-care system when the resources are less than one-tenth of what they used to be during peacetime? We took the risk of making fools of ourselves. Paradoxically, we sometimes succeeded because of the war by turning a wartime necessity into a virtue (although some of our critics found this unethical). The prescription-happy physicians of the former Yugoslavia could choose from a huge pharmacopoeia. Our kits taught them selectivity and parsimony. As the kits usually contained only one drug for a given condition, they did not enable the luxury of choice. Many doctors bitterly complained that humanitarian assistance forced them to practise second-rate medicine. Fortunately, the health authorities saw that they could not maintain the prewar bad habits and supported our efforts to develop a limited drug list. The Bosnian Ministry of Health first proposed a list of 1200 drugs. We convinced them that around 200 was enough. Gradually, also, the practising physicians accepted our list. The former Yugoslav Republic of Macedonia completely overhauled its drug legislation with WHO's help.

We sometimes unabashedly used our aid as a carrot to change prevailing practice. Tuberculosis treatment was a good example. It was based on active case-finding through radiological mass screening and long hospital treatment. WHO stressed full vaccination coverage of the new-born, passive-case finding and short but standardized and controlled treatment. The professors of pulmonary diseases and heads of tuberculosis sanatoria put up a stiff resistance. We were trying to ruin their life's work. We had, however, an effective weapon: a TB kit that contained all the drugs and supplies that, if one followed WHO's guidelines, were needed for the diagnosis and treatment of 50 patients. We also organized seminars where we tried to show that the approach worked. As our kits were just about the only source of drugs, local staff grudgingly started to use our guidelines.

Improving health – the real challenge. The former Yugoslavia, particularly Bosnia, had all the ingredients for major epidemiological catastrophes: poor nutrition and continuous stress lowered resistance; lack of water rendered personal hygiene and washing of clothes difficult; cold, humidity and overcrowdedness exposed people, particularly refugees, to diseases; and the ubiquitous mountains of uncollected garbage were infested with rats. Yet, there was not a single major epidemic. In fact, the incidence of epidemics was not much higher than before the war although the number of patients per epidemic increased. The years 1992–93 saw a five-fold increase in infectious diseases in Bosnia. The most common ones were enterocolitis, hepatitis A and scabies. The number of paediatric infections and pneumonias among the elderly as well as of food poisonings also increased. The situation was always worst in Sarajevo and the other Muslim enclaves. The overcrowding among the refugees and lack of safe water were the cause. Although we constantly heard of the difficult lot of patients with chronic diseases who did not have drugs, of children with congenital heart defects dying because they could not be operated on, of transplant patients rejecting their new organs in want of immunosuppressive drugs, of cancer patients unable to continue their chemotherapy and of tuberculosis running rampant, the official statistics and the evidence collected by our health monitors did not show any dramatic rise in mortality.

The war in Bosnia made history in war medicine in two ways: (i) in virtually all wars to date, health problems unrelated to the war have burdened the health-care system more than directly war-related casualties. In Bosnia, war-related problems had the upper hand; and (ii) the majority of the victims of the war were civilians. These tell of two characteristics of the Bosnian war, one encouraging, the other one discouraging: (i) the preponderance of war-related health problems shows that the health-care system, in spite of all the adversity, did not collapse but was able to cope with normal health problems; and (ii) the civilian majority among the war casualties tells of indiscriminate shelling of civilians; of long sieges of entire towns, including the capital of the country; of using public utilities (water and energy supplies) as weapons of war; and of the deliberate targeting of health-care institutions and personnel.

Did the humanitarian assistance help? War, hunger, cold and transport difficulties can be a deadly cocktail. Yet, the sombre predictions about tens or even hundreds of thousands of people dying from hunger and cold did not materialize. Although it certainly was cold and the population was starving – the weight of the adults in Sarajevo dropped an average 12kg during the first winter – there were few deaths. Some lonely elderly died from hunger and some 20–30 incontinent elderly persons from cold. There is no question that humanitarian assistance saved Bosnia: 80 per cent of the food in Sarajevo, almost 100 per cent of the food of the refugees in other parts of Bosnia and the bulk of the food for the rest of the population was humanitarian aid, mostly procured by WFP and distributed by UNHCR.

What about health? Did WHO's programme help? The regional health minister for the Zenica region summarized the impact of WHO's aid on the health-care system: 'You have kept our health-care system going'. As to health status, the assessment is more difficult. The best measure of the success of public-health measures is often a non-event (e.g., after vaccination, there are no epidemics). But are such non-events really attributable to the public-health actions or did the status quo survive because there was no need for intervention? In spring 1993, WHO worried about typhus breaking out among the refugees and started a massive delousing programme. Whether this prevented a single case of the disease will never be known, but had there been an outbreak of typhus and had WHO not done anything to prevent it, the world would have been unforgiving.

Yet we venture to say that our programme did make a difference. One can assume that WHO's winter survival guidelines saved at least some people from dying from cold. We can also assume that WHO's advice to UNHCR and WFP to add micronutrients to the food-aid basket probably prevented outbreaks of scurvy and rickets. In rehabilitation, the results are clearer: (i) nearly 1400 amputees can walk today thanks to WHO's programme and even more will benefit from the skills which WHO helped local prosthetic technicians to acquire; (ii) Croatia started designing handicapped-friendly buildings; (iii) the city of Tuzla in Central Bosnia launched, in the midst of the war, an ambitious policy for a handicapped-friendly society; and (iv) before WHO's mental-health programme, few professionals in the former Yugoslavia even knew what post-traumatic stress disorder was or how to recognize it, much less how to treat it. Now scores of psychologists, psychiatrists and primary health-care personnel are helping perhaps one million sufferers of this affliction, one of the most vicious and long-lasting scourges of the war.

In the summer of 1994, WHO became the first UN agency to invite a group of outside experts to evaluate our programme. While the group found reasons for criticism, it concluded:

> This programme has been highly successful in spite of its shortcomings, primarily WHO's rules and procedures that sometimes slowed down the operations and reduced flexibility. Even if none of the observed shortcomings were corrected before the next call for humanitarian action, this programme is well-worth repeating.

But was it justified?

The humanitarian agencies present in the former Yugoslavia can with justified pride show that, in spite of the war, they accomplished a lot. This has not, however, satisfied the critics. They may grudgingly admit the immediate results but keep on asking: Was it worth it and, more importantly, was it justified? Referring to the preponderance of civilians among the victims, they ask: Wasn't that a result of the humanitarian assistance? Didn't the aid just prolong the war? Thanks to emergency aid, the critics say, ruthless warlords and politicians could simply spend more resources on the war, safe in the knowledge that the international community would care for the sick and wounded, feed the hungry and give shelter to those who had been driven from their homes or seen them destroyed.

This is probably true. Sarajevo would have fallen early during the war without the airlift. The beleaguered Muslim enclaves of Szepa and Srebrenica would have succumbed much earlier than they did. Gorazde and Bihac would probably not have endured until the Dayton Accord. Although it would have meant military defeat, the besieged cities such as Sarajevo, Mostar, Tesanj and Maglaj might have been spared the horrors of continuous bombardment, sniping, hunger, cold, disease and the see-saw battle between hope and despair. Without humanitarian assistance, there might well have been peace in Bosnia much before Dayton.

But would the outside world, those with a conscience, have accepted the conditions of this peace? Before the fall of Szepa and Srebrenica, I used to ask myself how many more people would be butchered on all sides if the besieged areas were taken by force. How many tens or hundreds of thousands more people would be forced to flee their homes. How many thousands more children would become psychologically scarred, seeing their homes destroyed and their parents killed.

Unfortunately, these horror images materialized to a great extent in Szepa and Srebrenica and to some extent in the UN Protected Areas of Croatia when these fell to the enemy. But that was not the fault of the humanitarian assistance. It was the fault of the failure of politics and diplomacy. On the contrary, humanitarian assistance helped much of Bosnia, most notably Sarajevo and Bihac, to endure so that they had the chance of a peace that is acceptable to them and the international community. Although diplomacy played an important role, humanitarian assistance also contributed to the fact that the Dayton peace talks were attended by three groups instead of two, or even only one.

Thanks to humanitarian assistance, the international community can hold its head high after the war in Bosnia. Contrary to the claims of the Doubting Thomases, it showed that, in spite of war, humanitarian assistance can improve the technology for providing assistance, maintain high ethical principles, keep the health-care system going, contain the worsening health of the people and even introduce reforms. Perhaps most importantly, it showed that humanitarian aid can help to maintain human dignity although the price may have been prolonged misery. But without dignity, no war-inflicted wounds, including the deepest one, hatred between people, can heal.

Address for correspondence
Atatürk Bulvari 197, 06680 Ankara, Turkey
Tel: 90 (312) 428 40 31; Fax: 90 (312) 467 70 28; email: whotur@dominet.in.com.tr

55 FORENSIC MEDICAL INVESTIGATIONS IN KOSOVO

KARI KARKOLA

Forensic services are essential not only in cases of violent and obscure deaths under peaceful conditions but also during national and international conflicts. Material and documents have to be collected and interpreted to be available at tranquil times, when administration of justice is possible again. Alleged crimes against humanity and claims of ethnic cleansing have to be proved in court.

After the armed conflict in 1996 in Bosnia-Herzegovina, the Federal Republic of Yugoslavia, a Finnish forensic medical team was invited by the European Union (EU) to visit the country, with the task of investigating graves with remains of alleged civilian war victims. The Finnish system of investigating and reporting the cause of death turned out to fit well with this kind of work because of a clear division in Finland between medical and medicolegal investigations. The frequency of forensic autopsies is relatively high and these are carried out by specialized forensic pathologists. And the police and forensic pathologists, dentists and chemists and other experts have developed good and well-functioning cooperation. In the Finnish health-care system with its 5 million population, there are as few as 25 forensic pathologists, with the result that procedures and documentation are unified, reliable and well-controlled, both mutually and officially. It is also possible to gather quickly an expert team like this to work on a project when needed.

At one phase of the conflict in the Federal Republic of Yugoslavia, negotiations were carried out in the autumn of 1998 between President Slobodan Milosevic and Mr Richard Holbrooke, United Nations (UN) official negotiator, on dropping the economic sanctions set by the UN. An agreement was reached which included forensic medical investigation of alleged massacres in the Province of Kosovo. The question concerned alleged violation of human rights, for which the Serbian military, the special troops of the Ministry of Domestic Affairs and Albanian partisans or rebels were thought to be partly responsible. The problem was that the government of Yugoslavia did not allow the

International War Crimes Tribunal of the Hague to be involved in the events within its borders.

The project of the Finnish Forensic Expert Team was decided on the mandate of the EU. On the basis of the Finnish experience in Bosnia, the holder of the EU presidency at that time, Austria, asked the Finnish Government to find a forensic expert team to be sent to Kosovo. In December 1998, the EU allocated funds to the project.

Resources

A preliminary visit to the place of events was paid in October 1998 and the whole team arrived in Pristina, the capital of Kosovo, in early December. The team consisted of the leader of the group, four forensic pathologists, a forensic odontologist, an anthropologist, an oesteologist, a military security expert, six technical criminologists with different branches of expertise, five autopsy technicians and a secretary. The Human Rights Ambassador of the Finnish Ministry of Foreign Affairs and the Finnish Ambassador in Belgrade also participated in the on-the-site negotiations. The officials of the Austrian Embassy acted as intermediaries to the government of Yugoslavia and the administration of the EU project. The equipment and facilities of the forensic expert team were carefully planned and compiled and part of them were brought from Finland, among other things X-ray and dental X-ray machines, film-developing equipment, appliances for land clearing, autopsy tools and various protective devices. Premises for autopsies were acquired from the Department of Forensic Pathology at the University Hospital of Pristina, Kosovo. The premises were spacious enough but the local equipment was insufficient and hygiene and heating of the rooms were below the accustomed western level.

Ethical background

There have to be ethically accepted reasons for a forensic medical investigation. Distressing and emotionally hard work requires a conviction about the usefulness of the results, especially when the work is done in a foreign country and culture. In Yugoslavia, there was no war in Autumn 1998, only a conflict during which violent actions were taken. In a war, killing is part of the permitted activity, whereas during an armed conflict, killings have to be taken to court. It was evident that when a peaceful situation had been achieved, the alleged atrocities of both Serbs and ethnic Albanians would be investigated and settled either in a Yugoslavian or an international court, or possibly in a truth commission as in South Africa. When supposed killings are brought to court, reliable information must be available. This is important not only for an individual's legal protection, but impartial and examined facts are needed as evidence for alleged execution-type deaths of women and children. Identification of corpses and a thorough cause of death clarification are a good basis for this. The immediate investigation of alleged mass killings was also considered as sending a signal to both parties that events in Yugoslavia are followed internationally and trying to cover up the atrocities by burying the victims or destroying corpses is impossible. Investigation of mass graves is of course of great significance to family members, who do not know the fate of their relatives. It has to be admitted, though, that identifying hundreds or maybe even thousands of disappeared people by rather old remains is an almost desperate task. It is, however, significant work in the name of human rights, which is at least as important in an atmosphere of hatred and violence as in peacetime. The threshold of violence was supposed to become higher this way. However, this idea turned out to be naïve, when we think of the events in Kosovo in the spring of 1999.

The first trip

In early December 1998, the first investigations into alleged massacres in Kosovo were carried out at the invitation of the Yugoslav government and with the permission of the local court of justice. The inquiries were authorized and funded by the EU's General Affairs Council. The sovereignty of any nation cannot be violated and local laws have to be followed; that is why the forms of cooperation have to be negotiated with the local and national courts. Investigation of the identity and cause of death of the deceased is a duty of an independent state and cooperation with foreign parties can only take place by invitation. An agreement was reached with the national Yugoslavian and provincial Kosovar courts of justice and the respective departments of Forensic Pathology of the universities of Belgrade and Pristina. The investigation was to be made in cooperation but yet 'independently, impartially and objectively according to Yugoslavian law'.

The aim was to go to six different sites of mass graves and investigate the alleged killings. In three of them, the victims were supposed to be Serbs and in the three others ethnic Albanians. In practice, however, Serb officials brought material from two alleged mass graves of Serb victims in the villages Volyjak and Klecka. Background information was very scanty. The material consisted of about 200 pieces of skeletal remains, among them several skulls, bony parts of trunks and separate bones, some of them only broken and burned fragments. In many of them there were probable bullet wounds but only occasionally was it possible to determine the probability of life-threatening injuries, as in cases of bullet wounds through the skull or spine and pelvic bones.

The conclusions were not far-reaching. No individual background was available and thus no identification of victims was possible. The main discrepancy between the story and the findings concerned the number of victims. Instead of remains of more than 30 dead bodies only 8 individuals could be detected according to morphological and later, in Finland, DNA findings. No women or children were identified.

The next sites of investigation were supposed to deal with atrocities against ethnic Albanians. The Serbian officials did not, however, let the team enter the area controlled by ethnic Albanian fighters of the Kosovo Liberation Army (KLA), although an agreement had been reached and preliminary preparations made. The formal reason was that the judges from the provincial Kosovar court, controlled by the Serbs, had to be present when the graves were opened and this was not safe enough without sufficient military control. According to the Yugoslavians (Serbs), an armed confrontation was to be expected if they entered an area controlled by the KLA. The Finnish Forensic Expert

Team started out in a convoy early one morning in order to begin examination of an alleged mass grave of ethnic Albanians but was folloved by several military vehicles. After more than one hour's drive the KLA-controlled area was reached, but the Finnish team did not want to force their way to the grave sites in a convoy of Yugoslavian military vehicles because then their security could not be guaranteed. Serb officials did not let Finns continue on their own. The presence of ambassadors and diplomatic negotiations lasting three hours between EU officials and senior Yugoslav officials did not help. Representatives of the international mass media said later that KLA troops had been on standby not far from the road and that an armed fight had been close. The team returned to Finland before Christmas 1998. Part of their equipment was left behind for later work.

The second trip

In January 1999, another killing of several tens of people took place. Again, the different parties had different views on what led to the murders and what had happened. According to the Serbs, this event was an armed conflict between ethnic Albanian terrorists and the Yugoslavian army, where more than 40 people were killed. The ethnic Albanian interpretation was that the Serbs had attacked a peaceful village and killed unarmed civilians without reason.

The Finnish forensic experts were still analysing the material from the first trip, but were prepared to leave on a few days' notice. The presidency of the EU was now in German hands, and Germany suggested that the forensic expert team continue its work. Almost as big a group as on the previous visit travelled to Pristina, excluding the author of this chapter. They cooperated this time with local forensic pathologists, who had already performed autopsies on some of the deceased. The Finns became convinced of their local colleagues' professionalism and both their conclusions and thoroughness were reassuring. The cooperation was extended to Belorussian physicians who were invited by the Yugoslav authorities to join the team. There were a few bureaucratic and diplomatic difficulties but in the autopsy rooms a collegiate mutual understanding and consensus were predominant. The Finnish forensic pathologists performed part of the autopsies, carried out the forensic odontological investigations and took numerous X-rays in addition to taking samples for the DNA analyses. The forensic pathologists of different nationalities monitored each other's work and previous records were evaluated in a spirit of mutual understanding. There were 40 deceased and the team was informed that five more victims existed.

The investigation was thorough and multifarious. Each autopsy was documented by a narrative, photographs, X-rays and a video recording. Histological, forensic chemical, biochemical and DNA samples were taken, and the clothes and other items of the deceased were investigated and photographed. The protocols of each victim stated that in all cases bullet wounds were the cause of death; in many cases there were several angles and directions.

The report

After returning home from the second trip, some of the team stayed at the Department of Forensic Pathology of the University of Helsinki, where an office was established for its use. Their task was to write a summary of their findings, which included the protocols, results of the examined samples, photographs and X-rays, with interpretations. The text was translated into English and the whole report was copied to to be handed to all parties involved.

The report was eventually handed to the Yugoslavian government officials and to the EU. A press conference was arranged in Pristina on 17 March 1999.

Forensic medical needs in the future

When the Kosovo crisis culminated in an armed conflict, NATO began bombing and an unbelievably ruthless ethnic cleansing and expatriation of the Kosovars took place, it became evident that all further investigation and clarification of the course of events was impossible. It has to be accepted that it will take rather a long time before the team can return to investigate events that took place after the summer of 1998 and which still keep both the Kosovars and international observers engaged.

During a war human rights violations always take place, and these have to be investigated later. We know already, on the basis of refugee accounts, that while NATO was bombing Yugoslavia in the spring and summer of 1999, most probably numerous atrocities against civilians took place. We know that atrocities towards civilians, even in exceptional circumstances, are never accepted or forgotten. We see throughout history that family members and relatives want to know, even decades later, what happened to their brethren. Sometimes it is a question of compensation, sometimes of vengeance and most often just an unextinguishable desire to know the fate of their kinsfolk.

It is quite evident, therefore, that forensic medical investigations will be carried out extensively in Kosovo in the not-so-distant future, and international organizations must be prepared for this.

Address for correspondence
WEail: Kari.Karkola@ishl.intermin.fi

56 TRUST-BUILDING AMONG NATIONS IN CONFLICT THROUGH MEDICAL ACTIONS

The Case of the Middle East

ERNESTO KAHAN

The medical community has a responsibility to extend care and protect human lives and interests regardless of race, creed or colour. In this capacity, health-care professionals are in an ideal position to promote trust and understanding among people, particularly in the face of the hate, fear and misconceptions engendered by local or regional wars and conflicts. Chapter 56 deals particularly with the trust-building procedures that organizations such as the International Physicians for the Prevention of Nuclear War have instituted between Arabs and Israelis in the Middle East. I will also present guidelines for the development of mutual professional projects among physicians of countries at war based on the successful experience of the Middle East Cancer Society. The lessons learned in the region can serve as an example for all areas of conflict and hostility, worldwide.

On 12 May 1987, on the occasion of the conference of the International Association of Physicians for Prevention of Nuclear War (IPPNW), the then Israeli Deputy Prime Minister and Minister of Foreign Affairs, Shimon Peres, wrote the following far-reaching words:

> I see doctors as the bearers of the message of peace for mankind… There is today a real opportunity for opening negotiations that may bring us closer to a resolution of the Arab-Israeli conflict, in all its aspects. I trust you will join us in expressing your support for those countries and leaders that have already undertaken to pursue the course of peace and in urging others to do likewise… Your support will be an important contribution to the peace process in our region and will provide a stimulus to all those who still need to be encouraged.

Trust is the belief in the honesty and reliability of the other, and mediation is its operational companion.[1] N. Lewer defines mediation as:

> a process that first aims to remove obstacles such as misperceptions, prejudices and irrational

fears that prevent people in conflict meeting for constructive talks, including the creation of a context in which mediation attempts could be initiated. Should this primary task succeed, the mediator could act as a facilitator, allowing the disputants, talking face-to-face, to lay the groundwork that would enable substantive issues to be resolved. The mediator's task is not to negotiate directly, unless requested to do so by the disputants; direct negotiation is the job of professional diplomats and politicians.[2]

The resolution of conflicts and hostilities is the immediate responsibility of the governments involved and international agencies such as the United Nations. Nevertheless, a wide spectrum of national and international organizations and individuals has found that they too have a unique contribution to make, and more and more are taking up the gauntlet. The medical community has a sworn duty to protect the lives and health of all people without consideration of their social, racial or national affiliation.[3] That duty includes necessary actions against all types of crimes against humanity and violations of human rights, such as war, murder, slavery, prostitution, torture, and racial discrimination,[4] forced migrations and hunger,[5] the diversion of societal resources from welfare to arms purchases and development,[6] and genocide and the apocalypse of nuclear war.[7] To facilitate collaboration, physicians do not have to be diplomats, but they must be trained in diplomatic-type skills, and exercise tolerance and open-mindedness.[8] It is not within the scope of this chapter to deal with methods of conflict resolution or mediation. The recent past and potential future contributions of health professionals in building mutual trust among nations is the focus of this contribution.

> In the broader context of medical ethics, it is widely accepted that opposition to war does not permit the ethical health professional to refuse care to victims of war he or she is in a position to serve and that such care does not presume support by the professional of the war being fought. The ethical dilemmas arise when the professional actively supports the war effort by membership in a military medical service or by assigning priority to patient care based on military demands rather than patient needs. These issues and those associated with the role of the health professional in peacemaking and peacekeeping, often grotesquely distorted by the fervour that may accompany war and preparation for war, require dispassionate analysis and action in times of peace.[9]

The efforts of physicians and other health-care workers in the Middle East, in the midst of the region's numerous wars and, in particular, the difficult and protracted Israeli–Arab conflict, offer a good example of what can be done on the professional level to ease hostilities and resolve differences. Although this work focuses on the Middle East, the experience gained in this region can be adopted in all areas of regional conflict all over the globe. The end of the Cold War has effectively relaxed international tensions because of the diminished threat of nuclear war,[10] but it has at the same time heightened cultural and ethnic hostilities that had been dormant for generations, engendered economic crises and disintegrated age-old constitutional alliances in the former Soviet Union. Tribal wars have created millions of starving refugees in Africa, and religious differences continue to take their toll in Algeria, Afghanistan and the former Yugoslavia. Hatred, malice, misconceptions, confusion and obstinacy have blocked efforts at instituting rational-humanistic means of resolution and have disrupted interventions by national and international mediators and UN peacekeeping missions.

Role of the medical community

International Physicians for the Prevention of Nuclear War is a global federation of national physician organizations dedicated to safeguarding health through the prevention of war. The recent events in Israel and the region have made the responsibility of the IPPNW greater than ever. Regional organizations, such as the Israeli Physicians for Peace and Preservation of the Environment, the Israeli branch of the IPPNW, must work together in Israel and abroad with other peace groups to accelerate the peace process.

> When parties to disputes are locked in a frozen position and movement is restricted by domestic political considerations, outside impartial agents can be of significant benefit. As such, the IPPNW, in accordance with its duty and determination, must follow the initiatives of the Middle East Cancer Society and other such constructive forums. We must show that Syrian, Iraqi, Jordanian, Egyptian, Palestinian, Turkish, Iranian and Israeli physicians can meet in a positive atmosphere to discuss family medicine, or research in ambulatory medicine, or any other relevant topic that affects our region. We, as responsible doctors, must transmit a strong message supporting the peace process.[11]

The Middle East

The Middle East is a conglomeration of many countries: Egypt, Israel, Iran, Iraq, Jordan, Lebanon, Saudi Arabia, Syria, Yemen, Kuwait, Bahrain, Qatar, Oman and the United Arab Emirates, as well as Gaza and the West Bank. More than any other region, the Middle East epitomizes a living microcosm of the IPPNW's concept of the global macrocosm (Box 56.1).[12] For over five decades, this region has been a cauldron of war, unrest, violence, terrorism, insecurity and militarism, all consequences of religious, territorial and historical differences. The aftermath has been untold human suffering, with desperately-needed advances in transportation, trade, industry and technology delayed or blocked altogether. The last decades of the 20th century witnessed a lengthy Iran–Iraq war and the more recent Gulf War. But the most important and far-reaching conflict in the area is that between Israel and the Arabs on the issue of a Palestinian state. This dispute is well-rooted in both ancient history and in the Second World War (WW II) geopolitical events that led to the creation of Israel as a homeland for the Jewish people.

The Middle East has been described as the most overmilitarized region. The escalating arms race of the 1980s and 1990s has exerted a terrible financial and social cost. During the 1980s, military expenditures in the region totalled more than US$850 billion; in 1991 they accounted for 13.9 per cent of the GNP, as compared to 4.7 per cent for the rest of the world. By comparison, the social and economic outlay was poor. Health expenditures, for example, averaged only around 2 per cent compared to a world average of 4.7 per cent.

Medical action

Individual and organizational pressure to open a dialogue between the Israelis and Palestinians began long before the Oslo Peace Accords 1 and 2. Appeals were made to

56.1

Doctors Condemn the Massacre

As physicians, we were shocked by the massacre in Hebron today and by the fact that it was perpetuated by a doctor.

At this painful moment, we would like to express our condolences and identification with the pain of our Palestinian colleagues.

The Israel Association of Physicians for the Prevention of Nuclear War and its supporters call upon all doctors, nurses and health workers, Israeli and Palestinian, to use the influence of our humanitarian profession to advance the peace process. A peace settlement is the only solution which can prevent bloodshed, terror, war, and the arms race in our region.

The ongoing conflict between Israelis and Arabs creates conditions conducive to the growth of emotional disturbances and mental illnesses which not only drive nations and governments crazy, but also individuals.

We call upon the Government of Israel and the PLO leadership to intensify their efforts to promote a successful conclusion to the peace negotiations, to prevent further unnecessary killings on both sides.

Dr Ernesto Kahan
Chairman

Hillel Schenker
Spokesperson

Source: Press release of the Israeli chapter of the International Association of Physicians for the Prevention of Nuclear War expressing condolences for the massacre in Hebron in April 1993.

the respective leaders to recognize each other's right to exist, personally and officially. There was, of course, strong political opposition to these efforts, leading in Israel to the establishment of a law banning meetings between any Israeli citizen and members of the Palestinian Liberation Organization (PLO). Nevertheless, the lobby for peace continued.

During this period, many physician-diplomats on both sides took the brave initiative to open communications for the peaceful exchange of ideas. I cherish the memories of my groundbreaking encounter with Dr Fahti Arafat at the 1987 IPPNW Congress in Montreal. The meeting was arranged by Dr Bernard Lown, co-president of the IPPNW at the time, and others in order to bring Palestinians and Israelis closer, as doctors and as human beings. This is only one example of the steps taken by the medical community to build a bridge of trust and understanding. Since then, the IPPNW has made important contributions to the peace process in three major areas:

(1) The international and local chapters of the IPPNW have actively participated in the collaborative efforts of numerous peace groups and organizations;
(2) the IPPNW has consistently stressed the lethal relationship between the threat of nuclear war and the Israeli–Arab conflict and has made tremendous efforts in inculcating this message to all levels of the population. This contribution has been officially recognized by government leaders of the conflicting nations; and
(3) the IPPNW has maintained its role as a forum for dialogue for Israeli and Arab physicians. IPPNW interactions have yielded mutual objectives and common projects, and many friendly contacts have been established.

Pressure by example to inspire dialogue among politicians is only one way that physician-diplomats can be instrumental. Another approach is to implement on a community level what the politicians have already agreed to. The latter is particularly relevant to current relations between Israel and Egypt and Israel and Jordan. In these agreements, it was the political leaders who initiated the dialogue, and the governments of Egypt and Jordan were repeatedly and harshly criticized for doing so by the intellectual élite of their countries. It was only recently that Dr Ibrahim, founder and head of the Ibn Khaldoun Centre for Development Studies of Egypt, commented that:

> Egyptian doctors have rejected countless overtures from their Israeli counterparts for dialogue and cooperation. The same is true of Egyptian journalists, teachers, student unions, and a myriad of grassroots social organizations that have still not come to terms with the idea of peace with Israel.[13]

It is noteworthy that Dr Ibrahim now believes that the Egypt–Israel 'cold peace' will thaw as Israeli attitudes to Palestinian statehood change. However, Israel and Egypt still do not enjoy full peacetime relations. Medical diplomacy can do much to put the agreement into practice.

One major and very successful effort in this direction was the establishment of the Middle East Cancer Society (MECS). The evolution of the MECS, today composed of Cypriot, Egyptian, Israeli, Jordanian, Palestinian and Turkish doctors, has been slow and painstaking. The idea began in November 1994, at a meeting among a very small group of Egyptian, Israeli and Palestinian physicians at the 25th anniversary of the International Congress of Oncology, organized by the National Institute of Oncology of Cairo University. The physicians selected a steering committee of six doctors, and in March 1995 the National Cancer Institute (NCI) of the National Institutes of Health (NIH) invited the committee to meet American experts and authorities in Bethesda, Maryland. Joining the committee were other medical experts from the Middle East.[14] Together they designed the organizational structure and strategy of the new society and determined the type and amount of assistance it could expect from the NCI–NIH. The participants also decided to publish a common paper on cancer profiles in the Middle East, hold a Regional International Congress in Israel and to invite the members of the steering committee to the next Israeli Congress on Cancer Microenvironment.

At the 1995 Cancer Microenvironment Congress, the MECS committee set up a series of work sessions and meetings with the Israeli health authorities. These yielded several major results: assurances of financial support for the society from the Israel Ministry of Health, an agreement to draft a report with Israeli health organizations on cancer profiles and the formulation of three proposals for common research. The project received widespread recognition from both local authorities and renowned international organizations which provided further financial and institutional backing. As more people and countries joined, the society developed rapidly.

In November 1995, I had the honour of chairing the Regional International Congress of the MECS, aimed at promoting and coordinating efforts toward the exchange of information, knowledge and ideas bearing on cancer prevention and treatment. All major health organizations were mobilized, and hundreds of professional leaders from the Middle East, Europe and the United States participated. The high level of political representation (ministers of health) from Cyprus, Egypt, Israel, Jordan, the Palestinian Authority and the United States created a consortium of strong support for the society.

The establishment of the MECS was a major accomplishment for both the medical community and the whole region. It could not have been possible had we not followed a series of important and sometimes difficult steps to bring the concept to fruition. These guidelines were summarized at the Special Meeting of the Israel Public Health Association in November 1995 in a paper entitled 'Public Health in the Middle East in Times of Peace':[15]

1. Collaboration among institutions, not only individuals.
2. Equal status for all participants.
3. Major roles for existing agencies rather than the creation of new ones.
4. Clarification of the potential advantages of such activities for all participants.
5. Priority accorded to applied research.
6. Direction of initial collaborative efforts towards critical needs.
7. Focus on infrastructure and areas that affect the most people.
8. Election of well-recognized professionals to lead the society.

The meeting recommended that successful political steps be backed by rapid action on several levels, not only commerce and tourism, but also science in general and public health in particular. All expressed a strong belief that the time was right for such programmes and that United States and European participation would further facilitate cooperation.

As soon as more countries in the area join the peace process, they will be eligible to join the society; Qatar and Oman are next on the list of new members.

The future

The lessons learned in the Middle East have application to all areas of the world where terror, insecurity, distrust, hatred, exile and military occupation rage; where conflict and hostilities have given vent to disease, dislocation and death; and where regional nuclear, chemical and biological arms races escalate every day.

Peace in the Middle East is no longer a dream. The Israeli–Palestinian agreement, the Israel–Jordan peace treaty, the Israel–Syria–Lebanon negotiations and the Casablanca Conference for Middle East Development in Peace together constitute a dramatic breakthrough for our region.[16] The present peace process is fragile, however, because many people on both sides cannot surrender the land they believe is their historical legacy; it is incomplete because not all countries and territories in the area are included; and it is under fire by terrorists who instigate recurrent attacks against civilians. It needs to be reinforced and made more comprehensive, and it must be defended. In all of these, physicians and other health-care workers can help.[17]

To accomplish these objectives, it is essential that:

• more professional groups become actively involved in the promotion of a peaceful resolution of the Israeli–Arab conflict through dialogue, professional visits and meetings, and cooperative humanitarian activities, while avoiding all political themes;

- NGOs in war-torn areas collaborate to change misconceptions that engender hatred and enmity by encouraging citizens' groups, students, professional groups and others to meet as people, with common objectives of peace and development;
- medical groups such as the IPPNW, Physicians for Human Rights and other regional associations support their affiliates in areas of conflict, assist them in improving their infrastructure and communication facilities and bolster their programmes;
- medical students in the region should be encouraged to engage in grassroots and community level activities that focus on helping young victims of war; and
- common research and publication should be promoted among the professionals of countries in conflict.

The medical community has an instrumental role to play in world peace. The responsibility of all health-care workers everywhere provides them with common ground for establishing trust that goes beyond national, religious and ethnic boundaries. Medical actions like those described here are essential for effecting dialogue at all levels among nations.

REFERENCES

1. Hornby, A. S. (1974), *Oxford Advanced Learner's Dictionary of Current English*, Hong Kong: Oxford University Press, p. 928.
2. Lewer, N. (1997), 'Conflict Resolution and Mediation for Health Professionals', in (eds) B. S. Levy and V. W. Sidel, *War and Public Health*, New York: Oxford University Press, in collaboration with the American Public Health Association, p. 379.
3. Forrow, L. and E. Kahan (1997), 'Preventing Nuclear War', in (eds) B. S. Levy and V. W. Sidel, *War and Public Health*, New York: Oxford University Press, in collaboration with the American Public Health Association, pp. 336–49.
4. United Nations. (1991a), *Contemporary Forms of Slavery*, Human Rights Fact Sheet No. 14, Geneva; (1991b), *Methods of Combating Torture*, Human Rights Fact Sheet No. 4, Geneva; and (1991c), *Program of Action for the Second Decade to Combat Racism and Racial Discrimination*, Human Rights Fact Sheet No. 5, Geneva.
5. Levy, B. S. and V.W. Sidel (1997), 'The Impact of Military Activities on Civilian Populations', in (eds) B. S. Levy and V. W. Sidel, *War and Public Health*, New York: Oxford University Press, in collaboration with the American Public Health Association, p. 149.
6. Ibid.
7. Marmon, L. M., Seniw, C. M. and A.E. Goodman (1994), 'The Diplomat Physician in the Emerging International System', *Medicine and Global Survival* 1: 234–7.
8. Ibid.
9. Sidel, V. W. (1997), 'The Roles and Ethics of Health Professionals in War', in (eds) B. S. Levy and V. W. Sidel, *War and Public Health,* New York: Oxford University Press, in collaboration with the American Public Health Association, p. 291.
10. Renner, M. (1997), 'Keeping Peace and Preventing War: the role of the United Nations', in (eds) B. S. Levy and V. W. Sidel, *War and Public Health*, New York: Oxford University Press, in collaboration with the American Public Health Association, pp. 360–74.
11. Kahan, E. (1997), 'The Peace Process in the Middle East: present situation', *Medicine, Conflict and Survival* 13: 135–9.
12. See n. 3 above.
13. Goell, Y. (1996), 'Egypt's Intellectual Dove', *The Jerusalem Post*, 1 January: 7.
14. Vanchieri, C. (1995), 'Middle East Cancer Research Mirrors Peace Process', *Journal of the National Cancer Institute* 87: 9.

15. Kahan, E., Carel, R., Hart, J. and A. Kimhi (1996), 'Peace in the Middle East: the implications for public health', *American Journal of Public Health* 86: 1821.
16. Kahan, E. (1995), 'The Israeli-Palestinian Peace Process: a new lease on life for the Middle East. Medical and environmental perspective', *Medicine and Global Survival* 2: 49–52.
17. See n. 11 above.

Address for correspondence

Ernesto Kahan, Arazim street 7/4, Kefar Sava, 44456, Israel
Tel: 972-9-7671733; Fax: 972-9-7664644; email: ekahan@post.tau.ac.il

57 WORLD RELIGIONS, WORLD PEACE, WORLD ETHIC

HANS KÜNG

(1) The 21st century will not be a European one as was the 19th century, an American one like the 20th, nor an Asian one. It will be a world century. The age of imperialism and hegemonism is gone, and the damnation that is domination would be no less if it were Asian.

(2) But the world is faced with a new sense of east Asian self-worth, self-respect and empowerment; Asians today are aware of their own potential, their possibilities and their cultural values.

(3) We should avoid any silly confrontation, especially between the western world and Islam, and strive for a commonwealth of all nations where wealth is truly common: in other words, towards a single commonwealth of common wealth. We should aim for a universal civilization.

Challenges and responses

Some think we live in a time in which humanity is threatened by a clash of cultures, between Islam and the west. We are threatened not so much by a new world war but by all sorts of cultural and religious conflicts between specific nations or within a particular country, often even in the same city, the same street, or the same school. The reasonable alternative is peace among the world's religions. Without this there will be conflict among nations and civilizations.

But many people worldwide will ask: is it not religion that often supports and inspires hatred, enmity and war? We live in a time in which peace in the western and the Islamic world is threatened by all sorts of fundamentalism – Christian, Muslim, Jewish, Hindu, Buddhist, often rooted simply in social misery, in reaction to western secularism and in the desire for direction in life.

The alternative is dialogue between religions without which there will be no harmony among them. Many people will object: are there not too many differences and obstacles between the various faiths which make debate a naïve illusion? Better relations between religions are blocked by all sorts of assertions which exist within each creed. This is the reason for many clashes between dogmatism and pragmatism, fundamentalism and enlightenment.

The alternative is a global ethic without which there will be no new world order. The idea of a universal civilization does not imply the abolition of remarkable cultural and religious differences, whether in Europe or Asia, which is a geographical and not a political, ethnic, cultural or religious entity. A universal civilization means a universality in technology, economics, politics and, we hope, ethics. The globalization of markets, technologies and media demands the globalization of ethics. Nevertheless, we, in Asia or in Europe, shall and should not give up our specific cultures of particular tribes, regions or nations with their histories, languages, customs, beliefs, laws and art. A universal civilization does not mean a single unified religion, which would in any case be an illusion, but a culture of tolerance which respects cultural and religious minorities. Assuming the importance of both a universal civilization and cultural and religious differences, let us now talk about the emergence of a new political world order which, as I am convinced, needs an ethical basis.

New world order and ethic

Put negatively, a better world order will not be introduced on the basis:

- solely of diplomatic offensives which all too often are unable to guarantee peace and stability in a certain region and which are often, as in former Yugoslavia, characterized more by hypocrisy than by honesty;
- simply of humanitarian help which cannot replace political action and solutions. The European powers, by substituting humanitarian aid for political action in Bosnia, put themselves under the power of the aggressors and became complicit in their war crimes;
- primarily of military interventions. Of course non-intervention would allow a new holocaust, a new genocide but the consequences of military interventions tend often to be more negative than positive;
- solely of international law, as long as such a law rests on the unlimited sovereignty of states and is focussed more on the rights of states than on the rights of peoples and individuals. If moral convictions and moral intentions do not back a law, armistice or treaty, powers as in Bosnia are not even prepared to defend the principle that only peaceful and negotiated territorial change is acceptable in Europe.

In positive terms, a better world order will ultimately be brought about only on the basis of:

- common visions, ideals, values, aims and criteria;
- heightened global responsibility on the part of peoples and their leaders;
- a new binding and uniting ethic for all humankind, including states and those in

power, which embraces all cultures and religions. There can be no new world order without a new world ethic.

What is the function of such a global ethic?

- It is a not new ideology or superstructure;
- It will not make the specific ethics of the different religions and philosophies superfluous;
- it is therefore no substitute for the Torah, Sermon on the Mount, the Qur'an, the Bhagavad Gita, the Discourses of Buddha or the Sayings of Confucius;
- A global ethic is nothing but the necessary minimum of common values, standards and basic attitudes. It is in other words a consensus relating to binding values, irrevocable standards and moral attitudes, which can be affirmed by all religions despite their dogmatic differences and should also be supported by non-believers. It will be a decisive contribution to overcoming the crisis of orientation which has become a real world problem.

In recent discussion of human rights Asians have insisted rightly that in their traditions there has always been an insistence on duties, obligations and responsibilities, and that these rights are a relatively new development in Europe and America, originating with the Enlightenment.

One of the most astonishing and at the same time most welcome phenomena of the 1990s was the almost explosive spread of the idea of a world ethic, not only in theology, philosophy and education, but also in world politics and the world economy.

World politics discovers the global ethic

At the time *Projekt Weltethos* was published in 1990, there were hardly any documents on a global ethic from world organizations as sources of reference. There were declarations on human rights, above all the 1948 Declaration of the United Nations, but there were no conventions on human responsibilities. Three important international documents which not only acknowledge human rights but also speak explicitly of human responsibilities have since been published. These programmatically call for a global ethic and even attempt to spell it out in concrete terms.

The report of the UN Commission on Global Governance bears the title *Our Global Neighbourhood* and calls for a neighbourhood ethics: 'Global values must be the cornerstone of global governance'. For the 'ethical dimension of the world political order' this document gives the Golden Rule as the main basic principle: 'People should treat others as they would themselves wish to be treated'. To this end a request is made. The authors were presumably unaware that it had already been made in a discussion in the French Revolutionary Parliament of 1789, in Paris, at which time it could not be met. 'Rights need to be joined with responsibilities', for the 'tendency to emphasize rights while forgetting responsibilities' has 'deleterious consequences'. We therefore urge the international community to unite in support of a global ethic of common rights and shared responsibilities. Such an ethic, reinforcing the fundamental rights that are already part of the fabric of international norms, would provide the moral foundation for constructing a more effective system of global governance.

The international commission expresses the hope that:

> over time, these principles could be embodied in a more binding international document – a global charter of Civil Society – that could provide a basis for all to agree on rules that should govern the global neighbourhood.

The report of the World Commission on Culture and Development (1995) bears the title *Our Creative Diversity*.[3] Here the presupposition is a 'commitment to pluralism', but this statement is preceded by a chapter ‚A New Global Ethics', which stresses what is held in common rather than the differences that separate.

Why a global ethic? Because collaboration between people of different cultures and interests can be made easier and their conflicts diminished and limited if all peoples and groups 'see themselves as bound and motivated by shared commitments ... So it is imperative to look for a core of shared ethical values and principles'.[4] The commission emphasizes the agreement between its concern and the efforts of the UN Commission on Global Governance, and states:

> The idea is that the values and principles of a global ethic should be common points of contact which offer a minimal moral stimulus which the world must observe in its manifold efforts to overcome the global problems mentioned.

To this degree today there is a whole 'culture in search of a global ethics'. Such a search is already in itself an outstanding cultural activity. Questions such as: 'Who are we? How do we relate to one another and to humankind? How to we behave to one another and to humankind as such? What is our meaning?', stand at the centre of culture.

What are the sources of such a global ethic? Its formulation must draw content from 'the cultural resources, the insights, emotional experiences, historical memories and spiritual orientations of the peoples'.[5] Despite the differences between cultures, there are some themes which appear in almost all cultural traditions and which could serve as the inspiration for such an ethic.

The InterAction Council (1997), which consists of former presidents and prime ministers (Helmut Schmidt of Germany, honorary chairman, Malcom Fraser of Australia, Chairman) proposed in September 1997 that the United Nations accept a Universal Declaration of Human Responsibilities.[6] This declaration is based on the conviction that 'global problems demand global solutions on the basis of ideas, values and norms respected by all cultures and societies'. The Introductory Comment emphasizes that 'it is time to talk about human responsibilities'. The Universal Declaration of Human Responsibilities therefore:

> seeks to bring freedom and responsibility into balance and to promote a move from the freedom of indifference to the freedom of involvement ... The basic premise should be to aim at the greatest amount of freedom possible, but also to develop the fullest sense of responsibility that will allow that freedom itself to grow.

The comment stresses

> that a better social order both nationally and internationally cannot be achieved by laws, prescriptions and conventions alone, but needs a global ethic. Human aspirations for progress

can only be realized by agreed values and standards applying to all people and institutions at all times.

The responsibilities which 'should be taught and promoted throughout the world' contain Fundamental Principles for Humanity, Non-Violence and Respect for Life, Justice and Solidarity, Truthfulness and Tolerance, and Mutual Respect and Partnership.[7]

Contribution of religions

A communiqué of the InterAction Council bears the title *In Search of Global Ethical Standards*.[8] It openly addresses the negative role which religions have often played, and still play, in the world: 'The world is also afflicted by religious extremism and violence preached and practised in the name of religion'. But the positive role of religions is noted: 'Religious institutions still command the loyalty of hundreds of millions of people', and do so despite secularization and consumerism. 'The world's religions constitute one of the great traditions of wisdom for humankind. This repository of wisdom, ancient in its origins, has never been needed more'.

The minimal criteria which make it possible to live together are important; without ethics and self-restraint humankind would revert to the jungle. 'In a world of unprecedented change humankind has a desperate need of an ethical base on which to stand'.[9]

Now follow some statements on ethics and politics: 'Ethics should precede politics and the law, because political action is concerned with values and choice. Ethics, therefore, must inform and inspire our political leadership'.[10] To respond to the epoch-making change which is coming about, our institutions need a rededication to ethical norms:

> We can find the sources of such a rededication in the world's religious and ethical traditions. They have the spiritual resources to give an ethical lead to the solution of our ethnic, national, social, economic and religious tensions. The world's religions have different doctrines but they all advocate a common ethic of basic standards. What unites the world's faiths is far greater than what divides them.

This declaration defines much more precisely the core of a global ethic which can also be found in the other declarations. The InterAction Council achieves this precision by taking up the Declaration toward a Global Ethic passed by the Parliament of the World's Religions: 'We are therefore grateful that the Parliament of the World's Religions, which assembled in Chicago in 1993, proclaimed a Declaration toward a Global Ethic which we support in principle'.[11]

The Declaration toward a Global Ethic does not aim to invent a new morality and then impose it on the various religions. It wishes to make known what religions in west and east, north and south already hold in common but is so often obscured by numerous dogmatic disputes and self-opinionated intolerance. In short, the Declaration seeks to emphasize the minimal ethic which is absolutely necessary for human survival. It is not directed against anyone, but invites all, believers and non-believers, to adopt and live in accordance with it:

On the basis of personal experience and the burdensome history of our planet we have learned:

- that a better global order cannot be created or enforced by laws, prescriptions, and conventions alone.
- that the realization of peace, justice, and the protection of the earth depends on the insight and readiness of men and women to act justly;
- that action in favour of rights and freedoms presumes a consciousness of responsibility and duty, and that therefore both the minds and hearts of women and men must be addressed; and
- that rights without morality cannot long endure, and that there will be no better global order without a global ethic.[12]

The following two fundamental demands are developed:

- Every human being (white or coloured, man or woman, rich or poor) must be treated humanely.
- What you do not wish done to yourself, do not to others! [Or in positive terms] What you wish done to yourself, do to others! [found already in the Sayings of Confucius and practically in every great religious tradition on earth].

On this basis four irrevocable directives are developed. All religions agree on the following commitments:

- Commitment to a culture of non-violence and respect for life: 'You shall not kill!' (in positive terms: 'Have respect for life!');
- Commitment to a culture of solidarity and a just economic order: 'You shall not steal!' (in positive terms: 'Deal honestly and fairly!');
- Commitment to a culture of tolerance and a life of truthfulness: 'You shall not lie!' (in positive terms: 'Speak and act truthfully!'); and
- Commitment to a culture of equal rights and partnership between men and women: 'You shall not commit sexual immorality!' (in positive terms: 'Respect and love one another!').

According to the Parliament of the World's Religions we should commit ourselves to a common global ethic, to better mutual understanding, as well as to socially beneficial, peace-fostering and earth-friendly ways of life. This is the only efficient way to build a universal civilization. As far as religions are concerned this means making peace with one another. That must be done with every means available, including the media, and at every level: clearing up misunderstandings; working through traumatic memories; dissolving hostile stereotypes; working through guilt complexes, both socially and individually; demolishing hatred and destructiveness; reflecting on things that are held in common; and taking concrete initiatives for reconciliation.

The change of consciousness needed here is a task for the new millenium, the 'world century'. And it is for the young generation to realize decisively the sketch for the future. To quote Victor Hugo, the future has many names:

For the weak it is the unattainable. For the fearful it is the unknown. For the bold it is the opportunity.

REFERENCES

1. Küng, Hans (1991), *Global Responsibility in Search of a New World Ethic*, London and New York: SCM Press and Continuum.
2. United Nations (1995), *Our Global Neighbourhood. The Report of the Commission on Global Governance*, Oxford: Oxford University Press.
3. Commission on Culture and Development (1995), *Our Creative Diversity*, Paris: World Commission on Culture and Development.
4. Ibid.
5. Ibid.
6. InterAction Council (1997), *A Universal Declaration of Human Responsibilities,* Tokyo: InterAction Council .
7. Ibid.
8. InterAction Council (1996), *In Search of Global Ethical Standards*, No 2, Tokyo: InterAction Council.
9. Ibid.
10. Ibid.
11. Cf. Küng, H. and K.J. Kuschel (eds) (1993), *A Global Ethic. The Declaration of the Parliament of the World's Religions*, London and New York: SCM Press and Continuum.
12. Ibid.

FURTHER READING

Küng, Hans (ed.) (1996), *Yes to a Global Ethic,* London and New York: SCM Press and Continuum.
Küng, Hans (1997), *A Global Ethic for Global Politics and Economics,* London and New York: SCM Press and Oxford University Press.

Address for correspondence
Waldhäuser Strasse 23, D-72076 Tübingen
Tel: (0 70 71) 6 26 46; Fax: (0 70 71) 61 01 40; email: hans.kueng@uni-tuebingen.de

58 STUBBORN PEACE
Communities that Refuse to Fight

MARY-WYNNE ASHFORD

In order to prevent armed conflict, we in the international community must develop more strategies to intervene non-militarily in intra-state conflicts before violence escalates to war. A small number of communities that have resisted the call to war offer insights that may be helpful in such peace-building efforts by outsiders. The case studies presented here are followed by comments, including some by community members, about why they have been successful.

Studies of war usually focus on the causes and contributing factors in the conflict more than the protective factors that may help a community resist violence. Historical analysis, for example, describes the economic, political, social and cultural contexts that seemed to make war inevitable. Recently, however, some organizations, such as International Alert, have been examining the peace capacity of societies at high risk of armed hostilities, and attempting to enhance their inherent strengths to resist war. Some communities have taken grassroots actions to prevent armed conflict; these communities offer important lessons about what kinds of outside interventions might support and strengthen the indigenous initiatives. That is, in addition to studying what goes wrong, it is important to study what goes right when a community chooses not to take up arms. When people choose to stand in unarmed opposition to hate-mongering and tyranny, refusing either to fight or to submit, they demonstrate that alternatives can be found, even in desperate situations, and that the community itself is the source of power.

Chapter 58 outlines several examples of grassroots resistance: stubborn communities that refused to go to war. Fortunately, some of these communities have analysed the reasons for their success and provided their comments in discussions or publications. Their insights are valuable, particularly for non-governmental organizations (NGOs) working in the field of peace-building where outsiders try to offer assistance and international solidarity to peoples at risk.

Zones of peace

The Philippines

Until the 1980s the best-known example of the power of non-violent resistance was Gandhi's long, determined fight against British rule in India. Although many died in the struggle for independence, the moral authority of his methods undermined the rights previously accorded to colonial rulers and laid the groundwork for ending colonialism elsewhere. The lessons he taught were well-known in the Philippines when people were subjected to the rule of Ferdinand Marcos. Their struggle for democracy and the final velvet revolution is documented in Ed Garcia's book, *Pilgrim Voices: Citizens as Peacemakers*.[1]

Marcos was a brutal dictator known as the Hitler of the east, whose regime lasted from 1972 to 1986. In the Philippines, a predominantly Catholic country, the Church initially espoused what it called 'critical collaboration' with the government. As the Church became more and more critical and less and less collaborative, it eventually issued a pastoral letter advocating non-violent resistance. Many disagreed vigorously with the letter, but by 1984 people were participating in demonstrations and strikes despite the risk of jail, torture or murder at the hands of the army. In 1985, Marcos called a snap election and then moved to declare himself as president against the results of the vote. By this time there was a very active network of thousands of parish churches all over the country, sheltering and training a non-violent movement opposing him.

Corazon Aquino's opposition party used marches, petitions, trained poll watchers, rallies, vigils and civil disobedience to undermine Marcos's attempt to steal the election. Crucial defections from the government by two key leaders and a few hundred people precipitated the final crisis. Marcos ordered the army to capture the defectors. Cardinal Jaime Sin, the head of the Roman Catholic Church, rushed to the Church-owned radio station and called the people to gather on the streets to prevent the army from taking the rebel officers. Millions of people poured out in protest. Determined to stay as long as it took to depose Marcos, they prayed and sang, shared their food and drink, and somehow gave the occasion the atmosphere of a picnic. They remained on the streets for four days until Marcos finally fled.

After Aquino took over, the Filipino peace movement reflected on what made their non-violent revolution possible. They pointed to their common religious faith, and the support of religious leaders who had encouraged grassroots groups based in churches all over the country. They described their strength as coming from their faith and their bubbling sense of humour. The people shared common goals of social justice and had leaders who could articulate the issues and inspire others.

Ed Garcia, a political scientist and former Jesuit priest, was one of the leaders and, later, one of the writers of the new Philippines constitution. In discussing the role of the outside world, he comments that letters of support from outside the country sustained him while he was in prison and that international solidarity strengthened his commitment and showed him that he was not alone.

The images of the velvet revolution in Manila inspired people elsewhere to demonstrate against oppressive regimes. Only a few years later, in 1989, we saw some of the most memorable television footage of our time when soldiers, watching people dancing on the Berlin Wall, held their fire. In the months that followed, dramatic civil resistance toppled dictators in country after country in eastern Europe with little bloodshed.

Meanwhile, in the Philippines under Corazon Aquino, areas of civil war continued to flare, leading the peace movement to form the Coalition for Peace and the Multisectoral Peace Advocates. These groups met to help peasants and aboriginals who were caught between the army and the guerrilla forces. In the villages, first the army would come and execute those people they claimed were collaborating with the guerrillas. Then the guerrillas would return and execute those they accused of collaborating with the army. The strategy the farmers developed was to draw a map of their village with a circle around it. They took the map to both groups: 'This is a zone of peace', they said. 'Do not enter this area carrying weapons'. Surprisingly, both the army and the guerrillas respected the zones.

Colombia

Many international organizations have benefited from the commitment of Filipino peace groups to sharing their experiences through publications and conferences. After one conference, Eduardo Marino took the idea of zones of peace back to his own community in Colombia, an area called La India.[2]

In La India, peasants were caught between the army, the paramilitary groups supported by the government, and the guerrillas. Colombian peasants were being summarily executed, exactly as the Philippine people had been. They were told by the army: 'You have only these choices: join us, join the guerrillas, leave the area forever, or die'. The farmers devised another choice. They went to each group and asked: 'Who are you fighting for?' All of the commanders responded by saying, 'We are fighting for you!' The peasants answered:

> You have been fighting for us for 15 years, but we have been the only victims of this conflict. We ask you to stop fighting for us. We want to stay on the land and work for a living in a safe environment for our children.

As in the Philippines, the fighting ended and the farmers were able to grow and market their crops for the first time in many years. Today, despite frequent set-backs and horrifying massacres, 28 zones of peace persist in Colombia.

Another of those zones, San Jose de Apartado, is a very active *communidad de paz* (zone of peace) which has a website and opportunities for international membership to support the community.[3] San Jose de Apartado is a small hamlet where peasants had organized a cooperative to market and process cocoa beans. In February 1997 the paramilitaries came in and ordered everyone to leave, accusing the villagers of running a supply post for the guerrillas. They then dragged the four elected members of the board of the cooperative from their homes and executed them. Several hamlets combined to declare themselves a community of peace and committed themselves to a declaration:

- not to participate in the war in direct or indirect form;
- not to carry arms;

- not to manipulate or give information to any of the parties involved in armed conflict;
- not to ask any of the parties to solve conflicts; and
- each one commits him/herself to search for a peaceful solution to and a dialogue for solving the conflict of the country.

The idea for the community of peace originated with the Bishop of Apartado, Monsenor Isaias Duarte Cancino. The peasants began to have workshops with the Intercongregational Commission for Justice and Peace (CINAP). The ceremony to declare the community of peace was made in the presence of Pax Christi, the Diocese of Apartado, CINEP and the media. Five days later, the peasants were bombarded by the army and paramilitaries and several peasants were assassinated. The peasants were forced to leave the hamlets under the threat that, if they did not, more killings would follow. There were, however, two people from CINAP accompanying them when the exodus occurred and many of them, feeling supported in their stand, made the decision to stay in San Jose.

Since it has declared itself a *communidad de paz*, San Jose has seen the death of 35 members, 33 executed by paramilitaries and 2 executed by guerrillas. Nonetheless, the community is determined to continue with its policies of non-violent resistance as the only way forward. In March 1998, 240 people initiated the first return to the hamlet of La Union. The ultimate objective of the peace community is for all its members to be able to return to the hamlets from which they were displaced.

El Salvador

Zones of peace organized from outside a community can also contribute to a peace process.[5] For example, UNICEF's humanitarian ceasefires for the immunization of children established children as a zone of peace.

Under James Grant's leadership, negotiations with the government and the guerrillas in El Salvador permitted repeated three-day ceasefires during which international teams carried out primary health care and immunization of children in war zones. These ceasefires laid the groundwork for later peace negotiations in the country.

Kosevo Hospital in Sarajevo

Another example of a community that refused to fight is the Kosevo Hospital in Sarajevo. In 1995, as part of the UN 50th Anniversary celebrations, Friends of the UN recognized the hospital as one of 50 outstanding world communities.[6] Two doctors came to New York to receive the award just after the NATO strikes began, forcing the Serbs to withdraw. Before the war, Sarajevo was a cosmopolitan city with a thoroughly mixed population of ethnic and religious groups. People had intermarried for years. When the war began, the media incited hatred between groups, but the people of the city held to their pluralism and refused to turn against one another.

The hospital was the leading educational, diagnostic and therapeutic institution in the country, with 41 clinics and institutes, 2100 beds, modern diagnostics and therapy. Only

600 metres from enemy lines, it continued to work under impossible conditions. There was no electricity, water or gas and only minimal amounts of medical materials and medicines. Hospital staff treated thousands and thousands of wounded and sick in the besieged city. The hospital was under constant artillery barrage, receiving 1470 hits, of which 687 landed directly on clinics and institutes. Dozens of patients and staff were killed or wounded in hospital beds, in the hospital compound or while on duty.

Dr Mirza Dilic wrote in 1995 of their experience:

> How did we, exposed to the blockade and enemy attacks, maintain the universal principle of the Hippocratic oath and offer to help everyone, including enemy soldiers?
>
> Simply put, Kosevo Hospital had to succeed. If we had not succeeded in organizing the work and showing that one can work even under impossible conditions, what would have happened to the thousands of wounded civilians and the sick? We were simply doomed to success.
>
> We have succeeded thanks to the engagement of our people, thanks to a wish to help, thanks to the courage and devotion of the medical staff, thanks to respect for human rights, thanks to our efforts to preserve a multi-ethnic, and multi-religious community, thanks to the unselfish aid of many humanitarian and other organizations from the whole world.
>
> Unfortunately, the war in Bosnia continues. Sarajevo is still under a blockade, it has been encircled for 40 months. Already 1,300,000 (yes, you read correctly, one million and three hundred thousand) shells have hit the city. Civilians are still dying on its streets and squares. We are still struggling to help and save the wounded and sick. But fortunately, we know we are not alone. We have friends all over the world and we know that all those who help us now will one day be proud of the help they have given us.

When the doctors were asked to draw lessons from their experience, they emphasized solidarity in the face of adversity, the importance of altruism and a selfless call to help others: 'The path we take', they said, 'is always a choice to live according to our ideals or to join with the forces of violence and oppression'. Two other factors were significant: (i) Dr Faruk Konjhodzic, Professor of Surgery and General Manager of the Hospital, inspired his staff with his moral courage and persistence; and (ii) the hospital received international support in the form of letters and occasional supplies from outside.

Neve shalom/Wahat al-salam

There are other stubborn, non-violent communities within countries where violence is erupting today despite significant movement toward peace. In Israel, for example, there are more than 1000 peace organizations, most with both Jewish and Arabs members. There is an international community founded by Fr Bruno Hussar as an oasis of peace, called Neve Shalom/Wahat al-salam.[7] The community began slowly in the 1970s and continues today with active support from outside Israel. Fr Bruno wrote of his vision,

> We had in mind a small village composed of inhabitants from different communities in the country. Jews, Christians and Muslims would live there in peace, each one faithful to his own religion and traditions, while respecting those of others. Each would find in this diversity a source of personal enrichment.

The aim of the village: to be the setting for a school for peace. For years there have been academies in the various countries where the art of war has been taught. Inspired by the prophetic words: 'Nation shall not lift up sword against nation, neither shall they learn war any more', we wanted to found a school for peace, for peace, too, is an art. It doesn't appear spontaneously, it has to be learnt.

Lessons for the international community

The Friends of the UN invited the award-winning communities to a seminar in New York, where they offered insights into their successes.[8] They spoke of their sense of altruism, of being called to show the highest possibilities of being human, of a sense of dignity, identity and self-respect. They valued their ingenuity in designing initiatives that were home-grown, not handed to them by outsiders. The communities described their moral code of decency, equality, respect for life and the individual, and their rejection of raw power, threats and greed. The vast majority pointed to their spiritual strength, and their religious or cultural traditions as sources of resilience, perseverance and hope. Respect for nature was often a part of this framework. They spoke of their common vision and goal in social justice, and the importance of community ownership of programmes. Often there was a charismatic leader, but speakers were convinced that even if the leader had died, the people would have continued on the same path. Organizational structures were based on participation, equality and shared power. In fact, the people described the ideal structure as more circular than linear. They advised that communities should establish a culture of dialogue, build relationships across barriers, focus on practical results, lay the legal basis for equality, disseminate skills and knowledge, and hold on to courage, hope and humour. They stressed the importance of a legitimate economic base as essential to long-term success.

What strategies for outside support and intervention arise from the lessons of these communities?

(1) Showing concern provides those working for reform with a sense of solidarity that helps dispel the helplessness that often paralyzes action.

(2) The importance of education in moral values is clear in all the cases described. These values are often based in a deep religious faith or spiritual traditions that could well be supported by adherents in other countries.

(3) The development of structures and strategies such as zones of peace and training in conflict resolution can often be facilitated by outsiders who bring new ideas and materials to help organizers.

(4) Communication is key to successful action. The international community could take a powerful initiative in providing fax machines, cell phones, photocopiers and email access to organizers working toward social justice and democracy in communities at risk.

(5) Outside assistance can also be valuable in the establishment of a justice system and educating people about participatory democracy.

(6) A charismatic leader drew many of the communities to action. Whether outside support can nurture such a leader is not clear, but media attention may bring the

issues to the public sphere. Such attention is a two-edged sword, sometimes protecting prominent leaders, sometimes precipitating violence against them.

The above are only a few examples of communities that have chosen a determined stand against hatred and war. Their work is extremely dangerous, and some attempts have failed tragically.

Building the peace capacity of a community is one way to reduce the likelihood of violent conflict and war. Learning from those that have created resistance to war is an essential step in developing new ways to support the strengths of local initiatives and protect local activists in their work for social change.

REFERENCES

1. Garcia, E. (ed.) (1994), *Pilgrim Voices: Citizens as Peacemakers*, Manila: Ateneo de Manila University Press.
2. Seymoar, Nola-Kate and Juan Ponce de Leon (1997), *Creating Common Unity: models of self empowerment 50 award winning communities*, New York: Friends of the UN.
3. http://www.igc.apc.org/csn/sanjose/index.html .
4. http://nswas.com/index.html .
5. Langley, Winston E. (1997), 'Children, a Global Ethic, and Zones of Peace', *Peace Review: a Transnational Quarterly* 9 (2).
6. See n. 2 above.
7. See n. 5 above.
8. See n. 2 above.

Address for correspondence
Box 30143 Saanich Centre PO, Victoria, British Columbia, Canada V8X 5E1
Tel: 1-250-479-9189; fax: 1-250-479-9309; email: mashford@uvic.ca

59 PUGWASH

TOM MILNE

Pugwash conferences on science and world affairs

By 1955 both the United States and the Soviet Union had exploded thermonuclear weapons a thousand times more powerful than the atomic bombs that destroyed Hiroshima and Nagasaki. Bertrand Russell became intensely fearful for the future of mankind. He drafted a text appealing to scientists to help in combating this danger. In one of the last acts of his life Albert Einstein signed this text, which became known as the Russell-Einstein Manifesto.[1] The Pugwash conferences began in response to Russell's appeal. The movement is named after the small lobster-fishing village in Nova Scotia, Canada, where the first conference was held from 7–10 July 1957.

Pugwash started as a movement of natural scientists, many of whom had been or were involved in the development of nuclear weapons. It was based on the conviction that the ivory tower mentality in science had become dangerously irresponsible. The development of nuclear weapons was the starkest possible illustration of this fact. Since scientists would, in most cases, be the first to be aware of dangers created by scientific advance, there was an evident responsibility on them to be concerned about the consequences of their work.

A second reason for creating an international body of scientists working for peace was the belief that contacts between scientists from east and west might be possible at the height of the Cold War when there were few political interactions. The channel of communication between east and west that Pugwash provided turned out to be one of its most important early functions.

Nowadays half of Pugwash participants come from the social sciences (though many of them were originally trained in the natural sciences), and there are few hindrances to communication between persons from different parts of the world. Despite these changes the Pugwash movement is thriving. Since 1957 it has brought together well over

3000 scientists from more than 100 countries who wish to devote a part of their time to working for peace. *Scientists in the Quest for Peace*, the title of the official chronicle of Pugwash, sums up the movement.[2]

Those taking part in a Pugwash meeting do so in their private capacity, not as representatives of their governments or institutions. The meetings, usually involving 25–30 persons seated round a table, are held in private, and there is a rule that no-one should afterwards attribute a view or statement to any of the participants. These conditions make candid discussion easier. Imaginative ideas can be aired and what may seem far-fetched concepts can be discussed. In recent years, for example, one such far-fetched idea, the elimination of nuclear weapons, has become a distinct possibility.

Pugwash is not a campaigning organization and does not seek a high profile. The governing council issues a statement at the end of the annual conference, and takes an occasional public stand on an issue of major importance, but Pugwash operates mainly behind the scenes. It is effective in this way because many Pugwash participants occupy, or have occupied, professional positions that give them influence on official policy-making. Government scientific and arms-control advisers, senior figures in academies of science and universities, and former government and military officials are frequent participants at Pugwash meetings.

Although there is, of course, no single arms control or disarmament treaty for which Pugwash is directly responsible, it has, in different ways, helped to lay the groundwork for the Partial Test Ban Treaty (PTBT, 1963), the biological and chemical weapons conventions (1972 and 1993), and the Anti-Ballistic Missile (ABM) Treaty (1972). In addition, Pugwash has throughout its existence successfully promulgated arguments for eliminating nuclear weapons, and it continues to work on the practical obstacles to creating a nuclear-weapon-free world. To illustrate the way that Pugwash can influence events, it is helpful to outline a variety of the contributions it is known to have made.

Pugwash's contribution to the PTBT was revealed by Lord Zuckerman, chief scientific adviser to the British government at the time the treaty was being negotiated. The radiation hazards from nuclear testing had been taken up at the First Pugwash Conference and had become a central issue at subsequent meetings. In March 1963, three months before the PTBT was agreed, the secretary-general of Pugwash convened a special meeting in London, bringing together experts in seismology and other relevant disciplines from the USA, the then Soviet Union and the UK. All were close to their respective governments. In Zuckerman's words:

> the pressure brought to bear by Pugwash at that time on us officials – who were concerned as advisers to our governments – played a real part in pushing us along, and seeing the conclusion to a treaty.[3]

Chemical and biological weapons (CBW) were an important part of Pugwash work from the beginning. The 5th Pugwash Conference (1959), devoted to chemical and biological warfare, was the first meeting of scientists from east and west to assess, in depth, the dangers posed by chemical and biological weapons.[4] Throughout the 1960s, and until the Biological and Toxin Weapons Convention (BTWC) was ratified in 1975, regular Pugwash meetings focussed on aspects of detecting biological-weapons research, distinguishing between peaceful and military work, and building trust and promoting openness between laboratories involved in biological research for peaceful purposes.

A spin-off from the early Pugwash CBW work was a major study by the Stockholm International Peace Research Institute (SIPRI), *The Problems of Chemical and Biological Warfare,* that produced a six-volume series of books amounting to over 2000 pages. This was a comprehensive study of the CBW field written for those professionally involved as well as for interested scientists and lay people. The main contributor to the study was Julian Perry Robinson who, along with Matthew Meselson and Martin Kaplan, has been a mainstay of the Pugwash CBW work.[5]

After the entry into force of the BTWC, the Pugwash CBW study group switched its focus to achieving a convention banning chemical weapons. Annual meetings were held in Geneva, which allowed close contact between independent Pugwash scientists and those officially negotiating the Chemical Weapons Convention (CWC) at the Conference on Disarmament. The sustained interest and participation in Pugwash CBW work on the part of those negotiating the CWC indicates the useful background role that Pugwash played.

At a Pugwash Conference in Udaipur, India in 1964, two American scientists, Jack Ruina and Murray Gell-Mann, forcefully made the now familiar point that deployment of ballistic missile defence systems by either the USA or the then Soviet Union would be likely to provoke the other to make countervailing increases in their offensive potential.[6] It is known that one of the Soviet scientists present at this meeting, Mikhail Millionshchikov (a member of the Pugwash Council and for many years the leader of the Soviet Pugwash Group), together with another Soviet Pugwashite, Lev Artsimovich (a leading thermonuclear physicist and also a member of the Pugwash Council), who took part in Pugwash discussions on the anti-ballistic missile issue in following meetings, were influential in moving Soviet policy away from support for ABM systems.

In 1990 Pugwash began a research project that produced a ground-breaking book, *A Nuclear-Weapon-Free World: Desirable? Feasible?*[7] Among those who read the book and were persuaded by the arguments was Gareth Evans, then Australia's foreign minister. He convinced Prime Minister Paul Keating to establish the Canberra Commission on the Elimination of Nuclear Weapons (a group of 17 eminent scientists, politicians and military figures, of whom 8 were Pugwashites) which strongly argued for the elimination of nuclear weapons in its 1996 report.

These are a few of Pugwash's specific achievements. Similar contributions can be identified to the Intermediate-range Nuclear Forces Treaty (through longstanding study groups on European Security and Nuclear Forces), the development of the Non-Offensive Defence concept (notably, work by the Danish scholar Anders Boserup),[8] the Draft Code of Conduct on the Transfer of Technology (developed at a Pugwash workshop in April 1974 and accepted by the United Nations as a basis for discussion and negotiation).[9] The list goes on. More generally, Pugwash has encouraged thousands of scientists to devote a fraction of their time to working for peace, and educated a generation of scientists about the importance and practicalities of arms control and disarmament. The value of this is increased when these scientists take on roles as advisers to their governments, or when they inspire their students to be concerned with the wider implications of their work. During the Cold War, contact between Pugwash scientists had the specific benefit of increasing understanding between the USA and the Soviet Union across the whole spectrum of security issues.[10]

Recognizing all this, in 1995 the Norwegian Nobel Committee awarded the Nobel Peace Prize for 1995, in two equal parts, to Pugwash and to its president, Joseph Rotblat: 'for their efforts to diminish the part played by nuclear arms in international politics and in the longer run to eliminate such arms'.[11]

At least four major areas of current research in Pugwash can be identified: two traditional areas of work:

- the continuing dangers of nuclear weapons and practical means to eliminate them; and
- the implementation of the CWC and the strengthening of the BTWC;

and two expanding concerns:

- threats to international security stemming from degradation of the environment, and
- the ultimate need, if the human species is to survive, to eliminate war.

Taking these four areas in turn, foremost is the nuclear issue, with nuclear disarmament still Pugwash's paramount objective. The desirability of eliminating nuclear weapons is now more widely accepted than it has been since the years immediately after the end of the Second World War. Accordingly Pugwash works more on the feasibility of nuclear disarmament, including the difficulties involved in verification. It has also been concerned with the closely-related question of converting military research and development, in particular the need for the nuclear weapons-research laboratories (if they are not to shut down) to move to open research in non-military areas.[12]

In the CBW area, with the entry into force of the CWC in April 1997 Pugwash is now working on the implementation of the convention. The main activities in the biological warfare area are the efforts to strengthen the verification regime for the BTWC. In this connection the Pugwash Council made a detailed statement to the 4th Review Conference of the BTWC held in late 1996.[13]

As for environmental issues, the 1988 Dagomys Declaration of the Pugwash Council brought these concerns into the mainstream of Pugwash work:

> environmental degradation and large-scale impoverishment are already facts and can lead to massive catastrophe even if nuclear war is avoided.[14]

While it is widely agreed among Pugwashites that it is appropriate for their organization to work in this new area, its governing council is conscious that Pugwash must take great care in selecting specific areas to which the body is well-positioned to contribute. Two areas being researched by current Pugwash study groups are the problems (and opportunities for cooperation) caused by water shortages in the Middle East, and technical problems in implementing the Framework Convention on Climate Change.

Pugwash has recently returned to the most fundamental problem of all: the renunciation of war as a means of settling disputes. The need to end all war was the centrepiece of the Russell-Einstein Manifesto:

> Here, then, is the problem which we present to you, stark and dreadful, and inescapable: shall

we put an end to the human race; or shall mankind renounce war? ... People will not face the alternative because it is so difficult to abolish war.

The problem and the opposition to its solution are undiminished today, 40 years on. There are, however, trends making the world more interdependent which offer hope. There is increasing economic interdependence; increased cooperation for security: international nuclear safeguards, global bans on categories of weapons and global regulations to protect the environment; and deepening cultural links, driven by electronic communications, the mass media and international travel. All this may lead people to begin to see the advantages of and need for global cooperation. The need for a mass programme of 'education for world citizenship', to inculcate in everyone a 'loyalty to mankind', as an extension of the traditional loyalties to family, town and nation, was the subject of a recently completed research project.[15]

REFERENCES

1. *The Russell–Einstein Manifesto* (1982) in J. Rotblat (ed.), *Proceedings of the First Pugwash Conference on Science and World Affairs*, Pugwash Council.
2. Rotblat, J. (1972), *Scientists in the Quest for Peace*, MIT Press, supplemented in 1977, 1982, 1987, 1992 and 1997.
3. Zuckerman, Lord (1992), Opening address at British Pugwash Group Public Meeting, Egham, 20 September, in *Towards a Secure World in the 21st Century*, London: British Pugwash Trust.
4. *Biological and Chemical Warfare* (1959), Proceedings of the 5th Pugwash Conference, Pugwash, Nova Scotia, 24–29 August.
5. Stockholm International Peace Research Institute (SIPRI) (1996), *Continuity and Change 1966–1996*, official history of the Stockholm International Peace Research Institute.
6. Ruina, J.P. and M. Gell-Mann (1964), *Ballistic Missile Defence and the Arms Race. Current problems of disarmament and world security*, Proceedings of the 12th Pugwash Conference, Udaipur, India, 1964.
7. Rotblat, J., Steinberger, J. and B. Udgaonkar (eds) (1993), *A Nuclear-Weapon-Free World: Desirable? Feasible?* Boulder, CO: Westview Press.
8. Boserup, A. and R. Neild (eds) (1990), *The Foundations of Defensive Defence*, Basingstoke, UK: Macmillan.
9. Text is reproduced in *Pugwash Newsletter*, 11: 4, April 1974.
10. For example, Academician A.P. Vinogradov had the following to say in tribute to Mikhail Millionshchikov: 'Some of the problems which were raised by Pugwash scientists jointly with Millionshchikov were later considered at top government levels and became a basis for international agreements, the Non-Proliferation Treaty, the Moscow Test Ban Treaty, the international accord banning the use of the ocean floor for the emplacement of weapons of mass destruction, the Soviet-American Treaty on limiting ABM systems development and a temporary agreement on certain measures aimed at limiting the offensive strategic weapons – all of these stemmed from the joints efforts of Soviet and western scientists at Pugwash, with Millionshchikov always being the hub of all these activities', *European Security, Disarmament and Other Problems*, Proceedings of the 23rd Pugwash Conference on Science and World Affairs, Aulanko, Finland, 30 August–4 September 1973.
11. Norwegian Nobel Committee Communique, 13 October 1995.
12. Five monographs have resulted from Pugwash research projects relating to nuclear disarmament: (eds) F. Calogero, M.L. Goldberger and S.P. Kapitza (1991), *Verifying Disarmament*, Boulder CO: Westview Press; *A Nuclear-Weapon-Free World: Desirable? Feasible?*, see n. 7 above; (ed.) J. Rotblat (1998), *Nuclear Weapons: the Road to Zero*, Boulder CO: Westview Press; (ed.) J. Reppy (1998), *Conversion of Military R&D*, Basingstoke: Macmillan; (eds) F. Blackaby and T. Milne (forthcoming), *A Nuclear-Weapon-Free World: Steps along the Way*, Basingstoke: Macmillan.

13. For the text of the statement, issued on 23 September 1996, see *Pugwash Newsletter* 33: 6, December 1996.
14. Dagomys Declaration of the Pugwash Council: 'Ensuring the Survival of Civilization', in: *Global Problems and Common Security*, Proceeding of the 38th Pugwash Conference, Dagomys, USSR, 29 August–3 September 1988.
15. J. Rotblat (ed.) (1997), *World Citizenship: Allegiance to Humanity*, Basingstoke, UK: Macmillan.

Address for correspondence
London Pugwash Office
63A Great Russell Street, London WC1B 3BJ, UK
Tel: 44-20-7405 6661; Fax: 44-20-7831 5651; email: pugwash@qmw.ac.uk

60 A BRIEF HISTORY OF THE INTERNATIONAL PHYSICIANS FOR THE PREVENTION OF NUCLEAR WAR

MICHAEL CHRIST

International Physicians for the Prevention of Nuclear War (IPPNW) was founded in 1980 to bring together physicians from all parts of the world in common cause against the threat of nuclear war. IPPNW was the initiative of Dr Bernard Lown, world-renowned cardiologist and Professor Emeritus at the Harvard School of Public Health, and Dr Eugene Chazov, then Director of the USSR's National Cardiology Institute and later USSR minister of health under President Mikhail Gorbachev.

Drs Lown and Chazov, along with two other American doctors, James Muller and Eric Chivian, and two Soviet doctors, Mikhail Kuzin and Leonid Ilyin, met in Geneva in 1980 to lay the groundwork for an international physicians' movement against nuclear weapons. In that initial meeting, it became clear that in order to work together to prevent nuclear war, other important issues that divided east and west would need to be set aside to enable physicians to unite on a point of common understanding: that nuclear weapons posed an immediate threat to all of humankind.

The founders of IPPNW reasoned that physicians, regardless of nationality and ideology, shared a common commitment to health and life and, therefore, had a professional and moral obligation to work for the prevention of nuclear war. Prevention was deemed the only cure for the litany of medical horrors that would follow nuclear conflict. From the beginning, IPPNW physicians also campaigned against the diversion of resources needed to assure basic health and social development to satisfy insatiable military appetites.

A key moment in IPPNW's history came a year later, at a meeting held outside Washington, DC, when approximately 100 physicians from a dozen countries convened for IPPNW's First World Congress. Given the tenor of the times, with the Cold War deeply entrenched, the mere fact that Soviet and American physicians were able to launch an international movement defied long odds.

IPPNW's Early Work

IPPNW's early work was to document in rigorous detail the projected short- and long-term medical and public health consequences of nuclear warfare and to disseminate that information worldwide to the media, government leaders, the medical profession and the general public. IPPNW was, as former New Zealand Prime Minister David Lange put it, 'making medical reality a part of political reality'.[1] This work also gave substance to IPPNW's medical character. By focussing objectively on the consequences of nuclear war, physicians from east and west were able to work in a non-partisan fashion to educate the public and decisionmakers.

Though IPPNW began by detailing for the first time the full medical consequences of nuclear war and its impact on medical delivery systems, it soon began to focus on the health and social consequences of war preparations as well. Militarism, IPPNW argued, was keeping millions of people impoverished, retarding social progress and robbing tens of millions of even basic health care.

Following the success of its first world congress, IPPNW began holding annual conventions in different cities around the world, each year attracting greater numbers of participants from more countries. Intensive efforts to organize physicians into national affiliates around the world led to IPPNW's growth and extended its geographic reach.

In recognition of its efforts to educate physicians, political and military leaders and the public about the consequences of nuclear warfare, and to re-order world priorities away from militarism and towards health and development, IPPNW was honoured with both the UNESCO Peace Education Prize (1984) and the Nobel Peace Prize (1985). No other stripling organization (IPPNW was only five years old in 1985) had ever been so honoured.

IPPNW becomes an abolitionist movement

In 1986, IPPNW became one of the first international organizations to call unequivocally for the abolition of nuclear arms as a categorical, moral and medical imperative.

This position, first derided as unrealistic and unattainable, is now embraced by many governments, thousands of non-governmental organizations (NGOs) and scores of former military leaders from dozens of countries including General Lee Butler, former head of the US Strategic Command. The abolition of nuclear weapons has also been embraced by the Canberra Commission on the Elimination of Nuclear Weapons, a distinguished panel of experts that included both General Butler and IPPNW Co-President R.S. McCoy.

Documenting the impact of nuclear weapons testing and production

In the late 1980s and early 1990s, IPPNW's work emphasized the comprehensive documentation of the health and environmental impact of the nuclear arms race, spelling out in three books and numerous articles and op-ed pieces the tremendous price nuclear powers had paid in their pursuit of nuclear arsenals.[2] From uranium mining to nuclear testing, from Nevada to Kazakhstan, IPPNW collected and analysed data that began to provide the public with a frightening assessment of the health and human costs of pursuing security through nuclear weapons.

Bringing health information to the developing world

Also in the late 1980s, IPPNW launched an ambitious programme to utilize satellite technology to facilitate the transfer of medical and health information to health workers in the developing world where health-information resources are desperately needed. As then-President Reagan was developing his 'Star Wars' programme to extend the nuclear arms race into space, IPPNW proposed an alternative vision for the peaceful use of space technology. That project evolved into an independent, non-profit organization known as SatelLife which is today using satellite, computer and Internet technologies to provide communications and information services to more than 5000 health-care workers in the developing world.

The Cold War ends: the nuclear threat remains

As the Cold War ended, and the prospects of superpower nuclear war diminished, IPPNW gave heightened attention to the problems of nuclear proliferation, nuclear terrorism, the delegitimization of nuclear arms as instruments of politics and war, and the prevention of all war, not only nuclear war.

IPPNW was one of the most prominent and tireless proponents of a comprehensive test ban treaty (CTBT) over nearly two decades.[3] It was a principal sponsor of the World Court Project, a successful effort to secure an advisory opinion from the International Court of Justice on the illegality, under international law, of the use of nuclear weapons, a ruling that was a substantial step towards the delegitimization of nuclear weapons (see Chapter 48).

Despite these successes, the threat posed by nuclear weapons remains. Indeed, in addition to the possibility, through design, accident or miscalculation, that existing nuclear weapons will one day be used, there are the growing threats of proliferation and nuclear terrorism.

Today, IPPNW is engaged in research, education, advocacy and peace-promotion activities around the world. Its mission has been expanded significantly to include prevention of all war, the abolition of landmines and education and advocacy regarding the impact of small arms. Nevertheless, nuclear abolition remains IPPNW's most important commitment and the focal point of its international work.

REFERENCES

1. Keynote Address of Hon. David Lange to the 6th IPPNW World Congress, Cologne, Germany, 1996.
2. This work was undertaken by IPPNW in cooperation with the Institute for Energy and Environmental Research of Takoma Park, Maryland. Three books were produced: *Radioactive Heaven and Earth: the health and environmental effects of nuclear weapons testing in, on and above earth,* New York: Apex Press, 1991, 193 pp.; *Plutonium: Deadly Gold of the Nuclear Age,* Cambridge, MA: IPPNW, 1992, 178 pp.; and *Nuclear Wastelands: a global guide to nuclear weapons production and its health and environmental effects,* Cambridge, MA: The MIT Press, 1995, 666 pp. IPPNW's Russian affiliate also made a major contribution to this effort with the publication of *Atom Declassified: half a century with the bomb,* a two-volume study of the Soviet nuclear-weapons production complex.
3. For a thorough account of IPPNW's role in efforts to achieve a CTBT, see Philip Schrag (1992), *Global Action: nuclear test ban diplomacy at the end of the Cold War,* Boulder, CO: Westview Press.

Address for correspondence

IPPNW, 727 Massachusetts Avenue, Cambridge, MA 02139, USA
Tel: 617-868-5050; Fax: 617-868-2560; email: ippnwbos@ippnw.org

61 | MÉDECINS SANS FRONTIÈRES

TERHI HEINÄSMÄKI

At the end of 1960s some radicals of the French student revolution worked as doctors in Biafra and in east Pakistan (Bangladesh). They realized that most relief organizations tend to function too slowly in emergency situations because they are bound by international diplomacy. To protect civilian life efficiently it is sometimes necessary even to step on the toes of governments.

Back in Paris these active doctors raised a debate about the grounds of humanitarian aid. As the result of this discussion a new humanitarian association Médecins Sans Frontières (MSF – Doctors Without Borders) was founded in 1971. MSF also differs from other aid organizations in its awareness of the role of the media. Publicity brings the condition of people needing emergency aid to the attention of the world.

In the 1970s another aid group, Médecins du Monde (Doctors of the World) split from MSF, and in the 1980s the French MSF broke into five other operational sections. These are the headquarters for field operations situated in Amsterdam, Barcelona, Brussels, Geneva, Luxembourg and, of course, Paris. A further 14 sections, from Sydney to Stockholm, provide resources and support operations in the form of representation, recruitment of field volunteers, fund-raising and information. There are three MSF offices, in New York, Geneva and Brussels, with special administrative functions.

According to the MSF charter (see Box 61.1) the organization offers assistance to populations in distress, to victims of natural or man-made disasters and to victims of armed conflict, without discrimination and irrespective of race, religion, creed or political affiliation. MSF respects only medical and humanitarian ethics. MSF offers assistance to an afflicted population even without the support of local authorities.

MSF has grown to be the world's largest private medical aid organization. It is known for its bravery, entering emergency zones when other aid groups hesitate. International respect has broadened the role of MSF from a humanitarian movement to a guardian of human rights; the sole presence of its workers can prevent the violation of those rights.

47.1

Médecins sans Frontières

Médecins Sans Frontières offers assistance to populations in distress, to victims of natural or man-made disasters and armed conflict, without discrimination and irrespective of race, religion, creed or political affiliation. Médecins Sans Frontières observes strict neutrality and impartiality in the name of universal medical ethics and the right to humanitarian assistance, and demands full and unhindered freedom in the exercise of its functions. Médecins Sans Frontières' volunteers promise to honour their professional code of ethics and to maintain complete independence from all political, economic and religious powers. As volunteers, members are aware of the risks and dangers of the mission they undertake and have no right to compensation for themselves or their beneficiaries other than that which Médecins Sans Frontières is able to afford them.

Artsen zonder Grenzen, Max Euweplein 40, P.O.Box 10014, 1001 EA Amsterdam The Netherlands. Tel : ++ (31) 20 52 08 700; Fax: ++ (31) 20 62 05 170; e-mail: hq@amsterdam.msf.org

Medicos sin Fronteras, Nou de la Rambla, 26, E-08001 Barcelona, Spain. Tel : ++(34) 3 304 61 00; Fax: ++(34) 3 304 61 02; email: oficina@barcelona.msf.org

Médecins Sans Frontières, Artsen Zoonder Grenzen, Dupréstreet 94, B - 1090 Brussels-Jette Belgium. Tel.: ++ (32) 2 474 74 74; Fax: ++ (32) 2 474 75 75; e-mail:zoom@brussels.msf.org

Médecins Sans Frontières, Rue du lac 12, Case postale 6090, CH-1211 Genè;ve 6. Tel : ++ (41) 22 849 84 84; Fax: ++ (41) 22 849 84 88; email: office-gva@geneva.msf.org

Médecins Sans Frontières, 8, rue Saint Sabin, F-75544 Paris cedex 11, France. Tel : ++ (33) 1 40 21 2929; Fax: ++ (33) 1 48 06 6868; e-mail:office@paris.msf.org

Médecins Sans Frontières, 70, Route de Luxembourg, L-7420 Béreldange Luxembourg. Tel : ++ (352) 33 25 15; Fax: ++ (352) 33 51 33; e-mail:office-lux@luxembourg.msf.org

Its international aid work is heroic and its organization financially strong. In 1996, MSF's total resources were US$252 million, of which private donors (individuals, corporations and foundations) provided 49 per cent. In the former eastern Europe MSF is better known than Santa Claus and it is a habit to donate to it. A high percentage of private funding, provided by more than 1.5 million active donors, guarantees the organization's financial independence. In 1996, MSF also received grants from inter-national organizations and governments that represented 51 per cent of its total resources.

MSF has been criticized internally and externally for its rapid actions. Maybe that is why its spirit has remained alert and energetic. Growth in respectability and wealth may, however, lead to increasing bureaucracy. World politics have also become more complicated since Biafra. The crisis in Rwanda, for example, exposed contradictions in many humanitarian ideas. Information overflow shrinks the planet and new dilemmas arise in humanitarian work. What are the limits for international aid? How far can humanitarian help go?

MSF acts in over 80 countries. Every year approximately 1000 humanitarian aid workers are sent to the field. Medical doctors, nurses and other medical personnel represent a third of the staff. Almost half of the workers are non-medical: coordinators, logisticians, technicians and accountants. Thousands of local people are also hired every year in the host countries.

Humanitarian work is not taking place only on battlefields. Catastrophes sometimes last for years, as in Sudan or Afghanistan. Work with Thailand's AIDS patients or the homeless in European cities has gone on for years. Education in humanitarian work is given at every headquarters to staff with variable experience in the field. For further studies, there is the Epicentre in Paris, an education centre for epidemiology and public health.

In its 27 years of confronting reality, MSF has acquired highly valuable knowledge, knowledge that has been shaped by contact with the doctors, nurses and health workers of host countries. Manuals, guides and handbooks for MSF's field operations have been compiled from this accumulated experience and they are widely used in various humanitarian missions.

MSF usually requires two years of professional experience before taking a volunteer to the field, although it sometimes hires recently-graduated medical doctors who do not have much clinical experience. MSF has been criticized for using unqualified personnel, but a freshman always works with a more experienced staff member. Besides, experience in the field can only be obtained by working in the field. MSF does not want to stop the drive of young health professionals by declaring them inexperienced.

Recruiting starts by contacting the nearest MSF office, but the recruitment can occur in any MSF office. A human resources officer must interview potential field volunteers in one of the sections before they will be considered for a posting. After the initial interview, a volunteer is asked to take part in a training course of one to two weeks at one of the headquarters. The working language varies. Knowledge of French is helpful as the work team may have many native French speakers. The Dutch office has more English-speaking missions than the other sections.

During the first year no salary is paid, hence the term volunteer. However, the organization pays about US$700 a month during that year as an incentive. From then on remuneration rises gradually. Incentive and salary are usually paid into the bank account of the volunteer's home country. In the field MSF takes care of travel expenses, lodgings and insurance, and pays a daily allowance (*per diem*) ample enough to cover daily needs and short vacations in the country of mission.

Every third month a volunteer is allowed one week's vacation from the field. After a year, a month can be spent in the home country at the organization's expense. The duration of a mission varies from six months to two years.

More information about MSF can be found at its web site:
http://www.msf.org/index.htm

Address for correspondence

Liisankatu 19 E 20, 00170 Helsinki, Finland
terhi.heinasmaki@ktl.fi

62 PHYSICIANS FOR HUMAN RIGHTS

JONATHAN FINE and SUSANNAH SIRKIN

In 1986, a group of physicians in the United States, convened by Dr Jonathan Fine, founded Physicians for Human Rights (PHR). Their vision was to create a human rights fact-finding and advocacy organization to draw exclusively on the skills of physicians and other health professionals. Since its inception, PHR's reporting on the physical and psychological consequences of serious abuses has been its hallmark.

PHR's first international initiatives focussed on individual victims of violations in Chile, the Soviet Union and other nations where serious violations were prevalent and systematic. These early interventions concerned primarily torture, psychological terror and urgent missions to aid physician human-rights activists and other victims who had been detained, abused, or disappeared.

While its goals have remained constant, PHR has gradually broadened its objectives and operations.[1] By 1987, PHR had begun to address the health consequences of indiscriminate attacks on civilians in armed conflicts. Over the past decade, the use of chemical weapons against civilians, attacks on hospitals, health workers and patients, killing and maiming by landmines, refugee crises, massacres and genocide have become a primary focus of PHR's investigations and campaigns.

Origins and early history

PHR grew out of the Boston-based American Committee for Human Rights (ACHR) which had undertaken human rights missions to the Philippines, Chile and South Korea between 1983 and 1986. In the latter year, at the suggestion of Eric Stover and Richard Claude, both members of the ACHR board of directors, Fine agreed to attempt to transform the ACHR into an organization exclusively drawing on the skills of physicians and other health professionals. Fine found ready allies among several physicians in

Boston who in the summer of 1986 formed the initial board of directors. Stover and Claude, instrumental in the birth of PHR, were not alone in suggesting a role for such a specialty organization. In 1983, at the time that ACHR was launched, Aryeh Neier, then the executive director of Human Rights Watch, had made a similar suggestion to Dr Fine.

Also, by the spring of 1986, a group of Dutch physicians, human rights scholars and activists had launched a similar effort, founding the Johannes Wier Stichting. While not forming a separate medical organization, Amnesty International (AI) for some years had recruited physicians to join selected investigations concerned with allegations of torture and other abuses. Amnesty also established medical groups in several countries which intervened through letter writing and other appeals against torture, the death penalty and in support of individual victims of regimes in many nations.

Conflict situations

The human rights movement only gradually awakened to the enormity of the challenge of human rights documentation and advocacy against indiscriminate killing, atrocities the other human costs of armed conflict. In the late 1980s, almost alone among human rights organizations, America's Watch, a division of Human Rights Watch (HRW), began to report on the conflicts in El Salvador and Nicaragua, issuing a series of reports on civilian deaths from the indiscriminate use of weapons in the conflicts. Amnesty International and America's Watch repeatedly raised concerns about the training of combatants in these conflicts by the US military, and the use of US weaponry in the commission of gross abuses against the civilian populations of those countries. Beginning with a mission to the Republic of Korea in 1987, PHR's conflict work rapidly extended to many nations and a variety of abuses.

Tear gas in the Republic of Korea

The 1987 PHR mission to the Republic of Korea first presented to the organization the challenge of an investigation concerned with mass casualties. In June of that year, the world press had reported the use of massive amounts of tear gas in virtually all of that nation's major cities. Drawing on the skills of Dr Howard Hu, an epidemiologist at the Harvard School of Public Health, a PHR team traveled to Seoul and studied the indiscriminate use of CS gas against peaceful demonstrators and bystanders in that city. The investigators reported blindness, acute and sub-acute respiratory illnesses, penetrating fragmentation injuries and many second-degree burn injuries as the principal physical consequences. A search of the medical literature confirmed that the long-term consequences of the use of CS gas and other lacrimating agents had not been adequately researched. PHR cautioned against future indiscriminate use of these weapons.

Leading newspapers in South Korea endorsed the findings of the mission. *The Washington Post* gave the mission prominent coverage and the *Journal of the American Medical Association* published the findings of the mission participants.[2] Subsequent early PHR missions dealt with the use of poison gas by Iraq against its own Kurdish nationals and with an alleged chemical attack against unarmed civilians in Tbilisi, Soviet Georgia.

Land mines in Cambodia and the call for banning their use

With the growing realization of the potential of medical and forensic fact-finding in situations of armed conflict, in 1989 PHR joined with Asia Watch, a branch of HRW, in a landmark mission to Cambodia to establish the dimensions of the catastrophic use of landmines. The subsequent report estimated that one out of every 236 Cambodians died or had been crippled by landmines.

The two organizations called for a ban on the future manufacture, deployment and use of antipersonnel mines.[3] This call proved instrumental in the launching of the subsequent global campaign against landmines. PHR and HRW have served as leading participants in this campaign. PHR sent further missions in 1992 and 1993 to Somalia and Mozambique, documenting the extensive carnage from these weapons.

The two organizations subsequently co-authored a definitive study, *A Deadly Legacy*.[4] In 1996, PHR appealed to health practitioners and major medical associations to join the campaign. The result has been increasingly effective medical advocacy as a component of the remarkable international campaign calling for a total ban on antipersonnel mines.

Civilian casualties from the US invasion of Panama

In 1990, six weeks after the US invasion of Panama, PHR sent a delegation of three physicians to investigate the deaths from that conflict. The mission followed widespread allegations that the US had attempted to minimize the cost in civilian lives. By analysing morgue and hospital records, and through interviews with many eyewitnesses, the team concluded that there were more civilian deaths than reported from official US sources.[5] The US Department of Defense later conceded the accuracy of PHR's findings.

The Gulf War and its aftermath

In 1991, during the Gulf War, PHR missions to Iraq were among the first to observe and report on the devastating consequences of the economic blockade and the bombing, which disabled the national electrification grid and thus the potable water and sewage systems. The PHR studies, noted widely in the media, documented the consequent surge in infant and childhood deaths. At the same time, PHR reported on the assaults on the health infrastructure during the Iraqi attack on the Kurds in its northern provinces.

Concerned with reports of the crisis faced by more than a million Kurdish refugees fleeing the civil war in Northern Iraq, PHR next sent physicians to the mountainous regions of Turkey and Iran. These teams provided the first reliable estimates that, daily, between 400 and 1000 children were dying, mostly from diarrhoeal diseases due to polluted water sources on which the refugees were dependent. Influenced by these reports, international relief organizations promptly redirected their efforts to mitigate the tragedy.[6]

The Intifada

With the onset of the Intifada, another PHR mission documented that the Israeli military had carried out a policy of deliberately breaking the forearms and, in some cases, the legs of Palestinians suspected of throwing stones.[7] Examining many patients and reviewing X-rays and medical records, the delegation determined that the observed fractures could only have occurred with the victims' arms held outstretched, with palms facing up. Psychiatrist participants in these missions pioneered for PHR the bringing to light of the vast psychological consequences of the conflict during the Intifada for both the occupying Israeli forces and the Palestinians. Extensive media coverage followed publication of the findings of this investigation.

Forensic studies

Accountability was a key theme for the international human rights movement during the 1990s. Whether through truth commissions, domestic courts or international tribunals, some perpetrators of torture, extrajudicial executions, massacres and genocide were finally being confronted with the facts of their crimes and held accountable for their actions. PHR has pioneered the application of forensic sciences to provide court-admissible evidence of atrocities.

PHR's forensic work began during the Intifada, responding to appeals from Palestinian human rights organizations and lawyers to investigate deaths under interrogation. Working with Israeli counterparts in the military service, PHR's forensic pathologists conducted postmortem examinations which, in some instances, showed no evidence of trauma substantiating torture. However, other forensic missions helped the human rights community establish that a systematic pattern of abuse by the Israeli military and secret police interrogators took place. Some of the most severe beatings lead to the death of detainees. Other forms of cruelty were also documented.

Under the leadership of PHR's former executive director, Eric Stover, forensic investigations matured as a highly significant feature of PHR's work. In the early 1980s Stover had helped organize scientific investigations into the disappearances in Argentina for the American Association for the Advancement of Science. Together with forensic anthropologist, Clyde Snow and pathologist Robert Kirschner, Stover mounted PHR investigations into individual and mass graves in Honduras, Guatemala, Mexico and Iraqi Kurdistan. Dozens of scientists participated, sponsored by newly-organized forensic anthropology teams in Argentina, Chile and Guatemala.

When the UN Security Council established the International Criminal Tribunal for former Yugoslavia in 1993, the first such tribunal since Nuremberg, Chief Prosecutor Judge Richard Goldstone asked PHR to provide forensic teams for the investigation of mass graves. Subsequently, PHR carried out similar investigations for the United Nations in Rwanda. By 1996, over 100 forensic specialists from more than a dozen countries had participated in examination of the remains of the victims of massacres in Vukovar, Srebrenica and Kibuye for PHR under the auspices of the International Criminal Tribunal for the former Yugoslavia.

Current status and influence

By 1997, PHR's international and domestic investigations had created a core of over 100 medical and forensic specialists, who continue to serve the organization. Their expertise has also given the larger medical community a new discipline and faculty for the education of medical and forensic students on human rights fact-finding and advocacy. PHR's representatives and mission participants have lectured at several US universities and have helped establish courses and curricula on health and human rights at Harvard Medical School and the University of California at Berkeley, among other institutions.

The work of PHR has been an important factor in the growth of health and human rights organizations in several other nations. The year 1987 saw the birth of two additional national groups, PHR/UK and PHR/Denmark. The same year, these two joined with PHR of the United States and the Johannes Wier Foundation to found an international network that has met annually to coordinate work internationally, discuss medical human rights methods and extend cooperation within the health and human rights community. This network has gradually expanded. At the 1996 annual meeting in the Netherlands, representatives from organizations in nine nations founded the International Federation of Health and Human Rights Organizations. The new entity, as yet drawing on volunteer staff from its Dutch affiliate, has its headquarters in the Netherlands. All told, over its first 11 years, PHR has issued over forty reports based on international and domestic investigations. The organization's work takes place on all continents and encompasses the medical, forensic and psychological consequences of violations of many of the UN covenants.

Beginning with assessment of the needs of applicants for political asylum in the United States, physician participation in the death penalty and, later, investigations of brutality within the prison systems in the United States, the domestic agenda of this US-based international organization is also expanding, as is the organization's educational work. Holding the first post-graduate course in the United States on Health and Human Rights in 1993, the organization's leadership then urged the Harvard School of Public Health to establish its own programme in this field.

PHR has been a major influence within the medical profession, helping build a medical ethic for the protection of human rights and professional responsibility for proactive initiatives using all available skills from the medical sciences. Today, several national, subspecialty medical societies, including the American Academy of Paediatrics, the American Psychiatric Association and the American Public Health Association, offer health and human rights seminars and speakers at their national meetings. PHR edits a regular column on Health and Human Rights for *The Lancet*. Its findings and analysis are often published in other leading medical journals, bringing this new field of medicine to a global audience of health professionals.

Organizational development

While still modest in size, PHR's Boston headquarters house a staff of sixteen. A Washington DC office established in 1996 enables the organization to conduct effective advocacy on the International Campaign to Ban Landmines and other issues best handled in proximity to the policymakers of the US federal government, other human rights NGOs and foreign embassies. PHR's international forensic programme is based in Chicago under the leadership of Dr Kirschner. PHR also launched a genetics laboratory in 1996, under the direction of Dr Mary Claire King at the University of Seattle, Washington. The organization is directed by Leonard Rubenstein, its third executive director, and Susannah Sirkin, the deputy director. An active board of directors, currently led by Dr Charles Clements, sets policy for the organization and directs its programme and organizational development.

As a membership organization, PHR has sought the support of physicians and health professionals and has established as a major goal the development of a larger medical constituency for human rights in the United States. It has recently launched a nationwide campaign to promote the link between health and human rights during the 50th anniversary year of the Universal Declaration of Human Rights. While hundreds of individuals annually donate funds for its work, private foundations in the United States and abroad are the organization's principal source of income.

Conclusion

Only 11 years since its inception, Physicians for Human Rights has helped establish the indispensable role and influence of the medical sciences and of medical professionals in the protection of international human rights. While PHR will continue to concern itself with a broad spectrum of violations of the international human-rights covenants, the organization's participation in the monitoring of armed conflicts is in the ascendancy and has become a staple of its work and advocacy. The challenges ahead may be for the organization to demonstrate the efficacy of new and refined methodologies and, by example and precept, to assist in the development of health and human rights as an important field for all health professions and health practitioners in every nation.

REFERENCES

1. Physicians for Human Rights (1997), *10-year Report 1986–1996*.
2. Hu, Howard *et al.* (????), *Journal of the American Medical Association (JAMA)* 262: 660–3.
3. Asia Watch and Physicians for Human Rights (1991), *The Coward's War*, September.
4. Human Rights Watch (HRW), *A Deadly Legacy, PHR and the Arms Project*, HRW, October.
5. Physicians for Human Rights (PHR) (1991), *The Human Cost of Military Action in Panama*, PHR, October.
6. 'Initial Medical Assessment of Kurdish Refugees in the Turkey-Iraq Border Region', *JAMA* 991: 266: 638–40.
7. Physicians for Human Rights (PHR) (1993), *A Report on Emergency Measures and Access to Health Care in the Occupied Territories 1990–1992*, PHR, June.

Address for Correspondence
Physicians for Human Rights, 100 Boylston Street, Boston, MA 02116, USA; e-mail: hrusa@phrusa.org.

63 AMNESTY INTERNATIONAL
Research, Documentation and Action for Human Rights

JAMES WELSH

At the end of the 1950s and the beginning of the 1960s the London lawyer, Peter Benenson, was increasingly outraged by reports of the imprisonment of individuals solely for the peaceful expression of their political, social or religious beliefs. One such case was that of two students in Portugal who were arrested and imprisoned after an informer overheard them raising a toast to freedom in a public restaurant. Benenson decided to launch a one-year campaign, an 'Appeal for Amnesty 1961' and published an article to launch this campaign in the London *Observer*, on 28 May of that year. That article, 'The Forgotten Prisoners', is regarded as the starting-point of Amnesty International (AI).

The Appeal for Amnesty called for the release of men and women imprisoned because of the peaceful expression of their political and religious beliefs. Benenson called these people 'prisoners of conscience'. His plan was to encourage people to write letters to government officials in countries which had prisoners of conscience, calling for their release. The campaign grew rapidly, spread to other countries, and by the end of 1961 a permanent organization, Amnesty International, had been formed.

Amnesty International was founded on the principle that people have fundamental rights that transcend national, cultural, religious and ideological boundaries. Over the four decades of its existence, AI has maintained a core set of principles and continues to work for:

- freedom for prisoners of conscience (those who have been imprisoned solely for the non-violent expression of their political, religious or other conscientiously held beliefs, or by reason of their ethnic origin, sex, colour or other indicators of their status, provided they have not used or advocated violence);
  - an end to torture and cruel, inhuman or degrading treatment or punishment;
  - an end to disappearances and extrajudicial executions;
  - an end to the death penalty;

- prompt and fair trials in political cases;
- an end to the participation of children in conflict;
- non-refoulement of refugees;
- an end to the excessive use of force, and to deliberate and arbitrary killings and hostage-taking; and
- an end to military, security or police transfers which could contribute to human rights violations.

Amnesty International also opposes analogous abuses by armed opposition groups and is exploring its role in cases where governments fail to take action against abuses by private actors.

Amnesty International structure

At the present time, AI has more than 1 million members, subscribers and regular donors in more than 160 countries and territories and thousands of local AI groups. There are nationally organized sections in 56 countries in all continents.

The organization's headquarters is the International Secretariat in London, with more than 300 permanent staff and around 100 volunteers from more than 50 countries. The secretariat carries out research into human rights violations around the world, organizes and coordinates campaigning activities by its international membership, maintains relations with inter-governmental and non-governmental organizations and promotes human rights awareness.

Amnesty International is governed by a nine-member International Executive Committee made up of eight volunteer members, elected every two years by an International Council comprising representatives of the worldwide movement, and a member from the International Secretariat, elected by staff.

AI research and action

Amnesty International works on the basis that research and action must go together. Documentation is important but it must be translated into effective campaigning if it is to have an impact on the human rights situation. About half of the staff in the International Secretariat are involved in researching human rights violations and every country is under scrutiny. Staff carry out this work by maintaining contact with local activists, lawyers and human rights organizations, as well as by speaking or writing to families of prisoners, to released prisoners or to others with specific information about specific individuals. In addition, researchers travel, where possible, to the country on which they are working (or to adjacent territories) to interview victims, lawyers, human rights bodies and others, as well as to meet government representatives and officials to discuss findings. Where torture is alleged, medical evidence can be a vital adjunct to testimony and local medical reports as well as examination findings by medical delegates can strengthen documentation.

On the basis of the information gathered by research staff, the organization organizes appeals for individuals, as well as country or thematic campaigns involving parts of the AI membership and campaigning involving the whole AI membership. Every year, AI members from around the world join forces to campaign for several months on human rights issues in one country or on a particular human rights issue. These movement-wide campaigns involve the preparation and publication of reports on major human rights issues, lobbying governments and their embassies for change, publicizing human rights abuses and working closely with local human rights activists and other community organizations to achieve change.

In 1998, two major campaigns involved the entire AI membership in action for the promotion and protection of human rights. The first (Get Up! Sign Up!) was AI's campaign to mark the 50th anniversary of the Universal Declaration of Human Rights (UDHR). It surpassed its goal of getting 5 million people to pledge themselves to the rights in the UDHR and, at a ceremony on 10 December 1998 at the Palais de Chaillot (the building in Paris where the UDHR was adopted by the UN in 1947), AI's then Secretary-General, Pierre Sané, presented Kofi Annan, the UN Secretary General, with 13.2 million pledges from more than 130 countries around the world. This event was the culmination of a year of human rights promotion, lobbying and grassroots action.

In October 1998, AI launched a year-long campaign on human rights violations in the USA with a 150-page report, *USA: Rights for All*. The report revealed a persistent and widespread pattern of human rights violations in the USA, including police brutality, torture and ill-treatment of prisoners, and a spiralling rate of judicial execution. Racism and discrimination were shown to contribute to the denial of the fundamental rights of countless men, women and children. Amnesty International members worldwide joined civil rights activists inside the USA in demanding greater protection of rights for all US citizens. A number of issues were of particular relevance to health professionals, including medical participation in executions, the rights of asylum seekers to appropriate medical and psychological care and the rights of prisoners, including female prisoners, to effective medical attention. Apart from working to stop specific violations, the organization drew attention to the discrepancy between the human rights rhetoric of the USA in the international sphere and its domestic record, and pressed the US government to end its reluctance to apply to itself the international human rights standards it so often says it expects of others.

In October 2000 a one-year-long AI campaign for the abolition of torture commenced. The campaign underlined the role of discrimination as a basis for torture.

Working for individuals

In addition to major campaigns, AI members work for individuals or groups of people suffering the range of human rights violations in the organization's mandate – from imprisonment as prisoners of conscience to disappearance or extrajudicial execution. Working in local groups, members use, among others, techniques such as letter-writing, mobilizing support from other individuals or organizations, participating in embassy visits, publicity and petitioning on behalf of sick prisoners or detained health professionals.

In some cases very rapid action for prisoners or others at risk is needed. Support for those who are in immediate danger of serious human rights violations, such as torture or execution, is mobilized by the Urgent Action network. The network is made up of more than 80,000 volunteers in some 85 countries. Urgent Actions are distributed by AI's International Secretariat in London by email and fax to AI sections worldwide who then distribute them to members of the Urgent Action network asking them to send appeals to governments by the fastest means possible. Each case can generate between 3000 and 5000 appeals. In 2000 more than 800 Urgent Actions were issued, calling on supporters to take or to continue action, or to provide further information. About one third of cases featured in Urgent Actions see an improvement in their subject's situation.

Urgent Actions typically cover a variety of concerns on behalf of people who are either at risk or have been the victim of the following human rights violations: torture, disappearance, the death penalty, political killings and death threats, arbitrary arrest, prolonged incommunicado detention, detention without charge or trial, legal concerns, ill-health, deaths in custody, risk of forcible repatriation and forcible exile.

Contributing to the development of standards

Amnesty International plays an active role internationally in both inter-governmental and non-governmental fora in the area of human rights standards and protection. Over many years, AI has contributed to the evolving international and regional standards on torture, disappearances, the death penalty and refugee protection through its contributions to international discussions and standard-setting. For example, the organization joined many other NGOs in contributing detailed comments and suggestions to United Nations bodies during the preparations for the International Diplomatic Conference to inaugurate an International Criminal Court and it will continue to monitor the development and practice of the court.[1] Amnesty International was also active in non-governmental discussions concerning standards for the protection of non-combatants in conflict and the medical documentation of torture.

Specialist networks: the health professional network

Amnesty International has specialist networks – groups of medical professionals, lawyers and others – who use their expertise to campaign for victims of human rights violations.

The AI health professional network has members in around 35 countries. Utilizing materials prepared by the Medical Office within the International Secretariat, members take action on cases which usually (but not always) have a medical aspect. Examples include cases of denial of medical care, of torture, of infliction of corporal punishment or the death penalty, particularly where doctors or nurses are involved in the carrying out of the punishment. Other issues of concern to health professionals include hunger strikes by prisoners of conscience, harsh prison conditions, the use of repressive technologies such as electroshock devices, and the imprisonment of, or infliction of abuses against, health professionals for their human rights or professional activities or for the peaceful expression of their views.

The Medical Office of the International Secretariat also provides a range of documentation to Amnesty International members and to health professional bodies and individuals to assist in activities in favour of human rights. These include a compilation of codes and declarations on medical ethics and human rights,[2] a bibliography on health and human rights themes,[3] and occasional papers on subjects such as lethal injection executions and the health professions.[4] A fortnightly electronic newsletter is disseminated to any health professional or other interested individual requesting a subscription.[5]

Human rights education

Amnesty International aims to contribute to the observance of human rights throughout the world as set out in the UDHR. In pursuance of this aim, Amnesty International promotes awareness and knowledge of all human rights, in addition to its campaigning against violations of certain civil and political rights.

Amnesty International sections have adopted a range of approaches to human rights education. Recent activities have included lobbying governments to ensure that human rights are incorporated in official training and educational curricula in institutions ranging from schools and universities, to military and police academies as well as civil service and other professional training programmes.

Amnesty International's human rights education and other preventive work often forms part of a country strategy, aimed at enhancing the local impact of the organization's actions and helping the development of a wider and stronger human-rights movement. Health professionals play a part in the promotion of human rights education to students.

Exposing human rights violations

Amnesty International issues major public documents on human rights violations on 40 to 50 countries annually as well as reporting on more than 150 countries in its annual report. The 2001 Annual Report, which detailed abuses committed in 2000, is indicative of the kinds and levels of abuses against people every year. In gathering information for this report, AI sent delegations to more than 70 countries and territories during 2000. Delegates carried out a range of work which included discussing AI's concerns with government authorities, observing political trials and carrying out on-the-spot investigations into human rights abuses.

Financing human rights research and action

Amnesty International's funding reflects the movement's independence and its reliance on broad public support. No funds are sought or accepted from governments for AI's work investigating and campaigning against human rights violations. The hundreds of thousands of donations that sustain this work come from the pockets of its members, from the public and from organizations such as trusts, foundations and companies.

The international budget is spent on professional office-based and field research by

AI staff into human rights violations worldwide, on trial observations and representations to governments, and on the movement's international public information, campaigning and development activities.

The organization continues to review its programme, priorities, mandate and working methods in order to maintain its relevance and effectiveness, and the key event in this process is the biennial meeting, the International Council Meeting, the organization's decisionmaking body of delegates from all sections.

The patterns of abuse may have changed since Peter Benenson published his *cri de coeur* in 1961 but human rights violations remain a scourge of contemporary society. They occur in relatively peaceful societies as well as in those in turmoil and at war. There remains a need to mobilize public opinion and the international community to protest and demand an end to such violations. That is the goal of AI's work.

Amnesty International programme: a summary

Amnesty International works for the observance of rights set out in the Universal Declaration of Human Rights and opposes:

- the imprisonment, detention or other physical restrictions imposed on any person by reason of his or her political, religious or other conscientiously-held beliefs, ethnic origin, sex, colour, language, national or social origin, economic status, birth or other status, provided that he or she has not used or advocated violence;
- the detention of any political prisoner without fair trial within a reasonable time or any trial procedures relating to such prisoners that do not conform to internationally-recognized norms;
- the death penalty, and the torture or other cruel, inhuman or degrading treatment or punishment of prisoners or other detained or restricted persons, whether or not the persons affected have used or advocated violence;
- the extrajudicial execution of persons whether or not imprisoned, detained or restricted, and disappearances, whether or not the persons affected have used or advocated violence.

REFERENCES

1. Amnesty International (1997), *The International Criminal Court – Making the Right Choices: Part I*, (AI Index: IOR 40/01/97), January, and subsequent documents in the series.
2. Amnesty International (2000), *Ethical Codes and Declarations Relevant to the Health Professions* (4th revised edn), London: Amnesty International.
3. Amnesty International (1999), 'Publications on Health and Human Rights Themes: 1982–1998', in *Health and Human Rights* 4 (1): 215–76.
4. Amnesty International (1998), *Lethal Injection: the medical technology of execution*, London: AI Index: ACT 50/01/98.
5. Amnesty International, *Bulletin: human rights information and web links for health professionals*, fortnightly, available on request from medical@amnesty.org

Address for correspondence

Amnesty International, 1 Easton Street, London WC1X 8DJ, United Kingdom.
Tel: 44 20 7413 5500; Cell: 44 780 155 1927; Fax: 44 20 7956 1157; email: jwelsh@amnesty.org .

64 OPERATION HANDICAP INTERNATIONAL[1]

HANNA TAPANAINEN

Treatment, prevention, integration

Almost 10 per cent of the world's population suffer from some sort of handicap. In countries where the political and economic situation is uncertain, health services are often the first to suffer. The handicapped are particularly vulnerable in this situation.

Handicap International's vocation is to develop programmes for handicapped persons, especially in developing countries and situations of crisis. The organization helps the handicapped both physically (by providing equipment, such as prostheses, and rehabilitation) and economically and socially (through preventive measures and social rehabilitation). Handicap International is also actively involved in mine-clearing operations and develops programmes to alert the local population to the danger of mines in order to prevent future accidents. Handicap International was also one of the co-founders of the International Campaign to Ban Landmines.

Background

In 1979, two French doctors, Jean-Baptiste Richardier and Claude Simonnot, were practising in Cambodian refugee camps. They were struck by the situation of thousands of handicapped men, women and children, the victims of landmines, leprosy, polio and disabling conditions, abandoned by humanitarian aid. Later they met with other volunteers who had experience in producing equipment for the handicapped in Third World countries, and adapted from them the principle of manufacturing simple and inexpensive artificial limbs, using locally-available materials like wood and leather.

Handicap International (HI) was officially founded on 3 August 1982. It is a humanitarian, apolitical and undenominational non-governmental organization (NGO). It has offices or representation in France, Belgium, Denmark, Germany, Switzerland and the United States. In 1997 it had more than 140 rehabilitation and prevention programmes in 40 different countries, the largest ones being in Angola, Mozambique and Rwanda in Africa, Brazil and Nicaragua in Latin America, Cambodia in Asia and the countries of former Yugoslavia in Europe. Handicap International is financed by public sponsors such as the United Nations (especially UNHCR) and the European Union and by individual donations.

Fields of activity

Rehabilitation

Handicap International has over the years acquired invaluable experience in the field of rehabilitation. Artificial limbs enable a handicapped person to live on his feet again, rehabilitation enables him to regain the simple physical actions of everyday life and helps him to attain greater autonomy and integration into his community.

The organization has adopted simple techniques for manufacturing artificial limbs, crutches and wheelchairs. In many cases these are produced from locally-available materials, such as leather, wood, old tyres and rubber. Handicap International's volunteers work in close collaboration with local employees and authorities. They train technicians, physiotherapists and administrative staff in the local areas. By using simple techniques and local staff, and with the support of the country's authorities, HI aims at establishing a system which can be continued and maintained once the expatriates have departed.

Social reintegration

Apart from providing artificial limbs and other equipment to the handicapped, HI has different programmes that aim to help the reintegration of the handicapped in their community by providing economic assistance and developing activities which will provide income for the handicapped and their families. One example of this kind of activity is the Economic and Social Rehabilitation Programme in Cambodia which provides programme teams, composed mainly of physically handicapped people, who contact the handicapped in their homes.

The teams offers help in many ways: they provide moral support and listen to the problems that handicapped have to deal with; they assess the capabilities of the handicapped person and his family; provide economic assistance such as a loan for the purchase of equipment, tools or animals; and information and guidance about the programmes offered by the organization.

Prevention

Handicap International is also active in prevention programmes. In different community-based programmes HI tries to identify the origins of the disablement in the community, and teaches community members about the disabling effects of diseases such as leprosy and polio, and how to prevent these. Preventive work also covers awareness-raising programmes about the danger of mines. These aim to alert the population to the danger of landmines and teach appropriate ways to deal with them. This includes obtaining information on the location of mined areas and on accidents which have occurred in the region. Networking with other regional and international agencies and exchanging information helps to coordinate mine clearance and the provision of humanitarian and other aid to the victims. Handicap International Belgium, for example, has had the large Community Based Mine Awareness Programme in Afghanistan since 1996. The objectives of this are to limit the number of accidents and to put into place structures at the village and community level which will handle the problems of landmine and unexploded munitions accidents. The project is composed of three parts: (i) the recruitment and the essential role of the local trainers; (ii) raising mine awareness of the population and establishing mine committees of volunteers; and (iii) the establishment of a network that collects and disseminates information. From April 1996 to March 1998, more than 1500 villages and 160 schools received direct training, 251 mine committees were created, and more than 150,000 people followed the training.

International Campaign to Ban Landmines

Handicap International has been closely confronted with the problem of landmines, one of the principal causes of handicap in countries affected by war. The organization realized very quickly that repair was not sufficient; the number of mine victims grows more rapidly than the number of people provided with artificial limbs. HI decided, therefore, not only to add de-mining and mine awareness-raising to its orthopaedic activities, but also, since 1992, to launch an international campaign aiming at a total ban on landmines. The organization was one of the co-founders of the International Campaign to Ban Landmines, a campaign that since 1992 has brought together over 800 human rights, humanitarian, peace, children's, medical, development, arms control, environmental and women's groups in over 50 countries. Its work finally culminated in the signing of the Ottawa Agreement in December 1997 that bans the use, production, stockpiling and import or export of antipersonnel mines. The campaign against antipersonnel mines was awarded the Nobel Peace Prize in 1997. The work against mines didn't, however, stop at the signing of the treaty; now it is necessary to ensure proper enforcement of the agreement and respect for the deadlines that have been set.[2]

REFERENCES

1. Chapter 64 is based on the information available on the homepage of Handicap International, and on the campaign materials and newsletters of Handicap International Belgium.
2. More information can be obtained at: http://www.handicap-international.org/

Addresses
Handicap International France: Head Office, ERAC – 14 avenue Berthelot, F – 69361 Lyon Cedex 07
Tel: +33-(0)4-78 69 79 79; Fax: +33-(0)4-78 69 79 94
Paris office: 104-106 rue Oberkampf, F – 75011 Paris; Tel: +33-(0)1- 43 14 87 00; Fax: +33-(0)1-43 14 87 07
Handicap International Belgium:
67 rue de Spa 1040 Bruxelles; Tel: +32-(0)2-280 16 01; Fax: +32-(0)2-230 60 30
Handicap International Germany:
Hirschbergstrasse 3, D-80634 München; Tel: +49-(0)89-13 03 98 00; Fax: +49-(0)89-13 03 98 01
Address for correspondence
Topeliuksenkatu 35 A 34; 00250 Helsinki; Finland; Tel: +358-9-2419772; email: hanna.tapanainen@helsinki.fi

65 INTERNATIONAL PEACE RESEARCH ASSOCIATION

UNTO VESA

Modern peace research emerged in the 1950s as one of many different reactions in the academic community to the threat of global war. Peace research, according to its founding fathers, was to be interdisciplinary, international and applied. The International Peace Research Association (IPRA) was established in 1964 to respond to the growing need for international cooperation in this field. The basic activities of IPRA have been its general conferences, permanent research commissions and publications. Although the origins of the association were mainly in the countries of western Europe and North America, it has developed into a truly global scientific organization, which also has a role to play in the post-Cold War world.

The United Nations was established 'to save succeeding generations from the scourge of war'. The ambition to learn from past misery in order to prevent it from repeating itself has been quite common after great wars. After the Second World War (WW II) several different approaches stemming from that ambition emerged in the scientific community: one academic reaction was the effort to establish or strengthen ethical codes for scientific work, for example through the World Federation of Scientific Workers; another was the founding by scientists, especially those with expertise in atomic physics, of the Pugwash movement; still another reaction was the emergence of peace research, which in a well-known definition aims at the study of the causes of war and the conditions for peace, with the explicit normative ambition of abolishing war.

Although some of peace research's founding fathers (such as Quincy Wright) published pioneering works in the 1930s and 1940s, it arose as an organized intellectual movement in the early 1950s – first in the United States, Canada and some small west European countries. Many of its birthplaces had been strongholds of traditional pacifist peace movements, such as the Quakers. In the United States the first significant institutionalization took place around the *Journal of Conflict Resolution*, launched by famous social scientists at the University of Michigan in 1957. The first European peace research institution, later the International Peace Research Institute of Oslo (PRIO), was established by one of the leading figures of modern peace research, Professor Johan Galtung in 1959, and the journal of that institute, the *Journal of Peace Research*, in 1964. The process that led to the establishment of the Stockholm International Peace Research Institute (SIPRI) in 1966 was initiated by Sweden's Prime Minister Tage Erlander two years earlier as a pragmatic way of commemorating Sweden's 150 years of unbroken peace. All these are worth mentioning as indications of a wider intellectual climate and concern.

The intellectual mood and the ambitions of these pioneers are aptly illustrated by the first editorial of the *Journal of Conflict Resolution*:

> The reasons which have led us into this enterprise may be summed up in two propositions. The first is that by far the most important problem facing the human race today is that of international relations, more specifically, the prevention of global war. The second is that if intellectual progress is to be made in this area, the study of international relations must be made an interdisciplinary enterprise, drawing its discourse from all the social sciences, and even further.

In order to be of relevance, peace research was to be interdisciplinary, applied and international. This characterization was designed to dissociate peace research from unidisciplinary, nationally-biased, 'ivory-tower' approaches to the study of war and peace that have existed for centuries. The effort to organize research in this field as a joint international enterprise was programmatically motivated, but there were also pragmatic needs as new institutions, research centres, associations and journals emerged. The need for an international framework became more and more obvious, and the establishment of the International Peace Research Association (IPRA) in London in December 1964 was the response. It was founded with the principal aim of increasing the quantity of research focused on world peace and ensuring its scientific quality. Among the steps leading to that phase there had been preparatory contacts between the existing institutions; it is of some interest to note that the Quakers had some role in this process, and that the Pugwash conferences were taken as a model for IPRA.

The new organization emphasized the need for interdisciplinary work, stressing 'the inter-system approach', that is to say close cooperation between scholars from countries with different socio-economic philosophies, from east and west and from north and south.

According to its statute the purpose of IPRA is to advance peace research. Among the activities to be carried out the most prominent from early on were the organization of general and special conferences, the publication of scientific studies and the proceedings of IPRA conferences, and more general support to institutions, publications and researchers in this field. Although there have been changes, of course, in the procedures and emphases of the organization, the basic ambition and the basic activities have remained very much the same.

The Inaugural Conference was held in 1965 at the University of Groningen in the Netherlands. There have been general conferences since then, usually every second year, with the 18th conference in Tampere, Finland in August 2000. The proceedings of the inaugural conference, published in 1966, tell us that: 'there were 73 participants from 23 countries (Belgium, Brazil, Canada, Colombia, Czechoslovakia, Denmark, England, Finland, France, German Federal Republic, India, Israel, Italy, Japan, the Netherlands, Nigeria, Norway, Pakistan, Poland, Sweden, Switzerland, the USA and Yugoslavia) representing 19 disciplines'. From that relatively modest beginning IPRA has turned into a truly global scientific association, with hundreds of participants attending its conferences.

It is remarkable that most of the countries present in the first conference have remained strong peace research bases ever since. It is fair to note, however, that in the beginning the association was, despite representatives from Japan and some Third World countries, very much a European/North American organization. This is to some degree reflected in the person of the key functionary of the body, its secretary-general. Thus far eleven persons have served in that role, most of them Europeans and Americans.[1] While these lists might convey a very Western bias, this also reflects the financial fact that the association is dependent on the institutional support of its strong members; which can provide (for free) the infrastructure the organization needs.

The global character of IPRA is better illustrated by the list of the venues of its general conferences. Between Groningen (1965) and Tampere (2000) it held 16 such conferences.[2]

The global character of peace research and of the association is evident also in the regional organizations of IPRA. There are such affiliates for Asia and Pacific region, for Africa, for Latin America, for Europe and for North America. Some of these also have their own publications, but IPRA serves them all with its quarterly *IPRA Newsletter*. Throughout its history IPRA has been in close cooperation with the United Nations and especially with UNESCO, and the latter has been of great importance in promoting peace research worldwide.

Most of IPRA's work in the general conferences and between them is organized through its commissions. Their character and number have changed over the years. At present the association has 18 permanent commissions, the names of which tell us where the focus of today's peace research is: Conflict Resolution and Peace Building; Culture and Communications; Eastern Europe; Ecological Security; Global Political Economy; International Human Rights; Internal Conflicts; Non-violence; Peace Education; Peace History; Peace Movements; Peace Theories; Reconciliation; Refugees; Religion and Peace; Security and Disarmament; Women and Peace; and the Working Group on Indigenous Peoples' Rights.

Some old commissions and working groups have died when they have been perceived to have completed their mission, and new ones have been established for fresh needs.

It is perhaps not possible to submit any objective assessment of IPRA's performance – undoubtedly it has had its ups and downs, as most organizations have – but its role as the link between peace researchers and institutes around the globe is as vital today as it was at the time of its establishment. Although the world has changed fundamentally since then, especially with the disappearance of the Cold War system, wars and violent conflicts have not gone away. There is still need for peace research informed by the same ambition that animated the pioneers: that through interdisciplinary and international research on the causes of war and the conditions for peace it is possible to promote international harmony. The theme of the IPRA Tampere conference in August 2000, 'Challenges for Peace Research in the 21st Century. A Dialogue of Civilizations', paved the way for that research.

REFERENCES

1. 1971–75 Asbjörn Eide (Norway); 1975–79 Raimo Väyrynen (Finland); 1979–83 Yoshikazu Sakamoto (Japan); 1983–87 Chadwick Alger (USA); 1987–89 Clovis Brigagao (Brazil); 1989–91 Elise Boulding (USA); 1991–94 Paul Smoker (USA); 1995–97 Karlheinz Koppe (Germany); 1997–2000 Bjorn Moller (Denmark); and 2000– Katsuya Kodama (Japan).
2. The general conferences between Groningen and Tampere have been: Tällberg, Sweden (1967); Karlovy Vary, Czechoslovakia (1969); Bled, Yugoslavia (1971); Varanasi, India (1974); Turku, Finland (1975); Oaxtepec, Mexico (1977); Königstein, Germany (1979); Orillia, Canada (1981); Gyor, Hungary (1983); Sussex, England (1986); Rio de Janeiro, Brazil (1988); Groningen, the Netherlands (1990); Kyoto, Japan (1992); Valetta, Malta (1994); Brisbane, Australia (1996); and Durban, South Africa (1998).

Address for correspondence
TAPRI, FIN 33014 University of Tampere
Email unto.vesa@uta.fi

ABOUT THE AUTHORS

Dr Kingsley K. Akinroye, a physician and public health consultant, is at present a research fellow in the Department of Public Health and General Practice, University of Kuopio, Finland.

Kofi Annan was elected Secretary-General of the United Nations in December 1996. He has served in the UN since 1962, latterly as Under Secretary-General, Department of Peacekeeping Operations (1993–95) and as UN Special Envoy to former Yugoslavia (1995–96).

Mary-Wynne Ashford, a physician and an associate professor at the University of Victoria, Canada, is a co-president of International Physicians for the Prevention of Nuclear War.

Frank Barnaby, a nuclear physicist by training, is the former Executive Secretary of the Pugwash conferences and Science and World Affairs (1967–70) and Director of the Stockholm International Peace Research Institute (1971–81). He is currently a defence analyst and writer on military technology, nuclear weapons and nuclear energy. His most recent book is *Instruments of Terror* (London: Vision Paperbacks, 1997).

B.B. Bondarenko is a member of the St Petersburg branch of the Russian Committee of the International Physicians for the Prevention of Nuclear War.

Thomas A. Cardamone is Executive Director of the Council For a Livable World Education Fund in Washington DC. The organization's programmes are aimed at denying state and non-state actors the means to engage in arms races that can lead to the acquisition of weapons of mass destruction, waste finite resources and create global insecurity. He was previously director of the education fund's Conventional Arms Transfers Project, a programme which tracks and analyses arms-trade issues within the executive branch, in Congress and the defence industry, and editor of the project's newsletter, *Arms Trade News*.

Evgeni Chazov is an Academician and the Director of the Russian Cardiology Research Centre He was the co-founder and first co-president of IPPNW with Dr Bernard Lown. He is also a former Minister of Health of the USSR, and served as Vice-Minister of Health on several occasions.

Paul A. Chilton is Professor in Linguistics in the School of Language, Linguistics and Translation Studies at the University of East Anglia. He has worked for a number of years in the field of language and international relations. Initially concerned in the 1980s with the role of language use in the construction of the Cold War, he investigated 'nuke-speak', and has since published *Security Metaphors* (New York: Peter Lang 1966) which examines the cognitive processes involved in the conceptualization of international relations.

Michael Christ has been Executive Director of International Physicians for the Prevention of Nuclear War (IPPNW) since January 1998. He led IPPNW's World Court Project to persuade the World Health Organization and the United Nations to challenge the legality of nuclear weapons at the International Court of Justice.

Julie Cliff is an Australian physician and public health specialist who has worked in Mozambique since 1976. She now teaches in the Faculty of Medicine, Eduardo Mondlane University, having previously worked in Maputo Central Hospital and the Ministry of Health. She has been an International Epidemiologic Fellow at the US Centers for Disease Control and is an Associate of the Macfarlane Burnet Centre for Medical Research in Melbourne, Australia. She is a Fellow of the Royal College of Physicians in London, holds an Honorary Doctorate from Monash University, Australia, and is an Officer of the Order of Australia.

Merav Datan is programme director for International Physicians for the Prevention of Nuclear War. From 1994 to 1998 she worked for the Lawyers' Committee on Nuclear Policy in New York as research director, and for the World Order Models Project as director of the initiative on Comprehensive Arms Restraint. In between she worked as news analyst at the Ethiopian Consulate in Jerusalem. She is co-author of *Security and Survival: the Case for a Nuclear Weapons Convention* and principal drafter of the Model Nuclear Weapons Convention.

Kate Dewes has coordinated the South Island Regional Office of the Aotearoa/New Zealand Peace Foundation from her home in Christchurch for 20 years. In 1988–90 she served on the Public Advisory Committee on Disarmament and Arms Control. In 1992–96 she was an International Peace Bureau (IPB) executive member, becoming a vice-president in 1997. A pioneer of the World Court Project (WCP), she was on its International Steering Committee in 1992–96. She is currently on the International Steering Committee of the Middle Powers Initiative.

Klaus Dörner – professor, social psychiatrist and retired Medical Director of Rheinland-Westphalen Psychiatric Clinic in Guetersloh – has been called 'the Conscience of German Psychiatry'. Klaus Dörner has created the German–Polish cooperation in the field of psychiatry after the Second World War and started the reconciliation process between psychiatrists in those two countries. He established an organization for the relatives of persons killed by the euthanasia programme, and another for patients subjected to forced sterilizations. For an assessment of Professor Dörner's life and work, see M. Buchrig *et al* (eds), *Herr Dörner hat eine Idee* (Bonn: Psychiatrie Verlag, 1993).

Jonathan Fine served as the convener and first Executive Director of Physicians for Human Rights.

Richard Garfield, former chair of the human rights committee of the American Public Health Association, sits on the National Academy of Science Institute of Medicine Committee on Gulf War Studies Design, and on the boards of the Institute for the Study of Genocide and the Columbia University Center for the Promotion of Human Rights. He is an Academic Adviser to the Special UN Representative for Children and Armed Conflict.

Robert D. Green, a former commander in the British Royal Navy, was Personal Staff Officer to the Assistant Chief of Naval Staff (Policy), UK Ministry of Defence, who was closely involved in the replacement of the Polaris ballistic-missile submarine force from 1978 to 1980. In his final appointment he was Staff Officer (Intelligence) to Commander-in-Chief Fleet at Northwood HQ, in charge of round-the-clock intelligence support for Polaris as well as the rest of the fleet. Having taken voluntary redundancy in the 1981 defence review, he was released after the Falklands War. He is Chair of the World Court Project (UK) and was on the WCP International Steering Committee. He is currently chair of the Strategy Committee of the International Steering Committee of the Middle-Powers Initiative.

Pekka Haavisto was Minister of Environment and Development Cooperation in Finland from 1995 to 1999, and chairman of the United Nations Environmental Programme/Habitat Balkans Task Force, Summer–Autumn 1999.

Dr Joerg Haier is an Assistant Research Professor at the Institute for Molecular Medicine, Huntington Beach, California and an Assistant Professor of Surgery at the Wilheim University of Muenster, Germany.

Terhi Heinäsmäki is a physician and a specialist in internal medicine at the University Hospital of Helsinki. She is a member of the Physicians for Social Responsibility of Finland. She has worked for Médecins sans Frontières and Finnish Red Cross projects in various countries.

Ernst Jan Hogendoorn is a researcher in the Arms Division of Human Rights Watch–America.

Douglas Holdstock, consultant physician at Ashford Hospital, Middlesex, became a pacifist as a result of his school experience in the Army Cadet Force, and a peace activist with the escalation of the nuclear threat and the impact of arms spending on health care in the early 1980s. He is a member of the executive committee of MEDACT (the UK affiliate of the IPPNW), for whom he edits *Medicine, Conflict and Survival* (formerly *Medicine and War*).

Linda Hunt was, until 1996, Assistant Chief Inspector in the Social Work Services Group in Scotland. Her teaching, publications and policy work have focussed particularly on alcohol use in our society, the organization of practice in health and social care and the development of social work services and training. She now spends time in both Scotland and the Netherlands. Her current interests are in the development of new services for families and provision for older people.

Risto Hyvärinen was Special Representative of the UN Secretary-General to the Conference of the Committee on Disarmament in Geneva (1975) and President of the Union of Frontline Veteran Soldiers from 1992 to 1997.

Eva Isaksson has written about scientists and peace, women scientists, and women and war. She currently works as an astronomy librarian at the University of Helsinki. She has edited *Women and the Military System* (1988) and is currently involved in a project documenting the work and careers of Finnish women scientists and scholars.

Leo Jarho is a professor and specialist in neurology, especially brain injuries. He worked as the chief physician (now retired) at Kauniala Hospital for Disabled War Veterans, Finland, for over 30 years and as a member of the Expert Group of the World Veterans Federation.

Jussi S. Jauhiainen is currently Professor of Urban Geography at the University of Helsinki and Associate Professor of Human Geography at the University of Tartu (Estonia). He is a member of the management committee of EU COST A10 Action (defence restructuring and conversion). His research interests include regional aspects of defence conversion.

Søren Buus Jensen is Executive Director and Chair of Psychiatric Department P at Copenhagen University Hospital and Executive Director and Senior Mental Health Adviser at the European University Centre for Mental Health and Human Rights, Copenhagen. He was formerly senior Medical Health Adviser and Special Representative of the Regional Director of the World Health Organization's Emergency Assistance Programme to former Yugoslavia (1994–96).

Christian Jenssen is a physician and specialist in internal medicine at the Evangelisches Krankenhaus Königin Elisabeth Herzberge, Berlin. In 1982 he became a member of the council of the then East German section of International Physicians for the Prevention of Nuclear War (IPPNW) and founder of a medical students' anti-war group. He is currently a member of IPPNW-Germany. He is the author of a book (1991) on the history of the anti-war activities of physicians.

Kati Juva is one of the founding members of Physicians for Social Responsibility (PSR) Finland and was its secretary-general from 1990 to 1998. She is currently the chairperson of the organization. She has been a member of the committee of Finnish Physicians Against Nuclear War and participated in PSR's development cooperation project in Tanzania in the 1980s. She works as a consultant in neurology in the Psychiatric Department of Helsinki University Central Hospital.

Ernesto Kahan was director-general of the Ministry of Health in Argentina before migrating to Israel during the military coup in Argentina in 1976. In Israel he was head of the Department of Epidemiology at the Institute for Occupational Health of Tel Aviv University and director of the Medical Academic Branch of the International Institute. He is the founder and chairperson of the Israel Association of Physicians for Peace and Preservation of the Environment; vice-president of International Physicians for the Prevention of Nuclear War (IPPNW); founder of the Middle East Cancer Society and active in many medical associations related to epidemiology, cancer, public health and human rights. He was a delegate to the Peace Prize ceremony in Oslo (1985). In 1991 he was awarded the Albert Schweitzer Peace Achievement Award and appointed Peace Ambassador of the Youth of Uruguay.

Kari Karkola is senior medical examiner at the Provincial State Office of eastern Finland. He gained his international forensic experience at the Chief Medical Examiner's Office of New York City, USA and at the Department of Forensic Medicine, University of Uppsala, Sweden. He was part of the first Finnish Forensic Expert Team to Kosovo.

L. G. Kasyanenko is a member of the St Petersburg Branch of the Russian Committee of International Physicians for the Prevention of Nuclear War.

Laura Kauppinen is a research psychologist in the Department of Psychology at the University of Helsinki, Finland. Her major research interests are adolescence, social cognition, social behaviour and stress.

Meri Koivusalo is a researcher with publications in the areas of international health, environmental epidemiology and health, population issues and development policies. She is currently a research fellow in the Globalism and Social Policies Programme (GASPP) of the National Research and Development Centre for Welfare and Health (STAKES) in Finland.

Kolawole T. Raheem is a researcher in the Department of Biological and Environmental Sciences, University of Jyväskylä, Finland.

Sergei Kolesnikov is a member of International Physicians for the Prevention of Nuclear War–Russia. He is past co-president of IPPNW with Dr.Sidel. He is a cardiologist, an academician and a member of the Russian Duma (Parliament) and has been the chairman of the Health Commission of the Duma.

Mauno Konttinen is a medical doctor with specialist training in thoracic and cardiovascular surgery and in health-care administration. Since 1987 he has been engaged in administrative tasks, first at Helsinki University Central Hospital, and from 1994 in government central administration. In 1996/97 he worked for the World Health Organization (WHO) in Sarajevo, and in 1998/99 participated in an EU Phare project in Bosnia-Herzegovina as a senior part-time expert.

Hans Küng became president of the Foundation of Global Ethics in Germany in 1995, and in 1997 president of the Swiss branch of the same foundation. He has written about Christian existence, Church and Christian ecumenism, inter-religious dialogue and global ethics.

Jennifer Leaning is a senior research fellow at the Harvard Center for Population and Development Studies.

Barry S. Levy, is an Adjunct Professor of Community Health at Tufts University School of Medicine. In 1997 he served as president of the American Public Health Association. He has been a medical epidemiologist for the Centers for Disease Control; a professor at the University of Massachusetts Medical School, where he founded and directed its Occupational Health Program; and executive director, International Physicians for the Prevention of Nuclear War. He has worked in more than 20 countries, primarily developing countries of Africa and Asia and countries in Central and Eastern Europe. He is co-editor of *War and Public Health*, with Victor W. Sidel, published by Oxford University Press and the American Public Health Association in 1997.

Nick Lewer is research fellow and lecturer at the Centre for Conflict Resolution, Department of Peace Studies, University of Bradford, England.

Bernard Lown is co-founder and first president of Physicians for Social Responsibility (PSR-USA), co-founder with Dr Evgeni Chazov of Russia of International Physicians for the Prevention of Nuclear War (IPPNW) and the recipient of the UNESCO Peace Award and Nobel Peace Prize on behalf of IPPNW, founder and chairman of SatelLife, the global communication network to promote health information for developing countries, and founder and chairman of the Ad Hoc Committee to Defend Health Care, a body established to oppose the corporatization of medicine.

Ian Maddocks is Chairman of the Board of Directors of the International Physicians for the Prevention of Nuclear War (IPPNW), Chairman of the National Consultative Committee for Peace and Disarmament (Australia) and Secretary of the Medical Association for the Prevention of War (Australia).

P. Helena Mäkelä is a founding member of Physicians for Social Responsibility (PSR) Finland, and was its chairperson for 15 years from 1982 to 1996. PSR's work on development cooperation has been her special interest. She was one of the editors of the organization's textbook, *Health and Disease in Developing Countries*. In her professional life Helena Mäkelä is a bacteriologist interested in both the molecular genetics of bacteria and the use of this knowledge in the development and use of vaccines in the prevention of common infectious diseases. Now retired as former Head of the Division of Infectious Diseases in the National Public Health Institute in Finland, she continues work in vaccine research projects.

Saul Mendlovitz is Dag Hammarskjöld Professor of Peace and World Order Studies at Rutgers Law School, Newark, New Jersey. He is co-director of the World Order Models Project and a founding member of the transnational coalition, Global Action to Prevent War, Genocide and Internal Armed Conflict. Professor Mendlovitz has written extensively on problems concerning the development and promotion of a just world order. His recent publications include: *A UN Constabulary to Enforce the Law on Genocide and Crimes Against Humanity*; *A n Affirmative Appraisal of the Advisory Opinion on the Legality of the Threat or Use of Nuclear Weapons*; and *Preferred Futures for the United Nations* with Burns Weston. Forthcoming publications include: *Defensive Security and The Prospects for Abolishing War: a Proposal for the Twenty-First Century*. He is a former member of the executive committee of the *American Journal of International Law* and holds membership on various boards, including: Arms Control Association; Global Education Associates; Lawyers' Committee on Nuclear Policy; and International Association of Lawyers Against Nuclear Arms. Professor Mendlovitz is the representative of three civil society organizations at the United Nations: the International Peace Research Association; the International Association of Lawyers Against Nuclear Arms; and the World Federation of Future Studies. His teaching programme covers Law and a Just World Order and he also conducts a seminar on genocide.

Tom Milne is a researcher at the London Office of the Pugwash Conferences on Science and World Affairs.

William W. Monning is the former executive director of International Physicians for the Prevention of Nuclear War (1987–91). He is an attorney licensed in the State of California who currently serves as Director of the Negotiation, Mediation and Conflict Resolution Project at the Center for Trade and Commercial Diplomacy, Monterey Institute of International Studies. He has worked extensively in Latin America, and negotiated the release of political prisoners in Honduras, El Salvador and Guatemala in the 1980s. As the executive director of IPPNW, he was responsible for international governance of the federation, including development of regional and international campaigns. He represented IPPNW at the United Nations during the Test Ban Treaty Amendment Conference and was a member of the IPPNW delegation to the Middle East on the eve of the Gulf War. He has worked extensively in the Middle East, the former Soviet Union, Europe, Asia and the Americas.

Dr Marwan Nasralla Nasralla is the President of International Molecular Diagnostics, Inc. and an Associate Research Professor at the Institute for Molecular Medicine, Huntington Beach, California.

Garth L. Nicolson is the President and Chief Scientific Officer and Research Professor at the Institute for Molecular Medicine, Huntington Beach, California. He is also an adjunct professor of internal medicine and the former David Bruton Chair in Research at the University of Texas M. D. Anderson Cancer Center in Houston.

Nancy L. Nicolson is the Chief Executive Officer of the Institute for Molecular Medicine and International Molecular

Diagnostics of Huntington Beach, California.

Arto Nokkala held various officer and general staff officer assignments in the Finnish Defence Forces from 1970 to 1995. He is currently Visiting Research Fellow, Tampere Peace Research Institute (TAPRI), University of Tampere, Finland, where his main research interests are Finland's foreign, security and military politics, the post-Cold War military in Europe and security in northern Europe.

Abdul Razak Noormahomed was born in Mozambique. He studied tropical medicine and hygiene, at School of Hygiene and Tropical Medicine, University of Liverpool, and holds a post-graduate diploma in Health Planning and Administration from the Nuffield Institute for Health Services Studies, University of Leeds. He also holds degrees in public health and medical surgery. Since 1977 he has served the Mozambican health services in various capacities, and between 1994 and 2000 as Vice-Minister of Health. At present Governor of Nampula Province, since 1993 he has also worked as a professor in the Faculty of Medicine at the University of Lourenco Marques, Maputo. He is also a member of the Mozambican Public Health Association and the Mozambique Medical Association. His wide experience in health policy and planning is reflected in numerous published contributions to books, journals and conference proceedings.

Violeta Petroska-Beska is a professor of psychology and Director of the Ethnic Conflict Resolution Project, a training and research centre in the Faculty of Philosophy, Skopje University. Her work in the area of conflict resolution has been dedicated to educating and mobilizing Macedonian citizens to assume an active role in the resolution of seemingly intractable ethnic conflicts. She is the author of the first book and thus far the only conflict-resolution primer prepared by a Macedonian professional for a domestic audience (*Conflicts: Their Nature and Ways of Resolving Them*).

Lars Pohlmeier is a medical doctor and journalist. He is a member of the German IPPNW board of directors and currently works as speaker of the German IPPNW board in Berlin.

Matti Ponteva is a specialist in psychiatry and public health care with a particular competence in military medicine. He is Medical Director of Mental Health Work for the Finnish Defence Forces.

Eric Prokosch, an anthropologist, is an expert on antipersonnel weapons and was a staff member of National Action/Research on the Military Industrial Complex, a project of the American Friends Service Committee (Quakers). He now works at the International Secretariat of Amnesty International, but Chapter 7 reflects his own views.

Brian Rawson is a programme coordinator for International Physicians for the Prevention of Nuclear War, where he works on campaigns for nuclear weapons abolition and small arms control. He has an academic background in international development and has worked at the community level in the US and Latin America.

Michael Renner is a senior researcher at the Worldwatch Institute, Washington DC.

Julian P. Perry Robinson is director of the Harvard Sussex Programme at the Science and Technology Policy Research Unit, University of Sussex.

Ye N. Rose is a member of the St. Petersburg Branch of the Russian Committee of International Physicians for the Prevention of Nuclear War.

Professor Gunnar Rosén is former Deputy Secretary-General of the Finnish Red Cross and has served on numerous international Red Cross missions in South-East Asia, Africa and Saudi Arabia. He is also a historian and expert on the laws of war, who has published a centenary history of the Finnish Red Cross, a handbook and teaching guide on humanitarian law for the Finnish army, a study on the humanitarian aspects of the Finnish occupation of Soviet Karelia during the Second World War, and a great number of minor studies and articles.

Martin Scheinin is Armfelt Professor of Constitutional and International Law and Director of the Institute for Human Rights, both at Åbo Akademi University, Finland. He has published extensively in the field of human rights and comparative constitutional law. He is a member of the United Nations Human Rights Committee established under the International Covenant on Civil and Political Rights, and chairperson of the Committee on International Human Rights Law and Practice within the International Law Association.

Ruth Seifert is Professor of Sociology at the School of Social Work, Fachhochschule Regensburg, Munich. She worked for several years at German military educational institutions. She has published widely on gender, sexual violence and the military; gender and war; and the gendered aspects of armed conflicts.

Victor W. Sidel is Distinguished University Professor of Social Medicine at Montefiore Medical Center and the Albert Einstein College of Medicine in the Bronx, New York. He is president of the Public Association of New York City, past-president of the American Public Health Association and Physicians for Social Responsiblity (USA), and past co-president of International Physicians for the Prevention of Nuclear War, the recipient of the 1985 Nobel Peace Prize. He is co-editor of *War and Public Health*, published by Oxford University Press and the American Public Health Association in 1997.

Anna Sillanpää is a medical doctor who graduated in the year 2000 from the University of Oulu. She works in the Health Centre of Äänekoski, Finland, and hopes to become a specialist in otorhinolaryngology one day.

O.N. Simonova is a member of the St Petersburg branch of the Russian Committee of International Physicians for the Prevention of Nuclear War.

Jussi Simpura is a research professor and head of Alcohol and Drug Research (formerly the Social Research Institute for Alcohol Studies) and the National Research and Development Centre for Welfare and Health in Helsinki. He has worked in alcohol research since the 1970s, with comparative research on drinking patterns and alcohol-related problems as his main interest, and with empirical research on the Nordic and eastern European countries, the EU and elsewhere.

Susannah Sirkin is Deputy Director of Physicians for Human Rights and formerly served on the staff of Amnesty International USA.

Tytti Solantaus is a child psychiatrist at Helsinki University Hospital for Children and Adolescents. Her long-standing research interest is to help understand how societal phenomena are reflected in family life and child development. She has studied the impact of the threat of nuclear war on children and teenagers, and more recently the impact of economic recession and family economic hardship on parents and children.

Pär Stenbäck, born in 1941, served in different Red Cross positions for twelve years. He was appointed Secretary-General of the Finnish Red Cross in 1985, elected Secretary-General of the International Federation of Red Cross and Red Crescent Societies (IFRC) in 1987 and served until 1992. He was President of the Finnish Red Cross for four years, from 1996 to 1999. Stenbäck has also served as Finnish Foreign Minister and Minister of Education, as a Member of Parliament and as Secretary-General of the Nordic Council of Ministers (Copenhagen). Presently he is active in the International Crisis Group (ICG), as Vice President of the International Youth Foundation (IYF), and as a member of the advisory boards of the Humanitarian Affairs Review (Brussels) and the Institute for Human Rights at Åbo Akademi University. He has a degree in political science from Helsinki University and is a lifetime honorary Minister.

Paul Stubbs has lived in Croatia since 1993. He currently works as an Associate Senior Research Fellow with GASPP (the Globalism and Social Policy Programme) based in Sheffield, UK and at the National Research and Development Centre for Welfare and Health (STAKES), Helsinki, Finland. He was a founder member of the Centre for Peace Studies, a local non-governmental organization based in Zagreb, Croatia.

Ilkka Taipale, medical doctor and politician, is a founder of Physicians for Social Responsibility (PSR) Finland and currently its vice-president. He was re-elected to the Finnish Parliament in 2000.

Vappu Taipale is a professor of child psychiatry and a former Minister of Health and Minister of Social Welfare in the Finnish government. He is currently Director-General of the National Research and Development Centre for Welfare and Health (STAKES). He was vice-chair of Physicians for Social Responsibility, Finland from 1982 to 1992 and is the author of *Rauhan Lapset* (Children of Peace), and of several books and publications on issues of public health, mental health and child development.

Hanna Tapanainen is a board member of Physicians for Social Responsibility (PSR), Finland, and participated actively in IPPNW student programmes during her student years. Her special interest is health and development policymaking and she is currently involved in PSR's project on health and economic policies. She works as an intern in the Helsinki University Central Hospital, and is specializing in respiratory diseases and allergology.

Masao Tomonaga is Professor of Medicine, Department of Hematology, Molecular Medicine Unit, Atomic Bomb Disease Institute, Nagasaki University School of Medicine. Born in 1943, in 1945 he lived in an area at about 3 km from the hypocentre of the Nagasaki Atomic Bomb. After becoming a physician and hematologist, he has been engaged in US–Japanese cooperative epidemiological research activities, specializing in lukaemias induced by atomic bomb radiation. He has been an active member of IPPNW since 1983. At present, he is one of vice-presidents of IPPNW, representing the North Asia Region including China, North Korea, South Korea and Japan. He is also Director of the Atomic Bomb Disease Institute, Nagasaki University School of Medicine.

Tapio Varis is currently Professor and Chair of Media Culture and Communication Education at the University of Tampere, Finland. He is also a consultant on new learning technologies to the Finnish Ministry of Education, a member of the European Union's PROMETEUS Steering Committee and adviser to several international organizations. In 1996–97 he was UNESCO Chair of Communication studies at the Universitat Autonoma de Barcelona, Spain. He has also been a faculty member of the European Peace University, Communication and Media Scholar at the University of Helsinki and at the University of Art and Design in Helsinki. He is a former Rector of the University for Peace in Costa Rica and Professor of Media Studies in the University of Lapland, Finland. He has published approximately 200 scientific contributions – the latest being *Media of the Knowledge Age* (Helsinki University Press, 1995).

Unto Vesa serves as a senior research fellow at Tampere Peace Research Institute (TAPRI), Finland. He was one of the founders of the Tampere Peace Research Group in 1968, forerunner to TAPRI. He was also among the founders and was the first president of the Finnish Peace Research Association in 1971. From 1972 to 1990 he was the managing editor of *Current Research on Peace and Violence*, TAPRI's quarterly. In 2000 he was elected as President of the European Peace Research Association and a Member of the IPRA Board.

Lauri Vuorenkoski is a Finnish medical student with a specialist interest in child psychiatry. He has been the editor of the newsletter of PSR–Finland for four years and on its executive board for three.

Hannu Vuori is Director of the Department of Health and Social Welfare in the UN Civil Administration, Kosovo. After graduating in sociology (University of California, Berkeley) and in medicine (University of Turku, Finland), Dr Vuori chaired the Department of Community Health in the University of Kuopio, Finland. From 1979 until 1999, he has been with the Regional Office for Europe of the World Health Organization heading first the new primary health care programme and then programmes in research promotion and development, epidemiology and statistics, and health care management. He was Director of WHO's Humanitarian Assistance Programme for the former Yugoslavia during the Bosnia conflict in 1992–5. From July 1999, he has been the 'Minister of Health' in the UN Civil Administration, Kosovo. Dr Vuori has published 180 articles, mostly on quality assurance and health education, and ten books, including one on the Bosnian conflict. He has been visiting scientist at the Harvard Centre for Community Health and the National Centre for Health Services Research in the USA.

James Welsh is coordinator of Amnesty International's Medical Programme.

Arthur H. Westing, a forest ecologist, has been a senior research fellow at the Stockholm International Peace Research Institute (SIPRI) and at the International Peace Research Institute, Oslo. He has also been a consultant to the United Nations Environment Programme, United Nations Institute for Disarmament Research, the International Committee of the Red Cross and the Eritrean Agency for the Environment.

Aleksander Yemelyanenkov is a freelance journalist. In 1989 he was elected People's Deputy of the USSR from a constituency comprising the archipelago Novaya Zemlya and an active nuclear test site. Since that time ecological problems have been central to his professional and public activity. In 1991 the movement for ecological security, 'To Novaya Zemlya', was formed in Northern Russia. Yemelyanenkov was elected its co-chairman. His articles on ecological problems have been published by many national and foreign mass media. In 1992 he co-published with Vladimir Popov of IPPNW–Russia a collection of articles, *Atom Declassified*, to be followed by a sequel in 1996.

INDEX